Praise for *History of Africa, Third Edition:*

'The readability of the book, the valuable maps and illustrations, and the coverage of the precolonial period as well as more modern eras, make this textbook the best on the market.' – **David Chappell**, *University of Hawaii, USA*

'*History of Africa* provides extraordinary coverage of the basic history of the entire continent of Africa in a way that is accessible for new students.' – **Timothy Cleaveland**, *University of Georgia, USA*

'This new edition maintains Shillington's position as an expert who is adept at providing readers with an engaging and intricate portrait of Africa's past .... A master of the material, Shillington presents a volume that flows and informs. *History of Africa* is a compelling narrative of change over time on the continent .... There is an effective incorporation of new evidence in this edition that enhances our understanding of African history.' – **Elizabeth MacGonagle**, *University of Kansas, USA*

'Shillington's work is an excellent introduction for students who are new to African history.' – **Miles Larmer**, *University of Sheffield, UK*

Praise for previous editions:

'Shillington's coverage is comprehensive, his presentation clear, and his content well up to date with the latest research ...' – **J. B. Peires**, *University of Transkei (now Walter Sisulu University), South Africa*

'... a work with many virtues ... stylistic lucidity, profusion of clear maps and excellent illustrations.' – **International Journal of African Historical Studies**

Related titles from Palgrave Macmillan:

Bill Freund: *The Making of Contemporary Africa, Second Edition*
Paul Nugent: *Africa since Independence, Second Edition*

Other works by the author:

The Colonisation of the Southern Tswana (1985)
A Junior Certificate History for Zimbabwe (co-author, 1986)
Jugnauth: Prime Minister of Mauritius (1991)
An African Adventure: A Brief Life of Cecil Rhodes (1991)
Ghana and the Rawlings Factor (1992)
Causes and Consequences of Independence in Africa (1997)
Sowing the Mustard Seed: The Struggle for Freedom and Democracy in Uganda (editor, 1997)
History of Southern Africa, Second Edition (2002)
Encyclopedia of African History (editor, 2005)
History of Modern Seychelles (2009)
Luka Jantjie: Resistance Hero of the South African Frontier (2011)
Contributor to *Encarta Encyclopedia* (US and world editions)

History of Africa

Third Edition

KEVIN SHILLINGTON

 macmillan education palgrave

First Edition published 1989 by Macmillan Publishers
Revised Edition published 1995 by Macmillan Education
Revised Second Edition published 2005 by Macmillan Education
Third Edition published 2012 by
PALGRAVE MACMILLAN

Palgrave in the UK is an imprint of Macmillan Publishers Limited,
registered in England, company number 785998, of 4 Crinan Street,
London, N1 9XW.

Palgrave Macmillan in the US is a division of St Martin's Press LLC,
175 Fifth Avenue, New York, NY 10010.

Palgrave is a global imprint of the above companies and is represented throughout the world.

Palgrave® and Macmillan® are registered trademarks in the United States,
the United Kingdom, Europe and other countries

ISBN: 978–0–230–30847–3 paperback

This book is printed on paper suitable for recycling and made from fully
managed and sustained forest sources. Logging, pulping and manufacturing
processes are expected to conform to the environmental regulations of the
country of origin.

A catalogue record for this book is available from the British Library.

A catalog record for this book is available from the Library of Congress.

Printed in China

For Pippa

Contents

List of Maps   xii

List of Illustrations   xv

Acknowledgements   xxii

Preface   xxiv

	Introduction	**1**
	Historiography	1
	Geography, climate and vegetation	3
Chapter 1	**Early prehistory of Africa**	**9**
	Human evolution	9
	Homo sapiens, the hunter-gatherer	15
	Further climate change, adaptation and the ancestry of African languages	18
Chapter 2	**Later prehistory: farming and pastoralism in tropical Africa and Ancient Egypt**	**22**
	Crop cultivation, domestication and the origins of farming	22
	The impact of agriculture	23
	The origins of farming and pastoralism in tropical Africa	25
	Ancient Egypt	30
Chapter 3	**The impact of iron in north and west Africa**	**43**
	The spread and impact of early metal-working	43
	Origins of iron-working	44
	The Iron Age Kingdom of Meroe	48
	Iron Age north Africa and early trans-Saharan trade	54
Chapter 4	**The Early Iron Age in central, eastern and southern Africa**	**57**
	Evidence for the spread of iron-working	57
	Origins of the Early Iron Age in sub-equatorial Africa	60
	The spread of the Early Iron Age	61
	The development and organisation of Early Iron Age society	65
Chapter 5	**North and north-eastern Africa to 1000 CE**	**69**
	Northern Africa in the Graeco-Roman period	69
	The spread of Christianity in northern Africa	73
	The origins and rise of Aksum	76
	The Arab invasions: the Nile valley and the Maghrib	79

Chapter 6   **Trans-Saharan trade and the kingdom of ancient Ghana**   **85**
Trans-Saharan trade   85
The kingdom of ancient Ghana   88
Other early west African states and societies   93

Chapter 7   **Islam and the Sudanic states of west Africa**   **96**
The Almoravids   96
The Muslim states of north Africa, 1100–1500   98
The empire of Mali   100
The decline of Mali   107
The origins and rise of Songhay   108
The Fulbe (or Fulani)   113

Chapter 8   **Eastern Africa to the sixteenth century**   **114**
The Christian kingdom of Ethiopia, 850–1550   114
The Muslim penetration of Ethiopia and Somalia, 850–1550   118
Pastoralists and farmers of the east African interior   122

Chapter 9   **Trading towns of the east African coast to the sixteenth century**   **128**
The origins of east African coastal trading society   128
The growth of Swahili trading towns   134
The Portuguese on the east African coast, 1498–1600   137
Madagascar   143

Chapter 10   **Later Iron Age states and societies of central and southern Africa to 1600**   **144**
The emergence of Later Iron Age states north of the Zambezi   144
The development of Later Iron Age communities south of the Zambezi   151
The origins and character of the Great Zimbabwe tradition   154
Cattle-keeping peoples south of the Limpopo   160

Chapter 11   **North and north-east Africa to the eighteenth century**   **163**
The 'Arabisation' of northern Africa   163
From Fatimid to Mamluk: Egypt before the Ottoman conquest   164
Egypt under Ottoman rule   168
Nubia and the Funj Sultanate   169
Oromo migrations and the kingdom of Ethiopia   170
States of the Maghrib, sixteenth to eighteenth century   173

Chapter 12   **The Atlantic slave trade, sixteenth to eighteenth century**   **176**
Slavery in Africa before the Atlantic trade   176
The origins of European maritime trade with west Africa   177
The nature of the slave trade   180
Profit from the slave trade: the European dimension   185

Chapter 13   **West African states and societies, to the eighteenth century**   **187**
The fall of the Songhay empire   187
The sultanate of Borno-Kanem   189
The Hausa city-states   191

	Wolof kingdoms of Senegambia	193
	Kingdoms of the forest: Ife and Benin	194
	Oyo and Dahomey, savannah states of the seventeenth and eighteenth centuries	197
	The kingdom of Asante	200
Chapter 14	**Central and eastern Africa to the eighteenth century**	**203**
	Farmers, fishers and hunters of the Congo forest	203
	West-central Africa in the era of the slave trade	204
	Central African empires and the growth of trade	207
	The east African interior west of the Victoria Nyanza	212
	The east African interior east of the Victoria Nyanza	216
Chapter 15	**Southern Africa to the eighteenth century**	**218**
	Southern Africa before 1650	218
	The early Cape Colony: white settlement and Khoesan resistance, 1650–1770	218
	States and societies of the southern African interior, 1600–1800	225
Chapter 16	**West Africa in the nineteenth century and the ending of the slave trade**	**230**
	Islamic *jihads* in the western Sudan	230
	The ending of the Atlantic slave trade	237
	West African commerce in the nineteenth century	240
	Sierra Leone and Liberia	243
Chapter 17	**Central and east Africa in the nineteenth century**	**247**
	West-central Africa in the nineteenth century	247
	Kingdom of the floodplain	249
	The development of long-distance trade in east-central Africa	251
	Invasion from the south: the Ngoni	254
	The east African slave trade	256
	The trade in ivory and slaves in the interior of central Africa	258
	Madagascar: the rise of the Merina kingdom	262
Chapter 18	**Pre-industrial southern Africa in the nineteenth century**	**263**
	State-building and conflict: the *mfecane/difaqane* and its effects	263
	The British at the Cape	271
	The Boer Trek and African resistance	274
	Southern Africa in 1870	278
Chapter 19	**North and north-east Africa in the nineteenth century**	**280**
	The French in north Africa and Algerian resistance	280
	Egypt and Sudan to the Mahdist *jihad*	283
	The reunification of Ethiopia	291
Chapter 20	**Christianity and pre-colonial 'nationalism'**	**296**
	European Christian missionaries in pre-colonial Africa	296
	African Christians and pre-colonialism nationalism	298
	European 'explorers': the mapping of Africa as a prelude to Empire	303

Chapter 21	The European 'Scramble', colonial conquest and African resistance in east, north-central and west Africa	311
	The 'Scramble for Africa'	311
	Conquest and resistance	316

Chapter 22	Industrialisation, colonial conquest and African resistance in south-central and southern Africa	328
	The southern African mineral revolution	328
	The British 'Scramble' for south-central Africa	333
	Wars of conquest and resistance in Mozambique	337
	Conquest and resistance in Namibia	338
	The South African War (1899–1902)	340

Chapter 23	Consolidation of empire: the early period of colonial rule	343
	Raw materials and markets	343
	Peasant producers, railways and white settlement in British east Africa	349
	Rebellion in the German colonies	351
	Missionaries, Christianity and early expressions of 'nationalism'	353
	The First World War and Africa, 1914–18	355

Chapter 24	Africa between the wars: the high tide of colonial rule	361
	The economic impact of colonial rule	361
	The nature and impact of colonial administration	367
	The spread of Islam in tropical west Africa	370
	Education: from pre-colonial tradition to colonial reality	371
	African nationalism and protest movements in the inter-war years	374
	Segregation, nationalism and protest in South Africa	376

Chapter 25	The Second World War and Africa	379
	Fascist aggression and the Second World War in north and north-east Africa	380
	The impact of the war on Africa and Africans	384

Chapter 26	The winning of independence (1)	389
	Colonial development strategies	389
	The winning of independence in British west Africa	390
	The winning of independence in French West Africa and French Equatorial Africa	393
	The struggle for independence in the Maghrib	396
	Egypt, Sudan, Eritrea and Somalia	398

Chapter 27	The winning of independence (2)	402
	British east Africa	402
	Independence in Belgian-ruled central Africa	407
	Independence on the islands	413

Chapter 28	The winning of independence (3)	416
	Federation and independence in British Central Africa	416
	The winning of independence in Portuguese-ruled Africa	422
	The struggle for freedom in southern Africa	425

Chapter 29	**Africa since independence (1)**	**433**
	The political legacy of colonial rule	433
	The economic legacy of underdevelopment and dependency	436
	The early drive for economic development	438
	The role of the military in African politics	441
	Socialism and self-reliance: the Tanzanian course	443
Chapter 30	**Africa since independence (2)**	**447**
	The dilemmas of development: debt, climate change and international aid	447
	International cooperation and the Organisation of African Unity	453
Chapter 31	**Contemporary Africa (1)**	**458**
	Democratic progress in the 1990s	458
	North Africa	460
	West Africa	464
Chapter 32	**Contemporary Africa (2)**	**470**
	Eastern and Central Africa	470
	Southern Africa	477
	The HIV/AIDS pandemic	479
	China and Africa	480
Suggestions for further reading		482
Index		491

List of Maps

0.1	The physical geography of Africa	5
0.2	The vegetation of modern Africa	6
1.1	The evolution of humankind in Africa	13
1.2	The spread of African languages, 15,000–10,000 BCE	19
2.1	Africa, 7000 BCE: probable level of lakes and rivers in the last major wet phase	26
2.2	'Neolithic' farming and pastoralism, northern and central Africa: 5000–1000 BCE	27
2.3	The origins of farming: western Asia and north-east Africa	31
2.4	Ancient Egypt: 3500–1000 BCE	32
3.1	The spread of iron-working in Africa	47
3.2	Egypt, Kush and Meroe: 1500 BCE to 350 CE	50
3.3	Early trans-Saharan trade to 300 CE	56
4.1	The languages of Africa, c.1600 CE	58
4.2	The Early Iron Age in eastern, central and southern Africa	63
5.1	Northern Africa in the Graeco-Roman period	69
5.2	Africa according to Ptolemy	73
5.3	The spread of Christianity in northern Africa, first to sixth century CE	74
5.4	The kingdom of Aksum, 100–700 CE	76
5.5	The Arab conquest of north Africa, 640–711 CE	80
5.6	Muslim states of north Africa, 750–950 CE	84
6.1	Trans-Saharan trading networks up to 1200 CE	85
6.2	The kingdom of Ancient Ghana in the eleventh century (superimposed on modern boundaries)	89
7.1	The Almoravid empire in the eleventh century	97
7.2	The Almohad empire in the twelfth century	99
7.3	Muslim states of north Africa in the fifteenth century	99
7.4	The empire of Mali in the fourteenth century	102
7.5	The Songhay empire in the early sixteenth century	110
8.1	Solomonid Ethiopia in the fifteenth century and the Muslim penetration of north-east Africa	119
8.2	Conflict in the highlands: Ethiopia and Adal in the sixteenth century	120
8.3	Later Iron Age peoples of the east African interior to c.1500	123
9.1	The east African coast to 500 CE	129
9.2	The east African coast, 500–1000 CE	133
9.3	Indian Ocean trading networks, tenth to sixteenth centuries	134
9.4	Swahili towns and the Portuguese, fifteenth and sixteenth centuries	138
10.1	South-central Africa in the Later Iron Age	149

10.2	Later Iron Age states south of the Zambezi, 900–1600	153
10.3	The Later Iron Age south of the Limpopo	159
11.1	Migrations of Arab Bedouin into north Africa, 950–1350	164
11.2	Egypt under Fatimid, Ayyubid and Mamluk rule, 969–1517	165
11.3	Egypt under the Ottomans, sixteenth and seventeenth centuries	169
11.4	Ethiopia in the seventeenth century	172
11.5	The Maghrib in the sixteenth and seventeenth centuries	174
12.1	West Africa: Portuguese exploration and trade in the fifteenth century	178
12.2	The Atlantic slave trade, sixteenth to eighteenth centuries	185
13.1	Morocco and the fall of Songhay	188
13.2	Borno-Kanem in the sixteenth and seventeenth centuries	190
13.3	West African states and societies in the eighteenth century	194
14.1	Central Africa, sixteenth to eighteenth centuries	205
14.2	The Maravi and Rozvi: seventeenth and eighteenth centuries	210
14.3	The east African interior, seventeenth and eighteenth centuries	214
15.1	South-western Cape, 1650–1700	219
15.2	The expansion of Boer settlement in the eighteenth century	220
15.3	Southern Africa in the eighteenth century	225
16.1	Jihadist states of the western Sudan to c.1840	231
16.2	The Tukolor and Mandinka empires	234
16.3	West African exports in the nineteenth century	241
16.4	Sierra Leone and Liberia in c.1880	245
17.1	West-central Africa in the nineteenth century	247
17.2	East-central Africa in the nineteenth century	252
17.3	Long-distance trading routes of the east African interior in the nineteenth century	255
18.1	The rise of the Zulu kingdom and the *Difaqane* on the highveld, 1818–35	264
18.2	The Cape Colony and Xhosa resistance, 1811–36	273
18.3	The Boer Trek and African resistance, 1836–40	276
18.4	Southern Africa in 1870	278
19.1	Algeria and the Maghrib, 1800–80	280
19.2	The expansion of the Egyptian empire, 1805–80	286
19.3	The Mahdist Sudan, 1885–98	290
19.4	Ethiopia, 1855–96	292
20.1	Christianity and Islam in Africa, to 1885	297
20.2	European penetration of Africa before 1880	305
21.1	European territorial claims to Africa on the eve of the Berlin Conference, 1884	313
21.2	West Africa in the era of the 'Scramble'	316
21.3	The Congo Basin and Angola in the era of the 'Scramble'	322
21.4	British and German penetration of East Africa, 1884–1905	325
22.1	Southern Africa in the era of the 'Scramble'	330
22.2	South-central Africa in the era of the 'Scramble'	333
22.3	German conquest of 'South West Africa'	339
22.4	The South African War, 1899–1902	341

23.1	Sub-Saharan Africa in the early colonial period	345
23.2	The First World War and Africa, 1914–18	358
24.1	Colonial exploitation of sub-Saharan Africa in the inter-war period	361
25.1	Ethiopia and Eritrea, 1935–41	380
25.2	The Second World War in north Africa, 1941–3	383
26.1	Independence in western Africa	391
26.2	Independence in the Maghrib	396
26.3	Independence in north-east Africa	399
27.1	Independence in east Africa	403
27.2	Independence in Congo (Zaïre)	409
28.1	Independence in British Central Africa	417
28.2	Independence in Angola, Mozambique and Zimbabwe	423
28.3	Southern Africa: independence and resistance	426
29.1	The modern countries of Africa	434
29.2	The main features of Africa's export economies, showing principal sources of the major minerals and cash crops	437
30.1	Regional groupings: ECOWAS and SADCC/SADC	456
31.1	West African zones of conflict, c.1990–2011	466
32.1	Sudan/South Sudan, c.1990–2011	473
32.2	East-central Africa, c.1990–2011	476

List of Illustrations

0.1	The author at the Equator in 1995	4
1.1	Olduvai Gorge, UNESCO World Heritage Site, Serengeti, Tanzania	11
1.2	Microliths and other artefacts of early African pre-history	14
1.3	'Pygmy' boy sorting fishing nets in the Congo Basin	16
1.4	A modern photograph of the Kalahari San	18
1.5	A Khoesan hunter in Zimbabwe photographed c.1900	20
2.1	Modern pastoralists of the Sahel watering their cattle on the banks of the Niger River	24
2.2	Modern Ankole cattle, Uganda, thought to be descendants from the ancient domesticated cattle of the Sahara	25
2.3	Tassilin-Ajjer (Tassili Plateau, Sahara), prehistoric rock painting	28
2.4	Stone and pottery artefacts from the settlements and burials of Stone Age cultivators and pastoralists	29
2.5	Hieroglyphics carved in the tomb of Rameses II, c.1270 BCE	34
2.6	The fertile Nile Valley with the three great pyramids of the Old Kingdom period at Giza: Khufu (Cheops), Khefren and Mykerinos	35
2.7	Measuring and recording the harvest, an XVIIIth Dynasty wall-painting from a tomb in Thebes	36
2.8	The Great Pyramid of Khufu, IVth Dynasty	38
2.9	Nubians carrying tribute to the pharaoh, a wall-painting, c.1420 BCE	39
2.10	Tutankhamun's funeral mask in solid gold inlaid with semi-precious stones and glass-paste	40
2.11	The back of Tutankhamun's gold-plated throne	41
3.1	Smelting iron in Africa	44
3.2	Terracotta sculpture of the ancient Nok culture of Nigeria	48
3.3	Facsimile of an inscribed votive tablet of red slate from the Lion Temple at Naga	52
3.4	Engraving of a rural scene from the rim of a Meroite copper bowl	53
3.5	The pyramids of the Meroitic kings and queens in the north cemetery, Meroe, on a ridge overlooking the ruins of the city, 300 BCE – 400 CE	53
3.6	A racing chariot pulled by two horses: a Saharan rock-painting	56
4.1	A blacksmith at work in western Zambia in 1972, using the ancient technology of traditional double bellows	60
4.2	Early Iron Age copperbelt industry: rims of clay pots	64
4.3	Ceramic head from a site near Lydenburg, South Africa, dated c.500–700 CE	65

5.1	The Rosetta Stone, with hieroglyphics, cursive Egyptian and ancient Greek script	70
5.2	Part of the ruins of Roman Carthage (in modern Tunisia)	72
5.3	The tallest of the still-erect stelae at Aksum	78
5.4	The desert city of Nefta, described as the pearl of the Djerid (southern Tunisia)	82
6.1	Tuareg camel train travelling through the desert	87
6.2	A Saharan oasis	88
6.3	The archaeological site of Kumbi-Saleh (in modern Mali)	91
6.4	A bronze ceremonial wine bowl, Igbo-Ukwu and a 'lost-wax' cast vessel in the form of a shell eastern Nigeria, ninth century CE	94
7.1	The mud constructed mosque at Jenne with a souk in the foreground	103
7.2	Great Mosque, Timbuktu, the oldest mosque south of the Sahara	104
7.3	Detail from the Catalan Atlas, 1375, showing Mansa Musa, King of Mali, seated on his throne	106
7.4	Fisherman pulling net ashore, Niger River, Mali, West Africa	109
7.5	The tomb of Askiya Muhammad of Songhay at Gao	111
7.6	Timbuktu, from a German drawing dated 1858	112
8.1	A valley in the Ethiopian mountains	116
8.2	Portrait of King Lalibela, from an illuminated manuscript	117
8.3	The church of St George, one of the churches at Lalibela, Ethiopia, hewn from the living rock	118
8.4	Iron Age pottery of eastern Africa	125
8.5	Pastoralists of modern Sudan	126
9.1	Arab dhow used on the East African coast	131
9.2	The Mtambwe Mkuu Hoard, a scatter of tiny, locally minted silver and copper coins found on Pemba Island, photographed before cleaning and identification	133
9.3	The ruins of the Great Mosque at Kilwa	136
9.4	Portuguese ships of the sixteenth century	139
9.5	View of archway and walls from the fifteenth century ruined city of Gedi	141
9.6	Fort Jesus, Mombasa	142
9.7	A view to the sixteenth-century remains of the Portuguese fort at Kilwa	142
10.1	Potters of the Zambezi valley in the early twentieth century, decorating pots of the Late Iron Age type	145
10.2	A Kisalian grave	146
10.3	(a) Iron and copper artefacts from Upemba, in the classic Kisalian style; (b) and (c) Early Kisalian pottery from the Upemba Rift (Shaba)	148
10.4	Cotton-weaving in the Shire valley in the 1860s using Later Iron Age techniques	152
10.5	The Great Zimbabwe ruins	154–7
10.6	Shona girls in Zimbabwe, early twentieth century, wearing the sort of ornamental bangles and beaded leather skirts which were probably common in the Later Iron Age period	158

10.7	The stone foundations of a typical Sotho-Tswana dwelling of the Late Iron Age period	160
11.1	Arab Bedouins outside their tents in Tunisia, *c.*1935	163
11.2	Cairo: the citadel and Muhammad Ali mosque	166
11.3	Egyptian peasant working in the Nile valley	167
11.4	The state house of the king of Makurra (or Dongola), Sudan	170
11.5	The Ethiopian royal palace at Gondar	172
11.6	Skyline of a city of the Maghrib looking towards the Middle Atlas mountain range, Marrakesh (Marrakech), Morocco	175
12.1	Elmina Castle, Ghana, built for the Portuguese in 1482	179
12.2	Inside the ramparts of Elmina Castle looking towards the market chamber where slaves were sold	179
12.3	Diagram showing cross-sections of a trans-Atlantic slave ship	183
12.4	Armed guards watching a man being whipped outside a slave enclosure, *c.*1850	184
12.5	Slaves working on a West Indian sugar plantation, *c.*1870	184
13.1	Kano in the nineteenth century	192
13.2	Modern photo of the dye pits at Kano	193
13.3	Ife bronzes	195
13.4	View of Benin, Nigeria *c.*1846	197
13.5	Benin bronze plaque, formerly mounted on the wooden walls of the *Oba's* palace, and looted by the British in 1897	198
13.6	Benin ivory salt cellar	198
13.7	Some of the gold regalia of the Asante monarch	201
13.8	The Asantehene Opoku Ware II (r.1970–99), in full royal regalia	202
14.1	Fishers on the Congo River	203
14.2	Ndzinga, *Ngola* of Ndongo (1624–63) and Queen of Matamba (1629–63), negotiating with the Portuguese governor of Luanda on behalf of her brother *Ngola* in 1622	206
14.3	Cowrie shells (from the Indian Ocean) were widely used as currency in Africa from the sixteenth century	209
14.4	Pre-colonial mining in central Africa in the 1890s	212
14.5	The capital of Buganda, as seen by H.M. *Stanley*, 8 April 1875	215
14.6	Maasai women in eastern Africa, carrying their children on their backs, 1939	216
15.1	Khoesan-European trading at Table Bay, seventeenth century	219
15.2	Khoesan about to set up home, by the English artist Samuel Daniell, who was at the Cape 1801–3	222
15.3	Griqua men riding oxen	223
15.4	A typical Tswana house of southern Africa, painted by the English artist Samuel Daniell in 1804	226
15.5	The interior of a Zulu homestead on the Tugela River	228
16.1	The Segu palace of Ahmadu, ruler of the Tukolor empire after the death of al-Hajj Umar in 1864	234
16.2	Portrait of Samori Touré	235
16.3	Mandinka iron foundry, used for making and repairing guns to fight the French in the 1880s and 1890s	236

16.4	Portrait of the anti-slavery campaigner Olaudah Equiano by Daniel Orme, 1789	239
16.5	The British navy anti-slavery squadron attacks a slave establishment on the Solyman River, Sierra Leone, 1849	240
16.6	Trading canoes on the Niger River, nineteenth-century engraving	242
16.7	A trading station on the lower Niger in the 1890s	242
16.8	New settlers for Sierra Leone: a nineteenth-century engraving	244
17.1	The rubber industry in the Belgian Congo – thumping rubber to remove particles of wood and fibre	249
17.2	*Litunga* Lewanika I, in the early 1900s, aboard one of his smaller barges, preparing to depart from his summer dwelling as the annual floodwaters of the Zambezi rise	250
17.3	The Paramount Chief's royal barge, the *Nalikwanda*, Barotseland, Northern Rhodesia (now Zambia) in the 1950s	250
17.4	Yao slave-trader, southern Malawi, in the 1860s	253
17.5	The slave market at Zanzibar	257
17.6	Portrait of 'Tippu Tip' (Hamed bin Muhammed) (*c*.1837–1905), slave and ivory raider/trader and sometime agent of the sultan of Zanzibar	260
17.7	Mlozi and his slave-raiders, Karonga, Lake Malawi, 1890	261
18.1	Mgungundlovu, the Zulu capital in the reign of Dingane, 1838	265
18.2	Utimini, Shaka's nephew, in Zulu ceremonial battledress	266
18.3	Moshoeshoe's mountain stronghold of Thaba-Bosiu, water colour by Charles Davidson Bell, 1834	268
18.4	Moshoeshoe (in top hat) and counsellors in the 1860s	269
18.5	Ndebele town, showing cattle enclosure, in the 1890s	270
18.6	An incident in the Cape-Xhosa wars: the destruction of Stock's Kraal on the Keiskamma River, during the Eighth Frontier War, 21 June 1851	273
18.7	To escape British rule and secure 'free' land for themselves, Boer families emigrated northwards from the Cape Colony into what had hitherto been independent African territory. Here they cross the Drakensberg to enter the south-eastern lowveld where they came into conflict with the powerful kingdom of the Zulus	275
18.8	Portrait of Dingane, brother and assassin of Shaka, and King of the Zulus, 1828–40	277
19.1	An incident in the Algerian wars of resistance, 1830–79	282
19.2	Tuareg man working in his vegetable garden in the oasis, Djanet, Sahara Desert, Algeria	283
19.3	Muhammad Ali, *pasha* of Egypt 1805–49	285
19.4	Construction of the Suez Canal	288
19.5	Crowds watch a procession of ships on the Suez Canal, *c*.1874	289
19.6	The suicide of Emperor Tewodros II of Ethiopia, after his defeat by the British at the battle of Magdala, 1868	293
19.7	The battle of Adwa in which Menelik's Ethiopian forces defeated the Italians: Brigadier General Dabormida's troops encounter fierce resistance	294
20.1	Bishop Samuel Ajayi Crowther (*c*.1806–1891)	299

20.2	African Lakes Company (ALC) ivory warehouse, Karonga, 1904	302
20.3	The Ethiopian capital of Gondar, as observed by James Bruce in the 1770s	304
20.4	Richard Burton, traveller and fluent Arabic-speaker, in the costume he wore as a pilgrim to Mecca	306
20.5	Chuma, explorer companion to David Livingstone	308
20.6	Stanley on the Congo River	309
21.1	The German eagle swooping over Africa: a British cartoonist's view of German ambitions in east Africa, *Punch* 1890	315
21.2	A French gunboat suppresses African resistance in Dahomey (now Benin)	317
21.3	Soldiers of the British Royal Niger Company form a square to attack the camp of the Emir of Lapaie and subdue West African resistance to British colonial efforts	320
21.4	Plunder at Benin, 1897	321
21.5	Leopold II, King of the Belgians	323
21.6	The ruins of Zanzibar Palace after bombardment by British forces, as shown in a British magazine of 10th October 1896	326
22.1	The diamond mines at Kimberley	329
22.2	Workers following the compressed air drill in a gold mine at Johannesburg, South Africa	332
22.3	Rhodes straddling the continent, a *Punch* cartoon of 1892	223
22.4	*Litunga* Lewanika II (1878–84, 1885–1916) meeting with British officials at the Lozi capital, Lealui, October 1897	335
22.5	The trading station at Tete on the Zambezi, early 1900s	338
22.6	A group of Boers after a bushbuck hunt; a lull in the fighting during the South African War of 1899–1902	342
23.1	The lifestyle to which early colonial administrators aspired	343
23.2	The Belgian King Leopold II shown as a serpent whose rubber coils are crushing the people of the Congo (a *Punch* cartoon, November 1906)	346
23.3	Opening ceremony for a new Nigeria Railways station at Ibadan	348
23.4	The first copper-smelting furnace in Rhodesia in the early 1900s used African technology	349
23.5	Captured Herero, during the rising of 1904–6	352
23.6	John Chilembwe's Providence Industrial Mission, Mbombwe, Nyasaland (Malawi), *c*.1912	354
23.7	Chilembwe's Mission Church at Mbombwe, before and after its destruction by colonial troops, 26 January 1915	354
23.8	Rhodesian African Regiment on route march through Salisbury bound for east Africa, First World War	357
23.9	Von Lettow-Vorbeck, the undefeated German military commander, and his east African *askaris,* Kasama, northern Rhodesia, November 1918	358
23.10	Preparation of a troop train at Lome ahead of the Anglo-French conquest of Togoland (now Togo)	359
23.11	African machine-gun detachment, eastern Belgian Congo, 1916	359

24.1 Two advertisements published by the Empire Marketing
       Board 1927–33   362
24.2 Workers on a colonial cotton plantation, Magomero,
       Nyasaland (Malawi), 1908   363
24.3 Workers in the Nigerian tin-mines   365
24.4 Frederick Lugard (1858–1945), colonial administrator,
       established British military control of Uganda (1890–2)   368
24.5 The Sultan of Sokoto, the religious head of Hausaland, and
       spiritual leader of the nation's Muslims, 1903   369
24.6 The presentation of gifts to a chief by a colonial official as
       the British assume control of Zomba district in the Zambezi
       valley, Northern Rhodesia, June 1902   370
24.7 Lagos, Nigeria. Bird's-eye view of the port, c.1870   371
24.8 Marcus Garvey, then head of the Universal Negro
       Improvement Association and self-styled 'Provisional
       President of the Republic of Africa', rides through Harlem
       in his formal uniform   375
24.9 The African National Congress delegation to London, 1914   377
25.1 In the name of 'progress', the Italians conquered the
       Ethiopians in 1936 by dropping poison gas from the air:
       revenge for their humiliation at Adwa, 1896   381
25.2 Abyssinian officers in traditional dress, loyal to Emperor
       Haile Selassie, in Addis Ababa during the Italo-Ethiopian
       war, c.1936   382
25.3 British colonial troops in action on National Highway 1,
       also known as the road to Mandalay, Burma, c.1944   383
25.4 De Gaulle's Brazzaville conference, January 1944   387
26.1 Successful Nigerian businessman Louis Ojokwu worked on
       many Nigerian infrastructure projects in collaboration with
       the British firm Costain in the 1950s   390
26.2 Kwame Nkrumah (1909–1972), first prime minister and
       later president of Ghana, 1954–66   392
26.3 Prime Minister of Sierra Leone Sir Milton Margai (1895–1964)   394
26.4 A Félix Houphouët-Boigny (1905–1993)   395
       B Léopold Senghor (1906–2001)   395
26.5 A scene from the Algerian war of liberation   397
26.6 Gamal 'Abd al-Nasir (1918–1969)   399
27.1 Julius Nyerere (1922–1999)   402
27.2 Milton Obote (b.1924)   404
27.3 Arrested Mau-Mau suspects held by police in Kenya,
       Nairobi 1960   405
27.4 Jomo Kenyatta (c.1894–1978)   407
27.5 Tom Mboya (1930–69)   407
27.6 Ghanian UN troops in the Congo 1961   412
28.1 The opening session of the All-African People's Conference
       in Accra, Ghana, 8 December 1958   418
28.2 Front page of the *Nyasaland Times* at the time of the
       'state of emergency', 1959   419
28.3 Political 'education' in ZIPRA (Zimbabwe Independence
       People's Revolutionary Army) training in Zambia in the
       1970s   421

28.4   Portuguese soldiers talk with an Angolan man during a
       patrol on September 10, 1974 near Santa Eulalia   424
28.5   The Sharpeville massacre, 21 March 1960, marked a
       turning point in the political history of southern Africa 428
28.6   Frontline leaders at a conference on Namibia held in
       Lusaka, 1980   430
28.7   In one of the crowning events of twentieth-century Africa,
       South Africans of all races queued for many hours at polling
       stations across the country   431
29.1   Ghana's Akosombo Dam   440
29.2   Tanzanian *ujamaa* village committee   444
29.3   Women weeding crops in Zimbabwe   446
30.1   Loading hardwood for export at the Victoria Falls
       marshalling yard, Zimbabwe   449
30.2   The 'youth group' of Dlaba on their community-owned
       field hoeing the soil between millet plants by hand, a
       ccompanied by live music   453
30.3   The OAU summit in Tripoli, August 1982, was boycotted
       by one-third of the African heads of state. Leaders who
       attended included, seated here President Moussa Traore of
       Mali, *left*, and President Julius Nyerere of Tanzania with
       Colonel Gaddafi   454
31.1   Mathare informal township, Nairobi, Kenya, December
       2010   459
31.2   Abdoulaye Wade, elected president of Senegal in 2000,
       addressing the World Economic Forum in Davos,
       Switzerland, January 2004   465
32.1   Mwai Kibaki, leader of the National Rainbow Coalition
       (NARC) is greeted warmly by President Thabo Mbeki of
       South Africa in Pretoria, August 2003   470
32.2   A health education poster in Botswana, 1997   480

Acknowledgements

The author and publishers wish to thank the following for permission to reproduce their photographs and illustrations in *History of Africa*:

Figure 1.1 Copyright Jenny Pate/Robert Harding; Figure 1.2 © The Hunterian, University of Glasgow; Figures 1.3, 8.5 © Sarah Errington/Eye Ubiquitous/Hutchison; Figures 1.4, 6.2 © John Egan/Eye Ubiquitous/ Hutchison; Figures 2.1, 6.1, 9.5 © Tim Beddow/Eye Ubiquitous/Hutchison; Figure 2.3 akg-images/Erich Lessing; Figures 2.6, 7.3, 13.6, 20.6, 22.2 The Granger Collection, New York/TopFoto/TopFoto.co.uk; Figures 2.5, 2.7, 2.8, 2.9, 5.2 Michael Holford; Figures 2.10, 2.11 Copyright Robert Harding; Figures 3.1, 13.1 INTERFOTO/Sammlung Rauch/Mary Evans; Figure 3.2 Werner Forman Archive/National Museum, Lagos, National Commission of Museums & Monuments, Nigeria. Location: 02; Figure 3.3 Werner Forman Archive/Sudan Archaeological Museum, Khartoum. Location: 138; Figure 3.4 from *Meroe: A Civilization of the Sudan*, pp. 18–19, Fig. 3. by P. L. Shinnie, Thames & Hudson Ltd, London; Figure 3.5 Werner Forman Archive. Location: 138; Figure 3.6 Werner Forman Archive/Musee Bardo, Algiers. Location: 23; Figures 1.5, 10.1, 10.4, 10.6, 14.3, 14.4A, 14.4B, 14.4C, 14.4D, 17.2, 17.4, 17.7, 18.5, 20.2, 20.5, 22.4, 22.5, 23.1, 23.4, 23.6, 23.7A, 23.7B, 23.8, 23.9, 23.11, 24.2, 24.6, 28.2, 28.3, 28.6 National Archives of Zimbabwe; Figures 4.3 (University of Cape Town Collection), 11.1, 22.1, akg-images; Figure 5.1 © Bettmann/ CORBIS; Figure 5.3 Werner Forman Archive. Location: 70; Figures 5.4, 7.6, 9.1, 12.5, 13.4, 18.7, 19.6, 19.7, 20.1, 20.3, 20.4, 21.1, 21.2, 22.3, 23.2, 24.4, 24.7 Mary Evans Picture Library; Figure 6.3 Ghana Film Industry; Figure 6.4 (left) Werner Forman Archive/The Nigerian Museum, Lagos; Figure 6.4 (right) Werner Forman Archive/National Commission For Museums And Monuments, Lagos. Location: 03; Figure 7.1 © Thelma Sanders/Eye Ubiquitous/Hutchison; Figures 7.2, 7.5 Werner Forman Archive. Location: 30; Figure 7.4 Copyright David Poole/Robert Harding; Figure 8.1 © Ann Usborne/Eye Ubiquitous/Hutchison; Figures 8.2, 9.4, 17.6, 19.3, 19.4, 21.5 Hulton Archive/Getty Images; Figure 8.3 Werner Forman Archive/Location: 71; Figure 9.2 Mark Horton; Figures 9.3, 9.7 Werner Forman Archive. Location: 60; Figures 9.6, 13.3A, 13.3B, 14.1 © Eye Ubiquitous/Hutchison; Figure 10.2 PP.O.O.1643, coll. RMCA Tervuren, RMCA Tervuren ©; Figures 0.1A, 2.2, 4.1, 10.5A, 10.5B, 10.5C, 10.5D, 10.5E, 32.2 Kevin Shillington; Figure 10.7 Tim Maggs; Figure 11.2 © Jenny Pate/Eye Ubiquitous/Hutchison; Figure 11.3 © Robert Francis/Eye Ubiquitous/Hutchison; Figure 11.4 Copyright Andrew McConnell/Robert Harding; Figure 11.5 © Julia Bayne/Eye Ubiquitous/Hutchison; Figure 11.6 Copyright Michael Short/Robert Harding; Figures 12.1, 12.2 Werner Forman Archive. Location: 46; Figure 12.4 Rischgitz/Hulton Archive/Getty Images; Figures 12.3, 23.3 Universal Images Group/Getty Images; Figure

Preface

The purpose of this *History of Africa*, now in its third revised edition, is to provide a clear, basic and well-illustrated introduction to Africa's long and fascinating past, which is easily understood by the non-specialist general reader or student and at the same time is based upon the results of some of the most recent and up-to-date research. The book pays particular attention to social, economic, political and religious developments and the way in which these affect the lives of ordinary people. At the same time, I have sought to provide a critical but chronological narrative which covers most of the major developments and societies on the continent and touches on many of the themes that have most concerned historians in recent decades.

Starting from the earliest evolution of humankind, the book traces the history of Africa through the millennia of the Stone Age to the rise and decline of the states and societies of Africa in the ancient and medieval worlds. Through the more recent centuries of increasing European intervention, the focus has remained upon the indigenous African viewpoints, developments and initiatives. Finally, I have attempted to place the post-colonial problems of political, social and economic development in their proper historical context and so avoid the strongly negative tone of so much modern writing about contemporary Africa.

A number of important changes have been made to this third revised edition. Some of these changes have been based upon advice received by the publishers, Palgrave Macmillan, from academics who have used, or considered using, this text as a teaching tool for students, especially in universities in north America. I am extremely grateful to those historians and teachers who took the time to offer advice on ways to improve the previous edition and who have commented upon my proposed changes to the current edition. I have borne in mind their words of wisdom and have incorporated as many of their suggestions as I have considered practicable in a work of this scope. Many of these historians expressed a desire for greater coverage of historiographical debates, the complexity of historical interpretation and the point that history is so much more than a simple narrative of events. So as not to overburden the clarity of the text of this book, which I believe has been one of its strengths, these issues have been included in a companion website which now accompanies the text, for more of which, see below.

As in previous editions, I have made small revisions and clarifications throughout the book to reflect the findings of recent research and publications. But I have also expanded or extensively revised coverage in the following areas. There is a new introduction which provides a brief overview of African historiography, from the ancient recording and passing on of historical events and personalities through to the trends and influences that have characterised or stimulated the writings of modern professional historians. This is followed by a survey of the physical geography, climate and natural vegetation of the continent. Following the environmental theme, the initial chapter on human evolution and the Stone Age has been substantially rewritten and updated, especially in the light of recent research on the likely impact of climate change over the millennia of early human prehistory. The dynastic time-chart for Ancient Egypt has been moved to the website and there has been a substantial expansion in the treatment of Christianity in north Africa in the early centuries of the common era, thus clarifying the beliefs and significance of Donatists and Monophysites in the early Christian Church.

Oral history is reconsidered as a source of evidence for the empire of Mali. Coverage of the founding of Sierra Leone has been expanded, as has that of Somalia, throughout, from medieval to modern times in order to provide some understanding of the problems that have beset that state in recent decades. The Napoleonic occupation of Egypt now gets fuller coverage, along with its significance for the modernising state of Egypt and the study of Egyptology. There is a new section on the emergence of a nascent African 'nationalism', and even Pan-Africanism, among certain nineteenth-century west Africans in the decades before the colonial conquest. And there is expanded coverage of the First World War, including the significance for Africa of Woodrow Wilson's 'Fourteen Points', the Versailles Conference and the League of Nations.

Some of the more contemporary chapters have been reconfigured, with two additional chapters, bringing the total up to thirty-two. Within this coverage, both general themes and regional surveys have been brought right up to date, and besides expansion of the coverage on globalisation, there are new sections on international aid and the problems of aid dependence, climate change, the impact of HIV/AIDS, and the significance of China in contemporary Africa.

Perhaps the most significant innovation for this edition is the companion website, which is intended as an aid for students and teachers as well as a source of additional information and insights into historiographical debates and themes. The website contains chapter by chapter synopses, with key points to remember for each chapter and, where appropriate, cross-references to other chapters in the book which carry related themes or continuing narrative developments. Each chapter reference on the website contains essay and/or study questions, some related to illustrations and maps, as well as more extensive, partially annotated, bibliographies, to supplement those works listed at the end of the book.

The website contains digital copies of all 96 of the specially drawn historical maps that appear in the book. These will thus be available for comparative work across period and regions, and exercises have been designed to promote these possibilities. At certain strategic points in the margins of the book there are web pointers which refer the reader to further related information on the topic or to deeper discussion of historiographical developments, debates or controversies. The book thus relates the history, while the evolving companion website will not only help the student to understand and thus learn the history, but will also lead the reader through the process of historical construction. One thing that I hope any student will learn from this book and its website is that nothing in history is definitive: it is all subject to interpretation.

My debt to fellow-historians of Africa is immeasurable and ongoing – their works are referenced in the Further Reading list at the end of the book and chapter by chapter in the website. I have read widely of their work and only hope that my interpretation does some justice to their efforts. My thanks are due to Sonya Barker, my commissioning editor, and her team at Palgrave, for their deep commitment and enthusiasm for the project, and to Penny Simmons for meticulously copy editing the finished manuscript. Finally, as ever, I dedicate this book to Pippa, without whose unstinting encouragement and support I could never have undertaken yet another edition.

Kevin Shillington
Dorset

Introduction

Before we begin this particular history of the African continent, it is first of all useful to understand how the recording of Africa's history (its 'historiography') has developed. It is also beneficial to gain an appreciation of the physical makeup and climate of the continent, due to their impact on the humans who have lived there through the ages.

Historiography

The writing of Africa's history has taken many forms over the centuries. The Ancient Egyptians, who invented one of the world's oldest scripts, hieroglyphics, recorded their history on papyrus scrolls, on the walls of temples and tombs, and carved into solid pillars of rock. They certainly wanted people of the future to know about their history, even if it was often little more than king-lists and fantastic stories of the military prowess of their rulers. Ethiopians too were literate from at least the fifth century and aspects of their history were recorded in religious and regal texts and in works of literature. The most prominent recorders of Africa's history from the ninth to sixteenth century were Arabic-speaking north-African scholars. They wrote both the history of their own societies and that of the peoples of '*al-Sudan*' (the 'land of the black people'), south of the Sahara, whom they had heard about through trading contacts or had visited themselves. But it was not only outsiders who wrote the history of al-Sudan. In the seventeenth century a local Muslim scholar of Timbuktu, named 'Abd al-Rahman al-Sa'di, chronicled the history of the Songhay empire in the *Ta'rikh al-Sudan*. Similarly, in the trading cities of the east-African coast, local Swahili-speaking scholars recorded some of their history, using Arabic script. Much of these early forms of African history were heavily dependent upon the local oral traditions of the time. Today they form the basis of much of our understanding of those distant times.

Meanwhile in the pre-literate societies of much of sub-Saharan Africa, people had their own way of recording and interpreting their history, passing it from one generation to the next through the recitation of oral tradition. Some of this, such as the *Sundjata Epic* (see p. 100) took the form of performance art that persists to this day.

The modern discipline of history, based upon the strict rules of evidence and the principles of interpretation, only began to be developed in Europe from the late eighteenth century. There they had an abundance of written records dealing with all aspects of life, especially the affairs of government. And the kind of history that this emerging class of historians wrote assumed the primacy of official written records. Indeed, the prevalent belief among European historians of the nineteenth century was that without written records there was no history. They applied this principle to Africa during the period of colonisation from the late nineteenth century and concluded that Africa south of the Sahara had little or no history of significance before the coming of Europeans. This coincided with their views of racial superiority, which they used to justify their colonial conquests. These racist prejudices seriously impeded the study and writing of African history for at least the next half-century.

In spite of this atmosphere of European dominance, a small number of Western-educated Africans wrote some important works of history in this turbulent conquest period, for example Carl Christian Reindorf's *A History of the Gold Coast and Asante* (1895), Samuel Johnson's *History of the Yorubas* (1897) and Apollo Kaggwa's *The Kings of Buganda* (1901).

With the awakening of African nationalism after the Second World War, there was a great revival in the study and writing of African history. Centres of African studies were set up in European universities and new university colleges were established in east and west Africa. Together, African historians and their counterparts in Europe produced pioneering works on pre-colonial African history. A particularly important work of methodology in this period was Jan Vansina's *Oral history* (1961) which showed how oral tradition could be effectively utilised as a valid resource by the modern professional historian.

The ultimate inspiration for much of this 'Africanist' historiography of the independence period was twofold. First, it was to prove that Africa had a history at least the equal of that of Europe. This inevitably led to a focus on the great states and empires of the past at the expense of smaller societies that tended to be dismissed as 'stateless'. Second, there was a desire to produce 'national' histories to fit the new nation-states that were gaining their independence in the 1950s and 1960s. Part of the purpose of these 'national histories' was to reinforce the idea that the peoples within the new colonially created boundaries had a common history.

By the 1970s the euphoria of independence had begun to give way to disillusionment. The new political elites had followed European models of development that had clearly failed to deliver. At this point a Marxist school of history began to emerge. This saw African society in class terms and argued that Africa's problems stemmed from the exploitation of the capitalist system that had been forced upon Africa by colonialism. Indeed, Walter Rodney's highly influential *How Europe Underdeveloped Africa* (1972) argued that the roots of Africa's current problems of underdevelopment could be traced back to the slave trade, upon which Europe's industrial development was ultimately based. Although many historians of Africa did not subscribe to Rodney's radical view, his work and that of others in this period turned the focus away from that of great empires of the past and on to the history of the peasantry, migrant workers, domestic servants. Their 'heroic' struggles within the capitalist system, principally during the colonial period, had clear implications for the unresolved problems of the post-colonial present.

Since the collapse of the communist Soviet Union in 1991 and the consequent undermining of Marxist theory, historians of Africa have felt freer to study a wide range of social, economic and political issues, from the role of gender in African history to that of religion and ethnicity. Behind this movement has been a desire to better understand the problems in the Africa of the present. Thus, little of this work has been concerned with Africa's pre-colonial past, which perhaps is considered too distant to be of relevance.

One school of African historical writing particularly prevalent in North America is known as Afrocentrism or Afrocentricity. To some extent this is a reaction to the Eurocentric intellectual ideas that drove the Marxist class analysis of African history in the 1970s and 1980s. The inspiration for Afrocentrism has been the Senegalese historian Cheikh Anta Diop, whose work, originally published in French in 1954, was republished in English in 1974 as *The African Origin of Civilization: Myth or Reality?* Diop argued that Ancient Egypt was a black African civilisation upon which the civilisations of Greece, Rome and ultimately modern Europe were built. Diop certainly turned attention to the Africanness of the Ancient Egyptians, which subsequent research by others has largely borne out. But Diop went on to argue that all civilisations in Africa stemmed from Ancient Egypt, which implied that Africans elsewhere were not able to develop their own distinctive civilisations. Perhaps this is why modern Afrocentrism has not gained as much credibility as one might expect within Africa itself. As a school of history, it is more popular among African-Americans, which is perhaps more of a reflection on their own society in North America.

As the present book is a general introductory survey of the whole sweep of African history from ancient times to the present, it draws to some extent upon all of these approaches to the discipline. It can thus, for instance, be found within both the Africanist pre-colonial tradition as well as utilising elements of a Marxist critique in its analysis of modern African history.

Geography, climate and vegetation

The way that the globe is flattened out into the maps of a modern atlas tends to exaggerate the size of the northern hemisphere and disguise the true scale of Africa which straddles the centre of the globe. Africa is in fact the second largest continent, second only to Asia in size and far larger than the whole of North America. It is the only continent that encompasses both the northern and the southern tropics, 23 degrees north and south of the Equator. The (northern) Tropic of Cancer passes through the middle of the Sahara while the (southern) Tropic of Capricorn passes through the Namibian and Kalahari deserts, some 1200 kilometres north of the Cape of Good Hope. Africa thus experiences a huge range of climate between the temperate Mediterranean zone along the northern coastline to its equivalent at the Cape in the south.

The seasonal rainfall of tropical Africa generally occurs when the sun is overhead at midday, when heat and water evaporation from the oceans are at their highest levels. Then onshore winds from the Indian and Atlantic oceans carry moist air over the continent where it falls in heavy storms. The region near the Tropic of Capricorn thus experiences a single rainy season in the months around the summer solstice of late December, and an extended dry season from April through to October. The equatorial region – up to about 8 degrees latitude either side of the equator – sees the overhead sun in both the March and September equinoxes and thus experiences two rainy seasons, with much shorter dry periods in between.

The northern tropical region, like its southern equivalent, experiences a single summer rainy season and a prolonged dry winter season, at least as far as Latitude 15 degrees north – that is, approximately from the Senegal River

Figure 0.1 The author at the Equator in 1995

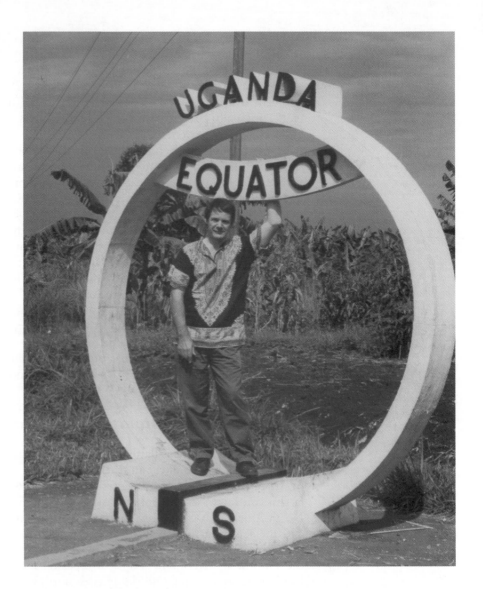

in the west to Lake Chad in the centre, to Khartoum on the Nile in the east. Further north the effect of the overhead sun is disrupted by cold Atlantic currents and offshore winds which deflect moist air away from north-western Africa just when temperatures are at their hottest. A consequence of this is the Sahara, the world's largest desert, which straddles the Tropic of Capricorn and dominates the northern third of the continent. In a similar fashion, in south-western Africa cold currents and offshore winds divert moist air away from the continent, resulting in the Namib and Kalahari deserts. Beyond these desert regions, the temperate coastal Mediterranean and southern Cape receive most of their rainfall in the northern and southern winter months.

The general pattern of Africa's vegetation is centred upon the equatorial rainforest of the Congo Basin and the southern coastal region of west Africa (see Map 0.1). North and south of the equatorial zone the forest gives way in turn to woodland savannah, grasslands and the dry scrub and thornveld of the desert margins. The equatorial rainforest does not extend into the east of the continent, however, as eastern and southern Africa are dominated by a

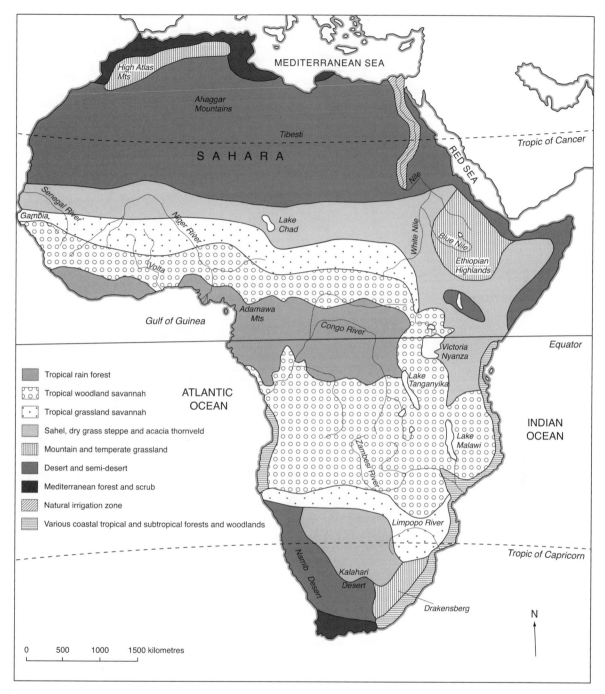

Map 0.1 The physical geography of Africa

plateau which, within a few hundred kilometres of the coast, rises to a height of between 1000 and 2000 metres above sea level. This ensures that the natural vegetation of equatorial east Africa is composed mostly of woodland savannah, grasslands and thornveld.

Africa has no massive mountain range like the Rockies, the Andes or the Himalayas that are so prominent in other continents. Africa's principal

5

Map 0.2 The vegetation of modern Africa

mountain ranges are the High Atlas of Morocco in the north-west, the Ethiopian Highlands of the north-east and the Drakensberg in the south-east. Other mountains of significance are the Adamawa highlands, situated in that great bend of Africa where the west–east coastline of west Africa turns southwards; and the highlands of Guinea, in the western region of west Africa. The latter giving rise to two great west African rivers, the Niger and the Senegal. Snow-capped Mount Kenya and Kilimanjaro are notable features of east Africa, while the Ruwenzori mountains mark the boundary between the Congo Basin and the east-African plateau.

The same forces that led to the world's continents drifting apart many millions of years ago also resulted in a geographical scar that cuts through the eastern side of Africa, known as the east-African Rift. The Rift Valley runs from the Red Sea and Djibouti in the Gulf of Aden, through the Ethiopian Highlands to Lake Turkana where it divides. The western Rift forms the string of lakes and highlands that divide east Africa from the Congo Basin, including the 600 kilometre length of Lake Tanganyika, while the eastern Rift cuts through the central Kenyan Highlands and extends into what is today northern Tanzania. The two branches of the Rift rejoin at Lake Malawi. Between the eastern and western Rift lies the shallow basin of Lake Victoria Nyanza, commonly held to be the source of the Nile, although the true source of that great river is beyond the lake in the mountains to the west.

At nearly 7000 kilometres, the Nile is the world's longest river and the only one of Africa's major rivers to flow northwards, out-flowing via a delta into the eastern Mediterranean. Halfway along its journey to the sea the slow-flowing main river, known as the White Nile, is joined by the Blue Nile which rises in Ethiopia. The latter, when in flood, carries fertile silt in a seasonal torrent from the highlands of Ethiopia and, in days gone by before the twentieth-century damming of the Nile, deposited it on the floodplain of the lower Nile Valley, literally bringing life to the arid desert of Egypt.

Africa's two other largest rivers, the Niger and the Congo both flow into the Atlantic. The Niger begins its journey in the highlands of Guinea, flowing north-eastwards through a multitude of channels, swamps and small lakes known as the 'Inland Delta' before reuniting into a single channel in the dry savannah lands south of the Sahara. Here, through the 'Niger Bend', the river flows round to the south-east, heading towards the forests of southern Nigeria, where it splits into a massive delta that pushes out into the Gulf of Guinea near where the coastline of west Africa turns south towards the equator.

The Congo River rises from the plateau south of the equatorial forest. Known as the Lualaba in its upper reaches, the river flows north through a series of cataracts in the east of the forest before turning west just north of the equator. There then follow 1500 kilometres of wide, navigable waterway, as the river flows south-westwards to the basin of Malebo Pool, picking up numerous major tributaries such as the Ubangui and the Kasai. From the historic trading terminus of Malebo Pool the river tumbles down 300 kilometres of cataracts into the Atlantic Ocean six degrees south of the equator.

Other African rivers worth noting include the Zambezi, which rises near the source of the Lualaba (Congo), but then flows south and east, away from the Congo Basin to enter the Indian Ocean on the east African coast. The Orange River rises in the high Drakensberg and flows westwards through the drylands bordering the southern Kalahari and Namib deserts, before entering the Atlantic on Africa's south-west coast. In west Africa the Senegal River rises in the Guinea highlands, flowing north-west and west to enter the Atlantic in the north of the modern republic of Senegal.

All of these rivers and their many tributaries have been integral to the history of humanity in Africa; not only as a source of water in arid zones or as a means of communication through thick forest, but their fertile flood deposits have also played a vital role in the origins and development of African agriculture, which in turn has played a part in the growth of urbanisation and the rise of states.

Early prehistory of Africa

Human evolution

The continent of Africa has a longer human history than any other continent in the world. When the English naturalist Charles Darwin first proposed his theory of evolution (*The Origin of Species*, 1859; and *The Descent of Man,* 1871), he suggested that the birthplace of humankind was probably Africa, and scientific research over the past three-quarters of a century has shown his supposition to have been correct.

Evidence: fossils, dating and climate change

Africa is the only continent in which evidence has been found for man's early evolution. The material evidence for human evolution depends largely upon the recovery and examination of ancient bones, fossils, stone tools and other artefacts.

Fossils are formed when animal or plant remains are trapped in mud that is then squeezed under great geological pressure to form rock. All that remains of the organic matter within the rock is an exact imprint (a fossil) that is revealed if the rock is broken open, by further natural process or by human intervention. Scientific geological methods can be used to give an approximate age to the formation of rocks and hence to their fossils.

The Potassium-Argon dating technique measures the changing ratio between these two elements during radioactive decay in rocks that are over a million years old. It is particularly useful for the volcanic rocks of Ethiopia and the East African Rift. Radiocarbon dating measures the radioactive decay of Carbon-14 atoms in dead organic matter such as bones and charcoal that is less than 40,000 years old. It cannot measure a precise age, but offers instead a probable age range and is most useful in providing a chronology rather than a particular date.

The modern study of genetics has also been an important tool for tracing relationships between ancient peoples and the movement of people both within and out of Africa.

Archaeologists have recently come to appreciate the importance of climate change as a potential influencing element in early human development and behaviour. The earth has gone through many changes in climate during the millions of years of its existence, and scientists are able to measure past climates by taking deep borings from the ice sheet, particularly in Greenland. From these, and from borings into the ocean floor, it is possible to measure the climate of the distant past.

At times the world's climate has been a lot colder than at present, with the ice-coverage of the poles being extended well into the temperate zones of

Europe, Asia and North America. These ultra-cold periods, often lasting for thousands of years, are commonly known as 'ice ages'. Africa lies beyond the range of the northern and southern ice-sheets, but during the ice ages of the past, with much of the world's fresh water – and thus potential rain – tied up in ice, Africa experienced these periods as times of extreme dryness. Deserts expanded and the rainforest contracted, sometimes into isolated 'islands' of forest growth in the heart of the Congo Basin. Many animals could not cope with the changed environment and became extinct, and early humans had to adapt or die.

There have been times, too, when climate has been a lot warmer than at present. In those periods, the ice-sheets melted, extra moisture was released into the air and Africa experienced much higher rainfall. Then the rainforest expanded, rivers flowed where today is only desert, and the Sahara itself was covered in savannah grassland.

The earliest hominins

In terms of evolution modern human beings belong to the primate family of 'hominins'. Hominin (formerly known as hominid) is a general biological name for human or humanlike creatures with enlarged brains and the ability to walk upright on two legs. For tens of thousands of years modern human beings have been the only surviving hominins. But in the early stages of human evolution there were a number of different species. From the evidence of fossils it appears that many millions of years ago the earliest species of hominin evolved away from the other main family of primates, the great African forest apes: the gorilla and the chimpanzee.

There are significant gaps in the fossil evidence and so little is known about the earliest hominins. But it appears that sometime between about ten million and five million years ago, perhaps during a glacial dry period when the tropical forest contracted, they moved into the more open savannah grasslands and woodlands of east Africa. There they began to develop the techniques of standing and walking on two legs. In terms of survival and evolution this had a number of distinct advantages. In the open savannah standing upright enabled them to see over the grassland and spot predators such as lion and leopard who hunted them for food. Those best able to stand upright survived longer, reproduced more and passed this advantage on to their descendants. A further highly important advantage of two-legged walking was that it left the hands free to carry food and use tools. Fingers no longer needed to be short and strong for hanging on to branches in the forest. The early hominins were able to evolve elongated fingers for performing intricate tasks and, eventually, for making their own tools.

The Australopithecines and early evolution of Homo (man)

The fossil record of the past five million years is continually being expanded with finds of early hominin fossils from eastern and southern Africa as well as the Sahara. The evidence up to 1.5 million years ago forms a complex story of the evolution and extinction of numerous related species of early hominin. Most of these belong to the genus known as *Australopithecus* ('southern ape'). They were largely scavengers, some vegetarian, others meat-eaters, and had a brain capacity less than a third that of modern humans. They were tool *users* rather than tool *makers*: they did not shape their own tools, but rather used whatever suitable sticks and stones they found available.

An important change occurred about 2.5 million years ago with the evolution of the first tool *makers*. Because of this important change these hominins

Figure 1.1 Olduvai Gorge, UNESCO World Heritage Site, Serengeti, Tanzania, East Africa

have been designated *Homo habilis* ('handy man'), the first of the genus *Homo*. A number of animals, such as chimpanzees, use sticks and other implements to assist in their foraging for food; but the ability to make and shape one's own tools and to use these tools for hunting as well as foraging does seem to set the *Homo* line apart from other animals and the Australopithecines. It is thought that modern humans may be descended from *Homo habilis,* although their brain capacity was still barely half that of modern human beings. Their stone tools, known as Oldowan (from the Olduvai Gorge in Kenya where they were first discovered), were simple chopping and cutting tools, made by chopping flakes off a volcanic pebble to form a sharp edge. Some of the flakes thus removed were probably also used for cutting or scraping skins and perhaps for whittling sticks. The final shape of the tool, however, was determined largely by the structure of the stone.

Some of the late species of *Australopithecus* continued to live alongside *Homo habilis*, but they found it increasingly difficult to compete for food with the more efficient *Homo* species. By the time of the next major evolutionary advance, 1.5 million years ago, the *Australopithecines* had all become extinct.

Technology and the 'Stone Ages' of Africa

From the middle of the last century it became customary for archaeologists and historians (including earlier editions of this book) to divide the period of stone tool-making in Africa into three 'ages', the Early, Middle and Late (or Later) Stone Ages. This periodisation placed the simple choppers and scrapers of the early *Homo* scavengers at one end of the spectrum and the precisely shaped and sharpened *microliths* ('tiny stones') of modern *Homo sapiens* ('wise man') hunter-gatherers at the other end. Archaeologists now, however, tend to consider this periodisation as too simplistic and even misleading. The system of ages necessarily implies primitivity for simple tools and advanced intellect for complex microliths. And yet, simple tools were often used alongside microliths, with no implication that they were evidence of the continued existence of more primitive people.

Thus, rather than slot a particular technology and its users into a particular 'age', the tendency nowadays among archaeologists and historians is to focus upon the technology and try to work out what it tells us about the people using the tools.

Climate change and the evolution of modern humans

Over the past two million years the earth has experienced numerous ice ages, some lasting a few hundred thousand years, others, just as severe, lasting only a few thousand, each age interspersed with warmer moist periods. With increasing evidence of the timing and extent of past climate change, archaeologists have come to appreciate the probable impact of these glacial cycles upon the evolution of the human species and their technology. For Africa the cool dry climate of the ice ages appears to have provided the greatest pressure for adaptation.

During the particularly long, dry glacial period of 1.8 million years ago to 1.6 million years ago, *Homo erectus* ('upright man') evolved and appears to have displaced the earlier *Homo habilis. Homo erectus* had a larger brain (two-thirds that of modern humans) and larger body, better able to roam great distances across the expanded open savannah. They were the first hominins to make specific and precise stone tools, to a predetermined shape. The tool for which they are best known is the handaxe, known as 'Acheulian' after the place in France where one was first discovered. The handaxe was a tough, sharp, heavy tool, chipped on both sides and shaped to a deliberate point (see Figure 1.2, p. 14). It could have been used for slicing, chopping or digging.

Archaeologists have found some beautifully made examples of the Acheulian handaxe which must have been the product of hours of skilled labour. Some may even have had symbolic ritual functions. There are certainly signs of some form of ritual or early religion with the beginnings of the deliberate burial of the dead. Furthermore, with *Homo erectus* we have the first sign of the use of regular, seasonal camps and cooperative hunting efforts as opposed to simple scavenging. They had also learned to control and use fire, possibly for hunting, certainly for roasting meat and probably also for warmth.

Homo erectus was the first hominin to move out of Africa into Asia and Europe. Evidence of their remains, or the tools they made between one million and just over half a million years ago have been found all over Africa, southern Europe and Asia, even as far away as China. Despite the French origin of the name, however, the vast majority of Acheulian tools have been found in Africa.

Between about one million and 500,000 years ago there was a great deal of climate and environmental instability. This must have put a great deal of pressure upon the African population of *Homo erectus* and by about 600,000 years ago they appear to have been replaced in the fossil record by the evolution of *Homo heidelbergensis*, the common ancestor of *Homo neanderthalus* and *Homo sapiens*. A skull found at Kabwe (Broken Hill) in Zambia in 1921 and dated to sometime after 400,000 years ago is a clear African example of *Heidelbergensis*. From the archaeological evidence of their camps we know

Map 1.1 The evolution of humankind in Africa

that about 500,000 years ago the social group size of *Heidelbergensis* had increased to about 150 individuals. This has given rise to the assumption that early forms of human language must have been developed by this time, language being the only way that a group of this size could have functioned together socially. Over the following 200,000 years their stone-tool technology became more complex, with stone, wood and bone being used in conjunction to make composite tools.

By 300,000 years ago *Heidelbergensis* had evolved the same brain size as modern humans and had begun to move into Asia and Europe. It was from these that the European Neanderthals evolved. Meanwhile, those Heidelbergs that remained in Africa gave way to modern *Homo sapiens* about 200,000 years ago.

Homo sapiens *populate the world*

The evolution of fully modern human beings appears to have occurred in the savannah woodlands of eastern and southern Africa. These people had the same brain capacity and ability to think as people in our own century. They were, in effect, the same as us. The only thing they lacked was our learned experience and accumulated knowledge. They were thus the original *pioneers* in the development of human thought, philosophy, religion and technology. Although population levels were still very low by today's standards, by 90,000 years ago *Homo sapiens* were to be found across most of the African continent. Modern DNA tracings show that all modern human populations stem from this African origin. They first migrated out of Africa about 60,000 years ago, during a particularly dry period when population levels in Africa were dangerously low. They appear to have crossed the Straits of Bab-el-Mandeb from Djibouti to Arabia and thence spread through southern Asia

Figure 1.2 Microliths and other artefacts of the African Stone Age
(a) Oldowan tools from the Olduvai gorge
(b) The characteristic Acheulian handaxe, from Kamoa, southern Congo
(c) (i) microliths; (ii) axe and arrow heads; (iii) decorated bored stone for weighting a digging stick; (iv) bone harpoon heads

to Malaysia and on to Australia. Other major migrations both in and out of Africa are thought to have occurred, via Sinai, between 45,000 and 40,000 years ago. By 12,000 years ago modern humans had spread to all the major regions of the world.

Since the earliest *Homo sapiens* came from tropical Africa, they were probably brown-skinned and similar in appearance to one or more of the many variations of African peoples today. As they spread throughout Africa and colonised the other continents of the world, they adapted to variations in climate and environment. Those in the heat of tropical Africa developed the darkest skin to protect them from the harmful rays of the direct tropical sun. Those moving to cooler climates developed paler skins in order to absorb more of the beneficial rays of the less direct sunlight. The so-called 'racial differences' between the various peoples of the world are thus literally only skin deep, local adaptations to climate and environment. All human beings belong to the same species, and the origins of that species are to be found in Africa.

The stone technology most closely associated with *Homo sapiens* is the *microlith*. Stone flakes were shaped and reshaped into tiny precise points and blades, sometimes in specific geometric shapes such as triangles and crescents. The thick edge of the blade was chipped back to make it steeper and stronger. These 'backed' blades were almost certainly hafted on to wooden shafts to form spears and arrows. One of the main advances in hunting technology during the period from 40,000 years ago was the development of the bow and arrow. This enabled a great improvement in hunting techniques. At the same time people made a wide range of fine bone tools: awls, needles, fish-hooks and barbs for arrows or harpoons. Furthermore, there is evidence of considerable artistic development from eggshell beads to adorn the person to the great works of rock painting and engraving found across many parts of Africa.

Homo sapiens, *the hunter-gatherer*

Until such time as people developed the techniques of growing their own food crops and taming their own animals, they relied for their livelihood upon hunting and gathering the wild animals and plants that grew naturally in the land. Even their tools and ornaments – made of stone, bone, leather or eggshell – were the product of natural materials gathered from the land.

Much of our knowledge about the way of life of these hunter-gatherers has come from extensive archaeological research, particularly over the past 40 years. Evidence of microlith technology has been found widespread throughout the savannah grasslands and dry woodlands of Africa. Perhaps the richest single source has been the excavation at Gwisho springs in the Kafue valley of central Zambia. Here in the waterlogged soils of the Kafue flats a unique range of vegetable matter as well as stone and bone materials have been preserved, together with as many as 30 human skeletons. The site dates to about 2000 BCE (Before the Common Era). This and other less dramatic sites in eastern, central and southern Africa reveal a fairly clear picture of a hunting and gathering way of life probably typical of many of the peoples of the savannah regions of Africa.

But perhaps the most vivid evidence surviving from these times is to be found in the paintings and engravings which the people themselves made on the rock walls of their caves and shelters. Examples of these have survived right across the drier regions of Africa from the mountains of the central Sahara in the north to the Drakensberg mountain range in the south. Their paints – mainly red, yellow, orange and white – were made from animal fats coloured with vegetable dyes and applied with sticks and feathers. Most show scenes of living creatures, animals and humans. Some appear to portray events such as hunting, fishing or dancing. Others are more abstract and may be inspired by religious beliefs about life, death and the spirit world.

Hunting

Careful study of the animal bones and stone artefacts recovered from their camp sites has revealed much about the hunting practices of these modern humans. In the savannah regions of Africa, they hunted a wide range of animals, large and small. Specially shaped microliths were glued and bound to wooden shafts to form multi-barbed spears, but perhaps the most important hunting weapon was the bow and arrow. The arrow shaft was tipped with a barbed point of stone or bone which had been treated with carefully

Figure 1.3 'Pygmy' boy sorting fishing nets in the Congo Basin

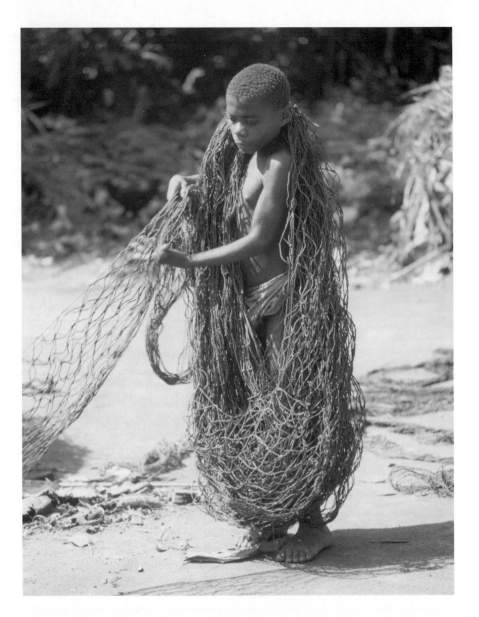

prepared vegetable poison. This enabled small groups of hunters to effectively hunt the large antelope and buffalo that ranged the plains of Africa. The poison, though slow to work, would eventually wear down even the largest animal. Many smaller animals were also caught in snares, traps and possibly nets. In the densely wooded areas of the tropical forest regions, the lightweight bow and arrow was not so widely used. Here larger, simpler tools and weapons were preferred as people hunted with traps, pits, spears and axes.

Hunted animals were not only a source of meat for diet: their bones were used for making tools and ornaments while the leather of their skins was a valuable raw material. Animal skins were scraped with sharp, thumb-sized stone scrapers. They were then dried, softened and used for clothing, shelter, leather thongs, gathering bags or slings for carrying babies.

Fishing

Most people took advantage of whatever food resources were readily available, including fishing in rivers and lakes. Fish are rich in protein and when abundant they are fairly easily caught in large numbers once the technology has been mastered. In some areas, such as western and southern Africa, shell-fish gathered from among the rocks along the coast became a dominant source of food, with important implications for the lifestyle of the communities involved. It demanded only a simple technology and encouraged the establishment of seasonal camps. Stranded seals were hunted at certain times of the year and bone-tipped harpoons, tidal traps and nets were also employed in active fishing.

Gathering

While the archaeological evidence for hunting and fishing is fairly easily interpreted, the evidence for gathering is not so obvious. Vegetable matter tends not to survive so well over the centuries as animal bones or the stone tips of spears and arrows. Twentieth-century studies of the few surviving hunter-gatherer communities, however, revealed that gathering accounted for up to three-quarters of the normal daily diet. There is no reason to suppose that gathering was any less important for the hunter-gatherers of the distant past.

Gathering was probably done mainly by the women, using digging sticks and carrying bags. They collected a variety of wild fruits, nuts and melons, and dug up edible roots and tubers from the ground. They also collected things like termites, caterpillars and locusts. In many ways the gathering of plant food was more reliable than hunting. The fruits of trees and bushes could be harvested each year and experienced gatherers could move around from place to place according to the seasonal harvests of various plants.

Social organisation

From the evidence of their camp sites it appears that hunter-gatherer communities usually lived in small family-sized groups. In drier regions these often comprised no more than about 20 individuals. In wetter regions where game and vegetable food was abundant, they seem to have lived in groups of up to 50 or even 100 people. But whatever the size of group, they were probably loosely organised on a family basis. Judging by the experience of recent hunter-gatherer groups, there was free movement between groups for marriage or other purposes. Where caves and overhanging rocks were available, they used these for shelters. In more open countryside they made temporary wind-breaks out of branches, grass and stones. In some areas, where seasonal camps were used for weeks or months at a time, conical shelters might be built of sticks bent and bound together and thatched with grass.

Recent studies of Khoesan (Khoisan) hunters of the Kalahari suggest that one of the most important aspects of hunter-gatherer groups was their dependence upon cooperative labour and communal effort for survival. Though there was a division of labour between men and women, neither one had higher status than the other. They recognised their equal dependence upon each other. At the end of the day gathered and hunted food was brought back to the camp and shared equally among the group. No special status was granted to the successful hunter. (See Figure 1.4 for a photograph of modern San people.)

Figure 1.4 A modern photograph of the Kalahari San

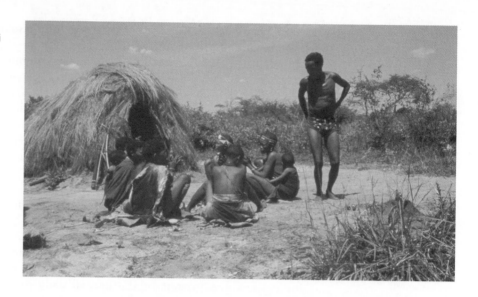

Further climate change, adaptation and the ancestry of African languages

In the period 20,000 to 16,000 BCE the climate and vegetation of Africa was similar to what it was until recent decades (see Map 0.2, p. 6). The Congo Basin was dominated by rainforest vegetation that stretched along most of the west African coastal region as far as southern Senegal. North and south beyond this lay drier forest, giving way to open woodland savannah, grassland savannah, dry steppe and then desert. On the plateaux of east and southern Africa, savannah woodlands and grasslands predominated. Between 16,000 and 11,500 BCE, however, Africa experienced a much drier climate: the rainforest contracted and the desert zones expanded. Human populations faced a crisis as old hunting and gathering techniques were found to be inadequate for the changed environment. It is thought that population levels dropped dramatically at this time. Those that did learn to adapt, however, spread their technology, and with it their cultures and languages, to the four corners of the continent. It is to them that the ancestry of the four indigenous language families of modern Africa can be traced.

Linguists who have studied the language families of Africa have traced the probable origins of at least three of the four to the general region of northeastern Africa and the middle and upper valley of the Nile (see Map 1.2). Between the Nile cataracts of Nubia (northern Sudan), the Red Sea and the Ethiopian highlands, ancestral speakers of the Afro-Asiatic language family specialised in collecting wild grasses and roots. They roasted the seeds and, using grinding stones, ground them and the dried roots into flour that they baked as flat bread. The Afro-Asiatic speakers expanded southwards into and around the Ethiopian highlands, through the 'Horn of Africa', and on to the east African plateau where they were the ancestors of Cushitic-speaking peoples. They also took their grass-threshing and grinding techniques northwards into Egypt and western Asia. In due course they spread westwards across north Africa where they assimilated the earlier Capsian hunter-gatherers and became the ancestors of the Berber-speaking peoples.

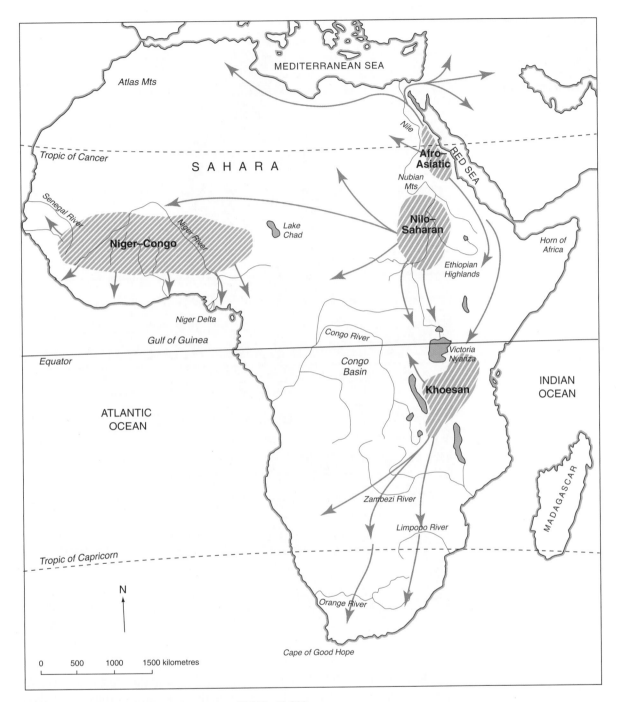

Map 1.2 The spread of African languages, 15,000–10,000 BCE

South of the Afro-Asiatic speakers, in the grazing lands between the Nubian Mountains and the middle Nile, the ancestors of the Nilo-Saharan language speakers are thought to have had their origins. They specialised in hunting the large antelope that grazed these favourable grasslands, using mainly throwing spears. Their prey probably included ancestors of the wild Saharan cattle that they were later to domesticate. They spread mostly

19

Figure 1.5 A Khoesan hunter in Zimbabwe photographed *c.*1900, one of the few such people to have survived in that region into the twentieth century

westwards along the grassland zone south of the Sahara towards Lake Chad and the Niger Bend. The Songhay-speakers of the middle Niger can be traced to this origin. Nilo-Saharans also spread southwards towards the Great Lakes, south-west of the Ethiopian highlands, and are ancestral to the Shilluk, Dinka, Nuer and Acholi of this region.

South and west of the Nilo-Saharans the ancestors of the Niger-Congo language family specialised in hunting the woodland savannah of west Africa armed with bow and poisoned arrow. They also dug for wild yams and fished with hook and line and probably baskets too. The languages of Kordofan, west of the middle Nile, are linked to the Niger-Congo family, which has prompted some linguists to suppose that Kordofan may have been the original ancestral home of the Niger-Congo group, that then migrated westwards to west Africa. Others, however, feel it was more likely the other way round, with Kordofanian being a remote offshoot of Niger-Congo. Stone Age hunters of the Congo forest, known to archaeologists as the Lupemban tradition, are probably ancestral to the Bambuti and Batwa hunters of modern times. Their ancestral languages have been lost as they were, from about 1000 BCE, absorbed into the Bantu-language sub-group of the Niger-Congo family (see below, Chapter 4).

Finally, the Khoesan family appears to have had its origins in the east-African region of Tanzania. Their main strength lay in the wide range of their hunting and gathering microlith technology, the bow and poisoned arrow and the bored-stone weighted digging stick for unearthing edible tubers. The Khoesan-speakers spread throughout south-central and southern Africa, assimilating earlier hunter-gatherers. Their technology was particularly suited to exploiting the dry, semi-desert zones of South Africa, Botswana and Namibia, which is probably why their hunting and gathering culture survived into modern times in these areas. In most of eastern, central and southern Africa the Khoesan were assimilated by Bantu-speakers of the Niger-Congo group from the beginning of the Common Era (see below, Chapter 4). Their only descendants surviving in Tanzania are the Hadza and Sandawe.

The spread of languages and cultures described in this section was a process of assimilation rather than displacement. In some cases it may have been the technology and its associated culture and language that spread rather than actual people in any great numbers. Their new techniques for surviving in adverse circumstances, however, were so successful that they resulted in two consequences of major importance for the later prehistory of Africa. In the first place their languages, social customs and religious beliefs came to dominate and assimilate all previous languages and cultures on the continent. The combination of the old and the new produced unique new regional cultures and dialects that formed the ancestral origins of Africa's historic peoples. Secondly, their knowledge and understanding of intensive hunting and gathering in adverse environmental conditions laid the foundation for the development of farming and pastoralism as soon as more favourable climatic conditions prevailed.

Later prehistory: farming and pastoralism in tropical Africa and Ancient Egypt

So far we have seen in Chapter 1 that by about 10,000 years ago human societies in Africa had developed stone-based technology to a remarkably high standard. But they remained essentially hunters and gatherers. They were still totally dependent for their food and general livelihood upon hunting wild animals and gathering the wild plants which grew in the land. Then, from about 8000 BCE (Before the Common Era), major changes in the age-old way of life were made possible by the development of farming and the herding of animals.

Crop cultivation, domestication and the origins of farming

The first movement towards crop cultivation probably began with the gathering of wild grain, as described in the previous chapter. There was a natural concentration on the heavy yielding 'grasses' usually known as 'cereals'. These were mainly wheat and barley in western Asia and Egypt and sorghum and millets in the summer-rainfall, savannah lands of tropical Africa. Cultivation began with the deliberate protection and weeding, saving seed and re-sowing of wild grains; and likewise with root crops. It was soon realised that seeds from the strongest plants were the best ones to plant for the heaviest crops next year. When this principle was pursued through many plant generations, the plant became reliant upon the assistance of human cultivators. In its new enlarged form it could no longer compete with weeds or survive in the wild without human intervention and protection. At this point the plant had become 'domesticated' and true farming had commenced. This process, from the cultivation of wild crops to the farming of domesticated ones, was gradual and one that is not easily discerned in the archaeological record.

A similar process occurred with animals and the origins of pastoralism. Initially the wild animals chosen as most suited to human needs were protected from predators and herded from one favourable feeding site to another. Well-fed and without the need to flee from wild predators, the animals gradually, over generations, became too large and ungainly to survive on their own. Their larger size suited both the human herder, who gained more meat or milk per animal, and the herded animals (cattle, sheep, goats or camels) that had a longer and more prolific life under human protection. When that point of dependence was reached, the animal in its new form could no longer survive on its own in the wild and had thus become 'domesticated'.

The impact of agriculture

With the development of farming, people began to live in larger, more permanent settlements. They no longer needed to be perpetually on the move in search of wild food. They were able to place their settlements in suitably fertile regions and grow their own food nearby. At the same time there was an increase in population. This was partly the result of an improved diet as food supply became more regular and abundant. And living in a more settled community, women were able to bear children more frequently. Small children were not such a burden as they had been in hunter-gatherer communities and they could be cared for by other members of the family within the safety of the home. Larger families meant an increase in agricultural labour. Children could work in the fields from an early age, scaring birds, weeding crops or tending domestic animals. Thus larger families could grow more food and this in turn made it possible to support an ever-larger population.

As people settled in one place for a longer period of time, they built more permanent houses. Often these were simple constructions, made of mud, poles, woven reeds and thatching; but sometimes too the houses themselves or the walls enclosing the settlement were built of stone. Now that they were farmers as well as hunters and gatherers, people needed a wider range of tools. And living in more permanent settlements, they now had the space to store these and other possessions. They made baked-clay pottery, useful for storing, carrying or cooking food and water. The remnants of their pottery and grinding stones, worn smooth from years of grinding grain, are often important items of archaeological evidence for the presence of early farming communities in ancient times. People gradually developed more sophisticated tools. A characteristic tool of this era was the ground stone axe. Instead of merely chipping a core stone into the required shape, as in Acheulian times, the toolmaker now ground the stone against another harder rock. The result was a smooth sloping surface with a sharp edge, more like a modern metal axehead. This new stone technology is sometimes referred to as 'Neolithic' (from the Greek words *neos* meaning 'new' and *lithos* meaning 'stone').

The development of farming brought important social as well as technical changes. Producing one's own food supply required social organisation, cooperation and planning within the community. People had to work together months in advance to plan future production: how much and when to plant, which crops where, and when to harvest. People had not only to plan for and store enough food to last from one harvest right through the year to the next. They were also now able to produce a *surplus* of food, that is, more than was actually needed to feed their own immediate family. If stored, this could be an important insurance against loss of future crops through natural disasters such as drought or flood. It also meant that a community could support a number of people not directly involved in food production: specialist craftsmen, ministers of religion or administrators and rulers who controlled and organised the planning of society. A surplus of food could be traded between neighbouring settlements in exchange for raw materials, luxuries or other items not produced within the community.

Finally, in agricultural and pastoral societies some of the equality and communal sharing of the hunter-gatherer was lost. With the production of a surplus, the existence of non-food-producing classes and a growth in personal possessions, there developed divisions between rich and poor in society. The extent of this varied from one society to another. In general those non-producers who controlled production were richer than those who produced the surplus upon which the former lived.

Pastoralism

The herding of domestic animals had similar advantages to crop cultivation. The animals were a real and potential source of food, particularly milk. They were often less frequently used for meat, but they could be so used if necessary; for instance, in times of drought and the failure of crops. Where the people were largely pastoralist (that is, animal herders) rather than crop cultivators or mixed farmers, their settlements tended to be less permanent. They needed to move in search of varying seasonal pastures. But with a reliable source of food ready to hand in their domestic animals, they could still live in large communities. Moving from one seasonal settlement to another they could carry their possessions and even housing materials such as poles and mats on the backs of their animals.

The 'agricultural revolution'

Traditionally the 'agricultural revolution' has been seen as just that. It was believed that once people discovered how to grow their own food, their lives were totally revolutionised. Clearly the potential changes and apparent advantages resulting from the development of farming were very great indeed. But this does not mean that all communities changed to a settled farming lifestyle as soon as they learned about it. Research in Africa has suggested that early moves towards crop cultivation may have been more gradual than previously thought. This is hardly surprising. Farming was not suitable in every environment and its disadvantages may have been apparent. Though farming could support a larger population, it left the people more exposed to the dangers of famine caused by natural disasters such as drought or flood. In any case, crop cultivation and the keeping of domestic animals was only one of several economic options. In many early farming communities hunting, gathering, and perhaps even fishing, remained important

Figure 2.1 Modern pastoralists of the Sahel watering their cattle on the banks of the Niger River sources of food and general livelihood. Indeed, as we shall see below, the Khoesan may have adopted herding because it fitted in with their migratory hunting practices, but they specifically did not develop cultivation. Probably, in their view, it would have involved a major and unnecessary break with the past.

Those who developed a dependence upon farming needed to accept a hugely changed world view. People were no longer working entirely within the confines of nature, and were much more dependent upon the vagaries of climate. New relationships needed to be developed with the spiritual world; and thus the origins of Africa's indigenous religions can probably be traced to this period. African religious thought, practices and shrines have traditionally been intimately connected with the spiritual fertility of the land and the seasonal rituals of 'rain-making', cultivation, sowing and harvest. Indeed, some scholars now think that the domestication of cattle in Africa may have been related to their religious significance, and that this may have been just as important as their being a source of food. Judging by the way some of them were buried in the Upper Nile valley – wrapped in matting and laid in the ground just like human burials – cattle appear to have been treated as sacred animals. This might have been a motivating factor leading to their initial protection and in due course domestication.

The origins of farming and pastoralism in tropical Africa

From about 11,000 BCE the particularly dry phase in the African climate, described in the previous chapter, came to an end with the return of higher levels of rainfall. By 9000 BCE a new 'wet phase', with more rainfall than today, had reached a peak that lasted until 6000 BCE. Thereafter the higher levels of rainfall began to tail off until, by 3500 BCE, rainfall levels had reached something similar to those prevailing today. During the wet phase the rainforest expanded, deserts contracted and the Sahara became habitable as an open grassland savannah. Rivers flowed from the Ahaggar and Tibesti mountains of

Figure 2.2 Modern Ankole cattle, Uganda, thought to be descendants from the ancient domesticated cattle of the Sahara

Map 2.1 Africa, 7000 BCE: probable level of lakes and rivers in the last major wet phase

the central Sahara, and Lake Chad became a huge expanse of water, many times larger than today. The swamplands of the upper Niger 'delta' and the upper Nile 'sudd' were probably lakes at this time (see Map 2.1). These increased wetlands opened up new opportunities for people to develop fishing settlements, for which there is evidence right across 'middle Africa' from the Niger Bend and Lake Chad as far east as Lake Turkana. And it is to the beginning of this wet phase that the origins of farming in Africa can be traced.

Nilo-Saharan beginnings

From 9000 BCE the Nilo-Saharans of the eastern Sahara adopted the grain-collecting and grinding practices of their northern neighbours, the Afro-Asiatics, and applied them to the tropical grasses of the middle Nile, sorghum and pearl millet. By 8000 BCE they had invented pottery in order to make porridge from these ground grains. Exactly at what point the sorghum and millet became domesticated is difficult to tell, but it was certainly before 7000 BCE. Between 8000 and 6000 BCE Nilo-Saharan cultivation practices and pottery-making spread north towards Egypt and westwards across the Sahara. By 5000 BCE the Nilo-Saharans had domesticated gourds and water-melons as well as cotton for weaving cloth. The Nilo-Saharans may also have been responsible for domesticating the wild cattle of the Red Sea hills between about 9000 and 8000 BCE, although so far there is only one piece of archaeological evidence supporting this idea. If true, however, this would have been 1000 years earlier than the domestication of cattle in Asia. They grazed the cattle on the grasslands bordering the Nile and their herding practices eventually spread westwards into the central Sahara.

The importance of tsetse fly in the early spread of pastoralism

One important factor in the spread of pastoralism in certain parts of tropical Africa was the presence or absence of a blood-sucking insect called the tsetse fly. A parasite carried in the saliva of certain tsetse causes 'sleeping sickness', a disease that can prove fatal both to cattle and to humans. Cattle as well as humans eventually develop some level of immunity to tsetse-borne

26

Map 2.2 'Neolithic' farming and pastoralism, northern and central Africa: 5000–1000 BCE

disease; but in general a tsetse-ridden area was one to be avoided when non-immune pastoralists moved in search of new pastures. The tsetse tended to congregate in the moist low-lying valleys and thickly wooded regions where they found plenty of wild game on which to prey. The drier open savannah grasslands of the southern Sahara and the eastern and southern African plateaux were thus generally the regions where specialised pastoralism tended to develop.

Pastoralists of the Sahara

The period from 4000 to 2500 BCE was the great age of pastoralism in the Sahara. Cattle-based pastoralism was well established in the mountainous Ahaggar region of the central Sahara by 4000 BCE. These pastoralists were probably mainly Nilo-Saharans, although they may have incorporated Afro-Asiatics from north Africa who probably brought west Asian sheep to the region. We know most about the Saharan pastoralists from the remarkable series of rock paintings that they left behind. Their paintings are to be found in what are today some of the driest parts of the Sahara. The largest number of paintings date to the period 3500–2500 BCE. The paintings depict nearly every aspect of domestic life. In particular they show their huge herds of long-horned cattle as well as sheep. The human figures depicted show a variety of mixed Mediterranean and negroid types. They are shown wearing woven cloth, and elaborate ornaments, hairstyles and body decoration. They used round-based pots for storing milk and cattle blood, skin bags for water

27

Figure 2.3 Tassilin-Ajjer (Tassili Plateau, Sahara), prehistoric rock painting: herd of cattle by a village (marked by white circles). Copy after a rock painting of the 2nd millennium BCE

and pack-oxen for carrying their possessions. The presence of grinding stones in their settlements suggests they also harvested grain.

Pastoralism and cultivation in north-east Africa

Meanwhile, in north-east Africa, the Afro-Asiatic Cushites took domesticated cattle from the Red Sea hills southwards around the foothills of the Ethiopian highlands and into the grazing lands of the east African plateau. By 3500 BCE Southern Cushites were herding cattle, sheep and goats south of the Ethiopian highlands in the region of Lake Turkana. There they met the south-eastern Nilo-Saharans who were cultivating sorghum, millet and beans. The Cushites adopted these cultivating practices as well as the Nilo-Saharan settlement pattern of round thatched houses surrounding a central cattle kraal that was enclosed within a hedge of thorns. They made the stone bowls that are characteristic of this culture and spread their settlements through east Africa between 3500 and 1000 BCE. Meanwhile the local Afro-Asiatic speakers of the Ethiopian highlands developed their own distinctive crops. Among the more important of these were *tef,* a small-seeded cereal still important in Ethiopia today; *noog,* an oil plant; and *enset,* the starchy fibrous stalks of a thick-stemmed banana-like plant.

Khoesan pastoralism in southern Africa

It is probably from these Cushite herders of east Africa that the Khoesan learned sheep- and cattle-herding techniques and spread herding practices southwards to the Khoe-speaking peoples of northern Botswana by about 500 BCE. By the turn of the Common Era, Khoe-speakers were herding cattle as far south as the Cape of Good Hope. Other than these herding practices in the dry grasslands of southern Africa, however, the Khoesan generally did not develop farming. This was perhaps because of the high efficiency and wide range of hunting and gathering technology and skills that they had developed. There was simply no economic or environmental pressure on them to make the huge change required by an agricultural lifestyle.

Figure 2.4 Stone and pottery artefacts from the settlements and burials of Stone Age cultivators and pastoralists

Farming in west Africa

The Niger-Congo peoples of west Africa, however, like the Nilo-Saharans, took advantage of the wet phase between 9000 and 5500 BCE to develop planting agriculture, especially yams, in the expanded woodland of the region. They developed techniques for making stone axes that were ground and polished to a smooth shape and fine point. These would have been used, by men, for clearing woodland for planting yams and other plants. The latter included the oil palm for oil and wine, peas, groundnuts and kola nut. By

3000 BCE they had domesticated guinea-fowl and were growing the raffia palm for making raffia cloth. In the wetlands of the inland delta of the upper Niger a west African rice was domesticated between 3000 and 1000 BCE and this was later spread to the high-rainfall forest margins of Guinea, Liberia and Côte d'Ivoire.

Women were the main planters of yams in Niger-Congo culture. This gave them a high status and may account for the development of matrilineal descent among the Niger-Congo peoples. In a matrilineal system, although positions of leadership and power in clan and village are held by men, these are inherited through the female line, from mothers and sisters.

The eastern branch of the Niger-Congo language family, the Bantu-speakers, began moving into the rainforest around the Gulf of Guinea to the east of the Niger delta. Travelling by dug-out canoe they established riverside settlements, fished in the rivers and hunted in the forest. They brought goats and guinea-fowl and colonised natural clearings in the forest. They cultivated yams and oil-palm, beans and gourds. Between 3000 and 2500 BCE they expanded their settlements rapidly southwards towards the Congo Basin, reaching the Congo River by 2000 BCE. Some travelled north-eastwards, up the Ubangui River, and eastwards along the northern edge of the forest. Others penetrated the forest south of the Congo, up great rivers like the Kasai and its tributaries, emerging in the woodland savannah of the plateau to the south of the forest by about 1000 BCE (see below, Chapter 4).

Ancient Egypt

Origins

We have already seen in the previous chapter (p. 18) that speakers of ancestral Afro-Asiatic languages were harvesting and grinding wild grains in the valley of the Nile from well before the wet climatic phase that began from 11,000 BCE. They spread their culture northwards, through Egypt and into western Asia where they and the people they assimilated, harvested and ground the wild wheat and barley that grew in these non-tropical zones. Between 8000 and 7000 BCE wheat and barley were domesticated in the 'fertile crescent' of western Asia and spread back through Egypt and north Africa as the main crop of cultivation. Domesticated sheep and goats also came from western Asia. At this stage cultivation would have been possible in Egypt at some distance from the Nile River itself, at what are now the oases of Bahriya, Dakhla and Kharga (see Map 2.4). The Fayum was also a major early site of farming settlement. It was only with the ending of the wet phase from about 5000 BCE and the encroachment of the desert from east and west that the early cultivators of Egypt fell back upon the unique resources of the Nile River itself.

As we saw in the previous chapter, in historic times the Blue Nile annually deposited a dark fertile silt in the widening valley of the Nile, from the third cataract to the Nile Delta in northern Egypt. The flood occurred in about August each year, when temperatures were at their hottest. As the waters receded in the ensuing months, seeds could be planted directly into this muddy silt, and with a little help from simple channel irrigation, crops could be harvested before the soil dried out. There was no need to worry about loss of fertility: each year the soil was 'miraculously' renewed by the

Map 2.3 The origins of farming: western Asia and north-east Africa

flood. In modern times the huge hydroelectric dams at Aswan affect the natural flooding of the Egyptian Nile and irrigation is done artificially, and without the natural renewal of the soil.

Between 5000 and 4000 BCE permanent settlements of full-time farmers became established in the valley of the Nile, with their farming techniques adapted to the river's annual flood. This period is sometimes referred to as 'Badarian' after the town of el-Badari, some 30 kilometres south of Asyut in central Egypt, where numerous graves and cultural artefacts were uncovered by archaeologists in the 1920s and 1930s. From about 4000 BCE some of these Nile-valley settlements began to form into recognisable states or kingdoms. This was developed initially in the upper Nile region of southern Egypt and Lower Nubia. River transport had been developed and the Nile was navigable all the way from Aswan in southern Egypt to the Delta on the Mediterranean coast. The people of Upper Egypt had access to the minerals of the eastern desert – copper, malachite and gold – and they traded these

31

Map 2.4 Ancient Egypt: 3500–1000 BCE

valuable items down the Nile where they were taken across Sinai by pack-donkey into Mesopotamia in western Asia.

The wealth gained from this trade stimulated the development of craft, art and manufacturing in Upper Egypt. And the elites who controlled the trade wielded political power over the people of the region. These elites gradually developed an economic and political system based upon the exploitation of large rural estates where those who wielded power were socially divorced from the bulk of the population who worked the land and mined the minerals. It was in effect what one historian, David Wengrow, has called 'an internal colonisation'. The elites were buried with grave goods – copper ornaments, ceramic pots, beads – that indicated their wealth and social status. Their graves show a large degree of cultural similarity throughout Upper Egypt and Lower Nubia. This extended as far south as the third cataract, the southernmost point of the Nile floodplain. From about 3500 BCE, however, as those of Upper Egypt became absorbed more closely into a wheat-based, bread-making culture, the Nubians developed their own distinctive cultural traits. These placed more emphasis upon grazing and hunting influences and less upon cultivation – a reflection of the limited arable land of their narrow upper floodplain.

By 3500 BCE local regional states north of the first cataract had become amalgamated into the two kingdoms of Upper and Lower Egypt. And in about 3100 BCE the King of Upper Egypt, Aha (also known as Narmer or Menes), conquered the delta kingdom of Lower Egypt. In doing so he founded what was to become known as the first 'Dynasty' of Ancient Egypt. Aha's unification of Egypt is generally recognised as marking the beginning of the 3000-year-long civilisation of Ancient Egypt: one of the most remarkable and certainly the longest-lasting civilisation in the history of humankind.

Writing and mathematics

From before the time of unification the Egyptians had transformed pictorial representations into a form of writing, known as hieroglyphics. Early writings were recorded on clay tablets or palettes, the writing being cut into the wet clay before it dried. Later they developed papyrus – the earliest form of paper, made from crushed papyrus reeds woven together – and wrote with inks made from various natural dyes. Hieroglyphics were also carved into the solid rock of temples and pharaohs' tombs.

There appear to have been two principal factors that impelled the development of writing. First, there was a need to record details of the passage of seasons and the annual flood in order to predict harvests and thus estimate and record the taxation of the peasantry. As part of this process, the Egyptian elite developed a remarkable knowledge of astronomy: with no modern light pollution and the clarity of cloudless Egyptian skies, conditions were ideal for studying the night heavens.

Through their study of the sun, the moon and the stars, Egyptian astronomers developed the world's first annual 12-month calendar of 365 days. They also developed some of the basic principles of mathematics – essential to their great architectural projects. These included the binary system, fractions, a formula for calculating the area of a circle and the common principles of a right-angled triangle.

A second impulse towards the Egyptian development of writing was a desire to record the names, chronology and deeds of their kings. Years were

Figure 2.5 Hieroglyphics carved in the tomb of Rameses II, *c.*1270 BCE. Rameses II used two cartouches. The symbols above the centre-left cartouche indicate he is 'King of Upper and Lower Egypt'. The symbols above the centre-right one refer to him as 'Son of Re' (the sun god)

recorded in relationship to the beginning of each reign, rather than as a continuous chronology. King-lists, found on fragments of ancient papyrus, have thus proved invaluable to modern historians in calculating a chronology of ancient Egyptian history.

Pharaohs, dynasties and kingdoms

The rulers of Ancient Egypt were known as 'pharaohs'. They claimed to be the earthly incarnation of their gods. Exactly how the idea of divine kingship originated is not known for sure, but it seems to have come from 'inner Africa' to the south. The rulers of the early farming communities are thought to have been religious leaders, 'rainmakers' and in due course controllers of the flood. As their power and kingdoms grew in strength and size, they exercised ever greater authority until they claimed direct descent from the gods themselves.

Historians have traditionally grouped the reigns of the pharaohs into a series of dynasties, 30 in all, spread over the period 3100–332 BCE. The framework of dynasties, however, is not as reliable as it might seem. It was not a system used by the Egyptians themselves. Their scribes recorded the names and deeds of specific reigns rather than a chronology of dynasties. The framework of dynasties was developed by historians trying to make sense of the king-lists many centuries later. Some of the problems are that the length of a reign is often not known and the grouping into dynasties is sometimes fairly arbitrary. Furthermore, several different names might be used for the

For more information see www.palgrave.com/ shillington

same pharaoh, who sometimes took on the name of his or her predecessor. There were a few female pharaohs, though they were a rarity and they often held power as a 'regent' for a male claimant.

Nevertheless, the grouping of dynasties into 'Old', 'Middle' and 'New Kingdoms' is still useful in discerning some chronological thread through the vast span of Ancient Egyptian history. The Old Kingdom (*c.*3100–2200 BCE), Middle Kingdom (*c.*2040–1670 BCE) and New Kingdom (*c.*1570–1100 BCE) were periods of enhanced royal power, separated by intermediate periods during which there was a general breakdown in royal authority.

Agriculture and the organisation of Egyptian society

The vast majority of the Egyptian population was made up of peasant farmers. It was they who produced the agricultural surplus upon which the wealth, power and fame of the Ancient Egyptian civilisation were built.

The peasantry lived in small mud houses built on sandy mounds above the flood plain. They subsisted on a diet of bread, onions, beer and fish. Their main crops were wheat, barley and flax. They also grew a range of vegetables and fruit such as figs and grapes. They herded cattle and goats, kept geese, fished perch from the Nile and hunted wild birds in the marshes. But the peasants ate little meat. Most of it was paid in taxes to the government for the consumption of the wealthy ruling classes. The fertile silt from the annual flooding of the Nile ensured that farmers were able to harvest a large surplus from their crops. But the peasantry themselves were not allowed to keep or accumulate that surplus. This was taken by the pharaoh's tax collectors. The peasantry were left with just enough to feed themselves until the next season's harvest.

Every stage of the peasants' labour was overseen by the pharaoh's civil servants: scribes and tax collectors. Government officials supervised irrigation projects. Taxes were assessed according to the annual level of the Nile at the height of its flood. The peasant farmers were thus instructed in advance how

Figure 2.6 The fertile Nile Valley with the three great pyramids of the Old Kingdom period at Giza: Khufu (Cheops), Khefren and Mykerinos much surplus they were expected to produce and pay to the government. During slack periods in the agricultural cycle the labour of the peasantry was still at the disposal of the government. They were used on communal projects: large-scale irrigation works such as draining marshes or digging canals, and the building of huge stone statues, temples and royal tombs.

Government

Agricultural surpluses were kept in huge government stores and were used to support the pharaoh and his family in luxury and comfort. They also paid for a large civil service, supported priests and their shrines and were traded abroad for luxury items or scarce raw materials. The day-to-day business of government was carried out by a huge bureaucracy of well-educated civil servants, the most important of whom were the scribes and tax collectors. The kingdom was divided into 40 local districts, each overseen by a governor appointed by the pharaoh.

For most of the time the pharaohs and their small clique of chief ministers were able to maintain strong control over this highly centralised system of government. Their position as divine kings gave power and respect to their authority, but they were helped by a number of other factors. Although the kingdom extended for 1000 kilometres from the first cataract to the sea, the width of habitable land was narrow. The Nile provided easy transport in reed and timber boats and every part of the kingdom was thus readily accessible to government officials. The population as a whole was predominantly rural; there were no regional fortified cities liable to challenge central authority. For 1500 years the kingdom suffered no foreign invasion, protected to some extent perhaps by the desert to east and west. Thus it was not until the New Kingdom period that the government felt the need to employ a standing army.

Figure 2.7 Measuring and recording the harvest, an XVIIIth Dynasty wall-painting from a tomb in Thebes

36

Art, architecture and religion

The art and architecture of Ancient Egypt were closely related to their religion. The Ancient Egyptians believed in many gods and each had its temple or shrine. Some represented the major forces of nature such as Re, the sun god, and Amun, the god of wind. In Middle Kingdom times these two were combined into the main state god of Amun-Re. Other gods were related to animals that were believed to hold particular powers, such as the hawk, the jackal, the snake and the crocodile. And there were numerous regional gods and shrines, stemming back to the gods of the old pre-dynastic communities.

The Egyptians believed that spiritual life continued after death and so great care was taken with their burials. The bodies of the wealthy were embalmed, wrapped in linen cloth and placed in a tomb. The tomb was then filled with offerings of food and drink and such personal possessions as might be needed for the next life. Egyptian burials were thus a clear reflection of social divisions within society. The poor peasant was buried with few possessions in a simple scoop in the ground. The pharaohs, by contrast, were buried in much grander style. Initially these were large underground chambers, topped with a building made of mud brick. By the time of the third dynasty, however, the building which covered the pharaoh's tomb had been developed into a vast stone pyramid, the chambers of which were filled with worldly goods representative of their great status in society. The religious belief that the pharaohs promoted was that the pharaoh himself was a constant link between the material and the spiritual worlds. It was thus necessary to provide for him in elaborate style in his tomb in order to maintain this essential link and ensure the well being of the Egyptian people.

The Egyptians were great builders in stone. Their temples, statues and pyramids were often built on a huge scale, still staggering in these days of modern technology. The great age of pyramid-building was during the third and fourth dynasties of the Old Kingdom period. Altogether over a period of 1500 years some seventy pyramids were built, stretched out along the low plateau overlooking the valley of the lower Nile. The largest and most famous of all, the Great Pyramid, was built in about 2600 BCE for Khufu (also known as Cheops), the first pharaoh of the fourth dynasty (see Figure 2.8).

Although the hard granite used to line the burial chamber of the Great Pyramid was brought from southern Egypt near the first cataract, the body of the pyramid was made from local limestone quarried from the edge of the Giza plateau. For a long time it was assumed by historians that the pyramids had been built with slave labour. The idea stemmed from the Greek historian Herodotus writing in the fifth century BCE. Herodotus was writing 2000 years after the event and he had simply *assumed* the use of slave labour because his own society and monument-building was based on slavery. Recent research by Egyptian archaeologists working at Giza, however, has uncovered the village of the workers who built the pyramids, and with it has destroyed the myth of slave labour. It appears that 1500 skilled stone masons cut and shaped the stone building blocks from which the pyramids were built. They acquired considerable status and were well fed and looked after. Even those suffering broken bones received expert medical attention. In addition the tens of thousands of unskilled labourers who dragged the blocks into position served several months at a time on a rotational basis, village by village, so as not to upset the labour of the farming calendar. The workers probably regarded it as a great honour to perform this national service on the pharaoh's project, almost as a right of passage for the young men who

Figure 2.8 The Great
Pyramid of Khufu, IVth
Dynasty

laboured and the women who looked after them. Khufu's Great Pyramid took 20 years to build and therefore required a lengthy reign to complete the project. This, combined with the enormous resources required, may account for the fact that after the pyramid of Khufu and those of his son and grandson, no subsequent pharaohs ever built such large pyramids, and many failed to complete them before they died.

The pharaohs employed many full-time craftsmen and artists in order to fill their tombs with beautiful examples of Egyptian craftsmanship: jewellery, fragile decorated pottery and elaborate ornaments of gold. The walls of some tombs were painted with scenes from everyday life such as ploughing, harvesting, hunting, feasting and the work of craftsmen and scribes (see Figure 2.7 and Figures 2.9 to 2.11 below). From these one can gain a vivid insight into life in ancient Egypt. In order to protect these valuable treasures, architects devised complex systems of tunnels and fake chambers to deceive the would-be grave robber. But in spite of these precautions, most of the pharaohs' tombs were raided by thieves in ancient times. In the New Kingdom period, pyramid building was abandoned. Instead the pharaohs were buried in massive stone caves hollowed out of the mountains in the 'Valley of the Kings' near the New Kingdom capital of Thebes (modern Luxor). One of these tombs, that of a minor pharaoh of the eighteenth dynasty called Tutankhamun, was only discovered in the 1920s, its coffin case and treasures still intact after more than 32 centuries. Now on display in Cairo Museum, the tomb's contents provide a magnificent example of the richness and highly elaborated art of the Ancient Egyptian world.

The Kingdoms of Ancient Egypt

The main features of Ancient Egypt's scientific achievement and artistic culture were established fairly early on in the Old Kingdom period. The basis of the pharaohs' power was the labour of the peasantry, to which was added the profits from international trade.

Figure 2.9 Nubians carrying tribute to the pharaoh, a wall-painting, *c.*1420 BCE. At times the Nubians of Kush were forced to acknowledge Egyptian power; at other times they asserted their independence and then trading between the two was on more equal terms

All foreign trade was conducted through the pharaoh's central government. Indeed, the desire for greater control over trade may have been an important factor prompting the unification of Upper and Lower Egypt in the first place. The main exports to western Asia were grain from the Nile valley and gold and copper from the Nubian mountains. Ebony, ivory and ostrich feathers were imported from the Nubian interior to the south, and much of this was also exported. Timber, especially Lebanese cedar, an important raw material not widely available in the Nile valley, was imported from Byblos in Palestine (present-day Lebanon). Luxury imports from western Asia included spices, incense and precious stones.

The unified kingdom founded by Aha lasted for nearly 1000 years. Over the centuries, however, foreign trade brought increasing wealth to the regional princes of the Nile valley and from about 2300 BCE they began to reassert the local powers that they had used to exercise before unification. With their increasing independence, central authority had collapsed in all but

Figure 2.10

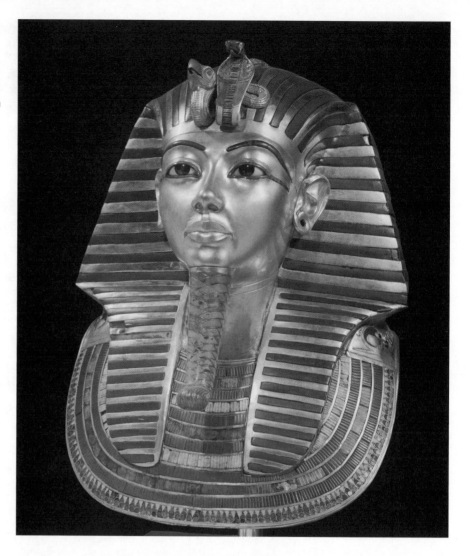

Tutankhamun's funeral mask in solid gold inlaid with semi-precious stones and glass-paste, from the tomb of the pharaoh Tutankhamun, discovered in the Valley of the Kings, Thebes, Egypt

name by 2200 BCE. Historians refer to this as the end of the Old Kingdom. At the same time the Sahara was drying out increasingly rapidly, prompting large numbers of Saharan pastoralists and hunters to push into the Nile valley. This would have disrupted the settled farmers whom they found there and provided a further challenge to central authority. During this intermediate period taxes were not paid to central government and the pharaohs' power was weakened, as shown by a temporary halt in pyramid-building.

In about 2040 BCE unity was re-established by the founders of the eleventh dynasty, who came from Upper Egypt. Historians refer to this as the Middle Kingdom period (2040–1670 BCE). Although the authority and prosperity of the pharaohs quickly recovered, trade was now largely in the hands of professional merchants who sought out new markets through the Mediterranean and Red Sea. Central government taxed the trade rather than controlled it. Nevertheless, taxes were paid, trade revived and pyramid-building was renewed. Irrigation was extended and a huge irrigation project was undertaken in the Fayum Depression as more land everywhere was brought into cultivation. This was possibly in response to the drying out of the

Figure 2.11 The back of the gold-plated throne, showing Queen Ankhesenamun putting the finishing touches to the King's toilet, from the tomb of the pharaoh Tutankhamun

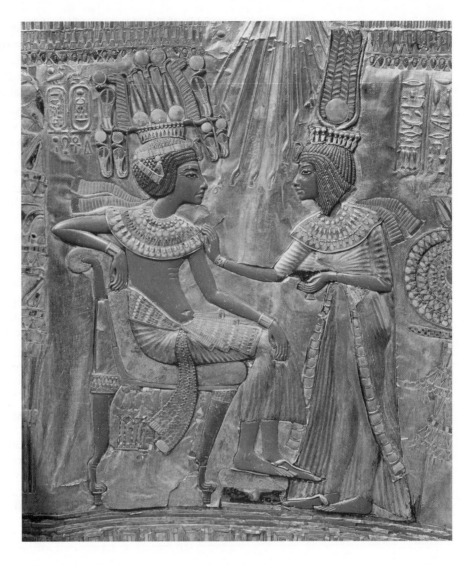

Saharan grasslands and an increasing dependence upon the resources of the Nile. At the same time the Middle Kingdom pharaohs extended their control southwards, as far as the second cataract, thus gaining greater control over the gold, ivory and ebony trade of Nubia.

The pharaohs of Old and Middle Kingdom times had never seen the need to maintain a standing army, as Egyptian control of the Nile valley remained unchallenged for nearly 1500 years. This situation came to an end in 1670 BCE when a people from western Asia called the Hyksos crossed the Sinai desert and invaded the Nile delta. They swept into Lower Egypt, riding horse-drawn chariots and wielding weapons of bronze (an alloy of copper and tin on a ratio of 8:1). Hitherto copper had been the only metal used for weapons and tools in the valley of the Nile.

The Hyksos dominated the delta region for more than a century. In doing so they cut off Upper Egypt from the wealth of foreign trade, thus weakening the power of the pharaohs.

The pharaohs of Upper Egypt, however, learned the lessons of the Hyksos invasion. They established a standing army, equipped with weapons of bronze – tin as well as copper was mined in the eastern desert. In about 1570 BCE the Theban kings of the seventeenth dynasty drove the Hyksos out of Lower Egypt and reunited the kingdom. In this 'New Kingdom' period which followed (1570–1085 BCE), Egypt became a major world power. Backed by the power of a standing army, the pharaohs of the New Kingdom were able to establish an empire, extending their rule by conquest into Palestine and Syria in the north-east and into Nubia as far as the fourth cataract in the south. The capital was moved from Memphis in Lower Egypt to Thebes in the heart of Upper Egypt. Trade in ivory, gold, incense and hardwood was expanded, especially down the Red Sea to the 'land of Punt' on the north-east coast of the Horn of Africa. The building of massive statues and temples along the valley of the Nile symbolised the power and wealth of the New Kingdom pharaohs.

In time, however, Egypt's foreign ventures began to rebound. In the years after 1100 BCE the empire was weakened and the New Kingdom brought to an end by attacks from outside: from across the desert in the west and the Mediterranean in the north. By 1050 BCE Palestine and Nubia had broken free. During this Late Period (1100–330 BCE) Egypt suffered a succession of foreign invasions; Nubian, Assyrian and Persian, and Libyan-Berber mercenaries dominated the army. Foreign dynasties were founded, to be ousted by native Egyptian ones. Compared with the previous 2000 years, these were centuries of relative turmoil. Nevertheless, there were periods of tranquillity and recovery, such as the twenty-sixth dynasty (664–525 BCE), during which the pharaoh Necho started work on a canal to link the Nile with the Red Sea. Necho was also reputed to have despatched a fleet of ships to sail around 'Libya' (Africa) to discover the size of the continent.

The last independent Egyptian dynasty fell to Greek conquest in 332 BCE. This brought Egypt into the empire of Alexander of Macedon (known in European history as 'Alexander the Great'). He gave control of the kingdom to his general Ptolemy. The Greek Ptolemaic dynasty ruled Egypt until the death of Cleopatra and the Roman conquest of 30 BCE (see pp. 69–70).

The impact of iron in north and west Africa

The spread and impact of early metal-working

We saw in the previous chapter how the development of crop cultivation and pastoralism brought important changes to the way of life of many of the Stone Age peoples of Africa. These changes were quickened by the development and spread of the knowledge and techniques of metal-working.

Metal provided early human societies with a superior raw material for making their tools, weapons and decorative ornaments. Metal could be shaped, joined, sharpened and decorated in a far wider range of ways than stone. One of the first metals to be mined and worked was copper. It is relatively 'soft' and is sometimes found in pure metallic form. It would not, therefore, have been too difficult for Stone Age craftsmen to develop the techniques for hammering and shaping it into their desired tools or ornaments. Most metals, however, including copper, are normally mined as ore, that is, metal-bearing rock. In due course early craftsmen learned how to extract their metals from this ore through heating. By a process known as 'smelting' copper or tin was, in effect, 'melted' from the rock. It was soon discovered that smelting copper and tin together produced a harder metal, an alloy which we know as bronze. Bronze was used for making a wide variety of effective tools and weapons.

One of the earliest known sites for the mining of copper was Sinai, that small piece of land in the north-eastern corner of Egypt which links Africa with western Asia. Early copper-workings in this region are thought to date to as far back as 4000 BCE. Copper and bronze were widely used in Ancient Egypt.

Metal as an item of trade

Besides providing metal-working societies with a basic raw material for their own use, metals in the ancient world became an important item of trade. Copper, tin and other valuable metals such as lead and gold were not widely available and were only found in a limited number of places. Societies that controlled the mining or production of these metals controlled a potential source of wealth which could be exchanged for luxuries or raw materials with other neighbouring societies. Some metals were so much in demand and thus so valuable that they were exchanged from one group of people to another, over huge distances, sometimes ending up many thousands of kilometres from their original source. Gold was one such metal.

Gold is particularly rare and is even softer than copper, too soft and too rare for making useful tools. But it is easy to work and does not tarnish or lose its lustre with age. These qualities, combined with its relative scarcity, have ensured over the ages that gold remained one of the most valuable and sought-after of metals. In Ancient Egyptian times, gold was mined in the Nubian mountains and taken down the Nile for trading with Mesopotamia. It is thought that Egyptian control of this trade was one important source of the great wealth accumulated by the pharaohs. In Egypt itself gold was widely used by the pharaohs' craftsmen for making fine burial goods for their tombs, and jewellery for the nobility.

Copper in western Africa

During the New Kingdom period of Ancient Egypt the use of bronze spread along the Mediterranean coastline of northern Africa. There is also evidence of early copper-working in western Africa, in the Aïr mountains of the southern Sahara. At Akjoujt, in present-day Mauritania, copper was worked and traded to local stone-using peoples between 1000 and 500 BCE. There is similar evidence of early copper-smelting at Azelik and Agades in central Niger where a number of copper objects such as spearpoints were used by otherwise Neolithic peoples. The skills of early copper-working in western Africa may have evolved locally. But it remained on a small scale and appears not to have had any dramatic effect on the way of life of the predominantly stone-using peoples of the region.

Origins of iron-working

The smelting of iron

The technique of iron-smelting is much more complex and difficult to master than that of other metals like copper or tin. Iron is chemically infused within its ore and its extraction involves a chemical process rather than merely melting it from the rock. Early iron-smelting furnaces were of two basic types: a trench dug below the ground or a circular clay construction raised a metre or two in height (see Figure 3.1). Crushed ore and hardwood charcoal were layered in the furnace in just the right proportions. A flux such as lime (sometimes in the form of seashells) might be added to aid the smelting process. The furnace was then lit and air was pumped in with the aid of

Figure 3.1 Smelting iron in Africa (wood engraving from *Buch der Erfindungen*, 1872)

bellows. Special clay pipes (*tuyères*) were sometimes inserted in the sides of the furnace to aid the flow of air. The air was both to raise the temperature within the furnace and to act as part of the chemical process.

After a number of hours of smelting, the furnace was broken open and red-hot iron was raked out of the bottom. The crude iron then needed to be frequently reheated and hammered to knock out its impurities and to prepare it for forging into useful weapons and tools. But iron easily rusts and so examples of iron tools and weapons have seldom survived from very ancient times. The main archaeological evidence for the early smelting of iron in Africa has thus often been the waste slag discarded from the smelting furnaces.

The advantages of iron

Although the smelting of iron is clearly a difficult and complex process, it produces, once mastered, tools and weapons far superior to those of copper or bronze. It is a much harder metal and can be sharpened to a finer edge. In addition, iron ore is widely available through much of tropical Africa. Its one drawback is that the smelting of iron ore needs large quantities of hardwood charcoal.

The origins of iron-working in Africa

Because of the specialised nature of iron-smelting, it used to be assumed that its techniques could not have been independently 'invented' in more than one place in the ancient world. The oldest known iron workings anywhere in the world are to be found in Anatolia (modern Turkey) and have been dated to 1500 BCE. Western Asian knowledge of iron-working was not taken to Egypt until 670 BCE and for a long time it was assumed that it must have spread to the rest of Africa from there. This argument of 'diffusion' from only one source of invention is no longer widely accepted among African archaeologists and historians. We have already seen in the previous chapter that numerous peoples independently 'invented' the domestication of various plants and animals. Indeed, agriculture was independently 'invented' in regions as far away as the Hwang Ho valley in China from 5000 BCE and central America from 3000 BCE. Thus there is no reason to suppose that ancient Africans were not capable of using the techniques of copper-smelting and independently applying them to the problem of smelting iron. Archaeological evidence can now confirm that this must indeed be what happened. There is evidence of the early smelting of iron from between 1000 BCE and 600 BCE in the region between Lake Chad and the Great Lakes of east Africa long before the western Asian technology reached Egypt (see Map 3.1). The knowledge and skills of iron-working did not spread further through east Africa until the turn of the Common Era (see Chapter 4); but the knowledge spread westwards, along old copper-trading networks, to the peoples of the west African woodland regions south of the Sahara.

The Early Iron Age in west Africa

Unlike copper ore, iron ore is fairly widespread throughout sub-Saharan Africa. All that was needed for the spread of iron-working was a knowledge of smelting technology. The woodland savannah of west Africa was ideal for this development. Not only did iron-tipped spears and arrows make hunting more efficient, but iron axes and hoes provided early farmers with a more efficient means of clearing woodland for cultivation. At the same time the wood itself provided the large quantities of charcoal needed for smelting iron. By 400 BCE iron-working was becoming fairly widespread in the savannah

45

woodlands of west Africa. Iron tools accelerated the spread of farming communities.

The floodplain of the middle Niger (the 'inland delta') produced a particularly interesting form of urbanisation during this period. The existence of the Niger's seasonal floodplain in the dry grassland of the west African savannah attracted iron-working settlements from at least 400 BCE. The settlements began as villages on mounds within the complexity of river channels and backwater swamps that characterise the floodplain. Their strength lay in local specialisation, adapted to the particular local circumstances of soil, rainfall and floodwater. They had at their disposal up to 42 varieties of African domesticated rice, besides sorghum, millet, cotton and livestock. Their clusters of villages reached urban density by 400 CE, rising to a peak of urbanisation in about 750 CE. The largest settlement was Jenne-Jeno, in the south-east of the region. Some of these settlements contained highly skilled iron-workers. The export of rice and cotton enabled them to import iron ore that they smelted locally into a high-grade metal, akin to steel.

The unique feature of this urbanisation was its lack of hierarchical control. It had no overhead ruler, no official state apparatus. The key to its success lay in local inter-dependence. Internal trade between many co-operating specialists ensured that the members of each local settlement satisfied their needs enabling the wider urban system to work as a complex whole. The level of co-operation across this complexity of settlements went into decline after 1100 CE, some mounds being abandoned and others becoming separate towns, but by then the informal unity of the whole had persisted for 1500 years.

Meanwhile on the Jos plateau of west Africa, north of the Niger-Benue confluence, iron-working was well established by 500 BCE. This centralised community is known to historians as the 'Nok Culture', after the site near Taruga where their artefacts were first discovered. The main items recovered from these sites have been a large number of beautifully constructed figurines of terracotta (baked clay) (see Figure 3.2). These represent human heads as well as elephants and other animals. It is thought that there are clear artistic links between the sculptures of the Nok culture and the later famous bronzes of Ife and Benin. There is evidence of fairly continuous occupation of this west African region from 'Stone Age' times right through to at least 200 CE. The makers of the Nok terracottas were thus almost certainly descendants of previous Stone Age farmers who added iron-working to their technology. Small, baked clay bowls and cooking pots have also been recovered from the site, as well as some iron implements and the remains of smelting furnaces.

In the centuries that followed, up to 1000 CE, the use of iron gradually spread to all the regions of west Africa. During this period there was a gradual rise in population and in some areas this led to the formation of large political units or states. The rise of the ancient empire of Ghana, which was part of this process, will be discussed in Chapter 6.

The origins of iron in north-east Africa

In north and north-east Africa the knowledge of iron-working spread from western Asia. The earliest smelting of iron in this region occurred in Anatolia (modern Turkey) from about 1500 BCE. The Hittites of Anatolia made strenuous efforts to keep the technique a secret. In this way their unique iron weapons gave them military superiority over their neighbours. Gradually, however, the knowledge of iron-smelting spread through western Asia.

Map 3.1 The spread of iron-working in Africa

47

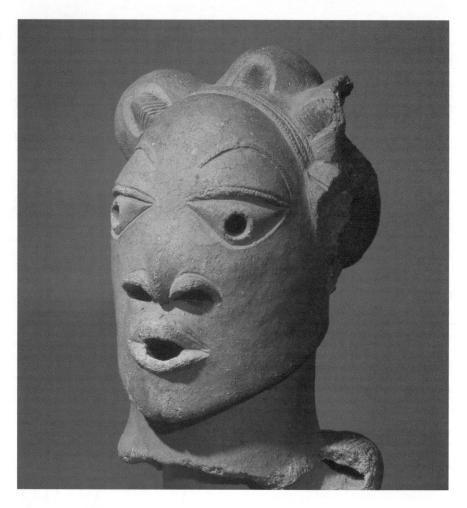

A few iron goods began to appear in Egyptian burials in the centuries after 1000 BCE, but these were rare and probably imported. The main factor preventing the Egyptians developing iron-smelting for themselves was the country's chronic shortage of timber for charcoal. Bronze therefore continued to be the main metal for their tools and weapons until the Assyrian invasion of 670 BCE. The iron weapons of the Assyrians proved too much for the Egyptian army which was quickly defeated. The Nubian rulers of the twenty-fifth or 'Ethiopian' dynasty were forced to withdraw their court to the Nubian region of the upper Nile, south of the second cataract. There, in the centuries that followed, tropical Africa's first truly Iron Age state was to develop.

The Iron Age kingdom of Meroe

Origins: the rise of Kush

A series of Nubian kingdoms had been established along the upper Nile since before the unification of Ancient Egypt (3100 BCE). During Old Kingdom times Egypt had imported gold, ivory, ostrich feathers and ebony from Nubia; but beyond that, very little is known about these early Nubian kingdoms. Middle Kingdom Egypt extended its boundary south to the second cataract in about 1900 BCE. The Nubians regrouped around a new capital at Kerma, just south of the third cataract. Soon after the beginning of the New Kingdom, however, in about 1500 BCE, direct Egyptian rule was extended deep into the Nubian heartland, beyond the fourth cataract. The aim was presumably to gain greater control over the region's trade. Egyptian towns and temples were built along this narrow ribbon of the fertile Nile. During the 500 years of direct Egyptian rule the local Nubian ruling class adopted many aspects of Egyptian culture, including their religion, language and writing.

With the decline of Egypt, following the fall of the New Kingdom dynasties, Egyptian administration was withdrawn from Nubia. Thus from about 1100 BCE local Nubian rulers were able to reassert their culture and independence. They built a new religious and political capital at Napata, near the fourth cataract. The new Nubian state was known to Egyptians as the Kingdom of Kush. This region from the third cataract southwards lay beyond the zone of the Nile floodplain and fell within the area of tropical summer rainfall. Kush's agricultural economy was therefore based on the cultivation of sorghum and millet and the grazing of cattle, away from the immediate vicinity of the Nile.

The rulers of Kush were still largely Egyptian in culture and their state was modelled on Egyptian lines. They expanded trade with Egypt and their kings gained steadily in wealth and power. In 730 BCE the king of Kush invaded Egypt itself and seized control of the kingdom at Thebes. There a line of Kushite kings ruled for more than 60 years, known in Egyptian history as the twenty-fifth or 'Ethiopian' dynasty. They were, however, so thoroughly Egyptianised that they brought no significant cultural change to Egypt. They wore the traditional double crown of Upper and Lower Egypt, worshipped Egyptian gods and had their names inscribed on Egyptian temples.

Following the Assyrian invasion of Lower Egypt in 670 BCE, the Kushite court withdrew again to Nubia and did not return to Egypt. Instead, they built a powerful and independent kingdom south of the second cataract.

The move to Meroe   Centred first at Napata near the fourth cataract, the kingdom soon shifted its administrative centre to the southern provincial town of Meroe. This may have occurred initially because of the threat of Egyptian invasion. In 593 BCE an Egyptian raiding army penetrated as far as the fourth cataract and sacked the town of Napata.

The 'island of Meroe', between the Nile and Atbara, had a number of distinct economic advantages. In the first place the land surrounding Meroe was rich in both iron ore and in the hardwood timber needed for making charcoal. Following their experience with the Assyrians, the Kushites were determined that their new kingdom of Meroe would be based on the production and use of iron. Besides improving their weapons of defence, iron provided the Meroites with spears and arrows for hunting. As we shall see shortly, the products of hunting formed an important part of the Meroitic economy. Iron also provided the Meroites with axes for cutting timber and clearing agricultural land and hoes for ploughing the soil.

Another economic advantage of the southern region of Meroe was its potential for extensive rainfall agriculture. In the Egyptian floodplain of the lower Nile, land clearance and ploughing were not a problem, so the development of iron tools had not been a necessity. But in the Nubian section of

Map 3.2 Egypt, Kush and Meroe: 1500 BCE to 350 CE

the Nile above the second cataract, the valley is much narrower and the extent of cultivable floodplain was therefore very small. It was soon realised at Napata that there was hardly enough agricultural land to support a large urban population. The 'island of Meroe', on the other hand, fell well within the region of tropical summer rainfall. Here it was possible to grow the tropical cereals sorghum and millet and to extend their cultivation away from the immediate region of the river. And in the plains to east and west, cattle and other livestock could be grazed. Thus, with the help of their iron tools, the people of Meroe were able to develop a mixed farming economy.

Finally, the southern town of Meroe was in a good position for the further development of trade. North of the fifth cataract trading parties *en route* to Egypt could strike north across the desert to rejoin the Nile near the modern town of Faras (see Map 3.2). By taking this shorter route they were able to avoid the perils of the third and second cataracts. In addition, when relations with Egypt became strained, as they did from time to time, Meroe had the further advantage of a trading outlet to the Red Sea. During the centuries of Greek and Roman rule in Egypt, the Red Sea increased in importance as a major trading artery between the Mediterranean, India and the Far East. By exporting its traditional products of ivory, leopard skins, ostrich feathers, ebony and gold, the tropical African kingdom of Meroe gained direct access to this expanding trade. It is no coincidence that the period of Greek and Roman prosperity saw the kingdom of Meroe reach the height of its wealth and power.

The development of a Meroitic culture

Initially the culture, language, writing and religion of the rulers of Meroe was highly Egyptianised in character. This was hardly surprising considering the deep association with Egypt over very many centuries. Indeed, the early rulers of Meroe still called themselves kings of Upper and Lower Egypt centuries after they had ceased to rule in Egypt. Egyptian was the official language of government, and inscriptions were in Egyptian hieroglyphics. Egyptian gods were worshipped in Meroe's temples, and pyramids were built over the tombs of their rulers.

Gradually, however, local indigenous influences came to the fore, and Meroe developed its own distinctive cultural forms. A local language, referred to by historians as Meroitic, came to replace Egyptian as the spoken language of the court. Hieroglyphics were adapted to this local language and in due course a flowing alphabetic-type script was developed. Unfortunately, since the Meroitic language is not known today, this distinctive Meroitic script has not yet been deciphered.

In their religion the Meroites retained Egyptian gods, especially Amun, but added their own local gods and shrines. The most important Meroitic addition was the Lion God, Apedemek. The ruins of the Lion Temple at Musawwarat are still visible to this day. Statues and engravings of Apedemek usually portrayed him as a lion's head on the body of a snake or a lion's head on the body of a man (see Figure 3.3). But there was one particular shrine at which the priests kept a number of live lions as symbols of the living god. The priests of Meroe's religious shrines were rich and powerful people in the kingdom. Indeed for centuries after the capital was moved to the south, new kings or queens of Meroe had to present themselves to the priests of the temples of Napata to obtain the official approval of the gods.

The art and architecture of Meroe similarly developed their own particular character. Prominent in Meroitic artforms were pictures, engravings or statues of tropical African animals such as lion, ostrich, giraffe and elephant. They produced two classes of pottery: fine, painted luxury ware, turned on a wheel; and a heavier, handmade domestic ware, for regular cooking and storage. The former was based on Egyptian shape and design but was clearly locally made and decorated in distinctive Meroitic style (see Figure 3.4). The latter seems to have been based upon an earlier Nubian tradition. Their pyramids too were

Figure 3.3 Facsimile of an inscribed votive tablet of red slate from the Lion Temple at Naga. It depicts a king of Kush dressed in a long robe making offerings to the lion-headed god Apademak. The inscription is in Meroitic. Second century BCE

distinctly Meroitic in style (see Figure 3.5). They were small, unpointed and regular in shape and size, quite unlike the royal tombs of the Egyptian pharaohs. Moreover they first appeared in Meroe several centuries after pyramid-building had altogether ceased in Ancient Egypt.

The economic and political organisation of Meroe

Economically and politically the kingdom of Meroe was quite distinct from Egypt. The economy was not based primarily upon the kind of irrigated floodplain agriculture practised in Egypt. As we have already seen, the extent of floodplain south of the second cataract was too narrow to support a large population. But living just within the northern boundary of the summer rainfall zone, the Meroites could grow their tropical cereals in extensive fields away from the river's edge. This pattern of agricultural production influenced the social and political organisation of Meroitic society.

The cattle-herders and peasant cultivators, who made up the vast majority of Meroe's population, were spread out over a wide area. They lived in mud and reed houses, clustered in small rural villages and ruled over by minor chiefs and heads of family clans. As such they appear to have been under less direct political control than their counterparts in the floodplain regions of the Egyptian Nile. They probably paid their taxes in the form of annual tribute to the king rather than the kind of detailed pre-assessed taxation demanded by Egyptian government officials. Cattle were grazed over a wide extent of savannah grassland to the east and west of Meroe. Herdsmen were semi-nomadic, moving their animals between summer and winter pastures. They probably had a fair degree of political

Figure 3.4 Engraving of a rural scene from the rim of a Meroite copper bowl

freedom from central government control, provided they paid an annual tribute in livestock.

The rulers, their government officials and full-time craftsmen, lived in the towns, of which the principal one was Meroe itself. Politically the king ruled as an all-powerful, absolute monarch, but there appears to have been a greater element of consent by the people than ever existed in Ancient Egypt. Although the choice of monarch came from within a single royal family, succession was not automatic. It required the agreement of the nobility and the final approval of the priesthood. An unpopular monarch was occasionally removed. The mother of the king was also an important figure in the government, which may have helped maintain stability and continuity from one reign to the next.

The personal wealth of the Meroitic kings came from their control of trade. The main exports from the kingdom were the products of mining and hunting. Both of these activities came under the direct control of the king. Hunting expeditions, armed with iron weapons, penetrated deep into the grasslands and woodlands to the south in search of elephants, ostriches and leopards. The hunters formed the basis of a standing army, and elephants were used in war. Indeed, trained elephants from Meroe were exported to Egypt for use in the Egyptian army.

The principal industrial craft in Meroe was the smelting of iron and the making of iron tools. To this day the huge mounds of waste slag from their smelting furnaces rise up alongside the modern railway to bear witness to the enormous iron output of the ancient kingdom of Meroe. Iron provided the farmers and hunters of Meroe with superior tools and weapons. The development and use of iron was thus partly responsible for the very success, growth and wealth of the Meroite kingdom.

Figure 3.5 The pyramids of the Meroitic kings and queens in the north cemetery, Meroe, on a ridge overlooking the ruins of the city, 300 BCE – 400 CE. Although much smaller than their Ancient Egyptian counterparts, the pyramids of Meroe had their own distinctive features and continued to be used to mark royal burials for more than a thousand years after they had ceased to be constructed in Egypt

53

The rise and decline
of the kingdom of
Meroe

During the final century before the Common Era (CE), the kings of Meroe expanded their rule into Lower Nubia between the first and second cataract. This led to clashes with the Roman rulers of Egypt. A Meroite army attacked the border town of Syene in 23 BCE and destroyed or seized a number of statues and other valuables. A bronze head of the Roman emperor Augustus, probably seized in this raid, was discovered by archaeologists at Meroe in 1912. The Meroite raid provoked a Roman counter-attack which penetrated as far as Napata and caused much destruction. When the Roman army finally retired to Egypt, they took with them several thousand captives whom they sold into slavery. Despite this military setback, under the leadership of King Netekamani, who ruled from 12 BCE to 12 CE, the Meroite kingdom recovered to reach the height of its power and artistic achievement. During Netekamani's reign the kingdom stretched from the Ethiopian foothills in the south to the first cataract in the north. The wealth of the period was displayed in the building of temples and palaces. Over the next two centuries relations with the Roman rulers of Egypt were normally cordial and Meroe contributed to the Roman expansion of trade through the Red Sea and into the Indian Ocean.

The kingdom of Meroe came to an end sometime after 300 CE. Royal burials ended soon after that date and sometime between 300 and 350 CE the town of Meroe was abandoned. A number of factors seem to have been responsible for the collapse of the kingdom. The former power of Meroe had been built on the strength of its iron industry and agricultural base and the wealth of its foreign trade. Between 200 and 300 CE, Meroe gradually lost the benefit of both these advantages. The agricultural base declined as the environment became worn out through over-exploitation. The mounds of waste slag suggest the scale of the former smelting industry and this would have consumed huge quantities of charcoal. Trees were cut down faster than new ones could grow. This led to erosion and loss of topsoil. The land, which had supported a thriving agricultural population for over a thousand years, lost its former fertility.

In addition Meroe lost its advantageous trade position. Its trade was closely tied to the wealth of Roman Egypt, through its connections down the Nile or along the Red Sea. As Roman wealth declined, there was less demand for Meroe's luxury goods. At the same time Meroe's Red Sea trade to the Indian Ocean was lost to her better-placed neighbour, the kingdom of Aksum. (The rise of Aksum will be considered in Chapter 5.) In about 350 CE the army of the Aksumite king Ezana invaded the 'island of Meroe'. By then the capital had already been abandoned and the region was in the hands of a people whom the Aksumites referred to as the Noba. It is not known exactly who the Noba were. They may have been an invading group of pastoralists from the south or south-west. On the other hand they may have been a subject Nubian people who regained control of the region when the power of their Meroite rulers collapsed.

Iron Age north Africa and early trans-Saharan trade

The Phoenicians were a seafaring people who originated from the region of present-day Lebanon. From about 1000 BCE the iron-using Phoenicians built their wealth upon the trade of the coastal region of the Mediterranean. In their search for valuable metals such as gold, copper, silver and lead, they penetrated the western Mediterranean and established a string of trading stations along the north African coast. By 800 BCE they had turned their principal settlements into colonies which in due course became virtually independent of the homeland of Phoenicia. The most famous of these was the colony of Carthage in modern Tunisia (see Map 3.3).

At Carthage the Phoenicians settled among the bronze-using Berbers of north Africa. In the Tunisian plains and the Algerian coastal lowlands, the Berbers were settled agriculturalists who supplied the Phoenician towns with food. In exchange the Phoenicians introduced them to iron-working. In time the Phoenicians, now 'Carthaginians', mixed with the Berbers to become an intricate part of north African society. Carthage became a base for further trading exploration of the Atlantic coast of north-west Africa. Their furthest settlement south, reached by about 400 BCE, was at a place called Cerne, believed to have been on the Mauritanian coast south of Cape Blanc.

Early trans-Saharan trade

By 600 BCE the Phoenician colony of Carthage had become a major power in the western Mediterranean. Part of their wealth was built upon a trade in tropical African products from across the Sahara. The Phoenicians themselves did not conduct this trade. They relied upon Berber pastoralists of the Atlas mountains and northern Sahara to act as intermediaries. The Berbers had long maintained tentative contact across the Sahara, possibly dating back to a time before it became a desert (see above in Chapters 1 and 2). Small settlements of desert-dwelling Berbers still clung to isolated natural wells, the oases of the desert. Communications between one group and another were maintained along certain lines of oases, stretching right across the Sahara. Trading contacts at this time were thus not directly across the desert but occurred by passing goods from one oasis to another. The main desert item traded to the south was salt, in exchange perhaps for food. But gradually, highly valuable trading items such as copper and gold were passed across the desert from tropical west Africa to the coastal dwellers in the north.

The rise of Carthage between 800 and 500 BCE provided a strong stimulus for the further development of trans-Saharan networks. The extent of these networks is revealed in a remarkable series of rock paintings at various sites across the Sahara. The paintings are of two-wheeled, horse-drawn chariots and for a time it was assumed that this was proof that wheeled vehicles were driven right across the Sahara, providing direct transport from one side of the desert to the other. It is now realised that this was not possible. In the first place, centuries of history have shown that horse-drawn wheeled vehicles would not have been able to negotiate the loose sands of the desert. In the second place, careful study of the detail of the paintings has revealed that they depict the 'racing chariots' used for sport by wealthy people in the Mediterranean towns of north Africa (see Figure 3.6). These were minimal in construction, built for speed and with no room for carrying any baggage. The chariot paintings do show that there was plenty of communication between north Africa and Saharan oases. Trade, however, was carried by pack-animals, probably donkeys, mules and horses. The Arabian camel was not widely used in north Africa until the first century CE and its impact will be discussed in Chapter 6. The early trade routes across the Sahara are shown in Map 3.3.

Trade across the Sahara in this early period was a dangerous and hazardous undertaking. Apart from the obvious environmental problems and the

Figure 3.6 A racing chariot pulled by two horses: a Saharan rock-painting. Chariots such as this were used for racing in Mediterranean north Africa, and not for transporting goods across the Sahara, as previously thought

dangers of not reaching the next oasis before water supplies ran out, traders were exposed to raids. People known as Garamantes living in the Fezzan were notorious for their raiding. They carried out raids not only on trading caravans, but also on the oases and peoples of the south in the direction of Lake Chad. Captives were used for mining salt in the Sahara or were transported and sold into slavery in north Africa. Slavery was a feature of trans-Saharan trade from its earliest beginnings. The main currency of trade, however, remained salt from the central Sahara. In addition cloth, beads and metal goods from north Africa were exchanged for west African gold and ivory as well as captives for sale into slavery.

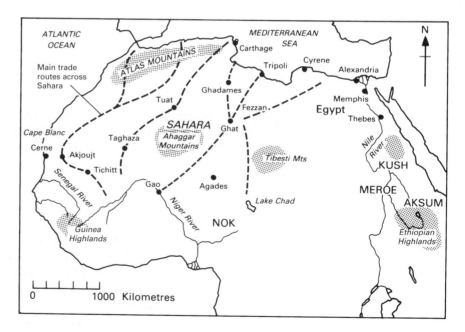

Map 3.3 Early trans-Saharan trade to 300 CE

4

The Early Iron Age in central, eastern and southern Africa

Evidence for the spread of iron-working

By the fifth century CE the knowledge and skills of iron-working and crop cultivation had been established right across the more favourable regions of central, eastern and southern Africa. The relatively rapid spread of iron-working to this vast region is generally believed to have been the work of small farming communities who spoke early forms of the Bantu family of languages. Historians have reached these conclusions by marrying the evidence of linguists on the one hand, with that of archaeologists on the other. Little, however, remains definite. Ongoing research continually reveals new evidence about the possible origins, nature, timing, direction and impact of 'Early Iron Age' farming. Thus as old theories are refined or new theories proposed, the spread of the Early Iron Age by Bantu-speaking farmers remains one of the great debates of African prehistory.

For more information see www.palgrave.com/ shillington

Linguistic evidence: the Bantu-speakers

All living languages are constantly changing and developing. In the days before the rapid and easy communications of the modern world, when one group of people moved away from another, they might well lose all regular contact with each other. Although they started with a common language, their languages would develop separately and in different ways. At first each group would form its own dialect, developing its own pronunciation and picking up or devising new words to suit changing circumstances. If in their new territory members of the group came into contact with other peoples and absorbed them into their society, this would bring further changes to their language. Finally, after the changes of many generations, the people of one group would no longer readily understand the language of the other. By then a new language could be said to have developed, though, stemming from a common parent language, they both belonged to the same basic language 'family'.

Linguists who study the features which various languages have in common are able to trace a family of languages back to their original parent language. Having established a language 'genealogy', or family tree, they can then demonstrate the development of its branches, and therefore *the movement of people*, away from the original language heartland. As more linguistic evidence becomes available, this movement is now being demonstrated with increasing accuracy for the Bantu family of languages.

'Bantu' is the name that modern linguists have devised for a particular family of African languages belonging to the wider Niger-Congo group

Map 4.1 The languages of Africa, *c.*1600 CE

which stretches across so much of sub-Saharan Africa. The word-stem *ntu*, or something very similar to it, is common to the languages of this family. It means 'person'. The prefix *ba-*, again common to most of these languages, denotes plural and so *ba-ntu* means literally 'people'. As can be seen from Map 4.1, the Bantu family is geographically the most widespread in the Niger-Congo group. But it should be stressed that the word 'Bantu' is not the actual name of any one language or people as such.

There are some 450 known languages in the Bantu family, from Kikongo and Gigikuyu in the north to Setswana and Isixhosa in the south. The original ancestor or 'parent' Bantu (referred to by linguists as proto-Bantu) is thought to have evolved in the region of present-day Cameroon. From there it is believed to have spread eastwards round the northern edge of the Congo forest and southwards through the forest to the savannah woodlands beyond. We shall return to the further spread of Bantu speakers later in the present chapter.

Archaeological evidence: smelters, potters and farmers

The main source of evidence for the development and spread of iron-working comes from archaeological sites. Radiocarbon and other scientific methods of dating ancient materials have made possible the ever-more-accurate dating of Iron Age settlements. The most useful materials for dating are charcoal and the waste slag produced as a result of iron-smelting. Another important kind of evidence is pottery.

Farming and pastoral communities need pots for carrying and storing milk and water and for cooking food, especially the porridge made from dried and pounded cereals. The presence of fragments of broken clay pottery in an archaeological site, therefore, is often an indication of a settled farming community. Iron Age farmers became skilled makers of baked-clay pottery. Their craftsmanship was so highly valued that they decorated their pots with carefully shaped grooves and regular stamped patterns. Their aim was to make the pot beautiful and the patterns adopted were dictated by local custom. The result was that related groups of people used similar styles and methods of pottery decoration. Thus the methods, shapes and styles of manufacture and patterning have enabled archaeologists to identify groups of people who were probably in some way linked or associated with each other. To some extent also, differing styles of pottery can be used to help date a variety of apparently linked archaeological sites.

The archaeological evidence for farming is not always direct. It is seldom that actual cultivated grains have survived the passage of time. But farming can be inferred from the presence of well-worn grinding stones or the remains of storage pits or bins. In some cases archaeologists have excavated whole villages such as Kumadzulo just north of the middle Zambezi or Kgaswe in the Toutswe region, east of the Kalahari. From these and other smaller excavations we can learn a great deal about the Early Iron Age way of life.

Bantu 'migrations'

Before the development of radiocarbon dating and the widespread archaeological research which has taken place since the 1950s, it used to be believed that Bantu-speakers spread across eastern, central and southern Africa in the comparatively recent past. The main source of evidence was oral traditions which seldom traced ruling lineages back more than 500 years. It was assumed, therefore, that to have so widely populated the subcontinent in so

Figure 4.1 A blacksmith at work in western Zambia in 1972, using ancient traditional double bellows

short a time there must have been large-scale conquering migrations of whole new peoples. It is now believed, however, that the initial spread of early Bantu-speakers was of very small numbers, infiltrating new areas and inter-marrying with and otherwise absorbing indigenous hunter-gatherer communities. And all this occurred over a very long period of time, stretching back at least to the early centuries of the Common Era. It is therefore nowadays generally considered misleading to refer to the spread of Bantu-speaking farmers as 'migrations'.

Origins of the Early Iron Age in sub-equatorial Africa

We saw in Chapter 2 that early Bantu-speaking farmers were already spreading through the Congo forest by the first millennium BCE. At this stage they still used stone tools and so, for easier cultivation, they sought out the natural forest clearings and forest fringes. Their main crops were palm-oil, nuts and root crops like yams, all suitable for the high-rainfall forest zone. They had not yet learned to cultivate the cereal crops more suitable for the drier, summer-rainfall, savannah regions which stretched to their south. Cereals such as millets and sorghum, however, had already been domesticated in the savannah regions of the Sudan. As we saw in Chapter 2, some form of pastoralism and cereal cultivation was established in the Rift Valley and Great Lakes (sometimes referred to as interlacustrine) region of east Africa during the same period. We have already seen in the previous chapter that iron-working was well established in central Nigeria by 500 BCE and in the Great Lakes region of east Africa by at least 600 BCE.

The spread of the Early Iron Age

Although the period of the initial spread of Bantu-speaking farmers through the southern half of the continent is known as the 'Early Iron Age', one must be careful not to assume that a knowledge of iron technology was the be-all and end-all of Bantu culture. Indeed, the fact that iron-working technology appears to have been known to the Bantu-speakers of east Africa for several centuries before their rapid spread across the region suggests another interesting possibility. It is important to remember that the earliest Bantu-speaking farmers had been forest-dwellers whose principal skills for living were gathering fruit and nuts, fishing and cultivating roots. In the dry savannah country to the east of the Congo forest they had come into contact with Sudanic and Cushitic-speaking peoples whose principal skills for living were herding cattle, hunting and cultivating cereals. It has recently been suggested that it may have been the Bantu-speakers' absorption of this savannah culture, and hence their mastery of a wide range of mixed farming practices and beliefs, rather than simply the adoption of iron technology, which accounts for the rapid spread of their settlements across eastern, central and southern Africa during the first few centuries CE (see Map 4.2). Another factor which may have influenced this rapid spread was the arrival on the continent of new crops from south-east Asia. Of particular importance were the banana and the Asian yam, brought to the east African coastal region by Austronesian sailors who colonised the island of Madagascar in about the second century CE (see p. 143). These crops were probably carried inland up the river valleys of eastern Africa such as the Rufiji or the Zambezi. The banana in particular soon became an important, high-yielding, staple crop in the moister regions of the continent such as the Congo forest and the lake-side region of southern Uganda.

The exact routes and directions of the spread of Early Iron Age Bantu-speakers, however, remain speculative. Archaeologists studying styles of pottery decoration and furnace construction have identified general differences between eastern and western traditions. This suggests the advance of Early Iron Age peoples along two broad fronts or 'streams'. The division between eastern and western streams seems to fall along the line of the Luangwa valley of what is today eastern Zambia. This corresponds roughly with linguistic evidence for the development and spread of eastern and western 'Bantu'. Further south, however, the evidence is less clear and it is more difficult to identify a division between eastern and western streams. Over much of central and southern Africa there was probably considerable inter-mixing and transmission of ideas between eastern and western peoples.

Since we cannot identify exactly who these Early Iron Age peoples were, in terms of their modern historical descendants, archaeologists and historians have generally found it useful to classify their settlements according to their traditions or styles of pottery.

The eastern stream

The earliest east African Iron Age pottery has been classified as Urewe ware. It has been firmly dated in the Lakeland region to between the second and fifth centuries CE, but its origins probably stem from well back in the BCE period, to the early origins of iron-working in the region. A distinctive characteristic of Urewe ware is an indentation on the base of its pots and bowls. For this reason it is sometimes referred to as 'dimple-based' pottery. To the east of the Rift valley a pottery style probably related to Urewe has been classified as Kwale ware. Here in the hills south-east of Kilimanjaro, Early Iron Age farmers making Kwale pottery settled from about the third century CE. Another important east African Iron Age site is at Uvinza, to the east of Lake Tanganyika. It has been dated to the fifth and sixth centuries. Its pottery is clearly Early Iron Age, but it is not dimple-based and is probably a local development. The site seems to have been a centre for the salt trade from nearby salt springs.

A remarkably early date of the first century CE has been identified for an Iron Age site near Maputo Bay in south-east Africa, but in general the main spread southwards of Early Iron Age farmers in the eastern region appears to have been in the third and fourth centuries. Between the fourth and seventh centuries settlements of Iron Age farmers became well established in the river valleys of the south-eastern regions of present-day South Africa. It used to be assumed that the Early Iron Age peoples of the Zimbabwe plateau belonged to the eastern stream. It now seems possible that they may have been part of the western or perhaps a combination of the two.

The western stream

Recent archaeological findings have revealed that iron-working farmers were living by the lower Congo near Malebo Pool by the first or second centuries CE. But archaeological research in this region and in present-day Angola is still in its infancy. The richest and most revealing Iron Age sites of the savannah woodland just south of the Congo forest are to be found around Lake Kisale in the upper Lualaba valley. Here there is evidence of copper- as well as iron-smelting from as early as the fourth century CE. While iron was used for tool-making, copper was used for necklaces and jewellery, trade or even currency. There seem to have been continuous and thriving farming and trading settlements in this area right through into recent historical times. We shall return to this region when looking at the growth of Later Iron Age states in Chapter 10 (pp. 145–6).

An important archaeological site for the Iron Age settlement of east-central Africa is in the Kalambo Falls region, between Lakes Tanganyika and Malawi. First excavated in the 1950s, this was one of the original sites to awaken historians to the antiquity of the central African Iron Age. Research has shown continuity of Iron Age village settlement in the Kalambo lake basin from the fourth to the fourteenth centuries. In the upper Zambezi valley a couple of very early first- to second-century dates have been identified. But most of the Early Iron Age settlement between the Kafue and

Map 4.2 The Early Iron Age in eastern, central and southern Africa

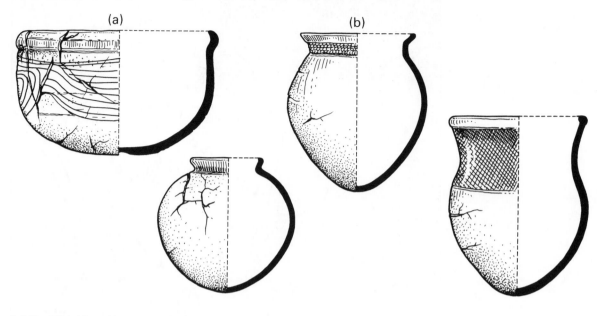

(a) Deep bowl from Urewe
(b) Pots from Mubende Hill, Uganda

0 1 2 cm

Figure 4.2 Early Iron Age copperbelt industry: rims of clay pots

Figure 4.3 Ceramic head from a site near Lydenburg, South Africa, dated *c.*500–700 CE

Zambezi rivers seems to have developed between the third and seventh centuries.

Early Iron Age occupation of the Zimbabwe plateau, south of the Zambezi, seems to have started with the makers of what is known as Bambata pottery who were settled at Mabveni in southern Zimbabwe in the second century CE before moving on south of the Limpopo. The main settlement of the Zimbabwe plateau by Early Iron Age farmers, whether of eastern, western or combined streams, occurred between the third and fifth centuries. Their pottery styles are generally grouped together as Gokomere-Ziwa ware. The earliest known Iron Age settlement of the famous Great Zimbabwe site was in the fourth century though the stone-walling of the area belongs to a later period (see pp. 154–9).

Makers of 'western stream' pottery colonised the Transvaal highveld, south of the Limpopo, between the fourth and fifth centuries. One of the most fruitful archaeological sites of this period has been near Lydenburg on the edge of the eastern Transvaal escarpment. Here archaeologists have recovered a number of remarkable pottery heads (see Figure 4.3). The hollow Lydenburg heads have been dated to about 500 CE and were probably used as ceremonial or religious masks. They show a considerable refinement of craftsmanship and suggest a settled, well-organised community which had the time and desire to develop such skills and ceremonies.

The development and organisation of Early Iron Age society

There appear to have been a number of stages in the development of the Iron Age in Bantu-speaking Africa. The earliest stage, from the second to the fifth centuries CE, saw the relatively rapid spread of iron-working farmers over much of the eastern, central and south-eastern part of the subcontinent. The fifth to eighth centuries were a period of consolidation. The resources of the more favourable regions were developed and exploited and adaptations were made to local environments. The eighth to twelfth centuries were a period of transition from what archaeologists and historians refer to as the Later Iron Age. In some areas this latter stage was a local development, while other areas seem to have received 'ready-made' Later Iron Age cultures from outside their area. This suggests a number of centres of development and expansion across the subcontinent which will be considered in more detail in Chapter 10. The concern of the remainder of this chapter is with the periods of the spread and consolidation of Early Iron Age communities.

The basis of the Early Iron Age economy was farming. The main crops were sorghum and millets, supplemented with various forms of pumpkin, melon and beans. Most also kept livestock though the numbers of cattle and sheep or goats were usually small in the early period. Some kept no livestock at all and those that did tended to use them for meat rather than milk and probably slaughtered them on ceremonial or religious occasions. The decision whether or not to keep cattle might be determined by the presence or absence of tsetse fly (for the importance of tsetse fly, see p. 26). Although they were farmers, hunting and gathering remained an important source of food for most peoples throughout the period. To some extent the relative importance of hunting depended upon the agricultural potential of the region. In some areas fishing was also an important source of food.

During the first few centuries of Bantu expansion, Iron Age farmers were moving into regions only thinly populated by small roving bands of pre-existing hunter-gatherers. They were therefore able to select the most suitable sites for their farming settlements. This freedom to choose the best sites – where the soil was most fertile, the grazing and the rainfall just right for their crops – probably explains their relatively rapid spread across the subcontinent in the early period. There was no need to clear thick forest or adopt new techniques to suit a difficult environment. New generations could simply move on to new areas. At first, therefore, settlements were usually confined to fertile river valleys and favourable rainfall regions – hence the general movement towards the south-east, avoiding the dry south-west.

Villages were typically small, with up to a dozen or so houses. In some areas, however, settlements were quite large, such as in Natal, where villages up to eight hectares in extent have been recorded. Houses were usually made of poles and clay though there was a wide variety of styles and methods of construction depending upon locally available resources. Their small round houses were usually arranged in a circular pattern enclosing a fenced livestock pen where cattle or goats were confined at night. Each village usually also contained a number of storage bins for grain. This might take the form of a clay-lined pit or a specially constructed bin, raised on stones or poles.

Politically, communities were probably organised on a simple village basis with each village containing an extended family and its dependants. There was a clear division of labour between men and women, with the women tending the crops, preparing the food and caring for the small children. The men meanwhile tended the livestock and hunted for meat and for animal skins for clothing. They conducted trade and other relations with neighbouring peoples where necessary and normally assumed overall control of production within the community. The dominance of men in this society is indicated by their exclusive burials in the ground beneath the central live-stock enclosure. Women and children were buried near their houses around the outer edge of the village.

An important factor in the early spread and siting of Iron Age settlements was the need to find sources of iron ore together with sufficient hardwood for the charcoal to fire their smelting furnaces. Experiments conducted in modern times, using techniques practised in the Later Iron Age period, revealed that a clay furnace with draught pipes attached for rapid ventilation consumed 1000 kilos of hardwood charcoal in the smelting of enough iron to make about three hoes. Iron-smelting under these circumstances was clearly an expensive business in terms of labour and timber. Nevertheless, in contrast to the later period when technical and craft specialisations were developed, most Early Iron Age villages smelted their own iron. But it was probably on a small scale and there is some evidence of continuing use of certain stone tools, for instance scrapers for preparing skins and of course grinding stones. Stone was also used for hammering the newly smelted iron during forging. And for a while stone axes may have continued to be used for some of the heavier tasks of cutting trees, before a harder, higher-quality iron was developed.

Most Early Iron Age communities were more or less self-sufficient, though there is increasing evidence of small-scale trade between communities from a very early period. This was most likely in areas where there was abundance of a particular natural resource such as copper and salt at Sanga in the Congo and salt at Uvinza in Tanzania. Some of the communities which were to develop a specialisation in iron-smelting were at places of rich ore deposits such as the Tswapong hills of eastern Botswana or Palaborwa in the eastern Transvaal.

As the more favourable sites were occupied, the rapid dispersal to new areas slowed down. Along the southern coast of South Africa, the most west-erly Early Iron Age settlement, dated to the sixth or seventh century, was just west of the River Kei. It is no coincidence that this was the westernmost limit of summer seasonal rainfall suitable for growing tropical cereal crops. To have expanded further west would have meant having to abandon their known agricultural practices or develop entirely new crops and techniques. During the middle period, from the fifth to the eighth century, therefore, Iron Age farmers throughout the subcontinent began to make fuller use of their resources in the regions already occupied. In the Natal region of the south-east, for instance, initial settlements were confined to coastal lowlands and valley bottoms. Gradually more use was made of the sour summer grazing veld of the Drakensberg foothills and cattle assumed a greater importance in the economy. Similarly, in the drier grassland highveld of the western Transvaal and bordering on the eastern Kalahari, where cereal harvests were not so reliable, an emphasis on stock-rearing is evident from an early period. In the denser woodland regions north of the Zambezi, however, the presence of tsetse fly ensured that domestic cattle did not so quickly become impor-tant to local economies. Here the regular hunting of wild game continued to provide an important supplement to the main agricultural diet of millet and sorghum.

Farmers and hunter-gatherers

Because the movement of the earliest Iron Age farmers was in relatively small numbers, they did not displace the pre-existing stone-using hunter-gatherers.

67

It was a while before Iron Age farmers came to dominate the hunter-gatherers. There is evidence of continued occupation of parts of the east African plateau by stone-using peoples until at least as late as 1000 CE. Initially there was enough room for both cultures to live alongside each other in relative harmony. Indeed, they probably benefited from each other's presence. The farmers were a source of food in times of hardship and were also a source of iron tips for hunting spears and arrows. In exchange the hunter-gatherers could offer hunting produce, medicinal herbs and skills, and other services such as livestock-herding. In this way a degree of inter-dependence built up between hunter-gatherer and farmer. Indeed, it has been suggested that Bantu-speakers of southern Africa may have acquired their cattle, or at least their cattle-herding practices, from the Khoesan themselves. As we saw in Chapter 2 (p. 28), the Khoesan were herding cattle and sheep or goats in the region ahead of the arrival of Bantu-speaking farmers. In addition, many of the words in southern Bantu languages that relate to cattle and cattle-herding practices are derived from Khoesan languages.

In central and southern Africa Iron Age farmers deliberately absorbed Khoesan hunter-gatherers into their ranks, and not just as client herdsmen or hunters. There is archaeological evidence of a clear Khoesan-negroid mix in skeletons recovered from Early Iron Age graves. There is also linguistic evidence in terms of characteristic Khoesan 'clicks' in certain Bantu languages, especially in the south, though this may have been a later development. The Early Iron Age farmers practised male polygamy and so always needed a surplus of women. Khoesan women were probably attracted into farming society through the payment of a brideprice or *lobola* of livestock or metal goods to the bride's family. The labour of women and their offspring increased food production and thus the security and wealth of the community. In the long term, therefore, iron-working farming communities were strengthened at the expense of the hunter-gatherers. But it was a slow process and for many generations the two lifestyles co-existed with each other. In some regions the process of absorption occurred more rapidly or more thoroughly than in others. In the agriculturally favourable regions north of the Zambezi, for instance, distinct groups of hunter-gatherers were absorbed much more quickly than in drier regions further to the south-west.

In the dry regions of south-western Africa, the herding and hunter-gathering economy continued to offer advantages over farming. Khoesan and Bantu-speakers met on more equal terms and absorption by Bantu-speakers was less marked and less inevitable. Indeed, in the sandveld regions of the western Kalahari and Namibia west of the Okavango Delta, Khoesan-speakers remained dominant until more recent centuries.

North and north-eastern Africa to 1000 CE

chapter

5

Northern Africa in the Graeco-Roman period

Egypt under Greek rule

We saw in Chapter 2 (p. 42) that the Greek army of Alexander conquered Egypt in 332 BCE and that his general Ptolemy founded a dynasty of Greek-speaking pharaohs who ruled Egypt for the next 300 years. The Greeks viewed their new conquest as a crucial, pivotal point in a vast trading network. Egypt linked the northern world of Mediterranean Europe with the riches of the African interior and the Indian Ocean. The valley of the Nile also had the agricultural potential to support a large and wealthy merchant class. One of the first actions of the new Greek rulers was to found the great trading city of Alexandria on the Mediterranean coast of the Nile delta. From there the ancient Egyptian trading system was developed and expanded – northwards into Mediterranean Europe and southwards through the Red Sea to the Indian Ocean. We have already seen how the expansion of Red Sea trade at this time probably stimulated the growth of the kingdom of Meroe in the African interior of the upper Nile. By 250 BCE

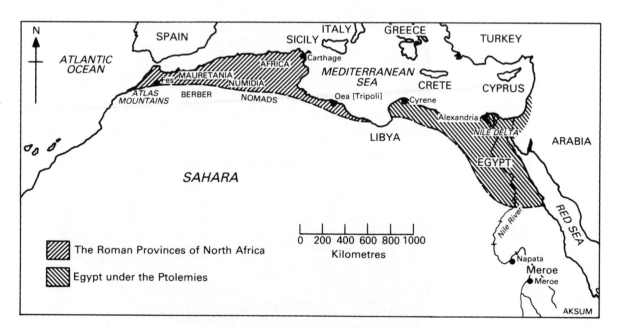

Map 5.1   Northern Africa in the Graeco-Roman period

69

the Greek rulers of Egypt had built up an Egyptian trading fleet of some four thousand ships.

It was during this period that the Arabian camel became widely used in Egypt. It was a larger pack animal than the Egyptian donkey and had already proved its effectiveness in the Arabian desert. Able to withstand heat and long periods without water, the camel was a valuable addition to Egyptian trading routes between the Nile and the Red Sea.

The Greeks brought to Egypt their own language and a faster-flowing, simpler form of writing. They built up a huge Greek-speaking bureaucracy of government officials who soon displaced the old Egyptian scribes. The more artistic but cumbersome Egyptian hieroglyphics fell out of use and were abandoned. With Greek the language of officialdom, the formal language of Ancient Egyptian fell into disuse. The Egyptian dialect of the common people evolved into what was to become known as Coptic. In later centuries this indigenous Egyptian language recovered some status as the language of the Coptic Christian Church (see below, p. 75).

Figure 5.1 The Rosetta Stone, with hieroglyphics, cursive Egyptian and ancient Greek script. The ability to read Ancient Egyptian hieroglyphics had been lost since about the fourth century CE. The discovery of the Rosetta Stone in 1799, and the realisation that it contained direct translations of the same passage, provided the key which enabled modern scholars to read and translate Ancient Egyptian hieroglyphics

To the mass of the Egyptian peasantry the main impact of the Ptolemaic dynasty was the introduction of a harsher, more efficient system of taxation. The new Greek-speaking tax collectors penetrated deep into upper Egypt, re-measuring the agricultural floodplain and reassessing taxes. They introduced a system of 'competitive taxation' whereby those peasants who promised to pay the heaviest taxes were awarded the most land. The system must have caused great hardship for the less fortunate or less efficient farmers. The profits of this taxation went to feed the prosperous merchants and ruling class in the expanding city of Alexandria.

For centuries before Alexander's conquest the Greeks had looked up to Egypt and admired its religion, arts and society. Greeks such as the historian Herodotus regarded the Egyptians as the cleanest, most religious and most 'civilised' of peoples. The word 'civilised' is of Greek origin. In general terms, and the way it is used here, it refers to an organised society in which people can practise their arts and culture and live together in harmony. (It is within this general meaning of the word that 'civilisation' is used with reference to Ancient Egypt in Chapter 2, p. 33.) In recent times the word has fallen into disrepute as European colonisers of the nineteenth and early twentieth centuries used it to suit their own racist ideologies. In their view only people of their own culture could be called 'civilised'. All other cultures they regarded as 'uncivilised', by which they meant 'inferior'.

Greek colonisation brought Egypt more thoroughly into the Mediterranean world. But in doing so the Ptolemies exploited the Egyptian peoples and hastened the decline of the distinctive Egyptian civilisation which had persisted for 3000 years. Nevertheless, the debt to the Ancient Egyptians remained and many of Ancient Egypt's ideas and achievements lived on in the arts, sciences and religion of the Greek and Roman world. The Greeks in their turn gave Africa two important names: Ethiopia and Libya. Ethiopian was the name they used to refer to the dark-skinned peoples living mainly to the south of Egypt. Libyan was the Greek name for the Berber peoples living to the west of Egypt.

North Africa under Roman rule

As we saw in Chapter 3, to the west of Egypt the north African coastal region was controlled by the Phoenicians from their trading capital at Carthage. In due course Greek and Phoenician domination of the Mediterranean gave way to that of Rome. By the middle of the first century CE the Romans, from their base in central Italy, had extended their empire over the whole of the Mediterranean world as well as much of western Europe. The Romans had begun their conflict with the Carthaginians in the middle of the third century BCE. After a century of drawn-out wars they finally conquered Carthage in 146 BCE and so took over the former Phoenician trading colony. The Romans called their new province 'Africa', a name gradually extended to refer to the continent in general. The origin of the word is uncertain. It may have been a Romanised version of a local Tunisian place or people. In due course it was adopted by Africans themselves and as such has persisted to this day.

In the mountainous and coastal regions to the west of Carthage lay independent Berber kingdoms. They were made up of a mixture of nomadic mountain pastoralists and settled coastal farmers. Their ruling classes lived in towns and were strongly influenced in their art and architecture by Greek and Phoenician culture. The Romans referred to these Berber kingdoms as

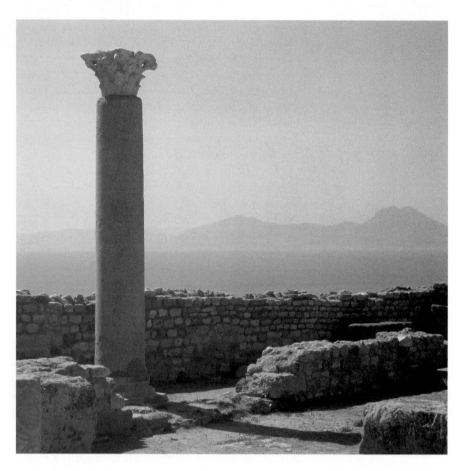

Figure 5.2 Part of the ruins of Roman Carthage (in modern Tunisia)

Numidia and Mauretania. By the time of the Roman conquest the ruler of Numidia, Massinissa, had extended his kingdom to cover most of the northern region of modern Algeria. The Romans initially formed an alliance with their powerful Berber neighbours. But gradually over the next two centuries they interfered in Berber politics, undermined Berber authority and finally, by conquest, brought Numidia and Mauretania within the Roman empire.

The Romans exploited to the maximum the agricultural potential of their north African possessions. Wheat production on the coastal plains was greatly expanded and groves of olive trees were planted in the dry rocky mountainous terrain further inland. But the agricultural producers of north Africa were very heavily taxed to feed the imperial city of Rome. Grain and olive oil was exported by the shipload to Rome where it was distributed free to the privileged citizens of the capital.

Society in Roman north Africa was sharply divided along distinct class lines. In the towns and coastal cities lived the ruling class of Roman administrators and wealthy Romanised Carthaginians (who were themselves of a Phoenician-Berber mixture). They owned large estates near the towns, which they farmed with slave labour: mostly Berbers traded or captured from Saharan nomads. Beyond the towns and large estates the population remained distinctly Berber in language and culture, and resentful of the oppressive Roman presence. The peasant farmers retained free access to their land but paid heavily in taxation. In turn they were supposed to receive

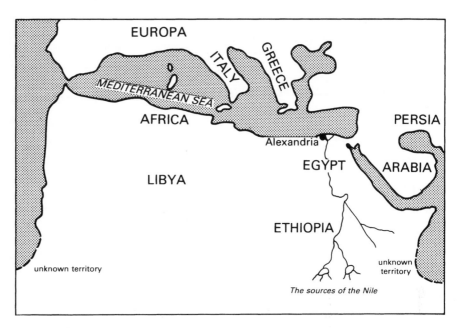

Map 5.2 Africa according to Ptolemy

Roman protection from raids by desert nomads. In practice they were sometimes better protected from Roman tax collectors by throwing in their lot with the raiding Berber nomads.

Beyond the region of settled farming communities, nomadic pastoralists herded sheep and goats and sometimes cattle. They lived on the very fringes of the Roman provinces, sometimes acknowledging Roman authority, at other times recognising the authority of independent Berber princes. The southern boundaries of Roman control were constantly under threat of raid from independent Berbers of the Sahara. Indeed it was in an attempt to regularly patrol a southern border that the Roman military introduced the camel to this region of north Africa. But the camels soon fell into the hands of the Berber nomads themselves. As a result, the Berbers' desert mobility and ability to conduct lightning raids was even further improved.

In the late 420s CE northern European Vandals crossed the Mediterranean and drove the Romans out of north Africa. By then, much of Mauretania and Numidia had already fallen to independent Berber chieftains.

In Egypt the period of Roman rule revived the taxation of the peasantry in an even more oppressive form. Egypt was regarded as little more than a source of grain for Rome. Indeed, the Roman exploitation of the peasantry in Egypt was so acute that many abandoned their fields and took to banditry.

The spread of Christianity in northern Africa

Of all the early centres of Christendom in the first century CE, Alexandria, the commercial capital of Egypt, was perhaps the most important. Alexandria was home to many of the early scholars who first defined the theology of the new religion. It was here that one of the earliest Christian bishoprics was said to have been founded by the apostle and gospel-writer Mark.

Map 5.3 The spread of Christianity in northern Africa, first to sixth century CE

Christianity quickly found an appeal among the oppressed population of first-century Roman Egypt. It offered hope with promise of a joyful afterlife to those suffering poverty and oppression in the present. Egyptian Christians soon developed a strong monastic tradition. There was something appealing in the notion of groups of religious people living in isolation, devoting their lives to prayer and wrestling with problems of the spirit. Perhaps it was prompted by a desire to turn their backs upon the intolerable material world of life in Roman Egypt.

From a slow beginning in the first century, Christianity gradually spread westwards during the second and third centuries to the Berber-speaking peoples of north Africa. As in Egypt the appeal again may have been partially a reaction to the harsh realities of life in Roman north Africa: an expression, perhaps, of a kind of anti-Roman Berber 'nationalism'. The Romans certainly viewed the early Christian Church as a dangerous and subversive sect, a threat to their authority. It threw a direct challenge into the face of the emperors, several of whom, in the fashion of the pharaohs, claimed to be gods themselves or were worshipped as such by their successors.

Right up until the early fourth century the Romans mercilessly persecuted the early Christian Church and martyred many thousands of its adherents. The final frenzy of persecution was ordered by Emperor Diocletian in 303 CE, during which many thousands of Christians, especially in north Africa, were martyred for refusing to sacrifice to the Roman gods. The Diocletian persecution did not end until the conversion of his successor Constantine (r.312–37) ten years later. Thereafter Christianity was officially recognised within the Roman empire although it did not become the state religion until 392 CE.

Donatists in the Maghrib

One of the edicts of Diocletian had been that Christian clergy must hand over all works of Christian scripture; and a majority of Christian clergy were coerced into submission. In Berber north Africa, however, there was strong resistance to the Roman persecution and a Numidian bishop, named Donatus, took the view that those who had submitted to the Diocletian edicts were no longer part of the true Church and should not be readmitted, even after the persecution was ended. Constantine and his successors urged the reunification of all branches of the Church, under Roman leadership. Donatus, however, held out against the readmission of apostate clergy into the Church; and his stand attracted the support of 400 north African bishops, who became known as 'Donatists'. The Romans attempted to bring the Donatists into line and in doing so continued to persecute the Christians of north Africa. Out of this conflict between Roman Church and Donatists there rose to prominence Aurelius Augustinus (354–430 CE), a Roman Christian convert from Numidia. An ardent opponent of the Donatists, he was destined to become, as Saint Augustine of Hippo, one of the founding Fathers of Roman Christian doctrine. In 411 CE the Roman Church officially declared Donatism to be a 'heresy', and this helped to weaken its hold in the urban centres of north Africa.

Within the independent Berber chiefdoms, Donatist Christianity blended with indigenous religious beliefs and practices and adopted many local variations in doctrine and in ceremony. As a result Christianity was not able to provide an effective force for unity in the face of the seventh- and eighth-century challenge of Islam from Arabia.

The Coptic Church in Egypt

In Egypt the bulk of local Christians similarly adopted the doctrine of Monophysitism, also unacceptable to the official Roman Church. The Monophysites, in emphasising the divinity of Christ, denied that He could also have been a normal human being. In 451 the Roman Church declared their doctrine a 'heresy' and unrepentant Monophysites were expelled from the official Christian Church that stressed the dual – divine and human – nature of Christ. Thereafter there were two Christian Churches in Egypt. The bulk of the Egyptian population stuck to the Monophysite doctrine and formed the 'Coptic' Church. In doing so they replaced the Greek of the official 'Melkite' Church with their own local Coptic language, a descendant from ancient Egyptian.

Christianity in Nubia

Between 500 and 600 CE, Monophysite Christian missionaries pushed southwards into Nubia, carrying with them their distinctive doctrine and strong monastic tradition. Nubia by this time was divided into three kingdoms. In the desert and floodplain zone between the first and third cataracts lay the kingdom of Noba with its capital at Faras. From the third to fifth cataracts was the kingdom of Makurra with its capital at Old Dongola. Finally, in the summer rainfall zone above the fifth cataract lay the kingdom of Aiwa with its capital at Soba on the Blue Nile just south of modern Khartoum. Little is known about the history of these Christian Nubian kingdoms.

Later Arab writers described the upper Nile valley of Christian Nubia as thickly populated with small agricultural villages. Date palms and vines were grown in the northern floodplain while cereals were cultivated further south. And throughout the region the grazing of cattle was widespread. Recent archaeological research has revealed that there was considerable prosperity within the Christian ruling classes. Their craftsmen made fine pottery, decoratively painted after firing. Artistic styles may have been influenced by earlier Meroitic origins. There is evidence too of numerous buildings of stone and wood: churches, monasteries and a range of large dwellings which may have been used as palaces. It is clear that along the upper Nile there flourished a distinct Nubian Christian civilisation that long outlived the seventh-century Arab invasion of Egypt.

The origins and rise of Aksum

Origins

Mixed farming in the highland border regions of northern Ethiopia, Tigray, Eritrea and eastern Sudan had been well established since at least 3000 BCE. Although the majority probably still lived in scattered homesteads, between 2000 and 1000 BCE a number of small centralised settlements were formed. The leaders or rulers of these emerging chiefdoms probably benefited from trade connections with Ancient Egypt, to whose merchants the region was known as 'the Land of Punt'. Traders of 'Punt' exported gold, timber, perfume oils and animal skins to Egypt via the Red Sea. Important burials in these Ethiopian chiefdoms were indicated by raised stone markers and some of their houses were constructed of stone, with timber-framed roofs. With the rise to power of the Nilotic kingdoms of first Kush and later Meroe after 1000 BCE (see above, pp. 48–51), the trade of 'Punt' declined in importance.

Some time during the sixth century BCE hunters and traders began crossing the Red Sea from Saba in south-western Arabia. They set up small trading

Map 5.4   The kingdom of Aksum, 100–700 CE

settlements on the Eritrean coast of north-east Africa. Already in their mountainous corner of Arabia the Sabaean-speaking people had developed the skills of terracing and irrigation which enabled them to farm in that otherwise largely desert peninsula. They had also learned to take full advantage of their strategic trading position between the Red Sea and the Indian Ocean. It was largely in search of ivory for the Persian and Indian trade that they crossed the Red Sea to north-east Africa. As skilled agriculturalists they soon realised the potential of the fertile valleys and foothills of Tigray and Amhara. By at least 500 BCE their hunting and trading settlements had expanded into colonies as they mixed and intermarried with the local population. In time their Sabaean language gave way to a locally evolved Ge'ez from which the modern Amharic of Ethiopia is descended. They were already a literate people and they developed their own Ge'ez script.

Though mainly based inland, these Ge'ez-speaking people developed a thriving sea port at Adulis. They took full advantage of the expansion of Red Sea trade that followed the Greek colonisation of Egypt. Indeed, initially it was traders from Saba and Adulis who carried much of the Greek trade through the Bab el Mandeb to the ports of the Indian Ocean. From there they returned with the luxury silks, muslins and spices of the East.

By the first century CE the Ge'ez-speaking farmers and traders of northeast Africa had developed their own powerful state, based inland at Aksum and politically quite independent of Arabia. The Greek shipping manual, *The Periplus of the Erythraean Sea*, reported that their Red Sea port of Adulis had become the most important ivory market in the whole of north-east Africa. It is clear from this that Aksum was already diverting the source of African ivory away from the interior kingdom of Meroe.

The rise of Aksum

Archaeological research has revealed that by the third and fourth centuries CE there was considerable prosperity at Aksum. The rulers were importing silver, gold, olive oil and wine. Their principal export was ivory and possibly also captives to sell as slaves. By 300 CE they had started minting their own coinage, which was a great aid to trading transactions at Adulis. This would have given them a further advantage over their Meroite neighbours, who never developed a coinage. Craftsmen at Aksum also manufactured luxury goods of glass crystal, brass and copper for export to Egypt and the eastern Roman empire. Other important exports to the Greek and Roman world were frankincense, used in burials, and myrrh which had important medicinal properties. Both these highly valued products were obtained from the resin of particular trees which grew mainly in the mountainous regions of Aksum and south-west Arabia.

The concept of stone buildings and burial monuments was already known to pre-Sabaean Ethiopians. However, the original Sabaean settlers introduced the practice of building with stone on a massive scale and in particular detailed carving on stone. The combination of the two traditions produced a unique Aksumite monumental culture. They built temples, palaces and tombs for the wealthy ruling classes. Among their most impressive stone buildings were huge monuments, some of which still stand to this day. Known to us as stelae, these tall, thin monuments of solid stone were placed to mark the tombs of their rulers and are thought to date from about 300 CE. They were carved in the unique form of a very narrow, many-storied house

Figure 5.3 The tallest of the still-erect stelae at Aksum. These 'multi-storied' structures, carved out of a single block of solid stone, were erected over the burial chambers of the kings of Aksum

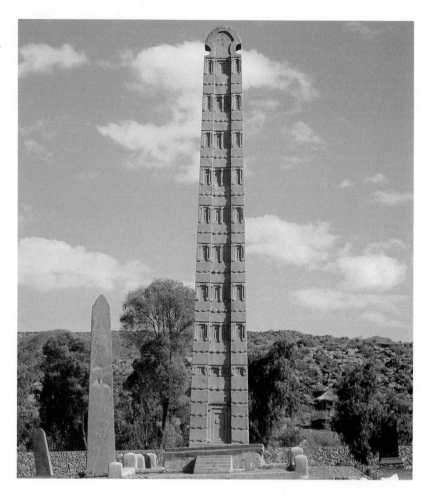

(see Figure 5.3). The tallest stelae, which has since fallen down, was made of 700 tonnes of rock and stood 33 metres in height.

In the fourth century CE Christian scholars from Alexandria brought Christianity to Aksum. The Aksumite king, Ezana (320–50 CE), adopted Christianity towards the end of his reign. It is thought that he may have been influenced by his desire to cement trading relations with the Greek-speaking world of the eastern Mediterranean. The influence of the Greek connection at this time is shown by the inclusion of Greek inscriptions alongside those in Ge'ez on the Aksumite monuments of the period. It was certainly a time of great prosperity and expansion for Aksum, and it was the army of King Ezana which invaded the 'island of Meroe' in about 350 CE. Two centuries later, at about the time that Nubia was undergoing conversion to Christianity, Monophysite monks from Syria also reached Aksum. There their monastic tradition was incorporated into the distinctive Aksumite Christian Church.

Within the Aksumite state the king exercised most direct power in the central region near the capital. Beyond the centre were regional rulers who paid tribute to the king. They were probably based on earlier pre-Aksumite chiefdoms. At times of weakness at the centre, the provinces were liable to assert their independence by refusing to pay tribute. The king's main wealth and power came from his control of foreign trade. At Adulis his officials charged taxes on all imports and exports. Apart from foreign trade, centred on Adulis, the economic basis of the state was its irrigated and terraced agriculture. But little is known about the relationship between the peasant farmers and the state.

The decline of Aksum

For a while in the sixth century Aksum was powerful enough to expand across the Red Sea to enclose the region of Saba (modern Yemen) within its borders. But by the end of the century they had been expelled from the Arabian peninsula by their great rivals in trade, the Persians. The rise of Islam and its rapid spread across western Asia and northern Africa in the seventh century further weakened the trading position of Aksum. Much of the trade between the Indian Ocean and the eastern Mediterranean now passed through the Persian Gulf rather than the Red Sea.

The decline of Aksum in the eighth century may have been largely to do with their loss of trade to the Persians and Arabs. But, as with Meroe, it is also likely to have been related to a deterioration in the environment. This was the result of the long-term cutting down of trees and over-exploitation of the soil, leading to the kind of erosion so typical of the region today. Although Aksum itself remained into modern times an important symbolic and religious site, by 800 CE the political capital of the much-reduced kingdom had been moved to the south, further into the central highland region of the Ethiopian interior. The kingdom's rulers still in theory laid claim to the coastal region of Adulis on the Red Sea. But the importance of external trade declined and the state developed in greater isolation as a highland agricultural community ruled over by a landed aristocracy. Greek and Arab influence was weakened and the more distinctly African Christian culture of Ethiopia came to the fore. Like Christian Nubia, it survived the Islamic onslaught which swept across northern Africa and western Asia in the seventh and eighth centuries.

The Arab invasions: the Nile valley and the Maghrib

Origins

The Islamic calendar begins in the year 622 CE. (The Islamic calendar is denoted by AH, the year of *Hijra*, the 'flight' from Mecca. For the sake of simplicity the Common Era (CE) calendar will be followed throughout this book.) That year the Prophet Muhammad withdrew into the Arabian desert from his birthplace Mecca to the small oasis settlement of Medina. But he soon returned to reconquer Mecca and by the time of his death in 632 the Prophet had united virtually all the Arabs of Arabia under the new Islamic faith. The subsequent expansion of Islam was remarkably rapid. Within less than a century of Muhammad's death the followers of Islam ruled from the Atlantic coast of Morocco and Spain in the west to the River Indus in the east (see Map 5.5).

For centuries the Arabs had been nomadic pastoralists in a largely desert land. As skilled horsemen, clan had fought clan for control of the oases and scattered pastures to graze their cattle, goats and camels. There had long been movements out of Arabia to more favourable lands beyond the fringes of the desert, but these had been small-scale and sporadic. At the same time the Arabian peninsula occupied a key trading position between the Mediterranean and the Indian Ocean, between the Red Sea and the Persian

Map 5.5 The Arab conquest of north Africa, 640–711 CE

Gulf, between Africa and Asia. Arabs had grown experienced at conducting trading caravans across the Arabian desert. ('Caravan' here means a group of pack animals and their leaders travelling together in convoy on long-distance trading routes.) Indeed, Mecca was an important desert trading junction and Muhammad himself had started life as a trader. Arabs in general were thus well aware of the rich and fertile lands of Mesopotamia and Egypt.

Before the time of Muhammad, Arabs had grown familiar with the notion of a single God, through contact with the Jewish and Christian faiths. One of the great strengths of the new Islamic faith was that its doctrine was simple and easily understandable. It lacked the exclusiveness of Judaism or the complex theology and heresies of Christianity. Belief in Islam required simply a belief in the One True God and an acceptance of His will as revealed by the Prophet Muhammad. And the words of the Prophet were recorded in the Qur'an. Islam lacked the mystery and ceremony of other religions. Nor was it ruled by an exclusive, upper class of priests. It called simply for regular private prayer and a strict regime of fasting before the holy feast of Ramadan.

The spirit of Islam was one of kindness and generosity. It brought the Arabs a new sense of brotherhood. Previously, the rival clans of Arabia had been linked only by a common language, Arabic. They had long looked to the wealth of new lands beyond the desert but had lacked the strength for conquest. Islam brought them the great power of unity with which to carry out that conquest.

Conquest of Egypt   By 640 CE the Arab army had conquered the 'Fertile Crescent' and swept into the fertile delta region of the lower Nile. Egypt at this time was ruled by Byzantium. (This eastern Roman empire, with its capital at Constantinople, modern Istanbul, had risen to prominence in the fifth century. That was when the western empire had fallen to the Vandals and other invaders of western Europe.) The oppression and corruption of Byzantine rule and

Byzantine persecution of the Coptic Church prompted the majority of Egyptians to offer no resistance to the Arabs. By 642 CE the Arab army had expelled the unpopular Byzantine administrators from Egypt. But the Byzantines still maintained a powerful navy which threatened the Arab presence at Alexandria. This led the Arabs to move their centre of administration inland to the head of the Nile delta. There, near the ruins of the Ancient Egyptian city of Memphis, they built their new Islamic capital of Cairo. From Cairo they were better able to dominate the Nile valley to the south as well as keep open their trading links with Syria and Arabia.

Arab conquest of Nubia, however, was halted by fierce opposition from the recently united kingdoms of Noba and Makurra. Nubians had long resisted the tendency of the various rulers of Egypt to try and extend their authority southwards into Nubia. In this instance a huge Nubian army of archers managed to confine the new Islamic rulers of Egypt to north of the first cataract. A treaty was agreed and this led to a lengthy period of peaceful co-existence and profitable trading between Islamic Egypt and Christian Nubia.

The Maghrib

The Arabs referred to the whole coastal region of north Africa west of Egypt as *al-Maghrib*, meaning 'the West'. Conquest of the Maghrib (or Maghreb) was by no means as easy as that of Egypt. The Arabs faced tough opposition from both the Byzantine empire and the north African Berbers. Their initial object was to seize control of Carthage and the fertile Tunisian plain. This was the Roman province of 'Africa' which the Arabs called 'Ifriqiya'. The Byzantines had recaptured Carthage from the Vandals in 533 and they now used their powerful navy to protect it from Arab attack. It was not until the 690s that the Arabs had built enough ships to defeat the Byzantine fleet. The conquest and destruction of Carthage soon followed. Near its ruins the victorious Arabs built their own city of Tunis.

Meanwhile Ifriqiya itself was under attack from Berber chiefdoms in the west and from desert nomads in the south. We have already seen how the Berbers of north Africa had long resisted the alien rule of the Roman empire. Now, in the Berber nomads of the northern Sahara the Arabs appeared to have met their match. The Berbers equalled the Arabs in their mastery of the camel and their conduct of lightning raids from the northern fringes of the desert. On one occasion 'rebel' Berbers from the central Maghrib drove the Arabs from the fortress of Qayrawan, which was their main base in Ifriqiya. But the Berbers were unable to sustain their resistance. Their main weakness was lack of unity and coordination. For the Arabs, on the other hand, unity was their greatest strength, and they used it to overcome the Berber chiefdoms one group at a time. By 711 CE the Islamic army had reached the Atlantic coast of Morocco and was poised to cross into Spain.

Arab rule in northern Africa

Initially the Arab presence in northern Africa was as an army of occupation. Their basic policy was that subject peoples should be given a choice: pay a poll-tax (which is a tax paid by each adult); convert; or die. Non-Muslims were thus a useful source of taxation and there was no widespread attempt at conversion. This enabled early Muslims in north Africa to be largely exempt from taxation.

Christianity had never been deep-rooted in Berber society and the established Christian Church in north Africa did not long outlive the initial Arab conquest. But though official Christianity was quickly abandoned, north

African Berbers as a whole did not readily accept the new Islamic faith. Indeed, for the best part of a century Arabs and Islam in the Maghrib were mostly confined to coastal towns. There they organised slave labour to work the nearby farming estates. Their slaves were drawn largely from Berbers captured in war and later from peoples raided or traded from the central and southern Sahara. The early Arab rulers of the Maghrib made little effort to conquer the highlands and desert fringes to the south. Provided some sort of tribute was paid, the Berber chiefdoms were left to their own devices.

One major way in which Islam was spread among the Berbers of north Africa was through membership of the army. From quite early on conquered or captive Berbers were recruited into the army where they were indoctrinated in the Muslim faith. They proved very able soldiers and ardent propounders of the new religion. As such they profited from the expansion of the Islamic empire. Indeed. it was a largely Berber Islamic army which crossed the Straits of Gibraltar in 711 CE and spearheaded the conquest of Spain where they were known as 'Moors' (people from Mauretania).

Within Egypt the Arabs quickly settled down as administrators, merchants and to some extent as landlords. On the whole, however, they left the majority of Coptic-speaking Egyptian peasants in possession of their land. The Egyptian population of the time has been estimated to have been as much as 15 million. As with earlier alien rulers of the Nile valley, the Arabs regarded Egypt as a major source of wealth for their empire, mainly in the form of food collected through taxation. But the Arab system of poll-tax was

Figure 5.4 The desert city of Nefta, described as the pearl of the Djerid (southern Tunisia). (By M. Blaizat in *Agenda PLM* for 1920)

82

less oppressive than the corrupt administration of the 'competitive taxation' of the Greeks and Romans before them. In addition the Arabs revived irrigation projects to improve agricultural production. At the same time increasing numbers of Egyptians learned that they could evade the burdens of taxation by becoming Muslims.

In Egypt the Arabic language and Muslim religion gradually spread through the local population. This was partly through the immigration of Arab peasants in the eighth and ninth centuries. It was also through a gradual process of education. From the beginning Arabic had quickly taken over as the language of administration, but it was also the language of the new religion as well as the language of literacy and education. Arabic, mass literacy and Islam were in fact all part and parcel of the same thing, taught through the study of the Qur'an. By the end of the ninth century the old Coptic language, the descendant of Ancient Egyptian, had become the language of a small minority. It was focused mostly on the remnants of the old Coptic Christian Church, which has survived into modern times. By the beginning of the tenth century the peoples of the conquered territories of the Maghrib as well as Egypt were predominantly Muslim.

The growth of Muslim states in northern Africa

The initial Arab Islamic unity of the seventh century did not long outlive the great era of conquest. At the heart of the empire, conflict arose over the succession to Muhammad. First the Umayyad and then the Abbasid dynasties seized control of the Caliphate (from *Kalifa,* meaning 'successor' to the Prophet). The capital was moved by the Umayyads to Damascus in 680 CE and then again by the Abbasids to Baghdad in 750 CE. Among the main opponents of the Umayyads and Abbasids were a group of people known as Shi'ites. They believed in the hereditary right of Muhammad's descendants to the leadership of the Islamic world. They criticised the opulence and corruption of the Caliphs and advocated a return to piety and strict observance of the Qur'an.

Meanwhile within the Maghrib, north African Muslims were asserting their independence from the Caliphs of the Arab world. Though Arabs had married into the local Berber population, Arabs as a whole retained a strong sense of racial and religious superiority which was greatly resented by the Berbers. This partly accounts for the fervour with which the Muslim states of the Maghrib defied the Arab authority of Baghdad and maintained a stout independence from the east. Conversion of the mountain and desert Berbers had been slow. But when they did turn to the Muslim faith they followed the unorthodox Shi'ite and Kharijite movements. The Kharijites were ardent opponents of the Baghdad Caliphate. They criticised the exclusive Arab culture of orthodox Islam and emphasised the equality of all professing Muslims, no matter what their racial, cultural or linguistic origin. Ironically the kind of equality they emphasised stemmed from those very principles which had originally united the rival clans of Arabia in the days of Muhammad. The Kharijite movement was reminiscent of the Donatist Christian movement in its rejection of alien authority. As such it provided a potent stimulus for Berber resistance to eastern Arab rule. A number of Kharijite Berber states rose and fell in the Maghrib during the eighth and ninth centuries, each asserting varying degrees of independence from the Caliphs of Baghdad.

Early in the tenth century a new dynasty arose in the central Maghrib which was to threaten the very existence of the Abbasids of Baghdad. This

Map 5.6 Muslim states of north Africa, 750–950 CE

was the Fatimid dynasty which, prompted by Shi'ite immigrants from Syria, claimed descent from Muhammad's only surviving daughter Fatima. By 950 CE the Fatimids had conquered most of the Maghrib region of northern Tunisia and Algeria, but their main object was the Abbasid empire itself. In 969 CE the Fatimids seized control of the Nile valley and declared Egypt independent from the alien rule of Baghdad.

chapter 6

Trans-Saharan trade and the kingdom of ancient Ghana

Trans-Saharan trade

We saw in Chapter 3 (pp. 55–6) that long-distance trade across the Sahara had gone on for many centuries before the introduction of the camel. Originally desert-dwellers sold Saharan salt in exchange for food grown by people living to north or south of the desert. The earliest trade goods were probably carried strapped to the backs of cattle, known as pack-oxen. Evidence for this is found in the Saharan rock paintings described in Chapter 2 (Figure 2.3). Cattle acclimatised to desert conditions could travel several days without water as they moved from the grazing and water of one oasis to another. We also saw in Chapter 3 that during the height of Phoenician trading from Carthage, desert-dwelling Garamantes rode horse-drawn 'chariots' across the desert. These were probably used more for racing than for trading.

Map 6.1   Trans-Saharan trading networks up to 1200 CE

One should not, however, gain the impression that trade across the desert was anything other than small scale and sporadic before the introduction of the camel. Pack-oxen continued to be used by some traders besides donkeys and horses. But with each of these animals the distance they could travel without rest and water was severely limited. Travel across the desert remained a risky business and most trade was passed through the hands of several groups of desert-dwellers before it reached its final destination. Small amounts of gold dust and red precious stones known as carbuncles filtered northwards across the desert to Roman north Africa. But the Romans did little to stimulate any regular or direct trade right across the Sahara. Until about 300 CE most of the Roman imports of African ivory, ostrich feathers and furs came from animals still to be found on the northern side of the desert. Trans-Saharan trade was mostly a local affair; its main stimulus was still desert salt in exchange for food.

The camel and the expansion of trans-Saharan trade

During the third and fourth centuries the camel spread among most of the Berber nomads of the northern Sahara. By the fifth century it had become the major form of transport in the desert. The introduction of the camel could be said to have revolutionised the scope and scale of trans-Saharan trade. The camel had a number of distinct advantages over other transport animals.

Though a single camel could not carry much more in weight than a good pack-oxen, the camel could maintain a steady pace over much longer distances. A fully laden camel, carrying 130 kilos, could maintain a steady regular pace of 25 to 30 kilometres a day. It could even on occasion travel a hundred kilometres or more in a single day. The fat stored in its hump and water stored in its gut enabled it to travel up to ten days without fresh water – twice the time and distance of most pack-oxen and horses. It could withstand both the daytime heat and the night-time cold of the desert. And with its large splayed feet it could negotiate the soft sandy conditions often found away from the main desert tracks.

With the camel, desert nomads could reach more distant oases and so open up whole new routes across the Sahara. Though never without risk, desert travel became a lot more reliable. For the first time it was possible for experienced desert travellers to seriously consider conducting large-scale and regular long-distance trading caravans right across the Sahara.

Desert transport itself remained largely in the hands of Berber nomads. The principal Berber groups involved were the Sanhaja in the west and the Tuareg in the central and southern Sahara. The latter were distinguished from the northern, Zenata, Berbers by their custom of wearing a veil to cover the lower part of the face. The precise origin of the veil remains unclear, but presumably it offered protection from desert winds and sandstorms.

Though many Saharan Berbers engaged in long-distance trade, it was seldom at this stage a full-time occupation. They remained primarily nomadic pastoralists. At the Saharan oases they harvested date palms and grazed their flocks of sheep and goats, camels and occasional cattle. Wealthy nomads also kept horses. These were a sign of status and were particularly useful in warfare. In the hottest, driest season of the year, desert nomads moved their flocks and herds to the better grazing of the Maghrib in the north or the Sahel to the south. This brought them into contact, and sometimes conflict, with more settled agricultural populations. (The Sahel is that

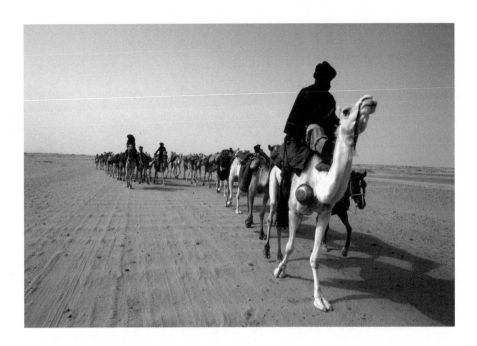

Figure 6.1 Tuareg camel train travelling through the desert

region of savannah grassland immediately to the south of the desert proper. The word comes from the Arabic *sahil* meaning 'shore'. The Arabs looked on the Sahara desert as an ocean, the *sahil* marking the boundary of that ocean of sand with the habitable grasslands beyond.)

Although the Sahara itself was mainly Berber territory, small groups of black, negroid peoples lived at some of the central Saharan oases. They harvested dates and dug salt to exchange for food, but they were often kept in a subordinate position by the Berber nomads who dominated most of the oases. They were possibly descendants from those earlier Neolithic fishermen and hunters discussed in Chapter 1. One of the principal salt mines of the desert was Taghaza in the centre of the western Sahara. There salt deposits were so thick that it was dug out in slabs which were then strapped to pack animals. With the expansion of trade in later centuries, the houses and mosques of Taghaza were even built out of blocks of salt and roofed with camel skins.

Historically the west African Sahel is sometimes referred to as the western Sudan and its inhabitants as Sudanese. The name comes from *al-Sudan,* the Arabic word for 'the black peoples' of tropical Africa

As the camel revolutionised desert transport, the products of sub-Saharan Africa became more readily available to the Mediterranean world. The trade in west African gold began to expand. At the same time the wild game animals of northern Africa were finally wiped out by over-hunting. This led to an increasing demand for ivory, ostrich feathers and furs from the sub-Saharan savannah. With all this expansion in cross-desert traffic a number of important trading settlements developed north and south of the Sahara. Here goods were exchanged and camel caravans off-loaded and reloaded for transport across the desert. Though the caravan traffic remained in the hands of desert nomads, the actual demand and exchange of goods was largely controlled by the peoples of the settled societies to their north and south. The next section of this chapter will consider one of the more important of those societies south of the Sahara.

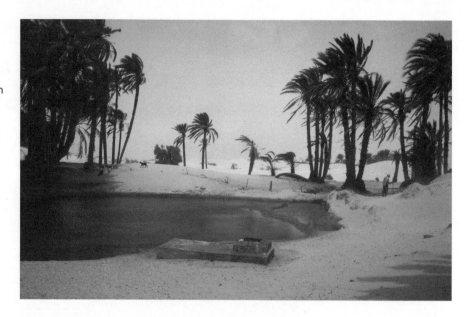

Figure 6.2 A Saharan oasis. It was the existence of water at oases such as this that enabled the development of regular long-distance trans-Saharan travel and trade. Here desert-dwellers harvested dates and mined salt which they traded in exchange for food, clothing and other goods

The kingdom of ancient Ghana

The kingdom of ancient Ghana is not to be confused with the modern republic of the same name. Though the name of modern Ghana was chosen in honour of the ancient historic state, there was in fact no direct relationship between the two. Ancient Ghana was several hundred kilometres north-west of the modern republic. It was one of the most important, and certainly the best-known, of the early west African Iron Age states. It dominated the southern border region of modern Mauritania and Mali between about the fifth and thirteenth centuries CE. The principal people of ancient Ghana were the Soninke, that is, speakers of the Soninke language, a division of Mande which, along with Bantu, was a major language family of the Niger-Congo group (see pp. 19–21 and Map 4.1). Ghana, the name by which the state was known to outsiders, was one of the titles of its king.

The origins of ancient Ghana

We saw in Chapter 2, when discussing the 'impact of agriculture' (pp. 23–4), that the development of farming enabled people to live together in larger, settled communities. The subsequent development of iron-working further increased farming and hunting efficiency. In west Africa this occurred in the last few centuries BCE and the early centuries of the Common Era (see above, Chapter 3, pp. 45–6). Many west African societies remained organised on a simple, small, village basis. In some cases, however, village clans grouped together to form larger chiefdoms. There were usually particular local reasons for this. In the Sahel grassland just south of the Sahara a number of such chiefdoms joined together to form a loose sort of empire – the empire, or kingdom, of Ghana. The origins of Ghana were thus, in the first place, an extension of the natural ability of iron-working farmers to form larger settled communities. But there were particular reasons why Ghana should have arisen as a relatively large state at the particular time and in the way and on the scale in which it did.

Map 6.2 The kingdom of Ancient Ghana in the eleventh century (superimposed on modern boundaries)

We saw in Chapter 2 that the Sahel was one of the regions for the early domestication of sorghum and millet. As the Sahara grew drier towards the end of the BCE period, farming techniques needed to be improved to make the most of limited fertile soil and rainfall. The ancestors of the original Ghanaians may have been descended from Neolithic fishermen who had long experience of living in large settled communities. They had taken the lead in developing new farming techniques. The farmers of the western Sahel quickly made use of new iron technology as it developed in west Africa. Iron swords and spears were used in the region from an early date. It is possible that the Soninke used superior iron weaponry to seize more farming and grazing land from weaker, less organised neighbours. Being near the southern fringes of the desert, the Soninke were also in contact with Saharan nomads from whom they received horses. This gave their rulers additional military advantage over neighbouring peoples of the savannah.

Contacts with Saharan nomads, however, were not necessarily peaceful. With the drying-out of the Sahara, desert nomads pressed further into the Sahel for their seasonal grazing. In years of drought their seasonal migrations took the form of raids on settled agricultural communities. As Sanhaja Berber nomads of the western Sahara raided deep into the Sahel, Soninke farmers may have been prompted to group together for their own defence. It thus seems likely that Sanhaja raids were at least one stimulus to the early formation of the Ghanaian state.

But perhaps more important even than this was Ghana's position with regard to trade. At the height of its greatness the Ghanaian state grew powerful and its rulers grew rich on the strength of the trans-Saharan trade. It therefore seems likely that trade was a major factor in the growth of the state from the very beginning.

The Soninke were ideally placed to exploit a growth in trade to and from the Sahara. From their position in the western Sahel they were midway between the desert – the main source of salt – and the territory of Bambuk – the goldfields of the upper Senegal River. Initially the Soninke could supply the desert salt-producers of Taghaza with their surplus grain in exchange for salt. Then the fifth-century introduction of the camel to trans-Saharan trade gave a great boost to cross-desert traffic. In particular it widened north African access to west African gold. As the trans-Saharan demand for gold increased, the Soninke were able to act as 'middlemen' in passing on Saharan salt to the gold-producers of the savannah woodland to their south. It would thus seem to be no coincidence that it is from the fifth century CE that the origins of the kingdom of Ghana seem to stem.

The expansion of the gold trade

During the course of the eighth and ninth centuries north African Arabs became more directly involved in the trade in gold. Islamic trading towns such as Sijilmasa to the south of the Moroccan High Atlas became important northern bases for the expanding trans-Saharan trade. There Arab merchants bought west African gold and financed further Berber caravans. Through closer Arab contact Berber nomads of the northern and western Sahara gradually converted to Islam. This eased their transactions with the Arab merchants of the Maghrib and also increased the sense of brotherhood and cooperation among the nomads themselves. Travel became safer, less subject to raids. At the same time, during the ninth and tenth centuries, there was a great increase in the demand for gold for minting into coins by the Islamic states of north Africa. As the volume of trade increased, many former nomads became full-time desert traders. By the tenth century the camels of a single trans-Saharan caravan might number several hundred. The expansion of the trans-Saharan trade in gold was paralleled by a growth in the state of Ghana.

On the southern side of the desert Islamic Berber traders had their own urban bases. Here southbound caravans were off-loaded and rested before the final stage of the journey to Ghana. It was also at the southern Saharan base that northbound caravans were loaded and stocked up for the two-month trek across the desert. One of the most important of these Islamic Berber towns was Awdaghust in the south-western Sahara. As trade expanded there was considerable rivalry between the Muslim Berbers of Awdaghust and the Soninke of Ghana. At the height of its power in the eleventh century Ghana expanded to enclose Awdaghust within its kingdom.

An important result of increasing Arab interest in the source of gold was the appearance of Ghana in the Arabic writings of the time. The non-Islamic peoples of sub-Saharan Africa were not at this stage literate so they produced no written records of their own. For written descriptions of the Ghanaian kingdom, the historian must rely on the accounts of outsiders. Some of these had never visited west Africa and merely recorded what they had heard passed on by word of mouth from distant merchants. The historian studying these Arabic accounts must also beware of their tendency to be biased against non-Islamic peoples. In other words, like most historical records, they cannot be taken as totally reliable. Nevertheless the best of these provide a useful insight into the kingdom of Ghana at its height.

The earliest written mention of Ghana was by the eighth-century Arab geographer al-Fazari who made a brief passing reference to 'the territory of Ghana, the land of gold'. Clearly Ghana was famed for its trade in gold as far away as the Asian Islamic capital of Baghdad. Later, Arabic writers provided more detailed descriptions of Ghana, and in particular of its capital Kumbi-Saleh. The fullest account was written by the eleventh-century Arab geographer al-Bakri. Based in Islamic Spain, al-Bakri obtained most of his information from Arabic-speaking merchants of the Maghrib. Judging by the extent of the detail recorded, some of these merchants had wide personal experience of travel in west Africa.

The eleventh-century Ghanaian capital, Kumbi-Saleh, was described as two separate towns situated a little distance from each other. One was a distinctly Islamic town, set aside for visiting Arab and Berber merchants and containing many mosques. Though the king's royal town was some 10 kilometres away, the area between the two was covered with the stone and wooden houses of the Soninke.

> The king's residence comprises a palace and conical huts, the whole surrounded by a fence like a wall. Around the royal town are huts and groves of thorn trees where live the magicians who control their religious rites. These groves, where they keep their idols and bury their kings, are protected by guards who permit no one to enter or find out what goes on in them.

Figure 6.3 The archaeological site of Kumbi-Saleh (in modern Mali)

None of those who belong to the imperial religion may wear tailored garments except the king himself and the heir-presumptive, his sister's son. The rest of the people wear wrappers of cotton, silk or brocade according to their means. Most of the men shave their beards and the women their heads. The king adorns himself with female ornaments around the neck and arms. On his head he wears gold-embroidered caps covered with turbans of finest cotton. He gives audience to the people for the redressing of grievances in a hut around which are placed 10 horses covered in golden cloth. Behind him stand 10 slaves carrying shields and swords mounted with gold. On his right are the sons of vassal kings, their heads plaited with gold and wearing costly garments. On the ground around him are seated his ministers, whilst the governor of the city sits before him. On guard at the door are dogs of fine pedigree, wearing collars adorned with gold and silver. The royal audience is announced by the beating of a drum, called *daba,* made out of a long piece of hollowed-out wood. When the people have gathered, his co-religionists draw near upon their knees sprinkling dust upon their heads as a sign of respect, whilst the Muslims clap hands as their form of greeting.

(Adapted from translation quoted in J. S. Trimingham, *A History of Islam in West Africa,* OUP, Oxford, 1970, p. 55)

Clearly the Muslim visitors to Ghana were impressed by the power and obvious wealth of the king and his court. In particular they were concerned about the source of the gold, but the Soninke managed to keep this secret from them. They themselves bought the gold in exchange for salt from the Bambuk miners to their south. The gold was then sold to Muslim traders at the capital Kumbi-Saleh in exchange for Saharan salt, clothing and other manufactured imports from the Maghrib. It was from the taxing of this trade that the kings of Ghana obtained most of their wealth. According to al-Bakri, the king charged a tax of one dinar of gold for each load of Saharan salt imported into the kingdom and a further two dinars on each load of salt re-exported to the goldfields of the south. (A dinar was an Arab gold coin with a weight equivalent to that of 65 grains of barley.) The import and export of gold itself was not actually taxed. But the king ensured his income from it by taking all solid nuggets of gold, leaving just the gold dust for the trade. This enabled the king and his courtiers to display their wealth in gold in the ways described above. The king employed literate Muslims as secretaries and ministers to keep account of trade and taxation.

The majority of the Ghanaian population got little mention from Arabic writers whose main concern was trade in gold. But we can assume that most people remained farmers, fishers and herdsmen. The king exercised little direct control over the outlying districts of his kingdom. Local government beyond the capital was left in the hands of local hereditary chiefs. These were required to recognise the overall authority of the king and send him regular tribute in the form of food and hunting produce. To ensure their cooperation the king kept their sons and heirs as hostages at his royal court. These were the 'sons of vassal kings' referred to by al-Bakri. In return for their tribute the king was expected to protect the people of his kingdom from raids by desert nomads. Though there was no regular standing army, the various districts of the kingdom sent young men for military service when the occasion demanded. According to al-Bakri, the eleventh-century Ghanaian king was able to summon an army of 200,000 men. The army was sometimes used to raid other less powerful peoples to the south. Captives from these raids were sold as slaves to Muslim traders. On the whole, however, this was not a major part of the trade conducted at Kumbi-Saleh. The main trade in captives across the desert to Muslim north Africa was from further east in the region of Lake Chad.

Decline of the kingdom of Ghana

For more information see www.palgrave.com/shillington

By about 1050 CE the kingdom of Ghana had expanded to take over the Islamic Berber town of Awdaghust. Some time after this the rulers and people of Ghana became Muslims. It has traditionally been claimed by Arab sources that this was the result of Islamic Berber conquest by followers of the Almoravid movement (see the next chapter for discussion of the Almoravids). But the sources are not at all clear on this matter. Several of those that refer to a conquest were written much later and may have been a little over-keen to boast of Islamic Berber victory over 'pagan' Sudanese. Careful study of the Arabic sources suggests that it may have been a peaceful conversion. Even if this were so, however, there was undoubtedly some level of conflict in the Sahel between Saharan Berbers and the Soninke of Ghana. This and the wider destructive wars of the Almoravids did much to weaken former trading links. For centuries the Ghanaian state had thrived on its domination of the gold trade of the western Sudan. By the end of the twelfth century Ghana had lost its domination of that trade. With their loss of trade the newly-converted Islamic rulers of Ghana lost the ability to hold together their loose and largely non-Muslim empire.

In the eleventh and twelfth centuries the Bure goldfields were opened up in the woodland savannah country to the south. At the same time new trans-Saharan routes were developed further east of Awdaghust. This gave the southern Soninke and Malinke chiefdoms of the south the chance to assert their independence. In the early 1200s the southern Soninke chiefdom of Sosso took over most of former Ghana as well as their southern neighbours, the Malinke. As we shall see in the following chapter, the struggle for Malinke independence from the tyrannical rule of the Sosso gave birth to the great empire of Mali.

A further reason for the decline in the kingdom of Ghana was a deterioration in the environment. The Sahel, between the savannah proper and the desert, was already a marginal zone for growing cereal crops. It seems that by the early thirteenth century the land was worn out and the region could no longer support a large settled population. At the same time Berber pastoralists were pushing southwards and overgrazing the region with their flocks and herds. In the early 1200s, therefore, the Soninke farmers and traders of the former Ghanaian kingdom dispersed from Kumbi-Saleh. They moved away in small groups to settle in the more favourable regions of the woodland savannah to their south and west. This Soninke dispersal further stimulated the development of trade and state formation already in progress in many parts of west Africa.

Other early west African states and societies

Of all the early Iron Age states of west Africa we know most about Ghana. This is mainly because it was most involved in the trans-Saharan gold trade and so literate Arabic-speakers visited it and wrote about it. But though we know less about them, elsewhere in west Africa populations were similarly growing. Metal-working and agricultural technology were being developed and people were organising themselves in numerous large and small communities throughout the breadth of sub-Saharan west Africa. The larger states seem to have developed near important trading routes and junctions. As with Ghana, rulers were able to increase their wealth and thus their local power by taxing this trade and importing luxury goods.

In the far west the state of Takrur in the Senegal valley is thought to have emerged as a powerful trading state even earlier than Ghana. Its rulers' wealth was similarly based upon trade in salt from nearby Awlil and gold from Bambuk (see Map 6.2). Takrur's connection with north Africa was along the western coastal route to Sijilmasa and Morocco. The rulers of Takrur adopted Islam as their official state religion early in the eleventh century, before the Soninke of Ghana. As such they sided with their Muslim Berber neighbours the Almoravids in their conflict with the Soninke.

Across the other side of the west African Sudan, north-east of Lake Chad, there arose the empire of Kanem. This began in about 900 CE with the grouping together of a number of nomadic pastoralist clans under the rule of a single dynasty known as Saifawa. The people of Kanem spoke Kanuri, a branch of the Nilo-Saharan group of languages (see Map 4.1, p. 58). Initially the Kanuri of Kanem remained nomadic. It was not until the eleventh century that their rulers established a fixed capital at Njimi. (The exact site of this capital has not yet been located.) As with Ghana and Takrur, the rulers of Kanem built their wealth and power upon their control of trade. Their main trading connection with the north was across the central Sahara to the Fezzan and thence to Tripoli and Egypt. Their main exports across the Sahara were ivory, ostrich feathers and captives to sell as slaves to the Muslims of north Africa. Their raids for captives brought them into frequent conflict

Figure 6.4 Left image: A bronze ceremonial wine bowl, Igbo-Ukwu, eastern Nigeria, ninth century CE; Right image: A 'lost-wax' cast vessel in the form of a shell surmounted by a leopard. Igbo-Ukwu, eastern Nigeria, ninth century CE

with their neighbours to the south. The further history of Kanem will be considered in Chapter 13 (pp. 189–91).

Elsewhere in west Africa a large number of metal-working, agricultural communities were developing. Some emerged as organised states, others remained small, essentially clan- or village-based communities. The latter were to be found scattered throughout the savannah and forest regions of west Africa. Living in small, family-based villages, they were usually subsistence farmers. That is, they grew food for home consumption rather than for taxation or trade. They had no bureaucratic government or ruling class as such, being of a small enough scale to settle disputes and make decisions on a purely family basis. Some of these peoples were linked together by common language and came together on occasion to defend themselves from outside attack. But they usually dispersed again as soon as the threat receded. From some of these small beginnings, state organisation emerged as guardians of religious shrines, military leaders or wealthy traders assumed the positions of rulers. The Yoruba and Hausa states, for instance, which were to emerge from early origins in this period will be discussed in Chapter 13.

Even in the smallest community, metal-working technology could be developed to a fine art. Fine bronze castings have been recovered from Igbo-Ukwo in the southern Nigerian forest (see Figure 6.4). These have been dated to as early as 900 CE and are believed to be the burial objects of a religious leader or ruler. The peoples of Nigeria had a long history of artistic modelling in clay dating back to at least the Nok culture from before the Common Era. The copper for the Igbo-Ukwo bronzes must have come from Saharan mines such as Azelik in modern Niger since there is no known source in the region of Nigeria. The methods of casting in bronze may have been developed from ideas passed southward along with the copper. The evidence of the Igbo-Ukwo bronzes proves that even deep in the forest people were to some extent connected with the long-distance trading networks of savannah and Sahel.

Islam and the Sudanic states of west Africa

The Almoravids

Origins

We saw in the previous chapter that by the end of the ninth century the Berbers of the western Sahara had largely converted to Islam. It was they who first brought Islam to the western Sudan. Islam provided Berber pastoralists and traders with a certain common sense of 'brotherhood'. It also gave additional purpose to their territorial rivalry with the Sudanese farmers of the Sahel. In the forefront of this rivalry were the Lamtuna branch of the Sanhaja Berbers and the Soninke of Ghana. Early in the eleventh century the Soninke of Ghana extended their control over the Muslim town of Awdaghust and the Lamtuna Sanhaja of the surrounding region. Certain Sanhaja leaders viewed this territorial rivalry in terms of a religious war, but they were unable to inspire their followers with the fervour of a *jihad* (a holy war).

It was not unusual by this time for wealthy Berber leaders to go on religious pilgrimage to Mecca. It was thus in 1036 that a certain Sanhaja chief on his return from Mecca visited the Muslim scholars of Qayrawan in north Africa. To them he appears to have poured out his troubles about the lack of Islamic fervour among his people and of their suffering at the hands of the 'infidel' Sudanese. The result of his visit to Qayrawan was that he brought home with him to the south-western Sahara a northern Berber scholar named Abdallah ibn Yasin.

Abdallah was shocked to find among these nominally Muslim Berbers so little observance of the teachings of Islam. Most were illiterate and knew little of the Qur'an. In addition they retained many of their pre-Islamic religious ideas and practices. Like later Sudanese converts to Islam, many of these southern Berber Muslims managed to combine belief in both the old religion and the new. To Abdallah it was clear that lack of strict Islamic observance was largely to blame for the Sanhaja's lack of unity and purpose and their loss of ground to pagan Soninke. But Abdallah's initial attempts to reconvert the coastal Juddala Sanhaja ended in failure. He then withdrew to a remote site on the Mauritanian coast. A fortress or place of retreat of this kind was known in Arabic as a *ribat*. There he built up a small but dedicated body of faithful Islamic followers referred to as *al-Murabitun* or 'the Almoravids'. Abdallah and the Almoravids preached the observance of strict Islamic law and the waging of *jihad* against the infidel (unbeliever).

The spread of the Almoravids

The message of the Almoravids found its greatest initial appeal among the Lamtuna, those Sanhaja nomads in greatest conflict with the Soninke. During the early 1040s the bulk of the Lamtuna joined the Almoravid movement. Prominent among the early converts were Yahya ibn Umar and his brother Abu-Bakr, the sons of a Lamtuna chief. They joined Abdallah ibn Yasin in leading the conquest and conversion of the Sanhaja of the western Sahara. The Almoravid movement brought the rival Sanhaja clans together in a new form of unity. It provided them with a chance to escape from the domination of the Zenata Berbers of Sijilmasa in the north and the Soninke of Ghana in the south. Within a few years Yahya and Abu-Bakr had moulded together a powerful mass army. What it lacked in discipline it made up for in speed and enthusiasm. Its conquests were fired by religious fervour and prospect of booty.

Map 7.1 The Almoravid empire in the eleventh century

By 1055 the Almoravid armies had taken Sijilmasa in the north and Awdaghust in the south. This gave them control of the trans-Saharan gold trade. The extent of their early success prompted these Sanhaja nomads to extend their conquests beyond the desert to the mountains and plains of Morocco. At this point, however, two of their principal leaders were killed in battle and some of the Almoravids' early unity was lost. Yahya died in 1057 and Abdallah in 1059. Abu-Bakr assumed the nominal leadership of the movement, but the conquered territory, stretching from north to south across the Sahara, had become too big for one leader to control. As Abu-Bakr returned to the south to carry the *jihad* against the Sudanese, he left his cousin Yusuf ibn Tashufin in control of the north. From then on the movement was effectively split in two as Yusuf carried the Almoravid army through Morocco and into southern Spain (see Map 7.1).

The southern Almoravids have usually in the past been credited with conquering the kingdom of Ghana in 1076. As we saw in the previous chapter, recent study of contemporary Arabic sources has thrown some doubt on the idea of an actual conquest. What is certain is that there was some armed conflict between Almoravids and Soninke. The latter were pushed back from Awdaghust and trade was disrupted. Sometime in the last quarter of the eleventh century the Soninke rulers of Ghana converted to Islam: whether by conquest or persuasion remains uncertain. It may have been a deliberate political tactic in order to re-establish trading links with the now firmly Islamic Sanhaja. Certainly in the early twelfth century Ghana was both Islamic and independent.

On the death of Abu-Bakr in 1087 much of the strength of the southern Almoravid army was drained away northwards. Many of their best fighting men were tempted to leave the southern desert and returned to join Yusuf in pushing forward the conquest of north Africa. Weakened by this desertion and the lack of further conquests the southern Sanhaja unity declined. This allowed the Soninke and later the Malinke to re-expand at their expense.

The Muslim states of north Africa, 1100–1500

Meanwhile in their northern empire of Morocco and southern Spain the former nomads of the desert were soon corrupted by the wealth and power of a settled existence. Their corruption and loss of religious piety provoked reaction among the Berbers of north Africa. In the 1140s this reaction erupted in a *jihad* against the Almoravids themselves. It was led by 'Abd al-Mu'min who united the north African Berbers, overthrew the Almoravid Sanhaja and founded the Almohad state. In effect the Almohad *jihad* continued the work of the Almoravids in unifying the whole of the Maghrib (see Map 7.2). This was complete by the end of the twelfth century. During this period the north African Berbers became more thoroughly Islamised and immigrant Arab nomads extended the Arabic language and culture into the rural areas.

One of the most important consequences of this was the spread of literacy through the Muslim world of north and west Africa. Literacy, usually in Arabic, was spread through the teaching of the Qur'an. The mosques thus became centres of learning. In this way the peoples of northern and western Africa were exposed to and contributed to the intellectual achievements of

Map 7.2 The Almohad empire in the twelfth century

the Muslim world. These achievements were considerable, especially in the fields of mathematics and science. It was people from this vast Muslim-Arab world who developed our modern numeral system based on counting from 1 to 10. They invented algebra, the use of the decimal point and the number zero – a mathematical concept missed by the ancient Greeks. They developed physics and astronomy. They studied chemistry and were the first people to separate medicine from religion and develop it as a secular science. As we shall see later in this chapter, the peoples of the western Sudan became part of this Muslim intellectual tradition.

The political unity of the Maghrib collapsed in the thirteenth century as the Almohad empire split into three rival states. At the same time Muslims were pushed out of Spain and into north Africa by the advancing armies of the Christian kingdoms of Aragon, Castile and Portugal. In 1415 the Christian Portuguese extended their 'Reconquista' to north Africa with the capture of the coastal fortress of Ceuta (see Map 7.3). In the century that

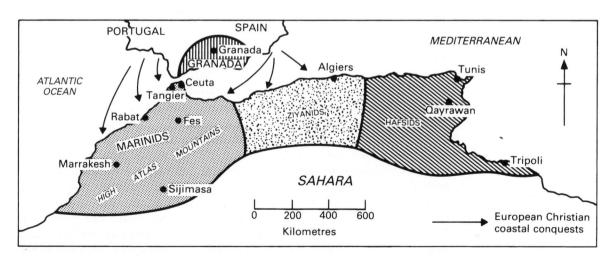

Map 7.3 Muslim states of north Africa in the fifteenth century

followed, Spain and Portugal established a number of trading ports along the north African coast.

Further expansion of the gold trade

The Almoravid and Almohad states of north Africa gave a great boost to the trans-Saharan gold trade. Like the Fatimids of Egypt in the tenth and eleventh centuries, the Almoravids and Almohads of the eleventh to thirteenth centuries minted their own gold coins. With increasing trade between Christian Europe and Muslim north Africa and Asia, Europe too by the thirteenth century began experiencing an economic revival. European kings and princes turned increasingly from silver and copper to gold for minting their coins. And most of that gold came from south of the Sahara. It has been estimated that as much as two-thirds of the gold circulating in Europe and north Africa in the fourteenth century came from trade with the western Sudan. Thus although initial Almoravid conflict with the Soninke of Ghana may have disrupted trading contacts, this was clearly only temporary. The Almoravid unification of the Saharan Berbers and the spread of Islam among west African rulers in fact did much to stabilise and expand the trans-Saharan trade in gold. As we saw in the previous chapter, new sources of gold were opened up and Ghana lost its domination of the trade. This opened the way for the rise of new west African states, and in particular the rise of Mali.

The empire of Mali

Evidence

Evidence for the history of this remarkable west African state is of two types: written accounts by contemporary north African Muslims and Mande oral tradition, in particular what is known as the *Sunjata Epic*. The principal written accounts, both fourteenth century, are those of the Tunisian-Berber intellectual and civil servant Ibn Khaldun and the great Algerian writer and traveller Ibn Battuta. Ibn Khaldun's history, mostly relating to north Africa, was derived from a wide range of sources, while Ibn Battuta visited Mali at the height of its power in 1352. His first-hand observations provide a vivid insight into life at both the Saharan oases and the Malian capital of Niani. He also recorded some of the oral traditions that he heard recited at the royal court.

Oral traditions in African society have in pre-literate days been the principal means of handing down the history and culture of a society from one generation to the next. Where powerful kingdoms were concerned, the traditions have been strongest, and they have been most faithfully learned and handed down, often through poetic recitations, through many generations. Many of these traditions started as praise poems, recited and sometimes sung, by official poets and musicians of the royal court. They recounted the exploits of the ruler and his antecedents. Such was the case with the *Sunjata Epic*, which still retains status in contemporary Mande society as a major work of oral history, literature and performance art. Presented in modern times primarily as performance literature, the *Sunjata Epic* has been passed down through many generations of griots or performers. And at each passing it has been subject to the interpretation and 'poetic licence' of the new performer. Nevertheless, the basic outline of the Sunjata story remains consistent and there are other sources that suggest that a figure similar to the Sunjata of the Epic really did expand the Mali kingdom sometime around 1200 CE.

The main new source of gold was at Bure in the savannah country of the upper Niger River. This brought the southern Soninke and Malinke-speaking peoples of the savannah more thoroughly into the great Sudanese trading network. The first to take full advantage of this were the Sosso, a branch of the southern Soninke. Under the leadership of Sumaguru of the Kante clan the Sosso quickly established a new and separate state, independent of Ghana. The Sosso state was built mainly on raid and conquest, killing rulers and seizing tribute. During the early 1220s Sumaguru's army raided the Malinke to his south and then attacked the northern Soninke of Ghana, sacking their capital in about 1224.

A Malinke survivor of the Sosso raids, Sunjata of the Keita clan, set about organising Malinke resistance. He brought a number of Malinke chiefdoms into an alliance under his authority. In 1235 he led a Malinke army against the Sosso of Sumaguru, whom he defeated in battle at Kirina near modern Bamako. With the defeat of Sumaguru, Sunjata took control of all the Soninke peoples recently conquered by the Sosso, including much of former Ghana.

Within a very few years Sunjata had built up a vast empire, known to us as Mali. The capital was built at Niani in the southern savannah country of the upper Niger valley near the goldfields of Bure. Even in Sunjata's lifetime the empire of Mali extended from the fringes of the forest in the south-west through the savannah country of the Malinke and southern Soninke to the Sahel of former Ghana (see Map 7.4). Awdaghust remained in the hands of the Sanhaja, but by then the more easterly town of Walata had become the main southern desert 'port' for the trans-Saharan trade. And whereas Ghana at its height had barely reached the upper Niger delta, Sunjata's successors extended the empire's boundaries to include Timbuktu and the middle Niger bend. At its height in the fourteenth century, the empire of Mali stretched from the Atlantic south of the Senegal River to the Songhay capital of Gao on the east of the middle Niger bend. In the south it reached the forest and included the goldfields of Bure and Bambuk while in the north it stretched across the Sahel to include the southern Saharan 'ports' of Walata and Tadmekka.

Religion and kingship

The traditional religion of the Malinke was like that of many west African agricultural peoples. The core of their belief was that it was the 'spirits of the land' who ensured the success of their crops. The earliest farmers to have settled in a particular region were believed to have made a deal with the spirits to ensure the successful production of their crops. And it was through spiritual contact with their ancestors that the people of the present were able to keep in touch with the original settlers and thus with the 'spirits of the land'. The village head or chief, the *mansa* in Malinke, was the person most directly descended from the earliest farmers. He was the most direct link with the 'spirits of the land' upon whom continued production of their crops depended. The *mansa,* as guardian of the ancestors, was thus both religious and secular leader of his people.

When Sunjata formed his Malinke alliance against the Sosso, he persuaded the other Malinke *mansas* to surrender their titles to him. He thus became the sole *mansa,* religious and secular leader of all the Malinke people and in due course of the whole of the empire of Mali. As the power of the *mansa* increased, so did his religious significance. The *mansa*'s central

Map 7.4 The empire of Mali in the fourteenth century

religious role within the empire was crucial to the people's survival and he was thus treated with exaggerated respect. He lived apart from his subjects, who approached him on their knees. He was surrounded by displays of great wealth and ceremonial regalia. This emphasised his power and dignity, and no doubt helped instil respect and obedience to his rule. But despite the misunderstanding of outsiders, he was not a 'divine king' as it was understood in Ancient Egypt.

Most of the rulers of Mali after Sunjata were Muslim, some more firmly so than others. A number made pilgrimage to Mecca, the most famous being the huge and lavish pilgrimage of Mansa Musa in 1324–5. Traders and court officials in the towns, those most detached from the traditional values of the land, accepted Islam more willingly and thoroughly than the bulk of rural commoners. The latter, most of whom were peasant farmers,

Figure 7.1 The mud constructed mosque at Jenne with a souk in the foreground

were still closely dependent on the goodwill of the 'spirits of the land'. Though the rulers of Mali accepted Islam, they never totally rejected their national traditional religion. To have done so would have lost them the support of their farming subjects, who largely adhered to indigenous religious beliefs and practices.

The administration of the empire

The political organisation of Mali was in many ways similar to that of Ghana. A number of literate Muslims were employed at court as scribes and treasurers to carry out most of the administrative work. In the outlying districts of the empire, traditional rulers were left in place provided they collected and forwarded tribute to the capital. The *mansa* kept a large standing army and the battalion commanders were among the more important officials at the royal court. Each army battalion consisted of a small elite corps of horsemen and a large body of footsoldiers armed with bows and spears. The army was used to protect the empire from outside attack, to patrol trading routes and to ensure that district chiefs paid their tribute to the king. The main source of royal income besides tribute was a tax on trade. As with the kings of Ghana, the *mansa* of Mali levied a tax on all goods passing in, out of and through the empire.

The economy

The main economic basis of the empire was the agricultural production of the rural areas. In this respect Mali was far better situated than its predecessor Ghana. It is significant that Niani, the capital of Mali, was centred in the south of the country in the heart of some of the most productive land within the empire. Unlike Sahelian Ghana, the empire of Mali stretched right across the southern savannah where rainfall was adequate to produce regular food surpluses. Different areas specialised in different crops. The main savannah crops were sorghum and millet with rice being produced in the Gambia

103

valley and around the upper Niger floodplain. This left the more northerly and drier Sahelian grasslands for the specialist grazing of camels, sheep and goats. Food was traded from one district to another and in particular from the savannah and Niger floodplain to the trading towns of the Sahel. Most of the empire's food was produced by independent peasant farmers living fairly close together in small family villages. They paid a proportion of the surplus to their traditional district chief who kept a portion and forwarded the rest to the government. At the same time the *mansa* and his army commanders controlled their own 'state' farms, where slaves were organised to produce food for the army and the court.

The main economic activity observed by outsiders was of course the gold trade. And control of this, as we have seen, was a major stimulus behind the founding of the state. But though the rulers of Mali taxed the trade that passed through the empire, they did not exercise direct control over the mining of gold. The peoples of the goldfields were particularly anxious to maintain their independence. They were prepared to send tribute of gold nuggets to the *mansa* and to pay a tax on their imports of salt. But whenever the rulers of Mali tried to interfere directly with their mining, the miners themselves simply ceased their production. They even ceased production when the *mansa* of Mali tried to convert them to Islam, so the project was abandoned.

There developed within the Mali empire a class of professional traders called Wangara in the west and Dyula in the east. They were Malinke, Bamana or Soninke in origin and were usually practising Muslims. They

Figure 7.2 Great Mosque, Timbuktu, the oldest mosque south of the Sahara. The mosque is constructed of round, dried, mud-bricks and stone rubble with clay rendering. The foundation of the mosque, in 1325, is attributed to Mansa Musa, king of Mali

carried the trade of the empire to the furthest corners of west Africa. They penetrated the forest to trade for kola nuts and they carried these and the food, hunting produce and gold of west Africa to the trading towns of the Sahel: Walata, Tadmekka, Timbuktu and Gao. It was Dyula traders from Mali who in the late fourteenth century penetrated south to the Akan forest of modern Ghana (see p. 200). From there they brought a whole new field of gold production into the trans-Saharan network. The opening of the Akan goldfields shifted the centre of the gold trade further eastwards enabling Timbuktu and Jenne to replace Walata as major 'ports' of exchange.

Sometime during the fourteenth century cowrie shells from the Indian Ocean were introduced as currency into the internal trade of the western Sudan. This appears to have been a deliberate move encouraged by the government. It improved the collection of taxation and eased the internal exchange of food and other goods. But gold dust and salt remained the main mediums of exchange in the long-distance trade of the Sahara.

Mali in the fourteenth century

The empire of Mali reached the height of its power and fame in the fourteenth century. Much depended in the kingdom on the personal power of the ruler. A series of dynastic struggles and short-lived reigns had temporarily weakened the power of the monarchy towards the end of the thirteenth century. When that happened outlying provinces asserted their independence and failed to pay tribute. But the monarchy recovered in the fourteenth century with the reigns of two particularly effective rulers: Mansa Musa (1312–37) and Mansa Sulayman (1341–60).

Mansa Musa brought Mali to the notice of the rest of the Muslim world with his famous pilgrimage to Mecca in 1324–5. He arrived in Cairo at the head of a huge caravan which included a hundred camel-loads of gold. There he was received with great respect as a fellow-Muslim by the Sultan of Egypt. Musa spent lavishly in Egypt, giving away so many gold gifts that the value of gold in Cairo fell and did not recover for a number of years. All who met him were impressed by his wealth, generosity and intellectual powers.

On his return from Mecca, Musa brought back from Egypt an architect who redesigned the mosque of Gao (which had recently been added to the empire). A number of other mosques were built during Musa's reign. He had always encouraged the development of learning and expansion of Islam. In the early years of his reign Musa had sent Sudanese scholars to the Moroccan 'university' of Fes. By the end of his reign Sudanese scholars were setting up their own centres of learning and Quranic study, particularly at Timbuktu.

The pilgrimage of Mansa Musa excited the interest of other Muslim scholars, among them a Berber geographer from Tangier, Ibn Battuta. After many years of travelling throughout the Muslim world of Asia, Ibn Battuta visited Mali during the reign of Musa's brother Mansa Sulayman. His account of his journey has become a major source for our knowledge of fourteenth-century Mali. Ibn Battuta set off in 1352, travelling via the salt-producing oasis of Taghaza and the Sahelian trading town of Walata.

> I set off at the beginning of God's month of Muharram in the year 753 [February 1352] with a caravan whose leader was Abu Muhammad Yandakan al-Masufi, may God have mercy on him. In the caravan was a company of merchants of Sijilmasa and others. After 25 days we arrived at Taghaza. This is a village with nothing good about it. One of its

marvels is that its houses and mosque are of rock salt and its roofs of camel skins. It has no trees, but is nothing but sand with a salt mine. They dig in the earth for the salt, which is found in great slabs lying one upon the other as though they have been shaped and placed underground. A camel carries two slabs of it. Nobody lives there except the slaves of the Masufa [a Berber people] who dig for the salt. They live on the dates imported to them from Dar'a and Sijilmasa, on camel-meat, and on *anili* imported from the land of Sudan [the land of the black peoples south of the Sahara]. ...

We stayed there for ten days, under strain because the water there is brackish. It is the most fly-ridden of places.

Water is taken on there for entering the wilderness which comes after it. This is a distance of ten days without water except rarely. As for us, we found plenty of water there in pools left by the rain. On one day we found a pool between two rocky hillocks with sweet water in it, so we renewed our water supplies and washed our clothes … .

In those days we used to go on ahead of the caravan and whenever we found a place suitable for grazing we pastured the beasts there. This we continued to do till a man named Ibn Ziri became lost in the desert. After that we neither went on ahead nor lagged behind.

(From N. Levtzion (ed.) and J. E. P. Hopkins (trans. and ed.), *Corpus of Early Arabic Sources for West African History*, Cambridge University Press, Cambridge, 1981, p. 782)

Figure 7.3 Detail from the Catalan Atlas, 1375, showing Mansa Musa, King of Mali, seated on his throne

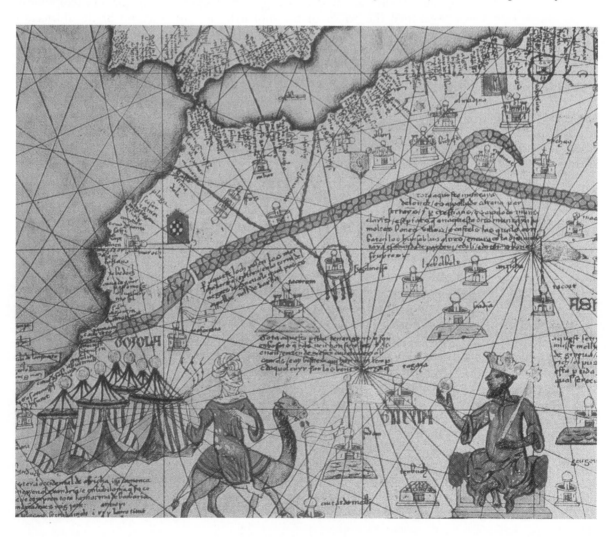

Ibn Battuta spent eight comfortable months at the Malian capital of Niani before returning home via Timbuktu, Gao, Takedda (Azelik) and Tuat (see Map 7.4). At first highly critical of what he saw as the Malinke's dull diet of pounded millet, honey and milk, Ibn Battuta soon warmed to them for their hospitality and love of justice. Of the latter he wrote:

> The negroes possess some admirable qualities. They are seldom unjust, and have a greater abhorrence of injustice than any other people. Their sultan (the *mansa*) shows no mercy to any one guilty of the least act of it. There is complete security in their country. Neither traveller nor inhabitant in it has anything to fear from robbers or men of violence.

(From a quotation in E.W. Bovill, *The Golden Trade of the Moors*, second edition, Oxford University Press, Oxford, 1968, p. 95)

The fame of Mali in the fourteenth century was such that it began to get particular mention in the maps which European geographers were producing at that time. In one map produced in 1375 the king of Mali is shown seated on a throne in the centre of west Africa (see Figure 7.3). He is holding a nugget of gold in his right hand and approaching from a tented settlement in the desert is a veiled Sanhaja Berber riding on a camel.

The decline of Mali

As we have seen, the strength and success of the Malian empire depended upon the strength of the ruler at the centre. In the late fourteenth century the power of the *mansas* declined through a series of weak rulers, brief reigns and dynastic struggle. The outer provinces seized the opportunity to assert their independence. Perhaps the most important of those to break away, as we shall see in the following section, were the Songhay of the eastern Niger bend. At the same time the wealth of the empire was sapped by raids from the Mossi in the south and the Tuareg in the north.

The Mossi

The Mossi came from savannah country south of the Niger bend. It was a region never brought within the empire of Mali. A ruling aristocracy had organised a number of Mossi states. They exercised control through their small but effective raiding bands of well-armed horsemen. With these armies the Mossi aristocracy exacted tribute from their peasantry and grew rich through further raids and pillage. They quickly seized on the opportunity of a weakening Mali empire. One of their northern raids reached as far as Walata in the early 1480s.

Timbuktu and Tuareg raids

Timbuktu had originally been founded as a tented settlement of Tuareg Berbers. It was a southern grazing settlement for their flocks and herds and also a link-up point with the trans-Saharan trade. During the reign of Sundjata or his successor it had been captured from the Tuareg and brought within the Mali empire. More permanent houses were constructed of mud brick and, as we have seen, Timbuktu became an important centre for Muslim traders and scholars, Sudanese as well as Berber. As central Malian authority declined, Tuareg nomads raided the town in the early 1400s, finally capturing it in 1433. The Tuareg appreciated that Timbuktu was a potential source of wealth. They did not disrupt the way of life within the town, but simply redirected its taxes from the Malian capital to themselves. In fact the economic and intellectual life of Timbuktu expanded as, in about 1450, further Berber Muslim merchants and scholars moved there from Walata. Timbuktu was to reach the height of its wealth and fame in the sixteenth century as it was brought within the expanding empire of Songhay.

Mali's loss of Timbuktu was a signal of its final decline and displacement by Songhay. By 1500 the formerly great Mali empire had contracted down to little more than its Malinke heartland. Most non-Malinke peoples had asserted their independence. By the seventeenth century even this Malinke federation had reverted into rule by individual village *mansas*. Even so, within the Malinke heartland the idea that the Mali empire might some day be revived was to live on right into the nineteenth century (see p. 236).

The origins and rise of Songhay

Origins of the Songhay state

The heartland of Songhay lay along the middle Niger River south-east of Gao (see Map 7.5). The principal peoples of the region were Do farmers, Gow hunters related to the Mossi, and Sorko fishermen. The latter were in the strongest position to dominate the region. From at least as early as the eighth century Sorko fishermen began to extend their territory upstream towards the Niger bend. Their canoes gave them mastery of the river which they used as a trading route, exchanging food from one region to another. As experienced fishermen and hunters of the hippopotamus it was easy for them to develop their canoes for military use. They set up trading villages along the middle Niger from which they dominated nearby communities of peasant farmers. By the ninth century this region of the middle Niger had been welded together into the single state of 'Songhay' with its capital at Kukiya. By then the people of Songhay were in regular contact with Muslim traders who had settled at Gao.

The trading town of Gao was founded by Berber and, possibly, Egyptian merchants who were attracted to the region by the Bambuk gold trade of Ghana. It became the trans-Saharan trading link of the central and eastern Sahara. The farmers and fishermen of Songhay provided the merchants of Gao with food in exchange for salt as well as cloth and other products from north Africa. Through these contacts the rulers of Songhay became at least nominally Muslim by the beginning of the eleventh century, earlier than either Takrur or Ghana. It was not long before Gao became the new capital of Songhay. Gao and other western parts of Songhay were brought within the boundaries of Mali during the fourteenth century. But the bulk of Songhay remained beyond Mali's tax-collecting armies.

With the decline of Mali in the fifteenth century, Songhay showed its independence. Its Sonni dynasty built up a powerful army of horsemen and war canoes. During the reign of Sonni Sulayman Dandi the Songhay army began to extend its territory upstream along the Niger bend. It was during the reign of Sulayman Dandi's successor Sonni Ali the Great (1464–92) that Songhay became an empire, totally eclipsing Mali.

Figure 7.4 Fisherman pulling net ashore, Niger River, Mali, West Africa

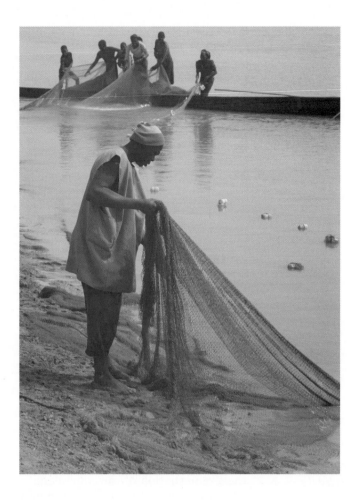

Sonni Ali and the founding of the Songhay empire

Sonni Ali began his reign of conquests by capturing Timbuktu from the Tuareg in 1468. Thereafter much of his reign was taken up with fighting off Tuareg raiders from the southern desert and extending the empire by military conquest. He built up a powerful army of horsemen backed up by a fleet of war canoes. His army had a reputation in Songhay oral tradition of having never been beaten. Certainly he was a formidable military general who extended the Songhay empire deep into the desert in the north and as far as Jenne in the south-west. The Mossi were pushed back south of the Niger in the late 1480s and Songhay's army raided deep into Mossi territory. Though it was a fruitful field for further raiding this turbulent savannah territory was never actually brought within the Songhay empire.

Sonni Ali's raids on Muslim Timbuktu, his relentless pursuit of the Tuareg and his general lack of respect for Islam led to his being highly criticised by Arabic historians. They portrayed him as a ruthless tyrant and oppressor. Scholarship in Timbuktu undoubtedly suffered during his reign, but Sonni Ali is remembered in Songhay oral tradition as a great conquering hero and founder of the Songhay empire. After Sonni Ali's death in 1492 his heir was quickly ousted by one of his generals, Muhammad Ture, a devout Muslim of Soninke origin.

Map 7.5 The Songhay empire in the early sixteenth century

Songhay under the Askiya dynasty

Muhammad Ture (1493–1528), founder of the Askiya dynasty, strengthened the administration of the empire and consolidated Ali's conquests. He used Islam to reinforce his authority and unite his far-flung empire. He thus justified a major raid against the Mossi in 1498 by declaring it a *jihad*. Askiya Muhammad recognised the importance of Islam to the trans-Saharan trade. He let the rest of the Muslim world know of his concern for the faith when he went on pilgrimage to Mecca soon after his accession. While in Cairo he persuaded the caliph of Egypt to recognise him as the 'caliph' of the whole Sudan. On his return from Mecca, Askiya Muhammad revived Timbuktu as a great centre of Islamic learning. But at the same time he did not force the Islamic faith upon the common people and the bulk of them retained their traditional religious beliefs.

Partly as a result of his promotion of Islam, Askiya Muhammad's reign saw a general revival of trans-Saharan trade. This in turn increased the wealth of Songhay. He ensured that Songhay benefited more directly from this trade by extending the empire further into the desert. His armies drove back the Tuareg of the southern Sahara, capturing Aïr in the east and the salt-producing centre of Taghaza in the north (see Map 7.5). And though Songhay exercised little direct control over the Hausa states to the south-east, these rich and varied communities were brought into the empire's broader trading network. (For the further history of the Hausa states, see pp. 191–3.)

The administration of Songhay was more centralised than that of Mali. As new provinces were conquered for the empire, traditional rulers were replaced by royal appointees. They were usually members of the royal

Figure 7.5 The tomb of Askiya Muhammad of Songhay at Gao

family or trusted servants. Their positions were not hereditary and these provincial governors were directly dependent upon the king for their appointment. Each governor recruited his own local army, which was used for ensuring the regular payment of tribute by the farmers of the province. The removal of traditional rulers and the centralisation of power helped prevent provinces from breaking away during periods of dynastic dispute or rule by weak kings. There were in fact frequent dynastic disputes after the ageing Askiya Muhammad was deposed by his son in 1528. But Songhay held together as a great trading empire until the Moroccan invasion of 1591 (see pp. 174–5).

The main sources of government income were, as in Mali, tribute from the provinces, royal farms in the Niger floodplain and the Songhay heartland, and taxes on trade. The principal currency of long-distance trade was salt. Cowrie shells were used for general internal trade. The items of trade were much the same as those for Mali. Gold provided the main impetus for the trans-Saharan trade, to which were added kola nuts from the southern forest and captives for sale as slaves in Muslim north Africa. The captives mostly came from raids into Mossi territory south of the Niger bend. Food was the main staple of internal trade while imports from north Africa, besides Saharan salt, included luxury goods, cloth, cowries and horses for the military. Cloth was widely woven from local Sudanese cotton, and in towns like Jenne, Timbuktu and Gao woollen cloth and linen from north Africa was unravelled and rewoven according to local preference.

Hassan ibn Muhammad al-Fasi, a young Moroccan educated at Fes visited the country in 1510 and again in 1513. Writing in Italian under the name of Leo Africanus (following his capture by Christians and forced conversion to Christianity) he published a vivid and detailed description of Songhay at its height under the rule of Askiya Muhammad. On the town of Timbuktu he wrote:

> Here are many shops of craftsmen and merchants, especially those who weave linen and cotton cloth. To this place Barbarie [Berber] merchants bring cloth from Europe. All the

111

Figure 7.6 Timbuktu, from a German drawing dated 1858

women of this region except maidservants go with their faces covered, and sell all necessary kinds of food. The inhabitants are exceedingly rich, so much so that the present king has married both his daughters to two rich merchants. There are many wells here containing very sweet water, and when the River Niger floods they convey its water by channels to the town. The region produces corn, cattle, milk and butter in great abundance, but salt is very scarce for it is brought here by land from Tegaza [Taghaza] which is five hundred miles [800 kilometres] distant. When I myself was here, I saw one camel's load of salt sold for 80 ducats [a gold coin widespread in Europe at the time].

The inhabitants are people of a gentle and cheerful disposition, and spend a great part of the night in singing and dancing through all the streets of the city. They keep great store of men and women slaves, and their town is in much danger of fire. On my second night there almost half the town was burnt.

The rich king of Tombuto [governor of Timbuktu] has many articles of gold, and he keeps a magnificent and well-furnished court. When he travels anywhere he rides upon a camel which is led by some of his noblemen. He travels likewise when he goes to war and all his soldiers ride upon horses. Attending him he has always three thousand horsemen, and a great number of footmen armed with poisoned arrows. They often have skirmishes with those that refuse to pay tribute, and as many as they take they sell to the merchants of Tombuto. There are very few horses bred here, and the merchants and courtiers keep certain little nags which they use to travel upon; but their best horses are brought out of Barbarie [north Africa]. And the king, as soon as he hears that any merchants have come to town with horses, he commands a certain number to be brought before him, and choosing the best horse for himself he pays a most liberal price for him.

Here there are many doctors, judges, priests and other learned men, that are well maintained at the king's cost. Various manuscripts and written books are brought here out of Barbarie and sold for more money than any other merchandise. The coin of Tombuto is of gold without any stamp or superscription, but in matters of small value they use certain shells brought here from Persia, four hundred of which are worth a ducat and six pieces of their own gold coin each of which weighs two-thirds of an ounce.

Leo Africanus then went on to Askiya Muhammad's capital, the city of Gao:

112

The houses there are very poor, except for those of the king and his courtiers. The merchants are exceedingly rich; and large numbers of Negroes continually come here to buy cloth brought from Barbarie and Europe … .

Here there is a certain place where slaves are sold, especially on those days when the merchants are assembled; and a young slave of fifteen years of age is sold for six ducats, and children are also sold. The king of this region has a certain private palace where he maintains a great number of concubines and slaves; and for the guard of his own person he keeps a sufficient troupe of horsemen and footmen … .

It is a wonder to see how much merchandise is brought here daily, and how costly and sumptuous everything is. Horses bought in Europe for ten ducats, are sold again for forty and sometimes for fifty ducats a piece. There is not any cloth of Europe so coarse, which will not here be sold for four ducats an ell [just over one metre], and if it be anything fine they will give fifteen ducats for an ell: and an ell of scarlet of Venetian or of Turkish cloth is here worth thirty ducats. A sword is here valued at three or four crowns [a European silver coin of smaller value than a ducat], and so likewise are spurs, bridles, with other like commodities, and spices also are sold at a high rate: but of all other commodities salt is most extremely dear.

(Adapted from Leo Africanus, *History and Description of Africa*, trans. J. Pory and ed. R. Brown, London, 1896, Vol. III, pp. 824–7, and quoted in E. W. Bovill, *The Golden Trade of the Moors*, OUP, Oxford, 1968, pp. 147–50)

The Fulbe (or Fulani)

One particular group of people inhabiting the sahelian and savannah grasslands of this period were the Fulbe (sometimes referred to as Peuhl and, more commonly known in the eastern regions of west Africa as Fulani). They were physically distinct from the bulk of negroid Sudanese, being of paler skin and more like the Berbers in appearance. But unlike the Berbers, they spoke a language belonging to the Niger-Congo group. In the eleventh century the Fulbe lived in the Senegambia region where they practised nomadic pastoralism among the predominantly agricultural Sudanese. Between the eleventh and sixteenth centuries the Fulbe gradually extended their grazing territory over much of the savannah of west Africa, from Futa Toro in the west to Borno in the east. They did not conquer or control the agricultural peoples but settled mainly in between them. Some Fulbe adopted settled agricultural practices and blended with the local population. Others remained distinctly pastoralist and as such retained a separate Fulbe language and culture. As we shall see in Chapter 16, the Fulbe were destined to play an important role in west African history in the early nineteenth century.

8

Eastern Africa to the sixteenth century

The Christian kingdom of Ethiopia, 850–1550

We saw in Chapter 5 that by 800 CE the capital of Ethiopia had been moved further south from Aksum to somewhere in the central highlands of the interior. External trade had declined with the rise of Muslim Baghdad and the subsequent diversion of Indian Ocean trade away from the Red Sea. By the early ninth century Ethiopia had become an isolated outpost of Christianity, a largely agriculturally-based economy, controlled by a landed aristocracy. Further expansion southwards had for the time being been halted by fierce resistance from the indigenous Agew communities of the Shoan plateau.

From about 1000 CE the fortunes of the Ethiopian kingdom began to recover. The period saw a revival of Red Sea trade, prompted by the growth of an independent Fatimid-ruled Egypt. Ethiopia exported a little gold to Egypt and probably some ivory. And the region remained one of the Muslim world's most important sources of the precious resins frankincense and myrrh. But one of the most profitable of Ethiopia's exports appears to have been captives, particularly women, for sale as concubines and household servants to the Muslims of Yemen, south-western Arabia. These captives were probably taken in warfare with highland communities south of Lake Tana. The principal trading link of the time was north of the old Aksumite port of Adulis to the Muslim-controlled offshore islands of Dahlak.

Ethiopia under the Zagwe dynasty, 1150–1270

The main period of Ethiopian revival followed the emergence of the Zagwe dynasty from among a group of Agew military officers who had been enlisted into the Aksumite elite. In about 1150 the founder of the Zagwe dynasty seized the throne from the descendants of the old Aksumite line of kings. The Zagwe kings brought in an era of more aggressive expansion by the Christian Ethiopian state. The capital was firmly established at Adefa in the central highlands. The Zagwe kings commanded a large army and Christian settlement and control was pushed south of Lake Tana to Gojjam and on to the Shoan plateau.

As the state expanded, traditional rulers were replaced by Christian military leaders or by members of the royal family or their trusted friends. These district governors were granted large personal estates and the freedom to tax the local people. They were expected to organise the military protection of their districts, ensure the safety of traders, provide central government with taxation and support the king in time of war. New conquests were backed up by the presence of Christian missionaries. They set up monasteries on land granted by the king. These became important centres of learning and Ethiopian Christian culture.

Ethiopian Christianity

The Zagwe rulers reopened links between the Ethiopian Church and the Holy Land of Palestine. Even in its centuries of greatest isolation the Ethiopian Church had maintained contact with the remnants of the Egyptian Coptic Church. Ethiopia was regarded as part of the ancient archdiocese of Alexandria. Throughout the period of the Coptic decline with the rise of Islam, the Ethiopian Church continued to have an Egyptian appointed as its most senior bishop. Despite this connection, the Ethiopian Church developed its own individual characteristics. Ethiopians saw themselves as an outpost of Christianity – a sort of chosen people of God – surrounded by pagans and Muslims. In their rituals and beliefs they developed close connections with the Old Testament. They believed themselves the true descendants of ancient Israel. At the same time the monastic tradition inherited from sixth-century Monophysite missionaries remained very strong.

Ironically the outward-looking policy of the Zagwe dynasty developed further this sense of connection between the Ethiopian Church and the Jerusalem of the Old Testament. By the early thirteenth century, trading relations between Egypt and Ethiopia had improved enough for Ethiopian Christians to travel freely through Muslim Egypt. Thus encouraged, Ethiopians began to make regular pilgrimages down the Nile and eastwards to the holy city of Jerusalem.

During the reign of Lalibela (see Figure 8.2), who ruled some time between 1200 and 1250, the monks in the region of the capital Adefa began building a most remarkable series of churches (see Figure 8.3). These were hewn out of solid rock and remain, unique to this day, a testament to the strength and fervour of the Ethiopian Christian Church. A total of 11 such churches have been found carved out of the mountains in the region of the capital, which was thereafter renamed Lalibela, after the monarch. A number of the churches were named after famous sites in Jerusalem such as Golgotha, the tomb of Christ. This has led at least one Ethiopian historian to suggest that the Lalibela churches were in fact an attempt to recreate Jerusalem itself in the mountains of Ethiopia. A large number of smaller and older churches have been found cut into the mountains and caves of the northern Aksumite region of Tigray. These offer sufficient proof that the Lalibela churches were a continuation of the artistic and architectural traditions of ancient Aksum.

Ethiopia under the Solomonid dynasty, 1270–1550

In 1270 the last Zagwe ruler was ousted by a new line of kings known as the Solomonid dynasty. The Solomonid kings justified their seizure of power by claiming descent through the rulers of ancient Aksum to the traditional union of biblical King Solomon and the queen of Sheba (Saba). The Solomonid rulers came from the central highland region of Amhara. Here early pre-Christian Ge'ez-speaking settlers had mingled with local Cushitic-speaking peoples to produce the Amharic language, the dominant language of modern Ethiopia.

The rise of the Solomonids brought an end to the architectural traditions inherited from ancient Aksum. There was instead a movement towards a style of architecture more typical of the common people in much of tropical Africa. The building of stone, rectangular churches and palaces ceased.

Figure 8.1 A valley in the Ethiopian mountains. In isolated valleys such as these local aristocratic landlords or district governors were often able to behave as though completely independent of central Ethiopian control

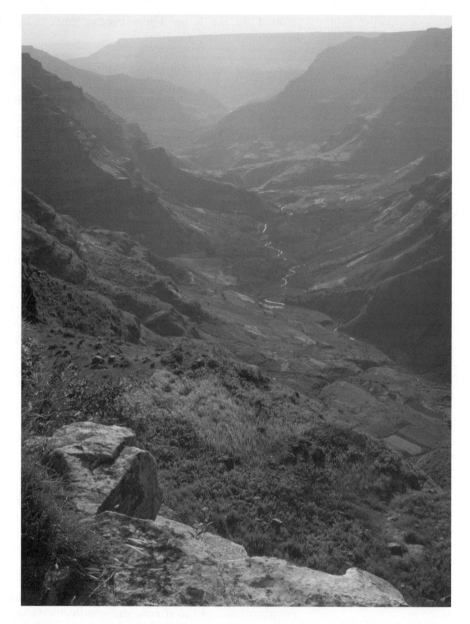

Further new monasteries were built in the less permanent, less grandiose style of domestic housing, namely, a circular design made of mud brick, pole and thatch.

The change in court and religious architecture was characteristic of a sense of impermanence within the court itself. Henceforth, the king abandoned the tradition of a permanent stone-built capital. The royal court, government officials and military personnel appear to have become too numerous for a single region to support for very long. In addition, the mountainous terrain made it difficult for the royal capital to receive sufficient food supplies from more distant parts of the kingdom. The king and his officials solved these problems of supply by living in a series of temporary, tented camps which were moved, sometimes two or three times a year, from one district to

Figure 8.2 Portrait of King Lalibela, from an illuminated manuscript

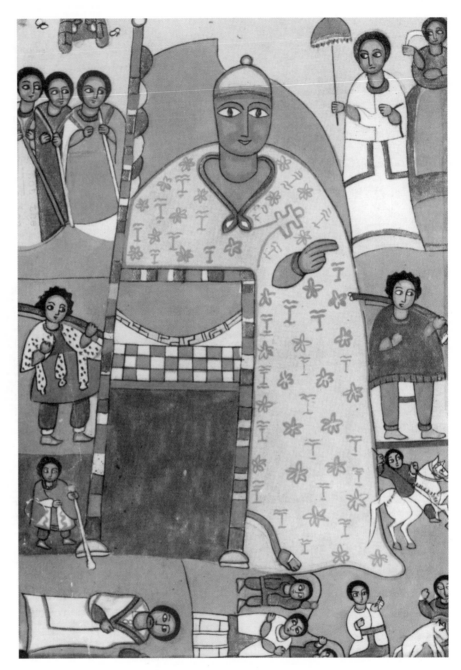

another. A European visitor to the Solomonid court in the sixteenth century observed that this temporary royal capital so depleted a region of its fuel and food supplies that the site could not be resettled for anything up to ten years. The royal capital was clearly a consumer rather than a producer of natural wealth. With this level of environmental exploitation, even on a small local scale, visions of late twentieth-century Ethiopia spring to mind. But there was a further advantage to the king, in this moving of his capital. It enabled him to keep in touch with otherwise isolated regions and so to reinforce their loyalty and ensure payment of taxation.

Figure 8.3 The church of St George, one of the churches at Lalibela, Ethiopia, hewn from the living rock

Following a period of civil war in the 1290s future problems of dynastic rivalry were solved by an unusual practice. As soon as a new king had succeeded to the throne, all possible royal rivals were imprisoned in the mountain fortress of Gishen. This novel device was so successful that Gishen remained a royal prison for the best part of two-and-a-half centuries, until the Muslim conquests of the sixteenth century.

The Solomonid dynasty looked to the south for the further expansion of the Ethiopian kingdom. This they achieved during the fourteenth and fifteenth centuries through a mixture of military conquest and the building of Christian monasteries as centres of conversion. In fact they achieved little real success in converting the bulk of the population in the more southerly parts of the kingdom. But at the same time, the Solomonids hoped to exploit the southern trading networks to the east of the Shoan plateau. This, as we shall see, brought them into conflict with the Muslim sultanates of the Awash valley. The conflict that followed was to dominate the life of Christian Ethiopia for the next two centuries, and almost destroyed it in the 1530s.

The Muslim penetration of Ethiopia and Somalia, 850–1550

We have already seen that the eighth-century rise of Baghdad as the Asiatic capital of the Muslim world shifted Indian Ocean trade away from the Red

Map 8.1 Solomonid Ethiopia in the fifteenth century and the Muslim penetration of north-east Africa

Sea and towards the Persian Gulf. This brought the Somali coast of eastern Africa (sometimes referred to as the 'Horn' of Africa) into closer contact with Muslim Indian Ocean trading networks. Arabs no longer looked to the Dahlak islands and other Red Sea ports as their main source of African trading products. By 900 at the latest Zeila, on the northern Somali coast just south of modern Djibouti, had become an important alternative Muslim trading settlement (see Map 8.1).

Muslim states of the interior

During the tenth and eleventh centuries Muslim merchants, probably mainly of Arab origin, began penetrating the Awash valley towards the highlands of Ethiopia. They set up small trading settlements from which they controlled the external trade of the interior. Initially they exercised little direct control over the surrounding non-Muslim, Cushitic-speaking communities. Gradually, however, they came to dominate the economic life of the region.

Initially competing against each other for the ivory and slave trade of the interior, Muslim merchants soon learnt the advantage of cooperation and unity. In the early twelfth century a merchant family from Mecca brought together a number of interior Muslim settlements to form the 'sultanate of

Shoa'. Other similar Muslim states followed and by 1300 the dominant position of the sultanate of Shoa had been taken by the 'kingdom of Ifat'. During the early 1300s Muslim merchants penetrated the highlands south of the Blue Nile. Driven by their search for new sources of slaves, they set up the small trading and raiding states of Dawara, Sharka, Bali and Hadya. This brought them into conflict with Christian Ethiopia, currently at the height of its power under the Zagwe dynasty.

Ethiopia was at a distinct advantage when it came to military conflict. The Zagwe kings ruled over a relatively united highland kingdom and could command a large and effective standing army. The Muslim sultans on the other hand were generally disunited and could not muster an efficient fighting force. Their armies, such as they were, were more accustomed to raiding for captives than fighting in defence of territory. Between 1320 and 1340 Ifat and the other Muslim states of the highland plateau were brought within the expanding empire of Christian Ethiopia.

The kingdom of Adal and the conflict with Ethiopia

The rulers of Ifat withdrew eastwards to the plateau of Harar where they founded the 'kingdom of Adal'. Here from a strategic position between the highlands of Ethiopia and the coastal port of Zeila, the Walaswa dynasty set about rebuilding Muslim power. They united the Muslims of the interior and began converting to Islam the pastoral Somali to their east and south-east. Somali pastoral nomads proved a useful source of manpower in the building-up of a more powerful Muslim army. In this way the Somali were gradually drawn into the heightening conflict between Muslim Adal and Christian Ethiopia.

Most of the battles between the two sides were little more than elaborate raids from which each brought home large booties of cattle and captives. In the early 1400s Ethiopia briefly occupied the Harar plateau, but they soon lost their advantage and by 1450 Adal had recovered. A near-perpetual state

Map 8.2 Conflict in the highlands: Ethiopia and Adal in the sixteenth century

of war persisted through most of the fifteenth century. This must have done much to disrupt peaceful trade and economic development in the region.

In 1526 a Muslim general named Ahmad ibn Ibrahim (also known as Gran, 'the left-handed') became effective leader of Adal. As a military man he saw Christian Ethiopia as a constant threat to Muslim security in the region. In his view the only way to end the disruptive pattern of raid and counter-raid was to embark on the final conquest and destruction of the Christian kingdom. To achieve this Ahmad summoned up Muslim unity and fervour in the name of a *jihad,* a holy war.

In the past the armies of the Muslim sultanates had been no match for the large, experienced and well-organised army of Ethiopia. But in now confronting the Christian kingdom in the name of a *jihad,* Ahmad ibn Ibrahim had two distinct advantages over his predecessors. In the first place the Ethiopian unity which had earlier been that country's great strength was showing signs of breaking up. This was especially so in the southern districts of Ifat, Shoa and Hadya. Christianity had never taken deep hold here, among the bulk of the local farming population who were sorely exploited by the Christian aristocracy. The latter often failed to respond to the demands of central government. Governorships, which had earlier been appointed, had become hereditary. And district governors treated the great estates that went with their office like their own private kingdoms. This tendency was encouraged by the mountainous terrain and steep-sided valleys which made communication between districts very difficult. Nevertheless, when confronted with invasion by Muslim Adal, King Lebna-Dengel was still able to summon up an enormous Christian army. This brings us to Ahmad ibn Ibrahim's second new advantage. The Muslim army was now supplied with up-to-date firearms traded from the Ottoman Turks who had recently extended their empire into Egypt.

Ahmad's army invaded the Shoan plateau and defeated a much larger Christian army at the battle of Shimbra-Kure in 1529. Both sides lost heavily in the battle, Adal's losses being estimated at 5000, Ethiopia's far higher. For many years much of southern Ethiopia had merely been held together by the overawing presence of the Ethiopian army. Now with the defeat of that army Ethiopian unity fell apart. Over the next six years Ahmad's army overran southern Ethiopia, burning and looting churches, killing Christian district governors and replacing them with Muslims. Lebna-Dengel evaded capture but was unable to organise effective Christian resistance. In desperation he appealed to Christian Europe for assistance against the 'common enemy' of Islam.

The Ethiopian kings had been in touch with the Portuguese for a number of years and Portuguese ambassadors had resided at Lebna-Dengel's court since at least 1520. The Portuguese responded by landing a small but well-equipped force in the north of the country. (Portuguese motives at this time will be considered in a later chapter.) The combination of Portuguese and Ethiopians managed to save the Christian kingdom by inflicting a sharp defeat upon the Muslim army in 1543. Ahmad himself was killed in the battle and with this loss his 'empire' collapsed. Not too much need be read into the contribution of the Portuguese to this important Ethiopian victory. The eventual defeat of Ahmad in Ethiopia was predictable, as his army was badly overstretched. He had not taken time to consolidate his conquests. And many of the Somali nomads who formed the bulk of the Muslim army had already returned home with their booty.

So far as the historian is concerned the major significance of the Portuguese connection at this time was that it resulted in some vivid written descriptions of sixteenth-century Ethiopia. Father Francisco Alvares, for instance, chaplain to the first Portuguese embassy to Ethiopia, commented upon the effects of the oppressive rule of the king and his nobility:

> There would be much fruit and much more cultivation in the country, if the great men did not ill-treat the people, for they take whatever they have. The latter are thus not willing to provide more than they require and what is necessary for themselves.
>
> In no part that we went about in were there butchers' shops, except at the Court, and nobody from the common people may kill a cow (even though it is his own) without leave from the lord of the country.
>
> The people speak the truth little, even when they make oath, unless they swear by the head of the King. They are very afraid of excommunication, and if they are ordered to do something that is to their disadvantage they do it from fear of excommunication.

(Adapted from C. F. Beckingham and G. W. B. Huntingford (eds), *The Prester John of the Indies,* Hakluyt Society, Cambridge, 1961, Vol. 2, p. 515)

Following the death of Ahmad, the Ethiopians under Galadewos (1540–59) recovered much of the Amharic and Shoan plateau over the next ten years. But two decades of destructive warfare had weakened the southern defences of both Ethiopia and Adal. This allowed the Oromo (Galla) pastoralists of the dry savannah grasslands north-east of Lake Turkana to encroach into the southern highlands towards the upper Awash valley. Further Oromo expansion and their impact on the subsequent history of the region will be examined in Chapter 11 (pp. 170–3).

Pastoralists and farmers of the east African interior

The evidence

We have seen that areas like Ethiopia and parts of northern and western Africa do have a certain amount of documentary evidence to back up archaeology and other sources of historical information. Unfortunately, the same is not true of the east African interior, that is, the inland regions of modern Kenya, Uganda, Rwanda, Burundi and Tanzania. Literate peoples were active on the coast, as we shall see in the following chapter, but they did not penetrate far inland. The peoples of the interior did not evolve their own system of writing and we do not have the written observations of outsiders until the nineteenth century. This leaves linguistics and archaeology as the principal sources of evidence for the early history of the east African interior. The character and limitations of language-study and archaeology as sources of historical evidence are described in Chapter 4 (pp. 57–9).

Fortunately, for the period from about the fifteenth century the historian is able to draw upon the oral traditions of the modern peoples of the region. These too, however, have their limitations, especially in the early period. They focus mainly upon the succession of rulers and tell us little if anything about how people lived. In addition it is known that chiefly genealogies have sometimes been distorted in order to justify the claims to leadership of a particular clan or chief. Nevertheless, much can be learnt by comparing the traditional history of one particular group with that of other neighbouring, and perhaps competing, peoples. The careful use of oral traditions can add a

Map 8.3 Later Iron Age peoples of the east African interior to *c*.1500

great deal to the otherwise impersonal and general observations arising from archaeology and the comparative study of languages.

East Africans in the Early Iron Age period

We saw in Chapter 3 (p. 45) that there is some evidence that the techniques of iron-smelting might have been developed independently in east Africa before the Common Era. But at the same time it is clear that iron-working technology was not actively spread through the east African interior until the early centuries CE. Then it was brought by Bantu-speaking farmers coming into the region from the west and south-west. These Early Iron Age farmers chose their sites carefully and settled the moist lakeside areas and fertile river valleys most suited to their crop cultivation. At this stage they had little reliance on cattle and so made little use of the drier upland regions more suited to cattle grazing and light cereal crops. Thus the dry open pastures of the central Rift Valley of Kenya and northern Tanzania remained largely undisturbed by early iron-working farmers. Here stone-using peoples continued their age-old practices of hunting and herding cattle until at least 1000 CE. It is thought that these were Cushitic-speaking peoples, probably descendants of the stone-using pastoralists described in Chapter 2.

We also saw in Chapter 2 that the presence of tsetse fly in thickly-wooded areas was often a barrier to the spread of cattle-keeping peoples. But where woodland was cut down and wild game driven away, the tsetse dispersed too. Thus the clearing of land for cultivation tended to make more grassland available for future grazing. The longer that mixed-farming communities, like the Early Iron Age Bantu-speakers, remained in a region, the greater were the chances that cattle-keeping could become more important in their economy. This is what had happened in the east African interior by about 1000.

Origins of the Later Iron Age

Archaeologists and historians of eastern Africa generally refer to this period after about 1000 CE as the 'Later Iron Age'. This is because between the eleventh and sixteenth centuries a number of distinct changes occurred among the Iron Age peoples of the east African interior. This is revealed in the archaeological evidence, which shows, on the one hand, a new emphasis upon cattle-keeping, and at the same time the introduction of a completely new style of pottery. The main evidence for the earlier period occurs in the 'inter-lake' region of central and southern Uganda. Here from about 1000 the drier upland pastures became more intensively occupied by people keeping cattle and cultivating cereals.

The explanation most widely proposed in the 1950s and 1960s was that these changes were brought about by the immigration of new populations into the region. In recent decades, however, linguistic research has pointed to the likelihood that these changes were locally evolved: new organisation of society rather than new populations. Furthermore, archaeological research has shown that the cumulative effect over many centuries of numerous Early Iron Age smelting and cultivating settlements had caused serious deforestation in the region to the west of the Victoria Nyanza. As forest was cleared, grassland suitable for cattle-herding became more widespread. This paved the way for the emergence of small, but powerful chiefdoms that based their political power on the authority of spirit mediums and their economic power on the control of cattle ownership.

The carefully made and skilfully decorated Urewe ware of the Early Iron Age was replaced throughout the region by a coarser, simpler style of pottery. This is known as 'rouletted' ware because its decoration was 'rolled' on to the outside of the rim with knotted ropes of grass while the clay was still wet. The adoption of new styles of pottery by pre-existing populations suggests important local changes in the organisation of domestic life. The more finely constructed Urewe ware was probably made by a small number of skilled craftsmen, specialists in the community who were rewarded with a relatively high social status for their craft. The adoption of coarser 'rouletted' ware suggests that Later Iron Age pottery in this part of Africa was probably made by a wider range of less specialised potters. In fact pottery-making had probably become a routine domestic task performed by the women while the men were engaged in the higher status task of looking after cattle.

As the Later Iron Age spread between the eleventh and fifteenth centuries a large number of small chiefdoms emerged throughout the inter-lake region. Some placed greater emphasis on pastoralism, others on cultivation. The choice depended on what was most suited to local conditions. There was

Figure 8.4 Iron Age pottery of eastern Africa (a) Early Iron Age of Rwanda: finely crafted pots from Remera and Sholi; (b) Later Iron Age of Rwanda: more simply constructed rim shreds with twisted cord decoration

considerable local trade between cultivator and pastoralist. Cultivators, being the iron-workers, were able to trade their iron tools and weapons for the cattle and hides of the pastoralists. By about 1450 a number of these chiefdoms had merged to form the state of Kitara in the south-west region of Uganda. For two generations they were ruled by the Chwezi dynasty from their capital at Bigo near the Katonga River. Who exactly the Chwezi were is not clear, but it seems that their rule was unpopular and they did not last long. In about 1500 the Chwezi clan of rulers were ousted by the Jo-Bito clan of Lwo-speaking immigrants from the northern border region of modern Uganda.

Immigration by Nilotic-speaking peoples

Between the fifteenth and seventeenth centuries a number of Later Iron Age pastoralists from the southern Sudan and south-western Ethiopia pushed down into the favourable grassland regions of the east African interior. Linguistic evidence shows them to have been speakers of the Nilo-Saharan group of languages (see Map 4.1, p. 58). For this reason they are generally referred to as the Nilotes. Why exactly they should move at this time is not known for sure. There may have been drought, or new, improved techniques of cattle-keeping may have led to increased numbers of cattle and the need for new grazing land. Initial migrations were not in large numbers and were probably in the form of small-scale seasonal movements in search of new pastures.

Though primarily pastoralists, most of the newcomers also practised cereal cultivation and so they moved mainly into the drier upland regions. In many cases they mingled and intermarried with their Bantu-speaking predecessors and with them developed new dialects. At the same time they brought with them a number of practices characteristic of the peoples of the southern Sudan. These included initiation ceremonies involving circumcision and the pastoralist practices of bleeding cattle and making greater use of cow's milk as a form of food.

There were three main streams of Nilotic-speaking immigrants into east Africa: the western or River-Lake Nilotes, the southern or Highland Nilotes and the eastern or Plains Nilotes.

The western Nilotes

The main western Nilotes were the Lwo-speaking peoples. They originated in the southern Sudan region of the Sudd. Here the Bahr el Ghazal meets the White Nile to form a seasonal floodplain. Migration of the Lwo-speaking Nilotes probably began with their seasonal movements to and from the pastures of the Sudd. By 1450 a number of Lwo-speaking clans had gathered at Pubungo near the northern border of modern Uganda. This appears to have been a hunting and raiding base for at least a generation. From there they dispersed in small clan groups through the inter-lake region and northeast of Lake Victoria Nyanza. One of these, the Jo-Bito clan, ousted the Chwezi from Kitara. From the remnants of the Kitara state, the Bito dynasty founded the kingdom of Bunyoro. Similar Lwo origins are traced in the oral traditions of other Ugandan states, in particular Buganda. The history of Buganda belongs to a later period and will be discussed in Chapter 14 (pp. 213–15). It is probably also to these western Nilote immigrants that the origins of specialist pastoralist groups such as the Hima of Nkore and the Tutsi of Rwanda and Burundi can be traced (see below, Chapter 14, pp. 215–16).

Even though Lwo-speaking immigrants often formed a ruling clan, they blended with the local Bantu-speaking population and adopted their language. Nevertheless, in a few cases they retained their own distinctive traditions and language, as with, for instance, the Luo to the north-east of Lake Victoria Nyanza.

Figure 8.5 Pastoralists of modern Sudan

The southern Nilotes   The southern Nilotes (sometimes referred to as Paranilotes) came from slightly further east in the southern Sudan. Their origins can be traced to the dry grassland zone to the north-west of Lake Turkana. Their initial southward movement into east Africa had occurred between about 200 BCE and 1000 CE. This was much earlier than that of the western and eastern Nilotes. In fact, it coincided more in time with the spread of Early Iron Age Bantu-speakers into the region. These early southern Nilotes had moved into the highlands to the east of Lake Victoria Nyanza. They came as iron-working cereal farmers and herdsmen and they absorbed the earlier stone-using southern Cushites of the region. From this combination there emerged the early Kalenjin peoples of the western Kenyan highlands. The Dadog of central Tanzania were similarly the result of a further extension of southern Nilotes and their absorption of southern Cushites.

The fertile valleys and upland pastures of the western Kenyan highlands were particularly suited to the combination of cereal farming and cattle-herding of the early Kalenjin. As a result the western highlands became a centre for further expansion in the period after 1000 CE. And as they expanded their settlements they came into contact with a number of other Later Iron Age groups. From this further contact and intermingling there developed a number of distinct groups, such as the Elgeyo, the Pokot and the Nandi, whose earlier origins can be traced to the southern Nilotes.

The eastern Nilotes   The eastern Nilotes (also sometimes referred to as Paranilotes) came from the same grassland zone north-west of Lake Turkana. The eastern Nilotes were much more of a positive intrusion than the earlier Nilotic groups, retaining their distinctive language and cultural traditions. From the eastern Nilotes stem the Ateker (Karamojong) of north-eastern Uganda and the Maasai of the central Kenyan and northern Tanzanian plains. But their intrusion into the east African interior belongs to a later period and as such will be considered further in Chapter 14 (pp. 216–17).

Trading towns of the east African coast to the sixteenth century

There have been periodic references to Indian Ocean trade in earlier chapters of this book. Most of these have been concerned with trading contacts between Egypt, the Red Sea coast and Aksum/Ethiopia on the one hand and the states of the Persian Gulf and western India on the other. The present chapter is concerned with the origins and growth of Swahili trading towns along much of the east African coastline and their contribution to the further development of Indian Ocean trade.

Historians in the past have sometimes tended to overemphasise the Arab input to the early growth of east African coastal trade. This view has placed all the initiative in the hands of Islamic Arab immigrants. Early research focused upon the Arab contribution to the language and culture of the Kiswahili-speaking peoples. Arabs were portrayed as the prime movers in developments. It was they who drew coastal Africans into their own trading culture, thereby creating the Afro-Arab combination that founded the Swahili trading towns. Recent research, however, has shown that past emphasis upon Arab input has been misleading. This is not to deny the extremely important contribution of Islamic Arab immigrants to the further development of Swahili culture and trading networks, especially in the eighteenth and nineteenth centuries. But what previously tended to be overlooked was the extent of the indigenous African input to the early development of coastal trade and the spread of Swahili culture and society.

For more information see www.palgrave.com/ shillington

The origins of east African coastal trading society

Azania: the east African coast to 500 CE

The east African coast was known to the Greek and Roman traders of the early centuries CE. They referred to the region as 'Azania'. The earliest known written reference to the land of Azania is in a first-century Greek handbook, *The Periplus of the Erythraean Sea* ('The Voyage of the Indian Ocean'). This was written in the great Egyptian trading port of Alexandria in about 100 CE. It was intended for Greek trading ships, as a guide to the known ports of the Indian Ocean. It refers to a series of market-towns along the Azanian coast from which overseas traders were able to obtain ivory, rhinoceros horn, tortoise-shell and a little coconut oil. In exchange traders from Arabia and the Red Sea provide the Azanians with iron tools and weapons, cotton cloth and a small quantity of wheat grain and wine. The author of the *Periplus* referred to 'Rhapta' as the most southerly known port on the coast of Azania. The exact site of Rhapta has not yet been identified, but it is thought to have

Map 9.1 The east African coast to 500 CE

been situated either somewhere in the Rufiji delta, in the central coastal region of modern Tanzania (see Map 9.1) or possibly close to Dar es Salaam.

The peoples of Azania were clearly experienced fishermen, well-practised in the use of small boats along the coastal waters offshore. They fished and caught turtles from dugout canoes and they sailed among the islands in small coastal boats made of wooden planks knotted together with lengths of coconut fibre. Each market-town was under the rule of its own chief, though the *Periplus* tells us little more about the people except that they were dark-skinned and they were tall. A few Arab traders were known to have settled in the region, intermarried with the local people and adopted their language. But there is no sign that these early Arab settlers had any significant impact or influence upon the Azanians. They were settling within already existing fishing and trading communities.

Who exactly these early Azanians were is not known for sure. Archaeological research has not yet revealed evidence of any of their early coastal market-towns. Future archaeological research might reveal pottery and other artefacts which would tell us more about them. In the meantime it seems likely that they were part of the developing east African Early Iron Age movement, probably Bantu-speaking, discussed in Chapter 4. The report of the *Periplus* that they imported iron goods need not contradict this. They may simply have found it easier to import manufactured iron goods rather than spend the time and effort smelting and making their own. They probably adopted the fishing techniques already developed by pre-existing hunting and fishing communities. The use of 'sewn' boats and the presence of the coconut suggest some early contact with the sort of Austronesian sailors who colonised Madagascar in the early centuries CE. But it does not appear that any Austronesians actually settled on the coast at this time. What is known for sure is that by at least the fifth century CE, Bantu-speaking farmers and fishermen were well-established along the east African coast.

The Land of Zenj: the east African coast to 1000 CE

Indian Ocean trade was given a great boost by the spread of Islam in the seventh and eighth centuries. The shift of the Islamic capital to Baghdad in 750 brought the Persian Gulf more firmly into Indian Ocean trading networks. A number of Shi'ite refugees from southern Arabia settled along the northern half of the east African coastline during the eighth century. They intermarried with the African population and learnt the local language. The increasing presence of Arabic-speaking peoples on the offshore islands greatly eased trading relations between the east African coast and the rest of the Muslim world. Arabic writers of the time referred to the main central region of the east African coast as 'the Land of Zenj' (sometimes spelt 'Zanj').

In the western Indian Ocean the monsoon winds blow towards east Africa between November and March and towards India and the Persian Gulf between April and October. This seasonal pattern of monsoon winds largely influenced the pattern of cross-ocean trade that developed between the east African coast and the Islamic world of western Asia. Most of the long-distance trade of the western Indian Ocean was carried in Arab sailing ships known as *dhows* (see Figure 9.1). The journey across the ocean could take several months. This did not leave them much time for trading along the east African coast before they had to turn for home on the south-west monsoon. The more northerly ports of Mogadishu, Barawa and Lamu islands thus became their most common ports of call. Local coastal trading was generally

Figure 9.1 Arab dhow used on the East African coast. (By Adolf Bock in *Allers Familj- Journal* [Sweden] 27 December 1927, No. 53)

left in the hands of east African traders who brought their goods to the principal market-towns. This enabled merchants from across the ocean to complete their business quickly without wasting valuable time calling between one tiny settlement and the next.

As the demand for African ivory, and later gold, rose, so more Muslim Arabs settled in the east African island towns to try and direct the local trade to their advantage. These early Muslim settlers developed good relations, often through intermarriage, with the local African ruling family. In this way they were able to ensure that their Muslim relatives, the overseas merchants, would be well received within the town.

By the ninth century there were a number of well-established market-towns along the coast of the 'Land of Zenj' (see Map 9.2). Most were situated on the offshore islands. There were several on the Lamu islands off the northern Kenyan coast and others further south on Zanzibar, Kilwa and the Comoro islands. Though clearly involved in overseas trade, they were nevertheless primarily local African towns. They housed cattle-keeping, mixed-farming communities who had added trade to their basic agricultural economy. Cattle were kept in central fenced enclosures and domestic houses were generally built on a circular pattern, made of mud-brick and thatch. Most of the pottery which archaeologists have found in these sites was locally made, on a general east African Iron Age pattern. Small quantities of imported pottery from the Persian Gulf, western India and China confirm the trading link. The style of local pottery is remarkably similar through the 3000-kilometre stretch of coastland from Mogadishu to Mozambique. This suggests close cultural links and regular sailing contacts between the various trading settlements along the coastal region.

The coastal towns of this period were mainly exporters of raw materials and importers of manufactured goods and luxuries, oriental pottery, glassware,

131

and Indian silks and cottons. The main African commodity sought by overseas traders was ivory. This was in particularly high demand in China, where it was used for making ceremonial chairs for the nobility. In India too it was widely used for making ornately-carved dagger-handles and sword-scabbards. The African elephant produces larger tusks than the Indian elephant and its ivory is of the finer 'softer' texture most suitable for carving. Other African exports included ambergris, a fossilised resin used for making perfume, and mangrove poles needed for building houses in the Persian Gulf. Captives were exported as slaves for the salt-mines of Basra and the farming plantations at the head of the Persian Gulf. The slaves were numerous enough at Basra to rise in revolt ('the Zenj revolt') in 868 CE. A small amount of gold was also exported. It was brought to the northern coastal towns by the Zenj from 'the land of Sofala', somewhere to the south. There is some evidence too of cotton cloth as well as glass and shell beads being manufactured in some of the main coastal towns. These were clearly intended for trading to peoples of the interior for ivory and other products. Beads of this type, dating back to the eighth and ninth centuries, have been found in numerous archaeological sites far across the central and southern African interior.

The historian of the east African coast is fortunate in being able to draw on the written accounts of several contemporary Arabic-speaking visitors to the coast. Among the more important of these were al-Masudi in the tenth century and Ibn Battuta in the fourteenth century. Al-Masudi visited the 'Land of Zanj' in 916. He came on an Arab *dhow* from Oman in south-eastern Arabia. He wrote:

> The land of Zanj produces wild leopard skins. The people wear them as clothes, or export them to Muslim countries. They are the largest leopard skins and the most beautiful for making saddles … . They also export tortoise-shell for making combs, for which ivory is likewise used … . The Zanj are settled in that area, which stretches as far as Sofala, which is the furthest limit of the land and the end of the voyages made from Oman and Siraf on the sea of Zanj. … The Zanj use the ox as a beast of burden, for they have no horses, mules or camels in their land. … There are many wild elephants in this land but no tame ones. The Zanj do not use them for war or anything else, but only hunt and kill them for their ivory. It is from this country that come tusks weighing fifty pounds and more. They usually go to Oman, and from there are sent to China and India. This is the chief trade route … .
>
> The Zanj have an elegant language and men who preach in it. One of their holy men will often gather a crowd and exhort his hearers to please God in their lives and to be obedient to him. He explains the punishments that follow upon disobedience, and reminds them of their ancestors and kings of old. These people have no religious law: their kings rule by custom and by political expediency.
>
> The Zanj eat bananas, which are as common among them as they are in India; but their staple food is millet and a plant called *kalari* which is pulled out of the earth like truffles. They also eat honey and meat. They have many islands where the coconut grows: its nuts are used as fruit by all the Zanj peoples. One of these islands, which is one or two days' sail from the coast, has a Muslim population and a royal family. This is the island of Kanbalu [thought to be modern Pemba].

(Adapted from a translation by G. S. P. Freeman-Grenville, *The East African Coast,* OUP, Oxford, 1962, pp. 15–17)

Map 9.2   The east African coast, 500–1000 CE

Figure 9.2   The Mtambwe Mkuu Hoard, a scatter of tiny, locally minted silver and copper coins found on Pemba Island, photographed before cleaning and identification. The coins are thought to date from between 980 and 1100 CE. Individually, they range from 7 to 12 mm in diameter and are so thin as to weigh less than a fifth of a gram each

133

The growth of Swahili trading towns

Origins of the Swahili

Kiswahili today is the most widely spoken of the African languages of eastern Africa. It is spoken all along the coastal region and in many parts of the interior. It has also been adopted as the official language of modern Tanzania. The name 'Swahili' came originally from the Arabic word sahil meaning 'coast'. Thus 'Swahili' means literally 'the people of the coast'. Kiswahili is basically a Bantu language to which has been added a number of Arabic words. It developed out of the language of the Early Iron Age peoples who appear to have lived in the region of the Tana valley and the Lamu islands. The Arabic additions came from Arab settlers who married into coastal society. They retained Arabic for writing and for communicating with overseas traders, but used Kiswahili in their normal daily speech. In due course Kiswahili was developed as a written language, using an Arabic script.

Between the tenth and fourteenth centuries the term 'Swahili' came to denote a distinctive coastal society that was Islamic in religion and culture, but primarily African in language and personnel. It was an urban, coastal trading culture and economy, and it is to the development of these Swahili towns that we now turn.

Map 9.3   Indian Ocean trading networks, tenth to sixteenth centuries

The period from about 970 to 1050 was one of renewed growth for the east African trading towns. This coincided with a rising demand for African ivory and gold in Byzantine Europe and Fatimid Egypt. There is evidence of further Muslim settlement on east African coastal islands. Al-Masudi's reference to the island of Kanbalu having a Muslim ruler suggests that that was unusual in the early tenth century. A century later it was more common, as Muslim influence increased. Mosques were built in some of the towns, as a number of African rulers converted to Islam or Muslim settlers married into local ruling families. Rectangular houses made of blocks of coral stone began to be built at some of the northern market-towns. This was in the style of houses on the Dahlak islands of the Red Sea, suggesting closer links through this trade route with Egypt and the Mediterranean. There were general signs of growing prosperity, at least among the ruling classes. A number of wealthy merchant rulers began to mint their own coins out of silver and copper (see Figure 9.2). The gold Fatimid dinar remained the principal currency of international exchange, but the small local coins were used for local transactions.

The gold trade and the rise of Kilwa

The period 1050 to 1200 saw further Muslim immigration from the Persian Gulf and Oman. Possibly because of pressure from newcomers, a number of northern Swahili Muslims, particularly from Shungwaya and the Lamu islands, moved south to settle on the islands of Zanzibar, Mafia, Pemba, Kilwa and the Comoros. Here they settled in existing trading towns and set up new dynasties which ruled the islands for generations to come. The leading members of these ruling families claimed to trace their Muslim ancestry to immigrants from Shiraz in the Persian Gulf. The dynasties they founded are therefore usually referred to as Shirazi. But there is no evidence of direct Persian immigration and it seems likely that some prominent northern Swahili families claimed the connection for added status. From the time of this so-called Shirazi 'migration', houses made of blocks of coral stone began to be built on the islands of Pemba, Zanzibar, Mafia and Kilwa.

Of all the new Swahili towns, Kilwa was destined to become the most important. Until this time the gold trade, such as it was, had been largely organised by the Muslim merchants of Mogadishu, the northernmost Swahili town, founded in about 1000 CE. Through their Muslim contacts along the coast the Mogadishu merchants arranged for gold dust to be brought north from the 'land of Sofala' far to the south. The new Shirazi rulers of Kilwa were now in a position to break Mogadishu's control of the gold trade. Kilwa was the most southerly point to which overseas merchants could sail in one season. It was therefore ideally placed to control the southern trade. The merchants of Kilwa sent ships south to form a small trading settlement at Sofala, just south of modern Beira. Here the peoples of the interior brought gold from the emerging societies of the Limpopo valley and the Zimbabwe plateau (see the next chapter, pp. 152–7). By 1200 at the latest, Kilwa had broken the hold of Mogadishu and established local control of the overseas trade in the gold of southern Africa. For the next two hundred years Kilwa remained one of the most important and perhaps the wealthiest of all the Swahili trading towns.

The political economy of the Swahili trading towns

There were in all some forty Swahili towns between Mogadishu and Sofala. Many were small, containing only a few stone houses, a mosque, a Muslim ruling family and a predominantly non-Muslim subject population. The larger towns such as Mogadishu, Pate, Mombasa, Malindi, Zanzibar and Kilwa were built almost entirely of coral stone and showed signs of great wealth.

Most of the towns acted independently, under the rule of their own Muslim sultan. At various times some of the larger towns exercised authority over their smaller neighbours. In the late fourteenth and early fifteenth centuries, for instance, the sultans of Kilwa claimed control over much of the coast between Sofala and Zanzibar. But their hold was weakened by a series of dynastic disputes, and by the 1490s most of the towns, including Sofala, were asserting their independence.

The ruling classes were mostly very wealthy. They lived in large stone houses and ornate palaces. They wore fine robes of silk and cotton and jewellery made of gold and silver. They ate off delicate imported porcelain from Persia and China. Though they owned large estates on which were grown millet, cotton, vegetables and fruit, their main source of wealth was the overseas trade. The sultan charged import and export dues of up to 50 per cent and more on all goods passing through the town. In spite of these heavy taxes, the merchants of the towns were able to grow wealthy on their trade. In some of the larger towns such as Kilwa and Mombasa, the merchants also organised the production of cotton cloth and glass and shell beads for trading in the African interior.

Below the merchants in wealth and status were the bulk of the towns-people, the Kiswahili-speaking Muslim craftsmen, artisans, clerks, minor court officials and captains of coastal ships. This part of the population was distinctly African in personnel with no claim to Arab or Persian ancestry. They tended to live in rectangular mud-and-thatch houses clustered inwards

Figure 9.3 The ruins of the Great Mosque at Kilwa which was founded in the thirteenth century and much extended in the fifteenth by Sultan Muhamed on the edge of the main stone town. Traditional African villages on the adjacent mainland housed non-Muslim farmers and fishers who provided the town with regular food, and visiting ivory hunters and traders from the interior usually stayed there.

Relations between the peoples of the mainland and the Swahili of the coastal and island towns varied considerably. In general it was in the interests of both to maintain good relations. The peoples of the interior supplied the Swahili with the ivory, furs and gold so essential to their trade and continued wealth. In return, the Swahili supplied them with cloth, beads, imported pottery and other luxuries.

At times, however, relations were not so good and mainland chieftains were known to attack or besiege coastal towns. The main cause of friction was raids by the Swahili themselves into the interior in search of livestock and other booty and captives to enslave. At the time of Ibn Battuta's visit in 1331, the sultan of Kilwa was conducting what he claimed was a *jihad* against the 'pagan Zanj' of the interior. The nature of his 'holy war' is revealed by Ibn Battuta's comment that the sultan 'frequently makes raids into the Zanj country, attacks them and carries off booty'. Some of this he kept for himself, the rest he put into a special fund for entertaining foreign visitors, such as Ibn Battuta himself. The sultan was surnamed Abu al-Mawahib ('the Father of Gifts') 'on account of his numerous charitable gifts'!

The sultans of Kilwa, who got much of their wealth from the gold trade of Sofala far to the south, could perhaps afford to antagonise the local mainland peoples in this way. Not so the rulers of many other towns. Later sultans of Kilwa re-established better relations with the mainland peoples. It is interesting to note that when the Portuguese attacked Kilwa in 1505 the local African chief sent archers across from the mainland to help defend the island.

Relations between the Swahili towns themselves were generally peaceable. There was great rivalry between them over trade, but they seldom attacked each other, and the violence of piracy was almost unknown before the coming of the Portuguese.

The Portuguese on the east African coast, 1498–1600

When the Portuguese rounded the southern tip of Africa and sailed north along the east African coast in 1498, they were the first western Europeans to enter the Indian Ocean from the south. Portuguese trading ships had for some years been sailing ever further south along the west coast of Africa in search of an eastern route to India. The motives behind these early European ventures will be considered further in Chapter 12 (p. 177). Basically they hoped that by entering the Indian Ocean from the south they could bypass their Muslim rivals who dominated north Africa and the eastern Mediterranean world of western Asia. The Portuguese hoped in this way to seize from Muslim control the fabulously wealthy trade in the spices, perfumes, silks and other luxuries of India. They knew little if anything of the existence of the east African Swahili trade.

When the Portuguese saw the wealth of the Swahili towns and the extent of their trade, they determined to seize control of it too, if necessary by force. The tactic they adopted was to sail with heavily armed ships into the

Map 9.4 Swahili towns and the Portuguese, fifteenth and sixteenth centuries

harbours of the more important towns. They then demanded that the ruler of the town become a Portuguese subject and pay a heavy annual tribute to the king of Portugal. If these demands were not met, the town was attacked, all its possessions were seized and any Muslims who resisted were killed. The whole process was justified in the name of a 'holy Christian war' against the 'Moors'. ('Moor' was the name used by European Christians at this time to refer specifically to the Muslims of north Africa. They also used it more generally to refer to all Muslims, whether African or Arab.) Even the larger island towns had not been used to defending themselves against determined attack from the sea. And they were so used to being rivals in trade that in their time of need, the Swahili towns failed to act together against the new threat from outside.

The sultan of Malindi hoped to avoid confrontation by quickly agreeing to pay tribute to the Portuguese. But the majority of coastal towns refused to surrender their independence so easily. Indeed, the sultan of Mombasa went so far as to declare war on Malindi, who had now apparently become an ally of the common enemy.

Zanzibar was the first Swahili town to come under serious Portuguese attack. In 1503 a Portuguese sea captain, Ruy Lourenço Ravasco, blasted at the townspeople with his ship's cannon until the sultan of Zanzibar agreed to pay an annual tribute of 100 *miticals*. This was in fact little more than a piratical raid on the Portuguese captain's own initiative. But it set the pattern for things to come. During 1503 Ravasco and his companions sailed up and down the Swahili coast, seizing ships and ransoming them for payment in gold. This was followed in 1505 by a more determined and official Portuguese assault. Francisco d'Almeida was sent with a fleet of 11 heavily

Figure 9.4 Portuguese ships of the sixteenth century

armed ships to seize control of the more important towns. That year Kilwa, Mombasa and Barawa were each attacked. The following Portuguese eyewitness accounts describe the sacking of Kilwa and Mombasa:

> From our ships the fine houses, terraces, and minarets, with the palms and trees in the orchards, made the city [Kilwa] look so beautiful that our men were eager to land and overcome the pride of this barbarian, who spent all that night in bringing into the island archers from the mainland … .
>
> [After some hand-to-hand fighting the following day the sultan fled and the Portuguese took the town.]

> Then the Vicar-General and some of the Franciscan fathers came ashore carrying two crosses in procession and singing the Te Deum. They went to the palace, and there the cross was put down and the Grand-Captain [d'Almeida] prayed. Then everyone started to plunder the town of all its merchandise and provisions … .
>
> [After two weeks spent securing the town, building a fortress and appointing a new 'puppet' sultan, the Portuguese fleet sailed up the coast to Mombasa.]
>
> The Moors of Mombasa had built a strongpoint with many guns at the entrance of the harbour, which is very narrow. When we entered, the first ship was fired on by the Moors from both sides. We promptly replied to the fire, and with such intensity that the gunpowder in their strongpoint caught fire. It started burning and the Moors fled, thus allowing the whole fleet to enter and lie at anchor in front of the town … .
>
> The Grand-Captain met with the other captains and decided to burn the town that evening and to enter it the following morning. But when they went to burn the town they were received by the Moors with a shower of arrows and stones. The town has more than 600 houses which are thatched with palm leaves: these are collected green for this purpose. In between the stone dwelling-houses there are wooden houses with porches and stables for cattle. There are very few dwelling houses which have not these wooden houses attached.
>
> Once the fire was started it raged all night long, and many houses collapsed and a large quantity of goods was destroyed. For from this town trade is carried on with Sofala and with Cambay [in western India] by sea. There were three ships from Cambay and even these did not escape the fury of the attack. It was a moonless night … .
>
> [Early the following morning the Portuguese stormed ashore.] The archers and gunners went ahead of everyone else, all going up the steep ascent into the town. When they entered, they found that some of the houses had been deserted as a result of the fire of the previous night. Further on they found three-storeyed houses from which stones were thrown at them. But the stones which were thrown fell against the walls of the very narrow streets, so that much of the force of their fall was lost. There were also many balconies projecting over the streets under which one could shelter.
>
> The Grand-Captain went straight to the royal palace where Captain Vermudez climbed up the wall and hoisted our flag, shouting: Portugal, Portugal. [Only four Portuguese were killed in the attack on Mombasa, but] … The death of these four was avenged by that of 1513 Moors … .
>
> The Grand-Captain ordered that the town should be sacked and that each man should carry off to his ship whatever he found: so that at the end there would be a division of the spoil, each man to receive a twentieth of what he found. The same rule was made for gold, silver and pearls. Then everyone started to plunder the town and to search the houses, forcing open the doors with axes and iron bars. There was a large quantity of cotton cloth for Sofala in the town, for the whole coast gets its cotton cloth from here. So the Grand-Captain got a good share of the trade of Sofala for himself. A large quantity of rich silk and gold embroidered clothes was seized, and carpets also; one of these, which was without equal for beauty, was sent to the King of Portugal together with many other valuables.

(Adapted from the eyewitness accounts of Joao de Barros and Hans Mayr printed in G. S. P. Freeman-Grenville, *The East African Coast,* OUP, Oxford, 1962, pp. 86, 102, 108–10)

Figure 9.5 View of archway and walls from the fifteenth century ruined city of Gedi

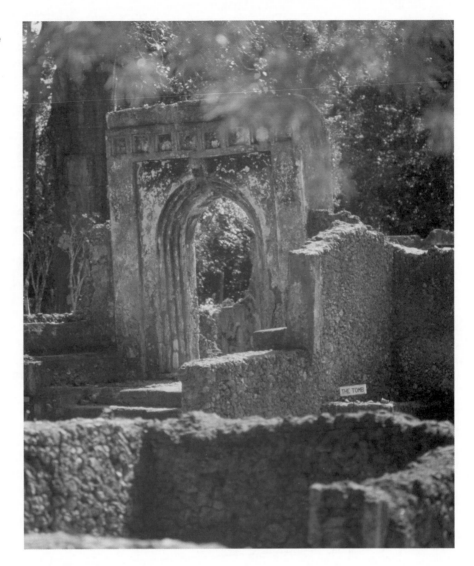

D'Almeida went on to become governor of Goa, a small Portuguese colony on the west coast of India. He met his death at the hands of the Khoesan of southern Africa whom he unwisely attacked during his return voyage to Portugal in 1509.

After sacking the Swahili towns that resisted them the Portuguese erected stone fortresses in the southern ports of Kilwa, Sofala and Mozambique. This provided them with a firm base on the African coast from which to sail across to their Indian colony of Goa. It also gave them coastal control of the gold trade which reached Sofala from the Zimbabwe plateau. (Portuguese relations in this direction will be considered further in the following chapter.)

The Portuguese hoped at the same time that their southern trading bases would divert trade away from the northern Swahili towns. But Swahili resistance continued in the north. The sultan of Mombasa refused to pay tribute to the Portuguese and continued to maintain direct trading contacts with Arabia and the Persian Gulf. As a result of this defiance Mombasa suffered two further Portuguese sackings, in 1528 and 1589. After the third and final

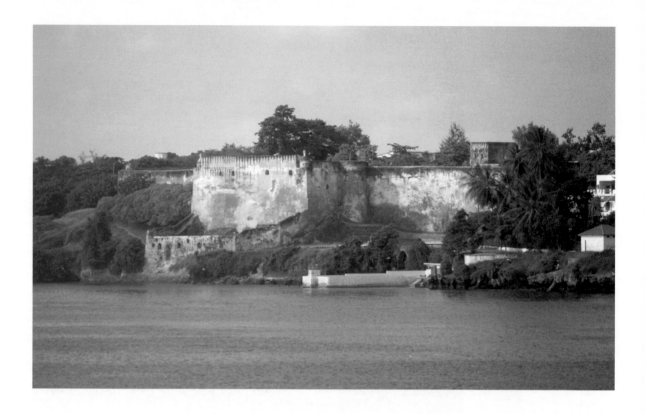

Figure 9.6 Fort Jesus, Mombasa

Figure 9.7 A view to the sixteenth-century remains of the Portuguese fort at Kilwa

sacking of Mombasa, the Portuguese realised that to dominate the trade of the western Indian Ocean they needed to control the northern cities as well. In order to do this they built a huge fortress at Mombasa which they called Fort Jesus. Completed in 1599, Fort Jesus became the main centre of Portuguese authority in eastern Africa for the next one hundred years. Its massive threatening walls (see Figure 9.6) aptly symbolised the violence with which Portuguese domination of the trade of the east African coast was maintained for much of the sixteenth and seventeenth centuries.

Madagascar

The huge island of Madagascar, which lies approximately 500 kilometres off the Mozambique coast of east Africa, was uninhabited until the early centuries of the Common Era. This long, north–south oriented island is dominated by a central plateau which has a fairly temperate climate, but not very fertile soil. To the east of the plateau is a narrow coastal strip that was in the past covered with thick tropical forest. On the west is a wider coastal plain, of mixed tropical vegetation in the north and drier, almost desert conditions in the south.

Madagascar was first settled by people of Austronesian origin (people of the Malasian/Indonesian/Australian/Polynesian group) and Bantu-speakers from the east African mainland, both of whom appear to have arrived at approximately the same time. Austronesians crossed the Indian Ocean in outrigger canoes to the east coast of Africa where they made no permanent settlement, but where they came into contact with Bantu-speaking farmers. It was contacts such as these which brought the banana to east Africa. They then settled on the northern coast of Madagascar, accompanied by Bantu-speaking east Africans, possibly as some form of slave labour. Linguistic evidence puts these events between about 100 and 400 CE, although the earliest direct archaeological evidence of settlement that has so far been found is dated to the eighth century. In subsequent centuries other east African Bantu-speakers followed and some established independent settlements in the western and southern parts of the island. Further occasional new arrivals of small numbers of Austronesians occurred until possibly as late as 1500 CE. Most early settlement was confined to the coastal lowlands. The interior plateau remained sparsely populated until later centuries.

Besides an obvious expertise in fishing, the Malagasy's Austronesian ancestors brought with them the cultivation of rice and bananas and a tradition of building rectangular houses; their African ancestors brought cattle and other farming practices. However, Indian Ocean trade remained an important aspect of the Malagasy economy. Following the expansion of Muslim-led east African coastal trade from the seventh century, Madagascar became part of the Swahili trading network. By 1000 CE small numbers of traders of Swahili, Arab and Indian ancestry were settled in the northern trading ports. The Arabic-speaking traders, known locally as Antalaotra, brought with them an ideology of kingship, and established ruling dynasties among the peoples of the north and west of the island. Along the east coast, which was relatively cut off from the trading networks of the western Indian Ocean, Austronesian contacts were maintained, and although some Antalaotra elites settled in this region, they adopted the dominant Malagasy language and culture. In the isolated valleys of the south, where concepts of kingship also took hold, Bantu languages were retained until at least the fourteenth century.

Later Iron Age states and societies of central and southern Africa to 1600

The cultural and economic changes that were observed with reference to eastern Africa after about 1000 CE (Chapter 8, pp. 122–4), occurred also in central and southern Africa around the same time. And as with eastern Africa, the transition is associated with a change in the style of pottery recovered from Iron Age settlement sites. It was now made of finer clay, decorated more elaborately and fired to a harder finish. Detailed study of this pottery and other archaeological artefacts has revealed a certain level of continuity between Early and Late periods. It appears that in some areas the development of Later Iron Age practices was gradual and evolved locally. In others the changes were fairly swift, suggesting the arrival of ideas or small numbers of influential people from outside that particular locality. The timing of the transition was equally variable, occurring sometime between the ninth and fourteenth centuries.

Characteristics of the Later Iron Age

As people learned to make the most of their local environment, agricultural and fishing techniques were improved and mining and manufacturing skills further developed. In some areas, particularly in southern Africa, there was increasing emphasis upon cattle-keeping, as people brought the drier grasslands into greater use. Certain communities specialised in mining, metal manufacture, food production or hunting. All of this regional specialisation helped promote inter-regional trade. The remnants of the stone-using hunter-gatherers were squeezed out or absorbed as populations expanded and more land was brought into regular use.

The emergence of Later Iron Age states north of the Zambezi

Religion and kingship in central Africa

With the development of Later Iron Age specialisations and population growth, people organised in larger political units and there was a rise in the power and importance of territorial chiefs.

The chiefs and kings that rose to power in the savannah woodlands south of the Congo forest could usually trace the origins of their authority to some religious practices. They may have been in a position to gain power through the control of trade. They may have possessed some superior metal-working or hunting knowledge or skill. But whatever their material source of secular power, they usually justified their right to rule through their role as mediators in traditional religion or their ancestral links with the spirit world. Thus the

Figure 10.1 Potters of the Zambezi valley in the early twentieth century, decorating pots of the Late Iron Age type

ancient rulers of Kongo were guardians of the 'spirits of the land' (for similar beliefs in west Africa, see p. 101). The original rulers of the Mbundu of modern Angola and the early Chewa of modern Malawi were guardians of religious 'rain-making' shrines. The people paid them tribute as religious leaders. They in turn ensured the success of harvest, hunt or rain. In a more secular role they protected the people from outside attack or maintained the safety of trade routes. In times of drought and famine they redistributed stores of food to the needy, raided neighbours or organised a move to a more fruitful and fertile site.

Origins and early growth of the Luba kingdom

One of the more important areas for the early growth of Later Iron Age chieftaincy was in the upper Lualaba valley, around Lake Kisale in the south-east of the Congo Basin. The Lake Kisale region had been continuously occupied by iron-working farmers since at least the fourth century CE (see p. 62–3). It was particularly well situated for the production of food surpluses. The savannah woodland on the southern edge of the Congo forest was a fertile region for the cultivation of cereal crops with sufficient rainfall to ensure a regular surplus. In addition, the woodlands were good for hunting and the river and lakes for fishing.

Figure 10.2 A Kisalian grave

The peoples of the Lake Kisale region made maximum use of the available resources. Over the centuries they developed the use of nets, harpoons and dugout canoes and cleared canals through reed-covered swamps. They learnt the techniques of drying fish which provided them with an important source of protein that could be traded to other peoples. They bought iron and salt from the north, and copper from the south where it was mined extensively in the region of the modern Zambian/Congo 'copperbelt'. They became expert craftsmen, especially in metal manufacture. They drew heated copper into fine wire for rings, bracelets and necklaces or cast it into cross-shaped ingots for trading or for storing wealth (see Figure 10.3).

By 1300 at the latest, the peoples of the Lake Kisale region were organised into a number of prosperous farming and trading chiefdoms: the ancestors of the modern Luba. Their prime farming and fishing grounds were, however, strictly limited. It was possibly competition for increasingly limited resources that led some village chiefdoms to group together into larger, more centralised states. Between 1300 and 1400 the Luba east of the Lualaba were organised into a single centralised kingdom under a dynasty known as Nkongolo. According to Luba oral tradition, the original Nkongolo came from the Songye peoples of the north. In the early 1400s the Nkongolo were ousted by a new dynasty. According to Luba mythology, the founding hero of this dynasty was a great huntsman called Ilunga Kalala. His father had come to Lubaland from the Kunda in the north and had married the Nkongolo's sister. Ilunga Kalala is portrayed in oral tradition as a heroic huntsman, possessing magical powers. He was probably the leader of a band of professional huntsmen who gained status and acceptance among the Luba by the introduction of new hunting techniques. These may have included the use of the bow and iron-tipped arrow not previously found in the region.

The Ilunga dynasty strengthened the centralised power of government and expanded the kingdom west of Lake Kisale. The central court of the kingdom was dominated by the royal dynasty. The king appointed provincial governors, often from the royal family, to collect tribute from local chiefs and headmen. The Luba kings had only a very small standing army but this was backed up by the powerful mystical and religious authority of the king. Within the court itself there was great family rivalry for power. Around the 1450s disappointed rivals from within the royal clan moved off to found their own kingdom among the Lunda to their west, astride the tributaries of the upper Kasai.

Origins of the Lunda empire

The Lunda at this time had no centralised chieftaincy, although they had a senior chief. The incoming Luba royals justified their position by marrying into the family of the senior chief. In Lunda oral tradition this is personified in the person of Chibunda Ilunga who married the Lunda queen Rweej (or Lueji). The descendants of this marriage produced a new Lunda dynasty which, during the sixteenth century, assumed the title Mwaant Yaav or Mwata Yamvo ('The Lord of Vipers'). In doing so they drew the loosely scattered Lunda chiefdoms into a single, centralised and expanding empire. The main period of growth and power of the Lunda empire was the seventeenth and eighteenth centuries (see below, pp. 207–9), but the foundations of the state had been laid by 1600.

The Lunda of the fifteenth century were less densely populated than the Luba. They lived in a large number of small villages where they practised farming, fishing, hunting and trading. Their technology, arts and crafts were less developed than those of the Luba. The small number of incoming royal Luba were thus able to bring to the region the finer elements of Later Iron Age metal-working technology. Luba ideas of centralised religious kingship, however, were adapted to local circumstances and as a result provided a firmer base for future territorial expansion. Lunda religious practices were respected and Lunda chiefs were left in place as the guardians of local spirits and 'owners of the land'. In return they were required to pay tribute to the newly centralised Lunda king, but were entitled to a position as advisers to the royal court. The king held the loyalty of this 'confederation' of Lunda chieftaincies by appointing a *cilool* or *kilolo* as royal 'adviser' and tax-collecting agent within each local chiefdom.

The spread of Lunda titles

From the time of the early founding of the united Lunda kingdom, royal rivals to the kingship moved away to found their own dynasties among the peoples to the south and west. Kingship among the Luena and Luyana (later Lozi) of the upper Zambezi of modern western Zambia was reputed to have distant Lunda origins. One of the more important of these Lunda 'dispersals' bore the title of *Kinguri*. The original *Kinguri* was reputed in oral tradition to be the brother of the Lunda queen Rweej. He founded a hunting and raiding state in the central highlands of modern Angola. Here there was no attempt to take over and utilise existing chiefly practices. Men and women from surrounding villages were incorporated into the new state by elaborate initiation ceremonies. By 1550 the rulers of this militarily orientated state had assumed the title of *Kasanje* and their people became the Imbangala.

Peoples of central and southern Angola

Meanwhile among the Mbundu-speaking peoples of modern Angola, chieftaincy and kingship were already developing along similar religious lines to those of the Luba and the Lunda. The principal Mbundu-speaking peoples were the Ndongo, Pende and Libolo. By the 1300s the guardians

147

Figure 10.3 (a) Iron and copper artefacts from Upemba, in the classic Kisalian style; (b) and (c) Early Kisalian pottery from the Upemba Rift (Shaba)

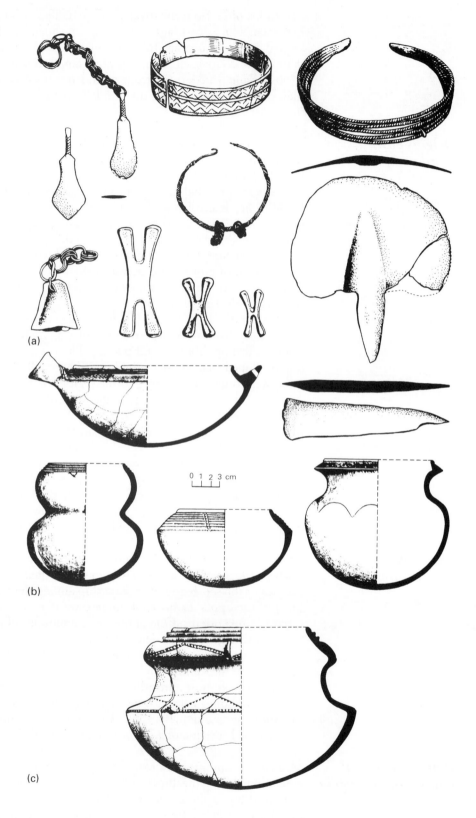

(a)

(b)

(c)

0 1 2 3 cm

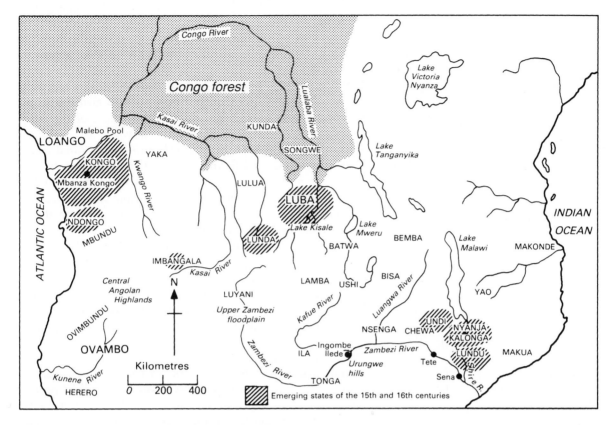

Map 10.1 South-central Africa in the Later Iron Age

of their rain-making shrines were assuming the positions of chiefs and exacting tribute for their services. In a number of Ndongo villages the guardians of the shrines were also known to possess important metal-working skills. They used the title of *Ngola*. It was possibly they who first introduced new Later Iron Age technology to the region. Whatever their source of power, they used it to weld the Ndongo chiefdoms together into a single united state. By 1500 there was a single *Ngola a Kiluanje* ruling over the Ndongo.

Very little is known of the peoples further south except that by the fifteenth century groups of Ovimbundu and Ovambo were practising mixed farming along the southern slopes of the central Angolan highlands. Further south still, in the dry grasslands bordering modern Namibia, the Herero were developing a mainly pastoral existence.

The kingdom of Kongo

One of the most important kingdoms to arise in west-central Africa was the kingdom of Kongo. The origins of the state are to be traced to a group of small prosperous farming villages just north of Malebo Pool on the lower Congo River. Here, like the Lake Kisale region of the upper Lualaba, was a particularly fruitful zone for the development of Later Iron Age skills and practices: the production of food surpluses, the promotion of manufacturing crafts and the development of trade. On the margins of forest and savannah woodlands, soils were fertile and rainfall plentiful. There were sources of copper, iron and salt within easy trading distance. The river and

149

its tributaries encouraged the development of fishing. In addition the Malebo Pool itself was a major trading crossroads. It was above the rapids of the lower river and had thousands of kilometres of navigable waterways stretching away upstream.

By the early 1300s the main group of Bakongo villages extended across the fertile uplands just south of the lower Congo. Being basically farming people their religious practices centred on their shrines to the 'spirits of the land'. The guardians of these shrines were called *mani kabunga*. By 1400 the Bakongo villages south of the Congo River had been loosely united into a single kingdom with its capital at Mbanza Kongo. The king bore the title *Manikongo*. Bakongo arts and crafts were highly developed. They were skilled metal-workers, potters and weavers. Fine cloth woven from the fibres of the raffia palm was widely traded as far as the Atlantic coast where it was exchanged for salt and sea shells for use as local currency. The tribute system operated by the Kongo kings stimulated an inter-regional trade. By the early 1500s the Manikongo held authority over the region from the Atlantic in the west to the Kwango River in the east.

The indigenous development of the Kongo kingdom was disrupted after the 1480s by the arrival of the Portuguese and their increasing demands for a trade in slaves. The consequences of this will be considered in Chapter 14 (p. 204).

Later Iron Age peoples of eastern Zambia and Malawi

Much of east-central Africa from central Zambia to Lake Malawi seems to have belonged to a single Later Iron Age culture known through its pottery as the Luangwa tradition. This seems to have spread fairly quickly between 1000 and 1200. There was a wider use of iron, especially axes to clear woodland for cultivation, and there was an increasing emphasis upon the herding of cattle. Ivory-hunting, copper manufacture and trade were also important. Though the origins and source of the Luangwa tradition remain unclear, there are clear cultural links between these Later Iron Age peoples and the Bemba, Bisa and Chewa of modern times.

In central and southern Malawi the concept of chieftaincy emerged from the religious cults that were guardians of the 'spirits of the land', especially those responsible for rain and soil fertility. Around 1400 the Phiri clan gained ascendancy among the chiefs of the Nyanja just south of Lake Malawi by marrying into the local Banda clan. They took the royal title of *Kalonga*. The Phiri clan's concept of religious kingship is believed in oral tradition to have come originally from the Luba. Whether they were direct migrants from Lubaland is not known for sure.

In the course of the sixteenth century, offshoots from the Kalonga dynasty founded the Lundu dynasty among the Manganja of the Shire valley and the Undi dynasty among the Chewa between the Shire and Zambezi. Fire played an important role in the religious rituals of the Phiri clan. The peoples of the Kalonga, Lundu and Undi kingdoms were known collectively as 'Maravi' meaning 'peoples of the fire'. The region was a rich field for ivory-hunting. Control of the ivory trade down the Shire and Zambezi to the Indian Ocean coast may have been an important source of power for the early Maravi kings. It was certainly exploited by the Kalonga kings of the seventeenth century, as we shall see in Chapter 14 (pp. 209–11).

The development of Later Iron Age communities south of the Zambezi

As we have already seen, one of the features of Later Iron Age societies was an increasing use of cattle. An area where this was particularly so and where it played an important role in early state-formation was in the open grassland zones south of the Zambezi.

The importance of cattle

In the first place, cattle were a useful source of food: both milk and meat. Although beef was not often eaten, except by the wealthy or on special occasions, it could be used in times of shortage. Cattle could also be traded with neighbouring communities in exchange for food or for iron and other necessary goods.

Secondly, cattle were a major source of wealth and social control. In general in Later Iron Age societies there was a growing division between rich and poor and a greater domination by men over women. This was especially so in cattle-keeping societies. Through a process of natural increase, a herd of less than 20 cattle could in favourable conditions multiply to several thousand within a single human generation. This enabled men to accumulate wealth for passing on to future generations. And it was men who controlled the social use of cattle.

Cattle provided men with their main source of bridewealth. Those with large herds of cattle could pay a dowry for several wives. And since women were the main cultivators of the soil, this increased a man's capacity to produce a surplus of food. This in turn could be used for trading as well as feeding his large family and their dependants. Those without cattle became dependent on the wealthy by herding their cattle in return for milk or borrowing cattle from them to pay their own bridewealth. Wealthy cattle-owners thus gained control over an ever-widening community. In this way cattle provided the material basis for the early development of chieftaincy.

One of the more important zones where specialised cattle-keeping developed at an early date was between Limpopo and Kalahari in the eastern-central region of modern Botswana.

Early cattle-keeping communities in eastern Botswana

The dry open grassland of this region, watered by springs and seasonal streams, was ideal for the rapid growth of cattle herds. Here between 650 and 1300 CE a complex system of hilltop settlements was developed. Archaeologists have named it the 'Toutswe tradition' after Toutswemogala, the largest of the sites.

On large, flat-topped hills, circular pole and clay houses thatched with grass were built around central enclosures where cattle were kept at night. The hills were probably originally chosen for defence from wild animals. They also gave the cattle-owners control over the surrounding area. The region was dominated by three large hilltop settlements, possibly representing chiefdoms. Each of these was surrounded by numerous smaller hilltop villages while herdsmen and cultivators lived within the valleys. The wealth of the hilltop dwellers is shown by their regular consumption of beef instead of game meat. Iron was imported from the iron-rich Tswapong hills of the south where specialist smelters operated over a long period of time. Other

Figure 10.4 Cotton-weaving in the Shire valley in the 1860s using Later Iron Age techniques

trading contacts stretched further afield and glass beads were imported, indirectly, from the Indian Ocean coast.

In about 1300 the Toutswe sites were abandoned. It was a period of persistent drought and the region was probably suffering from generations of overgrazing. Nevertheless, by then, cattle-keeping practices developed here had probably already influenced their adoption elsewhere. There is no evidence of large-scale migration from the region after 1300 though this may have been what happened. But with their herds decimated by the destruction of their pasture, the Toutswe people may equally well have reverted to a hunter-gatherer existence or become the dependants of other cattle-keeping communities. Several of these were rising in the damper grasslands further east.

Cattle-keeping, agriculture and the growth of trade: Leopard's Kopje, Bambandyanalo and Mapungubwe

On the Zimbabwe plateau a Later Iron Age, cattle-keeping culture had developed around the region of modern Bulawayo by about the tenth century. This is known as Leopard's Kopje after the site where it was first identified. The Leopard's Kopje people were in an area of slightly higher rainfall than that of the Toutswe people and so were able to develop more of a mixed economy of cattle-keeping and cultivation. In particular they developed the technique of terracing the hillsides on the southern slopes of the plateau in order to prevent erosion of the fertile soils. One such site was Mapela, where during the twelfth century a whole hillside was terraced with dry stone-walling for housing, defence and cultivation. These were prosperous communities, producing a surplus and engaging in long-distance trade.

Another feature of the Leopard's Kopje culture was the development of gold-mining. The western plateau was rich in gold-bearing rock and this was worked intensively by Iron Age miners between the tenth and eighteenth centuries. Narrow shafts were sunk, following seams down 30 metres or more until the seam ran out or the water-table was reached. The rock was cracked by alternate use of fire and water and broken out with iron wedges. Lightly built girls were often used to squeeze down the shaft and break out the ore.

Map 10.2   Later Iron Age states south of the Zambezi, 900–1600

A number of their skeletons have been found at the bottom of long-abandoned shafts. Once brought to the surface the ore was crushed and the gold panned out in the running water of nearby streams. Little is known about the organisation and control of mining labour, but it probably involved a considerable amount of coercion. As we have seen in earlier chapters of this book, the production and trade of gold provided those who controlled it with a major source of wealth.

The early Leopard's Kopje culture of western Zimbabwe reached its climax with the development of Mapungubwe on the southern side of the Shashe-Limpopo confluence. This community started at Bambandyanalo during the tenth century but had expanded to nearby Mapungubwe Hill by 1100. It was basically a farming and cattle-keeping community with sharp divisions between wealthy rulers and poorer dependants. The former lived in substantial clay-built houses on the top of the hill, their settlement dominated by a central cattle enclosure. Ivory-hunting, mining and trade were also very important to the rulers of Mapungubwe. It was strongly placed for the development of long-distance trade. Elephants were plentiful in the Limpopo valley, copper was mined locally and gold was brought down from the plateau to the north. The Limpopo valley itself provided a convenient route to the east African coast. The main exports eastwards were ivory and gold in exchange for glass and shell beads and brightly coloured Indian cloth. Small quantities of delicate Chinese celadon (green-glazed pottery) was imported

153

for their rulers. After 1300 Mapungubwe declined in favour of Great Zimbabwe, which was even better positioned for the development of cattle-raising, cultivation and long-distance trade.

For more information see www.palgrave.com/shillington

The origins and character of the Great Zimbabwe tradition

The modern republic of Zimbabwe is named after the stone enclosures of 'Great Zimbabwe' which were abandoned more than 500 years ago and now lie in ruins. They were originally built between 1200 and 1450 by the Later Iron Age ancestors of the Shona of the modern republic. The growth of Great Zimbabwe was a further extension of the Later Iron Age developments begun by the peoples of Leopard's Kopje and Mapungubwe. Great Zimbabwe itself was the centre or capital of a large and thriving early Shona state. The word *zimbabwe* (plural *madzimbabwe*) comes from the Shona *dzimba dzamabwe*, meaning 'stone buildings'.

The use of drystone-walling for cattle enclosures and encircling the houses of the wealthy was nothing very unusual among Later Iron Age cattle-keeping peoples of southern Africa. What was unusual about Great Zimbabwe was their elaborate development, first on the hilltop and later, from the early 1300s, in the valley. By 1400 the stonemasons of Great Zimbabwe had developed their craft to a fine art. The 10-metre high great enclosure in the valley (see Figure 10.5 C) shows early Shona stonemasonry at its finest. The techniques developed here for building walls to such a height without the use of mortar were unique in the whole of Africa.

The original stoneworks on the hilltop may have been intended for defence, or to impress potential enemies from afar. But it is unlikely that the later elaborate enclosures of the valley were ever built for defensive purposes. They encircled the clay-built dwellings of the country's rulers and their walls were tall and powerful, but there was no easy access to the top from which to

Figure 10.5 The Great Zimbabwe ruins

A. The hilltop had been an important early Shona religious site before it became a political capital. Building enclosures in stone began on the hilltop with the rise of political power from *c.*1200 CE. Centuries of weathering had split slabs from the rounded granite boulders, like the skin of an onion. These were roughly shaped to join the gaps between the boulders and thus form a series of stone enclosures

The Great Zimbabwe ruins
B. By *c.*1300 drystone-walling techniques had been refined and construction of a great royal enclosure was begun in the valley below – viewed here from the hilltop, in the middle distance. During the fourteenth century the whole of the intervening valley would have been cleared of bush and covered with small stone enclosures and circular mud and thatch houses

repel attackers. One is led to conclude that the main purpose of the Great Zimbabwe enclosures was to emphasise and enhance the mystery, power and prestige of the king.

The site for this capital was chosen for its valuable position on the south-eastern edge of the Zimbabwe plateau. Cattle were very important to the early Zimbabwean economy, and here at Great Zimbabwe was a wide range of upland and lowland seasonal grazing. Game was widespread, especially elephant for ivory-hunting. In addition, there was a plentiful supply of timber for firewood and building and well-watered fertile soil for cultivation. But perhaps most important of all for the growth of Great Zimbabwe's power and wealth was the capital's strategic position for trade. Standing at the head of the Sabi river valley it was ideally situated for exploiting the long-distance trade between the goldfields of the western plateau and the Swahili of the Sofala coast. It is no coincidence that the rise of Great Zimbabwe coincided with the rise of Kilwa. It was Great Zimbabwe that supplied the Swahili of Kilwa with the gold and ivory that made theirs the richest coastal town between 1300 and 1450.

The rise of Great Zimbabwe

The state of Great Zimbabwe probably started as a prosperous centre for cattle-keeping and farming peoples, with the ownership of cattle leading to considerable divisions between rich and poor. During the twelfth and thirteenth centuries much of the long-distance trade between western plateau and coast was diverted to pass via the Great Zimbabwe capital. Taxation from this trade was a major source of wealth in addition to the tribute paid by local Shona chiefdoms in ivory, gold and food. With this wealth the rulers of Great Zimbabwe were able to reward their supporters and feed their dependants and so increase their power.

The building of elaborate stone enclosures at the capital was extended into the valley during the fourteenth century. Within the great enclosure was the main residence or 'palace' of the king. Here he and his court lived in some luxury, surrounded by gold and copper ornaments and jewellery and eating off fine imported plates made in Persia and China. At the same time similar

**The Great Zimbabwe ruins
C.** The original perimeter wall of the royal enclosure (right) was later surrounded by an even larger wall (left), leaving a narrow passageway through which supplicants could approach the king

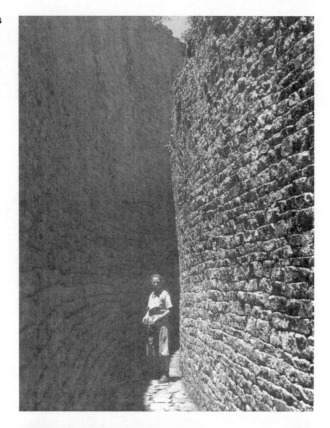

**The Great Zimbabwe ruins
D.** At the heart of the complex of royal enclosures lay a solid circular construction, thought to represent a grain storage silo that probably had symbolic religious or political significance

The Great Zimbabwe ruins
E. The final exterior wall of the royal enclosure was topped by a chevron pattern, which was to become a characteristic of the western capital of Khami, after Great Zimbabwe had been abandoned in *c*.1450. The Great Zimbabwe hilltop remained an important religious site until at least the end of the nineteenth century

smaller *madzimbabwe* were built over a wide area of the eastern plateau, probably as centres of provincial government. Great Zimbabwe itself became a major focus, not only of trade, but also of craft manufacture. Resident craftsmen at the capital worked gold and copper into fine jewellery and forged imported iron into a wide range of tools. There is also evidence from throughout the region of the extensive weaving of cloth from locally grown cotton. Even so, wealthy people still imported brightly coloured Indian cotton from the coast.

The abandonment of Great Zimbabwe

In about 1450 the site of Great Zimbabwe was abandoned. By then the cultivation, grazing and timber resources of the region were exhausted. Oral tradition also refers to a shortage of salt. Movement of settlement sites was a regular feature of Later Iron Age times, as it was necessary to allow agricultural land to recover. This had reached a critical stage at Great Zimbabwe by the fifteenth century. It has been estimated that in the early 1400s there were as many as 11,000 people living in or around the 'city' of Great Zimbabwe. By 1450 the region could no longer support them. At the same time the main focus of the region's long-distance trade was shifting northwards towards the Zambezi valley. It was during this period that Ingombe Ilede briefly flourished, as seen on the following page. This was quickly followed by the rise of the Mutapa state at the head of the Mazoe valley (see below).

The Torwa state

A close successor to Great Zimbabwe was the Torwa state founded at about this time in the Leopard's Kopje region of Guruuswa (or Butua). Its capital, Khami, was probably founded by fifteenth-century migrants from Great Zimbabwe. Here the stone-walling traditions of Great Zimbabwe were further developed and refined. Hills were terraced and drystone walls were elaborately decorated by the layering of carefully trimmed stones. Besides being the centre of the goldfields of the western plateau, the region was particularly healthy for the grazing of large herds of cattle. This was to provide the basis for the development of Changamire's Rozvi state in the seventeenth and eighteenth centuries (see Chapter 14, pp. 211–12).

The growth of the Mutapa state

According to Shona oral tradition, the Mutapa state was founded by Nyatsimbe Mutota, sent north from Great Zimbabwe to seek out a new source of salt. This is thought to have occurred in about 1420. Mutota settled among the northern Shona in the Dande area around the head of the Mazoe valley. Here was an apparently ideal site for the founding of an alternative state to that of Great Zimbabwe. It had fertile soil, good rainfall and plenty of woodland for building. In addition the Mazoe valley gave access to the Zambezi and the Swahili trading stations of Sena and Tete which were established at about this time.

The Swahili were probably originally tempted to penetrate the lower Zambezi by the wealth of copper and ivory coming down the valley from the inland trading town of Ingombe Ilede. This was an important fifteenth-century trading terminus and craft centre, situated 600 kilometres upstream from Tete. The craftsmen of Ingombe Ilede turned gold from northern Zimbabwe into beads and bracelets and copper into cross-shaped ingots for use as a trading currency.

Mutota and his son and successor Matope quickly took advantage of their favourable trading position. Using a small but powerful army they established control over the northern Shona of the region. Mutota and his successors took the title *Munhumutapa* (or *Mwene Mutapa*) meaning 'Conqueror' or 'Master-pillager', which can be taken as some sign of their relationship with their subject people. Ingombe Ilede went into premature decline, unable to compete, and in the 1450s Mutapa took over from Great Zimbabwe as the principal Shona state of the interior plateau. By the end of the reign of Matope in the 1480s the Munhumutapa's tribute demands extended eastwards into the coastal lowlands to include the states of Uteve, Barwe and Manyika.

Figure 10.6 Shona girls in Zimbabwe, early twentieth century, wearing the sort of ornamental bangles and beaded leather skirts which were probably common in the Later Iron Age period

There were a number of important differences between the Mutapa state and that of its predecessor Great Zimbabwe. The rulers of Mutapa came in as outsiders and used an army to maintain control over their subject peoples. This ensured that local village headmen paid them regular tribute. The northern Shona did not have a stone-building tradition and the Munhumutapa's *zimbabwe* of pole and clay houses was enclosed by a wooden palisade. Furthermore, unlike the rulers of Great Zimbabwe, who imported their gold from the west, the rulers of Mutapa had their own supply of gold ready to hand. The Mazoe region was a valuable source of alluvial gold which could readily be washed from the streams that cut through the gold-bearing rocks of the northern plateau. Peasant farmers of the gold-bearing regions were expected to provide a certain amount of regular labour, mining gold for the king. Most of the gold was used in foreign trade with the coast to purchase beads, coloured cloth and other luxuries for the country's rulers.

The Mutapa state and the Portuguese

We saw in the previous chapter that when the Portuguese arrived in the western Indian Ocean they tried seizing control of the Swahili trade in gold by building fortresses at Sofala and Mozambique. But, by then, the export of Zimbabwean gold had switched from the Sabi valley and Sofala to the Mazoe valley and the Zambezi. And from there the Swahili deliberately evaded Portuguese control by diverting their trade to their own coastal port of Angoche. The Portuguese responded by sending a small army up the Zambezi in the 1530s and seizing the Swahili trading posts of Sena and Tete. From there they established direct trading contact with the Munhumutapa's court and diverted the Zambezi valley trade to their own fortress town of Mozambique.

Map 10.3 The Later Iron Age south of the Limpopo

159

Initially the Portuguese were prepared to pay tribute to the Munhumutapa for permission to trade within his territory. But, frustrated by the small amount of gold they could legally buy, they determined to gain personal control over the Munhumutapa and operate the gold mines themselves. After an unsuccessful attempt to convert the Munhumutapa to Christianity, the Portuguese launched an all-out invasion in 1571. But the invading army never left the Zambezi valley. It was defeated by drought, disease and determined resistance from the local Tonga of the valley. Another invasion in 1574 managed to force the ruler of Uteve to agree to pay tribute to the Portuguese at Sofala. But the Mutapa state remained beyond Portuguese control and ended the century still the dominant independent state of the eastern plateau.

Cattle-keeping peoples south of the Limpopo

South of the Limpopo there was a general expansion of cattle-keeping as woodland was cleared and more upland grassland was brought into regular use. Later Iron Age developments between 1000 and 1400 CE saw the gradual emergence of chiefdoms in the region. As already observed for the Toutswe tradition (pp. 151–2), cattle often provided the material basis of chieftaincy. Certain clans wealthy in cattle established ruling lineages (or dynasties) over large numbers of dependants. The spiritual power of chieftaincy was based upon the chief's links with the ancestors. This stemmed largely from his reputed descent from the sometimes mythical founding hero of the clan. In practical terms his claim to chieftaincy was often assessed in terms of his rain-making powers.

The origins of the ancestral chiefly lineages of the modern Sotho-Tswana of the southern African highveld can be traced to about this time. The evidence of their settlements is shown in the large number of stone-walled enclosures and stone house foundations that have been found across the highveld north and south of the Vaal (see Figure 10.7). Some of these house

Figure 10.7 The stone foundations of a typical Sotho-Tswana dwelling of the Late Iron Age period foundations bear striking resemblance to the architecture of southern Tswana houses observed by European travellers in the early 1800s.

In the dry highveld grassland north-west of the Vaal the early Batswana lineages evolved fairly large chiefdoms based on central towns of several thousand people. Their concentrations of population were probably related to limited sources of water. When they became too large or were torn by succession disputes, chiefdoms split and subdivided. Wealthy rivals led their supporters and dependants away to found new chiefdoms and begin the process again.

South-east of the Drakensberg, rainfall was greater and the environment more varied. Within any one small area people had a wide range of hill and valley grazing, woodland and land for cultivation. As a result chiefdoms could be smaller and settlements more self-contained. Here the ancestors of the modern Nguni-speaking peoples founded a wide range of small chiefdoms stretching from the Kei to the Pongolo (see Map 10.3). Nguni is the name given to a southern sub-group of the Bantu language family. There is no such thing as 'the Nguni language' or 'the Nguni people' as such. It is merely a convenient modern term used by linguists and historians to refer to the linguistically related peoples of the south-eastern lowveld. In this way they can be distinguished from the Sotho-Tsawana of the highveld. These chiefdoms were often little more than groups of several extended family homesteads under the leadership of the senior clan head. Here too when population grew and disputes over leadership emerged, chiefdoms split and rivals moved off to found new settlements. As with the Sotho-Tswana of the highveld, although they were farmers, metalworkers, craftsmen and traders, the main source of their material wealth was their large herds of sleek, fat cattle. This point was clearly noted by a Portuguese sailor who was shipwrecked off the south-east coast in 1593. He travelled safely through the region all the way from the Mbashe River to Delagoa Bay and wrote of the peoples he observed:

> These people are herdsmen and cultivators … . Their main crop is millet which they grind between two stones or in wooden mortars to make flour. From this they make cakes, which they bake under the embers of the fire. Of the same grain they make beer, mixing it with a lot of water, which after being fermented in a clay jar, cooled off and turned sour, they drink with great gusto. Their cattle are numerous, fat, tender, tasty and large, the pastures being very fertile. Their wealth consists mainly in their huge number of dehorned cows. They also subsist on cows' milk and on the butter which they make from it. They live together in small villages, in houses made of reed mats, which do not keep out the rain … . The main clothing of these people is a cloak of calf-skin, rubbed with grease to make it soft. On their feet they wear shoes of two or three layers of raw hide, fastened together in a round shape and secured to the foot with thongs. With these they can run with great speed.

> (Adapted from C. R. Boxer (ed.), *The Tragic History of the Sea, 1589–1622*, CUP, Cambridge, 1959, pp. 121–2)

During the process of expansion of Later Iron Age chiefdoms, the Khoesan-speaking hunter-gatherers and specialist pastoralists were gradually absorbed. The presence of the characteristic Khoesan 'click' sounds in the southern Nguni and southern Sotho languages is evidence of this process. But Later Iron Age farmers did not extend their settlements beyond the region of regular summer rainfall. Thus in the drier south-western part of the continent, Khoesan communities retained their distinctive languages and cultures. But even here they did not develop in isolation. They traded with Bantu-speaking farmers, selling them sheep, cattle and hunting produce in exchange for copper, iron, dagga and tobacco. Khoekhoe clans of sheep and cattle pastoralists thrived in particular in the winter-rainfall grasslands of the extreme south-western Cape. And it was this source of meat which first attracted European shipping to the region, with consequences which will be discussed in Chapter 15.

11

North and north-east Africa to the eighteenth century

The 'Arabisation' of northern Africa

From the tenth to the thirteenth centuries large numbers of Arab pastoral nomads, known as Bedouin (from the Arabic *badawin,* 'desert-dwellers'), moved gradually out of Arabia and into northern Africa. Migration from the deserts of Arabia was nothing new (see p. 80). They were highly mobile communities, living in camelskin tented dwellings which they could easily dismantle and re-erect. They were frequently on the move as they herded their camels and goats from one source of pasture and water to the next. In general they travelled in small family-sized clans and there was little overall unity among them. At times they disrupted settled agricultural communities, but they were probably blamed for more chaos and disturbance than they actually caused. Though Muslim they were generally non-literate. This may partly account for the prejudice felt towards them by literate Arab scholars who accused them of widespread rural destruction in the Maghrib. Nevertheless, they spread the Islamic faith and the Arabic language and culture.

Figure 11.1 Arab Bedouins outside their tents in Tunisia, *c.*1935

Map 11.1 Migrations of Arab Bedouin into north Africa, 950–1350

Within a few decades of 1050 some quarter of a million Arab nomads moved from Egypt westwards into the Maghrib. Those taking a northern coastal route were known as the Banu Hilal, while the Banu Sulaym went inland, south of the Atlas. The latter absorbed large numbers of Berbers, though the Berber language survived in mountainous regions of the Atlas and among the Sanhaja and the Tuareg of the Sahara. In the thirteenth and fourteenth centuries Arabised Berber nomads known as Hawwara moved eastwards from the Maghrib into Egypt and pushed south up the Nile valley to the region of the first cataract. Earlier Arab nomads had already preceded them southwards into Nubia. It was during this period that the local populations of Egypt and the Maghrib became largely Arabic-speaking.

From Fatimid to Mamluk: Egypt before the Ottoman conquest

Egypt under the Fatimids, 969–1171 CE

The rule of the Fatimid dynasty in Egypt was initially a period of considerable prosperity, at least for the ruling class. Dams and canals were repaired and production of wheat, barley, flax and cotton increased. The delta region became a centre for the development of a thriving cotton and linen textile industry, though much of this remained under the direct control of the caliph. Trade revived along the Red Sea, and Egyptian merchants grew wealthy on the transit traffic between the Mediterranean and the Indian Ocean. The caliphs minted their own gold coins and the Fatimid dinar became a basic unit of international currency in the rising Swahili cities of the east African coast (see p. 135).

The Fatimid caliphs charged heavy customs duties on all imports and exports but, as usual in Egypt, the main source of government income was taxation of the peasantry. The collection of taxes was leased to Fatimid Berbers, who soon settled down in the role of a new landed aristocracy. They became in effect 'landlords' over vast areas of the fertile Nile valley. These 'tax-farmers' paid an agreed sum to the caliph and were free to keep any further taxes they could collect for themselves. It was thus in their interests to 'squeeze' the peasantry as hard as they could, and this they did. The system

Map 11.2 Egypt under Fatimid, Ayyubid and Mamluk rule, 969–1517

was open to abuse and corruption and powerful 'tax-farmers' often failed to pay their portion to the caliph.

The Fatimids had initially conquered Egypt with a small but effective Berber army. As the Berbers settled down into a new ruling elite, the caliphs resorted to the importation of slaves to boost the ranks of the army. The principal wing of this army was the cavalry, made up of free Berbers and Turkish slave horsemen known as 'Mamluks'. The footsoldiers were mostly black Sudanese slaves imported from south of the Sahara.

As government income from the tax-farming system declined through corruption, the caliph was unable to pay for the upkeep of his army. By the mid-twelfth century, discontented soldiery regularly looted the countryside. Faction fights between Mamluks, Berbers and Sudanese disrupted trade and cultivation, and seriously weakened the authority of the Fatimids.

In the 1160s Fatimid Egypt was in danger of being overrun by Christian Crusaders from western Europe who had already established the kingdoms of Antioch and Jerusalem in neighbouring western Asia. Egypt was saved from Christian conquest largely by the actions of Salah al-Din ibn Ayyub, the leader of a small band of professional soldiers who had originally come from Kurdistan, east of Turkey. He reorganised the Egyptian army, declared a *jihad* and expelled the Christian army from the borders of Egypt. He followed this up by recapturing Jerusalem for Islam in 1187, an action which prompted the Third Crusade from western Europe. He is known in European history as Saladin, the great Muslim opponent of the Third Crusade. On the death of the last Fatimid caliph in 1171 Salah al-Din became ruler of Egypt and founder of the Ayyubid dynasty.

The Ayyubid dynasty

Salah al-Din returned the government of Egypt to stability and prosperity. He brought Egyptians back to the orthodox Sunni Muslim faith and made Cairo an important centre of Arab and Islamic learning and culture.

Perhaps his most important innovation was that, in reorganising the army, Salah al-Din combined military recruitment with a reform in the system of taxation. He revived the regular importation of young Mamluk slaves from Turkey. Armed with bow and arrow and light curved sword and mounted on horseback, these were trained into a highly disciplined force. Successful Mamluks earned their freedom and became military commanders. At the same time, 'tax-farms', known as *iqta*, were taken over by the state and re-allocated to Mamluk officers. In return the latter used the income they gained from taxing the peasantry to supply the state with a certain number of full-time soldiers. The number depended on the size of the *iqta*.

In effect the Mamluks became a new military and landed aristocracy, the more powerful of them assuming the title of *amir*. In 1250 they challenged the authority of the sultan himself. A group of Mamluk *amirs* murdered the last Abbuyid sultan and took over the sultanate themselves. In doing so they founded the first of two Mamluk dynasties which ruled Egypt for the next 250 years.

Egypt under the Mamluks, 1250–1517

Egypt under the Mamluks was a powerful military dictatorship. The army was constantly strengthened by the importation of new Mamluks from Turkey and southern Russia. In the first few decades of the dynasty the Egyptian empire was extended into the western Asian territories of Palestine and Syria. The defeat of the central Asian Mongols and the European Christian 'Fourth Crusade' further strengthened Egypt's claim to be the

Figure 11.2 Cairo: the citadel and Muhammad Ali mosque

Figure 11.3 Egyptian peasant working in the Nile valley

intellectual centre of Islam. Mamluk 'protection' was extended over the holy cities of Medina and Mecca, and Cairo became a regular stopping-off point for pilgrims to Mecca, especially from the Maghrib and the west African Sudan. Mansa Musa's pilgrimage from Mali (1324–5) has already been referred to (see p. 105). Gold and emerald mines were developed with slave labour in the mountains east of Aswan, and Red Sea trade was expanded under Mamluk control.

It should not be forgotten, however, that the wealth of any Egyptian dynasty was always underpinned by the productive capacity of the Egyptian peasantry. The Egyptian *fellahin* (Arabic for peasant) were hereditary holders of their small family plots in the fertile floodplain of the valley of the Nile. Though a family plot was usually passed down from one generation to the next, a *fellah* who failed to pay the tax demanded was often expelled from his land. The productivity of a plot was calculated in advance and a tax was imposed on all crops: fruit trees, honey and wax, as well as field crops of barley, wheat and flax. Even domestic livestock, chickens, goats and cattle, were liable to an annual tax. The *fellahin* were squeezed particularly hard under the Mamluks as there were no restraints on the *iqta*-holder's power. Indeed, *fellahin* were so heavily taxed during this period that they often had to borrow back their own grain from their 'landlord' in order to get enough food to survive! And Mamluks imposed extra restrictions on the *fellahin* to prevent their 'desertion' to the cities. They were not allowed to leave their farms without the permission of their 'landlord'.

Not only were the Egyptian *fellahin* particularly heavily taxed by the Mamluks, they also had to provide their labour freely on demand for public works. Even then they had to supply all their own food, tools and draught-animals. During the fourteenth century there was a great expansion of public works. There was a general extension of irrigation in the valley and the delta as new dams and canals were built. This enabled new land to be brought into cultivation, which in turn meant new villages of *fellahin* to distribute as further *iqta* for the Mamluks.

The Mamluk *iqta*-holders lived mostly in the cities where their displays of great wealth were a stimulus to the trade in luxuries from the African interior, the east coast and the Indian Ocean. It has been estimated that in the early 1300s there were about 10,000 Mamluks in Egypt ruling over as many as four or five million Egyptians.

During the course of the fifteenth century the system of linking taxation with military service collapsed. Mamluks treated their *iqta* as their own hereditary possession. They ceased to provide military service. With increasing corruption among city-based Mamluks, public works ceased, canals became blocked and there was a decline in agricultural productivity. To this were added natural disasters of drought, locust-infestation and plague. Famine followed, and many farms were abandoned. The sultan, unable to rely upon the military service of the Mamluks, taxed trade more heavily to pay for his army. This prompted a general decline in Egyptian trade between the Mediterranean and the Indian Ocean. And this was just at a time when the Portuguese were moving round the southern tip of Africa to challenge Muslim trading domination of the western Indian Ocean.

The reputation of the Mamluk army rested mainly on their skilful use of horsemen armed with bow and arrow and sword. This was what had halted the Mongol advance into Palestine in 1260. Resting on their past reputation, the Mamluks failed to take account of the fifteenth-century revolution in warfare with the development of firearms and cannon. By 1500 the Mamluk army was disorganised and hopelessly out of date. It was no match for the modernised army of the Ottoman Turks who drove the Mamluks out of Palestine and conquered Egypt in 1517.

Egypt under Ottoman rule

The rise of the Ottoman Turks as a world power can be dated to their conquest of Constantinople in 1453. Changing that ancient city's name to Istanbul, they made it the capital of a vast empire. By the end of the sixteenth century the Ottoman empire stretched across much of south-eastern Europe, western Asia and northern Africa.

With the Ottoman conquest of 1517, Egypt lost its independence and became a province within a western Asian empire. The ruler of Egypt was henceforth a viceroy, appointed from, and answerable to, Istanbul. The Ottomans restored and reallocated the *iqta* system of land-holding, taxation and military service. Egypt's southern boundary was pushed into Nubia as far as the third cataract in the 1550s. Trade was revived and, in an attempt to counter Portuguese advances in the Indian Ocean, the Red Sea port of Massawa was seized. This prevented Portuguese access to the trade of the Red Sea and in particular to Ethiopia. But the Ottomans failed to regain for Egypt effective direct access to the Indian Ocean network.

During the course of the seventeenth and eighteenth centuries the hereditary Mamluk nobles gradually regained effective power in Egypt. The heads of the wealthy noble families were known as *beys*. The viceroys, known as *pashas*, had initially been expatriate Turks appointed from Istanbul. But by at least 1700 they had set up dynasties of *pashas* who operated independently from Istanbul in all but name for much of the eighteenth century. With so much power in the hands of a corrupt local nobility, Egypt lacked the unity

Map 11.3 Egypt under the Ottomans, sixteenth and seventeenth centuries

and strength to fend off serious foreign invasion. And as we shall see in Chapter 19 (p. 283), that invasion was to come in 1798 in the form of a French 'Army of the Orient'.

Nubia and the Funj Sultanate

The spread of Islam in Nubia

We saw in Chapter 5 that the initial Arab conquest of the Nile valley had been halted at the first cataract by the Christian Nubian kingdom of Makurra. The subsequent gradual spread of Islam though Lower Nubia was partly brought about by centuries of peaceful trading contact with Muslim Egypt. But the main process of Islamisation came in the fourteenth century. It was headed by the persistent southward pressure of Arab nomad pastoralist clans, the principal groups being the Banu Kanz and the Juhayna. In 1317 the King's palace was converted into a mosque (see Figure 11.4). During the fifteenth century, Arab nomads penetrated further south and west towards Darfur and the direction of Lake Chad. Though they continued to spread their Muslim religion, they intermarried with local Nubians and became heavily 'Africanised' in personnel and culture. By the end of the fourteenth century these Muslim Nubian pastoralists were raiding south of the eastern Sahara to capture non-Muslim men and women to sell as slaves and concubines to Egypt and western Asia.

169

Figure 11.4 The state house of the king of Makurra (or Dongola), Sudan, which was converted to a mosque in 1317

The Funj Sultanate

At about the same time as the Ottoman conquest of Egypt a new non-Arab power finally replaced the declining Upper Nubian Christian kingdom of Alwa. This was the Funj Sultanate. The Funj were cattle pastoralists and horsemen who originated somewhere to the south of Upper Nubia. Their exact origins remain obscure, but they came from among the numerous pastoral peoples who inhabited the grasslands between the floodplain of the upper Nile and the eastern foothills of the Ethiopian highlands. During the sixteenth century they gradually extended their control over the Nubian region of the Blue Nile as far as its confluence with the White Nile, near modern Khartoum (see Map 11.3). By 1600 they had become Muslim and were living in towns with their capital at Senna. The Funj remained essentially a ruling elite, owning huge herds of cattle and taxing the cultivators settled along the river banks. On the whole they left the local chieftains in power. But they used their small, effective army of mounted soldiers to collect tribute from a wide range of settled cultivators and nomad pastoralists. In the early 1600s their irregular rule of raid and tribute collection extended as far as the third cataract.

Oromo migrations and the kingdom of Ethiopia

The Oromo migrations

In the early sixteenth century the Christian kingdom of Ethiopia and the Muslim kingdom of Adal were struggling for control of the Ethiopian highlands (see pp. 120–2). As military defences in the south were destroyed and people fled the battle zones, a power vacuum was created in the southern highlands of the region. And into that temporary vacuum moved the Oromo from the south.

The Oromo (formerly known as Galla) were Cushitic-speaking cattle pastoralists who originated in the dry grassland zone to the north-east of Lake Turkana. Within little more than a single generation (1530–65) the Oromo had occupied the southern third of Ethiopia and were pushing towards the valley of the Awash and the plateau of Harar. But despite the

170

speed and relentless pressure of their occupation, the Oromo did not come as a single, organised mass-migration. To understand the nature of the movement one needs to understand something of the structure of their society.

The Oromo had no overall central authority. Like many pastoral peoples they lived in a number of loosely organised, extended-family clans. Within each clan Oromo society was organised into a series of five age-sets. As people grew older they steadily progressed from one age-set to the next. The fifth and oldest set was known as the *tuba* and its members were in principle the leaders of the clan. There was little social division between rich and poor and the leader of each adult age-set was elected by its members. The most important age-set was the third, the *folle,* in which the young men acted as military escort and protector of the clan and its cattle. It was they who spearheaded the search for new grazing land.

During the early decades of the sixteenth century the cattle herds of the Oromo seem to have undergone a rapid expansion. This may have been due to the Oromo's development of new cattle-keeping skills or simply that the southern foothills of Ethiopia were particularly well situated for intensive cattle grazing. Expansion up the Omo valley and into the southern foothills began as an extension of seasonal grazing migrations between winter and summer pastures. Each year the *folle* sought out new pastures further up the moister valleys. They moved on foot and were lightly armed with spears. Once the *folle* had settled the cattle in a new grazing zone, the rest of the clan moved their camp up to join them. Partly as a result of recent warfare, the region was initially lightly populated, and the Oromo were able to move into the open grazing zones between the old, established villages of the settled cultivators. Those cultivators who offered resistance were raided and driven out.

The clans that spearheaded the seasonal migration moved ever-further northward as they in turn felt the pressure of other Oromo clans who were moving up behind them. Once the movement had been allowed to develop, it was impossible to stop. The numbers were too large. And because there were so many separate clans, each with its vast herds of cattle and operating independently, it was impossible to 'defeat' them even if Ethiopians and Adalis had had the strength to try.

As they had already shown, in searching out new grazing territory, the Oromo were opportunists rather than 'never-changing' pastoralists. Those that came into contact with Muslim Adal converted to Islam, while others converted to the Christianity of Ethiopia. In the central highland zones of the Amhara and Sidama, many abandoned nomadic pastoralism in favour of settled agriculture. By the early 1600s the Oromo were the dominant population of the southern half of Ethiopia and were prominent among the Muslims of the Harar plateau.

The kingdom of Ethiopia

The Christian kings of Ethiopia in the late sixteenth century paid little attention to the Oromo incursions from the south. Sarsa Dengel (r.1562–97) concentrated his hold on the northern half of the kingdom and opened up trading contacts with the Ottoman Turks at Massawa. But apart from personal profit to the rulers, there was little to be gained for Ethiopia from this trade. The principal Ethiopian export was captives taken from southwest of Lake Tana and sold into slavery in Egypt and western Asia. It has been estimated that in the reign of Sarsa Dengel as many as 10,000 captives a year

Map 11.4 Ethiopia in the seventeenth century

were sold to Turkish traders on the Red Sea coast. The removal of so many people from the south-west merely eased the further expansion of the Oromo from the south.

Early in the seventeenth century Susenyos (r.1607–32) gave official recognition to the Oromo in the central and southern regions of the kingdom. He

Figure 11.5 The Ethiopian royal palace at Gondar. Construction of the palace was begun during the reign of Susenyos (1607–32), with architectural advice from a Spanish Jesuit priest, Pedro Paez

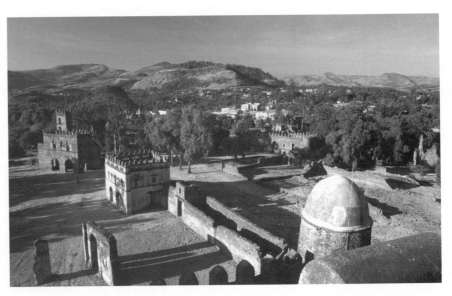

brought them in as mercenaries to serve in his army in return for permission to tax the local peasantry. This merely legitimised what the Oromo were already doing. The main concentration of seventeenth-century Ethiopian Christian power remained in the north. Under Fasiladas (r.1632–67) Tigray was brought more closely into the kingdom and a permanent Ethiopian capital was established at Gondar (see Figure 11.5). During the eighteenth century, however, the kings of Ethiopia lost all effective power over the provinces and the Christian nobility acted virtually independently.

States of the Maghrib, sixteenth to eighteenth century

The eastern and central Maghrib

A major feature of the sixteenth-century history of the Maghrib was the contest for control of the western Mediterranean between the Christian kingdom of Spain and the Muslim Ottoman empire. While the Ottoman empire was reuniting Islam in the eastern Mediterranean, the fifteenth century had been a time of Christian European revival in the west. The Spanish had ended nearly eight centuries of Muslim rule in southern Spain with the defeat of Granada in 1492. In the meantime, in the late fifteenth and early sixteenth centuries Portuguese and Spanish Christians seized a number of ports along the north African coast. Among the more important of these were Tangier, Algiers, Tripoli and Tunis.

Turkish corsairs (privateers or pirates who lived by the loot they gained from attacking other ships) responded by recapturing north African ports and using them as bases for raiding Christian shipping in the western Mediterranean. In the struggle that followed, Tripoli, Tunis and Algiers changed hands several times. The Turks suffered two major defeats, at the siege of Malta (1565) and the battle of Lepanto off the coast of Greece (1571). With these defeats the Ottoman Turks lost the chance to dominate Mediterranean shipping lanes. On the other hand they expelled the Spanish and Portuguese from their main north African bases and thus ensured that the Maghrib remained in Muslim hands.

Tripoli, Tunis and Algiers all became major Turkish bases from which their corsairs continued to raid Christian trading ships during the seventeenth and eighteenth centuries. They and the hinterland behind them became official provinces of the Ottoman empire. In practice there was no real control from Istanbul over rule within the territories. Booty captured from corsair raids provided most of the wealth of the coastal towns, particularly Tripoli and Algiers, which, unlike Tunis, had very little land for cultivation. Further inland the army, headed by Turkish officers, lived in the towns and periodically raided the pastoralists and cultivators of the countryside for tribute and taxation.

Tripoli also benefited from the trans-Saharan trade via the Fezzan. Direct relations were established between the *pashas* of Tripoli and the sultans of Borno. The latter imported horses, firearms and armour which were used for catching non-Muslim men and women for sale as slaves and concubines to the wealthy of the Ottoman empire. Though the Ottoman presence at Tripoli stimulated the development of this shortest route across the desert, the actual traffic of the trans-Saharan trade remained in the hands of independent Tuareg.

Map 11.5 The Maghrib in the sixteenth and seventeenth centuries

The rise of Morocco In the western Maghrib the sixteenth century saw the rise of Morocco as an independent state. During the first half of the century an Arab nomad clan called the Sa'dis (who claimed descent from Muhammad's daughter Fatima) gradually conquered and united the whole of Morocco. In doing so they not only prevented the Ottomans from extending their empire into the western Maghrib, they also drove the Christian Portuguese from their Atlantic coastal ports. When the Portuguese invaded Morocco in 1578 they suffered a major defeat at the battle of al-Ksar Kebir. In the battle the Portuguese king and the sultan of Morocco were both killed. This made way for the accession of Ahmad al-Mansur (r.1578–1603) whose vigorous rule brought Morocco to the height of its power.

The major event of Ahmad al-Mansur's reign was the conquest of Songhay in 1591. His aim in doing so was to outflank the Ottoman Turks and to gain exclusive control of Songhay's gold trade. By this time much of the trade in gold from south of the Sahara was being diverted to European traders who had become a significant presence along the West African coast. Through the 1580s al-Mansur had developed a thriving trade with Spain's great rival, Elizabethan England. Sugar was grown in the Sous valley inland from Agadir by slave labour imported from Songhay. This sugar was exported to England in exchange for English firearms. Al-Mansur then strengthened his army, which contained many slaves from Songhay, by recruiting Arab horsemen from the western plains. These were trained by European and Turkish mercenary officers into an effective cavalry force and al-Mansur was ready to launch his invasion of Songhay. (The Songhay end of this will be considered further in Chapter 13, pp. 187–9).

The conquest of Songhay brought al-Mansur initial rewards, mostly in the form of booty from the sacking of Gao and Timbuktu. But in the long run the Songhay part of the Moroccan empire was a drain on Morocco's resources. The regular trade in gold was disrupted and much of it diverted eastwards to Tunis, Tripoli and Cairo or southwards to Europeans on the

Figure 11.6 Skyline of a city of the Maghrib looking towards the Middle Atlas mountain range, Marrakesh (Marrakech), Morocco

coast of west Africa (see pp. 177 and 181–2). At the same time the occupation of Songhay cost Morocco heavily in military personnel and equipment. Morocco continued to interfere in the Niger Bend region during the seventeenth century, but real power there fell increasingly to local military governors.

Following al-Mansur's death in 1603 the Moroccan state was weakened by dynastic disputes between his sons, and for a while the country was split into the two rival sultanates of Fes and Marrakesh. Unity was re-established by Mawlay al-Rashid who founded the Alawid dynasty in 1669. His brother and successor Mawlay Isma'il (r.1672–1727) strengthened his control over the country by importing more Sudanese captives from south of the Sahara. Despite dynastic disputes after his death, Moroccan unity survived. For much of the eighteenth century, however, direct government control and taxation were confined to the regions near Fes and Marrakesh and the string of coastal towns from Tangier to Agadir. Beyond and in the Atlas mountains, independent nomad clans paid tribute on demand when threatened by action from the sultan's army.

The Atlantic slave trade, sixteenth to eighteenth century

Slavery in Africa before the Atlantic trade

Slavery has a long history in Africa, as well as in Europe and Asia. In ancient pharoanic times captives from Nubia were transported down the Nile to Egypt. Some were also transported across the Sahara to north Africa in Roman times, while others were sent out of north-east Africa to labour in the states of the Persian Gulf and India. All of these numbers were small, however, in comparison to the Atlantic trade that came later.

The trans-Saharan slave trade

Slave labour was used in the mid-Saharan salt mines from ancient times, but the scale of this increased dramatically with the expansion of trans-Saharan trade that coincided with the Muslim penetration of north Africa and the growth in the empire of Ghana. Islamic law did not allow the enslavement of fellow-Muslims, so north African merchants sought their slaves from non-Muslim societies south of the Sahara. Consequently, the transportation of captives for sale into slavery in north Africa became a regular, if initially small, part of expanding trans-Saharan trade networks from the eighth century. Nevertheless, it has been estimated that over the next 11 centuries as many as five million Africans were transported across the Sahara to be sold into slavery. And over a similar period, up to two and a half million people were transported from east and north-east Africa into slavery in western Asia.

Slavery in the Muslim world was not plantation slavery, such as was to become common in the Americas. Male slaves were often incorporated into armies and through this, and their conversion to Islam, they became an integral part of Muslim north Africa: some former slaves rose to high office. Female slaves, for whom there was a high demand, became household servants or concubines and were to be found right across the Muslim world of north Africa and western Asia.

Some form of slavery or subservient labour had long been a part of African society south of the Sahara. Usually originating as war-captives, in larger centralised states they were often thoroughly incorporated into the economy and society, almost as a way of strengthening and expanding the state. In small, decentralised communities, they tended to be treated more as outsiders, and on occasion were ransomed back to their origins. Slaves were sometimes sold in the markets of both large and small communities, but this was not a regular feature and their capture was not usually with intent to sell. Increasingly, however, from the eleventh century, as the rulers of states on the southern fringes of the Sahara converted to Islam, their armies raided their non-Muslim neighbours to obtain captives for the trans-Saharan trade. This trade in human beings continued until at least the end of the nineteenth century, with some reports of it occurring well into the twentieth century. In all it lasted some fifteen hundred years, but it was never on the massive scale that Europeans were to initiate for the trans-Atlantic trade.

The origins of European maritime trade with west Africa

The aims of Portuguese initiatives

When the Portuguese first sailed out on their voyages of exploration along the west African coast, the desire to reach India was a distant objective. Of more immediate concern was their attempt to bypass Muslim north Africa and gain direct access to the gold-producing regions of west Africa. This would provide the poorly-endowed state of Portugal with a major source of national wealth, for sub-Saharan west Africa was known to be the main source of gold for the coinage of western Europe (see Figure 7.3 on p. 106, a fourteenth-century European map of Africa, showing Mali as a major source of gold). Once access to this had been achieved, the wealth it provided could finance further exploration round the southern tip of Africa and on to India. Ultimately, by reaching India via a southern route the Portuguese would be bypassing the Muslim-controlled trading routes of western Asia. In doing so they hoped to reap rich rewards from the Indian trade in spices, perfumes, silks and other luxuries.

Early Portuguese trade on the west African coast

Portuguese sailing ships first reached the west African coast south of the Akan goldfields in the 1470s. They built a fort there, known as Elmina ('the mine'), to protect their trading post from rival European shipping (see Figure 12.1). At first the Portuguese traded copper, brass and European cloth in exchange for gold. They thus offered the forest peoples goods which they had previously got from Songhay and the trans-Saharan trade. The Portuguese also sold them a certain number of slaves brought from the forest kingdom of Benin near the Niger delta. It appears that for some time slave labour had been used to run the gold mines of the Akan forest region (see p. 201). In the early 1500s the Portuguese added cowrie shells and luxury cloths from the Indian Ocean trade to the range of goods they offered in exchange for west African gold. Cowrie shells quickly became a regular trading currency in west Africa. It was not long before half the produce of the Akan goldfields was being diverted southwards, away from Songhay and the trans-Saharan trade, and towards the European trading forts along the coast.

Origins of European-controlled plantation slavery

Meanwhile in the 1480s, the Portuguese had discovered the uninhabited equatorial islands of Príncipe and São Tomé. In the years that followed, Portuguese settlers developed thriving sugar plantations in the rich volcanic soils of these islands. They manned their plantations with slave labour drawn from the African mainland.

The plantation system for growing sugar cane had originally been developed in various Mediterranean islands and in southern Spain and Portugal

Map 12.1 West Africa: Portuguese exploration and trade in the fifteenth century

during the fourteenth and early fifteenth centuries. The slave labour for these plantations was drawn not only from north Africa but also from among the Slavs of southern Russia. Indeed the European word 'slave' comes from the use of Slavs for this kind of unpaid labour. As the Portuguese captured Atlantic islands from Madeira southwards to São Tomé, they extended to the tropics their plantation system for growing sugar.

In the early sixteenth century São Tomé became the largest single producer of sugar for the European market. Ultimately, the São Tomé plantation system, owned and run by European overseers and manned by African slave labour, was to become the model for plantation slavery in the Americas and the Caribbean.

Figure 12.1 Elmina Castle, Ghana, was built by the Portuguese in 1482 and used by them and later by Dutch and English traders as a base for dealing in slaves, gold and imported European products. Castles such as these were originally built to prevent rival Europeans from trading in that particular region, and to store slaves in the dungeons to await shipment across the Atlantic

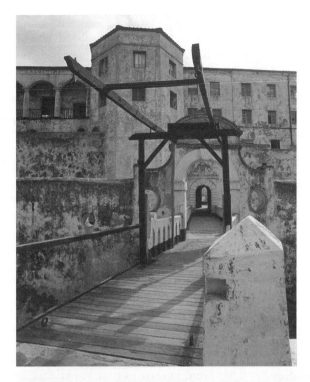

Figure 12.2 Inside the ramparts of Elmina Castle looking towards the market chamber where slaves were sold. Part of the coat of arms and monogram of the Dutch royal house can be seen on the wrought iron balustrade

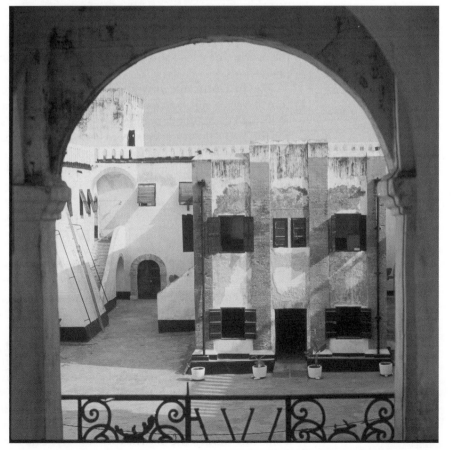

From early on in the Portuguese presence along the coast of tropical west Africa, captives were bought from local chiefdoms for sale into slavery. Initially, in the fifteenth and early sixteenth centuries, they came largely from the Senegal and Gambia region and were transported to the farms and plantations of southern Spain and Portugal. Those taken from the Niger delta and the Congo River region went mostly to the island of São Tomé.

Meanwhile, Columbus's pioneering trans-Atlantic voyage of 1492 had revealed a tropical 'New World' that Europeans, led by the Spaniards, were quick to colonise and exploit.

These European colonisers soon felt the need for a large imported labour force to work the gold and silver mines of the mainland and their tobacco plantations on the Caribbean islands. The local indigenous Amerindian population quickly succumbed to the harsh treatment of the colonisers and unfamiliar European diseases. By the end of the first century of European contact, 90 per cent or more of the Amerindian population of the Caribbean islands had been wiped out – victims of European violence or disease. Criminals and outcasts from Europe were transported to the Americas in the early sixteenth century, but their numbers were limited. Those that were sent did not long survive attacks of tropical disease. Faced with these problems the European colonisers of central and south America turned to Africa for their slave labour force.

Africans had developed a certain level of immunity to some tropical diseases. They were known to have experience and skills in metal-working, mining and tropical agriculture. Portuguese experience had already shown that there was always somewhere along the west African coast where African rulers were prepared to sell their war captives and criminals. And the example of São Tomé had shown the possibilities of using African slave labour on plantations.

The first African captives to be taken directly across the Atlantic and sold into slavery were transported in 1532. Thereafter a steady transatlantic trade in human cargo developed though annual numbers remained relatively small for the first 100 years. But from the 1630s, as first the Dutch and then the French and English became involved, there was a rapid expansion of sugar plantations in Brazil and the Caribbean. Demand for slave labour increased and the scale of the trade in captives from west Africa reached enormous proportions. There developed over the next 200 years the largest-scale forced transportation of captive people ever devised in human history.

The nature of the slave trade

Over recent years there has been considerable dispute among historians about the numbers involved in the transatlantic trade. Recorded statistics show that at least ten million Africans were landed alive and sold into slavery in the Americas and the Caribbean in the 300 years that followed 1532. Allowing for a further two million that died on the trans-Atlantic voyage, a total of at least 12 million people were taken captive out of Africa. Numbers which stood at only a few thousand a year in the sixteenth century rose to an average of 20,000 a year in the seventeenth and further rocketed to between 50,000 and 100,000 a year for much of the eighteenth century. Numbers tailed off during the nineteenth century, but the trade did not altogether cease until the 1870s and 1880s. Some historians argue that a huge amount of traffic went unrecorded and that the real scale of the trade was double the amount indicated here.

The African dimension

Although numbers taken out of Africa were clearly huge, they varied very widely from one region to another. Senegal in the sixteenth century was an important early source of slaves. The Angolan coastline was unusual in that it remained a major slave-exporting region for most of the period, from the sixteenth to the nineteenth centuries. The effects of this on the peoples of Angola will be discussed further in Chapter 14 (pp. 206–7). With the rise of Caribbean sugar plantations from the mid-seventeenth century, Dutch, French, English, Danes and other Europeans became more actively involved in the carrying trade. Then the so-called 'Slave Coast' (the western coast of modern Nigeria) became a major source of slaves. With the rapid expansion of slave exports in the eighteenth century, virtually every part of the Atlantic coastline from Senegal to southern Angola became involved in the human traffic. The greatest concentration of European trading forts was along the so-called 'Gold Coast', the coastline of the modern state of Ghana. Slaves continued to be taken from the 'Slave Coast' and Angola until well into the nineteenth century when many other regions had ceased their trade in people.

On the whole European slave traders were not active in the business of capturing their victims. European traders did not have the military power to go on their own extensive raiding expeditions. In any case, why go on expensive raiding expeditions when captives could be bought more cheaply and with less risk at the coast? When they did enter the interior, as in Angola, European armies either suffered military defeat or were weakened by disease. Nevertheless, in the Angolan case they stirred up warfare within the kingdoms of Kongo and Ndongo which provided ample numbers of captives for sale at the coast. European activity in the trade in Africans was usually restricted to their trading forts along the coast. And they sought permission to build these from local African rulers to whom they were obliged to pay tribute. In general it was African rulers who provided the captives, and specialist African and Afro-European slave dealers who conveyed them to the coast for sale.

The main source of people for sale into slavery was those captured in warfare. As we saw above (p. 176), slavery in Africa, and even the sale of slaves, had existed before the arrival of Europeans on the west African coast. A major difference with the European-initiated trade, however, was that the war-captives were being totally removed from their African societies, with a short life-expectancy in harsh conditions and with no hope of return.

It used to be assumed that most captives offered for sale at the coast were the product of wars deliberately waged for this purpose. This undoubtedly did happen on occasion, especially in the eighteenth century when prices offered by Europeans were rising. But research has revealed that there was considerably more local African initiative involved than was previously assumed to be the case.

A number of careful regional studies have revealed that the supply of captives at the coast was usually the result of specific local wars being waged in the interior. And the prime motive of these wars was the formation and expansion of states rather than simply a free-for-all in which the losers ended

For more information see www.palgrave.com/shillington

181

in slavery. Thus the forest state of Benin sold captives to the Portuguese in the late fifteenth century while they were undergoing a period of military expansion. Significantly, in the sixteenth century they refused to trade in people. The export of captives from Benin was only renewed in the eighteenth century as the formerly powerful kingdom went into decline. During the first half of the sixteenth century the Mane, a branch of the Mande-speaking peoples, colonised the highlands of Sierra Leone, making local people captive and selling them at the coast. In the early eighteenth century, the coastline of modern Guinea reached a peak of slave exports when the Muslim Fulbe of Futa Jalon created a new state and waged holy war against their neighbours. The result was a large number of captives for sale into slavery. Similarly, wars waged by the expanding states of Oyo (pp. 197–8), Dahomey (pp. 199–200) and Asante (pp. 201–3) in the seventeenth and eighteenth centuries produced specific local peaks in the supply of captives for sale to European slavers at the coast.

Basically, powerful African rulers provided captives when it suited them, and some of them became very rich in the process. But they rarely sold people from their own society, except unwanted criminals and outcasts. On the other hand, small societies, the weak states and 'stateless' village communities, the neighbours of the large expanding states, undoubtedly suffered greatly. Some disappeared altogether, their lands taken over by other, more powerful neighbours.

Wars in the west African interior may not have generally been waged deliberately just to produce captives for sale. But the presence of Europeans on the coast offering what appeared to be high prices for captives undoubtedly stimulated warfare. This was especially so in the eighteenth century when Europeans offered guns as their major trading item.

Impact of the slave trade

As a result of the slave trade, there was not only an increased level of general warfare in the west African interior. In purely economic terms, there was also a serious loss to the productive potential of the region. Previously war had produced tribute from the vanquished, and captives to work for the victors. But now the increased level of warfare produced a 'surplus' of captives. These were no longer kept, even as forced labour, within the African society that had captured them. They were no longer ransomed back to the society that had lost them. Instead, they were sold right out of Africa, and sold for goods which were worth a fraction of what those people might have produced within their own lifetime. In addition, those sold were the young, most productive sector of the population, mostly aged between 14 and 35. It varied from one region to another, but all areas of western sub-Saharan Africa were seriously affected at some time or other during the seventeenth and eighteenth centuries.

In an influential book, *How Europe Underdeveloped Africa*, first published in 1972, the Guyanese historian Walter Rodney argued that Africa's chronic poverty and underdevelopment at the time of political independence in the mid-twentieth century was a direct result of European action. He argued that the European slave trade out of Africa so weakened the continent that it left it open to Europe's mega-exploitation through colonisation in the nineteenth century and neo-colonialism in the twentieth (see later chapters in this book).

Figure 12.3 Diagram showing cross-sections of a trans-Atlantic slave ship. The drawing illustrates how space on board could be optimised to accommodate as many captives as possible, *c*.1800

The transatlantic trade

Whatever its effect in terms of depopulating or distorting the development of the continent, the greatest evil of the transatlantic trade in people was the extent of human suffering involved, and the callous disregard for human life and dignity displayed by those who dealt in slaves. When a person was captured in the interior and dispatched to the coast for sale, it marked the beginning of a short remaining life of appalling degradation and suffering. Captives were no longer treated as fellow human beings but rather as property, like domestic livestock, to be herded together, examined and bartered over.

Captives were chained together and marched to the coast where they were locked up in wooden cages to await the arrival of the next European trading ship. They were then stripped naked, men and women together, and examined minutely to see if they were fit, strong and healthy. Once a deal had been struck between African middleman and European slave merchant the most terrible part of their voyage began. On board ship they were chained together in rows and forced to lie on specially constructed 'decks' which were arranged like shelves barely half a metre one above the other (see Figure 12.3). This made it impossible for a person to sit up straight or to move freely. They lay like this for weeks on end, suffering in the stench of their own excreta and urine and given barely enough food and water to keep them alive. Those that died were simply thrown overboard. On average between 15 and 30 per cent could be expected to die from disease, maltreatment or exhaustion during the three to six weeks of the transatlantic crossing. Ships' captains allowed for this loss by packing in more people. In this way enough could be expected to survive the crossing for sale in America to make a handsome profit for the merchant who financed the voyage. On occasion disease would spread so rapidly in the terrible conditions below decks that it wiped out a whole shipload of captives. But this kind of misfortune was rare and on the whole the trade in human cargo was a highly profitable concern for the shipping merchants. If it had not been, the trade would not have continued on such an ever-increasing scale.

Figure 12.4 Armed guards watching a slave being whipped outside a slave enclosure, *c.*1850. The captives in the cage are awaiting transportation

In this manner tens of thousands of Africa's fittest young men and women were removed from the continent every year (see Figure 12.3), all in the name of profit for European merchants and plantation owners.

Plantations in the Americas and their demand for slave labour

The main plantations grew sugar and coffee in Brazil, sugar in the Caribbean islands and tobacco and cotton in the southern part of north America. The largest number of slaves were taken to the Caribbean islands. For most of the seventeenth and eighteenth centuries the number and size of plantations was constantly expanding. This meant an ever-greater demand for new slaves.

Figure 12.5 Slaves working on a West Indian sugar plantation, *c.*1870

Even on the long-established estates there was a persistent demand for replacements. Life on the plantations of the New World was hard and short. Some never survived the trauma and depression of leaving Africa and the transatlantic voyage. A third died within the first three years and few survived beyond ten years. The main causes of death were underfeeding and overwork.

The economics of the plantation system was such that until the end of the eighteenth century it was cheaper to import fresh slaves from Africa than it was to allow them to rear their own children. A woman in childbirth could no longer labour effectively on the plantation, and a child had to be fed for a number of years before it could be forced to work on the land. Thus in the British colony of Jamaica, for example, three-quarters of a million slave workers were imported from Africa over a period of some two hundred years; and yet, at the time of emancipation in 1834 the population of Jamaica was only a third of a million.

The productive wealth of the New World rested very heavily on the shoulders of African labour. And those who profited most from this wealth were the merchants of Europe who financed the whole system.

Profit from the slave trade: the European dimension

The 'triangular trade'

To European merchants involved in the slave trade the export of Africans across the Atlantic was only one part of a wider trading system. A single ship setting out from Europe completed three main stages in its voyage, each with its own separate cargo, before finally returning to its home port in Europe. At each stage of this three-sided or 'triangular' trade there was profit for the European merchant who financed the voyage. The first stage carried manufactured goods from Europe to Africa.

Map 12.2   The Atlantic slave trade, sixteenth to eighteenth centuries

185

Significantly; the original Portuguese imports into Africa had included raw materials such as copper and other metals in exchange for gold. By the seventeenth and eighteenth centuries this early pattern of trade had changed. Now the principal European imports into Africa were cheap manufactured goods – mainly cotton cloth and metal hardware, especially guns – in exchange for slaves. Indeed, in the late eighteenth century the special manufacture of cheap, substandard guns for the African market became an important source of profit for the new British industrial city of Birmingham. As dependence upon European manufactured imports increased, further development of African craft industries declined. At the same time, as we have seen, the import of European guns made African warfare more effective and increased the supply of slaves. This ensured that the price of slaves exported from Africa remained fairly static for most of the seventeenth and early eighteenth centuries. It was not until the 1780s that increasing European competition along the west African coast finally drove up the price of slaves. It was only then that European merchants began to question the trade's continued profitability (see below, pp. 237–8).

Across the Atlantic, slaves were sold for two or three times what they had cost on the African coast. Sometimes they were sold for cash which was then used to buy plantation crops. At times, especially on the sugar-producing islands, slaves were directly bartered in exchange for sugar, which was then sold in Europe.

Though risks were involved, as ships could be lost at sea, profits to the European merchants were generally huge. Profits from the 'triangular trade' largely accounted for the rising wealth of a number of major European port cities, such as Bristol and Liverpool in Britain, Bordeaux and Nantes in France, and Amsterdam in Holland. Merchants moved into banking and ultimately helped finance the capitalist factory system of the European industrial revolution. And as European merchants were well aware at the time, the key to their source of Atlantic trading profits was the systematic exploitation of African slave labour.

Slavery and the origins of racism

It has been argued that the roots of European racism are to be found in the European exploitation of Africans through the trans-Atlantic trade and the plantation slavery of the New World. The deep roots of racism are probably more complex than this, though European enslavement of Africans undoubtedly played its part. For some three hundred years Africans were viewed by Europeans almost exclusively as slaves, as though this was their natural state. Europeans argued that in taking Africans out of their native continent, they were 'rescuing' them from a 'primitive' and 'barbaric' existence. It was a short step from this to arguing that Africans were naturally inferior. And when Europeans sought to colonise the African continent in the late nineteenth century, they used arguments such as these to justify their actions in the name of spreading Christianity and 'civilisation'.

chapter 13

West African states and societies, to the eighteenth century

The fall of the Songhay empire

Songhay on the eve of the Moroccan invasion

The empire of Songhay had reached the height of its power in the early sixteenth century under the rule of Askiya Muhammad Ture (see pp. 108–9). During his reign Islam became more widely entrenched, trans-Saharan trade flourished and the Saharan salt mines of Taghaza were brought within the boundaries of the empire. During the course of the sixteenth century, however, this position of strength gradually declined. The power of the Askiya was weakened by a succession of short reigns and dynastic disputes which erupted in civil war in the 1580s. At the same time the general population and agricultural basis of the economy were weakened by drought and disease. There was a loosening of Songhay's control over long-distance trading networks. In the east the growth of Hausa states, Borno and the Tuareg sultanate of Aïr, was drawing trans-Saharan trade away from Songhay and the western routes. And from the south the supply of gold declined as the chiefdoms of the Akan forest diverted some of their trade to the newly arrived European traders on the coast.

The weaknesses of Songhay, however, seem more real in retrospect. The historian has the benefit of hindsight. At the time, despite the natural disasters of the 1580s, the empire appeared secure enough. Though rival states might draw away some of Songhay's trade, this was a gradual process which gave no immediate cause for alarm. With no great wars of conquest to finance, the rulers of Songhay had not unduly oppressed the peasantry to the point where they might revolt. And there had been no danger of external threat for the best part of a century. The Askiyas had seen no reason to 'modernise' their army with the importation of primitive and unreliable, European-manufactured firearms. Immediate neighbours to south, east and west were minor states. In the north the Sahara desert continued to provide an apparently impenetrable barrier to the armies of the Ottomans and Moroccans of the Maghrib: until, that is, the opening months of 1591.

The Moroccan invasion and the fall of Songhay

The main reason for the Moroccan invasion of Songhay was to seize control of and revive the trans-Saharan trade in gold. To this end the Moroccan sultan, Ahmad al-Mansur, sent across the desert the cream of his army – a small but highly disciplined band of professional soldiers, equipped with the most up-to-date muzzle-loading guns. The Moroccan army consisted of 4000 soldiers, 600 non-combatants and 10,000 camels to carry their equipment. It took them two months to cross the desert and up to a quarter of

Map 13.1 Morocco and the fall of Songhay

them perished in the attempt. Their arrival on the banks of the Niger took the people and rulers of Songhay by surprise. And at the battle of Tondibi, near Gao, on 12 March 1591 the massed charges of the huge Songhay army were thrown into confusion by the Moroccans' disciplined use of firearms.

After their deceptively easy victory at Tondibi, the Moroccans went on to capture Timbuktu and Jenne, but they failed in their conquest of the region as a whole. The bulk of the Songhay army had fled the Moroccan firearms at Tondibi and they now regrouped in the Songhay heartland of Dendi. They had quickly learned the futility of an open charge against guns. In the years that followed, Askiya Nuhu conducted a protracted and spirited guerrilla resistance which wore down the resources and resolve of the alien intruders. At the same time, Moroccan presence in the countryside beyond Gao, Timbuktu and Jenne was constantly threatened by raids from Fulani and Tuareg nomads.

Apart from the early years of looting and enforced payment of taxation, the invasion brought little long-term financial reward for the sultan of Morocco. In fact persistent Songhay resistance ensured that the cost of keeping an active army south of the Sahara became a serious drain on Moroccan resources. Moroccan presence on the Niger depended on a constant supply of guns and other expensive equipment, much of which had to be bought from Europe in exchange for west African gold. And the Moroccan government was not getting enough gold out of Songhay to pay for this expense.

After Sultan Ahmad's death in 1603, Moroccan enthusiasm for their empire declined, although some Moroccan presence remained on the Niger in the seventeenth century. The expatriate Moroccans, now known as *Arma,* married into the local population and settled down as military governors of the Niger Bend region. By the mid-seventeenth century they were acting independently and ceased sending tribute to the sultan of Morocco. The final pretence of acknowledging Moroccan authority ended in 1660 when the sultan's name was dropped from Friday prayers in the mosques of Timbuktu, to be replaced by the name of the local *Arma* governor.

In the late seventeenth and early eighteenth centuries Tuareg nomads pressed ever-further southwards. *Arma* rule finally collapsed in 1737 when the Tuareg seized Timbuktu itself and established their own control over the valuable grasslands of the middle Niger Bend.

The former empire of Songhay split up into a number of independent kingdoms. One of the more important of these was the Bamana kingdom of Segu, which developed in the region of the upper Niger delta. It came under strong Sudanic Muslim influence. The following observations on Segu were written by the Scottish traveller Mungo Park, who reached Segu from the Gambia in 1796:

> Sego, the capital of Bambarra [Bamana], at which I had now arrived, consists, properly speaking, of four distinct towns; two on the northern bank of the Niger, called Sego Korro and Sego Boo; and two on the southern bank, called Sego Soo Korro and Sego See Korro. They are all surrounded with high mud walls; the houses are built of clay, of a square form, with flat roofs; some of them have two storeys, and many of them are whitewashed. Besides these buildings, Moorish mosques are seen in every quarter; and the streets, though narrow, are broad enough for every useful purpose, in a country where wheel-carriages are entirely unknown. From the best inquiries I could make, I have reason to believe that Sego contains altogether about thirty thousand inhabitants.
>
> The king of Bambarra constantly resides at Sego See Korro; he employs a great many slaves in conveying people over the river, and the money they receive (though the fare is only ten cowrie shells for each individual) furnishes a considerable revenue to the king in the course of a year … . The view of this extensive city; the numerous canoes upon the river; the crowded population, and the cultivated state of the surrounding country, formed altogether a prospect of civilisation and magnificence, which I little expected to find in the bosom of Africa.
>
> (Adapted from Mungo Park, *Travels in the Interior of Africa*, originally published 1799, this edition Eland Books, London, 1983, pp. 149–50)

The sultanate of Borno-Kanem

The growth of Kanem

By the eleventh century the state of Kanem was becoming a powerful force to the north-east of Lake Chad (see pp. 94–5 for the origins of Kanem). It had been founded by Kanuri-speaking nomad clans who built up their wealth by raiding neighbours and engaging in the trans-Saharan trade. Much of their trading wealth came from the exchange of southern captives for horses from north Africa. The use of horses enabled the Kanem nomads to raid their neighbours more effectively.

In the second half of the eleventh century the Kanuri-speaking Saifawa clan established a new Islamic dynasty in Kanem. Islam had been an important influence in the state from as early as the ninth century. By the thirteenth century the Kanuri of Kanem were marrying into the local farming population. Taxation of the farmers near the capital, Njimi, became more regularised instead of the former irregular pattern of nomad raids and extortion.

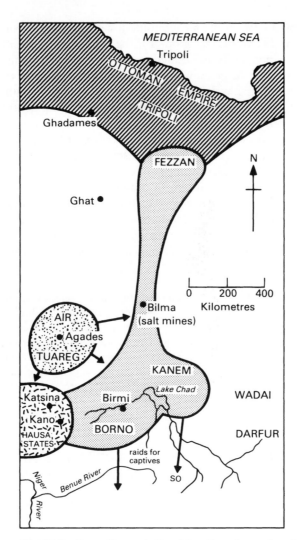

Map 13.2 Borno-Kanem in the sixteenth and seventeenth centuries

Kanem reached the height of its power during the reign of *Mai* Dunama Dibalami who ruled from 1210 to 1248. He commanded a cavalry force of 40,000 horsemen which he used to extend Kanem control over trans-Saharan trade as far as the Fezzan. Raids against the So, south-west of Lake Chad, were justified in the name of a *jihad* or holy war against the unbeliever. Captives taken in these raids were used to exchange for further horses from north Africa. Greater contacts across the desert prompted the growth of Islam among the Kanuri-speaking population, and pilgrimages to Mecca became a regular occurrence. A hostel was established in Cairo for pilgrims and students from Kanem.

The rise of Borno

By the end of the thirteenth century a tributary state had been established in Borno, south-west of Lake Chad. During the fourteenth century Kanem went into decline and Borno began acting independently, trading directly across the desert and refusing to pay tribute. Kanem itself was becoming overstretched. It lacked the natural resources for such a large state and was too dependent on the personal authority of the *Mai*. Pastures were drying out and becoming overgrazed. At the same time the Saifawa dynasty was struggling with a rival nomad clan, the Bulala, for the leadership of Kanem. In about 1400 the Saifawa dynasty saved their state from complete disintegration by moving their capital to the better grassland region of Borno. Kanem then officially became the tributary state, at times acting independently, at times acknowledging the authority of Borno.

By establishing their capital in Borno, the *Mais* of the Saifawa dynasty had access to a wider trading network. During the fifteenth century they established important trading links with the Hausa to the west, supplying salt and horses in exchange for Akan gold.

During the course of the sixteenth century, the *Mais* strengthened their grip on the people of Borno. There must have been considerable extortion of the peasantry because Borno was shaken by a series of internal revolts. These were savagely put down as the *Mais* waged *jihads* across the country. Firm control was established over the peasant population who, once they submitted, were no longer subjected to raids. The income of the state became based more firmly on the regular taxation of the peasantry and customs dues on trade. In the central Borno region taxes were assessed and charged on a village or family basis. Further afield traditional chiefs were left in charge provided they paid a regular tribute. Raids for captives now extended far to the south of Chad.

During the second half of the sixteenth century *Mai* Idris Aloma strengthened his army with the importation of firearms from north Africa. At a time when the Songhay army failed to 'modernise', Turkish mercenaries and advisers were brought in to train the new army of Borno. The *Mai's* tribute-collectors ranged as far west as the Hausa state of Kano. At the same time friendly relations were established with the Ottoman rulers of Tripoli. The dominance of Borno at this time helped drain trans-Saharan trade away from Songhay and the western routes.

We know little about the internal affairs of Borno in the seventeenth and eighteenth centuries. Until recently historians tended to assume it was a period of decline, but there is little firm evidence that this was so. Compared with the warfare of the sixteenth century it was a relatively peaceful period. Borno became a centre of Islamic learning, and written records of the time concentrate mainly on religious developments. Islam spread and the Kanuri language became dominant in the region. Slave-raiding further south remained an important source of royal income, and the eastern Hausa states continued to pay tribute until the end of the eighteenth century. But Borno's military superiority gradually declined as new firearms were no longer regularly imported. The Tuareg sultanate of Aïr asserted its independence and was operating freely at the salt mines of Bilma by the 1750s. Borno no longer dominated the trade of the central Sudan, but it was not deprived of access to trans-Saharan routes.

The Hausa city-states

The Hausa city-states first emerged between 1000 and 1200 CE. The Hausa developed from a mixture of southern Saharan nomads and local mixed farmers of the northern Nigerian savannah. Their basic political unit was a compact walled village. The wooden stockades of the early Hausa villages existed to protect the inhabitants from southern Saharan raiders. The stockades covered a large area enclosing not only the principal dwellings of the settlement, but also a considerable extent of cultivable land. In times of trouble the village enclosure could protect the Hausa of the district and their livestock through a lengthy siege. As the population increased, villages grouped together under the protection of the largest local Hausa town. In time these developed into walled cities which became the capitals of states.

The economic basis of the Hausa city-states was agriculture, manufacturing and trade, though each had its own particular specialisation. Gobir, the northernmost, had originally developed at Aïr though it moved south to Gobir under Tuareg pressure in the fifteenth century. From an early stage Gobir's strength came from its trans-Saharan trading contacts on the eastern fringes of the Mali and Songhay empires. Katsina, founded in the twelfth or thirteenth century, was also an important trading centre. Kano built its wealth on its craftsmen and manufacturing skills, especially in the weaving of cotton cloth. Later the Hausa of Kano developed the further skills of cloth-dying and leatherwork. Dark-blue cotton cloth from Kano was much sought after among the peoples of west Africa. And a large amount of so-called 'Moroccan' leather sold from north Africa to Europe originated from the Hausa craftsmen of Kano. Zamfara and Kebbi were other important Hausa states. The southernmost Hausa state, Zazzau, with its capital at Zaria, was founded in the sixteenth century. It was to become a major supplier of slaves to the other Hausa states, raided from the Kwararafa in the region of the Benue River. Some of these slaves were for internal Hausa use, others were for export to Borno and north Africa in exchange for horses, harness and guns.

Slavery was important in Hausa society. The Hausa of the cities were engaged in trade, warfare, manufacture and the elaborate bureaucracy of government. Slave labour, imported from outside, was used to build and maintain the city walls and to grow the food to feed the teeming cities. In addition, beyond the city walls were numerous free cultivators and herders

Figure 13.1 Kano in the nineteenth century (from a drawing dated 1851 by a German artist)

Figure 13.2 Modern photo of the dye pits at Kano. Cotton cloth dyed here was a major trade item from at least the thirteenth century, transported throughout western Africa and across the Sahara to north Africa

who paid taxes to the state. Growing trading contacts introduced the Hausa to the world of Islam. The ruling elite of the city-states became Muslim in the fourteenth century, though the bulk of the common people were as yet untouched by the Muslim faith.

The Hausa city-states flourished from the sixteenth to the eighteenth century. There was great rivalry between them and states rose and fell in relative importance. But no one Hausa state managed to subdue all the others. There was no single Hausa 'empire'.

The Hausa played an important role in the development of long-distance trade: at first between Songhay and Borno, and later between the Akan gold-fields, Borno and Aïr. But increasing rivalry and rising levels of warfare between the city-states had important consequences for their internal development. Warfare devastated the countryside, and yet to finance their wars the ruling class overtaxed the peasantry. And in their efforts to increase the supply of slaves the Hausa ruling elite resorted to 'illegally' enslaving Muslim commoners, often selling them to north Africa in exchange for firearms and horses.

With the eighteenth-century spread of Islam among the Hausa masses, there was a greater awareness of the principles of Islamic law, the *shari'a*. The corruption, oppression and Islamically 'illegal' actions of the Hausa rulers were called into question by Islamic religious leaders. The stage was set for the 'holy revolution' which was to sweep the region in the early nineteenth century (see pp. 230–6).

Wolof kingdoms of Senegambia

The break-up of the Ghana empire in the early thirteenth century enabled the Wolof-speaking people of the Senegambia region to form the Jolof empire, which lasted until the mid-sixteenth century. In 1549 the ruler of Kajoor province led a successful rebellion that resulted in the break-up of the empire and the formation of a number of independent Wolof kingdoms: Kahoor, Jolof, Waalo and Bawol.

During the seventeenth and eighteenth centuries the Wolof kingdoms engaged with Europeans in the Atlantic slave trade, although the numbers of slaves exported numbered hundreds a year rather than thousands. As many slaves were retained within Wolof society and worked to produce surplus foodstuffs both for the royal courts and for export to the coastal trading towns. The Atlantic trade created a thriving market for foodstuffs to feed the slaves gathered at Gore Island and St Louis awaiting export by European, mainly French, merchants. Wolof engaged in this trade became well established at the coastal towns, making Wolof the dominant urban culture and language of the Senegambia region. In playing an intermediary role between the coast and the riverine hinterland, Wolof merchants prompted the free peasants and slave-holding landowners of the interior to raise produce for the new urban markets. And as that market demand changed to groundnuts in the early nineteenth century, Wolof farmers and merchants were ready to respond rapidly.

Kingdoms of the forest: Ife and Benin

The Yoruba form one of the larger language groups in the western part of modern Nigeria. The word Yoruba originated as a Hausa name for the people of the Oyo empire (see below, pp. 197–9). In modern usage it refers to all those speaking the same language as the peoples of Oyo. In historic times the Yoruba-speaking peoples stretched from the savannah woodlands west of the lower Niger to deep into the forest towards the coast (see Map 13.3). They were basically mixed farmers, hunters and traders, living in small village communities.

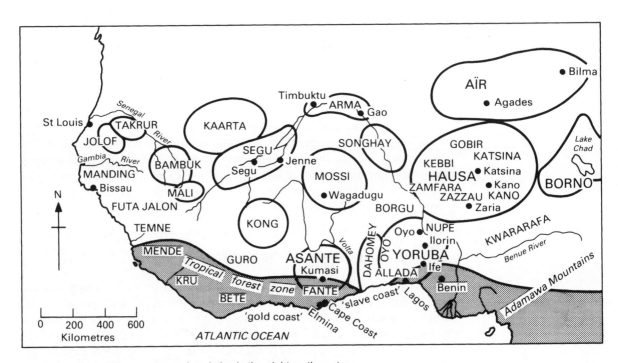

Map 13.3 West African states and societies in the eighteenth century

State-formation among the Yoruba seems to have begun in the eleventh and twelfth centuries. As with many other African societies, sources of state authority were related to religion. According to the myth of creation in Yoruba religion, the 'God of the Sky', Olorun, lowered the Yoruba founding ancestor, Oduduwa, down to earth at Ife. There he founded the original Yoruba state and his sons dispersed to head the other Yoruba kingdoms. The ruler, or *oni*, of Ife based his claim to kingship on his reputed direct descent from the founding ancestor, Oduduwa.

The economic basis of the early Yoruba states was their ability to produce a food surplus. This enabled them to feed, not only their non-productive rulers and officials, but also numerous court craftsmen and artists. As with many other states, profit from trade was soon added to taxation of the peasantry as an additional source of royal revenue.

It was no coincidence that Ife was the original Yoruba state and the one that produced some of the finest artistic artefacts in the whole of west Africa. Ife was perhaps the best placed of all the Yoruba states to produce a food surplus. It was founded on the borders of the savannah and the forest. Here the soil was fertile and the rainfall high. The varied environment was suitable for a range of root and cereal crops and the raising of domestic animals. We know little about the social or economic organisation of Ife, but its inhabitants certainly had the time and wealth to practise highly developed artistic skills, and it is for these that the forest kingdoms are best known.

The artists of Ife produced a wide range of wood and ivory carvings, terracotta sculptures, and bronze, brass and copper castings (see Figure 13.3).

Figure 13.3 Ife bronzes

Most of these, recovered by archaeologists, have been dated to the twelfth to fifteenth centuries. The terracottas and metal castings are remarkably realistic images of *onis* and were probably used in funeral ceremonies. The use of copper indicates trading links with Saharan mines. In exchange for copper, and possibly salt, the Yoruba probably traded food, kola nut and ivory to the peoples of the Sahel.

It is not, of course, surprising to find such highly developed artistic skills among the peoples of this region. We have already seen in earlier chapters (pp. 46–8, 94–5), with reference to the Nok culture and the Igbo-Ukwo bronzes, that the peoples of west Africa had an ancient tradition of fine artistic work in terracotta and copper alloys. Techniques of metal casting need not necessarily have been imported from afar.

To the south and east of Ife, towards the Niger delta and deep within the forest, were the Edo-speaking peoples. Though they mostly remained in small village chiefdoms, they too developed a centralised city-state, at Benin. Kingship at Benin dated from the eleventh century, at about the same time as it was developing at Ife. Indeed, the *Oba* (ruler) of Benin based his authority on claims to descent from Oduduwa, the Yoruba founding ancestor. Benin by the fifteenth century was a huge walled city, several kilometres across. A Dutch visitor to Benin city in about 1600 compared its wide streets and fine houses very favourably with his home capital of Amsterdam (see Figure 13.4).

Ewuare, *oba* of Benin in the mid-fifteenth century, built up a powerful standing army and expanded Benin into an extensive empire. By 1500 the empire of Benin stretched from the Niger delta in the east to the coastal lagoon of Lagos in the west. Ewuare strengthened his administration by selecting and appointing his own district chiefs. He established a stable system of *oba* succession by having his eldest son recognised as official heir.

When the Portuguese first contacted Benin in the late fifteenth century it was still undergoing a period of expansion. Thus the *obas* were prepared to sell their war-captives to the Portuguese who, as we saw in the previous chapter, exported them to the Akan in exchange for gold. Early in the sixteenth century, Benin expansion ended and with it the export of captives. Thereafter, during the sixteenth and seventeenth centuries the main exports from Benin to Europeans at the coast were pepper, ivory, gum and cotton cloth. The latter was resold to other west African societies further along the coast. Benin did not resupply the transatlantic slave trade until the eighteenth century when the ancient kingdom was wracked by dynastic dispute and civil war. The sale of its own citizens into slavery and the importation of firearms undermined the productive capacity of Benin and hastened its decline during the eighteenth century.

Benin, like Ife, possessed a highly-developed, official court art. Bronze, brass and copper heads and figurines were reproduced to honour and commemorate the *obas*. And on their wooden palace walls were nailed elaborate copper plaques showing their glorious deeds of the past (see Figure 13.5). Most of these artistic artefacts were looted or destroyed when British troops sacked the city in 1897 (see Figure 21.4 on p. 321). The court art of Benin reached its height in the sixteenth and seventeenth centuries as Portuguese traders provided a new source of copper. The Portuguese themselves were depicted in some of the copper plaques. Benin artists also made a number of ivory carvings, salt cellars and bangles, for sale to Europeans (see

Figure 13.6). These were probably specially commissioned by Portuguese merchants and form perhaps the earliest example of African artists catering for the European tourist market!

Oyo and Dahomey, savannah states of the seventeenth and eighteenth centuries

Though Ife was the oldest and most senior Yoruba state, it was soon surpassed in importance by the northern state of Oyo. Founded in the fourteenth century by a descendant of Oduduwa, Oyo, unlike its Yoruba neighbours to the south, was situated in the savannah woodland north of the tropical forest. The region was ideal for growing cereal crops and was also in a powerful trading position between the Yoruba of the forest and the Hausa of the north. In addition, being free of tsetse fly and other disease-carrying insects of the forest, the country was suitable for horses. And it was with their standing army of cavalry that the *alafins* (rulers) of Oyo were able to build their conquest state.

Because Oyo was unable to use cavalry effectively in the forest, its southward expansion was restricted to the south-west. Here from the west of modern Nigeria to the east of modern Ghana there is a break in the line of forest where the open savannah reaches down to the coast. Into this region Oyo's cavalry was able to intrude and extend the empire's authority. Towards the end of the seventeenth century Oyo invaded the coastal kingdom of Allada, forcing it to pay tribute, and so gaining access to the Atlantic trade of the Europeans.

The power and wealth of the *alafins* of Oyo grew enormously during the eighteenth century. The economic basis of this power and that which

Figure 13.4 View of Benin, Nigeria *c.*1846 (from Henrion, *Missions Catholiques,* vol 1.280 plate ix)

Figure 13.5 Benin bronze plaque, formerly mounted on the wooden walls of the *Oba's* palace, and looted by the British in 1897 (see p. 321)

Figure 13.6 Benin ivory salt cellar. Carved out of a single tusk of ivory, items such as these were specifically made for sale to Europeans financed the *alafins'* cavalry was the use of slave labour to work on royal farms. These were captives from warfare or traded from the Sahel. Other sources of income were tribute from the towns and villages of Oyo and from the country's neighbours. There was also a tax on the transit trade between the coastal states and Hausaland. In addition, the incessant wars of expansion produced more captives than were needed on the royal farms. The surplus was dispatched towards the coast to be sold to Europeans as slaves for the Atlantic trade. Firearms, cloth, metal goods and cowrie shells were imported from the coast. Part of this was kept within the empire, but much of it was traded to the north in exchange for horses and further captives.

With the enormous increase in the European demand for slaves in the 1780s Oyo became a major transit handler of slaves from north to south. But overdependence on the slave trade had important repercussions for the rulers of Oyo. When European wars between England and France reduced the trade in slaves in the 1790s, the *alafin* of Oyo lost a major source of income. There was less wealth to reward supporters, and the peasantry in turn were overtaxed. Royal authority declined and around the turn of the century there were a number of regional rebellions. As with the states of Hausaland, the scene was set for Muslim revolt in the early nineteenth century.

The rise of Dahomey

One of those neighbouring states forced to pay tribute to the *alafin* of Oyo was the kingdom of Dahomey in the modern republic of Benin. (Note that the modern republic of Benin, which changed its name from Dahomey in 1975, bears no direct relationship to the ancient forest kingdom of Benin.) Dahomey was founded in the early seventeenth century. A small group of Aja from the coastal kingdom of Allada moved northwards and settled among the Fon. The latter had hitherto lived in a loosely linked collection of rural villages such as those described in Chapter 6 (p. 95). Within a few years the Aja began to assert their authority over the Fon. In doing so they founded the new kingdom of Dahomey with its capital at Agbome. It was Wegbaja, who became king in about 1650, who organised Dahomey as a powerful centralised state.

Wegbaja declared that he, as king, was the ultimate 'owner of the land'. This entitled him to introduce direct taxation on the produce of the land, which was only 'lent' to its residents. Royal power was strengthened with the establishment of royal succession by primogeniture, that is, succession by the king's eldest male heir. This prevented traditional village chiefs from having any say in the succession, and so reduced their potential power. At the same time a 'cult of kingship' was developed. It was promoted by the introduction of annual human sacrifices to honour the royal ancestors. The victims of the sacrifices were usually captives taken in warfare.

Having come from the coastal 'slaving' state of Allada, the kings of Dahomey were determined to exploit to the full the profits to be gained from the slave trade. Firearms imported from the coast were exchanged for captives taken in Dahomey's wars of expansion. In the 1720s Dahomey conquered Allada and Whydah and so gained more direct access to the Europeans at the coast.

It has been suggested by at least one historian that in making these coastal conquests the Dahomian king, Agaja (r.1716–40), was in fact trying to suppress the export of slaves out of Africa. According to this account Agaja is reported to have asked Europeans to establish plantations in Dahomey, using slave labour, so that the labour of these slaves would not actually be lost to Africa. But Europeans at the time were not interested in the scheme. The transatlantic system was already very profitable for them and plantations in Dahomey would be beyond their control. Agaja did not press this policy and Dahomey's need for firearms was so great that he and his successors continued to sell captives to Europeans.

The hinterland of the 'Slave Coast' in the eighteenth century was dominated by Oyo and Dahomey. Rivalry between the two states, particularly over control of the coastal trade in captives, soon led to conflict. Oyo invaded Dahomey four times in the late 1720s. Agaja was unable to repulse the Oyo cavalry and in 1730 he agreed to pay tribute to the *alafin* of Oyo.

In spite of its new subservient position with regard to Oyo, the kingdom of Dahomey continued to expand and thrive during the eighteenth century. Most of the slaves exported from the state came from beyond the country's boundaries. The king himself was not the only dealer in slaves, he was just the largest. Other Dahomian slave dealers were heavily taxed from their profits. Taxes were mostly paid in cowrie shells which, by the eighteenth century, had become the most widespread currency in west Africa.

The majority of the Dahomian population remained little affected by the slave trade. They were mostly peasant farmers living in small rural villages. But the king's tax-collectors were thorough. They toured regularly through the countryside, assessing for taxation by making censuses of people, livestock, crops and possessions. There were taxes on just about everything. The royal household itself was fed from the produce of large plantations worked by slave labour. In due course, in the nineteenth century, these were turned to producing palm oil for sale to Europeans instead of slaves – the realisation, perhaps, of Agaja's eighteenth-century dream.

The kingdom of Asante

The origins and rise of Akan states

During the fourteenth century, when the empire of Mali was at its height, professional Malinke, Bamana and Soninke traders fanned out across the savannah in search of new trading opportunities (see pp. 104–5). In the region of the upper Volta rivers they were known as Dyula. Gold and kola nuts had filtered from the forest for many years, but only on a very small scale. Now, with the prompting presence of the Dyula, the Akan of the forest fringes began to exploit these products on a regular basis.

Until this time the Akan farmers had only entered the forest for hunting or for small-scale, seasonal gold mining. Permanent settlement and farming in the forest was difficult because of the large amount of labour needed to clear the land. It was more profitable for farmers like the Akan to remain on the forest fringes. From about 1400, however, the Akan began using slave labour to clear the forest for planting and to mine the gold. The slaves were bought initially from the Dyula in part-payment for the gold.

During the fifteenth century, permanent Akan settlement developed within the forest. An Akan who controlled a gold-mine used his slave labour both to mine the gold and to grow the food to feed the labour force. In time, free Akan farmers were attracted to settle in the clearings and become the subjects of the 'owners of the land'. Those who controlled the mines thus became the founders of new Akan chiefdoms.

At the end of the fifteenth century, as we saw in the previous chapter (p. 177), the Akan found both a new market for their gold and a new source of labour for their mines. In the 1480s the Portuguese set up trading bases on the coast and began buying Akan gold in exchange for slaves from Benin, cotton cloth, metals and other goods. Later the Akan of the forest were given a further boost to their economy when the Portuguese supplied them with new tropical crops such as maize and cassava from Brazil.

During the sixteenth century a number of Akan states emerged, the more important being Denkyira and Akwamu inland, and Fante near the coast. There was considerable rivalry between the rising Akan states as they competed for new land and new goldfields or for control of the trade routes to the coast. In due course all of these states were absorbed by the kingdom of Asante.

The rise of Asante

The kingdom of Asante was founded by Osei Tutu in the 1670s. Osei Tutu was a military leader and head of the Oyoko clan. He began by establishing control over a trading centre near Kumasi. He grouped other clan chiefs around himself and, using Kumasi as his base, he conquered the surrounding Akan chiefdoms. In doing so he took the title *Asantehene* and founded the Asante kingdom.

Initially, the kingdom of Asante was a loose grouping or federation of chiefdoms under the military leadership of Osei Tutu. The chiefs paid him tribute, collected from their villages and from the profits of their goldfields, and provided soldiers as part of the *Asantehene*'s standing army. Osei Tutu's authority over his fellow chiefs was strengthened when he gained the support of religious leaders. One of these religious priests magically conjured up a symbol of Asante kingship, a Golden Stool, which was presented to the *Asantehene*.

Figure 13.7 Some of the gold regalia of the Asante monarch: two finger rings and three wrist and/or knee bracelets. The ring with the elephant signifies the omnipotence of the wearer

201

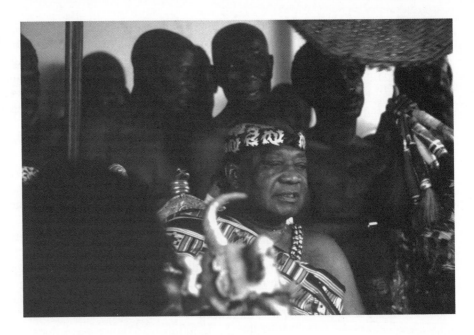

Figure 13.8 The Asantehene Opoku Ware II (r.1970–99), in full royal regalia

Osei Tutu's federation conquered Denkyira and other Akan states and by 1700 controlled most of the goldfields of the forest. His successor Opoku Ware I (r.1717–50) expanded the boundaries of Asante until it covered most of modern Ghana, from the forest on the coast to savannah in the north. During the eighteenth-century wars of conquest and expansion, the rulers of Asante sold their war-captives to slavers at the coast. But they never became very dependent on the trade for royal revenue.

In the late eighteenth century *Asantehene* Osei Kwadwo (r.1764–77) introduced a new, centralised administration. The federation of hereditary chiefdoms was done away with. Government officers were appointed or promoted by merit rather than by birth and much of the provincial collection of taxation was removed from local hereditary chiefs. The army too was restructured on a more centralised basis, with military officers appointed directly by the king.

Slave labour remained the basis of most gold-production. Some of these gold-mines were directly owned by the king and operated by his agents. Others were owned by Akan chiefs who paid taxes to the state. At the same time free Akan peasants washed alluvial gold from the rivers on a seasonal basis. This was sold to itinerant Akan traders, many of whom were direct agents of the king. The itinerant traders bought up cloth, metal and European firearms from the coast, or salt, cloth and other trading items from the north and travelled through the country selling them for gold. Even the remotest villagers were brought within this very extensive network. In this way the maximum amount of gold was extracted in Asante. And the king, either through taxation or from trading, was able to gain the greatest profit from the business.

14

Central and eastern Africa to the eighteenth century

Farmers, fishers and hunters of the Congo forest

The basin of the Congo river contains Africa's largest area of tropical rainforest. But this does not mean that the whole region is covered with unbroken galleries of dense vegetation. Apart from the navigable rivers there are a number of upland areas where the forest is broken by clearings of savannah. The varied environment allowed the peoples of this region to develop a variety of productive activities, though basically they were either farmers, fishers or hunters. Some peoples practised all three activities; others specialised in one or two. The best-known specialist hunters were the short-statured peoples of the denser forest zones, often referred to as 'pygmies'.

All these occupations required a level of cooperative effort that was not always quite so important elsewhere in the continent. The farmers needed the intensive effort of cooperative labour for clearing forest, often starting from the edges of a natural clearing, or for building mounds in the areas liable to flood. Hunters needed cooperative work digging pits and trapping animals. Fishing peoples joined together for building dams and netting rivers. The staple crops were bananas in the forest and millet or sorghum in

Figure 14.1 Fishers on the Congo River

the savannah clearings. In the seventeenth and eighteenth centuries the latter were largely replaced by the American imports of maize and cassava.

On the whole the people of the Congo forest lived in villages of between 30 and 200 adults. Any smaller would have left the people short of labour and any larger would have put too great a pressure on the natural resources of a region. The adults within a village were usually related, and exchange of brides from one village to another provided the basis of relationships between the two. Women, the main cultivators, were subservient to men but there were also within villages captives or hostages who were in effect slaves. In addition, some villages exercised a system of clientship over specialists like pygmy hunters who provided farming communities with meat in exchange for cultivated food.

River transport provided the key to trade between regions, and specialist craftsmen built a range of river canoes. At the downstream end of thousands of kilometres of navigable waterway lay Malebo Pool, which became a major trading junction.

Within the forest proper there were few large states, though there was a wide range of relationships between various villages. The most common linkages within a group of villages were alliances of marriage. Others were held together by a war-leader, or by common language or religious cult. Where kingdoms did develop, it was generally in the forest clearings, such as the Kuba in the mid-Kasai region, Loango on the coast or the Tio, north of Malebo Pool. It was usually these kingdoms that provided the link with the slave trade of the coast.

West-central Africa in the era of the slave trade

In the 1480s the Portuguese arrived off the coast of west-central Africa near the mouth of the Congo River. They soon established diplomatic relations with the kingdom of Kongo. The king of Kongo was interested in the foreign connection because he hoped the Portuguese would supply teachers and craftsmen to educate and train his people. He also wanted new weapons and Portuguese mercenaries to strengthen his army. The Portuguese, for their part, were delighted to form an alliance with what they considered to be a powerful African kingdom. They hoped it would provide them with a profitable trade in gold, copper, silver and spices. But they were soon disappointed. The kingdom could export a small amount of copper and local manufactured goods such as raffia cloth for resale elsewhere along the African coast. But it was not rich in the kind of minerals and spices which the Portuguese really sought. The most valuable item in the basically agricultural economy of west-central Africa was the region's labour.

The kingdom of Kongo

Within the kingdom of Kongo the Portuguese presence on the coast stimulated a dynastic dispute between those in favour of greater foreign contacts and those against. The former emerged victorious, with Portuguese help, and in 1506 a Kongolese Christian convert seized the throne and took the title Afonso I (r.1506–42).

Afonso exchanged letters with his 'brother monarch', the king of Portugal, and opened communication with the Pope in Rome. Within the Kongo Afonso developed Christianity along the lines of a royal religious cult. In this way he increased his own authority and undermined that of regional religious

Map 14.1 Central Africa, sixteenth to eighteenth centuries

leaders. On the one hand this rid him of the need for local regional support. On the other hand he now became heavily dependent upon the support of the Portuguese. Afonso used Portuguese mercenaries and guns to exert direct control over tribute collection and long-distance trade, and he expanded the kingdom by conquest as far as Malebo Pool. Afonso's wars of conquest produced plenty of captives and these were sold to the Portuguese for export to São Tomé as slaves. In exchange Afonso imported Portuguese priests, soldiers and metal manufactured goods.

For a while the Portuguese government was undecided as to whether it should continue to treat Kongo as a friendly ally or simply exploit the region as a source of slaves. The settlers of São Tomé had no such doubts. They even promoted local wars of resistance to Afonso in order to increase the supply of captives. With the development of the transatlantic trade from the 1530s there was further pressure on the king of Kongo to produce more captives for export.

In 1568–9 the kingdom of Kongo suffered an invasion from the east. The invaders, known as the Jaga, quickly overran the kingdom, laying waste the country and forcing the king into exile. There has been much historical dispute in recent years as to who exactly the Jaga were and why they invaded Kongo in 1568. It seems probable that a period of prolonged drought had prompted the settled farming peoples of the Kwango River region to resort to a life of raid and devastation. They may also have been reacting to increasingly heavy Kongolese demands for tribute or raids for slaves.

In 1574 the Kongo king, Alvaro I, was reinstated by the Portuguese with the aid of São Tomé mercenaries. But thereafter the king's authority among his people declined. He became ever-more dependent upon the export of captives in exchange for Portuguese military support. Dutch competition in the seventeenth century stimulated a further expansion in the demand for captives at the coast. Professional African and Afro-European slavers at Malebo Pool developed an alternative northern slaving route between the Kongolese interior and the Atlantic coast. They became known as *pombeiros*, after the Malebo port of Pumbo. Later the name *pombeiro* came to be used as a general term for most of the professional traders of west-central Africa. During the course of the seventeenth century central authority in Kongo collapsed and the kingdom disintegrated into rival regional factions, each fighting one another in the pursuit of war-captives.

Angola and the slave trade

From the 1530s São Tomé developed as a major transit point for captives being transported across the Atlantic to the new plantations in Brazil. With the hugely increased demand for slaves which this entailed, the São Tomé slavers evaded Portuguese royal control by establishing a slaving station at Luanda. From there they purchased captives from the *Ngola* ('king') of Ndongo, the southern rival kingdom to Kongo. The trade in captives from Ndongo strengthened the power of the *Ngola* during the course of the sixteenth century. The *Ngola* built up his army and expanded his kingdom by conquest in order to produce more captives for sale.

The Jaga invasion of Kongo had shown the Portuguese the precariousness of their position in the west-central African interior. Their subsequent relatively easy defeat of the Jaga encouraged them to take more direct control of the region. The rumour that there were rich silver deposits in the mountains around the upper Kwanza helped the Portuguese decide to try and conquer the kingdom of Ndongo (Angola).

Figure 14.2 Ndzinga, *Ngola* of Ndongo (1624–63) and Queen of Matamba (1629–63), negotiating with the Portuguese governor of Luanda on behalf of her brother *Ngola* in 1622. The Portuguese had refused her a seat and so she sat on the back of one of her attendants to indicate that the *Ngola* of Ndongo was of the same status as the King of Portugal. Ndzinga spent most of her life fighting wars of resistance against the Portuguese

The Portuguese invasion of Angola was defeated by a combination of stiff resistance by the Mbundu and the tropical diseases which decimated the Portuguese troops. As the invasion ground to a halt in the late 1580s, the remnants of the Portuguese army settled into the role of regular slave traders. The endemic warfare of the interior, stimulated by the Portuguese invasion, increased the supply of captives to the coast. Portuguese and Afro-European dealers, based at Luanda and later further south at Benguela, ensured that the Angolan interior became a regular source of slaves for the Atlantic trade for most of the seventeenth and eighteenth centuries. In the mid-eighteenth century Luanda alone was exporting more than 10,000 captives a year. If any part of Africa was dominated by the slave trade in this period, it was here in Angola. All the worst effects of the slave trade described in Chapter 12 could be applied to this region.

The Portuguese themselves made little further attempt to conquer the interior. There was no need, since the incessant wars of the region provided them with all the captives that they needed. Portuguese attempts to tax the slave trade at the coastal ports merely encouraged coastal dealers to sell to other European trading ships, especially Dutch, French and English. The sale of large quantities of cheap French and English guns in the eighteenth century further increased the level of interior warfare and the sale of captives at the coast. Other principal imports in exchange for captives from Angola were Indian cottons and Brazilian rum. The imports offered no hope for the indigenous development of African craft and industry.

Within the Angolan interior, various branches of Imbangala were widely active in the supply of captives for the coastal market. Dislocated from the central highlands through drought and warfare, Imbangala invaded the coastal lowlands in the 1570s and 1580s. After an initial period of raiding, many settled down to farming again. Others became regular slave-raiding mercenaries for the Portuguese at Luanda. Further Imbangala formed the raiding state of Kasanje (see p. 147), which became a major source of slaves in the seventeenth and eighteenth centuries. The peoples of the Angolan interior continued to be dominated by the wars of the slave trade until well into the nineteenth century.

In the early 1800s the Portuguese governor of Luanda dispatched two *pombeiros* to investigate the trading prospects of the central African interior. They traversed the continent, following well-established trade routes, which led to the capitals of the Lunda empires of Mwata Yamvo and Kazembe. These states had grown to dominate the long-distance trade of the interior during the course of the previous century.

Central African empires and the growth of trade

The Lunda of Mwata Yamvo

The Lunda empire of Mwata Yamvo reached its height in the second half of the seventeenth century. By then it had fathered many offshoots to the south and west such as the Imbangala kingdom of Kasanje in Angola. The latter provided a trading link with the Atlantic coast which was to gain in importance during the eighteenth and nineteenth centuries.

An important factor in the growth of the Lunda empire was the adoption of new American crops – maize and cassava – imported indirectly from the Portuguese on the Atlantic coast. In the dry savannah zones cassava rapidly became a major staple crop, displacing the indigenous African millet. Cassava was found to be heavy-yielding, drought-resistant and good for storage. It enabled the production of greater food surpluses, which added stability to the heartland of the Lunda empire.

The power of the Mwata Yamvo was based on the collection and redistribution of tribute and this in turn stimulated the development of long-distance trade. Near the capital, Musumba, tribute was paid in food, especially cassava, while further afield the chiefdoms of the empire paid in a variety of regionally specialised goods. These included salt, iron, copper, metal manufactured goods, raffia cloth, baskets, pottery and ivory.

The Mwata Yamvo used this tribute to redistribute as gifts to supporters or to exchange with other peoples for luxuries and essentials. As long-distance trade developed, two key items exported to the west were ivory and slaves, in exchange for woollen cloth and guns. The possession of guns helped the Mwata Yamvo to further extend his control over the trade and tribute of the region. Though the central African Lunda were thus drawn into the slave-trading system of the south Atlantic, this was never on the massively destructive scale found in Angola.

During the course of the seventeenth century Lunda tribute-collectors established chiefdoms to south, east and west of the central Lunda kingdom. Here they asserted authority over the local 'owners of the land', whom they taxed for tribute to send to the Mwata Yamvo. The most important of these new Lunda states was that of Kazembe.

The Lunda of Kazembe

In the early 1700s the Mwata Yamvo sent a small force of Lunda to capture the salt pans of the upper Lualaba. Their leader was given the title Kazembe with authority to extend the collection of Lunda tribute eastwards to the copper-producing region of the modern Zambian/Congo copperbelt. His successor, Kazembe II, extended Lunda authority further east until by 1740 he had established a new state in the valley of the lower Luapula (see Map 14.1). During the second half of the eighteenth century this new Lunda state expanded into an independent empire in its own right, paying only nominal tribute to the Mwata Yamvo.

The wealth of Kazembe's empire came from the rich natural resources of the region combined with his control over a well-organised, long-distance trading system. Like the Mwata Yamvos, the Kazembes left the 'owners of the land' in place but sent out tribute-collectors to bring into their own hands the surplus products of the region. These items were then turned to profitable, long-distance trade. And the Kazembe was even better-placed than the Mwata Yamvo to take advantage of this system. In the centre of the kingdom the fertile alluvial soils of the Luapula valley ensured the regular production of cassava and maize. To the north-west, salt was brought in from the upper Lualaba while copper came from the Shaba region of the copperbelt. A surplus of fish was produced from the Luapula and Lake Mweru, and tribute in iron was provided by the iron-workers of Chisinga and Ushi between Lakes Mweru and Bangweulu.

By 1800 Kazembe III's capital was at the centre of a vast trans-African trading network. Unlike the Mwata Yamvo, Kazembe was able to make use of both Atlantic and Indian Ocean systems. The main exports were iron, salt, copper, ivory and, later, slaves. These were sent westwards via Mwata Yamvo's empire and south-eastwards via Bisa middlemen to the Portuguese of the

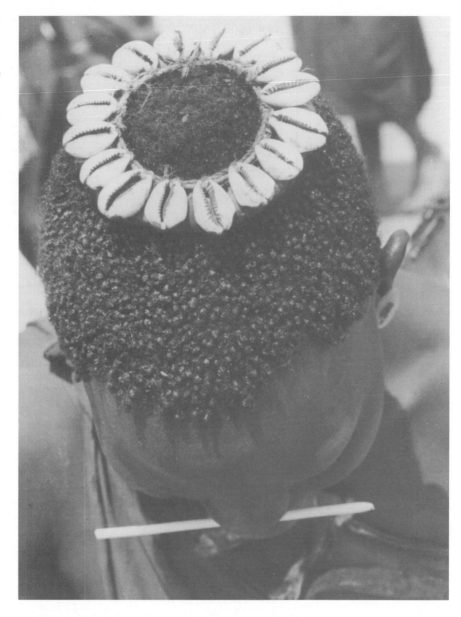

Figure 14.3 Cowrie shells (from the Indian Ocean) were widely used as currency in Africa from the sixteenth century, but by the end of the nineteenth century their value as currency was worthless and they were used only for decoration, as worn by this Tonga girl of the Zambezi valley, *c.*1900

Zambezi valley (see Map 14.1). The main imports were European woollens and guns, Indian cottons, glass beads and luxury manufactured goods for use at Kazembe's court.

The Maravi empire of Kalonga

We saw in Chapter 10 that by the sixteenth century the Maravi chiefdoms of modern southern Malawi were organised under three principal ruling dynasties (p. 150). The most senior of these, the Kalonga, was centred among the Chinyanja-speaking peoples around the southern end of Lake Malawi (see Map 14.2). To their south the Manganja of the Shire valley were ruled by the Lundu dynasty while further west the Chewa came under the Undi dynasty. Like the Lunda, they were in effect federations of chiefdoms who remained the 'owners of the land'. The kingship of the dynasties was recognised through the payment of tribute, mainly in food.

Map 14.2 The Maravi and Rozvi: seventeenth and eighteenth centuries

The Maravi were important manufacturers and exporters of iron while the valleys of the Zambezi and Shire provided them with important sources of ivory.

During the late sixteenth century the Portuguese tried to establish a monopoly of the ivory trade in the Zambezi valley. This provoked a violent reaction from the Lundu of the Shire valley. In the 1580s and 1590s the massed armies of the Lundu, known as 'wa-Zimba', sacked Sena and Tete and raided other Portuguese trading towns spreading terror among the peoples of the northern Mozambique coast. The exact origins of the wa-Zimba remain the subject of historical debate. The most likely explanation is that they were a mercenary band of refugees, possibly recently escaped from Portuguese slavery in the Zambezi valley, who put themselves at the disposal of the Lundu. The devastating invasions of the wa-Zimba may also have been prompted by the same extensive drought which dislocated the Imbangala of Angola at this time.

In the early 1600s Kalonga Masula reasserted authority over the Lundu kingdom and re-established peaceful ivory-trading with the Portuguese. Kalonga Masula ruled from about 1600 to 1650, during which time he built a powerful Maravi empire, largely by military conquest. By 1635 Kalonga's empire stretched from the Zambezi in the west to Mozambique island in the east. He had even tried extending his authority south of the Zambezi by invading Mutapa in 1623. Though he was forced to withdraw, he left with a large booty in gold. Kalonga Masula's rule was strong enough to ensure that the Portuguese did not interfere in his domination of the ivory trade north of the Zambezi.

Kalonga's Maravi empire, however, went into gradual decline after its founder's death in 1650. He had failed to set up an effective central administration, relying too much upon the energy of his personal leadership and the strength of his standing army. Chiefdoms asserted their independence, and the Yao from the east of Lake Malawi took over the main ivory-trading routes between the Shire valley and the eastern coastal ports of Mozambique and Kilwa. The lack of any powerful Maravian authority in the eighteenth century left the way open for the penetration of the violent slaving-caravans and raids of the early nineteenth century (see pp. 258–9).

The Changamire Rozvi of the Zimbabwe plateau

During the course of the seventeenth century the Portuguese gained increasing control within the Mutapa empire. The Mutapa's authority had been weakened by the Maravi invasion of 1623 and by succession disputes and civil war in the years that followed. Portuguese settlers (*prazeros*) from the Zambezi valley intervened in the civil war in exchange for the removal of restrictions on their mining and trading within the Mutapa empire. Between 1630 and 1670 they set up a number of trading fairs and tried forcing the local people to open up new gold-mines. The violence and oppression of the Portuguese provoked widespread resistance from among the local peasant population. Rather than work the gold-mines, people fled their villages and sought the protection of local powerful men.

The increasing level of violence in the late seventeenth century prompted the development of private armies within the remnants of the Mutapa state. Basically the poor sought the protection of the rich, and those who owned large herds of cattle attracted dependants into military service. Young men from poor families offered themselves for a number of years of military service in exchange for enough cattle to pay the brideprice for a later marriage. Wealthy cattle-owners were thus able to build up private armies both to protect their own cattle and grazing lands and to raid those of their neighbours as well as to resist the Portuguese.

One such wealthy cattle-owner, Dombo, who possessed a private army, acquired the title Changamire. He was reputed to have originally been a herdsman of the Munhumutapa. By the 1670s he was an important power in the north-east of the plateau region, rivalling that of the Munhumutapa. His highly-disciplined and well-trained army were known as *rozvi* ('the destroyers') and this in time became the proud title of the members of his empire. In the early 1680s Changamire led his army, herds of cattle and increasing body of dependants in an invasion of the south-west. He defeated the Torwa rulers of Guruuswa (or Butua), and took over their capital Danangombe.

Between 1684 and 1696 Changamire Dombo used his ruthlessly efficient army to expel the Portuguese from their trading fairs in Mutapa and Manyika, and made his Rozvi empire the dominant power of the Zimbabwe plateau. Mutapa became a minor state in the lowland north-east towards the Zambezi valley. The Portuguese of Sena and Tete were only saved by the death of Changamire Dombo in 1696. During the succession dispute which followed, the Rozvi armies were withdrawn from the Zambezi valley.

The power of the Changamire dynasty which dominated the plateau region throughout the eighteenth century was based upon a number of factors. Not least of these was the discipline and reputation of the Rozvi regiments. Their presence or threatened use guaranteed the payment of tribute by the various Shona chiefdoms. They were also used to tend and protect the Changamire's huge herds of cattle. Special government officials

Figure 14.4 Pre-colonial mining in central Africa in the 1890s

known as *banyamai* regularly toured the country, backed up by small military regiments. They collected tribute from the regions and approved or disapproved the succession of local Shona chiefs. Tribute was mostly in food, cattle, skins – the products of subsistence farmers – or game trophies such as ivory.

The mining and trading of gold was kept strictly under royal control and this helped prevent the Portuguese from regaining access to the gold-trade of the region. No Portuguese were allowed within the empire. They were restricted to their landholdings (*prazos*) and trading-posts in the Zambezi valley. In the eighteenth century the Portuguese were allowed to establish a small trading-post at Zumbo, but only their African agents (*vashambadzi*) were allowed into the Rozvi empire to trade at the Changamire's capital. Here gold-dust was exchanged for imported cloth and beads. Much of the country's gold, however, was crafted by local goldsmiths into jewellery for the royal court. The Changamires did not allow the empire's economy to become overdependent on foreign trade. The basis of the Shona economy remained cattle, hunting and subsistence agriculture.

The east African interior west of the Victoria Nyanza

As we saw in Chapter 8 our knowledge of east African history is really very limited, there being no contemporary written sources for the history of the interior until the nineteenth century. The area about which most is known for the period up to 1800 is the inter-lake region which saw the rise of the kingdoms of Bunyoro and Buganda.

Bunyoro under the Bito clan had taken over from the earlier Chwezi state as the dominant power in the region by the sixteenth century. The people of Bunyoro practised a mixed economy of farming, hunting and herding. For the most part they remained a loose confederation of village-based chiefdoms under the overall authority of the king, to whom they paid tribute. The chiefdoms provided military regiments which were used by the king to conduct raids against the country's neighbours. The principal aims of these raids were to seize cattle and to bring in additional tribute to the king. In the sixteenth and seventeenth centuries Bunyoro's raids extended south through Nkore to Rwanda and eastwards into Buganda. Indeed, the need to defend themselves from Bunyoro attacks may have been a contributing factor in the desire by the clans of Buganda to organise themselves into a close-knit centralised community in the seventeenth century.

The rise of Buganda

Buganda was in many ways quite the opposite of Bunyoro. It developed as a small compact state under the intensive control of a centralised government. The economy of Buganda was based upon its agriculture, and herein lay its strength.

The main agricultural crop in Buganda was the banana and its relative the plantain: grown as a starchy vegetable food rather than a fruit. The core region of Buganda, on the north-west shores of Lake Victoria Nyanza, was particularly suited to the growth of the banana. It had a rich, fertile soil and a high level of regular rainfall. Once a banana plantation was established, it yielded heavy crops with a minimum amount of labour. What was more, its harvested and rotting vegetation returned natural fertility to the soil. Its growth did not require the constant shifting on to new or fallow land that was characteristic of the low-technology cereal farming practised over so much of tropical Africa at this time. Buganda's banana plantations, therefore, provided the basis for a certain level of economic stability. They allowed the growth of a fairly dense population within a relatively small area. This, combined with the necessity to defend the territory from outside attack, promoted the development of centralised government.

The kings of Buganda took the title of *kabaka*. It was Kabaka Mawanga in the early eighteenth century who put Buganda firmly on the road to strong, centralised kingship. The system which he and his successors developed strengthened the power of the king at the expense of traditional clan chiefs.

Wealth and power stemmed from the productivity of the land and the labour of the peasantry. The *kabakas* of the eighteenth century ensured that ultimate control of this wealth and power remained within their own hands. The *kabaka* granted landed estates to regional territorial chiefs who were dependent for their position on loyalty to the king rather than any hereditary claim. They in turn granted minor chiefs control over smaller parts of those estates. The peasantry, the cultivators, provided the wealth through taxation, which was passed up as tribute from one hierarchical level to another. And because banana cultivation did not require their full-time labour, the peasantry were also required to perform public works such as road-building. A complex network of public roads was constructed in Buganda, with all roads

Map 14.3 The east African interior, seventeenth and eighteenth centuries

ultimately leading towards the capital (see Figure 14.5). This eased communications from the centre to the regions, which strengthened government control as well as aiding trade. The king was careful to keep the major territorial chieftaincies out of the hands of members of his own royal clan. In doing so he prevented the development of alternate power bases which might threaten his authority.

On this basis Buganda developed as a powerful and expanding centralised kingdom during the course of the eighteenth century. By 1800 it had surpassed Bunyoro in strength, if not yet in size.

Figure 14.5 The capital of Buganda, as seen by H.M. Stanley, 8 April 1875: 'It is sited on the summit of a hill overlooking a great and beautiful district. Great wide roads lead to it from all directions. The widest and principal road is that overlooked from the Durbar of the King's Capital. It is about 400 feet wide and nearly 10 miles long. Either side is flanked by the houses and gardens of the principal men.' *The Exploration Diaries of H.M. Stanley*, ed. R. Stanley and A. Neame, William Kimber, London, 1961, p. 73

Pastoralist kingdoms of the south-western highlands

To the south of Bunyoro and Buganda lay the densely populated fertile highlands of Nkore, Rwanda and Burundi. Here, in contrast to Buganda, the majority agricultural population were dominated by a minority of pastoralists. As discussed in Chapter 8 (pp. 125–6), the increasing importance of cattle-herding in the centuries before 1500 had led to the rise of numerous small kingdoms in the hill country west of the Victoria Nyanza. Mostly they were mixed-farming communities, but a few developed as specialist cattle-keepers. These were known as Ba-Hima in the north and Ba-Tutsi in the south. The Hima gained ascendancy over the peasant cultivators in Nkore and the Tutsi did likewise in the south-west region of Rwanda and Burundi.

Initially, they were able to take advantage of the natural upland grasslands which lay uncultivated by the farmers. Over the centuries they developed closer relations with the farming populations: at first trading cattle in exchange for food. But what had started out as balanced trade, the Hima and Tutsi clans distorted into positions of domination. As their herds increased in size, they lent out cattle to the farmers from whom they demanded herding services. And whereas cultivated food had previously been a trading item, it now became a form of tribute to be given as required to the cattle-owning rulers. The latter assumed the role of an aristocratic 'warrior' class who offered protection to their subjects from raids by rival Hima and Tutsi clans.

By the eighteenth century the Tutsi clans of the south had merged into two major kingdoms, Rwanda and Burundi, with northerly Rwanda emerging as the more powerful. Within these aristocratic kingdoms the Tutsi developed elaborate rituals and myths of ancient origin to justify their dominant position over the subservient 'Ba-Hutu' peasantry. Despite this and later twentieth-century distortions, it was not originally an ethnically based system. It was possible for Hutu to pass into the ranks of the Tutsi elite through accumulated wealth, marriage or prowess in war. Nevertheless, class distinction between cattle-owning ruler and cultivating subject was consolidated into a caste system, a system upon which ethnic antagonism was to be sharpened in the centuries to come.

The east African interior east of the Victoria Nyanza

To the east of the Victoria Nyanza the dominant development of this period was the expansion of the Maasai. They belonged to the final movement of Nilotic-speaking pastoralists who pushed southwards into the region in the sixteenth or seventeenth century. Referred to variously as the Eastern or Plains Nilotes or Paranilotes, these specialised pastoralists formed the Ateker

Figure 14.6 Masai women in central Africa, carrying their children on their backs, 1939

and Teso of north-eastern Uganda, the Turkana and Samburu of north-western Kenya and the Maasai of central Kenya and northern Tanzania.

Earlier Nilotic pastoralists had found central Kenyan grazing lands largely unoccupied and so had mingled peaceably with local farming and hunting populations (see Chapter 8, pp. 125–7). But as the Maasai pushed through the rift valley towards the plains of northern Tanzania they found the grasslands already occupied by cattle-herding peoples such as the Kalenjin of the central Kenyan highlands. An important part of Maasai expansion, therefore, was the seizure of grazing land by force. In justification of their action they maintained the belief that all cattle, by definition, belonged to Maasai. The raiding of cattle from other people was merely exercising their right.

Maasai society was organised on an age-set system developed along military lines. This was similar in some respects to that described for the Oromo in Chapter 11 (pp. 170–1). The Maasai had three main age-sets: children, young adults and elders. In their early teens boys were passed through tough initiation ceremonies, which included military training. They then served their young adult lives as full-time soldiers and herdsmen. Their duty was to protect their herds and grazing zones and to raid for more of both. The Maasai did not operate as a single coherent group; nor did they practise hereditary chieftaincy. Their various related groups were governed by councils of elders.

Though they raided other cattle-herding people and expelled them from their grazing lands, the Maasai developed peaceable relationships with neighbouring Bantu-speaking farmers. They traded with the Kikuyu and the Kamba for iron weapons and foodstuffs, and there was some level of intermarriage between Maasai and Kikuyu. The latter, who occupied the eastern ridges of the central Kenyan highlands, developed from Maasai practices their own age-set system and initiation ceremonies.

Over much of modern Kenya and Tanzania, Bantu-speaking farmers still lived in small clan-based chiefdoms. This was particularly so among the peoples of the dry scrub savannah country of the Tanzanian plateau. Some clans gained ascendancy over others, as in the higher-rainfall and mixed-vegetation regions of Kilimanjaro and the Usambara and Pare mountains. Here sizeable states emerged among the Chagga, the Pare and the Shambaa. Many of these peoples, like the Kamba and Kikuyu to their north, developed systems of age-set organisation and initiation ceremonies which were probably borrowed in outline from earlier Cushitic neighbours.

Though the Tanzanian plateau was generally lightly populated, parts of the interior were rich in two important raw materials: iron and salt. These provided the basis for the development of regional trading networks. In the western region the Nyamwezi in particular were, by the end of the eighteenth century, organising themselves as professional traders and ivory-porters. From south of Lake Victoria Nyanza they were well placed to develop long-distance trading routes between the inter-lake kingdoms and the east African coast. The trade in ivory, and later slaves, from the interior was to become an important feature of the region in the nineteenth century.

15

Southern Africa to the eighteenth century

Southern Africa before 1650

As we saw in Chapter 10, by the 1600s southern Africa had for some centuries been witnessing the development of Later Iron Age states and societies. In the north-west, Ovambo farmers and Herero cattle-herders already occupied the northern half of present-day Namibia. The central highveld to the east of the Kalahari was dominated by the distinctive ancestral Sotho-Tswana lineage groups which were to spread and develop into the Tswana, northern Sotho and southern Sotho states of the nineteenth century (see Map 10.3, p. 159). To the east of the Drakensberg the Nguni-speaking people were organised into many small, clan-based chiefdoms in the valleys and foothills of the south-eastern lowveld. The clans and chiefdoms of Khoesan pastoralists were to be found in southern Namibia and all over the south-western Cape, interspersed with hunter-gatherers. The latter were also still to be found in small family-sized groups among the Sotho-Tswana of the southern highveld and the Nguni east of the Drakensberg. The southernmost Nguni, the Xhosa, in particular were mingling with Khoesan sheep- and cattle-herders in the Fish River region to form new Khoe/Xhosa chiefdoms such as the Gona and Gqunukhwebe (see Map 15.1).

Most of these southern African societies were more or less self-sufficient though there was always a certain amount of inter-regional trade. The Khoesan of the south-west, for instance, received copper and iron from the Tswana to their north. Some of these metals were passed on to the Xhosa in exchange for dagga and local tobacco. The Xhosa, who were not themselves smelters, received most of their iron from the central Nguni to their north-east. The northern Nguni and Tsonga of southern Mozambique, meanwhile, sold ivory and furs to Portuguese traders at Delagoa Bay in exchange for beads and other luxuries which were in due course traded on into the wider regional network.

The early Cape Colony: white settlement and Khoesan resistance, 1650–1770

Foundation of the Colony

During the sixteenth century, European sailing-ships, mainly Dutch and English, began making regular voyages round the southern tip of Africa to trade in India, south-east Asia and Indonesia (known to Europeans as 'the East Indies'). The south-western Cape was about halfway on this long sea

Map 15.1 South-western Cape, 1650–1700

Figure 15.1 Khoesan-European trading at Table Bay, seventeenth century. (From *A Relation of Some Yeares Travaile, Begunne 1626* by Sir Thomas Herbert)

voyage between Europe and Asia, and by the seventeenth century Table Bay had developed into a regular port of call for ships needing to replenish their supplies of fresh water and meat bought from local Khoesan herdsmen.

It has been estimated that by the mid-seventeenth century there were up to 50,000 Khoesan pastoralists living south-west of the Olifants and Breede rivers (see Map 15.2). Those clans living nearest Table Bay at first welcomed the new trading opportunity as they were able to sell off their 'surplus' old and sick animals in exchange for iron, copper, tobacco and beads. Peaceable trading soon turned to conflict, however, as the Khoesan asked for higher prices and the Europeans turned to raiding. (See p. 141, for the fate of at least one European ship's captain who attacked the Khoesan in this way.)

The Dutch trading monopoly, the Dutch East India Company, sought to solve these problems by forming a small permanent settlement on the southern shores of Table Bay in 1652. They hoped this would regularise the meat trade with the Khoesan and so keep prices down. At the same time the settlement would grow fresh fruit and vegetables for their ships and provide a hospital for sick sailors. The Dutch hoped in this way to monopolise the provisioning trade at the Cape and so profit from selling supplies to ships from other European nations. A fortress manned by Company soldiers was built to protect the settlement from attacks by rival European shipping.

Early Boer settlement and Khoesan reaction

The Khoesan of the south-western Cape, who had initially welcomed trading contact with passing ships, quickly regretted the presence of a permanent white settlement at the Cape. In the first place the Company demanded far more cattle than the natural surplus which the Khoesan were prepared to sell. In exchange for the very economic basis of Khoesan livelihood, the

For more information see www.palgrave.com/shillington

219

Map 15.2   The expansion of Boer settlement in the eighteenth century

Company were only prepared to offer luxuries such as copper, beads, tobacco and alcohol. Iron was quickly dropped as a trading item in case the Khoesan made it into spears to turn against the white settlement, and guns were never offered for sale for the same reason. Khoesan who would not willingly sell their livestock under these terms had their cattle seized, often upon some flimsy pretext such as the theft of some tobacco.

Furthermore, it was not long before the Company began releasing some of its soldiers from their contracts and allowing them to set up as independent freeburgher 'Boers' (Dutch word for farmer) on Khoesan grazing land along the Cape Peninsula south of Cape Town.

Faced with an expansion of white settlement on to their traditional summer grazing lands, however, the Khoesan managed to unite in armed opposition in 1659. They quickly learned the limits of the Europeans' primitive muzzle-loading guns and drove the freeburghers back to the protection of their fortress. But despite several brave attempts, the Khoesan were unable to overrun the fortress itself. After months of stalemate and a complete suspension of trade, the Khoesan alliance fell apart and their leaders were forced to come to terms. Van Riebeeck recorded in his journal the minutes of his meeting with the Khoesan leaders:

They spoke for a long time about our taking every day for our own use more of the land which had belonged to them from all ages, and on which they were accustomed to pasture their cattle. They also asked whether, if they were to come to Holland, they would be permitted to act in a similar manner, saying, 'it would not matter if you stayed at the Fort, but you come into the interior, selecting the best land for yourselves, and never once asking whether we like it, or whether it will put us to any inconvenience.' They therefore insisted very strenuously that they should again be allowed free access to the pasture. They objected that there was not enough grass for both their cattle and ours. Are we not right therefore to prevent you from getting any more cattle? For, if you get many cattle, you come and occupy our pasture with them, and then say the land is not wide enough for us both! Who, then, with the greatest degree of justice, should give way, the natural owner, or the foreign invader?' They insisted so much on this point that we told them they had now lost that land in war, and therefore could not expect to get it back. It was our intention to keep it.

(Adapted from extract printed in D. Moodie (ed.), *The Record,* facsimile reprint, Balkema, Cape Town, 1960, Vol. I, p. 205)

Thus, claiming 'right of conquest', van Riebeeck simply overrode all Khoesan protests and the freeburghers remained in occupation of the Cape Peninsula. Thereafter, successive Company commanders and the freeburghers themselves simply assumed that all Khoesan land, no matter where it be, was free and 'empty land' and theirs to take.

The main significance of the Dutch settlement at the Cape was that it was not simply like another powerful pastoral group. The establishment of a European export market at the Cape steadily drained the region of its indigenous livestock. This stimulated the Company's traders, and raiders, into ever-deeper penetration of the interior. In doing so the Company exploited age-old rivalries between Khoesan clans, turning them against each other for the sake of the cattle captured as booty. The brief Khoesan unity of 1659–60 was never recaptured in the struggle that followed. The second Khoe/Dutch war of 1673–7 was mainly a series of cattle-raids, as Company officers persuaded impoverished Khoesan clans to unite with them in attacking the powerful Cochoqua clan who had rejected the Company's trading approaches. The war concluded, leaving the Cochoqua weakened and the Company with a large booty of cattle and sheep.

The expansion of white settlement: farmers and trekboers

Following the second Khoe/Dutch war, settlement of freeburgher Boers expanded rapidly. Moving across the Cape Flats they settled the favourable agricultural valleys of present-day Paarl and Stellenbosch. Direct immigration was promoted by the Company during the 1680s and 1690s, and in the early 1700s the white population reached a thousand. By then the colony grew enough wheat to feed itself and sell a surplus for export. The freeburghers' other crops included fruit, especially grapes for wine. Their main source of farm labour was therefore slaves imported from Madagascar, Mozambique and Indonesia. For much of the eighteenth century slaves were imported at the rate of two or three hundred a year until by the end of the century they numbered 25,000 compared with a total white population of 21,000.

White agricultural settlement was necessarily confined to the moist, fertile valleys nearest the Cape and it was not from them that the main territorial threat to Khoesan survival came. By the early 1700s the pastoral 'trekboer' had emerged as the spearhead of white settlement penetrating the interior. As the best agricultural land was bought up by the wealthiest freeburghers and Company officials, increasing numbers of Boers sought to make a living from pastoralism and hunting in the drier interior. They were called 'trekboers' from the Dutch word *trek*, meaning 'to pull (a wagon)' because, like other pastoralists, they were so often on the move, for much of the time living in their ox-drawn wagons. The Company allowed them to claim huge 'farms' of 2500 hectares or more and as these were grazed out, they moved on to new pastures. Each son, and they had huge families, regarded it as his birthright to claim his own farm when he reached adulthood. In this way trekboer

Figure 15.2 Khoesan about to set up home, by the English artist Samuel Daniell, who was at the Cape 1801–3

settlement expanded rapidly as can be seen from Map 15.2. And they stocked their farms with sheep and cattle, traded or raided from their Khoesan rivals.

Patterns of resistance: the loss of Khoesan independence

Faced with the challenge of rapid trekboer expansion, the Khoesan followed one or more of three basic courses of action: direct military resistance, withdrawal into the interior or acceptance of a subservient position within Boer society. From the start, the Khoesan were at a serious disadvantage and some moved through all three courses of action in succession. Apart from the Boers' superior weaponry of horse and gun, the Khoesan of the south-western Cape were nearly wiped out altogether by a series of smallpox epidemics brought to the Cape aboard European ships. The first of these occurred in 1713. Lacking natural immunity to the disease, thousands of Khoesan perished, especially among those nearest Cape Town.

Direct military resistance usually took the form of a kind of guerrilla warfare. Deprived of their pastoral livelihood, stockless Khoesan took the traditional course of reverting to full-time hunter-gathering, only this time they were more like hunter-raiders, preying on the livestock of the Boers who had dispossessed them. The trekboers countered by forming local voluntary militia groups generally known as 'commandos'. In the frontier districts of the colony mounted commandos used speed, treachery and ambushes to hunt Khoesan 'Bushmen' to near-extermination. The weakness of the commando system was that it left Boer farms and families unprotected and so commandos could seldom afford to spend long in the field. And as the commandos disbanded, the Khoesan renewed their attacks. In parts of the north-eastern Cape, Khoesan resistance prevented effective trekboer settlement for much of the eighteenth century.

A plausible alternative to direct military resistance was withdrawal into the interior, beyond the boundaries of the expanding colony. Many Khoesan who tried this at first were soon overtaken by the advancing frontier of white settlement. But the main line of trekboer advance was eastwards. Thus several

Figure 15.3 Griqua men riding oxen

groups of Khoesan – the Kora, the Oorlams and the Griqua – by withdrawing far enough north, were able to achieve some degree of independence (see Map 15.2). A number of these peoples were of mixed Khoe, slave and European parentage but had found themselves rejected by colonial society. Some of their leaders were fugitives from colonial justice, such as the German Jan Bloem who headed a group of Kora raiders along the middle Orange, and Jager Afrikaner who escaped to the Orange River to lead a group of Oorlams hunter-traders and raiders.

Gradually during the course of the eighteenth century more and more Khoesan resigned themselves to their loss of economic and political independence. By agreeing to work for the Boers, especially as herdsmen and hunters, they retained some access to land. Though paid very little, if anything, for their labour, they were usually allowed to keep a few animals of their own. But with the loss of Khoesan independence went the loss of their cultural roots and even their language as they adopted the clothing, Dutch language and other cultural trappings of their 'masters'. Many served alongside Boers on commando raids against other Khoesan and, in due course, against the Xhosa.

One of the commonest sources of Khoesan servants was 'orphaned' children captured on commando raids in which their parents had been shot. These were shared out among the commandos as 'apprentices' and forced to work as unpaid servants until well into adult life. After that they had nowhere else to go. Indeed, 'apprenticeship' was such an important source of trekboer labour that it was often reason enough in itself for going on commando raids against the Khoesan. It was a system which a later generation of Boers carried on to the highveld in the nineteenth century and pursued with the utmost vigour.

No matter how thoroughly Khoesan were absorbed into Boer society, they remained part of a servile class, never allowed the full rights of citizens (burghers) of the colony. As such they were lumped together with freed slaves and people of mixed Khoe, slave and European ancestry. It was during the nineteenth century that white colonists began referring to this whole Dutch-speaking Khoesan, freed-slave and mixed-race servile population as 'Cape Coloured'.

The eastern advance of trekboer settlement reached the westernmost territory of the Xhosa by the late 1760s (see Map 15.2). Contact between colonists and the southernmost Nguni had been gradually building up during the course of the eighteenth century. Even before 1700 reports reached the Cape of a fertile, well-watered land, rich in cattle and populated by black people, which lay to the east of the Great Fish River. The Xhosa too, soon heard of the presence of white settlers in the far south-western Cape; but they did not view their presence there with undue alarm. They saw the new white colonists as fellow-pastoralists who, like the Khoesan, could in due course be absorbed into an expanding Xhosa society. One of the earliest points of direct contact between white colonists and Xhosa, in 1702, was tainted with violence as a party of 45 freeburghers raided east of the Gamtoos, attacked a group of Xhosa and captured several thousand Khoesan sheep and cattle. But conflict was not inevitable. During the course of the eighteenth century a few notable trekboer individuals blended into Xhosa society, marrying Xhosa wives, polygamously in Xhosa fashion, and providing important hunting and trading connections between Nguni and the colony.

The real conflict, which began in the 1770s, arose over land. The arrival of the first trekboer settlers on to grazing veld known as the 'Zuurveld' east of the Sundays River coincided with a period of further Xhosa expansion westwards. The importance of the Zuurveld was that it provided ideal summer grazing, but was not so good during autumn and winter. Pastoralists using the Zuurveld needed freedom to move their livestock between the summer grazing of the Zuurveld and the sweet winter grasses of the valleys or the hills to the north. At first, though the trekboers laid claim to vast estates as their 'farms', they only used a portion of them and Khoe/Xhosa pastoralists were able to graze their livestock across the same land as well. But trekboer expansion was now no longer able to move eastwards because of the density of Xhosa settlement beyond the Fish River. The amount of unclaimed land between the original isolated Boer farms of the Zuurveld was thus soon used up. This situation quickly led to conflict as Boer and Khoe/Xhosa pastoralists accused each other of cattle-stealing and using each other's land.

In earlier conflict with Khoesan herders, trekboers had been able to take advantage of a general lack of Khoesan unity and the relatively small size of most Khoesan clans. The trekboer advance eastwards had built up a momentum between 1700 and 1760 which the Khoesan resisted but were unable to halt. The Xhosa by contrast had a much larger population with a more close-knit social organisation. Though often split by internal political disputes, the Xhosa showed a remarkable degree of unity and determination when their territory was threatened by expanding trekboer settlement. As such they presented the colonists with a formidable opposition which trekboer commandos alone were unable to overcome.

Unbeknown to the participants, the war which began in 1779 was only the first of what was to prove a long series of nine so-called 'Frontier Wars'. Fought between colonists and Xhosa, these were to continue on and off over much of the next 100 years. The first three Cape/Xhosa wars fought between 1779 and 1803 were inconclusive affairs, which left the Xhosa and their Khoe/Xhosa allies, the Gqunukhwebe, in possession of most of the Zuurveld.

States and societies of the southern African interior, 1600–1800

Namibia and northern Botswana

By 1500 CE the pastoral Herero and agricultural Ovambo had moved into northern Namibia from the Okavango region of south-eastern Angola and north-western Botswana. As their herds increased in size the Herero moved their small clan-based settlements in search of new grazing territory. Skirting the coastal desert (see Map 15.3), they pressed southwards into the upland grasslands of central Namibia. To their east the closely related Mbanderu expanded towards the Ghanzi and Ngamiland region of present-day north-western Botswana. Meanwhile, from southern Namibia, Khoe-speaking Nama clans were similarly moving northwards with their flocks of fat-tailed sheep into the dry grasslands of the central highlands. The Kalahari and Namib deserts prevented further expansion eastward or westward. During the eighteenth century, therefore, there was increasing competition between Nama and Herero for the scarce grazing resources of the central Namibian highlands. This conflict was to lead to a series of wars which dominated much of the nineteenth-century history of the territory.

The Kalahari itself was dry and sandy, a region of scattered thorn-scrub and sparse seasonal grassveld. The lack of surface water made it unsuitable for cattle and it remained largely an inhospitable hunting-veld. Peopled only by small groups of hunter-gatherers, it was crossed periodically by long-distance hunting and trading parties from the Griqua and Tswana of the south and

Map 15.3   Southern Africa in the eighteenth century

225

east. North of the Kalahari during this period, agricultural peoples such as Mbukushu, Subiya and Yei were being pushed ever further into the better-watered Boteti, Okavango and Chobe regions of northern Botswana by the expansion of the emerging Lozi state of the upper Zambezi floodplain (see pp. 249–51). There they developed a specialised riverine lifestyle based mainly on hunting, fishing and the cultivation of millet.

Peoples of the highveld

To the east of the Kalahari, the Sotho-Tswana of the southern African highveld had developed a complex social and political order. The large political unit, or state, was most clearly developed among the Tswana of the central and western highveld. In the larger states the chief, king or *kgosi* ruled over a large capital town of up to 15,000–20,000 people by the late eighteenth century. Crops of millet, sorghum, pumpkins and beans were grown in fields cultivated close enough to the town to receive regular attention and protection from wild animals. Beyond the agricultural lands lay the grazing veld for their large herds of cattle and beyond that the hunting grounds. There might be a number of other smaller towns and villages beyond the central capital which acknowledged the overall authority of the *kgosi* by sending annual tribute of hunting-produce or crops. Refusal to pay tribute was a common cause of dispute and was a test of a strong ruler.

Much of the oral tradition for this period is concerned with splits which occurred within the larger Sotho-Tswana states. These were usually associated with succession disputes and were led by a disappointed claimant who would take his dependants, relatives and other supporters to found a new chiefdom out of reach of the tribute demands of his rival. Splits often occurred at times of natural crisis such as drought and so were probably also prompted by a genuine need or desire to find new water resources, arable land, hunting territory or grazing lands for expanding herds of cattle.

The *kgosi* was a religious as well as political leader of his people. As such, one of his most important duties was the conduct of the annual rain-making

Figure 15.4 A typical Tswana house of southern Africa, painted by the English artist Samuel Daniell in 1804

ceremony. This was held between September and November and was intended to herald the early spring rains, which signalled the ploughing and planting season that followed the long. dry months of winter. A *kgosi's* success and power was often judged by his ability to 'make rain'. Prolonged periods of drought, therefore, promoted the cause of rival claimants to the chieftaincy and made splits within the *morafe* more likely.

Counterbalancing this disruptive tendency, however, were the initiation ceremonies and the regimental system which followed them. Initiates for the ceremonies, by which adolescents passed into adulthood, were summoned by the *kgosi* every few years, usually when his own son or daughter was of the appropriate age. On conclusion of the ceremonies, which included indoctrination in customary duties and social behaviour and male circumcision, initiates were formed into age-regiments. The female regiments were an important source of communal agricultural labour at the disposal of the *kgosi*, while the primary function of the male regiments was as a reserve army which could be called up to defend the *morafe* or go on cattle-raids against neighbours. The summoning of the regiments, drawn from similarly-aged men or women from right across the wards and villages of the *morafe,* was an important unifying factor within the state.

At the beginning of the seventeenth century the main Tswana states of the central and western highveld were those of the Rolong, Hurutshe, Kwena and Kgatla. By the end of the eighteenth century these early state groupings had expanded, spread and subdivided to rule over much of the territory between the Vaal and the Kalahari, as can be seen from Map 15.3.

The main branch of the northern Sotho were the Pedi, an earlier offshoot from the Kgatla. While sending out their own offshoots, the main Pedi stronghold of the eighteenth century was the Leolu mountains of the north-eastern Transvaal. Further north towards the middle Limpopo valley lay the chiefdoms of the Lobedu and Venda, with their origins stemming from the Shona of Zimbabwe to their north.

The southern Sotho chiefdoms south of the Vaal tended not to form the large centralised states so characteristic of the Tswana to their north. Their chiefdoms were smaller and more numerous, being by the late eighteenth century scattered over much of the present-day Orange Free State and Lesotho. There were particular concentrations of chiefdoms in the valleys of the southern tributaries of the Vaal and in the fertile valley of the Caledon which flowed southwards into the Orange. The oldest of the southern Sotho chiefdoms are thought to have been those of the Fokeng, who spread into this area from the central highveld in the fifteenth century. Further expansion and subdivisions from north of the Vaal in subsequent centuries brought Tlokoa, Koena and Taung chiefdoms into this southern Sotho highveld.

Finally there was movement of people between southern highveld and south-eastern lowveld across the narrow passes of the Drakensberg just north of present-day Lesotho. The Nguni-speaking Zizi had probably penetrated the eastern part of the southern highveld even before the arrival of the Fokeng. Some arrivals on the highveld, like the Ndzundza of the eastern Transvaal, retained a distinctive degree of Nguni culture and language. Other small groups of Nguni origin blended more thoroughly into Sotho-Tswana society, such as the Lete of the western Transvaal, while certain clans of present-day Lesotho are thought to have Nguni-related origins. Likewise it is probable that certain Sotho practices and customs, in relation for instance to cattle-keeping and initiation, were passed through the Drakensberg to the Nguni of the lowveld.

The south-eastern lowveld

Until the latter part of the eighteenth century the chiefdoms of the Nguni were generally smaller than those of the Sotho-Tswana of the central and western highveld. This may have been partly the result of the geography of the region. The lowveld to the south-east of the Drakensberg received generally higher rainfall than the highveld to the north-west. It was also much hillier territory. The region was cut by the deep valleys of numerous rivers flowing down from mountain to sea. There was thus a wide variety of arable and grazing resources in the region, from the drier but fertile valley-bottoms to the well-watered woodlands of the hills. Small family-sized homesteads were therefore able to live almost independently of each other, provided they were free to move their cattle between the differing grasslands of uplands and valleys according to season. While population levels and sizes of herds remained low, this presented little problem. Related homesteads were grouped into chiefdoms and when there were succession disputes, unsuccessful claimants were able to move off and found new chieftaincies in hitherto little-used regions. In doing so they tended to absorb into their ranks Khoesan whom they found there. In fact the relatively high rate of Nguni-Khoe absorption led to the development of distinctive Khoesan 'click' sounds in the Nguni languages.

We have already seen above how the southernmost Nguni, the Xhosa, were expanding westwards and absorbing Khoesan chiefdoms until they came into violent conflict in the late eighteenth century with the vanguard of the trekboers, expanding eastwards from the Cape Colony. For the central and northern Nguni the eighteenth century too was a period of significant developments which, in the long term, were to prove even more significant for the peoples of the southern African interior in the early nineteenth century.

During the course of the eighteenth century a number of northern Nguni chiefdoms in particular expanded and absorbed minor chiefdoms into their

Figure 15.5 The interior of a Zulu homestead on the Tugela River. The livestock are kept within the inner barricade. (Engraving by an unnamed artist in the *Illustrated London News*)

ranks. This appears to have been related to heightened competition over the resources of the region. Maize, introduced from America by the Portuguese through Delagoa Bay, had begun to be cultivated widely in the region. It yielded much heavier crops than native African sorghum, provided rainfall levels were high. And the latter half of the eighteenth century was a period of unusually high rainfall. With more food available, population expanded and more land was brought into cultivation. Cattle too thrived and multiplied on the much improved pasture and more woodland was cut down to expose new grazing veld. At the same time, the development of long-distance trade with the Tsonga and Portuguese at Delagoa Bay encouraged the growth of northern Nguni states. The desire to control the export of ivory heightened competition for the rich hunting grounds of the coastal forest belt.

Like the Sotho-Tswana of the highveld, the Nguni held initiation ceremonies and formed age-regiments, the practice possibly being adopted from the Sotho-Tswana in the first place. As chiefdoms grew in size and competition between them for limited resources became more marked, the role of the armed regiments grew ever more significant.

By the late eighteenth century the northern Nguni chiefdoms had amalgamated into three main centralised kingdoms, the Ngwane of Sobhuza, the Ndwandwe of Zwide and the Mthethwa of Dingiswayo (see Map 15.3). Among the number of small Nguni groups which by the turn of the century had been absorbed into the expanding Mthethwa federation was the chiefdom of the Zulu. In the closing years of the century the period of good rainfall was replaced by a prolonged drought and the expanding production of more than a generation was brought to a dramatic end. Control of scarce resources became vital for survival. That struggle for survival, and its repercussions which were felt throughout the breadth of the southern African interior, remain the subject of a later chapter (pp. 263–71).

chapter 16

West Africa in the nineteenth century and the ending of the slave trade

Islamic jihads in the western Sudan

Origins: the Fulbe (or Fulani)

In the early nineteenth century the political map of western Africa was dramatically changed as a succession of wars swept the savannah regions of west Africa. The political leaders of these military uprisings justified their wars in the name of Islam, claiming that they were waging Islamic '*jihad*'. This implied they were waging war against 'the unbeliever'; and yet, in many cases these wars pitched Muslim against Muslim. In reality, these were wars for the political control of an existing state or the creation of a new state out of the remnants of several former states. The Muslim leaders who formed the spearhead of this movement were drawn largely from people of Fulbe origin.

As we saw in Chapter 7 (p. 113), the Fulbe were a distinctive, mainly pastoralist people who had spread across much of the west African savannah by the seventeenth century. They retained their separate identity and usually took no part in the political life of the states or chiefdoms among whom they had settled. This may have suited them at first, but in due course they found themselves under increasing pressure from the settled agricultural population and their rulers. The Fulbe were often resented as intruders and their grazing lands and trading rights were restricted. At the same time they were subjected to increasingly heavy demands for tribute and taxation.

Their sense of isolation from the people among whom they were settled may help explain why many Fulbe at this time turned to Islam. This was partly through contact with the Muslim traders of the towns and partly through contact with Tuareg pastoralists of the Sahel. Islam gave the Fulbe an added sense of unity and purpose. And Islamic law, the *shari'a*, provided an alternative model of government with which to compare and confront their rulers. By the early eighteenth century a number of Fulbe Muslim clans were rivalling the Tuareg as the leading Islamic scholars of west Africa. Conversion of 'the unbeliever' was an essential part of Muslim duty and those Fulbe Muslim teachers who preached '*jihad*' against the infidel may have been drawing inspiration from earlier religious reforming movements such as the Almoravids of the eleventh century (see above, Chapter 7, pp. 97–8). Despite the fact that many of these '*jihads*' were not in fact against 'unbelievers', the waging of one war in the name of Islam frequently served to inspire the waging of another such war elsewhere.

The 'jihads' of Futa Jalon and Futa Toro

The west African '*jihadist*' movement of the eighteenth and early nineteenth centuries began in the highlands of Futa Jalon in what is now the modern

Map 16.1 Jihadist states of the western Sudan to *c*.1840

state of Guinea. Fulbe pastoralists had settled in these highlands from the early 1500s. The local farming population was organised in a series of small village chiefdoms. As their herds increased in size the Fulbe felt the pressure of the restrictions and taxation of the farmers, but in Islam they found their salvation. In 1725 the Fulbe rose in rebellion against their rulers and with the support of Muslim traders they waged holy war against the settled farmers who, for the most part, continued to practice their indigenous religion. It was 1750 before their conquest was complete. By then they had brought the region under Islamic law and created a Fulbe-dominated state. As we saw in Chapter 12 (p. 182), their wars of conquest produced a surplus of captives who were sold into slavery to European traders at the coast.

The Futa Jalon *jihad* inspired a similar movement to the south of the lower Senegal. Here between 1769 and 1776 Muslim Tukolor and Fulbe waged successful war against their neighbours until they had created their new Muslim state of Futa Toro and brought it under the rule of *shari'a* law.

Usman dan Fodio and the founding of the Sokoto caliphate

The eighteenth-century wars that saw the foundation of Futa Jalon and Futa Toro provided inspiration for later Muslim teachers elsewhere in western Africa. In the early nineteenth century a series of wars were waged in the name of '*jihad*' within the Hausa states of the northern regions of modern Nigeria. From these wars emerged the Sokoto caliphate or empire – the largest single west African state of the early nineteenth century. The leader and inspirer of the Sokoto revolution was Usman dan Fodio, son of a Fulbe Muslim teacher in the northern Hausa state of Gobir. (In this eastern region of west Africa the Fulbe were known by the Hausa name Fulani.)

Although Usman never went on pilgrimage to Mecca, he was widely educated as a Muslim scholar and undoubtedly knew about the west African '*jihads*' of Futa Jalon and Futa Toro. He completed his schooling at Agades under the influence of the revolutionary Tuareg holy man Jibril ibn 'Umar, who preached the value and importance of *jihad*. Usman began his preaching in Gobir as a young man in the 1770s. His two main concerns were the conversion of those Fulani pastoralists who still clung to indigenous religious beliefs, and the religious and social reform of the Muslim Hausa rulers, whom he judged to be failing to follow the strict principles of *shari'a*. At this stage he hoped to achieve his ends by the peaceful preaching of reform. However, he grew increasingly critical of the Hausa government whom he accused of corruption and injustice (see pp. 192–3). In this he had the support of Fulani pastoralists, Muslim and non-Muslim, who particularly resented the Hausa's taxation of their cattle.

Usman's reputation as a holy man and preacher quickly spread through the Muslim communities of Hausaland. It was even rumoured among some of his more enthusiastic supporters that he was the Mahdi, the prophesied Muslim leader who would prepare the faithful for the end of the world and the second coming of Muhammad. By the 1790s Usman had gathered a considerable following at Degel near the border of Gobir and Kebbi. His growing power and influence were resented by the rulers of Gobir, who tried to restrict his movements and prevent him making further conversions.

A crisis was reached in the early 1800s when the king, Yunfa, tried to assassinate Usman. In imitation of the Prophet Muhammad's *hijra* from Mecca in 622, Usman and his followers withdrew from Gobir. When Yunfa sent his cavalry against them in 1804, he suffered a severe defeat. This marked the beginning of Usman's '*jihad*'.

The revolution quickly spread through the Muslim and Fulani communities of Hausaland. It was not a single religious war, but a series of simultaneous uprisings against the rule of the Hausa aristocracy. The capital of Gobir was finally captured in 1808, by which time Kebbi, Zamfara, Zaria, Katsina and Kano had fallen to the '*jihadists*'. The Hausa rulers fell because they failed to gain the support of the oppressed Hausa peasantry, and because they did not act in unison. Centuries of inter-state rivalry had proved their final undoing.

Usman retired into religious life, and the active leadership of the new Islamic empire was taken over by his brother Abdullahi and his son Muhammad Bello. A new capital was built at Sokoto in Kebbi and the so-called *jihad* was pursued with vigour, particularly in the south and east. Western Borno was captured and Adamawa was added to the empire. By the time of Usman's death in 1817 the Sokoto empire stretched from Songhay in the west to the headwaters of the Benue in the east. There followed further extension in the south as Nupe and the Yoruba state of Ilorin were brought within the empire. It has been estimated that by the time of Muhammad Bello's death in 1837 the empire or caliphate of Sokoto had a population of some ten million people, larger than that of any west African state before it.

The Sokoto caliphate

The Sokoto empire had been achieved through a series of local risings, acting independently but with the support and approval of the caliph. The movement had been led by rural Fulani and Muslim Hausa townsmen. A number of Fulani pastoralists, of doubtful Muslim conviction, used it as an opportunity to loot the towns. This turned many of the Hausa against the movement. But once the conquests were complete and the Hausa aristocracy were removed, the empire settled down and the economic life of the region resumed.

The empire consisted of a number of separate Muslim emirates that acted independently in local matters, but took their religious authority from the caliph at Sokoto. And since it was an Islamic religious state, political power was equated with religious authority. The emirs visited Sokoto once a year to show their loyalty to the caliph and submit an annual tribute. Beyond that, the economy of Hausaland was soon re-established along the same sort of lines as before. The old Hausa aristocracy had been replaced by a new Fulani one, but they became increasingly 'Hausaised', adopting Hausa language and culture. They were careful not to become as corrupt as their predecessors, and greater respect for Islamic law ensured greater justice for the general Hausa population.

Islam and literacy spread more widely through the population, and the unity of Islam brought an end to the destructive wars of inter-state rivalry. Trade flourished and Kano in particular became a major market centre. Those who benefited least were the Hausa peasantry, who had merely exchanged one master for another. Slavery too remained an essential part of the economic life of the Sokoto caliphate: both in domestic service and working on the land to feed the towns. There remained, even within the empire, pockets of non-Muslim resistance and *jihads* against these provided a constant source of captives for pressing into slavery.

Borno in the nineteenth century

When Fulani pastoralists rose in rebellion against the Muslim sultanate of Borno, they quickly seized control of the western regions and even drove the *Mai* from his capital of Birni Ngazargamu. But Borno was not another Hausaland. It had a long and deep Islamic tradition: it was not ripe for political revolution in the name of Islam, and the Kanuri of Borno were not prepared to accept Fulani domination. Militarily, Borno was saved by a remarkable religious leader from Kanem known as Muhammad al-Kanemi. (In fact al-Kanemi was reputed to have been born in Fezzan, once the northernmost province of Borno-Kanem.) Al-Kanemi organised resistance and protested to the caliph of Sokoto that Borno was already an Islamic state, so there was no justification to wage *jihad* against it. At the same time, he backed up his protests by introducing religious and legal reforms in Borno.

Al-Kanemi ruled the sultanate of Borno in all but name, while the *Mai* remained little more than a figurehead. On his death in 1837, al-Kanemi was succeeded as *shehu* (religious leader) by his son Umar. In 1846 Mai Ibrahim tried to regain control by organising an invasion of Borno from the central Sudanic sultanate of Wadai, but his attempt failed and he was captured and executed. Ibrahim was last in the Saifawa line and with his death ended one of Africa's longest ruling dynasties.

Shehu Umar now became undisputed ruler, though Borno never regained its former position of wealth and prominence. In the west it had lost its hold of eastern Hausaland to the emirs of Sokoto. In the north and east it lost much of its access to the trans-Saharan trade to the sultanate of Wadai, which opened up direct links to Benghazi in north Africa. Within Borno itself this further emphasised the division between wealthy rulers and oppressed peasantry. With the loss of trading income, the *shehus* of Borno demanded ever higher taxes from the already hard-pressed peasantry.

In the final decade of the nineteenth century, as Borno was about to fall to European imperialism, it was conquered from the east by a military genius from the Nilotic savannah named Rabih ibn Fadl Allah. It was he who organised seven years of resistance to French imperial conquest.

233

Map 16.2   The Tukolor and Mandinka empires

The Tukolor empire of al-Hajj Umar

Meanwhile to the west of Sokoto, Usman dan Fodio's example had inspired further Muslim revolutions. In 1818 Fulbe in the upper Niger 'delta' region – both Muslim and non-Muslim – rebelled against their local rulers and created the Fulbe-dominated state of Masina. This new state was later to become part of the Tukolor empire which rose from further to the west. The revolution that created the Tukolor empire was led by a Muslim preacher from Futa Toro named al-Hajj Umar.

Umar was strongly influenced by the Usman revolution that had created the Sokoto caliphate. In 1826 Umar set off on a lengthy pilgrimage to Mecca. On his return he passed through al-Kanemi's Borno and then spent several years at Muhammad Bello's court in Sokoto, during which time he married at least one of the caliph's daughters.

Figure 16.1   The Segu palace of Ahmadu, ruler of the Tukolor empire after the death of al-Hajj Umar in 1864

During the 1840s Umar built up a large following on the borders of Futa Jalon. From there he traded non-Muslim captives in exchange for firearms with which to modernise his army. It was clear by this time that Umar was determined to create an Islamic state by force of arms. Unable to capture his home region of Futa Toro because of the French presence at Medina on the Senegal River, Umar pursued his '*jihad*' towards the north-east. By 1854 he had taken the Bamana kingdom of Kaarta and in the early 1860s he extended his conquests through the upper Niger states of Segu and Masina. But Umar's emphasis on conquest meant that he failed to establish a stable administration which would survive his death. And his policy of forced conversion to Islam provoked spirited resistance, especially among the Bamana of upper Senegal. Following Umar's death in 1864, the Tukolor empire was seriously weakened by internal revolts and lack of unity among his sons and closest followers. It was a situation which the French were able to exploit to their advantage in the 1880s and 1890s.

Samori Touré and the rise of the Mandinka empire

Meanwhile to the south of the Tukolor empire there arose the Mandinka empire of Samori Touré. He came from a non-Muslim Dyula trading family who lived in the region of the upper Niger basin to the east of Futa Jalon. As a young man in the 1860s he built up and trained a force of well-armed soldiers to protect the trading interests of his family. Theirs was one of a number of Mandinka-speaking states based on Dyula trading towns. (The Mandinka, like the Malinke, were a branch of the Mande-speaking peoples who had formed the heartland of the ancient empire of Mali; see above,

Figure 16.2 Portrait of Samori Touré

Chapter 7, pp. 104–8.) Samori's family were engaged in trade in gold-dust from Buré and cattle from Futa Jalon. Under Samori's leadership they used their extensive Dyula connections to import firearms from the coast and so to strengthen and modernise their army.

Between 1865 and 1875 Samori conquered surrounding Dyula states and built up a powerful Mandinka kingdom. The unity which he established in the region eased trade and brought greater prosperity to the merchants. At some time in his youth Samori became a Muslim, and while not pursuing a *jihad* in the manner of some of his contemporaries, he used Islam to unite and strengthen his kingdom. He promoted Muslim education and the building of mosques and he used Islamic law as a basis for his rule. During the late 1870s Samori extended his conquests to include the Bure goldfields in the north and down the upper Niger valley towards modern Bamako. By the early 1880s he had turned his trading kingdom into a huge empire, the third largest in western Africa (after Sokoto and Tukolor). In the view of many of Samori's Mandinka subjects he was reuniting the Mande-speaking peoples in the manner of the ancient empire of Mali.

Besides the spread of Islam, the strength of Samori's army was a major unifying factor in the creation of the Mandinka empire. He incorporated male captives into the army rather than selling them as slaves. This increased local loyalties to Samori and the state. He imported the latest quick-loading rifles from the Sierra Leone port of Freetown and he used local ironsmiths to repair and manufacture muzzle-loading guns.

Samori's Mandinka empire was tragically short-lived. Constantly engaged in defending his conquests from outside invasion, Samori had little opportunity to devote his considerable talents to further development within the state. As it was, the extent of peace and security within the empire impressed those visitors who saw it. But in 1881 the Mandinka had their first clash with the French, who were extending their colonial control westwards from the upper Senegal River (see pp. 314–18). Though the final struggle was postponed by a treaty with the French, the Mandinka army was one of the major forces of resistance to French conquest in west Africa in the final decade of the century.

The ending of the Atlantic slave trade

While the Islamic reformist movement of the early nineteenth century was changing the political pattern of the western Sudan, a reformist movement of a different kind was taking place within the European nations responsible for the promotion and conduct of the transatlantic trade in slaves.

During the course of the eighteenth century Britain overtook all other European nations as the single largest exporter of Africans from Africa. By the end of the century more than half the captives transported from west Africa were carried across the Atlantic in British ships. And yet, within a few years Britain had become in 1807 the first major European nation to abolish the trade in slaves. (The revolutionary government in France imposed a temporary French ban in the early 1790s, but this was soon lifted and French trading continued. The Danish government had in fact banned its citizens from the trade in 1805.) This did not abolish the institution of slavery itself, but it was an important first step in that direction. It made it illegal for British subjects to transport captive Africans across the Atlantic for sale into slavery. The newly independent United States of America officially banned its subjects from engaging in the trade in 1808 and Holland and France followed in 1814 and 1817 respectively.

The history of the abolition movement lies beyond the scope of this book. Nevertheless, it is important to understand something of the economic motivation that lay behind the abolitionists' cause. From it stemmed important changes in the relationships between Europeans and west Africans in the course of the nineteenth century. These were to culminate in the notorious 'Scramble for Africa' of the 1880s and 1890s.

For more information see www.palgrave.com/shillington

The American War of Independence against Britain (1776–83) and the French Revolution (1789) in the name of 'Liberty, Equality and Fraternity' provided important stimulation for the abolitionist cause. There was a growing belief among European intellectuals in the universal right of human beings to freedom and equality. But though a small body of high-minded Europeans argued long and hard against the institution of slavery, it was by no means an entirely humanitarian, or even a solely European initiative, which finally led to abolition. The African victims of slavery and the slave trade had struggled against their loss of liberty from the start and we shall consider their role in a moment. The most important factor leading to abolition was that by the early nineteenth century slavery and the slave trade were in many respects becoming uneconomic.

The economic background to abolition

A rapid expansion in Caribbean sugar plantations in the late eighteenth century had led to overproduction and a fall in the selling price of sugar. The French in particular, with huge new plantations and modern machinery, were flooding the market with cheaper sugar, which undercut their less-efficient British rivals. At the same time, west African rulers and merchants were charging higher prices for the sale of their captives. This reduced European profit levels still further. Plantation-owners were no longer able to pay their debts to European bankers. The latter, who had previously invested heavily in sugar and the slave trade, now found it more profitable to invest in new manufacturing industries at home. This was particularly the case in Britain, which was by then leading the world in the rising new 'Industrial Revolution'.

Once-powerful plantation-owners lost their influence with the British government in favour of the new industrialists. British manufacturers found that cheap wage-labour in European factories was more efficient and less expensive than plantation slavery. And, they argued, 'free' paid workers had to spend part of their wages on the clothing, pottery and metal goods manufactured by the industrialists. This provided the capitalist factory-owners with their own home markets. In due course, however, new machinery and steam-power produced even more and cheaper goods. The manufacturers and their bankers were soon seeking new markets abroad and they looked again at Africa. They saw that if Africans were left in Africa, instead of being removed by the slave trade, they would be able to do two things from which Europeans could profit. They could provide Europe with important raw materials and in exchange they could buy the goods produced in Europe's new factories. From the early 1800s, therefore, Europeans and their governments began to regard Africa as a source of raw materials and a market for manufactured goods rather than simply as a source of slave labour.

African resistance and the abolition of slavery

Another important factor prompting the abolition of slavery and the slave trade at this time was the struggle of Africans themselves to obtain their own freedom. This point is one that is often given little prominence in the history of Africa and the slave trade. In opposing their enslavement and the slave trade, Africans used both the pen and the sword.

In England the small band of eighteenth-century abolitionists were joined and stimulated in their struggle by the campaigns and publications of Olaudah Equiano (see Figure 16.4) and Ottobah Cugoano. Both men were ex-slaves from west Africa who had gained their freedom in England and became active in the anti-slavery movement. Broadly educated and anglicised in culture, both produced books in the late 1780s publicising the evils of the trade and strongly condemning the system of slavery. Equiano's autobiography became a best-seller in its day as he toured England making speeches and selling copies of his book. Cugoano proposed in 1787 that a British naval squadron should patrol west African waters to suppress the trade. It was to be another 30 years, however, before this idea was put into practice. Equiano and Cugoano had their counterparts in France and America. The eloquence of these Africans, speaking and writing from their own personal experience, played more than a minor part in the movement for abolition.

From the very beginning of the slave trade, captive Africans had, to the best of their ability, resisted their enslavement. Their attempts were often desperate and almost suicidal. On board ship for the transatlantic passage, revolts were not uncommon and sailors had to be heavily armed and constantly on their guard. Once in the Americas and Caribbean islands, enslaved Africans seized almost any opportunity to escape from their bondage. An example of successful early revolt and resistance occurred in Brazil in the seventeenth century. Here 'runaway' slaves set up an independent black republic known as 'Palmares'. It lasted for about a hundred years before it was eventually overcome by the Portuguese. In the eighteenth and early nineteenth centuries frequent slave revolts made the institution of slavery increasingly unsafe and expensive to maintain. In Jamaica, for instance, escapers known as 'Maroons' gathered in the central highlands where they established their own self-governing farming community. They survived frequent government attempts to oust them and their presence was a constant encouragement for those still enslaved to join them.

Figure 16.4 Portrait of the anti-slavery campaigner Olaudah Equiano by Daniel Orme, 1789. (Plate LVIII from *The Interesting Narrative of the Life of Olaudah Equiano, or Gustavus Vassa, the African … Second edition*)

The most dramatic of all slave revolts occurred in the French island colony of St Domingue (modern Haiti). This was France's major sugar-producing island. Plantation production had increased so rapidly in the late eighteenth century that by the early 1790s St Domingue contained some 400,000 slaves. Under the leadership of one of their number, known by the French name of Toussaint L'Ouverture, the slaves of St Domingue rose against and killed their white French masters in 1791. They beat off invasions by both French and British navies and established the independent 'Republic of Haiti' in 1803. The Haitian revolution had a major impact upon the willingness of European governments and bankers to continue to support the slave trade. Meanwhile, in the plantation colonies, especially in the Caribbean islands, the impact of the Haitian revolution cannot be overestimated. It was an inspiration for other enslaved Africans to revolt; and it was a powerful warning to the slave-owners and their governments as to what might happen if they continued to maintain their violent and inhumane system.

Once the British government had decided on abolition it was determined to force its decision upon other European nations. Only if the slave trade was altogether stopped or drastically reduced could British manufacturers and merchants hope to make significant future profits out of other trade with Africa. So Britain, which by then had the strongest navy in the world, set up an 'Anti-Slavery Squadron' to patrol west African waters and use force to stop

239

Figure 16.5 The British navy anti-slavery squadron attacks a slave establishment on the Solyman River, Sierra Leone, 1849. (From *Illustrated London News*, 14 April 1849)

the trade. Despite these efforts, large numbers of ships escaped the British patrols. The transatlantic slave trade continued so long as plantation slavery itself continued. Indeed, for a short period in the early nineteenth century imports of slaves into Cuba and Brazil actually increased. Slavery itself was not finally abolished until 1834 in British colonies, 1848 in French ones, 1860 in Cuba, 1865 in the southern United States and 1888 in Brazil. It has been estimated that a further 1.3 million Africans were transported into slavery across the Atlantic between 1807 and 1888.

West African commerce in the nineteenth century

For two or three centuries the slave trade had dominated trade along the west African coast. It had disrupted and distorted developments in the interior. The use of slave labour became more widespread, and local agricultural production was often disrupted by the greater level of violence and warfare. There were deeper class divisions in society between rich traders and rulers on the one hand, and the poor peasantry and the enslaved on the other. Nevertheless, beneath the surface there were important positive developments. African farmers experimented with, and developed, the growing of new crops from the Americas, especially maize and cassava. At the same time, trade in the age-old commodities of west Africa had continued to develop between African communities themselves, as well as to Europeans at the coast or across the Sahara to north Africa. Thus as Europeans gradually outlawed the slave trade, they found west Africa a fertile field for what they referred to as 'legitimate commerce'. The term was used to mean anything other than human trafficking, but it was a useful cover for the true nature of trading relations in west Africa in this pre-colonial period. As we shall see below, from the African viewpoint, European attempts to muscle in on their trading networks were anything but 'legitimate'.

During the first half of the nineteenth century a range of west African

Map 16.3   West African exports in the nineteenth century

commodities supplanted the export of captives. Production was organised by west African rulers and merchants, who often made use of internal slave labour for cash-crop plantations and for transport. Exports included gum arabic from Senegal. Gum arabic is a hardened-resin substance extracted from acacia trees found in the savannah woodlands north of the Senegal River. In the nineteenth century it was used for fixing coloured dyes in printed cloth in the textile factories of Europe. Other exports were groundnuts from Guinea and palm oil from most of the coastal forest zones. Now that Asante had completed its main period of expansion, its sale of captives declined and gold once more became that region's principal export commodity.

Some states, such as Dahomey, which lacked obvious alternatives, continued with the export of people for much of the nineteenth century. And the collapse of the old Oyo empire, torn apart by civil wars in the 1830s and 1840s, produced a major new source of war-captives for export at Lagos and Badagry. At the same time, a number of Niger delta states, such as Bonny and Brass, continued to export Igbo captives, despite vigorous attempts at suppression by British gunships and the local African exporters of palm oil. The large-scale export of captives from west Africa eventually ceased in the 1860s after the markets of Cuba and the United States had been closed.

By the middle of the nineteenth century, palm oil had become west Africa's major overseas export. It was used in industrial Europe for the manufacture of soap; and in the early part of the century it was a major lubricant for industrial machinery before the development of petroleum oil from the 1850s. Although oil-palm grew throughout the forest zone, the most important region for its large-scale production and export was the Niger River delta and the Cross River valley. The Efik of Old Calabar had been among the first to develop palm-oil plantations with the use of slave labour, even before the British abolition of 1807. In the Niger delta network the Ijo had long used their huge war canoes for transporting Igbo captives from the up-river

241

Figure 16.6 Trading canoes on the Niger River, nineteenth-century engraving

regions for sale at the coast. They now turned their energies to transporting palm oil. As such they became important middlemen in the trade between individual Igbo producers and the European traders at the coast.

With the vast increase in palm-oil trade that developed in the 1840s and 1850s British traders began to push up the Niger in order to cut out the Ijo middlemen and deal directly with the Igbo. As European demand for oil rose, heightened competition for the trade led to a series of wars among the delta states. British traders exploited these rivalries and with a mixture of

Figure 16.7 A trading station on the lower Niger in the 1890s persuasion and force they gradually extended control over the trade of the delta during the second half of the century. But this was only part of a more general trend that was developing along the west African coast by the mid-nineteenth century.

Thus the development of west Africa's export trade in raw materials did not provide African states with any real opportunity to develop their own economic strength and independence. In the first place, those that benefited from the trade were a small minority of wealthy rulers and merchants. There was little improvement in the social and economic well-being of the bulk of the population. Indeed, many saw their living conditions and levels of personal freedom decline as their labour was harnessed to increased production and transport for the export trade. Second, the three principal imports from Europe – cloth, alcohol and firearms – did nothing to strengthen indigenous African economies. The first item tended merely to undermine indigenous African craft industry, while the sense of well-being engendered by the second was purely illusory. The third item, firearms, may have enabled rulers to strengthen their grip over their subjects and neighbours. But they were never sufficiently modern and up-to-date to enable them to do much more than 'put up a good fight' against the machine-guns and artillery of the European armies sent against them at the end of the century. Finally, those states that did develop their export trade soon found their independence threatened by direct interference from their European trading partners.

As the century progressed, European traders, backed up by their governments, made increasingly strenuous efforts to control west Africa's internal trade. They sought to reduce their own costs and to maximise profits by cutting out both the African middlemen and their European competitors. It was this heightened level of European trading competition which in part was to lead to the 'take-off' of the 'Scramble for Africa' in the 1870s and 1880s. As such, the growing European mercantile penetration of west Africa will be discussed further in Chapters 20 and 21 (pp. 303–4, 316–21).

It remains in this chapter to say something about two important 'African' settlements which developed on the west coast of Africa in the early nineteenth century.

Sierra Leone and Liberia

The foundation and growth of Sierra Leone and Liberia were direct results of the abolition of slavery and the slave trade.

Sierra Leone was founded as a solution to the perceived 'problem' of the large number of unemployed black people who had settled in England, especially London, in the aftermath of the American War of Independence (1775–83). Many black, former slaves, had fought for the British in that war and had been forced into exile as a consequence of their 'loyalist' allegiance. The British had shipped most of them to Nova Scotia with lavish promises of land and freedom: promises that were not kept. Some of them had come to England, hoping for better treatment, but all they faced was unemployment and poverty.

Leading members of the British abolitionist movement, among them Olaudah Equiano, felt that they would face better opportunities in a free, Christian settlement on the coast of west Africa. The British Government provided some initial funding for the scheme and a ship to convey them. Threatened with prosecution for vagrancy if they did not go, 411 men, women and children boarded the ship bound for west Africa and an uncertain future. Nearly half of them died on the voyage and the survivors landed on the peninsula of modern Freetown in May 1787. They knew virtually nothing about how to survive in this tropical rural environment and by 1790, following a conflict with local inhabitants, most of them were dead.

Meanwhile the British abolitionists had set up a trading company to support the project and in 1792 they persuaded some 1200 free black 'loyalists' from Nova Scotia to join the settlement in Sierra Leone. These were followed in 1795 by a further settlement of 500 from Nova Scotia: this time they were former Jamaican Maroons who had been exiled to Nova Scotia following their unsuccessful rebellion in Jamaica in 1775. The British trading company, renamed the Sierra Leone Company, ran the colony and appointed its governors. The Nova Scotians found none of the representative government that they had been promised and their rebellion in 1800 against the British governor's dictatorial policies was firmly crushed. Conflict with the local Temne population turned to open warfare in 1801 and in 1807 the Temne were forced to sign over their rights to the land settled by the Sierra Leone Company.

In 1808 the British government took over the settlement from the Company and declared it a 'crown colony'. The previous year the British had banned the use of British ships in the transatlantic slave trade and they established a naval Anti-Slavery Squadron to patrol the west African coast and enforce the ban. In the years that followed, the British used their Sierra Leone colony as a base for settling freed blacks whom they released from captured slaving ships. The bulk of these 're-captives' originated from among the Yoruba

Figure 16.8 The harbour, Freetown: the ex-governor is leaving, which explains all the excitement. (Engraving by an unnamed artist in the *Illustrated London News*, 1854)

and Igbo peoples of modern Nigeria (the main source of west African slave exports in the early nineteenth century). The original settlers, known collectively as 'Creoles', were ardent Christians and strongly anglicised in character. Christian missionaries from Britain helped spread Christianity and European-style education among the new arrivals and the growing Creole population.

Sierra Leone had originally been founded as a settlement of farmers, but many Creoles quickly turned to trade as an easier way to make a living. Some made fortunes out of exporting commodities like timber, groundnuts and palm oil. Others became craftsmen, clerical workers, teachers and missionaries. Many travelled widely and were pioneers of Christianity and 'Western' education among the peoples of west Africa. The Yoruba scholar Samuel Ajayi Crowther, a founding student of Sierra Leone's Fourah Bay College, became west Africa's first African bishop and the leader of an important Christian mission to the Niger (see pp. 298–9). He also produced the first written grammar of the Yoruba language. He and others like him made a major contribution to the intellectual development of west Africa in the nineteenth century.

The neighbouring settlement of Liberia was founded in 1822 by freed African Americans from the United States of America. It was organised by the American Colonisation Society – a body of white Americans who believed that the increasing number of freed people in the southern states was a danger to the maintenance of other blacks in slavery. Representatives of the Colonisation Society forced local African chiefs in the Cape Mesurado area to sell them land by threatening them at gun-point. In the decade that followed, further settlements of freed African Americans were made along the coastline from Cape Palmas to Sherbo island.

Though originally organised by American whites, educated blacks soon

Map 16.4   Sierra Leone and Liberia in *c.*1880

245

took over the administration of the settlement. In 1847 they declared their colony the independent republic of 'Liberia'. (The name was derived from the Latin word *liber,* meaning 'free'.) It had a constitution modelled on that of the United States and its capital, Monrovia, was named after the American president, Monroe. Integration with the local population was gradually extended, though the original settlers and their descendants dominated the political, economic and intellectual life of the country. Education expanded and during the course of the nineteenth century, Liberia, like Sierra Leone, produced a number of outstanding African intellectuals. Trade in palm oil, coffee, ivory and camwood (from the wood of a west African tree, used for making red dyes in the European textile industry), became the country's major exports, though profits from these declined in the later nineteenth century. Individual Liberian merchants could not compete with powerful European rivals who established permanent bases and colonies along the west African coast. Nevertheless, despite internal political problems and corruption in the civil service, Liberia maintained a fragile independence. It survived even the European 'scramble' at the end of the century.

17

Central and east Africa in the nineteenth century

West-central Africa in the nineteenth century

Ever since the late sixteenth century much of the economic life of west-central Africa had been dominated by the European demand for captives for the transatlantic trade. Initially, European declarations of abolition applied only to the north Atlantic. So the export of captives from Angola to Brazil

Map 17.1 West-central Africa in the nineteenth century

continued freely for most of the first half of the nineteenth century. But as elsewhere in west Africa, even the ending of the transatlantic trade did not bring an end to slavery in the central African interior. Indeed, in some respects internal slavery increased as captives were turned to local production. This was partly to meet the need for more food to feed the growing population.

For centuries the notorious Atlantic trade had drawn off large numbers of fit young men. Though a proportion of women were also exported, the trade left on average a greater number of women than men in a number of African societies. With high female fertility and the widespread practice of male polygamy it was just about possible for local populations to reproduce themselves. But once slave exports ceased there was within the first generation a rapid increase in central African populations. This put a strain on the natural resources of the region, which was in any case subject to periodic drought and shortages of food. Enslaved populations, male and female, were turned to the production of food to meet rising needs.

At the same time, as in west Africa, enforced or enslaved labour was used for the production of alternative exports. This was needed to meet the continuing African demand for imported cloth, firearms and other manufactured goods. West-central Africa produced small amounts of palm oil and camwood. But the main export commodities that satisfied the European demand for 'legitimate' commerce were ivory and beeswax.

Chokwe

In the interior of the region old states crumbled and new groups emerged as a result of the changeover to production for a new type of export trade. The largest and most successful of these new groupings were the Chokwe.

The Chokwe originated as full-time hunters in the remote highland regions of Angola. Focusing their imports on firearms and excluding other luxuries, the Chokwe became specialised ivory-hunters and collectors of beeswax. They formed armies of professional hunters and strengthened their communities by incorporating captured women. These were pressed into cultivating food as well as collecting and processing wax. The Chokwe operated as a series of separate village communities. The maximum size of each group was about a thousand armed huntsmen together with their women, children and other dependants. Beyond that size they divided into new groups. In this way the Chokwe were in a state of perpetual expansion in search of new sources of ivory and wax. They expanded north and east towards the fringes of the forest and in doing so they absorbed much of the western portion of the crumbling Lunda empire.

As elephants were shot out and the availability of ivory declined in the 1870s and 1880s, the Chokwe turned to the production of rubber. The European market for rubber rapidly expanded in the 1880s with the invention of the pneumatic tyre for the bicycle (and later, from the 1890s and early 1900s, for the newly developed motor car). Chokwe women processed rubber from the sap of latex-producing bushes and creepers. They converted it into solid rubber balls for easy transportation (see Figure 17.1). The rubber harvest caused destruction of the environment as men cut down vines, bushes and woodland on the fringes of the forest.

Ovimbundu

As first the slaving and then the ivory frontier extended ever-deeper into the central African interior, a number of African peoples became specialists in

Figure 17.1 The rubber industry in the Belgian Congo – thumping rubber to remove particles of wood and fibre. (Illustration by Norman Hardy in the *Illustrated London News*, 2 October 1909)

long-distance trading. This role had been performed by the Imbangala of Kasanje at the height of the slaving period of the eighteenth century. In the nineteenth century their place was taken by the Ambaquista in the hinterland of Luanda and the Ovimbundu in the hinterland of Benguela. The Ovimbundu in particular organised huge trading caravans and penetrated as far as the upper Zambezi by the 1850s. The Ovimbundu were the main supply-link of firearms for the Chokwe exporters of ivory and rubber. Ovimbundu caravaneers who had earlier transported captives for sale used them now as porters in the carrying trade.

Kingdom of the floodplain

Origins and rise of the Lozi state

In its upper reaches the Zambezi River flows from north to south through an open grassy plain. During the second half of the summer rainy season (November to March) the river swells and floods the plain. The Lozi, originally known as Luyana, adapted their society to gain the maximum benefit from the natural resources of the floodplain. They built their settlements on a series of artificially constructed mounds dotted across the plain. When the surrounding land became flooded, they moved with all their belongings to winter-season settlements on the higher dry ground that bordered the western plain. As the waters receded they moved back to the plain to graze their cattle on refreshed pastures and plant crops in the fertile deposits of the flood.

Figure 17.2 *Litunga* Lewanika I, in the early 1900s, aboard one of his smaller barges, preparing to depart from his summer dwelling as the annual floodwaters of the Zambezi rise. Once he had transferred into the large, black and white-striped royal barge (the *Nalikwanda*), he would formally process along the river to his dryland winter quarters

Organised kingship had developed among the Luyana-speaking people at the northern end of the valley during the course of the seventeenth century. The origins of this development are not clear from Lozi tradition. It was possibly influenced by migrants or ideas from the Lunda (see p. 147), but it could also have been a local evolution based upon a religious shrine near Kalabo on the Luanginga tributary. The king used the title of *Litunga*. During the course of the eighteenth century the Lozi expanded their kingdom to cover much of the floodplain region. The *Litunga* and aristocracy who ruled the rising state organised enforced or slave labour to build the dwelling mounds and to cut canals for canoe transport and for controlling the waters of the flood. As the Lozi kingdom expanded in the eighteenth and early nineteenth centuries an increasing number of captives were used for cultivation and floodplain construction. Lozi commoners too were pressed into various labour projects as well as military service.

Figure 17.3 The Paramount Chief's royal barge, the *Nalikwanda*, Barotseland, Northern Rhodesia (now Zambia) in the 1950s

The movement from summer floodplain dwelling to dryland winter quarters was under the control of the *Litunga*. He led the move, riding in a huge royal barge. The whole procession was developed into an elaborate royal ritual which is still re-enacted each year in the western province of the modern republic of Zambia. A complex bureaucracy was developed in which promotion was based upon merit rather than royal connection.

The Kololo conquest

In the middle decades of the nineteenth century the Lozi kingdom experienced a major political crisis. The upper Zambezi floodplain was invaded by the Kololo in the 1830s. The Kololo were Sotho-speaking venturers who had fled from a period of turmoil in southern Africa that will be discussed in the following chapter. The Kololo, under the able leadership of Sebetwane, established their rule over the southern portion of the kingdom, driving the surviving Lozi royalty to the north. The Kololo supplanted the Lozi as the ruling aristocracy but otherwise left the political system largely intact. However, under the rule of Sebetwane's successor, Sekeletu, the Kololo treated the majority Lozi population as little more than agricultural slaves to farm the floodplain. They taxed them very heavily and sold a number to Ovimbundu slave traders in exchange for guns.

The Lozi kingdom in the later nineteenth century

In 1864 the Kololo were overthrown by a Lozi revolution, led by survivors of the Lozi royal family. An important impact of Kololo rule, apart from introducing the Sotho language to the region, was the extension of the boundaries of the kingdom in the south and east. There was a greater emphasis upon cattle-keeping and a more militaristic element was introduced into Lozi life. Raids against the cattle-keeping Ila of the Kafue valley became a regular practice of the Lozi army. By the 1870s the military were also being used for hunting elephants for their ivory. This was used to exchange for guns with African and European traders that were penetrating from the south. By the later nineteenth century the Lozi aristocracy were firmly re-established and lived in some luxury. As a sign of social prestige they grew their fingernails long to show that they did not engage in manual labour! It has been estimated that in the final decades of the century up to a third of the population of the kingdom were serfs or slaves. They worked for the aristocracy or were organised by the *Litunga*, Lewanika, digging irrigation canals in the floodplain.

The development of long-distance trade in east-central Africa

Kazembe's Lunda

An important feature of east-central Africa in the early nineteenth century was the development of long-distance trade. We saw in Chapter 14 (pp. 208–9) that by the end of the eighteenth century, the kingdom of Kazembe's Lunda had become the central pivot of a long-distance trading network that stretched from one side of the continent to the other. Kazembe accumulated goods for trade by collecting tribute from the regional chiefdoms of his kingdom. Copper was mined extensively in the Shaba/Copperbelt region of modern Congo and Zambia, and copper bars circulated within the kingdom as a form of currency. Kazembe's principal exports, apart from copper, were ivory and salt and an increasing number of

Map 17.2   East-central Africa in the nineteenth century

captives for sale into slavery. Imports from east or west included firearms, European woollens and Indian cotton cloth, shells and beads, and a range of metal manufactured goods from Europe.

Bisa and Bemba

Trade routes to the west were mostly through Mwata Yamvo's Lunda capital Musumba. In the east the Bisa provided Kazembe's kingdom with its principal trading-link to Portuguese traders and settlers in the Zambezi valley. The Bisa became professional traders, though Kazembe siphoned off most of their profits in customs dues and tribute. The Bisa were also subjected to raids by the Bemba. Starting from a region just to the east of Kazembe's kingdom the Bemba soon grew to dominate the northern region of modern Zambia. They developed a powerful military organisation and, based in stockaded villages, they lived largely from raiding others, especially Bisa trading caravans.

Yao

Meanwhile, south and east of Lake Malawi the Yao developed from specialist ivory-hunters into full-time, long-distance traders. They provided the trading link between the Shire valley and the coast at the Portuguese port of Mozambique. During the eighteenth century they opened up further routes to the Swahili port of Kilwa. The trade in ivory and slaves from this ancient Swahili port led to a revival of Kilwa in the early nineteenth century. By then the Yao were trading directly with the Bisa to the west of Lake Malawi.

Prazeros and Chikunda

In the Zambezi valley the main trading initiative was taken by the *prazeros* and their 'Chikunda' armies. The *prazeros* were descended from Portuguese and Afro-Portuguese hunters and traders who had settled in the valley in the seventeenth and eighteenth centuries. Breaking away from Portuguese control, they married local African women and set themselves up as virtual African chiefs. The *prazeros*' main sources of power were their large standing armies consisting mostly of captured slaves. These, known as Chikunda, were used for collecting local taxes as well as for hunting, raiding and trading. The *prazeros* controlled vast estates called *prazos* and treated the local African farmers, the 'owners of the land', as their subjects. They taxed them very

Figure 17.4 Yao slave-trader, southern Malawi, in the 1860s

heavily and expected them to grow enough food to support the *prazero* and his family and dependants as well as the Chikunda army.

With the decline of the Maravi empire in the eighteenth century the *prazeros* and their Chikunda grew to dominate the ivory trade of the lower Zambezi valley. Slaves too came to play an increasingly important role in this expanding trading system. Slaves were used both as porters to transport ivory to the coast and as soldiers to swell the ranks of the Chikunda armies. And, increasingly in the nineteenth century, slaves themselves became an item of the export trade (see below). By the 1860s independent Chikunda armies were extending their hunting and raiding frontier into the middle Zambezi valley to the west of the Caborabassa rapids. Well armed with guns and with no large African state to oppose them, the Chikunda had no need to trade for their commodities. Most of their ivory and slaves were taken by force. They shot elephants without regard to local hunting rights and they raided villages for their captives.

Nyamwezi and Kamba

In the region of modern Tanzania, between Lake Tanganyika and the coast, long-distance trading routes were developed and dominated by the Nyamwezi. They opened regular caravans from Zanzibar on the coast to their capital at Tabora (see Map 17.3). From there they penetrated north as far as Buganda in the lakeland region and south via the Bemba to Kazembe's Lunda and the copper-producing region to the west of the Luapula. The nineteenth-century development of regular Nyamwezi caravans from northern Zambia to Zanzibar drew off much of the Lunda's ivory and copper trade that had previously been carried south-eastwards by the Bisa.

Within the region of modern Kenya the principal trading nation was the Kamba. They developed important trading links between Kikuyu and the coast. But the Maasai domination of the central Rift valley tended to bar the Kamba access to Buganda and the lakeland kingdoms.

Invasion from the south: the Ngoni

In the 1830s the relatively peaceful development of trade in east-central Africa was disrupted by the Ngoni invasions from the south. The Ngoni, like the Kololo, were offshoots from the political turmoil that was going on in southern Africa at this time (see following chapter, pp. 263–5). The Ngoni impact was so dramatic partly because they introduced into the region an entirely new concept of centralised military organisation. This was based on a system of age-regiments which cut right across local loyalties and brought all young men into military service for the state. Conquered peoples too were absorbed into the structure. In this way the Ngoni regiments were formed into highly-disciplined and effective armies. Though they carried some guns they depended mostly on the short stabbing-spear and made full use of surprise and shock tactics. Most of their raids were made on unsuspecting villages at dawn or dusk. The Ngoni placed greater emphasis on cattle than on cultivation. When they settled in a region the regiments were sent out to raid for cattle and to collect tribute in grain and other food.

From about 1832 the Ngoni raided up the lower Zambezi and its Mazoe tributary to cause havoc among the Shona of the Zimbabwe plateau and the remnants of the Mutapa state. In 1835 Zwangendaba led the main body of

Map 17.3 Long-distance trading routes of the east African interior in the nineteenth century

Ngoni, several thousand strong, including Tsonga and Shona adherents, across the Zambezi. One branch of the Ngoni remained behind under the leadership of a remarkable woman named Nyamazana. She raided to the west and attacked the Rozvi capital Manyanga, in the process killing the last Changamire *mambo* Chirisamhuru II in 1836. Nyamazana settled in the region and went on to marry the conquering Ndebele king, Mzilikazi, after 1840 (see below, p. 271). She and her small band of Ngoni thus became part of the new Ndebele kingdom.

Zwangendaba, meanwhile, led the main body of Jere-Ngoni northwards as far as the Fipa country of south-western Tanzania (see Map 17.2). The success of the Ngoni was heavily dependent upon strong leadership, and following the death of Zwangendaba in 1848, the Ngoni broke apart into several separate groups. One raided north through Tanzania, causing considerable disruption and realignment of local peoples. Other Ngoni groups turned southwards and finally settled to the east and west of Lake Malawi.

Meanwhile, a separate branch of the Ngoni had moved up the eastern side of Lake Malawi before returning to settle in the Shire region to the south.

By absorbing local people into their ranks the Ngoni became in effect a small but powerful, centralised local African states. They retained the basic structure of the regimental system, and raiding neighbours and taking tribute by force remained an important part of Ngoni life. Their level of military organisation, discipline and experience enabled the Ngoni of east-central Africa to offer among the stoutest resistance to colonial conquest when it came in the closing decade of the century.

A number of eastern and central African peoples learnt from their Ngoni neighbours. Among the more successful of these were the Hehe of southern Tanzania. They adopted a Ngoni-style military structure based on the use of age-regiments. Under the leadership of Munyigumba the scattered Hehe chiefdoms united into a single centralised state. As such they were able to resist further Ngoni raids and later they offered firm resistance to German conquest in the 1890s.

The east African slave trade

We have already seen in earlier chapters of this book that a certain number of Africans had been sold into slavery from the east African coast for many centuries. Most of them had been taken as domestic servants, concubines or plantation workers to Arabia and the Persian Gulf. This trade in people from eastern Africa, however, was mostly on a fairly small scale and it certainly did not dominate the trading system of the east African coast, until, that is, the second half of the eighteenth century.

A number of factors intervened to transform the scale of the traffic in the late eighteenth and early nineteenth centuries. In the first place the French opened sugar and spice plantations on their Indian Ocean colonies of Mauritius, Réunion and Seychelles. Initially, they bought their slave workers from Portuguese and Indian traders in the Zambezi valley, at Quelimane and at Mozambique. With the rapid expansion of sugar plantations in the 1770s and the high death rate on the islands due to brutality, overwork and harsh conditions, the French looked further afield for their supply of slave labour. They turned to Arab and Swahili traders at Kilwa and Zanzibar. The Yao became major suppliers of slave labour raided from the Kilwa and Mozambique hinterland. The Yao were even known to sell fellow Yao into slavery.

In the early nineteenth century a second factor came into play. By then the Brazilians had found that they were not getting enough slave labour from the Atlantic coastline, partly because of the activities of the Anti-Slavery Squadron and partly because of an expansion of sugar plantations in Brazil itself. With the shortage of slaves for sale in the Americas the price of slaves rose. The higher profit margin now made it worthwhile for Brazilian slavers to make the extra-long trip to and from the Indian Ocean coast. Most of their slaves were purchased from the Zambezi valley and Mozambique region.

Finally, in the middle decades of the nineteenth century there was a rapid growth in the Arab demand for slaves to man their plantations on Zanzibar and surrounding islands. Arab domination of the northern coastal trade had

Figure 17.5 The slave market at Zanzibar. (From a sketch by Lieut. Henn of the Livingstone Relief Expedition, *Illustrated London News*, 8 June 1872)

been growing ever since their expulsion of the Portuguese from Fort Jesus and Mombasa in 1696–8. For most of the eighteenth century Portuguese traders were confined to the more southern coastal towns. By the early nineteenth century the sultans of Oman had extended direct control over many of the Swahili cities of the northern coastal region. In the 1820s Sultan Seyyid Said encouraged Arabs to set up clove plantations on the islands of Zanzibar and Pemba. The plantations, of course, were worked by slave-labour from the mainland. This part of the Omani economy became so successful that in 1840 Seyyid Said moved his capital to Zanzibar itself. There followed a rapid increase in the slave trade from the mainland to Zanzibar and the island became the largest slave market along the east African coast.

It has been estimated that at the peak of the trade in the 1860s, east Africa was exporting up to 70,000 slaves a year. The trade in people continued all along the coast, despite the activities of the Anti-Slavery Squadron.

In 1873 the British persuaded the sultan of Zanzibar to close the island's slave market. By then, however, the European demand for ivory was reaching a new peak. Previously most east African exports of ivory had gone to India and China. Now the highest demand came from Europe. The increasingly wealthy middle classes of industrialised Europe were using ivory for billiard balls, piano keys and the handles of their cutlery. By the 1870s the auction houses of London had become the world's largest single market for the sale of African ivory. Fewer human captives were now exported from east Africa. But all along the trade routes of the interior, innocent men and women were still raided, captured and forced to carry tusks of ivory to the coast.

The trade in ivory and slaves in the interior of central Africa

Between the 1860s and 1880s the east African markets for ivory and slaves pushed their destructive tentacles far into the interior of central Africa. Their agents transformed the nature of the region's long-distance trading networks and, unknowingly, prepared the ground for the colonial conquest that followed in their wake.

The *prazeros* of the lower Zambezi valley were quick to respond to the rising demand for slaves in the course of the nineteenth century. We have already seen above how independent bands of Chikunda had extended their hunting and raiding to the middle Zambezi valley. On the *prazos* of the lower Zambezi the *prazeros* resorted to selling their own subjects and even at times their own Chikunda armies. This hastened the break-up of the multitude of small-scale *prazos*. The few that survived had by the middle of the century consolidated into a small number of huge *supraprazos*, the main ones being Makanga, Massangano and Massingire. They became more firmly African in their content and outlook and as such provided strong opposition to Portuguese colonial conquest in the 1880s.

To the north of the lower Zambezi, Chikunda, Yao and Ngoni raids spread bloodshed and chaos over the previously prosperous farming regions of modern Malawi and eastern Zambia. By the 1870s and 1880s small-scale farming communities all over east-central Africa were having to live in stockaded villages for their own protection.

British Christian missionaries were attracted to the region, inspired by the anti-slavery appeals of David Livingstone. But their failure to replace the violence of the slave and ivory trade with 'Christianity and commerce' led the missionaries to appeal for British government intervention. The role of these and other missionaries will be discussed in Chapter 20.

Swahili traders in the east African interior

The Arab input into eastern African trading in this period has at times been oversimplified. The issue is confused by the writings of contemporary European travellers whose 'journals of exploration' (see below, Chapter 20, pp. 303–10) are the principal source of evidence for interior traders at this time. They tended to refer to all long-robed Muslim traders from the east coast as 'Moors' or 'Arabs'. Tippu Tip, for instance (see Figure 17.6), was referred to by both Livingstone and Stanley as an 'Arab', though he was in fact of mixed Arab, Swahili and Nyamwezi ancestry. There was undoubtedly a considerable increase in the number of Arab immigrants to Zanzibar and coastal towns during the nineteenth century. And some of those penetrating the interior trading networks at this time were indeed of Arab origin. But any focus on ethnicity is a distraction from the fact that the overwhelming majority of coastal east Africans were Swahili, in both language and culture, even if many Swahili liked to trace their family lineages to Arab or Persian ancestors. So the term 'Swahili' will be used here to refer to Muslim traders of coastal origin whatever their particular ancestry. However, although coastal Swahili were often the leaders of long-distance interior trading expeditions, the vast majority of the members of their caravans – hunters, raiders and porters – were local recruits, captives or volunteers.

As coastal demand for slaves and ivory rose, Swahili and Nyamwezi hunter/traders moved ever-deeper into the interior in search of these 'commodities'. Financed by Zanzibari or Indian merchants, they travelled in well-armed caravans of several hundred or even a thousand men and women. They exploited the weaknesses of old-established states and set up permanent bases in the central African interior. Like the Yao in the south, the Nyamwezi were the pioneers of this movement north of Lake Malawi. Swahili carava-neers followed Nyamwezi routes and were well established at Ujiji on the shores of Lake Tanganyika by the late 1830s. From there they crossed the lake in the 1840s to collect ivory and captives from the eastern fringes of the Congo forest. By then the Nyamwezi were penetrating far to the west of the Tanganyika-Malawi corridor (see Map 17.3).

Msiri and the Yeke

In the 1850s a Nyamwezi trader, Msiri, established a permanent inland base west of the Luapula. The Kazembe kingdom was suffering the crisis of a civil war which Msiri was able to exploit to his advantage. From his capital at Bunkeya he expanded his initial holding into a raiding/trading state composed of a number of heavily fortified villages. As the Nyamwezi expanded their control they absorbed other peoples and began calling them-selves by the local name 'ba-Yeke'. From their position in the heart of the copper-producing country, Msiri's Yeke drew off most of the tribute from the western regions of the Kazembe kingdom. They established contact further west with Chokwe and Ovimbundu. In this way they benefited from both eastern and western connections as Kazembe's Lunda had before them. Msiri used the region's resources of ivory and copper to build up a considerable arsenal of firearms which he bought from Ovimbundu in the west and Swahili in the east. It was his command of the copper resources of the region that attracted British and Belgian colonists to Bunkeya in 1890–1.

Tippu Tip and the eastern Congo basin

Meanwhile the most famous of the Swahili traders of the central African inte-rior had established himself west of Lake Tanganyika. His name was Hamed bin Muhammed, commonly known as Tippu Tip. He started his hunting and raiding experience among Msiri's Nyamwezi. During the 1860s he estab-lished himself at the Swahili bases of Nyangwe and Kasongo on the Lualaba (upper Congo) River. From here he was able to maintain direct trading contact through Ujiji and Tabora to Zanzibar. This kept him supplied with firearms with which to hunt in the forest and raid surrounding villages. In doing so he virtually destroyed the ancient Songye towns of the upper Lualaba and seriously weakened the declining Luba empire.

Considering his 'kingdom' as the western outpost of the Zanzibari sultanate, Tippu Tip built a trading empire for himself which stretched from the Luba in the south to the great westward bend of the upper Congo River (see Map 17.3). By the early 1880s Tippu Tip's army was several thousand strong. But he was merely the overlord of an informal federation of hunting-raiding bands. His close companions were Swahili and Muslim Nyamwezi who commanded their own bands of armed retainers. Tippu Tip and his companions hunted elephants deep into the Congo forest, and raided villages for food and captives. Captured women were taken as concubines while men were used as porters and despatched along the route to Zanzibar. Both men and women were used as agricultural labour to tend the plantations of sugar-cane, rice or maize which surrounded the towns of Kasongo and Nyangwe. Any 'surplus' captives were usually ransomed locally in exchange for ivory. The cheapness of human life to Tippu Tip and his companions is illustrated

Figure 17.6 Portrait of 'Tippu Tip' (Hamed bin Muhammed) (*c*.1837–1905), slave and ivory raider/trader and sometime agent of the sultan of Zanzibar

by an observation in the journal of the Anglo-American traveller H. M. Stanley:

> Halt at Mpotira [downstream from Nyangwe], to allow a winding caravan under our escort to come up with hundreds of sheep and goats which they are taking to Tata for trade. A sheep is said to purchase one [tusk of] ivory, 12 slaves purchase an ivory. In Ujiji 6 slaves purchase an ivory.
>
> 'Slaves cost nothing,' said Hamed bin Mohammed, 'they only require to be gathered.' And that is the work of Muini Dugumbi and Mtagamoyo [Tippu Tip's companions].
>
> These half-castes of Nyangwe have no cloth or beads or wares of merchandise. They obtain their ivory by robbing … . They attack the simple peoples of Nyangwe right and left, 12 or 15 slaves then caught are sold for 35 pounds (16 kilos) of ivory. Muini Dugumbi has one hundred to one hundred and twenty women. Mtagamoyo has 60 … .

(R. Stanley and A. Neame (eds), *The Exploration Diaries of H. M. Stanley,* William Kimber, London, 1961, p. 134; entry for 7 November 1876)

Stanley himself, it should be noted, was not averse to shooting Africans dead at the slightest provocation.

Swahili penetration of the lake regions of eastern Africa

By the 1870s and 1880s Swahili traders from the coast were dominating the major trading routes between the coast and the interior. By then they had virtually taken over the Nyamwezi trading capital of Tabora. Well-armed

Figure 17.7 Mlozi and his slave-raiders, Karonga, Lake Malawi, 1890

Swahili trading caravans even penetrated beyond Kikuyu country and through the northern fringes of Maasai territory to do business with cattle pastoralists and ivory-hunters to the west of Lake Turkana.

From the 1860s a small number of Swahili traders were allowed to settle at the Baganda capital north-west of Lake Victoria Nyanza. But, they were never able to develop there the sort of freedom to raid and trade which they exercised elsewhere. The powerful Baganda ruler *kabaka* Mutesa I (r.1856–84) kept their activities strongly under his control. The Baganda aristocracy were keen to acquire the cotton cloth and guns that the Swahili traders had to offer. So they themselves sent out their own hunters and raiders to collect the ivory and captives which the Swahili sought. The latter played the role of middlemen between Buganda and the coast. At the same time Baganda canoeists were opening up further trading contacts on the southern shores of the Victoria Nyanza.

Within western Tanzania the Nyamwezi responded to increasing domination of their trading routes by Swahili from the coast. Mirambo created an extensive Nyamwezi trading empire which operated over much of west-central Tanzania while a further Nyamwezi leader, Nyungu, established central political control over the previously disunited Kimbu further south. Both were successful trading states whose activities confined the Swahili in western Tanzania to the well-worn trading routes and towns such as Tabora and Ujiji.

For much of the nineteenth century the economic life of east-central Africa had been disrupted and dominated by the violence of the trade in firearms, ivory and captives. Apart from the wealth gained by individual traders and rulers, the vast majority of central African peoples gained little benefit from the trade. And the persistence of slavery and the slave trade and the dislocation of people that went with it provided potential European colonists with both opportunity and excuse to intervene in the region. Then the peoples of east and central Africa found to their cost that they were exchanging one form of slavery for another.

Madagascar: the rise of the Merina kingdom

The arrival of Europeans in the Indian Ocean from the sixteenth century transformed power relations on the island of Madagascar. The southern Malagasy kingdoms had hitherto played little direct role in the Indian Ocean trading networks. The development of European shipping to India via southern Africa gave the southern Malagasy rulers the opportunity to provide visiting ships with food (especially rice) and slaves. A further international boost to the Malagasy economy occurred with the eighteenth-century French development of plantation slavery on their island colonies of Mauritius and Réunion.

Supplying the provisioning and slave trade for these French colonies prompted the growth of the Merina kingdom in the central plateau from the late eighteenth century. The Merina kings used a regulated system of forced labour to service their growing imperial state. Forced labour provided military service as well as state-controlled agricultural and industrial production. The latter, the most systematic attempt to establish an industrial revolution in pre-colonial Africa, used the water-power of the country's numerous mountainous rivers to drive machinery. Industrialisation focused mainly on the production of military hardware: muskets, cannon and ammunition. A large centralised industrial complex was built by 20,000 forced labourers and maintained by a permanent workforce of 5000.

By the mid-nineteenth century the Merina empire extended to the whole of the central highlands and eastern half of Madagascar. But at the height of its power, the imperial nature of the Merina state contained the seeds of its own downfall. Christianity had been adopted as the state religion in the 1820s, and Church and schools both recruited forced labour for the state.

The ban on slave exports and increasing direct competition from French trading settlements on the north coast weakened the Merina economy during the mid-nineteenth century. The military struggle against persistent French incursions from the north bankrupted the Merina state from the 1870s. Their Malagasy subjects seized the opportunity to foment numerous rebellions against the state's forced-labour demands. The oppressive Merina ruling class became so discredited and unpopular that when the French finally entered the Merina capital in 1895, they did so unopposed.

The Menalamba revolt of 1895–7 has commonly been portrayed as one of the first great nationalist rebellions against French imperialism. Recent historical scholarship, however, has pointed out that the rebels did not attack the French as such. Rather, they attacked the structures and personnel of the Merina administrative system, which the French proposed to re-establish. Thus they attacked the Church, the schools and the administrators of the forced-labour system.

For more information see www.palgrave.com/shillington

chapter 18

Pre-industrial southern Africa in the nineteenth century

State-building and conflict: the mfecane/difaqane and its effects

In the early decades of the nineteenth century the former societies of the southern African interior were torn apart by a series of wars which raged across the breadth of the subcontinent. These were aptly described by the Nguni of the south-east as *mfecane*, meaning 'the crushing', and by the Sotho-Tswana of the highveld as *difaqane* or *lifaqane* meaning 'the scattering'. Between 1816 and 1840 the *mfecane/difaqane* transformed the political map of the southern African interior.

The 'myth' of the mfecane

During the 1980s a group of South African historians began questioning whether or not the *mfecane* ever really happened. They suggested that the whole idea of the *mfecane* was no more than a propaganda myth, invented by colonially-minded whites and their modern racist sympathisers. The purpose of the myth, argued these historians, was to provide a justification for nineteenth-century colonisation and, by implication, the modern *apartheid* state. There is little doubt that white colonists in the past, and their modern equivalents, deliberately distorted certain aspects of the *mfecane* period. Their purpose has been to try and prove, for instance, that Africans were naturally prone to irrational 'tribal conflict' and that as a consequence much of the southern African interior was vacant land in the 1830s, just waiting for white settlement. Much of the modern critique of the *mfecane* appears to have been a reaction to this distorted version of events, a distortion which still persisted in official school histories of South Africa in the 1980s. The critique, however, pays little heed to the very different interpretation of the *mfecane* which had been developed and taught in universities and schools beyond South Africa since the 1970s. Nevertheless, their critique has caused historians of the period to re-examine the evidence and to rethink certain aspects of this very important period in southern African history.

The mfecane east of the Drakensberg

The movement known as the *mfecane* originated in the south-eastern lowveld among the emerging northern Nguni kingdoms of the Mthethwa, Ndwandwe and Ngwane. The most likely roots of this conflict have been outlined in Chapter 15 (pp. 228–9). Basically, it stemmed from increased competition for the region's limited natural resources. Initiation age-regiments had for

For more information see www.palgrave.com/shillington

Map 18.1 The rise of the Zulu kingdom and the *difaqane* on the highveld, 1818–35

some years been increasingly used for military purposes: to expand a chiefdom's range of grazing, cultivating and hunting land, and to defend their holdings from the raids of rivals. Now, with rising competition between the three kingdoms, regiments were almost permanently in the field, defending territory and raiding neighbours. Weak chiefdoms sought the protection of more powerful neighbours and were incorporated into the major kingdoms, voluntarily or by force. Initiation ceremonies themselves were dropped and regiments were brought increasingly under the centralised authority of the powerful kings. A crisis of drought in 1802–4 was turned into famine by the disruption of military action: in other words, it was a man-made famine – a concept that has echoes in our own modern times.

Competition in the region culminated in a period of intensive warfare between 1816 and 1819. Sobhuza's Ngwane were expelled north of the Pongola valley and in the final showdown between Ndwandwe and Mthethwa the Ndwandwe at first appeared victorious. Dingiswayo, the leader of the Mthethwa, was killed and his forces scattered, but a new leader, Shaka, quickly rose to challenge Ndwandwe domination. Shaka, a former commander in Dingiswayo's army, was the leader of the Zulu, a minor chiefdom of the former Mthethwa federation. After a prolonged and devastating war Shaka's regiments defeated their enemies and drove the broken Ndwandwe army north of the Pongola. The Ndwandwe and other northern Nguni, fleeing from these and later battles with the Zulu, carried the *mfecane* northwards. Known as 'the Ngoni', they raided through east-central Africa in the middle decades of the century (see previous chapter).

Shaka and the rise of the Zulu kingdom

By the middle of 1819 Shaka had established himself as the all-powerful ruler of a single kingdom which dominated the region between the Tugela and Pongola. For most of the next decade he vigorously expanded his kingdom. He extended his control through the Drakensberg foothills and sent his regiments to exact tribute from the peoples of the southern region between the Tugela and Umzimkulu Rivers (see Map 18.1). By the mid-1820s his kingdom covered most of modern KwaZulu-Natal, although the Zulu heartland remained north of the Tugela.

A vital factor in the rapid expansion of the Zulu kingdom at this time was the important military changes introduced by Shaka. These were not entirely his own innovation but were based on developments which had taken place within the armies of Ndwandwe and Mthethwa over the previous decade. Shaka refined them and made them more efficient. The Zulu regiments were closely drilled and highly disciplined. Their principal weapon was a short stabbing-spear which replaced the former ,less-efficient, long throwing-spear. But success ultimately stemmed from the use of speed and surprise, combined with a ruthless determination to destroy the enemy. It was regiments drilled in this style of warfare which Ngoni and Ndebele carried northwards into central Africa with such effect in the 1830s and 1840s.

Shaka's use of regiments was closely linked to political control. He developed a centralised form of government in which the king had absolute authority. In newly conquered regions hereditary chiefs were replaced by royal officials (*indunas*), directly responsible to the king. Any who did not submit were simply destroyed; at times whole villages, men, women and children,

Figure 18.1
Mgungundlovu, the Zulu capital in the reign of Dingane, 1838

Figure 18.2 Utimuni, nephew of Shaka the late Zulu king, in ceremonial battledress. (Plate 13 from 'The Kafirs Illustrated', 1849)

were literally wiped out. Sometimes the *indunas* were the former hereditary chiefs themselves, if they had been quick to show a very willing submission. But even where this happened, chiefs lost a major source of independent power. They lost the right to summon their own regiments. The young men and women of newly conquered chiefdoms were now incorporated into the regiments of the king. Mzilikazi, chief of the Khumalo, was a rare exception. He was allowed to remain both hereditary chief and military commander at the head of his own regiments. He proved the wisdom of Shaka's general policy when he defied the Zulu king's authority and withdrew with his fighting regiments on to the highveld (see below p. 270).

Besides performing military duties, male and female regiments were also involved in production for the state. The men herded the king's cattle and hunted for ivory while the women cultivated the king's fields. Regimental towns, based on the pattern of a central cattle enclosure (see Figure 18.1), were placed at strategic positions around the kingdom. It was only after a number of years in the king's service that regiments were disbanded and their members allowed to marry and set up their own homesteads. Even then they remained always liable to military call-up. In this way the regimental system served to break down regional identities and foster loyalty to the Zulu king. Before the end of Shaka's brief reign, all the people of the kingdom had begun to think of themselves as 'Zulu'.

To the north of the Zulu kingdom the *mfecane* had given rise to a number of new and powerful states. In the mountains north of the Pongola Sobhuza's Ngwane founded what was to become the Swazi kingdom, named after Sobhuza's successor Mswati I (r.1839–65). In the southern region of modern Mozambique the former Ndwandwe military commander, Soshangane, founded the powerful raiding-state of Gaza. Further Ndwandwe offshoots, the Ngoni of central Africa, have already been referred to.

Meanwhile, to the south, Shaka continued to expand his area of control. His army raided the Mpondo south of the Umzimkulu in search of cattle and other booty. It used to be argued by contemporary colonists and early twentieth-century historians that vast areas south of the Tugela (colonial Natal) were completely depopulated by Zulu raids and that everywhere, destitute refugees fled the wrath of Shaka's regiments. Modern research, however, has questioned this myth of depopulation. Careful rereading of contemporary European sources confirms a fairly even population of 'Natal' during the 1820s, and even in the few areas that were temporarily depopulated due to specific raids, the people had returned by the 1830s.

Nevertheless, it appears clear that the Hlubi of Mpangazitha and the Ngwane of Matiwane suffered a number of raids in the foothills of the Drakensberg that prompted them to leave the region. In 1821–2, first the Hlubi and then the Ngwane crossed the high passes of the Drakensberg, carrying conflict onto the Sotho highveld (see below).

The end of Shaka's reign

In 1828 Shaka was assassinated by his half-brother Dingane, who proclaimed himself king. It had taken Shaka a mere ten years to create the Zulu kingdom. Yet within ten years of his death it had reached the verge of destruction. Dingane lacked the military genius and leadership qualities of Shaka; but it is doubtful whether even Shaka could have coped any better with the problems that confronted his successor. Some of Dingane's major problems were inherited. The power and unity of Shaka's kingdom had been built very largely upon the success of a perpetual state of war and a continual supply of booty. By the final years of Shaka's reign that success was becoming increasingly difficult to sustain. Potential enemies were ever further afield and they were learning to defend themselves. Indeed, the army was returning from defeat by the Gaza state of Soshangane when they learned of Shaka's death. But the greatest problem which Dingane had to face was not of Shaka's making. This was the invasion of the lowveld in 1837–8 by armed and mounted Boers who had emigrated from the Cape Colony and came in search of new land to take for white settlement (see below, pp. 274–7).

The *difaqane* on the highveld

In the early nineteenth century the Sotho of the southern highveld lived in numerous small and independent chiefdoms. There was a particular concentration of settlements in the fertile and well-watered valley of the Caledon. Each chiefdom had its own system of initiation age-regiments. These were used for public works as well as military purposes, but they were only summoned as need arose. The raiding of cattle between one chiefdom and another was fairly common, but warfare of this kind was not particularly destructive. Chiefdoms were seldom totally impoverished by the raids.

When the Hlubi and Ngwane burst on to the highveld in 1821-2, they found the small Sotho chiefdoms easy prey. Initially the Hlubi fell upon the Tlokwa, who in turn attacked the Sotho chiefdoms of the upper Caledon valley. Although these raids undoubtedly caused much destruction and instability, the extent of devastation has in the past often been exaggerated. Conflict and cattle raids were nothing new to the area. The new, and most dangerous, element of the time was raids from the south by small bands of mounted Griqua and Kora armed with guns from the Cape Colony. They raided up the Orange and Caledon valleys, looting villages, seizing cattle and taking people captive to sell into slavery in the Cape Colony.

This period has traditionally been referred to as the *difaqane,* 'the scattering', and there was indeed widespread conflict; but at the same time there emerged a number of strong leaders who seized the opportunity to build powerful new states in the region. Far more devastating in the long term was the invasion of Boer settlers from the Cape Colony who caused havoc on the highveld from the late 1830s and, in effect, extended the *difaqane* by several decades (see below).

Moshoeshoe and the rise of the Sotho kingdom

In the troubled times of 1821–3 Moshoeshoe of the Mokoteli clan established his headquarters on the slopes of a mountain to the east of the upper Caledon. Here he quickly gained a reputation as an able military leader and refugees fled to his protection. In 1824, after suffering several major attacks from Tlokwa and Ngwane, Moshoeshoe moved his following of several thousand people to the larger, flat-topped mountain of Thaba-Bosiu. This was a strong defensive position, able to withstand a lengthy siege. It had access to good grazing and fresh water and commanded the surrounding valley.

From this secure central capital, Moshoeshoe built up a new and powerful Sotho kingdom. It was not a centralised state in the style of Shaka's Zulu; it was more of a confederation of semi-independent chiefdoms. As chiefdoms sought the protection of Moshoeshoe, they were incorporated into the expanding kingdom. Hereditary chiefs were left in place and remained responsible for raising their own age-regiments. They were merely required

Figure 18.3
Moshoeshoe's mountain stronghold of Thaba-Bosiu, water colour by Charles Davidson Bell, 1834

Figure 18.4 Moshoeshoe (in top hat) and counsellors in the 1860s

to acknowledge Moshoeshoe's overall authority, support the kingdom with regiments when required and send tribute to the capital. Moshoeshoe cemented relations within the kingdom by a complex system of marriage alliances. He himself had many wives and children, and most Sotho chiefly families were related to the king in one way or another.

Moshoeshoe was not averse to raiding weaker neighbours to build up his herds of cattle, but at the same time he recognised the strength of certain powerful neighbours. Thus he paid tribute in cattle to Matiwane's Ngwane and sent feathers and furs as presents to Shaka. He even sent a gift of cattle to the Ndebele after repelling one of their attacks. It was only after Zulu attacks had weakened the Ngwane in 1827 that Moshoeshoe scattered the remnants of this enemy and drove them southwards into Thembuland.

In the early 1830s Moshoeshoe invited missionaries from the Cape Colony to come and settle in his kingdom. His motives were political and economic rather than religious. He recognised that the main threat to Sotho security came from the raids by bands of mounted Griqua and Kora from the northern border regions of the Colony. Moshoeshoe hoped that friendly relations with white Christians from the Colony would help stave off these attacks as well as provide the Sotho with access to a trade in firearms and horses. In the latter respect Moshoeshoe's policy succeeded. In the 1830s and 1840s Sotho imports of horses and guns enabled the kingdom to become one of the most formidable African powers in southern Africa.

The difaqane on the western highveld

While the growth of the Sotho kingdom brought a certain level of stability to the eastern highveld, the *difaqane* was spreading to the Tswana of the western regions. Attracted by the southern Tswana's large herds of cattle, dislocated groups of Fokeng, Hlakoena and Taung converged on the Tlhaping capital of Dithakong in 1823. The Tlhaping appealed to the missionary Robert Moffat to bring the Griqua and their firearms to their assistance. In the event a hundred armed and mounted Griqua managed to disperse the Sotho from the environs of Dithakong. The reputation of the missionaries, as allies of the men with guns, was greatly enhanced by this event.

Following their repulse from Dithakong, Hlakoena and Taung raided further among the Tswana before returning to resettle south of the River Vaal. A group of Fokeng, however, under the able leadership of Sebetwane, raided northwards through the northern Tswana states between the Kalahari and Limpopo. Known as 'Kololo', Sebetwane's compact band of raiders overcame many difficulties and near-destruction in the desert before conquering and settling in the Lozi kingdom of the upper Zambezi valley (see Chapter 17, p. 251).

Mzilikazi and the founding of the Ndebele kingdom

The only major Nguni state to be founded on the highveld was the kingdom of the Ndebele. They originated from the Khumalo clan, former allies of the Ndwandwe. Following the defeat of the Ndwandwe, the Khumalo came nominally under the authority of Shaka. Rather than submit to the Zulu king, the chief of the Khumalo, Mzilikazi, led the core of his fighting regiments on to the highveld in 1822. Here they raided among the northern and central Sotho before settling in the 1830s around the Marico River basin. The Sotho called them 'Matabele', a name which the Khumalo themselves adopted as 'Amandebele' or 'Ndebele'.

Mzilikazi built up a powerful centralised kingdom through a combination of Zulu-style regiments and fighting methods and the absorption of large numbers of Sotho-Tswana men and women. A number of regimental villages were established to keep order in the districts, to collect tribute from the villages and to tend the king's herds. Neighbouring independent states were

Figure 18.5 Ndebele town, showing cattle enclosure, in the 1890s expected to offer tribute, and if they did not pay, they suffered crushing raids. The core of the Ndebele kingdom was relatively calm and peaceful; but raids in search of tribute ranged far among the Tswana and reached the southern Sotho south of the River Vaal.

The Ndebele expulsion from the highveld in 1837 was the culmination of a series of raids against them from the south. Some of these were far-reaching attacks from Dingane's Zulu regiments. But those that finally expelled them were a combination by Griqua, Rolong and Boers mounted on horseback and armed with guns. In 1838–40 the Ndebele withdrew north of the Limpopo, where they overcame the Shona Rozvi state which was already weakened by earlier assaults from the Ngoni. There Mzilikazi absorbed subject Shona and re-established his kingdom on much the same pattern as on the Sotho-Tswana highveld.

The British at the Cape

The British government seized control of the Cape Colony from the Dutch East India Company in 1795. Though they handed it over to the Dutch government in 1803, the British retook the colony in 1806 and this time they retained control. Like the Dutch before them, the British needed a supply-station for their ships to India and a naval base from which to protect their shipping from attacks by rival Europeans. In their attempts to turn the Cape into a secure and profitable British colony, the British introduced a number of social and economic changes to the territory. The net result of these changes was to prompt a large number of Dutch-speaking colonists, Boers, to trek northwards out of the colony in the 1830s and 1840s.

Economic expansion

At first the early years of British rule seemed to offer a lot that favoured the interests of the Boers. The wine farmers of the western Cape now had freer access to British markets. The large British garrison at Cape Town and the increasing number of British ships calling at the port provided better markets both for local wheat-farmers and for the pastoral trekboers of the interior. There was an expansion in the farming of Merino sheep, grown for their wool rather than just their meat; and trekboer hunters of the interior benefited from the rising British market for African ivory.

Labour

Though the abolition of the slave trade in 1807 created an initial shortage of labour, British proclamations soon tightened up controls over 'free' labour in the colony. According to the so-called 'Hottentot Code' of 1809, all Khoesan and 'free-black' men in the colony had to carry 'passes' showing where they lived and who their employer was. Any without a pass could be contracted to the nearest white colonist who needed labour. At the same time, however, employers had to issue written contracts to their workers. And the latter were allowed access to the courts, where they could challenge their 'masters' for breach of contract or assault. In 1812 a number of judges toured the rural districts of the colony to hear the large number of cases brought by servants against their employers. Though very few convictions were obtained, the circuit courts caused outrage among frontier Boers who had previously felt free to use and abuse their workers as and when they saw fit.

While these changes were taking place, a number of Christian missionaries arrived from Europe to work among the 'heathen native' population of the colony. Missionaries very soon became champions of the poor and oppressed Khoesan of the Cape. They pursued their interests in the courts and encouraged them to develop independent peasant farming at the mission stations – much to the annoyance of local Boer employers.

The activities and writings of the missionaries were a strong influence on the British government at the Cape. In 1828 the government issued Ordinance 50 which removed the restrictions of the 'Hottentot Code' of 1809. This allowed Khoesan and 'coloured' workers the basic right and freedom to move around the colony and choose their own employer or become independent peasant farmers. Ordinance 50 and the abolition of slavery in 1834 were based upon the belief that a free waged labour force was in the long term more efficient and contented than a restricted or enslaved one. Both measures were resented by the Boers of the eastern frontier regions. The poorer Boers were unable to afford good enough wages to attract workers to their farms. Wealthier, slave-owning Boers complained of the poor compensation which they were offered for their 'slaves'. The labour policies of the British at the Cape were thus a strong incentive for frontier Boers to consider emigrating northwards beyond the boundaries of the colony.

The eastern Cape frontier and the conflict with the Xhosa

The most important innovation which the British brought to the eastern Cape frontier was the presence of a standing army at Cape Town which could be quickly summoned when the need arose. On the one hand this brought the frontier trekboers under closer government control. But ultimately it strengthened the position of the white settlers in their continuing struggle with the Xhosa for possession of the Zuurveld.

The pattern of the first three Cape-Xhosa or 'Frontier' wars had been one of raid and counter-raid between two fairly evenly-matched opponents (see above, Chapter 15, p. 224). The Boers' weakness, despite their advantage of guns and horses, had been the temporary nature of their voluntary 'commandos'. In time of war their attention was torn between pursuing the enemy and protecting their own farms and families. The professional forces of the British army had no such problem. Local volunteers were still widely used, but they now had the back-up of the garrison at Cape Town, and, if necessary, reinforcements from overseas.

In their first conflict with the Xhosa, the British introduced the concept of total warfare, more akin to that of Shaka's Zulu, and totally alien to the Xhosa. In the 'Fourth War', of 1811–12, the British brutally cleared the Xhosa from the Zuurveld and expelled them east of the Fish River. In the overcrowded conditions which resulted, civil war soon erupted among the Xhosa east of the Fish. The British seized the opportunity and intervened in what became the 'Fifth War' (1818–19). Despite a daring Xhosa invasion of the Zuurveld, the British eventually pushed them even further back, beyond the Keiskama.

Determined to protect the colony from any future 'invasion', the British attempted to create a barrier of 'empty land' between the Fish and Keiskama and built a number of military forts to patrol the region. An attempt at a 'human barrier' was added to the northern part of the region when the British allowed a group of Khoesan and 'coloured' (mixed-race) peasant farmers to settle in the Kat River valley. But the British then ruined this

Figure 18.6 An incident in the Cape-Xhosa wars: the destruction of Stock's Kraal on the Keiskamma River, during the Eighth Frontier War, 21 June 1851

settlement's chances of economic success by using it as a dumping-ground for unemployed 'coloureds' from the colony. Furthermore, the general land-shortage in the region ensured that the 'empty land' policy did not last for long. Xhosa quickly returned to the region and clashes soon erupted between them and trekboer squatters who ignored British restrictions on the territory. In the resultant 'Sixth War' (1834–5) the British pushed even further east and annexed the rest of Xhosa territory west of the River Kei.

As a result of this annexation, Boers of the eastern Cape looked forward to a whole new region being thrown open to white settlement. But the

Map 18.2 The Cape Colony and Xhosa resistance, 1811–36

273

British government disappointed them by deciding that the security of the new province would be too expensive to maintain. To the disgust of frontier Boers and eager British land speculators, the territory between the Keiskama and the Kei was handed back to the Xhosa. The 'loss' of this new province decided many Boers to join the growing number of their compatriots who were packing up their belongings and trekking northwards from the colony.

The Boer Trek and African resistance

The Boer Trek

In the late 1830s several thousand Boer families and their servants trekked northwards from the eastern Cape, on to the southern highveld and away from the Cape Colony. Modern Afrikaner historians and nationalists have glorified this movement as 'the Great Trek': the founding event in Afrikaner culture, the earliest expression of Afrikaner nationalism. In fact it was a series of relatively small, separate treks, with poorer families grouped together under the protection and leadership of richer patriarchs. There was little overall unity of purpose and direction. Indeed, there was considerable rivalry among the various group leaders. This was reflected in the lack of unity and cooperation between the first generation of trekker republics that were founded on the highveld. The one issue on which they were united was their desire for freedom from British government control, combined with free access to vast stretches of new land.

Most of the 'Voortrekkers' (meaning, literally, 'front trekkers') of the 1830s and 1840s came from the eastern Cape districts, where they experienced a severe shortage of land. The Xhosa had effectively blocked the trek-boer movement eastwards, and the British had shown an unwillingness or inability to extend the colony further than the Keiskama. In addition, Xhosa invasions of the Zuurveld in 1819 and 1834 had emphasised the continuing insecurity of white settlement in the frontier districts. On top of this came the increasingly restrictive policies of the British government. Rents were rigorously collected. The freedom of the old loan-farm system was being replaced by a system of land tenure that led to the ownership of land as private property, which poorer Boers could not afford. Locally elected Boer officials were replaced by British-appointed magistrates from Cape Town. English was used in education and the law courts, and Boer employers found their traditionally violent treatment of their servants was being interfered with. The 'free labour' policy of Ordinance 50 and the abolition of slavery added greatly to Boer dissatisfaction, especially in the eastern frontier districts. The British failure to provide them with further Xhosa land east of the Keiskama was the final straw for many.

The impact of the Boer Trek and African resistance

For more information see www.palgrave.com/shillington

The Boer Trek of the 1830s and 1840s extended permanent white settlement firmly into the interior of southern Africa. Many historical maps and some historians of South Africa have tended to assume that within a few years the Voortrekker 'republics' controlled the whole of the modern provinces of the Orange Free State and Transvaal. In fact this was not the case. The direction of the treks and the positioning of the 'republics' were determined very largely by patterns of African settlement and resistance. Initial Boer settlement was concentrated in areas temporarily depopulated by the upheavals of the recent *mfecane/difaqane*. The further expansion of settle-

Figure 18.7 To escape British rule and secure 'free' land for themselves, Boer families emigrated northwards from the Cape Colony into what had hitherto been independent African territory. Here they cross the Drakensberg to enter the south-eastern lowveld where they came into conflict with the powerful kingdom of the Zulus. (Painting by R. Caton Woodville in *Harper's Magazine*, June 1897)

ment was slow and largely dependent upon the extent and nature of African cooperation or resistance.

The Voortrekkers aimed initially for the relatively underpopulated southern highveld in the region of the middle Vaal. At Taba 'Nchu they were befriended by the Rolong who welcomed them as useful allies. The Rolong hoped to use the Boers' military advantage of guns and horses against the Ndebele who had recently expelled them from their traditional 'homeland' region around the upper Molopo basin. The Rolong thus joined with Boers and Griqua in attacking the Ndebele in 1837. As we saw above, the Ndebele were eventually driven into abandoning the region in order to regroup further north on the Zimbabwe plateau. The Boers then claimed right of

Map 18.3 The Boer Trek and African resistance, 1836–40

conquest to the former Ndebele kingdom and established their main settlements north and south of the middle Vaal. Those Rolong and other Tswana who returned to their former territory found themselves subjected to frequent Boer demands for labour and taxation.

Further north and east small groups of Voortrekkers established tiny 'republics' in the far northern Soutpansberg and at Ohrigstad and Lydenburg. But these were largely hunting and trading bases and the extent of effective Boer settlement was kept in check by the strength of Swazi, Pedi and Venda resistance. The latter eventually succeeded in expelling the Boers completely from the Soutpansberg in the 1860s. The Pedi by then were sending migrant workers to the Cape Colony to stockpile firearms for future conflict with the Boers.

Meanwhile the most dramatic conflict had occurred in the south-eastern lowveld. Access to this well-watered and fertile grassland had been a primary aim of many early Voortrekkers. They hoped to settle south of the Tugela. But first they had to come to terms with the powerful Zulu kingdom.

The Zulu king, Dingane, used the traditional Zulu tactics of speed and ruthlessness to try to remove this new potential threat. Having at first allayed Boer suspicions by apparently agreeing to come to terms, Dingane suddenly unleashed his Zulu regiments. Most of the early south-eastern trekkers were wiped out in the early months of 1838. By the end of the year, however, the Boers had regrouped and in a decisive battle they proved the superiority of their weaponry. Protected behind a tight circle of wagons (known as a *laager*), the guns of 500 Boers successfully beat off the massed attacks of the cream of the Zulu army. The Ncome River was said to have run red with the blood of the 3000 Zulu killed. Even after this dramatic victory, however, the Boers dared not occupy the densely populated region of the Zulu heartland. Their 'republic of Natalia' was founded to the south of the Tugela.

The Zulu suffered a civil war in 1840 during which Dingane was killed. Under the rule of his brother Mpande (1840–72) the Zulu kingdom recovered, and strengthened its northern boundary at the expense of the Swazi and remnants of independent Nguni. Further conflict with their white neighbours to the south was deliberately avoided.

In 1843 the British annexed the trekker 'republic' of Natal, primarily in order to prevent it falling into rival European hands. With that, many of the original Voortrekkers moved back on to the highveld and much of the land of Natal passed into the hands of British land speculators. The British briefly took control of the southern highveld in 1848 but then decided it was not worth the expense. At the Sand River and Bloemfontein Conventions (of 1852 and 1854 respectively) the British recognised the political independence of the Boer republics north of the Vaal and Orange Rivers.

Further expansion of Boer settlement on the highveld continued at the expense of their neighbours, in some regions with more difficulty than in others. In the south-eastern highveld of the Caledon River valley they were fiercely resisted by the powerful Sotho kingdom. During the 1840s the Sotho had strengthened their position by buying in guns and horses from the Cape

Figure 18.8   Portrait of Dingane, brother and assassin of Shaka, and King of the Zulus, 1828–40. (From *Narrative of a journey to the Zoolu Country* by A F Gardiner)

Colony. They became expert horsemen and the 'Basuto pony' became a characteristic breed of southern Africa. Full use was made of the mountainous terrain and some Sotho defensive positions were virtually impregnable. Nevertheless, in a series of wars in the 1850s and 1860s the Boers of the 'Orange Free State' gradually occupied the lowlands and reduced the size of the Sotho kingdom. In 1868 Moshoeshoe was driven to ask for British annexation. This saved the remnants of the Sotho kingdom from complete annihilation. But the most productive and valuable part of the kingdom had already been lost to Boer conquest.

Southern Africa in 1870

After further wars in the eastern Cape in the 1840s and 1850s, colonial authority had been extended as far as the River Kei. Xhosa resistance had shown the futility of simply expelling Africans from their land, and 'reserves' were set aside for African occupation in the eastern Cape. Much of the best land, however, was sold to white colonists who used it for grazing Merino sheep. The 'reserves' were inadequate for the subsistence of the western Xhosa and many families began to depend on meagre wages earned on white-owned farms. In Natal, where the African population of 250,000 outnumbered that of whites by nearly 15 to one, Africans were 'reserved' a mere 15 per cent of the land. In Natal, however, most of the white landowners were absentee. In practice, therefore, Africans occupied much of the land as peasant farmers,

Map 18.4   Southern Africa in 1870

paying rent or a share of their crops to the official white 'owners'. Within the Boer republics of the highveld, Africans living on white-owned farms were allowed to keep a few animals and grow their own crops, but in return they were expected to provide unpaid labour services to the Boer landholders.

The majority of the people in the southern African interior, black or white, in republics, colonies or kingdoms, were still, by 1870, largely dependent on a self-sufficient mixture of pastoralism and small-scale crop cultivation. The products of hunting – skins, ivory and ostrich feathers – were their main export commodities. These were exchanged for guns, ammunition and manufactured luxuries. British merchants at the coastal ports of Cape Town, Port Elizabeth and Durban made large fortunes out of what was known as 'the interior trade'.

By 1870 a certain political balance had been achieved between black and white in southern Africa. The rapid white expansion of the early years of the Boer Trek had ended. White settlement had become firmly established in the areas most weakened by the *mfecane/difaqane,* but elsewhere African kingdoms had recovered and emerged militarily stronger than before. They were now importing guns from the Cape and Natal and would be better able to defend themselves against future white challenge. Any further large-scale extension of white settlement in the interior would require the kind of military resources which only a major European power such as Britain could provide. But so long as the hunting trade, furnished primarily by willing African hunters, remained the interior's principal export, the British had no particular incentive to intervene.

All that was about to change with the discovery of huge deposits of valuable minerals in the southern African interior: diamonds just north of the Orange River in the 1870s and gold in the heart of the Boer republic of the Transvaal in the 1880s. The impact of these discoveries transformed the course of southern African history, as will be discussed in Chapter 22.

chapter

19

North and north-east Africa in the nineteenth century

The French in north Africa and Algerian resistance

The whole of the north African coastal region, apart from the western kingdom of Morocco, was still nominally part of the Ottoman empire in the early nineteenth century. But the Turkish regents of the north African provinces ruled their territories with no direct reference to the sultan at Istanbul. Even in the territories themselves, regency authority did not extend far beyond a narrow coastal fringe. Algeria was typical in this respect. Here the ruler, the *dey*, was drawn from the ranks of the Turkish officers of the coastal and garrison towns. Beyond the towns the Berbers remained virtually independent, especially in the mountains. The *dey* periodically intervened in disputes between rival Berber groups, but otherwise had little effective influence in the rural areas. Nominal Ottoman rule in Algeria was ended by the French in 1830 when they occupied the coastal towns of Algiers and Oran and sent the *dey* into exile.

The French invasion of Algeria

Relations between France and the rulers of Algeria had been under strain for some time. Algeria had been exporting grain and olive oil to France since the eighteenth century. In 1798 the Algerian *dey* supplied grain to the French army for Napoleon's invasion of Egypt – an indication of the degree

Map 19.1 Algeria and the Maghrib, 1800–80

of independence exercised by these supposed provinces of the Ottoman empire. Subsequent French governments, however, refused to pay the debt for the grain. Disputes over this and other matters led to a break in diplomatic relations between France and Algeria in 1827.

The excuse for the French invasion in 1830 was to bring an end to the piracy of the corsairs of Algiers (see p. 173). In fact corsair piracy, which had been rife in earlier centuries, was no longer a serious threat to powerfully protected European shipping in the Mediterranean. In reality the French invasion and occupation of Algiers in 1830 was an attempt to raise nationalistic fervour in support of a corrupt and unpopular French monarchy. Subsequent French governments viewed the territory as a potentially wealthy colony for white settlement and as a market for the products of French factories. From the beginning, however, the French faced the formidable opposition of the Arab-Berber Muslims of the interior.

'Abd al-Qadir and Algerian resistance

The French invasion of Algeria prompted one of the continent's hardest-fought and most protracted wars of African resistance against nineteenth-century European colonial conquest. The nomadic and semi-nomadic clans and Muslim brotherhoods of the Algerian interior were notorious for their rivalry and the frequent raids and warfare between themselves. But they had at least the pattern of their economic life, their Arabic language and their Islamic religion and cultural values in common. There thus always existed the seeds of an underlying unity which might emerge when faced with an outside threat to their whole way of life. The French invasion of 1830 was just such a threat. Alien rulers had exercised their power from the coastal towns for centuries, but the Turks were at least Muslim and their rule was to some extent informed by Islamic law and practices. The French, on the other hand, threatened not only conquest and foreign rule, but also the imposition of a completely alien religion, culture and legal system. Resistance to the French, therefore, took the form of a *jihad* or holy war against the infidel (the 'unbeliever'), and as such, the struggle continued for almost fifty years.

Early Algerian resistance was organised and led by 'Abd al-Qadir (the title 'al-Qadir' means 'the Great' in Arabic), a gifted and energetic young *marabout* ('holy man') from western Algeria. Like his jihadist contemporaries south of the Sahara, 'Abd al-Qadir used the stimulus of the *jihad* to unite the Arab-Berber clans and Muslim brotherhoods of Algeria into a single, powerful Islamic state. He overcame the problems of local rivalries by dividing the country into a number of administrative districts and holding each district chief responsible for his own defence. Administrative headquarters were heavily fortified and were used as bases for raiding French columns and towns. Though guns were imported from Europe, many were also made and repaired by the Algerians themselves. Much of the central authority of the state was exercised by 'Abd al-Qadir himself. As 'Commander of the Faithful' he regularly toured the administrative districts, coordinating military operations and dispensing justice according to the strict laws of the Qur'an.

In the end the French prevailed, but only at the cost of tens of thousands of French lives and possibly hundreds of thousands of Algerian ones. The massive French army of occupation numbered more than 100,000 by the end of the 1840s. They used scorched-earth tactics, destroying animals and crops and massacring villagers. They exploited local rivalries and promised support

Figure 19.1 An incident in
the Algerian wars of
resistance, 1830–79

to those who resented the authority of 'Abd al-Qadir. Al-Qadir himself was
finally captured and exiled in 1847. But the strength of the movement he had
founded was shown in the continuance of resistance long after his removal.
The mountainous region of Kabylie was not occupied by the French until
1857 and was disrupted by rebellion for most of the 1870s. It was 1879
before the French could finally consider that they had battered the Algerians
into submission. But they never conquered the sullen resentment which their
occupation engendered.

*The French
occupation*

In the wake of French conquest came white settlers, not only from France but
also from Spain and the poor rural districts of the Mediterranean islands. As
Arab-Berber farmers and pastoralists were cleared from their land, the white
settlers moved in, taking over olive plantations and vineyards along the
coastal hillsides and wheat farms in the plains around the towns. When the
military government had no more land to give out, the European immigrants
bought further land for a pittance from impoverished peasant farmers. In
1871 the European colonists in Algeria, known as *colons,* numbered 130,000:
by the end of the century they had reached a million, 13 per cent of the total
population. By the closing decades of the century, most of the cultivable land
in the country was in the hands of European landowners, the majority of
whom were absentees, living in the towns. The land itself was worked by the
dispossessed Arab-Berber peasantry, who were poorly paid and overtaxed.
Muslim Algerians were brought under strict control and their freedom of
movement was restricted, much in the manner of the Khoesan of the Cape
Colony in the early nineteenth century (see pp. 271–2). To add to the
humiliation of conquest, Islamic law was overridden by French law. In their
own country Muslim Algerians were regarded by the French *colon* government as alien and inferior. The arrogance of French administrators added
insult to injury.

Figure 19.2 Tuareg man working in his vegetable garden in the oasis, Djanet, Sahara Desert, Algeria

Egypt and Sudan to the Mahdist jihad

The French occupation of Egypt

In late June 1798 a French army, 25,000 strong, landed on Egypt's Mediterranean coast and seized Alexandria. At the time Egypt was loosely controlled by two Mamluk *beys*, Ibrahim and Murad. Their power was based upon the loyalty of local *beys*: Ibrahim commanding Cairo and the Delta and Murad most of Upper Egypt.

Underlying French designs on Egypt was an old Anglo-French rivalry that stemmed back to at least the Seven Years War (1756–63) when France lost out to Britain in both India and North America. Although Britain had lost the American War of Independence (1776–83), she still had Canada, many Caribbean colonies and, above all, India. France, on the other hand, was in the process of losing her most profitable Caribbean sugar colony to the slave revolt in Haiti. It was under these circumstances that French attention turned to Egypt. The French already had trading interests in Egypt, through which they received grain and cotton, but by the 1790s they were suffering competition from British traders. French colonisation of Egypt would secure them a reliable source of cotton and grain as well as potentially provide sugar plantations to supplant those lost in the Caribbean.

The colonising expedition was led by the young, impetuous French general Napoleon Bonaparte. Napoleon's ambition far outstripped the designs of the French Government in Paris. He modelled himself on Alexander ('the Great') of Macedon who had conquered Egypt and led his armies through western Asia as far as the valley of the Indus. Napoleon aimed to create a similar 'Empire of the Orient', with himself as its leader. He even saw it as potentially, like an 'America of the East', ultimately gaining its independence from France. And in order to create his eastern empire of French civilization, Napoleon took with him 200 civilians from among the best intellectuals in France – scientists, mathematicians, geographers, artists and linguists. He called them his 'savants'.

On 21 July 1798 the French fought the main Egyptian army north of Cairo in what Napoleon pretentiously termed 'The Battle of the Pyramids'.

Napoleon's army was substantially outnumbered, but the courageous charges of the cream of the Mamluk cavalry were no match for the tightly disciplined French infantry squares. By the end of the day the Egyptian army had been put to flight with the loss of many thousand men, including up to 2000 of the Mamluk's elite cavalry, with the French loss of barely 150 casualties. Murad Bey retreated into Upper Egypt from where the Mamluks conducted regular attacks against the French occupying forces. Ibrahim Bey withdrew into Syria (the contemporary name for the whole of the territory between Turkey and Sinai).

Days after the French victory outside Cairo the British navy annihilated the French fleet as it lay at anchor in a bay to the east of Alexandria. Cut off from supplies and reinforcements, Napoleon's attempt to extend his conquests into Ottoman Syria were defeated. The following year he abandoned his army in Egypt and made his way back overland to Paris to seize power in the French capital. In 1801 an Ottoman army, with British naval support, forced the remnants of the French army out of Egypt.

The French three-year occupation of Egypt is important for a number of reasons. In his brief year in Egypt Napoleon undermined Mamluk feudal power and began laying the foundations of a modern civil state which would be taken up by his successor, as we shall see below. Second, the French invasion marked the beginnings of an Anglo-French rivalry in Egypt that was to dominate much of that country's history in the century that followed. Indeed, it prefigured the late nineteenth-century European 'Scramble for Africa' that was largely led by France and Britain. Finally, in meticulously recording Ancient Egyptian religious and artistic work, as well as finding the 'Rosetta stone' (see p. 70), Napoleon's 'savants' laid the foundations of modern Egyptology.

Egypt under Muhammad Ali, 1805–49

Out of the chaos which followed the French evacuation of Egypt in 1801 there rose to power in Egypt a remarkable man named Muhammad Ali. He dragged the Egyptian state out of the sands of weakness and corruption into which it had sunk during the eighteenth century. Within a mere twenty years Muhammad Ali transformed Egypt into the most powerful province of the Ottoman empire, able to challenge the authority of the sultan himself.

Muhammad Ali came from the Ottoman province of Albania, north-east of modern Greece. He came to Egypt with an Albanian contingent as part of the Ottoman army which forced the French out of Egypt in 1801. With the backing of his Albanian troops, Muhammad Ali soon made himself the master of Cairo, and in 1805 the Ottoman sultan recognised him as *pasha* (viceroy) of Egypt.

Muhammad Ali's initial aim, like that of so many of the alien rulers of Egypt before him, was to found his own dynasty. He wanted the *pashalic* of Egypt as a hereditary position for himself and his family after him. He sought to make Egypt the richest and most powerful state in all of northern Africa, independent in all but name from the Ottoman empire, and secure from all internal or external enemies. Muhammad Ali recognised that in order to achieve these aims he needed to implement some pretty drastic reforms and in particular, in the wake of the French evacuation, he needed to prevent the Mamluks from re-establishing their corrupt tax-farming system.

In implementing his reforms Muhammad Ali favoured European advice and technology. He developed a salaried civil service and a modern professional

Figure 19.3 Muhammad Ali, *pasha* of Egypt 1805–49

army, both modelled on European rather than African or Asian lines. Because of these leanings European historians have often praised him as a 'moderniser', and indeed many Egyptians themselves view him as 'the founder of modern Egypt'. It is important to remember, however, that for all his reform and modernisation, Muhammad Ali was not motivated by any desire to better the lot of the Egyptian people as a whole. The Egyptian population in the 1820s was 2.5 million, 90 per cent of whom were *fellahin* (peasants), despised by Muhammad Ali as 'barbarians'. The Egyptian *fellahin* had always been grossly exploited, especially during periods of Egyptian 'greatness'. But even by these standards, during Muhammad Ali's reign they suffered particularly harshly. On top of their usual taxation and forced labour, they were conscripted into the army. When the *fellahin* responded with a series of revolts in the 1820s, these were brutally suppressed.

The basis of Muhammad Ali's power was the army: first the Albanians who brought him to power, then Sudanese slaves, and finally conscripted Egyptian *fellahin*. For centuries the Egyptian army had consisted of irregular feudal levies, raised and controlled by Mamluk *beys* (commanders) in return for vast estates ('tax farms' or *iqta*) from which they drew the tax. The system had been open to corruption and abuse as *iqta* became hereditary and the Egyptian central government lost control of both the army and the country's tax. In its place Muhammad Ali built a professional salaried army, organised in specialised regiments of cavalry, artillery and infantry, disciplined and drilled by Turkish and European officers. He disposed of his principal opponents, the Mamluks, with characteristic ruthlessness. In 1811 he organised the massacre of several hundred Mamluk *beys* and the remainder fled the country to take refuge at Dongola, south of the Egyptian frontier in what was to become known as Sudan.

Muhammad Ali took over for himself the estates of the Mamluks. He abolished the tax-farming system, so that taxes were now paid directly to the state. He introduced a new land survey, the first for several centuries, so that taxes could be reassessed and more efficiently collected. He developed a reformed and salaried civil service answerable only to central government. At

Map 19.2   The expansion of the Egyptian empire, 1805–80

the same time he introduced agricultural reforms. As with so many of his predecessors, reform of agriculture in Egypt was motivated by a desire to raise greater revenue for the state. In Muhammad Ali's time irrigation was extended, the work being done by the traditional forced labour of the *fellahin*. More land was brought under cultivation and long-fibre cotton, imported from Sudan, soon became a major Egyptian cash crop. Taxes were paid in kind, mostly wheat and cotton, and these were exported to Europe at a good profit to the state.

The Egyptian invasion and occupation of Sudan from the 1820s will be considered shortly. It is sufficient to note here that it was initially prompted mainly by a desire to increase the supply of Sudanese slaves for the Egyptian army. Muhammad Ali's reign saw a revival of trade through the Red Sea to the Indian Ocean which had suffered since the opening of the south Atlantic route. Muhammad Ali's forces reasserted Ottoman power in the Red Sea and defeated the Wahhabi Arab clans of central Arabia who had occupied the holy cities of Mecca and Medina. This reopened the holy places to international Muslim pilgrimage, to the benefit of the merchants of Cairo who, as in earlier times, did brisk business with the pilgrims. Muhammad Ali reached the height of his personal ambition in 1841 when the Ottoman sultan recognised the *pashalic* of Egypt as a hereditary position within Muhammad Ali's family.

The growth of European power and influence in Egypt to 1882

There was increasing European interest in Egypt during the reign of Muhammad Ali and his immediate successors. European advisers, army officers and bureaucrats were all employed in the effort to 'modernise'. European merchants began to operate in the country after their governments had put pressure on Muhammad Ali to drop his restrictions on foreign traders in 1838. French and British merchants were particularly interested in expanding the ivory trade from Sudan. Britain began to use Egypt and the Red Sea as a shorter and alternative 'overland' route to her colonial territories in India. There followed heavy British investment in railway construction in the 1850s connecting the Mediterranean port of Alexandria to Cairo and the Red Sea port of Suez. In the early 1860s French engineers began work on a canal linking the Mediterranean to the Red Sea at Suez.

Muhammad Ali was succeeded by two short reigns, during which French and British influence increased still further. In 1863 Muhammad Ali's grandson, Isma'il, succeeded to the *pashalic* and shortly afterwards upgraded his title to that of *khedive* (an ancient Persian title meaning 'king'). It was a time of major boom in the state's finances, as Egyptian cotton exports benefited from the shortage of American cotton caused by civil war in the United States (1861–5). On the strength of this boom Isma'il invested heavily in extending the railway up the Nile and in updating his army to expand the Egyptian empire further into Sudan. But with the decline that followed the cotton boom of the 1860s, Egypt's vast indebtedness to Europeans began to tell. With the opening of the Suez Canal in 1869, more and more of Egypt's trade was dominated by European shipping. The canal had been jointly financed by France and Egypt, with the Egyptian government paying three-quarters of the £19 million costs. As Egypt's finances became overstretched in the 1870s, Britain seized the opportunity to buy the Egyptian share of the canal in 1875 for a mere £4 million, a fraction of its true worth. With this action Britain safeguarded its route to India and at the same time became deeply committed to the security of its investments in Egypt.

Figure 19.4 Construction of the Suez Canal. Before work on the canal could begin the Egyptian government excavated and re-flooded a 3000-year-old canal from the time of the Pharaohs, linking the Nile to the Red Sea, in order to provide fresh water for the workers

In 1876 Isma'il was forced to admit that his country was bankrupt, unable to pay its foreign debts. In order to safeguard their heavy financial involvement in Egypt the French and British forced the deposition of Isma'il in 1879 and the installation of his son Tawfiq as a puppet *khedive*. In an action that prefigured late twentieth-century World Bank and IMF policies in Africa, Britain and France formally established 'Dual Control' over Egypt's finances in order to ensure the payment of Egypt's debts to European banks.

This aroused the passion of Egyptian nationalists who opposed the Turko-Albanian ruling clique almost as much as they opposed this new European interference. Led by the son of an indigenous Egyptian *fellah* (peasant), Colonel Ahmad Urabi (sometimes referred to as Urabi Pasha), the nationalists and their supporters in the army pressured Tawfiq into appointing two of them to key government posts. Thus in 1881, Urabi became Minister for War and Mahmud al-Barudi became Prime Minister. Urabi's 'National Party' gained wide popularity under the slogan 'Egypt for the Egyptians'. The British and French pre-empted the establishment of an independent nationalist republic by sending a naval force to blockade Alexandria in May 1882. The French had done the same thing before occupying Tunisia only a year previously. Urabi strengthened the defences of Alexandria in which anti-imperial riots left 50 Europeans dead. In July 1882, while the French were busy quelling resistance in Tunisia, the British invaded Egypt. Four weeks later they defeated Urabi's army at the battle of Tel el-Kebir and occupied the country. Urabi was captured and exiled to Sri Lanka (the British-ruled Ceylon). Although Britain now in theory ruled the country in the name of their appointed *pasha,* Egypt had in practice become a British colony. A genuine attempt to establish an independent, modern nationalist Egyptian state had been deliberately thwarted in an action that some historians regard

Figure 19.5 Crowds watch a procession of ships on the Suez Canal, *c.*1874

as the first act in the notorious European 'Scramble for Africa'. Certainly, to the extent that inter-European rivalry fuelled the 'scramble', the French greatly resented the permanence of Britain's unilateral action of 1882 and Egypt became a thorn in the flesh of their imperial rivalry in the decades to come.

Egypt in Sudan to the Mahdist jihad

The principal aims of Muhammad Ali's invasion of Sudan were to crush the Mamluk stronghold of Dongola and to obtain Sudanese slaves to reinforce the Egyptian army. The invading force of 1820–1 consisted of only 4000 men but it was heavily armed with imported European guns and artillery. They occupied Dongola and scattered the remaining Mamluks. The Funj sultanate had been disintegrating for some years, and so was able to offer little effective resistance. The Egyptians took the Funj capital, Sennar, without much difficulty and founded Khartoum as an administrative capital at the junction of the two Niles. During the 1820s Egyptian control was extended over Kordofan to the south-west of Khartoum.

Egyptian forces raided for slaves to east and west, and particularly into the Nuba mountains to the south of Kordofan. Hopes of rediscovering the gold-mines of ancient Egypt were quickly disappointed, but ivory soon became an alternative source of wealth. In the early 1840s the Egyptians finally overcame fierce Shilluk resistance on the upper Nile and thus gained access to the rich elephant-hunting region of southern Sudan. The European, Egyptian and Sudanese merchants based in Khartoum, however, found it more profitable to raid than to trade and the Egyptian government placed no restrictions on their activities on the upper Nile. So the private armies of these mostly alien merchants literally plundered the southern Sudanese in their search for ivory and to a lesser extent for slaves.

In the 1860s and 1870s *khedive* Isma'il made further efforts to extend the Egyptian empire in the south. Garrisons were built among the Shilluk and Dinka of the upper Nile. European administrators Samuel Baker and Charles Gordon were employed in the 1870s in an unsuccessful attempt to bring the lakeland kingdoms of Bunyoro and Buganda under Egyptian control. Darfur was conquered in 1874. All this military activity provoked great hostility among the Sudanese and added considerably to Egypt's crippling foreign debt.

In 1881 a Muslim holy man from Dongola, Muhammad Ahmad, declared that he was the Mahdi, 'the Guided One', the saviour who would restore Muslim purity to the faithful of Islam. His call for a *jihad* prompted an enthusiastic response in Sudan. Attempts by Gordon to suppress the slave trade in the 1870s had been strongly resented by Muslim traders who had for generations profited from the traffic. The cattle-owning nomads of Kordofan hoped to throw off the heavy burden of taxation imposed on them by the bankrupt Egyptian administration. The holy men of the Sudanese Muslim brotherhoods were scandalised by the corruption and lack of Islamic observance practised by Turkish and Egyptian administrators. The increasing use of European Christians in the administration merely emphasised the alien quality of the Egyptian presence in Sudan.

The Mahdist state of Sudan

The bravery and fervour of the Mahdist forces won them some impressive early victories over the better-armed, 'modern' Egyptian armies sent against them. In 1885 they took Khartoum, killing Gordon and the remnants of the Egyptian soldiers and officials in the city. Five months later Muhammad Ahmad died, to the consternation of his most fervent supporters who

Map 19.3 The Mahdist Sudan, 1885–98

290

believed the Mahdi was immortal. For a while the unity of the Mahdist movement lay in the balance, but the situation was saved by the determined rule of his successor, *khalifa* 'Abdallahi. This man set up a strong administrative system of appointed district governors, responsible for collecting taxation in strict accordance with the rule of the Qur'an. This was paid fairly willingly as it was far less arduous than the demands of former Egyptian tax-collectors. The administration of the Mahdist state covered most of the region of the modern republic of Sudan. Communications were maintained over this vast area by a regular system of camel-mounted couriers. Unfortunately, most of the energies and revenue of the state were spent on wars with its neighbours: Ethiopia to the south-east and British-controlled Egypt in the north. The Mahdist state was finally destroyed by a huge Anglo-Egyptian army sent against it in 1898. At the battle of Omdurman 11,000 Sudanese were slaughtered by British and Egyptian machine-guns and artillery at the cost of merely 48 killed in the Anglo-Egyptian army. The Mahdist state of Sudan became an Anglo-Egyptian condominion – in effect, a British colony. The remote western sultanate of Darfur, however, which had only ever been loosely attached to the Mahdist state was not included in this British conquest. Indeed, it remained for the time being one of the few African states to survive – through neglect – the 'Scramble for Africa' of 1880–1910.

The reunification of Ethiopia

Ever since the eighteenth century the emperor residing at Gondar had been little more than nominal head of the Ethiopian empire. The very title 'king of kings' indicated that the emperor was ruler over many separate 'kings' and in this, the 'era of the princes', the provincial rulers of this 'federation' asserted their independence. In the northern and western borderlands it was left to the local nobility to defend their 'territory' from persistent Egyptian raids.

The power of the nobility and the position of the peasantry is indicated in a revealing observation by the British consul to Ethiopia in 1854:

> The prosperous or adverse condition of a village depends almost entirely upon the rapacity or moderation of its immediate chief … . The imposts are numerous, but vary according to the traditional customs of each village. They pay a certain portion in kind to the Ras, or other great chief, and sometimes a regular tax in money; besides this they must furnish oxen to plough the King's lands: their immediate governor then takes his share in kind of every grain – say a fifth, and feeds besides a certain number of soldiers at the expense of each householder; he has rights to oxen, sheep, and goats, butter, honey, and every other requisite for subsistence; he must be received with joy and feasting by his subjects whenever he visits them, and can demand from them contributions on fifty pretexts – he is going on a campaign, or returning from one; he has lost a horse, or married a wife; his property has been consumed by fire, or he has lost his all in battle; or the sacred duty of a funeral banquet cannot be fulfilled without their aid.

> (Great Britain, Parliamentary Papers, Correspondence respecting Abyssinia, 1846–68 (London 1868), 107, Plowden to Clarendon, 9 July 1854. Quoted in *Cambridge History of Africa,* Vol. 5, p. 70)

In the early 1850s the governor of the western province of Qwara, Lij Kassa Haylu, learnt from the experience of his clashes with the Egyptians. He reformed his army of irregular feudal levies into a trained and disciplined regular fighting force, equipped with firearms and artillery. In 1855 Kassa invaded the central provinces and seized the imperial throne for himself. He took the title Tewodros (Theodore) II. Though the 13-year reign of Tewodros was to end in disaster and suicide, it was nevertheless crucially important for the future survival of Ethiopia as an independent state. It was Tewodros who revived the concept of effective centralised government. His reforms brought him the hostility of Church and nobility alike. But in trying to tackle these reforms Tewodros laid the foundations for unity and revealed the nature of the problems to be faced by his successors.

Tewodros attempted to cut the independent power of the regional nobility by appointing district governors and judges, who were paid a salary by central government. In the past these positions had been in the hands of the local hereditary nobility, who supported themselves from the labour of their peasantry. At the same time, Tewodros eased his dependence on the irregular feudal levies of the powerful nobility. He expanded his own regular military force into a national army, drilled, disciplined and salaried, and trained in the use of modern firearms and artillery. Between 1855 and 1861 there were a number of regional rebellions as the local nobility tried to assert their independence from

Map 19.4 Ethiopia, 1855–96

Figure 19.6 The suicide of Emperor Tewodros II of Ethiopia, after his defeat by the British at the battle of Magdala, 1868 (by Emile Bayard, in Cassell's *Illustrated History of the World*)

centralised government control. Hostility towards the emperor was raised still further when Tewodros, in attempting to suppress these rebellions, allowed his soldiers to loot and massacre and mutilate their captives.

Tewodros might have survived these problems had he retained the support of the Church. But in attempting to abolish the grosser privileges of the clergy, he confiscated many of the huge Church estates, leaving each parish with just enough land to support a minimum handful of clergy. Tewodros's loss of Church support lost him the legitimacy of his imperial title. It was largely Church influence which persuaded a majority of Ethiopians to desert their emperor in his time of greatest need.

The crisis came in 1868. In a minor diplomatic dispute with British consular officials, Tewodros arrested the local British consul. The British, anxious to assert their position as a major world power, sent a huge British army of 30,000 men to rescue the consular 'hostages'. As the British army penetrated the highlands, support for the emperor melted away. At the battle of Magdala Tewodros was only able to field 4000 troops and these were quickly overcome. Tewodros himself committed suicide rather than face capture. The British withdrew, their honour satisfied, and Europeans were left with a false sense of the ease with which Ethiopia might be conquered in the future.

The reunification and expansion of Ethiopia to 1896

Dej Kassa of Tigray, who had assisted the British in their march through northern Ethiopia, declared himself Tewodros's successor. He had rivals to defeat and battles to win, but in January 1872 he had himself crowned as Johannes IV in Axum's Church of Mary, following elaborate ancient rituals to show his faith in Ethiopian tradition.

Johannes abandoned the practice of appointing salaried officials as district governors and judges and returned much of their former power to the regional nobility. This regained him the support of most of the powerful princes of Ethiopia, though it left the feudal system firmly entrenched in Ethiopian society. With the wide support that he could now command, Johannes was able to summon a large Christian army to repel the threat from Muslim Egypt in the north. The other main external threat came from the east where the Italians had declared a colony over the ports of Assab and

Figure 19.7 The Battle of Adwa in which Menelik's Ethiopian forces defeated the Italians: Brigadier General Dabormida's troops encounter fierce resistance. (Illustration in *L'Illustrazione Italiana*, 29 March 1896, p. 200)

Massawa in 1882 and 1885 respectively. Johannes defeated a force of 500 Italians at the battle of Dogali in 1887. Johannes, however, never established complete control over the whole of Ethiopia. He faced constant opposition from his rival to the throne, Menelik of the southern Christian kingdom of Shoa.

Menelik had for years been strengthening his position in the southern regions of the empire. He built up a large and powerful army, equipped with rifles and artillery bought from French and Italian traders on the coast. While Johannes was still on the throne and defending the empire from the Italians, Menelik was expanding his power to the east. He captured the Muslim city of Harar and made it the centre of his arms trade with the French at the Gulf of Tadjoura (Djibouti).

Menelik succeeded to the imperial throne on the death of Johannes in 1889. He established his capital in the Shoan heartland at Addis Ababa and proceeded to expand the empire in the south by military conquest. Non-Christian Oromo, Sidama and Somali were brought within the empire and vast estates in the region were given out to Shoan military governors and notables.

In the north Menelik was confronted by the imperial ambitions of Italy. He was forced to recognise the Italian coastal colony of Eritrea, over which they had extended their authority between 1887 and 1890. But an Italian attempt to extend their conquests into the Ethiopian heartland was faced with resounding defeat by Menelik's vastly superior army. Menelik's victory at the battle of Adwa in 1896 effectively saved Ethiopia from European colonial conquest during the era of the 'Scramble for Africa'.

chapter
20
Christianity and pre-colonial 'nationalism'

European Christian missionaries in pre-colonial Africa

Early Christian missionaries to sub-Saharan Africa

Roman Catholic Christian missionaries from Portugal had closely followed the early Portuguese coastal penetration of tropical Africa. In the late fifteenth and early sixteenth centuries Catholic missionaries were sent to Africa to convert a number of African rulers. These, it was hoped, would become useful allies of the Portuguese. But once African rulers realised the strong political motivation behind their presence, the missionaries' initiative was doomed to failure. In one African state after another, Portuguese missionaries were expelled or even killed. This was largely because they and their handful of converts offered a direct challenge to the established political and religious order. African rulers were interested in contact with Europeans, but they wanted new trading openings, technical assistance and firearms. They did not want new ideas that threatened to undermine the traditional religious basis of their authority.

Portuguese missionaries made little headway in Benin, and attempts to convert the *Oba* were abandoned in the early sixteenth century. Christianity left little lasting impression there, beyond such things as the adoption of the cross as a symbol within Benin artwork. Greater success was achieved in Kongo where a Christian convert became king in 1506. But with the growth of the slave trade the Portuguese soon gave up even the pretence of treating the king of Kongo as a fellow-Christian monarch. Foreign missionaries became increasingly alienated from the communities they were supposed to serve, as Christianity itself was absorbed into traditional Kongo culture. In Ethiopia missionaries of the newly founded Jesuit order followed hot on the heels of Portuguese military assistance to Galadewos in the early 1540s. But they had little success in converting Ethiopian Christians to the Roman Catholic version of the faith. In the mid-seventeenth century they were expelled for political interference. Further south, in the Mutapa state of modern Zimbabwe, Portuguese Catholic missionaries tried in the 1560s to convert the Munhumutapa and his court. They hoped in this way to control the kingdom and the region's gold trade. As elsewhere, their activities provoked a political and religious reaction and in this case the missionary and some converts were killed.

Looking back from the perspective of the late eighteenth century it was clear that European Christianity, as a vehicle for religious and cultural change, had made virtually no impact at all on the peoples of sub-Saharan

Africa. By contrast, the Christian revival of the early nineteenth century was a very different matter. Though initially slow to take effect, eventually its impact proved to be both far-reaching and permanent.

The evangelical Christian revival

The evangelical Christian revival arose in late eighteenth-century and early nineteenth-century western Europe and north America. It was closely related to the humanitarian movement for the abolition of the slave trade (see above, p. 237). It had arisen out of a desire to bring moral and spiritual salvation to the oppressed working classes of the new industrial cities of Europe and north America.

The evangelical movement contained a strong missionary purpose, it being the duty of every devout Christian to spread the faith to the wider 'heathen' world. And in their ignorance of Africa, European Christians believed that non-Muslim Africans had no religion. What rituals they observed, they dismissed as superstition. Africa was therefore seen as a fruitful field for

Map 20.1   Christianity and Islam in Africa, to 1885

Christian missions. Here missionaries could play their part in preaching against the evils of slavery and the slave trade. Europeans were quick to overlook their own central role in the promotion of the slave trade.

The evangelical missionaries saw their Christianity as part and parcel of their own European cultural values – even to the extent of insisting that African converts adopt European clothing. They preached a strict puritanical moral code. They opposed dancing, drinking, non-religious singing and any form of sexual freedom outside monogamous marriage. Applied to Africa, this meant condemnation of much of the essential fabric of African society. In particular, they condemned what they saw as the sexual laxity of polygamy and anything that contained an element of non-Christian ritual such as initiation and rain-making ceremonies. On the positive side, Christianity offered a sense of spiritual salvation to those who for one reason or another had lost faith in the security and comforts of traditional African beliefs. And since belief in the written word of the Bible was an essential ingredient of their faith, the spread of Christianity also meant the spread of basic education for literacy.

During the course of the nineteenth century, a large number of European Christian societies sent their missionaries to Africa. Among the more important were the British-based Anglican Church Missionary Society (CMS), which was prominent in Sierra Leone; the Wesleyan Methodist Missionary Society, which had bases and schools along the West African coastal region; and the London Missionary Society (LMS), which initially worked mainly in southern Africa. Protestant missions also came from France, Germany, Holland and the United States. French Catholic missions followed later in the century.

African Christians and pre-colonial nationalism

West Africa

The most successful early fields of mission enterprise in tropical Africa were Sierra Leone and Liberia (see pp. 243–6). Sierra Leone in particular had two distinct advantages. In the first place, the dislocated 'recaptives', settled there in large numbers from the 1820s, had for the most part been torn violently from the security of traditional African cultural practices and religious beliefs. In this position they were particularly receptive to the teachings of European missionaries. European cultural values and Christianity gave them a new sense of spiritual security and social purpose. Second, European missionaries found themselves cut off from much of the tropical African interior by barriers of language, culture and tropical disease. Sierra Leone presented the ideal training ground for educating Africans themselves as the missionaries who would carry the Christian message into the heart of tropical Africa. Thus, much of the early Christian mission-work in the interior of tropical West Africa was in fact carried out by Africans themselves. Among the most important of these was Samuel Ajayi Crowther (see Figure 20.1 and caption), West Africa's first black Anglican bishop and the leader of the successful CMS mission to the Niger delta.

More significant in terms of African political thought in this period was Edward Wilmot Blyden, a Liberian settler, born (in 1832) of free parents in the slave society of the Caribbean Virgin Islands. Having been refused entry to an American university in 1850, he took ship to Liberia, the newly independent

Figure 20.1 Bishop Samuel Ajayi Crowther (*c.*1806–1891). Ajayi, an enslaved Yoruba from south-western Nigeria, was 'liberated' from a Portuguese slaving vessel off Lagos in 1821 by a ship of the British Anti-Slavery Squadron that transported him to Sierra Leone. He was one of the first students of Fourah Bay College, converted to Christianity, taking the names Samuel Crowther after a CMS benefactor, and became a CMS missionary. A founding member of the CMS mission to southern Nigeria in 1845, Ajayi Crowther was consecrated bishop of the Niger Mission in 1864. He published numerous influential books in English and translated the Bible into Yoruba. (Unattributed engraving in *Missionary Heroes of Africa*)

(since 1847) African-American republic on the west African coast. There, as a school and university teacher, a prolific writer and the editor of *The Liberia Herald*, Blyden became the most influential African intellectual of his generation. His writings showed great pride in the African empires of the past, but like many of his African Christian contemporaries, Blyden believed that what Africa now needed was a new 'civilising mission'. This sounded a lot like the white paternalistic American Colonisation Society (the ACS, which had founded Liberia), of which he was a great admirer. Unlike the ACS, however, Blyden's civilising mission – spreading the enlightenment of Western knowledge and ideas – was to be brought to Africa by Westernised black people like himself. In effect, he believed that the republic of Liberia, or something very like it, should be extended all along the west African coast. In these ideas one can see the first traces of a new African 'nationalism' – distinct from indigenous African authority and independent of white control. It was also one of the earliest expositions of Pan-Africanism being applied to West Africa. Like many of his contemporaries in the 1850s and 1860s, however, Blyden had a misplaced faith in British imperialism as a source of enlightenment in Africa.

Another important intellectual of this generation, and one who was to try and put some of Blyden's ideas into practice, was James 'Africanus' Horton. Born of Igbo 're-captive' parents in Sierra Leone in 1835, James Horton showed early intellectual promise and became a student of the new Fourah Bay College in Freetown in 1853. The British army at the time, aware of the high mortality rate among European medical officers in West Africa, was keen to recruit African officers into its West African medical corps. Horton became one of their star recruits, gaining his doctorate from the University of Edinburgh in 1859. On the title page of his thesis on west African medical topography, he inserted the middle name 'Africanus', so that nobody would doubt from the rest of his name that he was African. He rose to become a renowned surgeon-major in the British army in West Africa, serving mainly in the Gold Coast, and published numerous works on tropical medicine. Even while serving in the British army, however, Horton also involved himself in politics and particularly in the emerging ideas of African nationalism and Pan-Africanism, as espoused by Blyden.

The 1860s was a vibrant time among educated Africans on the Gold Coast and Horton helped in the formulation of their ideas. It was a time when the British Protectorate of the Gold Coast was under threat from the powerful inland empire of Asante that wanted to assert control over trading at the coast. The British had encouraged the coastal Ga and Fante states that were supposedly under their protection to assert their independence from Asante, thus ensuring British domination of coastal trade. Tension between Britain and Asante soon led to the war of 1863–4, in which Horton served.

Following British defeat in this war, the British parliament considered withdrawal from direct involvement in west Africa. It proposed that Britain's coastal protectorates should become self-governing under some loose form of British oversight. Although this was never implemented, it coincided with African nationalist ideas of the time and the Ga and Fante set up confederacies in anticipation of British withdrawal. The Accra and Fante Confederate constitutions were influenced and largely drawn up by James Africanus Horton. They proposed a series of self-governing states, working in collaboration in a broad federal system, a combination of the best of traditional and modern. Traditional rulers would be incorporated and would rule as equals alongside the educated elite. Government would be representative and the profits of trade would be used for the development of roads, schools, health, agriculture, industry and the exploitation of minerals. Most importantly, these modern states would be independent of both Asante and the British.

It was believed by Horton and others that modernising ideas such as these could be spread throughout west Africa, thus ultimately forming a Pan-Africanist federation. The British feared the concept and did their best to suppress the Confederacies, arresting some leaders on charges of treason. Horton's best-known political book, published in 1867, was *West African Countries and Peoples: A Vindication of the African Race*. It was a powerful attack on European notions of racial superiority that were then becoming prominent. In 1873 war broke out again between Britain and Asante. This time the British invaded and sacked the Asante capital of Kumasi. Although they withdrew from the occupation of Asante, Britain followed up its military victory of 1874 by declaring that the Gold Coast Protectorate would now become a full Crown Colony. This left the British in complete control of the coastal region and killed off any hope of a modern African independent confederation.

Southern Africa

Another prolific field of early nineteenth-century mission enterprise was southern Africa (see p. 265). Like Sierra Leone it contained, in the Khoesan, a large number of dislocated people. It was thus among the poor and dispossessed communities of Khoesan, freed slaves and mixed-race peoples that

LMS and Moravian missionaries founded their most successful early missions. The best-known African Christian of this period, however, was a Xhosa, Tiyo Soga. Born in independent Xhosa country, Soga was sent to mission school by his mother, a Christian convert. He caught the eye of Scottish missionaries and was brought to Scotland on two occasions for further education. In 1856 he became the first African from South Africa to be ordained. He returned to South Africa with a Scottish wife in 1857 and worked as a missionary in the eastern Cape region. He translated much of the New Testament into the Xhosa language. In other writings he urged his fellow-Africans to take pride in their African heritage in the dominant colonial world. In tackling such issues he was perhaps an inspiration to later African journalists in South Africa, such as J. T. Jabavu and Sol Plaatje.

In general, beyond the borders of the Cape Colony, missionaries were welcomed mostly for their technical and literary expertise and their access to firearms. This was particularly the case at Kuruman, the LMS mission to the southern Tswana, north of the Cape Colony. Luka Jantjie, born in the 1830s, the son of a rare Christian convert from within the southern Batswana ruling family, sought throughout his life to reconcile the duties of a modern indigenous ruler with the aggressive demands of advancing colonialism. It was a struggle he was doomed to lose following the discovery of diamonds in his people's territory in the 1870s. Most African rulers, like Moshoeshoe of the Basotho, valued European missionaries as technical advisers and literary secretaries, but resisted their religion. They viewed Christianity as a threat to the religious basis of their political authority. A notable exception, the northern Batswana *Kgosi* Khama III, managed to use Christianity as a state religion to strengthen his authority.

Missionaries as agents of imperialism

Apart from a few special places like southern Africa, Liberia and Sierra Leone, it was clear by the third quarter of the nineteenth century that the Christian mission in tropical Africa was making slow progress (see Map 20.1). Mission stations were still largely confined to coastal regions, working among Africans already in cultural contact with Europeans through trading activities. Certainly less than 1 per cent of non-Muslim Africans (outside Ethiopia) had been converted to Christianity by the early 1880s. It was largely because of this relative lack of initial success that European missionaries turned more and more to their European governments for assistance. In doing so they appealed for European intervention to help change African society and make it more amenable to missionary enterprise.

Few Christian missionaries were directly active agents of European imperialism. But they were an essential ingredient of the increasingly assertive European presence which was a forerunner of imperial control. In a number of cases Christian missionaries played a significant role in promoting and shaping the advent of European colonialism. At times, especially in the final quarter of the century, European missionaries appealed to their home governments for various degrees of political or military 'protection'. This was usually in the face of local political conflict which threatened the safety of their missions. Nevertheless, when European governments responded positively to these appeals, it was usually due more to their own wider strategic or commercial interests.

In the region of modern Malawi, Scottish missionaries had been established to the west of the lake and in the Shire highlands since the mid-1870s.

Figure 20.2 African Lakes Company (ALC) ivory warehouse, Karonga, 1904. The ALC was funded by missionaries to promote the commercial side of the anti-slavery mantra: 'Christianity and commerce.' The warehouse was in fact built on the site of the headquarters of the slave and ivory-trader Mlozi (see p. 261)

They were aided by a small group of fervent Basotho Christians from Lovedale College in South Africa. Attempts to establish 'Christianity and commerce' as an alternative to the continuing slave trade of the area was aided by the African Lakes Company. This was a British trading company with strong links to the Scottish evangelical movement. They supplied cotton cloth and other British manufactured goods in an attempt to undercut the Arab, Swahili and Yao slavers who were still active in the area. The company hoped to make a handsome profit from the large-scale export of locally hunted ivory (see Figure 20.2).

The slave-traders of east-central Africa, however, were well-armed and firmly established. The missionaries had little success in promoting Christianity, and the African Lakes Company was unable to break the slavers' control of the ivory trade. In the early 1880s the missionaries and their sponsors in Britain began a series of appeals for some undefined form of 'British protection' to help suppress the slave trade. But the British government did not act decisively until the late 1880s. Then, they were mainly concerned to prevent the Portuguese of the lower Zambezi valley from restricting British trading access to the Shire highland region. Nevertheless, it was the joint pressure of British missionary and trading interests that helped promote and justify the British declaration of a 'protectorate' over the Shire highlands in 1889.

Similarly, German missionaries in Namibia appealed to their home government for 'protection' in the early 1880s. During a territorial war between Nama and Herero in 1880 their mission and trading activities were badly disrupted. A mission station was destroyed and one German missionary was lucky to escape with his life. Again, it was to safeguard commercial rather than missionary interests that the German government declared a 'protectorate' over 'South West Africa' in 1884. But the long-term presence of German missionaries in the interior provided some degree of public justification for German interest in the region.

In the wider scramble for southern Africa (see next chapter), British missionaries played an active part in promoting the extension of British imperial control. They saw this as preferable to white-settler control from colonial South Africa. In Bechuanaland LMS missionaries urged Tswana rulers to seek British protection as the only way to safeguard their land from seizure by Boers from the Transvaal. The Christian king, Khama, needed no persuasion. One LMS missionary, John Mackenzie, briefly acted as the British government's Deputy Commissioner for southern Bechuanaland in 1884. He tried, unsuccessfully, to prevent the alienation of Tswana land to white land-speculators from the Cape Colony and the Boer republics.

The most ignoble act of missionary imperialism in southern Africa was that of the LMS missionary to the Ndebele. In 1888 the Reverend Helm deliberately mistranslated a document for the Ndebele king, Lobengula, in order to cheat him into signing away his territory to a group of South African commercial speculators. But Helm was only reflecting the widely held opinion of Christian missionaries in general. After years of unsuccessful mission effort in Zimbabwe, the LMS missionaries openly advocated the overthrow of this powerful 'pagan' king as the only way to achieve a Christian breakthrough. It was only later that they realised the true nature of the monster they had helped unleash in the form of the British South Africa Company (see pp. 333–5).

In the meantime, in Buganda Christian missionaries faced the insecurity of threatened civil war; much of it, incidentally, promoted by recent Christian converts seeking to assert political control. The Anglican CMS, fearing for the survival of their mission in Buganda, set about raising money in Britain. This was used to pay half the cost of maintaining a British military force in the country from 1890 to 1891. The region was already declared a 'sphere of British influence', through agreement with other European powers. But with lack of military back-up the precise future of the territory remained uncertain. The CMS action undoubtedly saved their mission, promoted Protestant Christianity and helped smooth the way for the formal declaration of the British 'Protectorate' of Uganda in 1894.

European 'explorers': the mapping of Africa as a prelude to Empire

In 1768 an eccentric Scottish nobleman named James Bruce set off on a lengthy journey to Ethiopia to see for himself the source of the Blue Nile. On his return to Europe in 1783 Bruce found that few would believe his stories of the splendours of Ethiopia and in particular its royal court at Gondar. Bruce's revelations did not fit the prejudiced European view of Africa as a mass of primitive and disorganised societies, little more than a source of slaves. Despite centuries of coastal trading contact, Europeans were still remarkably ignorant of Africa, its peoples and their history. European interest in Africa, however, was about to be awoken.

It was the movement for the abolition of the slave trade which provided the stimulus for a revival of European interest in Africa. If Europeans were to benefit and to profit from the development of 'legitimate' commerce with Africa (see pp. 240–3), they needed a far wider knowledge of the continent. They needed knowledge of the transport potential of its great river-systems.

Figure 20.3 The Ethiopian capital of Gondar, as observed by James Bruce in the 1770s. On his return to Europe, readers of his book refused to believe that such grand and complex buildings could possibly have been built by Africans

They needed to know the raw materials which Africans had to sell, and they needed to locate the main centres of population which would form the new markets for European manufactured goods.

In 1788 a group of wealthy and influential Englishmen formed the African Association. Their immediate object was to send an expedition to visit the fabled city of Timbuktu and to investigate the course of the River Niger. Africa was still known to Europeans as the principal source of gold in medieval times. The Malian king Mansa Musa's famous fourteenth-century pilgrimage to Mecca had seen to that. His lavish gifts of gold in Cairo had helped to raise Timbuktu in European mythology as a city of immeasurable wealth where even slaves wore gold. As we have seen in earlier chapters, Timbuktu itself was never a source of gold. And its position as a major trading terminus had seriously declined in recent centuries. Nevertheless, this was the direction in which initial European journeys of exploration were aimed.

Between 1788 and 1877 an enormous number of European 'explorers' set out into the heart of Africa in an attempt to rectify their ignorance of the continent. It seems that once the movement got under way, barely a year went past without there being at least one European expedition engaged in exploring the interior of the continent. It can be argued, of course, that these European adventurers were not explorers in the strictest sense at all. The word 'exploration' implies the investigation of something previously unknown, whereas there was no part of Africa that was not known to some local African inhabitants. And many parts of Africa, especially the Sahara and Sahel, had been well known to the Arabic-speaking world for hundreds of years before European explorers 'discovered' them. European explorers, for the most part, followed well-worn long-distance trading routes, some even disguising themselves in Muslim dress in order to accompany trading caravans (see Figure 20.4). It is also worth observing that virtually every European explorer was dependent on African hospitality and travelled with

Map 20.2   European penetration of Africa before 1880

the aid of African guides and servants. Some travelled with their own massive caravans of porters and armed retainers. Had these indispensable African assistants been literate and recorded their adventures, their fame within Africa today might have equalled that which their employers achieved in nineteenth-century Europe.

The European explorers of Africa before the 1850s have usually been portrayed by historians as motivated by a spirit of pure, disinterested, scientific enquiry. Many of them may have seen themselves in that light. Others were attracted by sense of adventure, desire for fame or both. But it was taken for granted among those who financed the journeys, praised their 'discoveries' and avidly read their books, that their major benefit to Europe was the chance of greater trading profit in the future. The constitution of the African Association even allowed for information gathered to be kept secret, if that was likely to be to the commercial advantage of Britain. And the Association's first successful explorer, Mungo Park, clearly understood the prime intention of his journey. He described it as 'rendering the geography of Africa more familiar to my countrymen, and … opening to their ambition and industry

Figure 20.4 Richard Burton, traveller and fluent Arabic-speaker, in the costume he wore as a pilgrim to Mecca (unnamed photographer)

new sources of wealth, and new channels of commerce' (*Travels into the Interior of Africa,* first published London, 1799; this edition, Eland Books, 1983, p. 2).

Mungo Park visited the Niger twice (1795–7 and 1805–6), though he died in his attempt to follow the course of the river to the sea. Others followed his initiative, but it was 1827 before the Frenchman René Caillé became the first European to return with a first-hand account of Timbuktu. Ironically Caillé was disbelieved because his description of drab and dusty Timbuktu failed to live up to Europe's golden expectations. This was in direct contrast to James Bruce who had been disbelieved in 1783 because his description of Ethiopia had been too full of praise! In 1830 the Lander brothers finally traced the Niger to its mouth by sailing downstream from the inland town of Bussa. In doing so they revealed to an excited Europe that the fever-ridden swamplands known as the 'Oil Rivers' were in fact the delta of the mighty Niger River. Here at last, thought European merchants and manufacturers, was a navigable waterway into the heart of the west African interior. But the high mortality rate from malarial fever managed to hold European explorers and traders at bay for a further two decades. The turning-point came in the early 1850s when it was discovered that doses of quinine provided reasonable protection from malarial fever. With this useful medical discovery, European exploration of Africa quickly gathered pace.

The main objects of European exploration in the 1850s, 1860s and 1870s were the courses of the other major rivers of Africa: the upper Nile, the Zambezi and the Congo. This intense interest in Africa's rivers was not fired simply by detached scientific curiosity. The rivers of Africa were viewed by Europeans as the primary trading arteries to and from the heart of the continent. They were the 'highways' through which Europeans could 'open up' the continent to European trade and exploitation.

Burton, Speke and Grant traced the source of the Nile to Lake Victoria Nyanza and showed the river's navigable possibilities upstream from Khartoum. Further south, Livingstone traversed the continent from Zambezi to the west coast at Luanda and back again to the east coast at Quelimane. He led a later expedition up the Shire River to Lake Malawi and devoted much of the remainder of his life to the exploration of the lake and river systems of south-central Africa. A former missionary himself, Livingstone was driven by a burning sense of mission. He preached that Christianity and European commerce were the only possible antidote to the evils of the slave trade which still survived in the region (see pp. 240–3). Meanwhile the Germans Barth and Nachtigal had explored the major trade routes of the Sahara and Sahel. Barth's detailed five-volume description of his travels remains a major source for historians of Sokoto and Borno.

Because of the wealth of information in his detailed published journals, Barth has sometimes been portrayed as the last of the great disinterested scientific explorers. And yet the prime purpose of his journey into sub-Saharan Africa (1850–5) was to assess for European merchants the trading potential of the Borno, Sokoto, Niger Bend region. Though German in origin, Barth was partly sponsored by a group of British merchants. On their behalf, he sought from the sultan of Sokoto 'a letter of franchise guaranteeing to all British merchants entire security for themselves and their property in visiting his dominions for trading purposes'. The sultan readily agreed to the request, though Barth was doubtful about his ability to meet the guarantee.

Earlier, while in Bagirmi, south-east of Lake Chad, Barth had been imprisoned as a spy and spent a few days shackled in leg-irons. The experience gave him time to reflect:

I came to the conclusion that it would be absolutely necessary, in order to obtain the desired end, to colonise the most favourable tract of the country inclosed by the Kwára, Benuwé, and the River Kadúna [most of modern northern Nigeria], and thus to spread commerce and civilisation in all directions into the very heart of the continent.

(From H. Barth, *Travels and Discoveries in North and Central Africa,* first published 1857, this edition Minerva Library, Ward Lock, London, 1890, p. 50)

Figure 20.5 Chuma, explorer companion to David Livingstone. On Livingstone's death in the Lake Bangweulu region of modern Zambia in 1873, Chuma supervised the embalming of the body and then he and a helper, Susi, led a caravan of 60 men to the coast for its transportation and burial in England. The journey to Bagamoyo took them ten months. They received little thanks and no reward from a parsimonious British government

Despite his misgivings about the ability of local African rulers to ensure the security of European merchants in the African interior, Barth was thankful for the extent and success of local trade which he observed in the capital of Sokoto:

Friday, April 22 [1853]. – It was the great market-day, which was of some importance to me, as I had to buy a good many things, so that I was obliged to spend there a sum of 70,000 shells ... . The market was tolerably well attended, and well supplied, there being about thirty horses, three hundred head of cattle for slaughtering, fifty takérkere, or oxen of burden, and a great quantity of leather articles (this being the most celebrated branch of manufacture in Sókoto), especially leather bags, cushions, and similar articles, the leather dressed and prepared here being very soft and beautiful. There were more than a hundred bridles for sale, the workmanship of which is very famous throughout all this part of Negroland; but especially a large quantity of iron was exposed for sale, the iron of Sókoto being of excellent quality and much sought for, while that of Kanó is of bad quality. A good many slaves were exhibited, and fetched a higher price than might be supposed – a lad of very indifferent appearance being sold for 33,000 shells; I myself bought a pony for 30,000. It being just about the period when the salt-caravan visits these parts, dates also, which usually form a small addition to the principal merchandise of those traders of the desert, were to be had; and I filled a leather bag, for some 2,000 shells, in order to give a little more variety to my food on the long road which lay before me.

(From H. Barth, *Travels and Discoveries*, pp. 163, 184)

Figure 20.6 Stanley on the Congo River. Battle between Stanley's expedition party and Bangala war canoes, 14 February 1877. (Contemporary line engraving)

It was Stanley who completed Livingstone's work by unravelling the mystery of Africa's remaining major river. In 1874–7 he crossed the continent from Zanzibar and in doing so sailed down the Congo from its upper tributary, the Lualaba, to its mouth at Boma. (From the late nineteenth century and throughout the colonial period Europeans referred to this great equatorial river as the Congo, after the Kongo people and kingdom to the south of its lower reaches. Formerly Portuguese sources had referred to it as the Zaïre, presumably from a local African name at the river's mouth. Local African names for the river varied widely throughout its length. For 20 years from the mid-1970s the river and the republic were renamed Zaïre, but both reverted to the name Congo in 1997.) At the head of a heavily armed expedition Stanley ruthlessly blasted his way downstream against fierce opposition from numerous riverine peoples (see Figure 20.6). The latter rightly saw their control of ancient trading routes perilously threatened.

For some years European merchants had pushed their contacts and control over trading routes further into the continent from their coastal bases. In the case of the French on the Senegal River, they had the military support of their home government which by the 1860s had established a narrow riverine colony as far east as Medina. Similarly, the British government declared the Fante states a Crown Colony when the kingdom of Asante challenged the British trading monopoly on the 'Gold Coast'. The British position in this coastal colony was further secured by a military victory over the Asante army in 1874. Meanwhile, British merchants were exploiting the disunity of the Niger delta states and extending control over much of the trade of the lower Niger River. Now Stanley suddenly revealed the vast navigable possibilities of the Congo River basin. The Belgian king, Leopold, seized the opportunity and sent Stanley back to the Congo mouth with orders to construct a roadway linking Boma with Malebo ('Stanley') Pool. It was in effect a colonising expedition.

The Belgian king's initiative merely added impetus to the already gathering pace of European competition for control of the natural wealth and trade of Africa. Much of Africa remained to be 'mapped', but from now on European 'explorers' were generally direct agents of colonial expansion.

21

The European 'Scramble', colonial conquest and African resistance in east, north-central and west Africa

↖ For more information see www.palgrave.com/shillington

The 'Scramble for Africa'

Ever since the emergence of so-called 'legitimate commerce' in place of the Atlantic slave trade in the early nineteenth century, European merchants had been increasingly interested in gaining control over the trading systems of the African interior. As we saw in the previous chapter, it was with this in mind that European, especially British, merchant classes supported and often financed the investigation of Africa's river systems by European 'explorers'. The rivers of Africa were viewed by Europeans as the primary trading arteries to and from the heart of the continent. They were the 'highways' through which Europeans could 'open up' the continent to European trade and exploitation. The British African Association had financed Mungo Park's investigation of the middle Niger at the turn of the century. Others followed, the Frenchman Caillié visiting the fabled city of Timbuktu in the 1820s and the British Lander brothers tracing the outflow of the Niger to its delta in 1830. Likewise, the main objects of exploration by people like Burton, Speke, Grant, Livingstone and Stanley in the 1850s, 1860s and 1870s were the courses of the other major rivers of Africa: the upper Nile, the Zambezi and the Congo.

By the early 1870s European trading companies were pushing up the major rivers of Africa's western coastline. But they still generally recognised African authority and operated through alliances with local African rulers. Apart from British and Boers in South Africa, the French in Algeria and nominal Ottoman rule in north Africa, foreign incursion into tropical Africa was generally confined to small coastal enclaves (see Map 21.1). The authority of the Arab rulers of Zanzibar did not extend much beyond the adjacent coastal towns and islands of east Africa. Portugal had long maintained claims to an African empire in Mozambique and Angola, but their authority extended little beyond the coast or river valley. In west Africa the French had pushed up the Senegal valley in support of French trading interests, but theirs was still at this stage a narrow riverine colony. The British meanwhile controlled Sierra Leone and a small coastal colony at Lagos; and they were on the verge of annexing their Protectorate of coastal modern Ghana as the crown colony of Gold Coast. But even with these foreign incursions, the vast majority of the African continent remained under indigenous African rule in the early 1870s.

Between 1880 and 1900, however, the whole tone and tempo of Afro-European contact changed. By the end of the century a massive colonial onslaught, known as the European 'Scramble for Africa', had brought most of the continent within the sphere of some European colonial empire. But what led to this dramatic turn of events, and how was it possible that independent Africa was apparently so quickly overrun? Historians have argued long and hard over the relative importance of various 'causes' and no doubt they will continue to do so. It is only possible here to refer to some of the principal background factors.

The European background

Britain's position as the leading industrial nation in the world had remained unchallenged until the second half of the nineteenth century. During this time it suited Britain to promote a policy of European 'free trade' in Africa. That is, no one European nation was to interfere with the right of another to freely trade in Africa. In practice this meant British domination of Africa's external trade. For Britain produced the cheapest European manufactured goods in the largest quantity and had the largest merchant navy for shipping them to Africa. By the late 1860s, however, it was becoming clear that France, Germany and the United States had caught up with Britain in terms of industrial technology and manufacturing. By the 1870s, western Europe's factories were producing so many cheap goods that they were running out of people to sell them to. With their home markets saturated, European manufacturers and merchants turned more and more to Africa. Cloth, clothing, alcohol, guns and metal manufactured goods were poured into the continent in search of new markets. With European industrial and trading competition approaching more equal terms, 'free trade' gave way to 'protectionism'. Britain's main trading rivals, France, and later Germany, realised that the way to beat British competition was to establish colonies or 'protected' areas in Africa. From these the trade of other European nationals could be excluded or heavily taxed.

A further economic factor in the scramble was the European belief that vast stretches of the African interior contained huge quantities of untapped wealth and raw materials. The tropical forests of western Africa had already proved a valuable source of vegetable oils. Ivory was a fast-wasting asset, but rubber from the tropical forests was about to enter a boom. And finally, the discovery of huge quantities of diamonds and gold in southern Africa in the 1870s and 1880s heightened expectations for the whole of the continent.

Even less-industrialised European nations joined in the rush to stake a claim to part of Africa. Theirs was in anticipation of quick profits or to safeguard markets for the future. European partition of the continent would clearly only happen once. The possession of colonies in Africa became a point of national prestige within Europe.

The rapid colonial conquest of Africa was only possible, however, because of two important factors. In the first place colonists were able to exploit traditional and long-standing rivalries between African states. Thus some African rulers accepted a European alliance or treaty of 'protection' in the belief that it would protect them from traditional African enemies. It was only when those traditional enemies had been brutally conquered that the full implications of European 'protection' became clear. No African leader knowingly and willingly signed away his birthright, though this was how the 'protecting' European power usually chose to interpret the treaties.

In the second place, Europe gained an important advantage in military technology. In earlier centuries African rulers had generally been able to hold

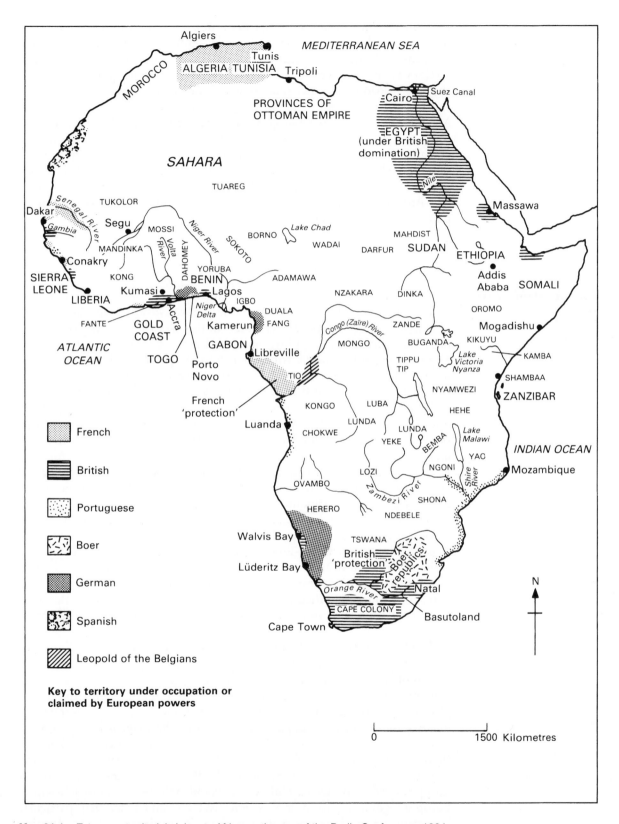

Map 21.1 European territorial claims to Africa on the eve of the Berlin Conference, 1884

their own against invading European armies. They built up their own arsenals of muzzle-loading guns and made skilful use of more traditional weapons and guerrilla tactics. In the 1870s and 1880s, however, African armies were rapidly overtaken by advances in European weaponry. First came the breech-loading repeater rifle, to be followed in 1889 by the Maxim-gun, the world's first highly mobile modern machine-gun. Possession of the Maxim-gun transformed European military fortunes in Africa. Its use was often crucial in the final crushing of resistance. Old, outmoded European guns had for years been freely sold to Africans, but restrictions were placed upon the sale of the latest models. Though most African armies of resistance acquired a number of breech-loading rifles, none acquired a Maxim-gun. The British anti-imperialist poet Hilaire Belloc summed up his countrymen's position in the famous sarcastic couplet:

> Whatever happens we have got
> The Maxim-gun; and they have not.

The 'Scramble' takes off

In 1879 the French threw down a challenge to European 'free trade' in Africa. They started constructing a railway from Dakar to link their colony of Senegal with the upper Niger valley. In this way the French government hoped to gain control of a huge protected market across the Sahelian and savannah regions of west Africa. In 1882 they proclaimed French protectorates over Porto Novo and the north bank of the lower Congo. The former lay between the British coastal colonies of Gold Coast and Lagos, and thus broke Britain's near-monopoly of west Africa's south-facing coastline. The latter opened up the whole question of 'free trade' on the navigable Congo River. Stanley had already established claims along the south bank on behalf of the 'International Association', which was a front for King Leopold of the Belgians. The British responded by supporting Portuguese claims to Angola and the Congo mouth. By this time it was becoming clear that Britain's 'temporary' occupation of Egypt (since 1882, see p. 288) was likely to be fairly permanent, much to the annoyance of French investors in the country. The German leader, Bismarck, saw the direction in which Anglo-French rivalry was leading and decided to act while there was still some of Africa left to colonise. In 1884 he proclaimed German protectorates over Togo, Kamerun (Cameroon) and South West Africa (Namibia). He then invited the major European powers to Berlin to discuss the issue of maintaining free navigation along the Niger and Congo Rivers.

The Berlin West Africa Conference (1884–5) was an attempt by European leaders to add some kind of international European agreement to the carving-up of Africa that was already under way. It did not decide on any colonial boundaries as such, but it did settle two important principles. In the first place it recognised Leopold's so-called 'International Association' as the legitimate authority in the Congo basin. In return the Belgian king agreed to allow European traders and missionaries free access to the area. Based on this Berlin recognition, Leopold proclaimed his own personal kingdom, the 'Congo Free State', in 1885. Secondly, the Berlin Conference agreed that a European claim to any part of Africa would only be recognised by other European governments if it was 'effectively occupied' by that particular European power. This was a deliberate tactic by Bismarck to undermine

Figure 21.1 The German eagle swooping over Africa: a British cartoonist's view of German ambitions in east Africa, *Punch* 1890. Although the British and Germans had divided the territory east of Victoria Nyanza in 1885–6, land north and west of the lake was still unallocated. In 1890 the Germans announced that their agent Carl Peters had signed a treaty with King Mwanga of Buganda. The British were horrified: the kingdom controlled access to the source of the Nile, the life-blood of British-occupied Egypt, hence the cartoon. Later that year an Anglo-German treaty settled the Uganda-Tanganyika boundary well to the south of Buganda. In partial exchange the British offered a narrow strip of land north of Botswana, linking German South West Africa with the Zambezi. Named the Caprivi Strip, after Bismark's successor as German Chancellor, this was supposedly to provide navigable access to Germany's east African colony. In fact, as such it was worthless, being just upstream of the largest waterfall in the world, a fact well-known to the British who thirty years previously had named it Victoria Falls

PUNCH, OR THE LONDON CHARIVARI.—April 26, 1890.

ON THE SWOOP!

British claims to vague informal 'spheres of influence'. Within days of the ending of the conference in February 1885, Bismarck put this principle into practice. He proclaimed a German protectorate in the heart of Britain's east African 'sphere of influence'. The grounds on which he claimed 'effective occupation' were that a German agent, Peters, had recently travelled the region and collected a handful of 'treaties' from local rulers. The result of

315

Bismarck's proclamation was the colony of 'German East Africa', later renamed Tanganyika (modern mainland Tanzania).

A series of European treaties during 1890–1 confirmed many of the internal colonial boundaries of the African continent (see Figure 21.1). The Sahara and Sahel were still largely not defined and most of the territory 'acquired' was far from being 'effectively occupied' by Europeans. Africans did not lightly lay down their independence and the 1890s was a period of widespread African resistance to European conquest.

Conquest and resistance

The French in west and north-central Africa

The French colonisation of Senegal had been built originally around the trading ports of Dakar and St Louis. In the 1850s and 1860s Governor Louis Faidherbe had extended French control up the Senegal valley to secure French trading interests and to forestall the westward expansion of the Tukolor empire. He achieved these conquests by building up a highly disciplined Senegalese army, locally recruited and trained in the use of the most up-to-date weaponry from Europe. It was this Senegalese army, commanded largely by local Afro-French officers, which provided the French with their main frontline troops for the conquest of western Africa in the 1880s and 1890s.

Between 1879 and 1881 the French began an aggressive policy of widespread colonisation in west Africa. They pushed towards the upper Niger,

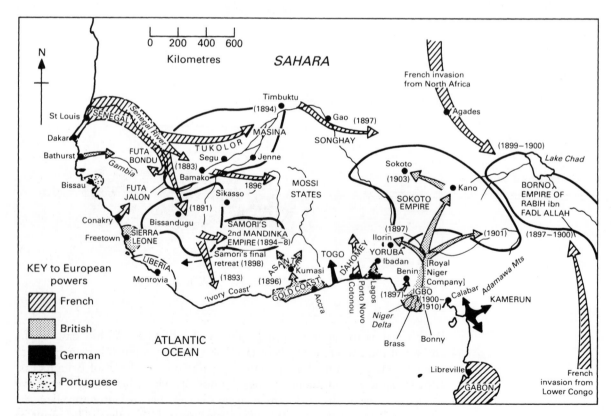

Map 21.2   West Africa in the era of the 'Scramble'

316

building a series of forts between Senegal and Bamako. They started constructing a railway along this route, thus hoping to draw off through Senegal the bulk of the trade of the western Sahel.

The principal opponents of French expansion in the western Sahel were the Tukolor empire under the rule of Ahmadu Seku, the son and successor to al-Hajj Umar, and the new expanding Mandinka empire of Samori (see pp. 235–6). Both Ahmadu and Samori initially tried diplomacy rather than military conflict with the French Senegalese army. The main weakness of Ahmadu and Samori was that they could not unite in their opposition to this new foreign intrusion from the west. They had for too long been rivals for power in the western Sudan.

Ahmadu concluded an alliance with the French which he believed secured him French recognition of the Tukolor empire. By 1883, however, the French, in defiance of the treaty, had constructed a line of forts right across southern Tukolor as far as Bamako (see Map 21.2). Ahmadu still showed his good faith in the alliance. In 1885–7 he supported the French in their war against Mahmadu Lamine's Muslim state of Futa Bondu, between upper Gambia and Senegal. But it soon became clear that the French had never had any intention of respecting treaties with independent west African states. A further Franco-Tukolor treaty in 1887 gained the empire little more security, and two years later the French launched an assault upon Tukolor's border fortresses. As was to happen so often over the next decade, French use of artillery firing explosive shells proved decisive in securing them victory over opposing west African forces. But even after the French took Segu in 1890, Ahmadu's army refused to surrender. They conducted a fighting retreat as far as Masina where they held out until 1893. Ahmadu was only finally defeated because the French were able to exploit political divisions within the empire. They formed an alliance with Ahmadu's brother whom they made puppet ruler of Masina once Ahmadu had been removed. Although Ahmadu died in exile in Sokoto, many of his scattered forces moved south to join Samori and so continue the unequal struggle against the invading *infidel*.

Figure 21.2 A French gun-boat suppresses African resistance in Dahomey (now Benin). (Illustration by H. Meyer in *Le Petit Journal* 20 August 1892)

Samori was France's single most formidable military opponent in western Africa. He commanded an army of 30,000 men, mostly footsoldiers, but containing an elite corps of cavalry. They were well armed with muskets and rifles, imported from Sierra Leone or manufactured and repaired by his own Mandinka metalworkers. In addition the state was strengthened by a unifying sense of Mandinka nationalism which recalled the glories of the ancient Malian empire.

After initial border clashes in the early 1880s a Mandinka-French treaty was concluded in 1887. This was supposed to secure Samori's north-eastern boundary along the line of the Niger. But as with their Tukolor treaties, the French regarded such alliances as only temporary tactics. At this crucial period in Mandinka-French relations Samori's grip on the region was critically weakened. His army suffered heavily in an exhausting siege of the Sikasso capital on his north-eastern border. And in 1888 he was faced with an internal revolt against his abortive attempt to force-convert the Mandinka to Islam.

In 1891 the French invaded from the north. Samori had no desire to meet the French Senegalese army in full open battle for he had no answer to their heavy artillery and machine-guns. Instead he ordered a 'scorched-earth' policy as he conducted a tactical withdrawal from the capital Bissandugu. The result was devastating for the heartland of the empire, as standing crops and whole villages were left in smouldering ruins. But it meant that the French army ran short of supplies and had to abandon their invasion in 1892. Realising the insecurity of his military position, Samori then commenced an amazing undertaking. Between 1892 and 1894 he shifted his entire empire to the east, to a region on the northern borderlands of modern Côte d'Ivoire and Ghana. But even here there was no peace for the Mandinka, for they themselves were now foreign conquerors and faced the internal opposition of a subject people. Further retreat eastwards was blocked by Asante, which fell to the British in 1896. Unable to secure a protectorate from the British, Samori was forced to fight it out with the French. In spite of being cut off from their Sierra Leone arms-suppliers, the Mandinka army still scored some important victories over the French. In the end it was famine which finally defeated Samori's troops in the mountains north of Liberia in 1898. Samori gave himself up to the French and was exiled to Gabon, where he died aged 70 in 1900.

In the central Sahel the main resistance to French conquest was led by Rabih ibn Fadl Allah, the conqueror of Borno. Originating from the Nile valley of Sudan, Rabih rose to prominence as the military commander for a Sudanese raider-trader who dealt in ivory and slaves. Following the founding of the Mahdist state in 1885 (see pp. 290–1), Rabih set up his own military state in the Bahr el-Ghazal. The basis of his power was the army, the core of which was highly mobile cavalry, armed with imported rifles, which he used to raid and subdue the surrounding countryside.

Seeing himself as a disciple of the Mahdi, Rabih gradually pushed his conquests westwards until, in 1893, he reached Lake Chad and conquered the state of Borno. There he set up a form of military dictatorship which was in many ways fairer and less corrupt than the rule of the Borno aristocracy which had preceded it. Taxes were at least fixed and charged only once a year. And most of the state's income was spent on the army and defence rather than on personal luxuries for the ruler. But Rabih remained a foreign conqueror, and for most of his short reign he faced internal opposition to his rule. Villages were constantly raided by the army for supplies of food, which led to a serious decline in agriculture. The main threat to Rabih's rule, however, came from invading French forces which, by the end of the century, were challenging his independence. The French knew little about Rabih and were surprised by the strength of his resistance, but in April 1900 two major French armies converged upon Borno. Though Rabih himself was defeated and killed, the struggle was continued by his son, Fadl Allah ibn Rabih. He withdrew the remnants of his forces into north-eastern Nigeria, hoping for British recognition as the ruler of Borno. But the British offered him no protection. He was pursued by the French and killed in battle in 1901.

Dahomey was conquered by a French Senegalese army in 1892–4 in a move which was initially welcomed by many Yoruba as a liberation from Dahomeyan tyranny. Côte d'Ivoire was proclaimed a French colony in 1893, but its military subjugation was not so easily achieved. There was no centralised authority for the French to overthrow and it was more than twenty years before the numerous forest-chiefdoms were forced into submission.

The British in west Africa

Although the British did not conquer as much territory as the French, they ended up with two of the wealthiest states in the region, Gold Coast (Ghana) and Nigeria. Both of these were based on coastal trading enclaves in which the British were already well established.

In the early 1870s the British acquired a trading monopoly along the Gold Coast, having bought out the last remaining Dutch and Danish trading forts. Now they were in a position to charge customs duties on imports and exports without fear of losing trade to Dutch or Danish competition. This provided finance for a colonial administration, and in 1874 they proclaimed a colony over the coastal Fante states.

On a number of occasions earlier in the century the British had done battle with Asante, who wanted to prevent foreign domination of the coastal trade. In order to assert their new authority at the coast, therefore, the British invaded Asante in 1874, defeated the Asante army and burnt their capital Kumasi. On this occasion, wishing to avoid the expense of formal colonial administration, the British withdrew their forces from Asante. By 1895, however, under the rule of Asantehene Prempe, Asante power had revived. At the same time the British found it necessary to assert their claims to the Gold Coast hinterland in the face of French advances against Samori. So in 1895–6 the British again invaded the Asante kingdom. In the face of British military superiority the Asante military leaders tactically avoided battle. The kingdom was occupied and a British Protectorate was proclaimed over most of the region of modern Ghana. But the Asante army had remained intact and in 1900 they seized their opportunity and rose against the British. In the war that followed, the Asante scored a number of victories and nearly expelled the British from Ghana. Eventually, however, British reinforcements arrived from Sierra Leone and Nigeria. The Asante army was overcome and the colony of Gold Coast was proclaimed. Prempeh, his family and retainers were all exiled to the Seychelles.

Until the 1880s the only official British possession within what was to become Nigeria was a small coastal colony at Lagos. By the time of the Berlin Conference of 1884–5, however, the British had obtained a virtual trading monopoly over palm-oil exports from the Niger delta and the lower Niger

Figure 21.3 Soldiers of the British Royal Niger Company form a square to attack the camp of the Emir of Lapaie and subdue West African resistance to British colonial efforts. Note the British use of machine-guns. (Illustration drawn by S. T. Dadd from a sketch by Major Arthur Festing, reproduced in *The Graphic*)

River. Several British trading companies had been united by George Goldie into the National African Company. This company alone controlled virtually all the palm-oil exports between the Niger/Benue confluence and the Delta. Goldie was thus able to keep prices down and secure large profits for the company. After Berlin the British government quickly affirmed its position in the region by declaring a Protectorate over the Delta. At the same time she granted a royal charter (document of approval) to Goldie's company to rule the lower Niger in the name of Britain. The company now became known as the Royal Niger Company. Rival African traders like the men of Brass were excluded from the oil trade by force. And Delta merchant princes, such as Jaja of Opobo, who refused to trade on British terms, were threatened with gunboats and deposed.

Between 1892 and 1902 most of the vast inland territory of modern Nigeria was gradually brought under British rule. But much of the region had to be taken by force, for the various Nigerian peoples fought hard against their conquerors. Like the French, the British used African soldiers for the bulk of their frontline troops. Under the command of British officers these were turned into highly disciplined, full-time professional battalions, equipped with the latest rifles, heavy artillery and machine-guns. And traditional lack of African unity in the region meant that British forces were able to take on one African state at a time. Most of Yorubaland was conquered in 1892–3, though the Royal Niger Company did not manage to conquer Ilorin, the Yoruba province of Sokoto, until 1897. Meanwhile it took the British two years to oust Nana, ruler of Benin River, from his defensive position in the forest swamps. The state of Benin City was taken in 1897 after fierce fighting. The British ruthlessly sacked the city and looted its most valued treasures (see Figure 21.4).

The Sokoto Caliphate was overcome between 1900 and 1903. The organisation of the empire as a federation of semi-independent emirates meant that the British general, Lugard, was able to attack first one emirate and then another. The massed charges of Hausa cavalry were no match for Lugard's disciplined squares of riflemen and machine-gunners, and the walls of their cities were easily breached by British artillery. In 1903, with only Sokoto itself remaining unconquered, Caliph Attahiru conducted an orderly *hijra*, withdrawing eastwards towards the modern republic of Sudan.

In the end the British in Nigeria, like the French in Côte d'Ivoire, faced some of their toughest opposition from those small groupings of 'stateless'

Figure 21.4 Plunder at Benin, 1897. Hundreds of bronze plaques that had decorated the walls of the *Oba's* palace since medieval times (see p. 198) were ripped off, collected here and sold to private European individuals and museums, most of them ending up in the British Museum in London

peoples who had no large centralised authority that could be overthrown. Thus the British spent years of exhaustive campaigning in the forest country of south-eastern Nigeria. It was 1910 before all the villages of Igboland were finally forced to accept the reality of British overrule.

The Congo basin and Angola

French claims to the Congo basin stemmed from a treaty concluded in 1880 between the French explorer de Brazza and the Tio chief Makoko just north of Malebo Pool (see Map 21.3). De Brazza claimed that Makoko ceded his sovereign rights to France. We have no clear record of Makoko's understanding of the agreement. If, indeed, he did agree to any form of French 'protection', it is possible that he sought a European ally in the face of encroachment from Leopold's agent Stanley. Nicknamed *bula matari,* 'breaker of rocks', Stanley was busy using forced-labour to build a road from Boma to the Pool. His reputation during his violent descent of the river in 1876–7 was well known to the peoples of the lower Congo. It is likely, therefore, that Makoko saw Stanley's return to the region in 1879 as a direct threat to the safety of his people.

At Berlin in 1884–5 the French used de Brazza's treaties to establish claim to territory north of the lower Congo. In the late 1880s de Brazza was sent out to conclude further treaties in the region. He used a small Senegalese force to push French claims and plant administrative and trading posts up the lower Congo and its northern tributary, the Ubangui. No large-scale African resistance was organised at this stage and, with no major African kingdom to conquer, initial French presence in the region was not unduly aggressive. Treaties were signed in exchange for trivial 'gifts' of metal goods, cloth and alcohol, and it is unlikely that their implications were explained or realised by the African chiefs concerned. By the early 1890s the French had established their equatorial colonies of Gabon, Moyen ('Middle') Congo and Ubangui-Chari (modern Central African Republic). Widespread African resistance came later when private French companies were granted authority to exploit the region (see p. 344).

Map 21.3 The Congo Basin and Angola in the era of the 'Scramble'

South of the French sphere the bulk of the Congo basin fell to the Belgian king, Leopold, and his 'Congo Free State'. The state was only 'free' in the sense that it was not subject to any government control from Europe. It was the personal empire of Leopold himself (see Figure 21.5). It was in reality anything but free for its African population, who suffered under Leopold one of the continent's most oppressive colonial regimes. The nature of this regime and the opposition it provoked will be discussed in Chapter 23. It is sufficient to record here the initial establishment of colonial authority in the region. According to the Berlin Conference and subsequent European agreements, the authority of Leopold's Congo state extended over most of the Congo basin south of the Ubangui and as far as the Zambezi watershed. The main potential opponents of Leopold's authority within this vast equatorial empire were Tippu Tip's Swahilis in the east and Msiri's Yeke kingdom in the south-east region of Katanga (modern Shaba).

Tippu Tip's Swahili federation dominated the Lualaba/Lomani region, which covered about a third of Leopold's potential Congo state. Tippu Tip attempted to head off the Free State challenge from the west by claiming that he owed allegiance to the sultan of Zanzibar. By the late 1880s, however, the sultan of Zanzibar's authority had been seriously curtailed by British and German action in east Africa (see below). It was clear that Tippu Tip would receive no diplomatic protection from that quarter. In 1887 Tippu Tip was persuaded to throw over his supposed allegiance to Zanzibar and to accept the governorship of the Free State's eastern provinces. This solution saved both sides a costly war and was of great advantage to the Free State. The region's profitable ivory trade was no longer drained off towards the Zanzibari coast. From now on it passed westwards, through Free State merchants' hands and subject to Free State customs dues.

The arrangement may have kept Tippu Tip in power but it did not suit his fellow Swahili merchants. They resented the restrictions placed upon their raiding activities and in particular the intrusion of rival European traders and the increasing presence of the Free State's motley mercenary army. The latter, the *Force Publique,* was officered by Europeans of various nationalities and was recruited from the local African population anxious to avenge the oppression of Swahili raiders. Relations were severely strained by the time Tippu Tip retired to Zanzibar in 1891. The following year the local Belgian officer launched an all-out attack upon Swahili strongholds. There followed 18 months of particularly brutal warfare before Swahili resistance was finally overcome.

Meanwhile in the south, when it came to confrontation, Msiri's Yeke kingdom of Garenganze offered little effective resistance. Leopold was awoken to the region's great potential mineral wealth by the British South Africa Company (see following chapter) which sent its agents to Bunkeya in 1890. Msiri realised only too well the meaning of their treaties and he promptly sent them packing. When Leopold's own agents arrived in 1891, Msiri refused to allow the hoisting of the Free State flag, declaring, 'I am the master here, and so long as I live, the Kingdom of Garenganze shall have no other.' In the dispute which followed, a Belgian officer promptly shot him dead. Perhaps surprisingly there was no attempt to avenge Msiri's death, apart from the spearing of the man who shot him. Famine was in the land; the region was wracked by several years of drought; and Msiri's increasingly tyrannical rule in recent years had robbed him of his former loyal support.

The crucial importance of this Katanga region to the future colony of the Congo was revealed the following year when Free State officers visited a local copper-mine and carried samples of the copper back to Europe.

In terms of its own industrial development Portugal was weak, compared with her fellow European colonists in Africa. But because of this very weakness, Portugal could not afford to lose its ancient claims to colonies in Africa. Manufacturers needed their own protected markets for they could not compete in the open market with their more powerful European rivals. Portuguese industrialists therefore pushed their government into more assertive action to try to make good her claims to the vast inland hinterland of Angola.

Portugal had not the wealth to mount huge effective armies of occupation. So, in attempting the conquest of Angola, it adopted the old technique of exploiting local rivalries. Punitive expeditions were often little more than African raiding parties, locally recruited from political rivals, armed with Portuguese guns and officered by Portuguese ex-convicts. Bakongo, Mbundu, Ovambo and Chokwe continued to defy Portuguese tax-collectors

Figure 21.5 Leopold II, King of the Belgians, whose employees brutally exploited the peoples and resources of most of the Congo basin, and who ruled the territory as his personal fiefdom from 1885 to 1908. The brutality of his rule was so excessive, even by colonial standards of the time, that he was forced by international pressure to hand over control of the country to the Belgian government in 1908

until well into the twentieth century. This was partly because of the great rubber export boom of 1890–1905, which enabled Africans of the interior to buy guns from local Portuguese traders. It was only with the collapse of the rubber trade in 1910 and the ban on arms sales to Africans in 1912 that the Portuguese government was finally able to make its authority felt throughout the colony of Angola.

British and Germans in East Africa

Until the 1870s, British policy in east Africa had been to support the sultan of Zanzibar's claim to much of the coastal territory of modern Kenya and Tanzania. This policy gave British merchants and missionaries free access to the region while preventing rival Europeans from gaining a foothold on the mainland: all at no expense to the British government. British support had enabled the Saidi royal family to retain the throne of the sultanate against internal opposition in both Oman and Zanzibar. In return, however the sultan had to bow to British demands for the gradual curtailment of the slave trade. This and the increasing interference of British consuls in Zanzibar created resentment towards the sultan by his Muslim subjects.

By the time of the Berlin Conference, however, this policy no longer ensured British supremacy in the region. The sultan's power was negligible when faced with a determined European challenge. As we have already seen above, Germany declared a protectorate over the Tanganyika mainland in February 1885. The British and German governments settled between them the northern and south-western boundaries of 'German East Africa' in 1886 and 1890, while a narrow coastal strip was officially leased from the sultan of Zanzibar (see Map 21.4).

Bismarck gave the administration of the territory to a private commercial company whose violent demands for taxation and labour soon provoked spirited resistance within the colony. A Swahili rising in 1888 was joined by reinforcements from the Hehe and the Yao, and the German colonists were nearly expelled from the territory. The rising was only finally overcome at the end of 1889 after the German government had taken direct control of the colony and brought out imperial reinforcements.

The Germans continued to face widespread resistance to their authority in the Tanganyikan interior and for years their trading caravans had to be heavily guarded by military patrols. In south-central Tanganyika, the Hehe conducted a successful campaign of guerrilla attacks against German patrols and trading caravans which lasted until 1898. Finally, facing defeat, their leader, Mkwawa, chose suicide rather than surrender. In the far south-east the Yao held out until 1899. The Maasai in the north were considered serious potential opponents, but their power was rudely shattered by the spread of the deadly cattle disease, rinderpest, which wiped out most of their economic livelihood. Initial conquest in east Africa gave the Germans only a short breathing space. In the early 1900s they were faced once again with widespread armed resistance in what has become known as the 'Maji Maji rising' (see pp. 351–2).

In an Anglo-German treaty of 1890 the region of modern Uganda was confirmed as falling within the British sphere. The British began by granting the administration and exploitation of their sphere to a private merchant company, the Imperial British East Africa (IBEA) Company. The Company sent Captain Lugard (of later Nigerian fame) to establish their authority in the most powerful kingdom of the region, Buganda. Lugard persuaded

Map 21.4   British and German penetration of East Africa, 1884–1905

kabaka Mwanga to accept British overrule. As we saw in the previous chapter, Mwanga was the leader of a Christian faction at the Baganda royal court. The Muslim Baganda and their Swahili merchant allies had recently been ousted and had retired to the rival kingdom of Bunyoro. With few government resources at his disposal, Lugard allied himself firmly with Buganda and in particular the Christian aristocracy. He used Baganda levies in a campaign against Bunyoro and their Muslim allies in 1891 and established forts in Toro and Nkore.

The British government formally took over the administration of the territory from the Company in 1894. Kabalega of Bunyoro continued guerrilla warfare against the occupying British forces for a further four years. The British faced mutinies in their army and had to import troops from India before they were finally able to overcome resistance in the territory in 1898. Kabalega and Mwanga, who had recently fallen out with the British, were deported to the Seychelles. The importance of Baganda support to British overrule was symbolised by their calling the whole territory the Protectorate of 'Uganda'.

Within Kenya the British, who took over the territory from the IBEA Company in 1895, faced an early rebellion from the coastal Swahili and their

458   *BLACK AND WHITE*   OCTOBER 10, 1896

IN THE SMOKING-ROOM

BY BARRY PAIN.

"I SAW the other day," said the Eminent Person, "in the *Daily Mail* an account of a meeting of waiters who are anxious to abolish the tipping system. The public's equally anxious, I suppose—but it will never be done."

"Why not?" asked the Ordinary Man.

"It's too old—too inveterate: the roots have struck too deep. It will never be abolished."

"For my part I can't see why a stupid absurdity cannot be abolished merely because it is old as well as stupid. After all, the public is the master of the business. If the public can only be got to understand that it never tips a waiter at all—that it only tips the proprietor—the eleemosynary twopence will go."

"The public can never be got to understand anything," said the Poet pessimistically.

"It's simple enough. The waiter pays the restaurant proprietor for the holy privilege of waiting in his restaurant. This money which goes to the proprietor is taken from the tips given by the public. The system is an indignity to the waiter and an imposition on the public. The only person who profits is the restaurant proprietor, and he does quite well enough without it."

"Don't imagine the way out of it is so easy," said the Journalist. "I have watched that London restaurant proprietor for years, and had faint glimpses of the naughti-

SAID KALID
THE ZANZIBAR PRETENDER

as the public puts up with it, and always has put up with it, the public presumably can do nothing."

"Excellent!" said the Poet; "a fine, generous, impassioned enthusiasm. It shows where your heart is."

"I do not complain of the food alone. I complain of the supremacy of the restaurant proprietor. Any twopenny-halfpenny Italian confectioner's refreshment-room thinks it has a right to stick up a notice that 'Pipes are not allowed in this saloon,' in order to force the customer to take the proprietor's penny packet of pestilence, call it a cigar, and pay sixpence for it. That sort of thing would be impossible if the proprietor did not *know* that he was master of the situation."

"This is very gloomy," said the Eminent Person, "and you tell us that there is no hope—that, even if we abolished tips, we should get higher prices and no advantage."

"I don't say that you would get no advantage—you would get the steady civility of a club servant, which is what you want."

"And what would the waiters get?" asked the Ordinary Man.

"They should get thirty shillings a week."

"Thirty shillings!" said the Mere Boy. "The memory of Loisette and Stokes, the agility of the *pulex irritans*, the temper of Job, the smile of a Venus, the steady civility of a club servant—and all at thirty shillings a week! It's an awful world."

Figure 21.6 The ruins of Zanzibar Palace after bombardment by British forces, as shown in a British magazine of 10th October 1896

neighbours. Known as the 'Mazrui rebellion', it started as a succession dispute within the Mazrui clan in which a local IBEA official had intervened against the wishes of the Muslim majority. It soon developed into a general coastal rebellion against British overrule which the colonisers took nine months to crush. Following this rebellion the British abandoned their attempts to rule the coastal towns through the local aristocracy. Instead they promoted Zanzibari and Omani Arabs to positions of local power in the Kenyan coastal towns.

Meanwhile there was little effective resistance to the initial establishment of British authority in the Kenyan interior. The IBEA Company had regarded it as little more than a route to Uganda. As in Tanganyika, the Maasai and others had been seriously weakened by the rapid spread in the early 1890s of the deadly cattle pandemic rinderpest. The Nandi offered a brief challenge to Company trading caravans in 1894, but this was soon defeated. Significantly, from an early date the Company began to raid the Kikuyu for labour and for food. But the full effects of British rule did not begin to be felt within the country until the building of the Uganda railway and the beginnings of European settlement in the central highlands in the early 1900s.

Somalia

For many centuries before the nineteenth, the clan-based Somali had survived on a mixture of camel and goat herding and international trading. In northern Somalia they had been active coastal traders since the Greco-Roman period, famous for their exports of frankincense and myrrh. From the eighth to fourteenth centuries they had expanded south and west, spreading Islam and absorbing Oromo and earlier Bantu-speaking settlers. They turned Mogadishu into the most important northern town of the Swahili coastal trade before the Portuguese intrusion. Nevertheless, Mogadishu remained an important trading city, exporting cinnamon from India to the Red Sea; while the southern Somali interior produced cotton for export until the trade was killed off in the nineteenth century by cheap, slave-grown imports from America. Weakened economically by the late nineteenth century and lacking any centralised form of government, the Somali were able to offer little initial resistance to foreign overrule.

In the era of the 'Scramble' the Somali suffered more division than any other peoples on the continent. In the 1870s the British encouraged the Egyptian *khedive* Ismail to take control of northern Somalia, thus safeguarding the British route through the Suez canal to India. The Egyptians pressed into the interior and took the historic inland Muslim city of Harar. When forced by the Mahdist revolt to evacuate Sudan in 1885, however, the Egyptians also withdrew from Somalia. Two years later Menelik of Ethiopia moved in to take over where the Egyptians had departed. Capturing Harar in 1887, he added the Ogaden to the Ethiopian empire. The British took the northern region of Somalia as a provisioning colony for their important Yemini refuelling port of Aden on the route to India, while the French claimed the northern coastal enclave that was to become Djibouti. Meanwhile, the Italians, who with British approval had taken Eritrea following Egyptian withdrawal in 1887, occupied southern Somalia.

From 1895 a Somali religious scholar named Muhammad Abdile set up an Islamic school in Berbera in British Somaliland where he criticised growing Western and Christian influences. Moving into the interior, he gathered around him a large following, several thousand strong. In 1899 he declared that he was the Mahdi, the holy one who would expel the infidels from Somalia. The British mounted annual military expeditions against him, but each time, through guerrilla tactics of withdrawal and ambush, Abdile avoided capture and remained a constant thorn in the side of the British colonial government. In 1909 the British ordered their forces to evacuate the interior and withdraw to the coastal regions. As the apparent conqueror of the British, Abdile's reputation spread throughout the interior, and he gained a further reprieve during the First World War (1914–18) while the British were occupied elsewhere. In 1920, however, the British renewed their campaign against the man they now called the 'mad mullah'. Assisted by aerial bombardment, they took Abdile's stronghold of Taleh, though Abdile himself escaped and lived on in freedom until his death from pneumonia in 1921.

Industrialisation, colonial conquest and African resistance in south-central and southern Africa

chapter

22

The southern African mineral revolution

1870 was a turning point in southern Africa's history. It ushered in an era of dramatic change prompted by the discovery of first diamonds and then gold in the southern African interior. The industrial mining cities which developed to exploit these valuable minerals transformed the social, economic and political life of the subcontinent. This transformation is known to historians as the southern African 'mineral revolution'. It began with the discovery of huge quantities of diamonds in the region of modern Kimberley in the period 1869–71.

The diamond-fields dispute

The diamond fields lay to the north of what was then the British Cape Colony, in territory claimed by the Boer republics of the Orange Free State and the Transvaal as well as by the rulers and representatives of local Griqua, Tswana and Kora residents. Thousands of people, black and white, from all over southern Africa, as well as miners and speculators from Europe, America and Australia, converged on the region. The British were determined to add this valuable territory to their southern African possessions. Ignoring the claims of the local Batlhaping people, a branch of the southern Tswana, the British set up a court of enquiry which found in favour of the Griqua chief Waterboer. The latter meanwhile had been persuaded to ask for British protection from the Boer republics. This provided the British with their justification and they promptly annexed the territory. Thus, by the end of 1871 what was then the richest known diamond-bearing territory in the world had become the British colony of Griqualand West.

> For more information see www.palgrave.com/ shillington

The development of mining

From the start, white people dominated the exploitation of the diamond fields. They had the advantages of technology and capital. They also had the important backing of British political power. Initially, the mines were exploited by thousands of individual 'diggers', most of them white, but a number of them black. Each digger staked out his own tiny 'claim', which he worked with hired black labour. By the late 1870s the principal diamond-mines had become huge open pits needing expensive steam machinery to haul earth to the surface and to pump out floodwater. Individual claimholders gave way to companies which could raise the necessary capital. During the 1880s one company, De Beers, grew to dominate all the others. It was owned by Cecil Rhodes, an English immigrant who had made an early fortune at the diamond fields in the 1870s. By 1889 De Beers had bought

328

Figure 22.1 The diamond mines at Kimberley. Early labour relations in industrialising South Africa are revealed in the bottom left foreground. (Wood engraving from *The Illustrated London News*, Supplement, 31st August 1872)

out all its rivals and so obtained a complete monopoly of diamond mining at Kimberley.

With the De Beers monopoly the role of Africans at the diamond fields was confined to that of manual labourer. De Beers used their monopoly to keep down wages. Those seeking work had to accept six-month contracts at lower wages than before and live confined in fenced compounds, separated from their families and deprived of the opportunity to find alternative income.

Social and economic impact of the mineral revolution

The sudden rise of a city of 30,000 people in the southern African interior had important consequences for the people of the region. In the first place Kimberley provided a ready market for agricultural produce. Farmers from all over the region, black as well as white, responded eagerly to the new opportunities. Though many prospered in the short term, ultimately it led to greater competition for the best agricultural land. In the Boer republics white landowners made new demands upon the labour of their tenants. Throughout the region the 1870s and early 1880s saw a revival of conflict over land.

The other major impact of the diamond fields was the development of migrant labour. The mines of Kimberley in the 1870s employed up to 50,000 black workers in a year. They came from the colonies and republics and from the kingdoms beyond. The wages, though low by today's standards, were higher than could be got anywhere else in southern Africa at the time. The price of a gun could be earned within a month. It was this which attracted so many to make the long trek on foot to Kimberley, so as to return home with the guns to defend their territory from further white encroachment.

Kimberley brought many in touch for the first time with a cash economy, whether they were farmers selling their crops, woodcutters selling fuel or individuals selling their labour. They returned home with cash, wagons, guns or imported cloth and cheap metal manufactured goods from Europe. The latter tolled the death knell for the independent Iron Age of the southern African interior.

The political impact of the mineral revolution

One of the most important consequences of the mineral revolution was the increasing level of conflict between black and white which dominated the region in the 1870s and 1880s. It ushered in a new era of aggressive white colonialism which extended white control and settlement over much of the remaining independent African-ruled territory of the region. At the same time, Africans were better armed and often better organised for resistance than they had been in previous conflicts with white colonists. The first signs of this were in a war between Pedi and Boers in the eastern Transvaal in 1876. The Pedi drove invading Boers back from their mountain stronghold in a conflict which nearly bankrupted the government of the Boer republic.

The driving force in the revival of colonial ambition in the 1870s was the British. They hoped to amalgamate the white-controlled states of southern Africa into a new, British-dominated federation, the prosperity of which would be guaranteed by the wealth of the diamond fields. An essential part of the plan was the destruction of the remaining independent African kingdoms of the region, in particular the Zulu, the Xhosa and the Pedi. This would provide security for further white settlement and at the same time turn armies of African soldiers into labourers on white-owned farms and mines. Though there was little local white enthusiasm for the planned federation, ultimately it was African resistance which defeated British schemes.

In the ninth and final war with the Xhosa beyond the Cape's eastern borders (1877–8) the British faced unexpectedly tough opposition. By the time it was finally over, the strength of Xhosa resistance had decided local colonial authorities against seizing any more Xhosa land for white settlement. The Xhosa were thus left with a substantial 'reserve' of land east of the River Kei.

Map 22.1 Southern Africa in the era of the 'Scramble'

In January 1879 the British confronted their principal African opponents, the Zulu. A large British army advanced in three columns into the heart of the Zulu kingdom. Cetswayo, who had ruled the kingdom since 1872, launched the full weight of his army against the central British column and overran it at the battle of Isandhlwana. This Zulu victory, more than any other single event, eclipsed British plans for federation. It took the British an eight-month campaign and thousands of reinforcements before they defeated the Zulu army and captured Cetswayo. Subsequent British attempts to weaken Zulu unity by dividing Cetswayo's kingdom into a number of artificial chiefdoms ultimately succeeded. Factional disputes between supporters and opponents of the British plan led to civil war and the disintegration of the kingdom in the 1880s. In 1887 a devastated and famine-struck Zululand became a British colony.

In the meantime the British had annexed the bankrupt republic of the Transvaal in 1877 and, with Swazi help, had finally defeated the Pedi in 1879. In 1877 the Boers of the Transvaal had been too much weakened by the Pedi war to resist the British action, but they greatly resented their loss of independence. By 1880 they no longer needed British protection from Pedi or from Zulu, and they began to resent the burden of British taxation. In 1880–1 the Boers rose in rebellion against the British in the Transvaal. British schemes for federation had already been abandoned, so after the Boers had scored some early military victories, the British agreed to withdraw from the Transvaal and returned it to Boer authority.

The gold-mining revolution and its consequences

In 1886 the southern African mineral revolution entered an entirely new phase with the discovery of huge quantities of gold at the Witwatersrand in the central Transvaal. The massive industrial development which followed the founding of Johannesburg in 1886 dwarfed even the diamond revolution of Kimberley. Within a few years the gold-mining city of Johannesburg had grown from a few tents on the *veld* to being the largest city in sub-Saharan Africa. Almost overnight the economic centre of southern Africa shifted from Kimberley and the British colonies to the heartland of the Boer republic.

The social and economic effects of the industrialisation of the Witwatersrand (sometimes known simply as 'the Rand') were similar to those observed for Kimberley though on a far larger scale. Mining capitalists from Kimberley and bankers from Europe quickly bought up gold-mining claims and formed them into companies. It soon became clear that the bulk of the gold-bearing ore lay deep within the ground and the long-term future lay in deep-level mining. This required huge quantities of capital investment, so by the early 1890s gold mining on the Witwatersrand had become dominated by a handful of very powerful companies, among them Cecil Rhodes's own Consolidated Goldfields.

Labour recruiting agents drew migrant workers to Johannesburg from all over the subcontinent. The development of regular labour migrancy to the Rand was helped by further white seizure of African land in the 1880s and 1890s. At the same time the rapid growth of Johannesburg as a market for agricultural produce was a great source of new wealth for the rural Boers of the Transvaal. African tenants on the white-owned farms were forced into tougher tenancy agreements. This meant they provided more and more free labour to the Boer landowners in return for the right to remain on what had originally been their own land.

Figure 22.2 Workers following the compressed air drill in a gold mine at Johannesburg, South Africa (stereograph, late nineteenth century)

Although not many Boers were directly involved in the gold-mining process, the government of the Transvaal profited enormously from the new industrial developments. They taxed the mining industry hard, and charged heavy import duties on essential mining equipment. The Transvaal government, previously bankrupted by the Pedi war of 1876, was now able to afford the powerful regular army that was needed to continue the Boer conquest of the northern highveld region. Punitive military expeditions were sent out east, west and north in the 1880s and 1890s against those African chiefdoms that still defied Boer authority. By 1898 the Transvaal Boers had reconquered the Soutpansberg from the Venda and so made good their claims to territory as far north as the Limpopo.

In the British sphere the last resistance of the century came from the southern Batswana following the outbreak of rinderpest which threatened to decimate the remnants of their economic independence. White-settler colonists, eager for further African land, did not wait for rebellion; rather, they actively sought it out, driving those who resisted into the remote Langeberg mountain range, near the southern edge of the Kalahari desert. After a six-month siege, the defenders were defeated by starvation and a fresh 2000-strong colonial force. Their heroic leader, *kgosi* Luka Jantjie, died in the final shootout. His body was mutilated for colonial souvenirs, while his people were 'ethnically cleansed' from the region: their land confiscated for sale to white settlers and the several thousand survivors transported to the south-western Cape to serve as indentured labourers.

The British 'Scramble' for south-central Africa

The annexation of Bechuanaland

In 1884 the Germans had declared a protectorate over 'South West Africa' (Namibia) as part of their initiative in the wider 'Scramble for Africa' (see previous chapter). The British responded by annexing 'Bechuanaland' – the Kalahari and Tswana territory north of the Cape Colony. Various Tswana leaders had for years requested some form of British protection from increasing Boer encroachment on their narrow strip of fertile land between Transvaal and the Kalahari desert (see Map 22.2). But the British declaration of the Bechuanaland Protectorate in 1885 was in their own interests rather than that of the Tswana concerned. It was mainly to prevent the possibility of a German link-up with the Transvaal Boers across the strategically important 'road to the north'. This was the trade and labour route to and from the northern interior which was so important to the continuing prosperity of Kimberley and the Cape Colony. The annexation of Bechuanaland also ensured that future British colonists would not be deprived of access to the possible mineral wealth of the south-central African interior. Within a few years the mining magnate Cecil Rhodes had devised a scheme to exploit this opportunity.

The colonisation of Zimbabwe

Rhodes and those who invested in his scheme had heard of the ancient gold-mines of the Rozvi and Mutapa empires. They believed that a private British company using modern mining techniques could turn the Zimbabwe plateau into a 'second Rand'; and one not subject to the restrictive taxation policies of a Boer republic. The main opposition to such a scheme was the kingdom

Map 22.2　South-central Africa in the era of the 'Scramble'

333

of the Ndebele which dominated the western half of the Zimbabwe plateau. In 1888 the Ndebele king, Lobengula (who had succeeded Mzilikazi in 1870), was tricked into signing away his kingdom to one of Rhodes's agents. Lobengula believed he was allowing a mere handful of prospectors to enter his country. But the concession which he signed was deliberately mistranslated by the resident British missionary, the Reverend Helm (see p. 303). In practice it gave Rhodes's agents a free hand to take 'whatever action they consider necessary' to exploit the minerals of the kingdom. Despite Lobengula's vigorous protests, the British government accepted the fraudulent concession and approved the colonisation of Zimbabwe by Rhodes's newly formed British South Africa (BSA) Company.

In 1890 Rhodes sent in a heavily armed 'pioneer column' which skirted the south of the Ndebele kingdom and occupied Mashonaland on the eastern plateau. The 'pioneers' then dispersed to stake out farms for themselves

Figure 22.3 Rhodes straddling the continent, a *Punch* cartoon of 1892. He holds in his hands a telegraph wire. It was Rhodes's ultimate ambition to build a railway through 'British Africa', from the Cape to Cairo and to exploit the abandoned gold-mines of the former Mutapa empire. They soon discovered, however, that the ancient Shona miners had been more thorough than they had supposed and there were very few exploitable mines left. In their desperate search for valuable gold artefacts, these early white colonists vandalised and looted many ancient historical sites, destroying hundreds of years' worth of irreplaceable archaeological evidence.

Meanwhile, at his capital in Bulawayo, Lobengula tried every available diplomatic tactic to ward off the attack that he felt certain was inevitable. When it came in 1893, the Company's advantage of mounted troops and Maxim-guns was clearly evident. Within a matter of days Bulawayo fell to the invading column. The subsequent death of Lobengula threw the Ndebele into disarray. The Company, considering they had won, confiscated all Ndebele cattle and carved up the country into white-owned farms. In 1896–7, however, both Ndebele and Shona rose against the oppression of their conquerors. With the encouragement and leadership of religious spirit-mediums, they very nearly expelled the white colonists from their country. But Rhodes was able to call upon the assistance of reinforcements from the Cape Colony, and Ndebele and Shona resistance was eventually overcome. Nevertheless, their struggle for freedom in the 1890s was an important inspiration for a later generation who fought for their country's independence in the 1970s (see pp. 420–2).

Lewanika, Barotseland and the BSA Company

After the old Lozi aristocracy had ousted the Kololo in 1864, the Lozi court suffered a lengthy period of dynastic dispute and palace revolutions. It was not until 1885 that one contestant, Lubosi, emerged in final control of the kingdom. He assumed the title, Lewanika, meaning 'conqueror'.

In 1889 Lewanika sought a British protectorate for his kingdom (known to the British as 'Barotseland'). He was encouraged by the example of the Bechuanaland Protectorate. There the British offered the Batswana protection from Boer aggression without, as yet, interfering in any way with internal Batswana affairs. Lewanika sought protection from the constant threat of

Figure 22.4 *Litunga* Lewanika II (1878–84, 1885–1916) meeting with British officials at the Lozi capital, Lealui, October 1897. Major Robert Coryndon of the British South Africa Company (and soon to be the first Resident Commissioner of North-Western Rhodesia) seated centre; Lewanika seated to his right with hat and fly-whisk, with his eldest son and successor, Litia, later King Yeta III (1916–45), seated to his right (on extreme left of picture)

Ndebele raids; and he believed a British resident at his court would strengthen his personal position over any potential rivals to the throne. He also wanted British aid in setting up schools to teach his people literacy and technical skills. In 1890 Rhodes's agent, Lochner, promised all of this and £2000 a year in return for a concession to exploit the minerals in the kingdom. Believing he was dealing with an agent of the British government rather than with a private British company, Lewanika signed the concession. But he was soon disillusioned. Though Ndebele power was ultimately crushed by the Company, it was not before another Ndebele raid on Barotseland in 1893. It was 1897 before the BSA Company paid Lewanika any money or sent even a temporary resident. And no industrial schools were ever financed by the Company. Nevertheless, Barotseland was one of the few parts of south-central Africa to which colonisation came peaceably, and very little Lozi land was lost to white settlement.

The Central African Protectorate and North-Eastern Rhodesia

In 1889 the British government proclaimed the Central African Protectorate over the region, which eight years later they renamed Nyasaland. (*Nyasa* is a local African word for 'lake'. Hence the British colonial names 'Lake Nyasa' and 'Nyasaland', changed since independence to 'Malawi'.) The British government's action had been prompted by Portuguese attempts to deprive British traders of access to Lake Nyasa and the Shire valley region. Harry Johnston, a friend and associate of Cecil Rhodes, was appointed administrator.

Johnston's administration faced determined African resistance and for most of the 1890s he was engaged in military action, firstly against Yao (1891–5), then Swahili (1895), Chewa (1895) and Ngoni (1895–9). Most of his wars were in the name of 'the suppression of the slave trade'. To this end he did receive the keen support of the Shire valley Nyanga who for years had suffered from the raids of Yao slavers. But in reality Johnston's wars in the Central African Protectorate were a crude military conquest of the principal African authorities in the territory. He confronted each ruler in turn with a treaty of submission for him to sign and a demand for taxation. Those that rejected this interpretation of 'protection' faced conquest, death and taxation of the survivors. A senior British government official of the time aptly likened Johnston's demands to those of a highway robber: 'Treaty or compulsion; your money or your life!' Ultimately it was Maxim-gun, artillery, gunboats on the lake and a hardened professional corps of 300 Sikhs from India which finally ensured British control of the territory. A number of defeated Malawian resistance leaders committed suicide rather than submit to British captivity.

Johnston also acted as an agent of Rhodes's BSA Company in the neighbouring territory of 'North-Eastern Rhodesia'. Rhodes supplied Johnston with a £10,000 'pacification subsidy' for his work in Nyasaland. In return, Johnston supported Rhodes's interests by despatching treaty-making agents into the eastern and central districts of modern Zambia. The main resistance to Company rule in the region came from Bemba and Ngoni. In their conflicts with these, Rhodes's agents were able to call upon the military support of British government forces in Nyasaland.

In initial battles with the British, the well-armed Bemba had been able to hold their own. But the wealth and authority of the principal Bemba chiefs was gradually undermined. This was partly caused by British and German conquests in Nyasaland and Tanganyika, which were disrupting the long-distance trading caravans upon which the Bemba used to prey. They were further weakened by a leadership crisis within the Bemba hierarchy. Finally, in the confusion which followed the death of one claimant to the paramountcy in 1898, a French Catholic missionary declared himself king and welcomed the Company's forces into the Bemba capital.

Meanwhile, in the south-east, the techniques which had ensured the Ngoni two generations of military superiority in south-central Africa proved no match for the ruthless British use of Maxim-guns. In military confrontation in 1898 British machine-guns mowed down thousands of Ngoni soldiers. In launching their attack from neighbouring Nyasaland, the British claimed to be ridding the district of a tyrannical raiding state. Yet they themselves seized large tracts of land for white settlement in the region and forced surviving Ngoni into wage-labour by confiscating all their cattle and demanding taxation.

Wars of conquest and resistance in Mozambique

Resistance to Portuguese authority in Mozambique was particularly widespread and prolonged. The Portuguese faced opposition from the Gaza empire in the south, the Barwe kingdom in the foothills of the Zambezi escarpment, and the huge *prazos* of the Zambezi valley with their local Tonga, Manganja and Chewa allies. In the northern territory, resistance was led by Yao, Makonde and Makua – many of them well armed through years of trading in ivory and slaves with coastal merchants. Those in longest contact with European and Goan (Indian) traders tended to offer the toughest resistance to Portuguese demands for taxation in the 1880s and 1890s. They had the arms, and were used to defying the attempts of local Portuguese officials to assert their authority. This was particularly true of the *prazos* of the Zambezi valley, some of whose stockaded towns were defended with artillery.

The largest single state, the Gaza empire, was already in decline by the 1880s. One reason for this was the expansion of Gouveia's Gorongoza *prazo* which partly induced the Gaza ruler Ngungunyane (or Gungunhane) to shift his capital further south in 1889. More fundamentally, however, the authority of the Gaza *indunas* was being undermined by the development of migrant labour to Kimberley, Johannesburg and Natal. This not only removed large numbers of potential soldiers, herdsmen and hunters from the territory. Young Shangane men earned wages outside the Gaza state and so, on their return, they no longer depended on their elders to supply them with *lobola* for their brides.

Anticipating the Portuguese threat, Ngungunyane sought an alliance with the British, but his appeals were ignored. In 1891 an Anglo-Portuguese treaty placed most of the Gaza empire firmly within the Portuguese sphere. It was one of those deals so typical of the wider European 'Scramble', in which European governments drew the colonial boundaries of the continent without regard to African interests or requests. In 1894 Gaza took the offensive and raided the Portuguese port of Lourenço Marques. But the Portuguese response was more than the weakened Gaza state could bear. In two decisive battles the Shangane armies were defeated and Ngungunyane was captured.

In this instance it was primarily a Portuguese army of conquest, utilising the Maxim-gun to best advantage. In most of the rest of Mozambique the

Figure 22.5 The trading station at Tete on the Zambezi, early 1900s. Founded as a Swahili trading village in the days of the Mutapa empire, it was seized by the Portuguese in the sixteenth century and remains as an important crossing point of the Zambezi in modern times

Portuguese were very heavily dependent on local African armies for their conquests. In fact it has been described as not so much a 'Portuguese' conquest, but rather a series of African inter-state or 'civil' wars, exploited and directed by Portuguese officers. In the early 1880s it was the *prazeros* Kanyemba and Matakenya who extended Portuguese authority over the Nsenga and re-established a Portuguese trading post at Zumbo on the middle Zambezi. In the later 1880s the Portuguese exploited ancient rivalries to turn the *prazos* themselves against each other. In 1888, for instance, the Portuguese used the army of Gouveia, estimated at 12,000, in their conquest of the rival *prazo* Massingire. And 6000 Ngoni mercenaries were used against the *prazo* of Makanga north of Tete in 1901. In northern Mozambique, where resistance lasted longest, the Yao were only finally overcome when the ban on arms sales to Africans was enforced in 1912.

In most cases African mercenaries, conscripts and allies of the Portuguese saw themselves as exploiting a local advantage, reacting to ancient inter-state rivalries or seizing opportunities for loot. The Portuguese had been around for centuries; they were only one local power among many. Their authority could usually be defied in the end. There was no particular reason to suggest that this time the Portuguese would eventually come to dominate the whole region.

Conquest and resistance in Namibia

In central Namibia, between the Namib desert in the west and the Kalahari in the east, lies the dry grassland region of the central plateau. Though too dry for regular cultivation, for the peoples of Namibia it remained an essential resource for herding cattle, sheep and goats, and for hunting. Much of the nineteenth-century history of this region was dominated by intense conflict between Nama and Herero pastoralists and hunter/traders. By mid-century the region had been penetrated by British traders and German missionaries. Both Nama and Herero competed for the trade, exporting cattle, ivory and ostrich feathers in exchange for guns and ammunition.

In 1884 the Germans declared a protectorate over the coastal region from the Orange to the Kunene rivers. It was part of a deliberate new German policy to stake out colonies in Africa. On the face of it they claimed to be protecting the interests of German missionaries and traders, in particular a German merchant named Lüderitz who had set up a trading-post at Angra Pequena in 1883. Lüderitz claimed to have 'bought' huge tracts of coastal territory from local Nama chiefs in exchange for guns, alcohol and paltry sums of cash.

When the Germans moved on to the central plateau in 1890 they were able to exploit the age-old rivalry that existed between Nama and Herero. They offered the Herero a treaty of protection and in return proposed to help them in their long-term territorial conflict with the Nama. The Nama leader, Hendrik Witbooi, understood the nature of the German threat only too well. He wrote to the Herero chief, Maherero, warning him of the reality of his new alliance:

> You think you will retain your independent Chieftainship after I have been destroyed … but my dear Kaptein you will eternally regret your action in having handed over to the White man the right to govern your country. After all our war is not as serious as you think … . But this thing you have done, to surrender yourself to the Government of the White man, will be a burden that you will carry on your shoulders. You call yourself Supreme Chief, but when you are under another's control you are merely a subordinate Chief.

(*The Diary of Hendrik Witbooi,* Van Reibeeck Society, Vol. 9, p. 77)

The German commander set up a military base at Windhoek and launched an attack on Witbooi's home town of Gibeon. But Witbooi withdrew his

Map 22.3 German conquest of 'South West Africa'

troops from Gibeon and waged a successful guerrilla campaign against the German supply lines. For months the Germans were penned in at Windhoek until the arrival of heavy reinforcements from overseas in 1894. Though the Nama were then militarily defeated, the Germans were obliged to allow them to keep their weapons.

The position of the Herero, meanwhile, had been weakened by the death of Maherero and the succession dispute that followed. The Germans proved the truth of Witbooi's warning and took advantage of the situation. They set up a military garrison at the Herero capital, Okahandja, and declared their recognition of Samuel Maherero as Herero chief. They then ignored the new chief's authority and started allocating vast tracts of land for white settlement in the Windhoek area. This included much of the best grazing land in the central plateau region. When the eastern Herero and Mbanderu resisted German tax and labour demands in 1896, their 'rebellion' was crushed, their leaders executed and more land was seized for white settlement.

By the turn of the century the Germans had extended their control over most of the territory of 'South West Africa', apart from Ovamboland in the extreme north. The spread of rinderpest in 1896–7 crippled the pastoral economies of Nama and Herero and eased the rapid spread of German settlement after. German attempts to turn the whole territory into a colony of white settlement, however, was to provoke one of the great wars of African resistance between 1904 and 1907 (see pp. 352–3).

The South African War (1899–1902)

We saw earlier in this chapter that the development of gold mining on the Rand brought a great deal of wealth to the Boers of the Transvaal. Most of the actual mining remained in the hands of *uitlanders* (European 'outsiders'), mostly British, who had the expertise and capital to develop deep-level mining. The Transvaal president, Paul Kruger, pursued a deliberate policy of taxing the mining industry very heavily in order to benefit his political supporters, the rural Boers (now beginning to refer to themselves as 'Afrikaners'). Kruger also ensured that vital supporting industries, such as the manufacture of dynamite for blasting rock, the supply of water to Johannesburg and the building of railways, all remained in the hands of Boer monopolies. These charged the *uitlanders* high prices for their products and services. The policies of Kruger's government thus imposed a heavy cost on the British-dominated mining industry. At the same time the *uitlanders* were denied political rights. This was because there were so many of them that if they were allowed to vote, they might outnumber the Boers themselves and so take over control of the state.

In 1895 Rhodes, who was then prime minister of the Cape Colony (1890–6), hatched a plot to overthrow the Transvaal government by force. He hoped to raise the *uitlanders* of Johannesburg in rebellion and then send in the BSA Company police from 'Rhodesia', via neighbouring Bechuanaland. But the rising failed and the raiding force, led by Jameson, was captured and its leaders imprisoned. The Jameson raid provoked great anti-British feeling in the Boer republics and among Afrikaners of the Cape Colony. Rhodes was forced to resign from office and the Transvaal and

Map 22.4 The South African War, 1899–1902

Orange Free State formed a military alliance against any further British threat to their independence.

Where Rhodes and private capitalists had failed, the British government now directly intervened. There was a very real danger that the Transvaal would form an anti-British alliance with Germany. And Britain was determined that the gold-mines of the Rand should not fall into rival European hands. Between 1896 and 1899 tension mounted as the British demanded Kruger introduce reforms which would favour the British-dominated mining industry. In particular they demanded that the *uitlanders* be allowed full political rights. To back up their demands the British moved troops up to the Transvaal's borders. Kruger, realising war was inevitable, decided to strike first. He declared war in October 1899 and Boer commandos stormed across the republics' borders into the British colonies of the Cape and Natal.

The British suffered some initial humiliating defeats but they imported an army of up to half a million troops and by mid-1900 they had captured the principal Boer towns. Kruger fled into exile in Europe but his commando leaders continued a guerrilla campaign for a further two years. They were eventually forced into surrender only after the British had practised a devastating 'scorched-earth' policy. Boer farms were burnt and their families imprisoned in appalling 'concentration' camps where thousands of women and children died from disease. It was a legacy which the Boers would not easily forget. The harsh treatment meted out to Boer women and children during the South African (or Anglo-Boer) War was a strong

Figure 22.6 A group of Boers after a bushbuck hunt; a lull in the fighting during the South African War of 1899–1902

stimulus for the development of Afrikaner nationalism during the early decades of the twentieth century.

During the war both sides had officially taken the view that it was 'a white man's war' and Africans should not be involved. Basically the war was about who should dominate South Africa, the British or the Boers. It was feared that if Africans were armed and encouraged to shoot whites, then after the war they would no longer resume the subordinate position that both sides intended they should take. In practice, however, Africans were very much involved in the war, as victims and participants. They too suffered from the scorched-earth tactics and thousands likewise died in concentration camps. They were employed as support-personnel to British armies and Boer commandos, serving them as labourers, wagon-drivers, scouts and messengers. They also grew much of the food that supplied both the armies. Some took up arms, in support in particular of the British cause. It was believed by many Africans that this support would be rewarded by the British. They occupied deserted Boer farms and expected that the British would confirm their ownership of this land, much of it seized from them by the Boers in an earlier generation. They believed also that a British victory would ensure for black people generally a more equal share in the political and economic life of the region.

Their trust and expectation, however, were sadly misplaced. After the war the British were mainly concerned to placate the Boers, and to establish unity and understanding between Boer and Briton. In 1910 the former Boer republics and British colonies were joined into a single 'Union of South Africa'. A principal purpose of this was to ensure the security and continuation of white domination in South Africa.

23

Consolidation of empire: the early period of colonial rule

Raw materials and markets

We saw in Chapter 21 that two of the prime economic reasons for European empire in Africa were the need for new markets for manufactured goods and the search for raw materials for European industry. In theory the two should have gone hand in hand, and at times they did. Africans themselves produced the raw materials and sold them for cash, much of which they spent upon imported manufactured goods. Too often, however, European governments, merchants and colonists abused the power that went with recent conquest and looked to their own short-term gain. Land was seized and raw materials extracted from the continent with little or nothing given in exchange.

Concessionary companies

In many parts of Africa European governments used concessionary companies to colonise their new-found empires. By this system private European companies were granted vast stretches of African territory to exploit and colonise at their own expense in the name of the European country concerned. It was an attempt by Europe to colonise 'on the cheap'. We have already seen that the British used the system in Nigeria (the Royal Niger Company), in 'Rhodesia' (the British South Africa Company) and east Africa (the Imperial British East Africa Company). Concessionary companies were also widely used in the

Figure 23.1 The lifestyle to which early colonial administrators aspired. A postmaster and tax collector in 'Nyasaland' in 1891 being carried in a *machila*, with game trophies at his side

343

early exploitation of German, French and Portuguese colonies. In theory the company would 'open up' the territory, set up a rudimentary administration, invest in railways and introduce Africans to a cash economy. This would in due course build up markets for European manufactured goods. But in practice the system was widely open to abuse, mainly because it was motivated purely by short-term private profit. There was little long-term investment in administration, roads or railways. Instead, the companies concentrated upon the violent exploitation of the people and their natural resources. Persistent African resistance, however, ensured that early high profit-levels could not be sustained and many companies went bankrupt. In most of the continent, apart from Mozambique, administration by concessionary company had given way to direct European imperial control by the early 1920s. The worst abuses of the system were observed in the Congo River basin, that is, in the Congo Free State and French Equatorial Africa.

The Congo Free State

Leopold had declared that all land not actively occupied and cultivated by its inhabitants was 'vacant land' and as such belonged to him and his Free State government. In the sparsely populated forest, where hunting, gathering and shifting cultivation were predominant, this meant the bulk of the land in the territory. Some of this 'vacant' land Leopold kept for himself; the rest he leased to private concessionary companies. One Belgian company, for example, was granted 8000 square kilometres of land in return for building a railway from the coast to Malebo Pool. Another, the Katanga Company, got a third of the 'vacant land' and exclusive mineral rights in the south-eastern quarter of the state. In return, the Free State government was to get a third of the company's profits.

The main object of concessionary exploitation in the tropical forests from the 1890s to the early 1900s was wild rubber. The spread of the bicycle and motor car in Europe and north America stimulated a boom in the world market for rubber which only subsided with the development of plantations in south-east Asia between 1905 and 1910. Company agents took their private armies of African ex-slaves into the Congo basin and forced the local people to collect rubber from the forest. In a report published in a British newspaper in 1895, an American missionary working in the Congo, Reverend J. B. Murphy, described the barbarity of the system he had witnessed:

> It has reduced the people to a state of utter despair. Each town in the district is forced to bring a certain quantity [of rubber] to the headquarters of the commissaire every Sunday. It is collected by force. The soldiers drive the people into the bush. If they will not go they are shot down, and their left hands cut off and taken as trophies to the commissaire. The soldiers do not care who they shoot down, and they more often shoot poor helpless women and harmless children. These hands, the hands of men, women and children, are placed in rows before the commissaire, who counts them to see that the soldiers have not wasted the cartridges. The commissaire is paid a commission of about 1d. a pound upon all the rubber he gets. It is therefore to his interest to get as much as he can … .
>
> I have been in the interior and have seen the ravages made by the State in pursuit of this iniquitous trade … . Let me give an incident to show how this unrighteous trade affects the people. One day a State corporal, who was in charge of the post of Lolifa, was going round the town collecting rubber. Meeting a poor woman whose husband was away fishing, he said, 'Where is your husband?' She answered by pointing to the river. He then said, 'Where is his rubber?' She answered, 'It is ready for you,' whereupon he said, 'You

Map 23.1   Sub-Saharan Africa in the early colonial period

lie,' and, lifting his gun, shot her dead. Shortly afterwards the husband returned, and was told of the murder of his wife. He went straight to the corporal, taking with him his rubber, and asked why he had shot his wife. The wretched man then raised his gun and killed the corporal. The soldiers ran away to the headquarters of the State and made misrepresentations of the case, with the result that the commissaire sent a large force to support the authority of the soldiers; the town was looted, burned, and many people killed and wounded. In November last [1894] there was heavy fighting upon the Bosira, because the people refused to give rubber, and I was told upon the authority of a State officer that no fewer than 1,890 people were killed.

(*The Times,* London, 18 November 1895)

These and other incidents like them were brought to public attention in Europe, but little was done about it for a further decade. In the meantime Africans resisted the crude and brutal exploitation as well as they were able. Desertion of their villages was the most readily available form of resistance, though this in turn resulted in great hardship, as Reverend Murphy explained:

345

Two of the most flourishing towns in Mr H.M. Stanley's time, situated at Stanley Pool, viz. – Kintamo and Kinchassa – are now no more, and the people have gone over to the French Congo. ... Many people have left the main river and gone into the interior in order to escape the arbitrary demands of the State ... . The people of the district of Lake Mantumba, of Irebu, and Lokolala and all the Mobangi towns have crossed over to the French side ... . The people did not run away without great provocation, for it meant starvation to them, all the gardens and their homes being upon the State side. Going over to the French side meant that they would become homeless and hungry wanderers. Even then the State could not leave them in peace; they heard that they came over at night to their old homes to get food, and they stationed canoes and lay in wait for them, with orders that the soldiers should shoot as many as they caught, and to my knowledge they shot seven people in one night.

Increasingly, people resorted to armed resistance. Those in the lower Congo region obtained rifles from traders on the coast and in their many conflicts with the Free State forces they learned to use these weapons to great effect.

Figure 23.2 The Belgian King Leopold II shown as a serpent whose rubber coils are crushing the people of the Congo (a *Punch* cartoon, November 1906)

By the early 1900s open rebellions were becoming widespread and colonial authority was in danger of collapse. Growing African resistance, combined with international condemnation of the regime and the falling price of rubber, led Leopold to abandon his private venture in 1908. That year he handed over the Free State to a reluctant Belgian government. The latter ended the worst abuses of the system, though private European companies remained in control of most of the territory's resources. The Union Munière company, for instance, continued with its sole right to exploit the Katanga copper-mines. And in 1911 the British company of Lever Brothers (later Unilever) was granted the monopoly rights to purchase all palm products from an area covering three-quarters of a million hectares.

French Equatorial Africa

Across the river in Gabon, Middle Congo and German Kamerun the concessionary system was open to similar abuses. As much as 70 per cent of French Equatorial Africa was allocated to 41 private concessionary companies. Company agents raided the forest people, seizing hostages and forcing villagers to hand over fixed quotas of ivory and rubber. In the middle Congo many thousands of men were forced to work as porters for very low wages, carrying supplies for the French army of conquest in Chad. Forced-labour was also used in the building of a railway from the coast at Pointe Noire to Brazzaville on the northern shores of Malebo Pool. Living and working conditions of the forced-labour camps were appalling and in the railway project alone an estimated 16,000 African workers died through brutality, disease or malnutrition. It is significant that in the early colonial decades in this part of Africa population levels fell dramatically. In the short space of a few decades the people of this region probably suffered worse than in any similar short period during the whole of the slave trade era.

Peasant production and railways in west Africa

The savannah and forest zones of sub-Saharan west Africa were the regions where African initiative was best able to respond to the new market opportunities of the early colonial period. Forced labour and the plundering of forest resources by European agents were characteristic of parts of the region. Rubber and hardwood, for instance, were plundered from the Côte d'Ivoire forest in the face of continued armed African resistance right up to 1915. On the whole, however, the production of raw materials in the region was left in the hands of African peasant farmers. They were quickly found to be more efficient producers than European plantation-owners, dependent as the latter were upon the inefficient use of forced-labour. In both French and British zones, African farmers were 'encouraged' to turn away from food crops and produce cash crops for the European markets. Production for export was stimulated by a combination of colonial demands for cash taxation, the building of railways for inland transport to the coast, and individual African initiative.

Groundnuts and palm oil, the main export crops of the pre-colonial nineteenth century, were carried forward into the colonial period. The production of groundnuts in Senegal expanded greatly with the building of the railway which reached from Dakar to Bamako on the upper Niger by 1905. Senegalese peasants migrated seasonally into the less densely populated Gambia river valley to cultivate the crop and sell their exports downstream to the coast at Bathurst (modern Banjul). Palm oil remained the principal export of Igboland in eastern Nigeria, though palm-oil exports from the

French colony of Dahomey never recovered to the scale of the pre-conquest period.

The development of cocoa as an export crop from Gold Coast (Ghana) was a striking example of African initiative. It was originally brought to Gold Coast from Fernando Poo by a Ga metalworker called Tetten Quarshie in 1879. He set up a cocoa nursery on the Akwapim ridge north of Accra, and by the 1890s was selling cocoa seedlings by the thousand to local peasant farmers. The British governor of Gold Coast set up a similar cocoa nursery in the 1880s, but the initiative for the rapid spread of inland cocoa plantations lay firmly in the hands of local peasant farmers. From the Akwapim ridge, industrious farmers migrated northwards into the relatively undercultivated forest zone. There they bought land from local Akan chiefs and developed a thriving peasant-operated cocoa plantation system. Cash from the sale of cocoa, apart from the payment of taxes, was spent on imported manufactured goods, the local building of houses, roads and bridges, and the education of children in mission schools. By 1914 Gold Coast had become the world's largest single producer of cocoa.

The British, meanwhile, had pushed their Nigerian railway system inland from Lagos in 1896 to reach Ibadan in 1900 and Kano in 1911. Cocoa production became an important peasant cash crop in Yorubaland south of Ibadan. The British expected the Hausa of northern Nigeria to become major producers of cotton, but to their surprise the farmers in the Hausa region turned instead to groundnuts. They had sufficient agricultural expertise to realise that cotton was a greater-risk crop, more susceptible to drought and requiring greater labour to produce. The prices offered for groundnuts by European merchants at the Kano railhead were more attractive than those offered for cotton. Experienced local Hausa traders quickly spread the word and organised the local marketing networks. Within two years the peasant farmers of Hausaland were producing so many tonnes of groundnuts that the railway was unable to cope with the traffic. As a result, the European merchants in Kano had to stockpile sacks of groundnuts in the streets.

Figure 23.3 Opening ceremony for a new Nigeria Railways station at Ibadan. A crowd of European and African people gather on the platform beneath an array of flags. Ibadan, Oyo State, Nigeria, 5 March 1901

Figure 23.4 The first copper-smelting furnace in Rhodesia in the early 1900s used African techniques

Peasant producers in many parts of tropical Africa undoubtedly benefited from the vastly improved transport facilities – roads, railways and harbours – which were developed in the early colonial period. But this was not without considerable cost to themselves. European governments expected their colonies to be self-financing. Thus the construction of railways and harbours had to be paid for out of local funds. Apart from providing a large amount of free labour, however unwillingly, Africans ultimately paid for their own railways and harbours through direct taxation and customs duties on imports. In many cases railway construction companies received huge free grants of African land. European merchants and manufacturers, who benefited most from the increased trade, paid nothing for the transport infrastructures of the colonies from which they profited.

Peasant producers, railways and white settlement in British east Africa

The peasant farmers of west Africa had not taken to the growing of raw cotton on the scale that British or French manufacturers had hoped. Their agents in Africa, such as the British Cotton Growing Association (BCGA), had failed to entice the farmers of west Africa to grow much cotton for export. The prices they offered were too low compared with other cash crops such as cocoa, palm oil or groundnuts. In Egypt and Uganda, however, the BCGA met with greater success. The completion of the Aswan Dam in 1902 meant that year-round irrigation was now possible in the lower Nile valley. Encouraged by the BCGA and British administrators in Cairo, the peasant farmers of Egypt developed an over-dependence upon cotton at the expense of food crops.

Uganda

The most dramatic development of cotton production in sub-Saharan Africa was in Uganda. We saw in Chapter 14 (pp. XXX–X) that the Baganda were already used to intensive agricultural production. In the early 1890s the British had used an alliance with the Christian aristocracy of Buganda to establish a protectorate over the whole region. In 1900 the British made a further agreement with the Baganda aristocracy, which laid the foundations for British rule throughout Uganda. They agreed not to take any land for white settlement and introduced a system of private land tenure. This meant that much of the agricultural land of Buganda became the privately owned estates of the Baganda chiefs with the peasantry as their tenants. The Buganda king, the *kabaka*, lost his former control over land-allocation and with it most of his effective power. He became a figurehead, appointed by the colonial administration, which now assumed the power to appoint and dismiss chiefs. This system was extended to the other former kingdoms of the territory.

It was against this background that the Uganda Railway from Mombasa to Kisumu on the shores of Lake Victoria Nyanza was completed in 1901. A short trip across the lake brought the Baganda into touch with a cheap and easy transport system to the coast. Once the BCGA had introduced seed in 1903, cotton production for export from Uganda took off on a rapidly increasing scale. The spread of peasant cotton production in Uganda was helped by the recently established system of land tenure. Seed was initially distributed through the chiefs, who organised their tenants to grow the crop. In this way cotton-growing spread rapidly through Bunyoro and Busoga as well as through Buganda. Chiefs were enticed on to the governing board of the Uganda Company which was founded to organise the marketing of cotton within Uganda. Within Buganda, in particular, peasant farmers began producing on their own account as well as for their chiefs. Soil and climate here was sufficiently suitable for farmers to be able to produce the cotton crop for cash in addition to tending their banana plantations for their food. This left them with a level of security not experienced elsewhere in the continent, where the production of single cash crops for export grew to dominate over basic food production.

Kenya

From an early period the British viewed their East African Protectorate (renamed 'Kenya' in 1920) as a potential colony for white settlement. The highlands east of Lake Victoria Nyanza offered a favourable climate and fertile soils and the region was served by the newly completed Uganda Railway. Much of the best land lay within the Uganda Protectorate where white settlement had been precluded by agreement in 1900, but this problem was easily overcome. In 1902 a huge section of Uganda's territory, from the Rift Valley to Lake Victoria Nyanza, was transferred to the East African Protectorate. The dense population of Africans included in this transfer was viewed by the British as so many more taxpayers for their colony and potential workers on white-owned farms.

The African peoples of the region refused to give up their land and freedom without a struggle and they engaged the British in a series of wars of resistance between 1901 and 1908. British military superiority and widespread use of violence, however, eventually prevailed and plans for white settlement went ahead. The highlands were set aside for white ownership only. Indian traders who had come inland with the railway were prevented from buying land in the region. Africans already on the land were classed as 'squatters', only allowed to remain so long as the white 'owner' needed their labour. Particularly badly affected in this respect were the Gikuyu agriculturalists whose steady expansion into the fertile Rift Valley region was halted and pushed back by the influx of white settlement. From the mid-1900s white settlers were brought in from Britain and South Africa in a determined effort to turn the highlands into 'white-man's country'. The administrative capital was shifted inland to Nairobi and from an early period the white settlers were allowed a powerful voice in the administration of the colony.

Rebellion in the German colonies

The Maji Maji rebellion (1905–7)

Across the border in German East Africa, colonial conquest seemed complete by the late 1890s. It had been a long-drawn-out struggle and inland administration centres were in reality little more than a series of small military fortresses. From 1898 head tax was levied on all adult Africans in the colony and a high level of violence and intimidation was used in its collection. Experiments with European-owned plantations were tried in the north near Kilimanjaro, but for a while most of the rest of the country was regarded by the Germans as little more than a source of ivory and taxation.

In July 1905 rebellion broke out in the southern part of the colony, in the hinterland of Kilwa. It began in the Matumbi hills, when the local people resisted government attempts to force them into growing cotton for export. The revolt spread rapidly throughout the region with attacks on all foreigners: missionaries, administrators and their Swahili clerks.

It was a spontaneous rising with no previous planning and no central leadership. And yet the peoples of southern Tanzania came together in a way that is unique in the history of African resistance to colonialism. Instinctively they turned to their beliefs in the powers of the spirit world. It was a deliberate attempt to overcome the problems which had crippled earlier African resistance to European conquest, namely, lack of African unity and the European machine-gun. They sprinkled their bodies with magic water known as *maji-maji* which they believed would turn the bullets of their enemies into water. It was a simple device and one which brought the people together. The Germans were staggered by the rapid spread of the revolt and initial 'rebel' successes strengthened the belief in *maji-maji*. But the turning-point came at the end of only four weeks. Armed with nothing but spears and the protection of *maji-maji*, the 'rebels' stormed a German machine-gun post, only to be mown down in their thousands. Though the revolt continued to spread, it had lost its initial momentum. The power of *maji-maji* had been weakened and political unity gradually fell apart.

By the end of 1905 the Germans had brought in reinforcements, recruited from Somaliland and New Guinea. During 1906 the Germans gradually brought back the central highland region under their control. They pursued a 'scorched-earth' policy, destroying villages and laying waste vast stretches of southern and central Tanzania. While official German figures claimed that 26,000 'rebels' were killed in military action, an estimated further 50,000 Tanzanians died in the famine which ensued.

In the immediate aftermath of Maji Maji the Germans reduced their use of violence in enforcing their authority, for fear of provoking another rising.

They encouraged mission-school attendance and made European employers accept some responsibility for the health of their workers. But, more important in the long term, the Maji Maji rising had shown the possibility of a wider African anti-colonial nationalism across the old pre-colonial divides. The sacrifice of the thousands of Tanzanians who died in Maji Maji was an important inspiration to a later generation of nationalists who brought their country to independence in the early 1960s.

The Herero and Nama risings (1904–7)

Meanwhile in their colony of South West Africa the Germans were vigorously pushing forward a policy of white settlement in the central highland region. Nama and Herero pastoralists had suffered heavy cattle-losses in the rinderpest epidemic of 1896–7. White settlers took advantage of this misfortune and moved on to valuable African grazing land which was now temporarily underused. At the same time, white traders systematically stripped African pastoralists of their few remaining cattle in order to stock the newly acquired white-owned ranches. Traders extended loans of food and clothing to impoverished African stockowners and then insisted upon repayment in the form of their few remaining livestock. The arrival of labour recruiters from Johannesburg in the early 1900s was regarded by the Herero leadership as a deliberate white conspiracy to destroy the Herero nation by stripping it of its able-bodied young men.

In 1904 the Herero rose in revolt, killed over a hundred German traders and settlers and reoccupied much of their former territory. But they failed to persuade the Nama to join them until it was too late. By then the Germans had brought in reinforcements from abroad and had isolated the Herero in the Waterberg. When the Herero broke out of their encirclement, the German general, von Trotha, issued his notorious 'extermination' proclamation:

> The Herero are no longer German subjects. They have murdered and plundered … . The Herero nation must leave the country. If it will not do so I shall compel it by force … . Inside German territory every Herero tribesman, armed or unarmed, with or without cattle, will be shot. No women and children will be allowed in the territory: they will be driven back to their people or fired on. These are the last words to the Herero nation from me, the great General of the mighty German Emperor.

(Quoted in H. Bley, *South-West Africa under German Rule,* Heinemann, London, 1971, pp. 163–4)

Figure 23.5 Captured Herero, during the rising of 1904–6

The retreating Herero were driven westwards into the Kalahari desert, where tens of thousands died of thirst and starvation. By the time von Trotha's proclamation was withdrawn at the end of 1905, a mere 16,000 Herero were left alive within the territory out of a previous population of 80,000. Only 2000 refugees reached neighbouring Bechuanaland.

In the meantime the Nama too had risen in revolt. Under the able leadership of Hendrik Witbooi they waged a successful guerrilla campaign. They managed to tie the German forces down until at least the end of 1905, when the ageing Witbooi was killed. Thereafter Nama unity gradually fell apart. Other Nama leaders continued the resistance into 1907, but the Germans gradually reasserted their control.

At the end of the war the Germans destroyed any remaining Nama and Herero independence by confiscating all their cattle and deposing all their chiefs. The survivors were forced into the position of a subordinate, low-paid workforce, serving the German farms and mines. But so many Nama and Herero had been killed during the war that German labour agents had to seek new recruits from Ovamboland in the north. By the outbreak of the First World War hatred of German rule had become so intense that some of the southern Nama welcomed the South African army when it invaded the territory in the early months of 1915.

Missionaries, Christianity and early expressions of 'nationalism'

African political and religious authority were generally very closely allied. Even in the smallest-scale society the chief was usually the guardian of religious shrines or protector of ancestral spirits. So European destruction of African political authority also weakened the authority of traditional African religion, opening the way for the spread of Christianity. The opening decades of the twentieth century were thus a major growth period for Christian missionary expansion. An important factor in this growth was the mission provision of some small degree of elementary education and rudimentary health clinics. These were services to which the new colonial governments paid little or no attention. It was probably these badly needed services that attracted Africans in their thousands to the mission establishments in the 1910s and 1920s.

Already by then, however, some of the earlier converts to Christianity had felt the yoke of a religion so closely tied to European culture and political power. In the 1880s and 1890s in South Africa, African Christian clergymen had rebelled against European domination of their Churches. A number of them formed their own independent Christian Churches, encouraged in many instances by American evangelists. The movement was known as the 'Ethiopian Church' movement, after the use of 'Ethiopia' as a name for Africa in the Christian Bible. The tendency to reject European control and to form independent African Churches spread to central Africa in the wake of the spread of European colonialism.

African Church leaders took the teachings of the Bible more literally than some of their European colleagues. They saw in the Bible the doctrines of justice and the equality of humankind. The promise of a 'second coming' was seen by many as heralding an end to the oppression of the new colonial

Figure 23.6 John Chilembwe's Providence Industrial Mission, Mbombwe, Nyasaland (Malawi), *c.*1912. Chilembwe (seated right, in glasses) and some of his congregation in front of their newly constructed church. By 1915 the Mission's roll contained 1160 'Baptised Believers'

regimes. In this respect the Independent Church movement can be seen as an early expression of African nationalist sentiment against European colonialism. One of the strongest voices of African Christian protest came from Elliot Kamwana's Watchtower sect, founded in Nyasaland in 1908. Kamwana preached a 'second coming' which would liberate all of Africa. Colonial taxation would be ended and Africans would achieve political self-government.

Figure 23.7 Chilembwe's Mission Church at Mbombwe, before and after its destruction by colonial troops, 26 January 1915

Even after the arrest and deportation of Kamwana, the Watchtower movement grew in strength in neighbouring Rhodesia where the colonial impact was particularly severe.

Perhaps the most famous African Christian 'rebel' of the period was John Chilembwe, also from Nyasaland. He had founded his own mission station in the Shire Highlands, an area of white plantation settlement. In 1915 he led his followers in a brief rebellion against specific local and general injustices of the colonial regime. He objected in particular to the shedding of innocent African blood in the First World War conflict in the northern borderlands of Nyasaland (see below). Chilembwe had resolved to 'strike a blow and die', and he did indeed die, shot while escaping into Mozambique. But the blow he struck was symbolic, an inspiration to a later generation, which earned him an honourable place in the folklore of the Malawian nationalist movement.

The First World War and Africa, 1914–18

When war broke out in Europe in August 1914 it was at first essentially a European conflict. But the fact that the major European powers had colonies in Africa meant that the war had a considerable impact in Africa itself. The British joined their French allies in invading the German colonies of Togo and Kamerun. Togo was easily overrun, but the struggle for Kamerun went on until February 1916. This left four-fifths of the country occupied by the French and one-fifth, bordering Nigeria, occupied by the British. Meanwhile the forces of the newly united white government of South Africa had occupied the German colony of South West Africa. The longest conflict was in German East Africa. Here South African forces joined with British east and west African troops in a campaign which lasted for the duration of the war. Once the territory had been occupied, by the British from the north and the Belgians from the west, the German general, von Lettow-Vorbeck, led his troops in an undefeated campaign through Mozambique, Nyasaland and north-eastern Rhodesia.

The destruction caused by the Kamerun and east African campaigns caused severe hardship to the rural peoples of the region. Their villages were often burned and their food supplies and labour were indiscriminately requisitioned by the opposing armies. Both sides used scorched-earth tactics, destroying crops and villages to deprive their opponents of support and supplies. Cattle, whose numbers were just beginning to recover from the devastation of the rinderpest pandemic of the 1890s, were a particular target of the military campaigns, providing food for the armies and depriving their owners of the means of subsistence. Famine became widespread in 1916–18, even in Rwanda which was not in the direct theatre of war. An estimated one million Kenyans and Tanzanians served as porters for the armies of the east African campaign. And up to 100,000 of these died of disease, malnutrition or overwork. Similarly in Egypt, British troops requisitioned Egyptian corn, cotton, camels and labour in their campaign against the Ottoman allies of Germany.

At the same time it should be borne in mind that most of the troops on either side of the war in tropical Africa were in fact Africans, recruited or pressed into service by their European rulers. The Germans in east Africa recruited their *askaris* (Swahili word for 'soldiers') from among Africans whom they had recently conquered, such as the Ngoni. The British recruited 50,000 troops from Sierra Leone, Gold Coast and Nigeria for their east African campaign, while the South Africans recruited blacks but did not allow them to carry rifles for use against whites. The British were somewhat hesitant about recruiting Africans for direct use in the European theatre of war. Not so the French. In total some 600,000 Africans were recruited or conscripted into the French army. 150,000 of these served in the trenches of the European Western Front, of whom 30,000 were killed in action. A further 40,000 African troops died fighting for the French around the eastern Mediterranean and in Africa. One Moroccan regiment that featured regularly in the casualty lists became the most highly decorated regiment in the whole of the French army. The French also conscripted 140,000 labourers, mostly from north Africa, for service in the war.

When the French tried to enforce military conscription in west Africa, they were faced with widespread rebellion, especially in the Sahelian and desert regions of their vast African empire. In 1916 the Tuareg of French Soudan (modern Mali) rose in open revolt, a rebellion which it took French legionnaires more than a year to suppress. The Germans and their Ottoman allies tried stoking these rebellions, but their provision of firearms was sporadic and rebellious attacks were ill coordinated. In fact, the years of the war were a period when the French completed their conquest of the remaining independent peoples of their vast African empire, both in the desert regions and in the forests of Cote D'Ivoire.

The British, too, used the war years to take firmer hold of Egypt and to seize control of Darfur. In Egypt they gave up their pretence of merely providing support for Ottoman rule in the territory, for Britain was now at war with the Ottoman empire. The British deposed *Khedive* Abbas, declared a formal protectorate over Egypt and turned the delta region into their principal military base in the eastern Mediterranean. Meanwhile, south of Egypt and to the west of Sudan, the sultanate of Darfur had remained until now one of the few remaining un-colonised states on the continent. The sultan of Darfur had been a close ally and tributary of the Mahdist state that had driven the Egyptians out of Sudan in the 1880s. When the Anglo-Egyptian force under General Kitchener had conquered Sudan in the late 1890s, they had left Darfur as an insignificant Saharan sultanate to their west. But on the outbreak of war in 1914, Sultan Ali Dinar declared an alliance with the Ottomans and also with the Sanusiyya who were fighting the Italians in Libya. In 1916, therefore, the British military ruler of Sudan, Sir Reginald Wingate, invaded Darfur, brought it under military occupation and incorporated it into colonial Sudan.

Away from the direct African theatres and zones of intense conscription, the impact of the war varied enormously across the continent. Soon after the outbreak of war, shipping lanes became badly disrupted with the result that exports of cash crops and other raw materials were severely curtailed. Prices paid for cash crops fell, while the cost of imports rose sharply. This resulted in a sharp recession for the newly emerging colonial economies. Peasant producers and industrial workers were impoverished and their health status declined. From 1916 allied shipping lanes were generally restored, which was a great boost for cash crops such as the groundnuts and palm oil of Nigeria. At the same time African clerical workers gained access to jobs vacated by whites called up for military service. South Africa, already Africa's foremost industrial economy gained a further boost as it geared up to meet wartime demands for food, minerals and engineering maintenance for shipping. Economic and social wartime gains were few compared to the losses suffered by Africans across the continent. And immediate political gains were non-existent.

There were, however, two significant social consequences of Africa's wartime experiences that were ultimately to have political implications later in the century. One was a wearing away of much of the aura of European invincibility that had accompanied the speed and ruthlessness of colonial conquest in the preceding decades. The other was the emergence of urbanisation in tropical Africa. Mediterranean north Africa had long had an urban culture, as had parts of South Africa and west Africa. But the vast majority of tropical Africans had hitherto lived a predominantly rural life, in relatively small towns and villages that were intimately connected with the local production of food and trading goods. Heavy wartime pressures on rural communities, however, destroyed or seriously weakened indigenous rural economies and prompted many to seek work in coastal ports or new colonial administrative centres. A generation later those who had grown up in these burgeoning urban centres and colonial capitals were to provide the backbone of the mid-century resistance to colonial rule on the continent.

The general ravages of the First World War were compounded by famine and the influenza pandemic which followed in 1918–19. Spread along the coast and inland along the new railway lines, influenza struck hardest where people were already weakened by warfare, hunger or poor working conditions. Vast areas of east, west and central Africa lost up to 3 per cent of their population while in southern Rhodesia an estimated 7 per cent of black mineworkers succumbed to the disease.

In January 1918, shortly after the United States entered the war, President Woodrow Wilson pronounced 'Fourteen Points' that ought to form the basis of any post-war settlement. These included the right of 'self-determination of nations', and general freedom from oppression. He also proposed the setting up of 'a general association of nations' that would help prevent future wars and would protect the smaller nations from foreign

Figure 23.8 Rhodesian African Regiment on route march through Salisbury bound for east Africa, World War I

Figure 23.9 Von Lettow-Vorbeck, the undefeated German military commander, and his east African *askaris,* Kasama, northern Rhodesia, November 1918

Map 23.2 The First World War and Africa, 1914–18

Figure 23.10 Preparation of a troop train at Lome ahead of the Anglo-French conquest of Togoland (now Togo). In August 1914 a combined British and French force conquered Togoland and established a joint protectorate while another Anglo-French force overran Cameroon, but here the German forces did not surrender until 4th March 1916

occupation. Wilson's 'self-determination' referred principally to the main theatres of war in Europe and western Asia that had been under German and Ottoman occupation. But his declaration encouraged educated Africans to believe that the settlement after the war might be the first step on their own road to freedom from colonial occupation. Consequently, after the war ended in November 1918, a number of African political parties applied to be represented at the peace conference that assembled at Versailles in France in the early months of 1919. Among these was the forerunner of the African National Congress, the South African Native National Congress (founded in 1912). They were seeking freedom from white domination (see p. 376). Similarly, the Egyptian nationalist party, the Wafd, was seeking an end to the British wartime 'Protectorate' and the restoration of Egyptian independence (see p. 376). Neither party, however, was allowed to attend the Versailles Conference.

Figure 23.11 African machine-gun detachment, eastern Belgian Congo, 1916

The most important outcome of the Versailles Conference for Africa was the setting up of the League of Nations, of which Ethiopia was the only independent African founder member. The League took over responsibility for the former German African colonies and delegated this responsibility to their French, British and Belgian occupiers. Thus the French and British shared Togo and Kamerun (Cameroon in English, Cameroun in French), the Belgians got Rwanda and Burundi, the British kept Tanganyika and the British delegated responsibility for South West Africa (Namibia) to its occupying Dominion, the Union of South Africa. The League of Nations 'Mandate' under which these occupying powers held their new territories bound them to safeguard the interests of their African inhabitants and prepare them for eventual self-government. In practice the European victors treated their new acquisitions much like any other colony.

chapter

24

Africa between the wars: the high tide of colonial rule

The economic impact of colonial rule

The expansion of white settlement

The most prominent colonies of white settlement in tropical Africa were Kenya and Southern Rhodesia. It used to be assumed that these were the only ones 'chosen' for extensive white settlement because of their favourable highland climate. The implication of this notion of choice was that the lowland west and central African zones were deliberately avoided by white

Map 24.1   Colonial exploitation of sub-Saharan Africa in the inter-war period

settlers because of their uncomfortable heat and humidity and the prevalence of tropical disease. In fact Europeans did try to establish white settlement in most tropical African colonies. Where European settlement failed to become the dominant economic force, it had more to do with African than with European initiative.

In many parts of tropical west Africa, for instance, land was extensively occupied by African farmers already engaged in cash-crop production. The French persistently attempted to push forward white-settler agriculture in Guinea and Côte d'Ivoire. But European-run plantations in west Africa were not a great success, dependent as they were on forced and unwilling, low-paid labour. Generally they could not compete with the more numerous, more efficient, small-scale production of the African peasant farmers. In some colonies European settlement was prevented by direct African political opposition. In Gold Coast, for instance, educated African Christians had got together with traditional rulers to form the Aborigines' Rights Protection Society. In 1898 they had successfully petitioned the British government against allowing the alienation of African land to Europeans. Similar African opposition had prevented the early alienation of African land in southern Nigeria. Meanwhile, at the other end of the continent, the Tswana chiefs of Bechuanaland had successfully petitioned the British government against their territory being handed over to the white colonists of Rhodesia.

Even in the French colony of Algeria white-settler agriculture only succeeded because it was heavily subsidised by the majority Muslim population. In the first place European settlement had only been made possible by extensive and costly military conquest in the nineteenth century. By the 1920s white settlers 'owned' most of the decent arable land in Algeria north of the Sahara. 'Native' Algerian Muslims had to resort to cultivating marginal, former grazing land. The result was rapid land deterioration and famine in times of drought. Under pressure from government taxation, Muslims were therefore forced to accept the low-paid seasonal labour offered on white-owned farms. At the same time the income from this taxation was spent on government loans, grants, research advice and marketing facilities for the white-settler farmers.

A similar system of subsidies drawn from 'native' taxation was what established white-settler agriculture in Kenya and Rhodesia. African peasant production was deliberately discriminated against in both settler colonies. Africans were forced off the best land and only allowed back if they worked

Figure 24.1 Two advertisements published by the Empire Marketing Board 1927–33

EAST-AFRICAN TRANSPORT–OLD STYLE

EAST-AFRICAN TRANSPORT–NEW STYLE

362

Figure 24.2 Workers on a colonial cotton plantation, Magomero, Nyasaland (Malawi), 1908. Many of the cotton-pickers of this estate became involved in the Chilembwe uprising of 1915 (see p. 355)

as labour tenants. The dreaded pass system, known in Kenya as *kipande*, placed severe restrictions on African freedom of movement outside the 'reserves'. In Kenya, Africans were forbidden to grow *arabica* coffee, the country's most profitable cash crop. By the 1920s there was a general decline in the productivity of Kenyan and Rhodesian peasants in favour of the white settlers, who received marketing help and cash subsidies. Even so, not much more than 10 per cent of white-owned land in either colony was ever actually cultivated, a point much resented by Africans restricted to poor-quality and overcrowded 'reserves'. Ugandan peasants produced more in export crops – cotton and groundnuts – than all the white farmers of the Kenyan highlands.

European-run plantations were a feature of parts of Mozambique, Angola and the Belgian Congo. But these were not the individual settler estates of Kenya or Rhodesia. Large commercial companies employed European managers to run their huge plantations, such as Unilever's palm-oil estates in Belgian Congo and the Mozambique Company's sugar plantations in northern Mozambique. Little was invested in research, technology and transport. Production was often fairly inefficient and a high level of violence was used to force labour on the projects.

Cash crops and peasant production

Small-scale peasant farmers still dominated cash-crop production in much of tropical Africa. Groundnuts remained the dominant cash crop of northern Nigeria and Senegal. Coffee was developed as a profitable peasant crop in Côte d'Ivoire, Angola, Tanganyika, Uganda and eastern Belgian Congo. Cocoa was even more successful and remained the principal export crop of the Gold Coast and south-western Nigeria. Cotton, low-priced and labour-intensive, was usually only produced under pressure from Europeans. In an effort to satisfy the demands of the French textile industry, peasant production of cotton was made compulsory in certain parts of Ubangui-Chari (Central African Republic), Upper Volta (Burkina Faso), Soudan (Mali) and

Niger. In the Djazira plains of Sudan, between the Blue and White Nile, the British government sponsored a vast irrigation scheme to promote the peasant production of cotton in the area. African tenants of the scheme, however, lost access to other land for growing food and only received 40 per cent of the profits from their cotton.

Successful cash-crop production did not necessarily mean widespread rural prosperity. African peasant farmers still grew most of their own basic foodstuffs. But the importation of mass-produced, European manufactured cloth and metal goods was undermining African industrial self-sufficiency. African peasants still built their own homes out of locally available material and some still wove their own cotton cloth. The woman's hoe, harvesting basket and water-pot might still be locally manufactured, but the man's machete and axe were likely to be imported. And former luxuries of diet, such as imported sugar, were becoming a necessity. Cheap rice from French Indo-China was imported into French west African colonies and sold at rates which undercut local food producers. African peasant farmers, who had often started the growth of cash crops for export under pressure from colonial taxation, rapidly became dependent upon the imports which their crops might buy. And this was where they fell into a poverty trap, for the prices paid for exports and the prices demanded for imports were beyond their control.

Marketing at the coast was in the hands of a small number of large European merchant companies. They ensured that prices paid to African producers were maintained at the lowest possible level. If higher prices were obtained in Europe, the merchants kept the difference as extra profit for themselves. Those same merchants controlled the sale of manufactured goods imported from Europe; when prices rose in Europe, the increase was immediately passed on to the African buyer. In general then, during the 1920s and 1930s, African farmers were paid less for what they produced, but had to pay more for what they bought. This was particularly the case after the 'Great Depression' which struck Europe and the United States in 1929–30. With falling real incomes and the constant pressure of colonial taxation, African peasants had to bring more and more land into cash-crop production. Food crops were neglected, soil became exhausted and in times of drought, famine struck. In 1931 famine killed nearly half the population in some areas of Niger.

Mining

The sector of the colonial economy most profitable for capital investment was mining. Colonial authorities assumed all rights over minerals within their territories. These were then leased for European-owned companies to exploit. The British thus took over the gold fields of Asante. The Bure gold fields of nearby Guinea were found to be of too poor a quality to attract French companies and individual Africans were allowed to continue mining gold in Guinea on a small scale. Other major mineral outcrops which attracted European mining capital to west Africa were the ancient tin-mines of the Jos plateau region in northern Nigeria. These were exploited by low-technology, open-caste mining using huge quantities of unskilled African labour. The Niger famine of the early 1930s brought thousands of impoverished people to northern Nigeria and enabled the mining companies to lower the wages that they offered. By then Nigeria had become the world's fourth-largest producer of tin.

Figure 24.3 Workers in the Nigerian tin-mines

The richest part of tropical Africa for European mineral exploitation in this period was the central African region of Katanga (Shaba) and the Northern Rhodesian 'Copperbelt'. The Union Munière company had obtained exclusive control of copper mining in Katanga. They drew much of their initial labour from nearby Northern Rhodesia, where BSA Company agents were vigorously pressing demands for cash taxation. Katanga copper mining was financed mainly by Rhodesian and South African capital and the railway through Northern Rhodesia was built to serve the Katanga mines. The settlement of white farmers along the Northern Rhodesian line of rail was to grow maize and cattle to feed the Katanga miners.

In the 1920s mining began in earnest on the Northern Rhodesian side of the Copperbelt, and the Congo border was then closed to labour recruiters from Katanga. The Northern Rhodesian mining companies pursued a deliberate policy of maintaining workers on a migrant labour basis. Workers were employed on short-term contracts and were paid just enough to support a single man. Employers assumed that the man's family was supported by his wife's subsistence farming in the remote rural areas, though this was often not the case. Migrant workers were employed as unskilled labour, the better-paid skilled jobs being reserved for whites, mostly from South Africa.

When Union Munière lost its source of labour from Northern Rhodesia, the company began recruiting from within the Congo and from Rwanda/Burundi. But unlike their Northern Rhodesian neighbours, Union Munière stabilised its labour force by offering three-year contracts and encouraging wives to settle near the mines. The company paid Catholic missionaries to provide basic primary schooling. They allowed African workers to develop certain mining skills and thus move into slightly better-paid jobs. Even so wages were still very low and wives were expected to supplement the family income by growing their own food.

Southern Rhodesia was another important zone of European mining enterprise. Besides the coal of Hwange which provided the Copperbelt/Katangan mines with most of their industrial fuel, Southern Rhodesia became a major producer of gold, copper and asbestos. The dominant industrial mining centre of southern Africa, the Witwatersrand, will be considered further in the final section of this chapter (p. 376).

Labour and taxation

A major feature of the colonial economies in this period was the development of migrant labour. Colonial authorities almost universally imposed a head tax upon all adult men: usually about £1 a year, or its equivalent. This amounted to at least a month's wages on white-owned mines or two months or more on a white-owned farm. The purpose of the tax was twofold: to pay for colonial administration and to force all adult men into the cash economy, in particular, to work for low wages for European colonists. It was a deliberate attempt to break African rural self-sufficiency. It was no longer enough for a community to feed, clothe and house itself. Cash had to be found to pay taxes, regardless of a family's income. In areas where cash crops could not be readily grown and profitably sold, this meant migration to places of wage employment. But European employers, in the towns and in the mines, only offered very low wages, not enough to feed and clothe a whole family. Accommodation, when it was provided, was only ever for a single person. The worker's family must therefore remain at home in some far-off rural area and try to grow enough food to feed themselves. When the worker returned home, he was left with little for his family after he had paid his taxes.

Reference to Map 24.1 (p. 361) will give some idea of the range of migrant labour movements over the continent in this period. It should be noted that some of those in west Africa and Uganda went for work on African agricultural projects. These included the cocoa and coffee farms of Gold Coast, Côte d'Ivoire and Nigeria, the groundnut zones of Gambia and Senegal, or the cotton and groundnut farms of the lakeside region of Uganda. The work was seasonal and payment was usually by a portion of the harvest. In west Africa many of those seeking work of this kind were fleeing from French attempts to enforce the compulsory cultivation of cotton in Soudan, Niger and Upper Volta.

From all the major centres of European employment – mines, farms and plantations – recruiting agents were sent out to hire large amounts of unskilled labour at the lowest possible wage. A wide range of methods were used to persuade, cajole or force people into entering labour contracts lasting anything from three months to a year. Recruiting agencies were granted monopolies over certain zones. The agents were then able to fix wages at very low rates for there was nowhere else where a man seeking work could get employment. The Portuguese authorities of Mozambique, for instance, granted a recruiting monopoly to the Witwatersrand Native Labour Agency, WNLA ('Wenela'). In return the mining companies agreed to use the Portuguese railway to the Mozambique port of Lourenço Marques. As a result, under pressure from the Portuguese, southern Mozambique became little more than a vast pool of labour for the gold-mines of Johannesburg. Similarly, Nyasaland was treated largely as a pool of labour for the farms and mines of Southern Rhodesia. The recruitment of Copperbelt/Katangan labour has already been discussed above. From northern Angola Portuguese agents recruited labour for the new coffee plantations on São Tomé. In this instance recruitment was little different from slavery, for workers were paid a pittance and few were ever allowed to return to their families.

All over the continent chiefs were pressured into acting as unofficial agents to serve the labour needs of European farming and mining enterprises. In areas of high European settlement Africans were pushed into wage labour as a result of being forced off their land. Those allowed back on the land were expected to perform various unpaid labour services for the white landowner.

In addition, in most colonies Africans were expected to work for no pay on local public works such as road and bridge construction. In the French-controlled colonies this was known as *corvée* labour and was regulated to a minimum of seven to 14 days a year. Forced-labour was one of the most hated aspects of colonial rule.

Conditions were little different in the independent west African state of Liberia. In 1925 the Firestone Rubber Company of the United States leased nearly half a million hectares of potential plantation land from the government of Liberia. Firestone professed to be helping the development of the country. They did improve the port facilities at Monrovia and arranged an American loan to help Liberia with its foreign debts. But Firestone paid only a nominal rent for their rubber plantations and paid no income tax on profits in Liberia. In fact their main motive in setting up business in Liberia was to take advantage of what they saw as the 'practically inexhaustible' supply of indigenous labour in the country. Also it was the only lowland tropical African country not under some form of European colonial control. Under the terms of the agreement the Liberian government undertook to supply the Firestone plantations with up to 50,000 workers a year. These were drawn mainly from the Kru population of the interior. As elsewhere, chiefs were used to round up recruits and force them to sign contracts with Firestone for very low wages. The chiefs were backed up by the Liberian army, which raided villages that were slow to produce recruits. Army raids were also used in the same period to 'recruit' contract workers from Liberia for the Spanish cocoa plantations on Fernando Poo.

The nature and impact of colonial administration

For more information see www.palgrave.com/shillington

Historians have for years argued over the merits and demerits, similarities and differences, of the French and British 'systems' of colonial administration: French '*Assimilation*' and British 'Indirect Rule'. In recent years less emphasis has been given to the theory and more to the impact these systems had on the majority of African colonial subjects. At the local level, and from the point of view of the African subject majority, all 'systems' of colonial administration were remarkably similar in practice.

The French originally sought to 'assimilate' their colonial subjects into cultural Frenchmen, regardless of their skin colour. They were to have the full legal and political rights of French citizenship, including the right to send representatives to the French parliament in Paris. This may have worked in the mid-nineteenth century while their tropical African colonies consisted of a mere handful of trading-posts on the coast of Senegal. But once large-scale colonisation of the continent began in the later nineteenth century, the French abandoned 'assimilation' for all but the citizens of the original four Senegalese towns (Dakar, St Louis, Gorée and Rufisque) and a select few highly educated, French-speaking Africans. The French continued to hold up potential 'assimilation' as an ideal which all Africans should strive for. But French authorities made the educational qualifications for African 'assimilation' extremely difficult to achieve. And few Africans sought the status, for it involved a total rejection of their African personality and culture. By the 1930s the assimilated of the 'Four Communes' of Senegal numbered 50,000, while the few additional 'selectively assimilated' Africans never numbered more than 500. The remaining 15 million people of France's tropical African empire were classified as *sujets* ('subjects'), and as such were denied virtually any legal or political rights at all.

The French broke up the large pre-colonial states like Dahomey, Tukolor and Futa Jalon and made use of African chiefs at the lower levels of local government. District and village chiefs were appointed or dismissed at will by provincial French administrators. It was the duty of these French-appointed 'chiefs' to collect taxes, recruit labour, especially forced *corvée* labour, and to suppress rural African opposition. Any who failed to perform to French satisfaction were replaced. As a result many of these so-called 'chiefs' had little if any 'traditional' chiefly title. Their qualification for office was more likely to be an ability to speak French than familiarity with the language and customs of their 'subjects'. They became in effect French government officials, denied any independent religious or legal authority. In this way the French effectively destroyed African customary law. The law to which Africans were most commonly subjected was the *indigénat*. This notorious colonial law entitled French provincial administrators to imprison any African *sujet* indefinitely and without charge or trial.

In north Africa the French ruled the settler-colony of Algeria as though it were a part of mainland France, though with the important distinction that the majority Muslim subjects were denied the rights of citizens. In the neighbouring 'protectorate' of Morocco, the French ruled in theory in the name of the sultan, their own nominee. In practice they were occupied for most of this period in military conquest of the peoples of the mountainous interior.

The British, too, made use of 'traditional' African rulers at local-government level, but they raised the practice to a 'theory' of colonial administration. They called it 'Indirect Rule'. The theory was most clearly formulated by Frederick Lugard (see Figure 24.4), former Governor of Nigeria, in his book *The Dual Mandate in British Tropical Africa,* published in 1922. Lugard described the system of government he had worked out for the administration of the Sokoto emirates of northern Nigeria. He recommended its application to all British tropical African colonies. 'Indirect Rule' was believed by the British to be the cheapest and most effective way of administering vast populations stretched over even vaster territories with the minimum of European personnel. But 'Indirect Rule' was far from being a clear-cut system. Its application varied enormously from colony to colony.

Like the French, wherever possible the British used 'traditional' African rulers to carry out the basic functions of local government, in particular the collection of taxes, the recruiting of labour and the controlling of potential African unrest. Uncooperative chiefs were dismissed and suitable replacements were found. In this case the British paid slightly more attention than the French to a candidate's 'legitimate' claim to the chieftaincy. Nevertheless, the British had no scruples about inventing new chieftaincies in former 'stateless' societies, such as the Igbo of Nigeria and the Kikuyu of Kenya, where chiefs had previously not been known above the local village level.

Unlike the French, the British made greater use of African 'customary law'. Chiefs were allowed to judge local civil disputes and to try minor criminal cases, though they were never allowed to try serious criminal cases or any dispute involving a European. British attention to 'customary law', however, was not because of any particular respect for things African, but rather because of its administrative convenience. The chief performed a whole range

Figure 24.4 Frederick Lugard (1858–1945), colonial administrator, established British military control of Uganda (1890–2). As British High Commissioner to Northern Nigeria (1900–6), he pragmatically and successfully negotiated a system of 'indirect rule' with the emirs of Sokoto. His unification of Northern and Southern Nigeria, as Governor-General, 1912–19, was less successful, leaving the country with deep cultural and political divisions. (Photo by Downey in the Cabinet Portrait Gallery)

Figure 24.5 The Sultan of Sokoto, the religious head of Hausaland, and spiritual leader of the nation's Muslims, 1903. He is wearing a *hassa* or turban. It was with Sokoto that Lugard evolved his system of 'indirect rule'

of legal duties which would otherwise have been costly and inconvenient to the colonial administration. And retaining the chief as the mediator between ruler and ruled helped blunt the impact of colonial over-rule. When the chief was presented with unpopular colonial laws to enforce, it was the chief who received the full weight of local African hostility. At the same time, British colonial administrators did not hesitate to adapt, change and if necessary *invent* African 'customary law' when it suited their own purposes.

The whole colonial emphasis upon the role of chiefs exaggerated so-called 'tribal' differences. The very word 'tribe' was deliberately used in a derogatory sense by European colonists who looked down upon African societies as 'primitive' and 'inferior'. The British based their local administration upon what they saw as a series of minor but totally separate pre-colonial chiefdoms. In order to make this a reality, they emphasised differences of dialect and redefined them as totally separate languages. They described customary differences of dress, housing and religious practices in terms of rigid 'tribal' distinctions. In many pre-colonial African societies there had been considerable overlap between the peoples, languages and customs of a region. Where competition and conflict between groups had existed it was for political power or economic advantage rather than simply because they were of different 'tribes'. Indeed, it has been argued that colonial authorities *invented* 'tribalism'. By insisting on the strength of 'tribal' differences and rivalries, colonists made it more difficult for Africans to achieve unity in opposition. This was particularly so among the rural population of settler colonies such as Southern Rhodesia where each 'tribe' was isolated in its own separate 'reserve'. The British in particular thus made use of the age-old imperial maxim: 'divide and rule'.

Portuguese administrative policy was similar to the French in principle. A tiny number of select individuals who had adopted Portuguese language and culture were classified *civilisado* (later renamed *assimilado*) and were excused

Figure 24.6 The presentation of gifts to a chief by a colonial official as the British assume control of Zomba district in the Zambezi valley, Northern Rhodesia, June 1902

the tax and labour demands made on their fellow African subjects. But they were never allowed the kind of voting rights in local or central government enjoyed by French assimilated 'citizens' in Senegal. The *civilisados* were only ever a very small minority, in this period mostly of mixed-race origin. They lived in the towns and worked as clerks, teachers and petty traders, totally divorced in culture and outlook from the majority '*indigena*' population.

The Belgians used a mixture of French and British systems for their colonial administration. They recognised the cultural 'assimilation' of a tiny minority of mission-educated Africans, known as *évolués*, but like their Portuguese counterparts, these were never allowed any participation in local politics. Education above rudimentary primary level was actively discouraged. Appointment and use of chiefs in local government was fairly arbitrary, dependent upon local circumstances and administrative convenience. On the other hand, where there still existed a clearly defined pre-colonial authority structure, as in Rwanda and Burundi, this was utilised in a form of controlled 'indirect rule'.

The spread of Islam in tropical west Africa

We saw in the previous chapter how European conquest opened the gates for the spread of Christian mission influence. Ironically the period of consolidated European colonial rule witnessed a parallel and even greater spread of Islam in tropical west Africa. The colonists' use of Muslim emirs under the guise of 'indirect rule' strengthened the position of Islam in the northern savannah regions. European colonial rule may have ended the nineteenth-century period of conversion by conquest; but by confirming Islamic rulers as 'traditional' African authorities, it eased the gradual conversion of the mass of their 'subject' people. In places like the Sokoto province of Ilorin, for instance, Muslims were only recent conquerors. European over-rule

Figure 24.7 Lagos, Nigeria. Bird's-eye view of the port, *c.*1870. (Engraving by an unnamed artist)

confirmed their position and eased the mass conversion of the Yoruba of Ilorin.

In addition, the reorientation of trade away from the desert prompted Muslim penetration of the southern savannah, forest and coastal zones of west Africa. During the colonial period Islam became an important element in all the major ports such as Lagos, Dakar, Freetown, Conakry and Accra. Islam had an advantage in that, unlike Christianity, it was not associated directly with the European colonial power. Furthermore, Islam did not insist on the abandonment of important African customary practices such as polygamy. Under European colonial rule, Islam thus had greater success than Christianity in terms of numbers of new converts. In Senegal, where Islam had a long tradition, Muslim brotherhoods flourished, uninterrupted by colonial authority. And across the continent in Sudan the British positively discouraged the work of Christian missionaries in the northern half of the country as likely to disrupt the relative calm of existing Islamic domination. As it was, the British had problems suppressing a serious 'Mahdist' revolt in Darfur in 1921–2.

Education: from pre-colonial tradition to colonial reality

Education in pre-colonial Africa was of two principal types. In north Africa, the Sahara, the Sahel and the east African Swahili coast where Islam predominated, basic education was widespread and closely connected to religion. Children (mostly boys), aged between six and 12, attended Qur'anic schools where they learned, by rote, Arabic verses from the Qur'an. This provided them with basic literacy in Arabic, to which was added some elementary numeracy. Levels of learning varied enormously at these schools. Those who did well, and whose parents could afford it, went to study under a learned *marabout* or *mallan*. A few, who mastered Arabic, might go on to study theology and Islamic law at the universities of Jenne or Timbuktu in west Africa, or at Qayrawan in Tunisia or Cairo's al-Azhar.

371

In the pre-literate societies of sub-Saharan Africa education in pre-colonial times was generally less formal, but it was universal and compulsory for both boys and girls. Although there was enormous variation in the content of this education from one part of the continent to another, the methods and principles were generally similar. Boys and girls learned their religious beliefs and their economic and social skills for life from their parents and other older relatives. From the elders of their extended family they learned the history of their ancestors and the oral traditions and customs of their community or nation. Children were brought up to value the wisdom of their elders, a vital component of a pre-literate oral culture, and much of what they absorbed from their elders was instilled by rote-learning. Some time after puberty, boys and girls separately attended initiation schools where they were housed for a number of weeks, isolated from the rest of the community. Here their informal education was consolidated with formal instruction in religious beliefs and practices, gender-related social and sexual mores, moral behaviour, and tests of personal character, such as courage and endurance. This culminated in an initiation ceremony, often involving circumcision, and sometimes including facial or bodily scarification. On emerging from initiation school, 'graduates' were expected to assume the duties and responsibilities of adults, though at a low social level, in accordance with their age and marital status.

In parts of sub-Saharan Africa where Islamic penetration was slight or only recent, the two systems of education, Qur'anic and indigenous, existed side by side, with many children attending both.

French and British imperialists decided not to interfere with existing Muslim systems of education, especially in northern Africa where Islam was almost universal. Similarly, Qur'anic schools flourished in colonial west Africa. They spread with the general spread of Islam, discussed above, aided by the colonial destruction or weakening of indigenous societies. At the same time Christian missionaries attacked indigenous social mores, and the initiation schools: partly for their sex education, but primarily for their religious content. This turned many people towards Qur'anic schools, specifically because they were *not* associated with the European intrusion.

Apart from their toleration of Qur'anic schools, in the early decades colonial governments generally left education to the Christian missionary societies, some of whom had a considerable history in the region (see Chapter 20, pp. 296–8). Like the Qur'anic schools, Christian mission schools provided a basic education in religion and literacy. The Protestant missionaries based their teaching on the Bible, parts of which they translated into local languages. Catholic missionaries based theirs on the Catechism, translated into the local language and taught by rote.

By the 1920s, colonial governments began to take a more active interest in education. In French West Africa and French Equatorial Africa they began subsidising the mission schools; but with the subsidy came control of the curriculum, which now focused on literacy, numeracy and the French language and culture. Anything to do with African history or culture was definitely not on the curriculum. In French West Africa a small number of state schools were set up at primary level, most of them in Senegal where the William Ponty School, founded in 1903, offered a three-year post-primary training for teachers. In French Equatorial Africa there was no state secondary education until the 1930s when one secondary school was established in Brazzaville. Basically, colonial governments were only interested in training a small elite to fill the lower rungs of the administrative service. They saw mass education as a danger to be avoided. Thus, aside from the Qur'anic schools, in French West and Equatorial Africa in the 1920s a mere 3 per cent of school-aged children attended school, mission or state.

Within the British sphere 'western' education had a somewhat longer history. Mission education, with its emphasis upon literacy for religion, still predominated until at least the 1930s. However, in Sierra Leone, Fourah Bay College, owned by the CMS as a seminary and teacher-training college, had been affiliated to the University of Durham since 1876. In the early colonial period many of Fourah Bay's students came from the Gold Coast, where Governor Guggisberg made a concerted effort to make education a cornerstone of colonial policy. He founded west Africa's first state secondary school, Achimota. Nevertheless, the British, like the French, based their educational provision primarily upon providing financial support to pre-existing mission schools, with the result that even in the Gold Coast fewer than 10 per cent of school-age children attended state-aided schools in the early 1920s. In Nigeria, with a far larger population, colonial funds to aid mission education were pitifully inadequate. Governor Gifford complained in 1920 that in the whole of northern Nigeria, where Qur'anic schools predominated, there was not one person with the level of English and educational qualifications to fill the lowest rungs of the colonial administration. In southern Nigeria and Kenya, so-called 'hedge schools' proliferated where basically educated individuals passed on their literacy, numeracy and English-language skills to the local population in informal outdoor settings. The very independence of these informal schools, however, caused considerable concern to colonial authorities who feared they might become hotbeds of anti-colonial intrigue.

In 1921 the US-based Phelps-Stokes Commission reported on education in British tropical Africa. Despite being independently funded and committed to African-American education in the United States, their report reflected British colonial thinking of the time. They recommended an increase in educational provision, but made the dated assumption that Africans lived primarily in rural, subsistence-based communities. Thus for the foreseeable future Africans would need only basic literacy and numeracy, combined with a little vocational training in agriculture, building and carpentry. The Phelps-Stokes Report took no account of the rapid urbanisation and labour migrancy that was increasingly part of African daily living, even as early as the 1920s. What Africans needed and were increasingly demanding was access to secondary and higher education, with curricula that paralleled the academic education available to Europeans. By the end of the 1930s colonial authorities were beginning to take these realities on board. Nevertheless, until the very last decade of the colonial period, curricula for African education reflected a deliberate rejection and denigration of African culture, language and history. Africans were taught the superiority of European technology, culture and civilisation. They learned the history of France and of England, or that of 'heroic' Europeans in Africa; but they were taught nothing of their own historical past.

In the decades either side of the Second World War, Africans who were determined to seek further education had to go abroad. French-speakers went to France, while English-speakers went mostly to African-American institutions in north America. In the 1930s and 1940s more than a hundred west Africans went to US universities, among them Azikiwe ('Zik') of Nigeria and Nkrumah of the Gold Coast, both of them graduates of Lincoln University. From among these overseas graduates came most of the leaders of the nationalist and independence movements that followed in the decades after the Second World War.

African nationalism and protest movements in the inter-war years

African acceptance of colonial domination in this period was anything but calm. A rebellion in Mauritania that had begun with the assassination of the French governor in 1905 was not finally suppressed until 1934. Nevertheless, large-scale rebellion was now less common. An important and little-known exception was a rebellion by 350,000 Baya in French Equatorial Africa in the late 1920s. The slaughter that accompanied the violent suppression of this revolt in 1928–31 was one of the great atrocities of colonial rule in tropical Africa.

Independent Christian Churches continued to spread. In the Belgian Congo, Simon Kimbangu founded his own Church in 1921 and declared himself a prophet. He preached that God would soon deliver the Congolese people from colonial oppression. Though the Belgians quickly imprisoned him, 'Kimbanguism' persisted through the 1920s and 1930s, with his followers refusing to pay taxes or grow export crops for the government. Periodic revivals of Kimbanguism occurred at times of drought and particular rural hardship. Kimbanguists believed in the imminent and miraculous return of their Prophet Kimbangu, though the latter in fact remained in prison until his death in 1951.

On the whole, Africans in the inter-war years were learning how to come to terms with the new order, and in due course how to overthrow and transform it. Formation of workers' unions was still in its infancy and all forms of trades union activity was proscribed as illegal. Nevertheless, workers staged a number of spontaneous strikes for better pay and working conditions. The more significant of these were on the mines and railways of Guinea, Sierra Leone and Gold Coast in the 1920s and on the Copperbelt of Northern Rhodesia in 1935 and 1940. The cocoa farmers of the Gold Coast gave an early demonstration of the potential impact of effective African unity. During the First World War they withheld their cocoa harvests until prices offered by coastal merchants were increased. They subsequently formed a cocoa farmers' federation and used the same tactics again in the 1930s.

Meanwhile, all over tropical Africa in the 1920s and 1930s Africans were forming self-help welfare associations and these were used increasingly to protest against specific local injustices. At the same time in the ports and administrative towns of east, west and central Africa, there was the steady growth of a new, educated African elite: clerks, interpreters, traders, teachers and clergymen. These people were particularly conscious of the social and economic injustices of colonial society and their own exclusion from the politics of their country. Few as yet, however, outside Algeria and Tunisia and the coastal towns of British west Africa, thought in terms of political independence as the solution to their problems.

An important influence upon the educated elite was the Pan-African movement that was awakening a new self-confidence among people of

Figure 24.8 Marcus Garvey, then head of the Universal Negro Improvement Association and self-styled 'Provisional President of the Republic of Africa', rides through Harlem in his formal uniform. Garvey, born in Jamaica in 1887, was an early exponent of justice and equality for blacks. He died in England in 1940

African descent in north America and the Caribbean in the 1920s. A particularly influential African-American Pan-Africanist was the writer and intellectual W. E. B. Du Bois. He had taken part in a Pan-African Conference in London in 1900 and between 1919 and 1927 he was involved in the organisation of no fewer than seven Pan-African Congresses in London, Paris, Brussels, Lisbon and New York. Although they called for the end of racial discrimination and the colonial empires in Africa, these congresses attracted little attention within Africa itself. There the most influential of the Pan-Africanist voices was that of Marcus Garvey (see Figure 24.8). Jamaican-born founder of the Universal Negro Improvement Association and the widely circulated newspaper the *Negro World,* Garvey never visited Africa himself. Yet his flamboyant style and confident preaching of 'Africa for the Africans' and the expulsion of all Europeans was an important inspiration for many young, educated Africans who were to rise to prominence in the nationalist struggles of the 1940s and 1950s.

Similarly, French-speaking writers from the Caribbean and west Africa developed a new sense of black self-respect through a movement known as *Négritude.* Thus the writings of the Senegalese poet Léopold Senghor celebrated the

African's 'blackness' and a deep pride in the ancient cultures of Africa. *Négritude* was an important psychological boost in a time of European cultural dominance, a clear rejection of French 'assimilation' policy.

It was only in Egypt that the rising wave of African nationalism achieved any substantial political gains in this period. The rapid rise of Egyptian nationalism in 1918–19 was prompted by the oppression which Egyptians had suffered from British demands for food, animals and labour during the war. Peasants, lawyers, civil servants, landowners, Christians and Muslims displayed a rare spirit of unity in their demands for an independent Egypt. The lead was taken by a group of intellectuals who formed a political party known as the Wafd, under the leadership of Sa'ad Zaghlul. When the British failed to respond to the Wafd's demands, demonstrations, strikes and riots forced their hand. But the British managed to defuse the situation by briefly exiling Zaghlul to the Seychelles and, in his absence, by agreeing to a declaration of Egyptian independence in 1922. Sultan Fu'ad became King of Egypt and a form of parliamentary government was established. In practice the British army remained in occupation of Egypt and still the real source of power behind the throne. Then, in the 1930s the 'Muslim Brotherhood' awoke a new generation of young Egyptians to a wider Islamic 'nationalism'. Their immediate appeal was a reaction to European influence and materialism and the political corruption of parliament and monarchy.

Segregation, nationalism and protest in South Africa

Various forms of African nationalism have, since the 1950s, overthrown European colonial or white minority rule throughout the continent. Ironically, since ultimately they were the last to achieve political liberation (in 1994), it was the peoples of South Africa who led the growth of African nationalism in the early decades of the twentieth century. It was in South Africa that some of the continent's earliest independent Christian Churches and African-owned and edited newspapers were founded in the 1880s, 1890s and early 1900s. These were followed in 1912 by the formation in South Africa of the continent's first modern African nationalist political party. But these pioneering African nationalists failed to achieve their goals. Their growth was paralleled by a steady strengthening of white political and economic domination, especially Afrikaner domination. ('Afrikaner' was the name used by the descendants of the seventeenth- and eighteenth-century Dutch settlers, formerly referred to as Boers.)

Between 1910 and 1940 the successive white governments of the Union of South Africa passed a series of laws which imposed a system of racial segregation in the country. This segregationist legislation laid the foundations on which the Afrikaner nationalist government, which came to power in 1948, built the system of *apartheid* (see pp. 426–9). Segregation was basically to do with maintaining white domination in the two main sectors of the economy: mining and land.

Under pressure from white mineworkers between 1913 and 1922, the government legalised a job 'colour bar' in the mining industry. This reserved all skilled and better-paid jobs for whites while confining blacks to the unskilled, lowest-paid jobs. The Natives Land Act of 1913 restricted blacks

For more information see www.palgrave.com/shillington

to a mere 7 per cent of the land in the Union (increased to 13 per cent in 1936), despite the fact that they outnumbered whites by five to one. This led to widespread evictions from white-owned land. Blacks were pushed into the already overcrowded 'reserves' or migrated to the towns in search of work. The government sought to control the movement of labour and to prevent too many unemployed blacks from settling in the towns, by tightening up its 'pass laws'. This forced blacks to carry a 'pass' at all times indicating their 'tribal' origin and the name of their employer. If found without a valid pass, blacks could be arrested, fined or imprisoned, forced to sign a low-paid work contract with a white employer or expelled to some remote rural 'reserve'. Finally, in 1936 the white government abolished the right of 11,000 blacks to vote in the parliamentary elections of the Cape Province (formerly Cape Colony). Until this time well-educated blacks who owned property or had well-paid jobs had been allowed to vote in this one province of the Union. Now that right was removed.

Black resistance to these assaults on their political, social and economic freedom took many forms. In the rural areas peasants resisted government regulations on the dipping and movement of their animals and fled from their homes to avoid paying taxes. In the urban area of Johannesburg, municipal workers went on strike for better pay and conditions. There were huge anti-pass demonstrations in 1919, and 40,000 black mineworkers struck in 1920. On each occasion, however, police used violence to break up the strikes and demonstrations, and thousands of workers were sacked. In 1919 a clerk from Nyasaland, Clements Kadalie, founded the Industrial and Commercial Workers' Union (ICU) among Cape Town dockworkers. When their strike for higher wages was successful, the fame and membership of the ICU spread like a bushfire right across South Africa, especially among rural workers who were facing eviction. By 1926 the ICU claimed a membership of 100,000. But the union's leadership did not know how to make use of

Figure 24.9 The African National Congress delegation to London, 1914 (*left to right*): Thomas Mapikela, Treasurer (eastern Cape businessman); Rev. Walter Rubusana, Vice-President (Congregational minister and only black member of Cape provincial council); Rev. John Dube, President (Natal school principal and newspaper editor); Saul Msane, Vice-President; Sol T. Plaatje, General Secretary (northern Cape newspaper owner and editor)

their potential power and were reluctant to call for widespread strikes. As a result the union fell apart having achieved little beyond proving the existence of a national worker-consciousness and the possibilities for future union movements.

Meanwhile, in 1912 the educated African elite of teachers, clerks, clergymen, lawyers and journalists had formed their first national political party, the South African Native National Congress, renamed the African National Congress (ANC) in 1923. But they, too, were cautious in their tactics. They worked strictly within the law, confining their actions to meetings, protests and petitions to the government. All to no avail. The South African government ignored their protests and pressed ahead with its racist legislation. Nevertheless, the conferences and meetings of the ANC in this period, and their cooperation with the representatives of Indian and 'coloured' (mixed-race) political parties, laid the foundations for the later development of more widespread mass political action.

25

The Second World War and Africa

When Britain and France declared war on Hitler's Nazi Germany in September 1939, their African colonies were once more drawn into a European conflict which was not of their making. Fascist dictatorships were established in Italy, Germany, Portugal and Spain in the 1920s and 1930s. Fascist political parties believed in the seizure of power by military force, the denial of democratic freedoms, and the racial inferiority of subject peoples (which all sounds a bit like certain aspects of European colonial rule in Africa). Fascists were particularly dedicated to the destruction of all aspects of socialism and communism. In May 1940 German armies overran Holland and Belgium and drove the British army out of northern France. With German victory in sight, Mussolini, the fascist dictator of Italy, brought his country into the war on the side of Germany on 10 June 1940. By then the militarist government of Japan had already joined them in what was known as the 'Axis' pact. By the end of June the German army had occupied north-ern France and installed a puppet government at Vichy in southern France. A French colonel, Charles de Gaulle, formed a 'Free French' government in exile. This division into 'Vichy' government in France and 'Free French' government in exile was to have an important impact upon France's African colonies, as we shall see below.

Hitler's invasion of Russia in June 1941 brought the Soviet Union into the war. Meanwhile Japanese forces were busy occupying western China and French south-east Asia. In the early months of 1942 Japan overran British-ruled Malaysia and Burma, and Dutch Indonesia. By then the Japanese attack on the United States Navy in Pearl Harbor, Hawaii (December 1941), had brought the United States into the war. Against the Axis Powers were now ranged the Allied forces of the United States, the Soviet Union, Britain and the latter's colonies and dominions. The war had assumed a truly worldwide dimension. But what of Africa in this conflict?

While Europe, Asia and north America were drawn into full-scale war between 1939 and 1941, for Africa the war against fascist aggression had in fact begun as early as 1935 with the Italian invasion of Ethiopia. (Ethiopia was known to Europeans as Abyssinia, a name thought to be drawn from an old Arabic name for the Aksumite kingdom.)

Fascist aggression and the Second World War in north and north-east Africa

Background: the Italian conquest of Libya

Italy, a relatively new European power, had competed in the Scramble for Africa with rather less success than her main European rivals. In the 1880s she had occupied the Eritrean and southern Somali coasts, but her invasion of Ethiopia had been repulsed at the battle of Adwa in 1896. It was not until 1911–13 that Italy seized Libya, the last-remaining independent Ottoman territory in north Africa. The Sanusiyya Muslim Brotherhood of the eastern Libyan desert, however, organised a brilliant guerrilla campaign which kept the Italian invaders at bay until 1931. In the end Italy only conquered Sanusiyya resistance through the employment of tens of thousands of Italian troops, combined with aerial bombing of civilian targets, the imprisonment of hundreds of thousands of civilians in concentration camps, and the construction of massive barbed-wire fences across the Libyan desert. An estimated 100,000 civilians died in the appalling conditions of the concentration camps. The Sanusiyya leader, 'Umar al-Mukhtar, was finally captured and executed in September 1931. With his death, Libyan resistance finally collapsed. Italian forces were now free for Mussolini's long-awaited plan, the re-invasion of Ethiopia and revenge for the humiliation of Adwa.

The Italian invasion of Ethiopia

Apart from Liberia, colonised by African-Americans in the 1820s and 1830s, Ethiopia by the early 1930s was the only remaining independent African

Map 25.1 Ethiopia and Eritrea, 1935–41

Figure 25.1 In the name of 'progress', the Italians conquered the Ethiopians in 1936 by dropping poison gas from the air: revenge for their humiliation at Adwa, 1896 (see p. 295). Although critical of the Italians, as this cartoon from *Punch* (April 1936) shows, the British took no effective action in support of the Ethiopians until Italy declared war on Britain in June 1940

THE DAWN OF PROGRESS.

"BUT HOW AM I TO SEE IT? THEY'VE BLINDED ME."

state which had not come under some form of European control. Ras Tafari, a Shoan aristocrat and distant relative of Menelik (d.1913), had become regent to the empress in 1916. In 1930 he succeeded as emperor and took the title Haile Selassie. Ethiopia was by then a member of the League of Nations (forerunner of the United Nations Organisation) and Haile Selassie expected the other member states to protect his country from Italian aggression. But in this he was to be sorely disappointed. In October 1935 an Italian army of 120,000 men crossed the Somali and Eritrean borders into Ethiopia. This time the Italians had the military advantage of aeroplanes, armoured cars and modern artillery. Even so it was many months before their conquest of the Ethiopian army was complete. By then they had wreaked havoc on the Ethiopian countryside, bombing villages and spreading poison gas from the air.

Although the Italian army occupied Addis Ababa in May 1936, they never subdued the whole country. Pockets of guerrilla resistance continued throughout the five-year Italian occupation. During this relatively short period the Italians directed the building of a considerable amount of modern transport infrastructure; but their rule was characterised by a great deal of violence. When an unsuccessful attempt was made to assassinate Viceroy Graziani in February 1937, for example, Italian reprisals killed up to 6000

Ethiopians in three days in Addis Ababa alone. This strengthened the Ethiopian resistance movement, which was now joined by large numbers of women who had been raped by the Italian army.

Ethiopia and the League of Nations

In May 1936 Haile Selassie went into exile in Europe where he addressed the General Assembly of the League of Nations in Geneva. He reminded them of their inaction during eight months of Italian aggression against Ethiopia. The very purpose of the League, he argued, was to establish the international equality of all member states, and, in particular, to protect the smaller states from aggression by more powerful ones. He warned that 'International Morality' was at stake: 'God and history will remember your judgement .... Are the States [of the League] going to set up the terrible precedent of bowing before force?' But Britain and France, the major powers of the League, did nothing effective. Ethiopian 'Patriots' had to continue guerrilla resistance on their own. Nevertheless, they managed to keep some parts of Ethiopia free from Italian control. Meanwhile, Hitler's Germany followed Mussolini's example, going on to commit acts of international aggression which were eventually to lead to war in Europe in 1939. British policy did not change until Italy declared war on Britain following the fall of France in 1940.

The liberation of Ethiopia

During August and September 1940 Italian forces occupied British Somaliland and invaded British-controlled Egypt from their base in Libya. Recently expelled from continental Europe and facing a direct threat to her Suez Canal route to India, Britain finally reacted to Italian aggression in north Africa. By December the British had pushed the Italians back into Libya and in January 1941 they began the invasion of Ethiopia. Haile Selassie returned to southern Sudan to head a force of Ethiopian Patriots. The British summoned thousands of troops from Nigeria, Ghana and Sierra Leone. The Belgians dispatched a small force of African soldiers from the Congo, while the Free French governor at Brazzaville sent a small contingent

Figure 25.2 Abyssinian officers in traditional dress, loyal to Emperor Haile Selassie, in Addis Ababa during the Italo-Ethiopian war, *c.*1936

Map 25.2   The Second World War in north Africa, 1941–3

from Equatorial Africa. Volunteer forces were sent up from Rhodesia and Nyasaland to join those assembling in Kenya. And from South Africa came a force of 200,000 volunteers, a third of them black. While the black troops from British east, west and central Africa were armed and provided the bulk of the fighting forces, those from South Africa, as in 1914–18, were not allowed to carry arms. By May 1941 the Ethiopian capital, Addis Ababa, had been retaken and Haile Selassie re-established on his throne. The British, somewhat reluctantly, recognised Ethiopia's independence, though they remained in occupation of the Ogaden and Eritrea.

The war in north Africa

In February 1941 Hitler sent a German army, the *Afrikakorps*, to support the Italians in Libya. They forced the British back into Egypt and came within 100 kilometres of Alexandria. The immediate German aim was to seize the Suez Canal and beyond that the oil fields of the Persian Gulf. Before the war began, Hitler had declared that Germany would regain its 'rightful place in the tropical sun.' Thus as part of his occupation of north Africa, Hitler had

Figure 25.3   British colonial troops in action on National Highway 1, also known as the road to Mandalay, Burma, *c.*1944

383

longer-term plans for striking south across the desert, seizing the strategically important French territory of Chad and re-occupying the former German colony of Kamerun, lost in 1916. But he never got the chance to put these plans into action. The Allied forces finally broke through the German lines in western Egypt at the battle of El Alamein in October 1942. At almost the same time American and British troops landed in Morocco and Algeria. Attacked from both sides, the Germans and Italians were pushed back to Tunisia. Here the remnants of Germany's *Afrikakorps* was forced to surrender in May 1943.

The war on African soil was finally over. The destruction of the warfare in north Africa, especially the urban areas of Tunisia, had been very extensive. Apart from the massive army losses, countless thousands of Libyan and Tunisian civilians lost their lives and homes. From Tunisia, Africans joined British and American troops in the Allied invasion of Sicily and Italy in July and September 1943. And African troops from French and British colonies went on to serve with distinction against the Japanese in the forests of Burma and south-east Asia.

The war in French-speaking Africa

On the outbreak of war in Europe, 80,000 regular African troops were sent from French West Africa to defend French soil from German invasion. Here they suffered heavy casualties and many were captured and imprisoned by the Germans. On the fall of France in 1940, the colonial officials of French north Africa and French West Africa declared their loyalty to the Vichy government. This effectively took them out of the war for the next two years. The black governor of Chad, on the other hand, Félix Eboué from French Guiana in South America, declared his loyalty to the 'Free French' government in exile. In due course the governors of the other French equatorial territories followed his example and for a while Brazzaville became the capital of 'Free France' in exile. A number of French Equatorial Africans served in the Ethiopian campaign of 1941. At the end of 1942, with the Allied invasion of Vichy north Africa, the colonial authorities of French West Africa abandoned their Vichy allegiance and declared for the Free French government of de Gaulle. Once more the Africans of French west Africa supplied soldiers and raw materials for the Allied war effort. At one time, in 1943, Africans from French West Africa and French Equatorial Africa made up more than half of the total of the Free French army.

The impact of the war on Africa and Africans

Manpower and materials

We have already noted the important contribution of African soldiers to the Ethiopian, north African and south-east Asian campaigns. Throughout the war Africa remained an essential source of men and materials for the Allied war effort. Once Ethiopia had been liberated (in 1941), however, it was more difficult to persuade Africans that they should help the Allied cause. The British officially recruited African soldiers on a volunteer basis and used chiefs as the main recruiting agents. Recent research, however, has shown that at times a considerable amount of pressure was used to 'persuade' Africans to volunteer. The French relied more openly upon forced conscription to supply men for the war. Between 1943 and 1945, for instance, over 100,000 soldiers were conscripted from French West Africa.

Africa's importance as a source of raw materials for the Allied armies was greatly increased by the fall of south-east Asia to the Japanese in 1941–2. Colonial administrators used a mixture of force and persuasion to get Africans to produce more goods for the Allied cause. French West Africans were pressured to produce more groundnuts and cotton. The forest zones of western Africa became the sole Allied source of palm oil. The forced-labour of up to 18,000 men was used in the tin-mines of Nigeria. Following the loss of the Malayan plantations, the forced collection of wild rubber from the forests of the Congo basin was reminiscent of the earlier decades of the century. And all over British east, central and southern Africa village chiefs were required to organise the cultivation of special fields for growing extra food for the war effort.

Before the war it had been left to the major European merchant companies to control the marketing of African produce and to restrict the prices paid to African peasant farmers. During the war the colonial state moved in to take a more prominent role. All over east, west and central Africa, particularly in the British sphere, colonial authorities set up marketing boards to organise African production for export. At the same time they used the political power of government to impose official price controls. Thus, although African palm oil, rubber, sisal, groundnuts, cotton, coffee, tea and cocoa fetched high prices in Europe because of wartime shortage, African producers received no benefit from this. Prices paid to African producers were kept at low fixed rates. Colonial governments were able to pocket the difference and even send subsidies to the Allied war effort. At the same time, with the inflation of manufactured goods from Europe, Africans had to grow more and more export crops just in order to buy the same amount of imports.

Nevertheless, the war did not only have a negative impact so far as African peasant farmers were concerned. It was a period of increasing division between rich and poor peasants, between those who had land and those who had not. Growers of some higher-priced crops like cocoa and coffee gained more than growers of cotton or groundnuts. In addition, there were ways of getting round the restrictive prices of the marketing boards. In Kenya, for instance, where higher-priced markets were kept open for European settler-farmers, some African peasants were able to smuggle their goods on to the open market and so gain the rewards of higher prices for their produce. Among those who benefited from this were some Kikuyu peasants in the so-called 'white' highland district of central Kenya. Competition for land and markets intensified between Kikuyu and white settlers, with potentially explosive results, as we shall see in the following chapter.

The commercial and military demands of the Second World War stimulated colonial governments into investing in African harbours and airports on a scale not seen since the initial colonial investment in railways. In a number of west African ports, such as Freetown and Lagos, docks were deepened and harbour facilities improved. Freetown became a major port for the Allied command of the south Atlantic. Accra airport became an important terminus for the transportation of Allied troops to the north African battlefront. During this period more Africans moved into the growing urban centres in search of wage employment, some escaping forced cropping in the rural areas, others attracted by the wages offered in naval harbour constructions.

Within the Union of South Africa the war stimulated a tremendous growth in manufacturing industry. With a shortage of imports from Europe,

South Africa began to manufacture her own food, clothing, chemicals, machinery and tools. The need for Allied shipping repairs gave a great boost to South African steel manufacturing. By 1943 manufacturing had overtaken mining as the largest producer of wealth and employer of labour. With increasing land restrictions and poverty in the rural areas, blacks were already pouring into the rising manufacturing centres of the Witwatersrand, Cape Town and Port Elizabeth. It was a major period of black urbanisation in South Africa. It was a time of great job opportunities for some. But it was also a time of growing black urban poverty and unemployment as the numbers seeking work far outstripped the numbers of new jobs available. It was a situation approaching crisis point when the 200,000 whites and 100,000 blacks serving in Allied armies overseas returned to South Africa after the war.

The political and psychological impact of the war

In the First World War the colonial powers had used a considerable amount of force to coerce Africans into supporting their colonists' interests in the war. In the Second World War, on the other hand, while some degree of force was still applied, there was a greater tendency to *encourage* and *invite* African support for the European war effort. Many of the methods of persuasion used would now be defined as blatant misinformation and propaganda. Nevertheless, it marked an important break with the methods of the past. The British, in particular, used films, radio and officially sponsored newspapers to spread wartime propaganda. They sought to *persuade* Africans to cooperate with the colonial authorities, to volunteer for war service or to produce more food and raw materials. In seeking to persuade in this way, rather than relying on naked force, colonial authorities were admitting a need to explain their policies and to open a discussion with their African subjects. Literate Africans were quick to respond.

The voice of the minority of educated Africans – clerks, teachers, lawyers, clergymen and journalists – could no longer be ignored in the wartime French and British colonies. They saw their local newspapers and their pre-war welfare associations as a means of expressing their opinions and in particular their criticisms of many aspects of colonial rule. A number of African-run newspapers had appeared in the 1930s. The influence of these grew rapidly in the war years. A single copy of a newspaper would very likely reach a wide audience as it was read aloud at markets and village meeting places far from the major urban centres.

In contrast to the First World War, Africans were widely informed about the course and issues of the Second World War. The *West African Pilot*, founded in Nigeria in 1938, for instance, published a report on the Atlantic Charter of August 1941. This was an agreement between the British prime minister, Churchill, and the United States president, Roosevelt, which laid out the basic principles of what their governments hoped the war would achieve. Relevant to Africans was Clause Three of the Charter: '... They [the British and US governments] respect the right of all peoples to choose the form of government under which they will live; and they wish to see sovereign rights and self-government restored to those who have been forcibly deprived of them.' The *West African Pilot* noted critically that Churchill had quickly claimed that the principles of Clause Three did not apply to Africa. All over the continent literate Africans bombarded their local newspapers with letters protesting that the clauses of the Atlantic Charter should indeed apply to Africa. For the first time demands for political independence began to become a dominant theme of the emerging African political organisations.

The Italian invasion of Ethiopia in 1935 had shocked Africans and those of African descent on both sides of the Atlantic. Hitherto Ethiopia had been held out as a symbol of African self-respect and independence from European cultural and political domination: a proud link with Africa's historic roots and ancient cultures. The liberation of Ethiopia by a British-led, but largely African force in 1941 was an inspiration to many Africans: if Ethiopia today, why not the rest of Africa tomorrow? This was the tone of the Fifth Pan-African Congress held in Manchester (England) shortly after the end of the war in 1945. The main theme of the Congress was an end to colonial rule and political independence for Africa. The timing and means of achieving this were not yet clear, but African delegates such as Nkrumah of the Gold Coast and Kenyatta of Kenya dispersed to their home countries with a clear goal in mind.

Even in the remotest rural regions of Africa, the forced cropping, conscription and inflation of the wartime period served to heighten peoples' dissatisfaction with the colonial regimes. Into this atmosphere came the returning ex-servicemen with their vastly broadened view of the world beyond the village and the petty tyrannies of the local colonial magistrate. Previously, the only Europeans that most Africans had seen had been wealthy, well educated and in positions of authority. During the war Africans had worked and

Figure 25.4 De Gaulle's Brazzaville conference, January 1944. He is seated second from the left. By this time all France's African colonies had declared allegiance to the 'Free French'. The conference, to which no Africans were invited, made declarations in favour of reforming the colonial system, at least in the social and economic sphere. Political reform leading to self-government, was, however, ruled out for the foreseeable future. Nevertheless, political reform followed fairly rapidly from 1945

fought alongside a wide range of working-class Europeans, and found them little different from themselves. They had fought against and killed Europeans, in the name of freedom and democracy. They had observed European poverty in Europe and savagery in warfare. Africans with their range and level of experience would never return to their home countries as a docile and subservient colonial labour force. Few ex-servicemen actually played a significant role in the leadership of the ensuing independence movements. But their influence in undermining the aura and prestige of Europeans in Africa was considerable.

The Second World War also helped change the attitude of Europeans themselves towards their colonies in Africa. Allied Europe, especially France, was made acutely aware of its indebtedness to Africa during the war. In order to ensure continuing African support, European administrators had been obliged to promise that social, economic and political reforms would follow Allied victory in the war. At a Free French conference held at Brazzaville in 1944 de Gaulle had specifically promised a 'new deal' for the subjects of the French African territories. Significantly, there were no African delegates at the conference and there was no suggestion yet of African political independence. But the promises of Brazzaville were followed up in 1946 with the abolition of the hated *indigénat* and the *corvée* labour system. In British west Africa the war years saw educated Africans being brought increasingly into higher administrative positions and on to elected local councils. British colonial administrators began to contemplate a time in the distant future when Africans would be allowed some degree of self-government. Significantly, Portugal, which had remained neutral in the war, felt no such obligation to introduce reform in her African colonies.

chapter 26

The winning of independence (1)

As we saw in the previous chapter, Europe's dependence upon Africa during the Second World War helped change the attitude of the main colonial powers, Britain and France, towards their African colonies. Portugal and Belgium, at this stage, had no plans for any significant changes. The economic value of the French and British colonies, on the other hand, had been clearly revealed and this was reflected in the development strategies for the colonies in the post-war period.

Colonial development strategies

The British Colonial Development and Welfare Acts of 1940 and 1945 and the French equivalent, known by its initials as FIDES (Fonds d'Investment pour le Développement Economique et Social, 1946), established funds for colonial economic and social investment. Much of the economic investment, however, went directly to sectors already controlled by European colonists. These included projects such as mining in the Gold Coast and Nigeria, settler farming in Kenya and Southern Rhodesia, and mechanised timber felling in Guinea and Gabon. There was little effective investment in African production in the rural areas where most of the population still lived. In the Rhodesias and Nyasaland the British tried to promote a class of African 'master farmers', using modern machinery and the advice of scientific researchers. But the numbers involved were relatively very small. Where government tried to *organise* and *improve* peasant production on a larger scale, its plans were often ill conceived and unsuccessful.

British investment in extending Sudanese irrigation works increased cotton production on the Djazira scheme between Senna and Khartoum. But French attempts to develop a similar scheme for cotton and rice on the upper Niger failed, largely through lack of proper consultation with the peasant settlers who were supposed to operate the scheme. Similarly, a British groundnut scheme in Tanganyika failed because of insufficient research and lack of forward planning in consultation with local peasant farmers. In Ubangui-Chari (modern Central African Republic) the French resorted to forced-labour as they tried to convert the country into a cotton-exporting region, despite enormous transport problems.

Colonial governments were generally too intent upon *ordering* and *instructing* rather than *consulting* and *supporting* local African initiatives. With an eye to Europe's needs, colonial post-war economic initiatives were still mainly

Figure 26.1 Successful Nigerian businessman Louis Ojokwu worked on many Nigerian infrastructure projects in collaboration with the British firm Costain in the 1950s, seen here at Lagos airport in 1957 with his daughter Grace and the wife of the Managing Director of Costain. His son Emeka Ojokwu was to become the leader of the Biafran secessionists in 1967

concerned with developing Africa as an exporter of raw materials and an importer of manufactured goods. There was certainly no intention in the late 1940s of developing African self-reliance in preparation for economic and political independence from Europe. Nevertheless, with rising demand for African products in Europe, the early 1950s was a boom period for the export of Africa's minerals and agricultural raw materials. But such African peasant prosperity as was achieved in this period was generally *in spite of* government marketing and land-use restrictions, *not because of* government investment.

Despite the shortcomings of colonial economic investment at this time, an increasing amount of government money was spent on African social welfare. Much of this was in response to the rising demands of African nationalists. For the first time colonial governments began seriously to invest in expanding African educational and health facilities. New hospitals were built in the main administrative centres, though in the field of health, government's main concern was with disease prevention. Important advances were made in the spraying and control of tsetse fly and malaria-carrying mosquitoes.

Most of the educational emphasis was still on primary schooling. Barely 3 or 4 per cent of Africa's teenagers were attending secondary school by 1960. Nevertheless, there was a need to cater for the growing demand for teachers and higher civil servants. A number of new universities were opened in British east Africa and British west Africa: Ibadan (Nigeria), Legon (Gold Coast/Ghana), Khartoum (Sudan) and Makerere (Uganda). In line with assimilation policy, the French assumed that Africans seeking higher education would attend universities in metropolitan France.

Politically, the post-war aims of both Britain and France were to introduce reforms which would *gradually* lead to African internal self-government, but at a pace determined by the colonial power. It was assumed that the former colonies would remain within the wider French or British empires. In this way Europe's economic domination of Africa would be maintained. But the major colonial powers soon learned that they could no longer dictate the pace of political change in Africa. It was the rising tide of African nationalism which now forced the pace of change and led most African states to political independence by the early 1960s. (The failure of most of these states to achieve effective economic independence will be discussed in Chapter 29.)

As will be seen in the following regional survey, there were, in the French and British colonies, two contrasting routes to independence. In general terms, the greater the number of white settlers, the greater the likelihood of war. In most west African states, for instance, European settlement was minimal. Here, with the notable exception of Portuguese Guinea, colonial authorities responded positively, if at times reluctantly, to African demands for a greater share in their own self-government. By contrast, in colonies of extensive white settlement, such as Algeria, Kenya and Southern Rhodesia, the white settlers themselves intervened to stop the process. As a result, in these colonies African freedom and independence was only won after prolonged and violent wars of liberation.

The winning of independence in British west Africa

Ghana

The movement towards the independence of India in 1947 heralded the break-up of the British empire. Self-government for Africans could not be far

Map 26.1   Independence in western Africa

behind. In British west Africa the movement towards independence was led by the colony of Gold Coast, soon to become the independent state of Ghana. (For the origin of the name 'Ghana', see above, Chapter 6, p. 88.) In 1946 the British revised the Gold Coast constitution, establishing an African majority in the Legislative Council. Most of the African representatives, however, were nominated by the country's chiefs. Though committed to the development of African self-government, the British still believed this could be done by the gradual reform of the existing system of 'indirect rule'. This excluded the small but influential body of educated Africans who were determined to win a greater share in government.

In 1947 a number of prosperous businessmen and lawyers from Accra and other coastal towns formed the United Gold Coast Convention (UGCC). They wanted the revision of the 1946 constitution to increase the number of *elected* rather than *nominated* African members of government. Kwame Nkrumah, a former teacher from southern Gold Coast, was invited to become secretary of the new party. Nkrumah (Figure 26.2) had recently returned from some years of higher education in the United States, where he had been inspired by the ideals of the radical Pan-Africanist Marcus Garvey

Figure 26.2 Kwame Nkrumah (1909–1972), first prime minister and later president of Ghana, 1954–66

(see p. 375). Nkrumah saw this as the chance to fulfil the aims of the Pan-African Congress of 1945 which he had attended in Manchester (see p. 387).

In February 1948 an event occurred in Accra which quickened the whole tempo of events. Police opened fire on a peaceful demonstration by African ex-servicemen protesting at the rapidly rising cost of living. The shooting prompted widespread rioting in Accra, Kumasi and other towns. The government suspected that UGCC was behind the disturbances. Nkrumah and leading members of the party were arrested and held in prison for several months. The extent of the disturbances prompted the British government into reviewing the constitution of 1946. This in turn demonstrated to Nkrumah the power of mass action. Following his release from prison, Nkrumah founded his own, more radical, Convention People's Party (CPP). He pursued a vigorous drive for widespread mass membership with the attractive demand of immediate independence. He called for a campaign of 'Positive Action' in support of these demands and a wave of demonstrations and strikes swept the country. Nkrumah was promptly re-arrested for subversion. His tactics, however, proved successful.

The British revised the 1946 constitution, bringing in a larger, African-dominated, Legislative Council. In elections held in 1951 the CPP won a clear majority and Nkrumah was released from prison to become leader of government business in parliament. The 1951 constitution, however, still reserved half the parliamentary seats for chiefly nominees. Nkrumah spent the next three years negotiating with the Governor, Arden-Clarke, for a new constitution which brought fully-elected, internal self-government to the territory in 1954. CPP won the new round of elections and Nkrumah became prime minister.

Gold Coast became independent as the new state of Ghana in March 1957. But it was clear that support for CPP, though widespread, was far from universal. An important sector of the population, the cocoa farmers of Asante, resented the way Nkrumah's government still maintained the marketing boards which brought in large profits for the government while restricting prices paid to farmers. A regionally-based party, known as the National Liberation Movement, had been founded in Asante. They did not trust Nkrumah and the southern Fante, who dominated coastal towns and government. Clearly, serious problems loomed ahead, but, for the moment, Nkrumah's Ghana was an inspiration for African nationalists in the rest of the continent.

Nigeria

Ghana set the pattern for the transition to independence in the rest of British west Africa. Ghana, however, was a relatively small, compact country with a population of about five million in the early 1950s. Nigeria, by contrast, was a large and disunited territory of 35 million people (in 1953). Northern and southern Nigeria had been governed as two separate territories until 1946. And within southern Nigeria there were sharp regional divisions between the Yoruba west and the Igbo-dominated east.

The African nationalist initiative in Nigeria was taken by the National Council of Nigeria and Cameroons (NCNC), founded in 1944. Among its founders was Nnamdi Azikiwe, the outspoken editor of the *West African Pilot* (p. 386). Azikiwe sought to make the NCNC a nationwide organisation, though the party's main base of support was in the Igbo country of the south-east. Other regionally-based parties followed in 1949, with the formation of the Yoruba Action Group (YAG) and the (Hausa/Fulani) Northern Peoples Congress (NPC). Independence was delayed as the various parties could not agree upon a suitable constitution. Should the country have a single unitary government, should it be a federation of self-governing regional states, or should it split into three or more completely separate states? The conservative Muslim northerners feared domination by the culturally 'Europeanised' southerners. Within the north itself there was conflict over the continued aristocratic domination of society. Eventually a federal solution was evolved and Nigeria became independent in October 1960, with northerner Sir Abubakar Tafawa Balewa as prime minister. But the tensions which were to lead to future regional conflict and civil war were already clearly evident.

Sierra Leone and The Gambia

Independence for Sierra Leone in 1961 was a victory for the educated elite of the Mende peoples of the interior over the formerly dominant Freetown Creoles. Independence for the tiny state of The Gambia was delayed during discussion over its possible union with its more powerful neighbour Senegal. Gambian nationalists resisted these moves and the territory became independent in 1965.

The winning of independence in French West Africa and French Equatorial Africa

The French West and Equatorial African territories followed a slightly different route towards political independence. The French were determined from the start to dictate the pace of reform and to keep their African colonies as part of 'Greater France'. The culturally assimilated African nationalists accepted this in principle but expected to be treated equally with French citizens. It

Figure 26.3 Prime Minister of Sierra Leone Sir Milton Margai (1895–1964) arriving at Marlborough House, London, for the Commonwealth Premiers Conference, 19 September 1962. He was the first Sierra Leonean to qualify as a medical doctor (1926), was elected Chief Minister in 1954, and first prime minister of Sierra Leone from 1956–64

soon became clear that this was not to be the case. Under the reforms of 1946 the French abolished the hated *indigénat* and *corvée* labour system. French West Africa and French Equatorial Africa were together allowed to send ten delegates to the French National Assembly in Paris. But this gave them only 2.5 per cent of the seats in the Assembly. If they had been treated equally with metropolitan France, the African territories should have been allowed about 50 per cent of the seats.

The African delegates formed a political party, the *Rassemblement Démocratique Africain* (RDA), under the leadership of Félix Houphouët-Boigny from Côte d'Ivoire. Differing regional interests over such a vast stretch of Africa, however, ensured that unity among the various nationalist politicians did not last for long. In 1948 the Senegalese nationalist and poet of the *Négritude* tradition, Léopold Senghor, broke away from RDA to found the *Bloc Démocratique Sénégalais* (BDS). In 1951 BDS won both Senegalese seats to the French National Assembly.

The main point of dispute among the African nationalists was about what course to pursue in negotiations with France. Senegal supported the poorer territories like Niger, Chad and Soudan (Mali) in favouring a federal solution. The French West African territories would form one federation and French Equatorial Africa another. Each would then be powerful enough to hold its own in future negotiations with France. In addition, Senghor expected Senegal to be able to dominate the economically weaker partners of French West Africa. Dakar, capital of Senegal and seat of the colonial governors of French West Africa, could expect to remain the capital of such a federation. Houphouët-Boigny, on the other hand, opposed federation, for he feared that it would lead to Côte d'Ivoire's wealth (from coffee, palm-oil and cocoa exports) being used to subsidise the poorer territories of the Sahel.

A

B

Under pressure from the Algerian war of liberation (see below), which began in 1954, the French introduced further reforms in West and Equatorial Africa. These led to fully elected, internal self-government for the various territories of the region by 1956. African representation in the French National Assembly was maintained, and Houphouët-Boigny joined the French Cabinet in 1956. But France retained control over African military and foreign affairs and economic development planning. It was certainly far short of 'independence'. Furthermore, under the influence of Houphouët-Boigny, the *Loi Cadre* (Outline Law) of 1956 ensured that plans for effective African federation were abandoned.

As the French came under increasing pressure in Algeria, de Gaulle, who came to power in 1958, determined to rid himself of the burden of potential future conflict in West and Equatorial Africa. He gave the colonies an ultimatum. Vote '*Oui*' ('Yes') to maintaining the link with France, or vote '*Non*' ('No'), to break all links with France and become completely independent. Confronted so suddenly with such a stark choice, a majority of French-speaking Africans, while hoping for a greater level of reform, voted for maintaining the link with France. Only Guinea, under the leadership of the trade-unionist Sekou Touré, voted '*Non*' and became immediately independent. France responded by attempting to cripple the 'rebel' territory so as to prove to the others the depth of their 'debt' to France. All French civil service personnel, economic aid and equipment were withdrawn from Guinea, even down to removing government files and filing cabinets and ripping out office telephones. Guineans serving in the French army were promptly dismissed without their pensions and returned to the streets of Conakry, a potential source of dissatisfaction and unrest. Guinea, however, survived with emergency aid from newly independent Ghana and the Soviet Union. The former soldiers of the French army were usefully employed by Sekou Touré's government on economic development projects.

With the gathering momentum of the independence movement in British west Africa, the leaders of the other French African territories soon pressed de Gaulle for their own independence. In an attempt to ensure continuing French economic ties with Africa, de Gaulle agreed to their demands and in 1960, the 'Year of Africa', 13 French African territories became independent (see Map 26.1).

The struggle for independence in the Maghrib

Morocco and Tunisia

The French had used a form of 'indirect rule' to govern Morocco, ruling the country as a 'protectorate' in the name of the sultan. In the post-war period, however, Sultan Muhammad V sided with the Muslim nationalist movement, which demanded independence. The French tried to tackle the problem by deposing the sultan and exiling him to Madagascar in 1953. But the tactic rebounded. Muhammad V became a national hero and a Moroccan 'Liberation Army' was founded to fight for independence. By late 1955 the French were feeling the rising pressure of the liberation war in Algeria. In order to concentrate their forces on their major settler colony, the French bowed to the inevitable and agreed to independence in both Morocco and Tunisia. Muhammad V returned to Morocco in triumph, the Tunisian nationalist leader Habib Bourguiba was released from imprisonment, and both territories became independent in March 1956.

Western Sahara

The Spanish meanwhile continued to occupy their mineral-rich desert colony of Rio d'Oro (Western Sahara). In 1976 the Spanish agreed to a withdrawal and this territory of 100,000 people was partitioned between Morocco in the north and Mauritania in the south. Both countries sent their

Map 26.2 Independence in the Maghrib

396

Figure 26.5 A scene from the Algerian war of liberation: a captured Algerian surrounded by Algerians who fought for the French, 1961

armies to occupy the coastal regions. The indigenous Arab-Berbers of the desert who had formed the Polisario Front in the early 1970s were determined to resist this foreign occupation of their country. With military aid from Algeria, the Polisarios waged a bitter guerrilla struggle against Mauritanian and Moroccan occupation. Mauritania withdrew in 1979, but the struggle continued with Morocco. This caused a worsening of relations between Morocco and Algeria and disagreement among the leaders of other African states over whether or not to recognise the Polisario Front as the legitimate government of an independent Western Sahara.

Fighting between Morocco and the Polisario escalated in 1979–81 as first Cuba and then 36 other countries, most of them African, recognised Polisario's Sahara Arab Democratic Republic (SADR). International recognition, however, did not help the situation as Morocco refused to relinquish its claims or withdraw its occupation. In the meantime, Morocco encouraged thousands of Moroccans to take up residence there in anticipation that one day the United Nations might force a referendum on the territory's future.

Algeria

In Algeria the French were determined not to grant independence. It was France's principal colony of white settlement, there being as many as two million French settlers (*colons*) in the country by 1945. That year the Muslim population was fired with a new sense of nationalism. It began in May 1945 when colonial police opened fire upon a peaceful Muslim nationalist demonstration in the inland town of Sétif. In the rioting and colonial retaliation which followed, a hundred Europeans and up to 8000 Muslims were killed. It was a day of awakening for the people of Algeria. Reforms offered by the French government in 1946–7 were no longer enough. Increasing numbers of Algerians became committed to the need for an all-out war of liberation.

The war was launched by the Front de Libération Nationale (FLN) in November 1954. The FLN found its initial base of support in the isolated regions of the Aurès mountains. In August 1955 the uprising moved down into the town of Constantine, where up to 70 European *colons* were killed in a single day. Following this incident the French realised they were facing full-scale revolution and they began to pour tens of thousands of troops into the country from mainland France. We have already seen elsewhere that the escalation of the war in Algeria played an important role in forcing the French to concede independence in her other African territories.

By 1958 there were up to half a million French troops in Algeria. But each French attempt to suppress the uprising brought more recruits to the liberation armies. It was a long and bitter struggle. Thousands of French troops were killed and they in turn killed literally hundreds of thousands of Algerians, most of them non-combatant civilians, accused of helping the guerrillas. The FLN suffered from internal disunity as each regional command operated virtually independently of the others. Nevertheless, by 1962 their combined efforts had forced the French government to override the protests of the *colons* and negotiate independence.

The first president of the independent republic was Ahmed Ben Bella, a political leader of one of the FLN's principal factions. He had been captured and imprisoned by the French during the war. Now, after independence, he relied heavily upon the FLN's armed forces, under the command of Colonel Houari Boumedienne, to enforce national unity. He became so dependent upon the support of Boumedienne that the colonel was able to replace Ben Bella in a virtually bloodless *coup d'état* in 1965. (A *coup d'état*, or coup, means the overthrowing of a government, by force.)

Libya

Libya, occupied by the British since 1943, became independent in 1951 with the leader of the Sanusiyya Muslim brotherhood, Idris, as king. Following the discovery of rich reserves of oil in the Libyan desert in the 1960s, Idris was overthrown by Colonel Mu'ammar al-Qadhdhafi (Gaddafi) in a military coup in 1969. Gaddafi sought to mount a radical Muslim revolution. This involved a wider distribution of Libya's wealth among its Muslim population combined with a return to non-materialist Muslim values, guided by the Qur'an and Gaddafi's own 'little green book' of revolutionary principles. Gaddafi's revolution took the form of *a jihad* against anti-Muslim forces. He was determined to rid the country of 'Western' (European and US) influence and exploitation of the country's mineral resources, and to establish Libya as a major unifying force in the Arab Muslim world. Some political leaders in northern and trans-Saharan Africa feared that Gaddafi planned the Libyan domination of a grand Muslim empire on the scale of former centuries.

Egypt, Sudan, Eritrea and Somalia

Egypt

In 1944 Britain ended its wartime occupation of Egypt and the country regained its independence. The corrupt and oppressive regime of King Farouk and the old Ottoman landed aristocracy was overthrown by a military coup in 1952. The army officers had been prompted into action by the recent humiliating Egyptian defeat in the first Arab-Israeli war of 1948–9, the blame for which was laid squarely upon the shoulders of King Farouk's government. By 1954 Colonel Gamal 'Abd al-Nasir (usually written in English as Abdul Nasser) had taken over the ruling military council as president of Egypt.

Nasir was of humble origin and was determined to rectify the gross injustices of the Farouk regime. The main problem was that of land distribution. Much of Egypt's precious supply of cultivable land was in the hands of a small

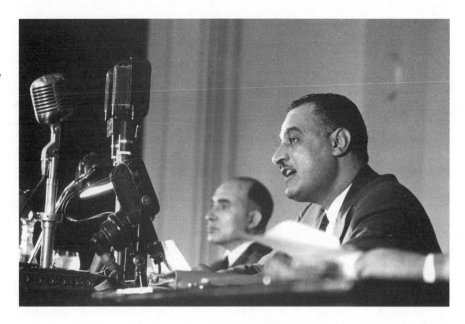

Figure 26.6 Gamal 'Abd al-Nasir (1918–1969), colonel in the Egyptian army, leading member of the Council of Revolutionary Command that overthrew King Farouk in July 1952, president of Egypt, 1954, elected three times unopposed, 1956–69. Here addressing a conference in Cairo 25 August 1956

Map 26.3 Independence in north-east Africa

number of very wealthy landlords. The vast majority of Egypt's 20 million population remained landless and desperately poor. Nasir ordered the breaking up of the large estates and the redistribution of land among the peasantry.

In 1956 Nasir's government seized the Suez Canal from the French company that owned and operated it. In part this was a deliberate anti-colonial move aimed at the continuing dominance of France and Britain in the region. But Nasir also intended using profits from the canal to benefit the peoples of Egypt. In particular, he needed funds for his ambitious scheme to raise the Aswan Dam in order to increase the amount of irrigable land in the lower Nile valley. Britain and France responded to the nationalisation of the canal by invading Egypt in an attempt to occupy the canal zone. But they were forced to withdraw by a combination of Egyptian resistance and international opposition from the United States and the Soviet Union. Following the humiliating withdrawal of French and British troops in 1956, the Egyptian government nationalised all remaining French and British companies in Egypt. Nasir's 'victory' in the 'Suez War' ended a century or more of western European domination of the Egyptian economy. Egypt under Nasir now became the undisputed leader of the Arab world, assuming the title 'The United Arab Republic'.

Sudan

In 1954 Egypt gave up its claim to authority in Sudan, a claim which dated back to the pre-colonial conquests of Muhammad Ali. Britain then negotiated an independence constitution for Sudan which came into effect in 1956. It was a hasty arrangement and the problem of internal unity remained unsolved. The British had ruled the Muslim-dominated north and the non-Muslim south as two separate territories for most of the colonial period. After independence the northerners began a positive Islamisation campaign in the south as a means of reinforcing national unity. But the non-Muslim southerners regarded rule by the northern Sudanese as no more acceptable than rule by the British. The result was civil war which nearly tore the country apart for much of the 1960s and again in the 1980s and 1990s.

Eritrea

The former Italian colony of Eritrea came under British occupation after 1941. The Muslim Eritreans of the coastal plain favoured complete independence, but their ambitions were thwarted by the intervention of Ethiopia. The government of this landlocked empire saw the period of decolonisation as an ideal opportunity to regain an outlet to the sea. (Massawa had been lost to Turkish occupation in the sixteenth century.) The British responded favourably, keen to build a strong alliance with Christian Ethiopia during a period of rising Arab Muslim power in Egypt and Arabia. The British therefore denied the Eritreans complete independence, preferring to hand the territory over to Ethiopia in 1952 as a self-governing state within an Ethiopian federation. Subsequently, Emperor Haile Selassie denied the Eritreans even this limited level of political independence by annexing Eritrea as a province of Ethiopia in 1962. Muslim and Marxist Eritrean liberation movements soon began an armed struggle against what they regarded as the imperialism of Ethiopia. It was to be 30 years before they finally achieved their independence.

Somalia

Somalia, the country with the greatest ethnic unity, was destined to suffer more division and conflict than almost any other country in Africa, with the notable exceptions of Sudan and the Congo. Divided five ways by colonisation, the predominantly pastoral Somali population found the historic seasonal grazing patterns for their cattle, goats and camels radically restricted. Ethiopia had seized the Somali Ogaden while the French had occupied the principal northern Somali port (Djibouti). The British had not only taken the northern Somali region opposite the Gulf of Aden, but had also incorporated the valuable south-western Somali grazing lands into its colony of Kenya as the Northern Frontier District. This left the Italians with the most economically productive southern region that bordered the north-western Indian Ocean. After the Second World War, the latter became a United Nations Mandate, administered by the Italians, but committed to independence by 1960.

The main aim of Somali nationalists, both before and after independence, was to achieve the unity of a 'Greater Somalia'. The five-starred emblem on their national flag represented the five parts that needed reunification. At independence in 1960, the Somali Republic united only two of these, British and Italian Somaliland. The decade following independence was dominated by attempts to 'liberate' the other three parts, resulting in destructive border wars with Ethiopia and Kenya. In fact the Somalis had never historically acted as a single 'nation'. Theirs was an informal cultural unity, with power exercised by local clan leaders with their own local priorities. This was reflected in their democratic politics, as in the late 1960s a thousand candidates, representing 68 parties, competed for 123 parliamentary seats. The highly personal nature of Somali politics, combined with a lack of development focus, allowed for the early emergence of widespread nepotism and corruption. It was supposedly in an attempt to solve these problems that General Siad Barre staged a bloodless coup in October 1969.

Barre committed his government to 'scientific socialism' and nationalised foreign-owned banks, businesses and land. With Soviet and Chinese financial support, Barre brought a sense of unity, purpose and development to the country which lasted for a few years. The aim of a Greater Somalia, however, overshadowed all else and attacks into the Ethiopian-occupied Ogaden continued, especially after the overthrow of Emperor Haile Selassie in 1974. Once Brigadier Mengistu had established a Marxist regime in Ethiopia by 1977, however, the Soviet Union switched sides, giving its support to the strategically more significant Ethiopia in the on-going Ogaden conflict. In a hugely destructive war in the aftermath of drought, Somali troops were expelled from the Ogaden in 1978. At which point, in one of the more cynical moves of the Cold War, the United States threw its weight behind 'socialist' Somalia, supplying Barre's government with massive military aid in exchange for a US military base at Berbera. Meanwhile, the drought of 1974–5 had dealt a devastating blow to Somalia's predominantly pastoral economy, and the country was awash with refugees from the Ogaden.

Siad Barre's rule became steadily more oppressive through the 1980s and a separatist movement grew in the northern region as government development projects were increasingly concentrated in the southern region around Mogadishu. Heavy government retaliation against the north left the city of Hargaise almost destroyed, with tens of thousands killed and hundreds of thousands fleeing as refugees into Ethiopia. By 1990 Barre's oppression throughout the country had provoked such opposition that people reverted to old clan-based loyalties. In January 1991 Barre fled the country, leaving behind chaos and national disintegration.

chapter 27

The winning of independence (2)

British east Africa

British east Africa was a region of contrasts so far as the route to independence was concerned. The lead was taken in Tanganyika. The event which spurred Tanganyikan nationalists into mass political activity was the eviction in 1951 of thousands of Meru farmers to make way for a handful of white settlers. Following protests against this action by the Tanganyikan African Association (TAA), Julius Nyerere led Tanganyikan nationalists in forming the Tanganyika African National Union (TANU) in 1954.

Nyerere had been educated at the new University of Makerere in Uganda and at the University of Edinburgh in Scotland. He quickly turned his organisational talents to making TANU a countrywide political party, modelled on Nkrumah's CPP. He was helped by the extent of rural dissatisfaction with heavy-handed government attempts to change and 'improve' the agricultural practices of peasant farmers. Government schemes to enforce the terracing of

Figure 27.1 Julius Nyerere (1922–1999), '*Mwalimu*' (teacher), political philosopher, international statesman; elected Chief Minister of Tanganyika, 1960, became prime minister of independent Tanganyika, December 1961, resigned during 1962 to work on a new constitution, elected president of the Republic of Tanganyika, 1962. Negotiated union with Zanzibar, 1964, and thus became president of the Republic of Tanzania, 1964–85

mountain-slopes, for instance, provoked violent rioting in 1955. The rapid spread of TANU membership was also helped by the widespread use of the Kiswahili language in Tanganyika. Kiswahili had become the language of long-distance trade in the pre-colonial period. Throughout the colonial period, Kiswahili was used by missionaries and officials in their schools and civil service because they found it more convenient to learn and use just one 'native' language. As a result, Nyerere had to hand an African language which could be used to help create a sense of national unity among the many African peoples of the territory.

For a while the British tried to establish what they called a 'multi-racial' constitution. In fact it was a racist constitution which guaranteed a powerful say in government for the tiny minority of Asians and Europeans. The British were influenced in their attitude by their attempts to uphold more extensive white settlement in neighbouring Kenya. But under Nyerere's leadership TANU won the support of a number of influential white-settler politicians. As a result, TANU won a clear majority in the parliamentary election of 1958, even under the terms of the 'multi-racial' constitution. By the end of 1961 Tanganyika had become independent under a totally non-racial constitution.

The British conceded independence to Zanzibar in December 1963, but the island-state remained under Arab domination with the Sultan still as

Map 27.1 Independence in east Africa

head of state. Within weeks of independence, the Sultan's regime was overthrown in a violent revolution on behalf of the long-oppressed African majority. In April 1964 Tanganyika and Zanzibar amalgamated into the Republic of Tanzania.

Uganda

Nyerere's Tanganyika (Tanzania) provided a lead which inspired the nationalist movements in the rest of British east and central Africa. In Uganda, however, political unity in opposition to colonialism was not so easily achieved as it was in Tanganyika. During the colonial period the British had treated the 'kingdom' of Buganda as though it were a distinct separate unit within the Protectorate of Uganda. At the same time the British use of 'indirect rule' had emphasised the continuing role of the *kabaka* (king) in Baganda political life. Kabaka Mutesa II was determined to retain Buganda's special status in any future independent Ugandan state. Under the terms of the independence constitution of 1961 Buganda was allowed to exercise its own internal self-government, separate from central government and under the direct control of the *kabaka*.

The government which took Uganda to independence in October 1962 was a political alliance between Milton Obote's northern-based Uganda People's Congress and the Buganda royalist party, the Kabaka Yekka ('King Alone') Movement. Obote became prime minister and the following year Kabaka Mutesa was installed as ceremonial president. Support for Obote's party strengthened after independence and he was soon able to dispense with his political alliance with the Buganda royalists. In April 1966 Obote declared a new constitution in which he himself became executive president. The special status of Buganda ended violently the following month when government troops attacked the *kabaka*'s palace. The palace was destroyed and many of its inmates were killed, though Mutesa managed to escape into

Figure 27.2 Milton Obote (b.1924), founder of Uganda People's Congress (UPC), prime minister of independent Uganda, 1962; abrogated the constitution and declared himself president of the Republic of Uganda, 1966; exiled by Idi Amin's coup, 1971; re-elected president, 1980; exiled by coup again in 1985

exile. The military commander who led the attack was Colonel Idi Amin, who was later to oust Obote himself in a military coup in January 1971.

Kenya

The road to independence in Kenya was a rough one. White settlers from the central highlands dominated the colonial government in Nairobi. Because of this it took a period of guerrilla warfare before political negotiation for African majority rule and independence was possible. Though not on the scale of the Algerian war, the Kenyan armed rising, usually referred to as 'Mau Mau', was nonetheless a hard-fought and bitter struggle.

The main support for Mau Mau came from African 'squatter' tenants, mostly Gikuyu, but including Embu and Meru, who had been expelled from white-owned farms in the fertile highlands north of Nairobi. The white settlers sought to prevent their African 'squatter' tenants from becoming successful peasant farmers who might compete with the white 'farmers' themselves. They wanted to ensure that the only Africans remaining in the fertile 'white highlands' were those who were entirely dependent upon white 'farmers' for their very low wages. Large numbers of Gikuyu 'squatters' had been evicted from the highlands in the 1930s. Many had been pushed into dry, infertile resettlement areas or overcrowded 'reserves'. Others had abandoned the struggle to remain on the land and moved to the urban area of Nairobi in search of work, or the easier pickings of petty crime.

The Mau Mau struggle began in the early 1940s with a campaign of violent rural action which included labour strikes, setting fire to farm buildings and crops and the maiming of livestock. By the late 1940s their action had become more organised with the 'Land and Freedom Army' introducing secret oathing ceremonies to enforce unity and loyalty to the cause. The aim of the campaign was not to engage the colonial government in full-scale war, but to frighten the settlers into abandoning their farms, and ultimately leaving the country. Only then, they believed, could political freedom be

Figure 27.3 Arrested Mau-Mau suspects held by police in Kenya, Nairobi 1960

achieved. To rural Gikuyu 'political freedom' meant an end to oppressive land and labour laws and a radical redistribution of white-owned land.

The conflict accelerated during 1952 with a series of attacks on white settlers themselves and on African chiefs who were seen as collaborators with the colonial regime. In October the colonial governor declared a State of Emergency. A hundred known African political leaders were arrested and British forces were flown in from abroad. But Mau Mau was a grassroots movement which had developed out of severe oppression in the so-called 'white highlands'. It was not, as colonial authorities assumed, a movement invented and led by African nationalists in Nairobi, though their ultimate aims were similar and some nationalist party members had sworn the Mau Mau oaths. The arrest of African nationalist leaders did not end the struggle. The Mau Mau freedom fighters, however, were forced back to the Aberdare forests from where they fought a defensive war for the next three years.

Severe government anti-Gikuyu oppression deprived the fighters of more widespread support as thousands of potential rural sympathisers were rounded up and forced into concentration camps. Total Mau Mau casualties probably exceeded 10,000. As usual in African colonial conflicts, Africans bore the brunt of frontline casualties on the government side. Some seventeen hundred African 'loyalists' died while barely a hundred Europeans were killed. British use of torture and the abuse of prisoners in the camps was commonplace, British written evidence of which was concealed for more than 50 years. Only uncovered in a British government building in 2005, these documents have enabled a few elderly Kenyan survivors to initiate legal action in the British High Court in London in 2011.

Although the Mau Mau freedom struggle had technically been defeated by the end of 1955, the war won for Kenyans as a whole the possibility of major political reform. In the first place, it persuaded the British government to abandon the extreme demands of the local white settlers whose oppressive laws had clearly provoked the crisis. By 1960 the British had accepted the principle of African majority rule for a self-governing Kenya.

Before the outbreak of Mau Mau, the African nationalist movement in Kenya had been led by Jomo Kenyatta (Figure 27.4), a former secretary of the Kikuyu Central Association, who had recently returned from some years in Britain. In 1947 Kenyatta became president of the newly formed Kenya African Union (KAU) which began pressing for political reform and independence. As an outspoken opponent of the government, Kenyatta was one of those imprisoned under the State of Emergency in 1952. With the lifting of the State of Emergency in 1959 and the British acceptance of the principle of majority rule in 1960, nationalist political parties could again be formed. Two main parties emerged: the Kenya African National Union (KANU) and the Kenya African Democratic Union (KADU). The former was founded by Oginga Odinga and the influential trades unionist Tom Mboya. Among KADU's founders was the future Kenyan president Daniel arap Moi. Kenyatta was released from prison in 1961 to become president of KANU and leader of the African majority in the Legislative Assembly. After further constitutional negotiation Kenya finally became independent in December 1963.

Figure 27.4 Jomo Kenyatta (*c.*1894–1978), '*Mzee*' ('the Old Man'), General Secretary of the Kikuyu Association in the 1920s, campaigned in Europe for the restoration of Kikuyu (Gikuyu) land, 1929–46, published *Facing Mount Kenya* (1938), imprisoned during the 'State of Emergency', 1952–61, prime minister of independent Kenya, 1963–4, president of the Republic of Kenya, 1964–78

Figure 27.5 Tom Mboya (1930–69), General Secretary of the Kenya Federation of Labour, 1953–62, the leading Kenyan nationalist politician during the 'State of Emergency' of the 1950s, key political ally and minister in Kenyatta's government, 1963–9. Assassinated 5 July 1969

Independence in Belgian-ruled central Africa

Background

The road to independence in the Belgian Congo was unlike anywhere else in Africa. In the immediate post-war years the Belgian government was determined to hang on to its major African colony. The possibility of transfer to African self-government was not even discussed in official Belgian circles until 1956 and even then it was assumed to be in the distant future. With this in mind, the Belgian authorities deliberately tried to keep the Congolese people isolated from the radical political ideas sweeping the rest of the continent. State aid to education was restricted to the primary level only, though achievement of literacy at this level was more extensive than in most of Africa in the late-colonial period. But there was no higher education for Africans, apart from those training to become Catholic priests. The Belgian authorities forbade the formation of political parties and there was no independent African newspaper in the colony until 1957. There was no African representation in any Legislative Assembly, even in an advisory capacity, and Africans in the civil service were restricted to the very lowest grades.

By 1956, however, the tiny educated minority of clerks, teachers and shopkeepers in the main urban centres were raising demands for the abolition of the racial discrimination which dominated all aspects of social and economic life in the colony. The Belgians believed they could satisfy this group by permitting them to take part in open elections for local government in the principal towns of Leopoldville (Kinshasa), Stanleyville (Kisangani), Elizabethville (Lubumbashi) and Luluabourg (Kananga). The elections, held in late 1957 and early 1958, opened the gates to a flood of African political activity. Most of the political parties subsequently formed, however, were locally-based regional organisations, drawing their main support from single ethnic groups. The most prominent of these was the Bakongo cultural organisation ABAKO (Alliance des Ba-Kongo) under the leadership of Joseph Kasavubu. In the Katangan copper-producing region the principal party was CONAKAT (Confédération des Associations Tribales du Katanga) founded by Moise Tshombe and based mainly upon Lunda support. Only the MNC (Mouvement National Congolais), founded by Patrice Lumumba, made any determined effort to create a nationwide political party. Even the MNC, however, was dependent for most of its support upon the peoples around Lumumba's home town of Kisangani (Stanleyville), capital of Orientale province (see Map 27.2).

During 1958 these aspiring African politicians quickly transformed their local interests into demands for political independence. Most of them indicated a fairly generous timescale: from 1961 to 1965 for independence. They were strongly influenced by events elsewhere in Africa, especially the granting of self-government to the peoples of French Congo-Brazzaville just across the river from the Belgian colony. In December 1958 Lumumba returned to the Congo, inspired by the All-African Peoples' Conference which he had attended in newly independent Ghana. The political rallies which followed in Kinshasa (Leopoldville) in January 1959 quickly degenerated into widespread and uncontrolled rioting, particularly by unemployed youths in the country's main towns. Attacks were concentrated mainly upon government buildings, Catholic missions and European-owned property.

Problems of historical Interpretation

The traditional interpretation of the events surrounding Congo's independence, including in earlier editions of this book, has been faced with a radical re-interpretation in the light of new evidence hitherto unavailable to the general public. The traditional story of events can be summarised as follows.

Faced with a general breakdown of law and order throughout the country in 1959, the Belgian government panicked, fearful of provoking an Algerian-type war of liberation. Having only officially legalised African political parties in August 1959, the Belgians summoned the colony's main political leaders to a 'Round Table Conference' in Belgium in January 1960. Lumumba, who had been imprisoned since November 1959 on charges of inciting violence, was released to enable him to attend. African politicians later admitted that they had been prepared to negotiate anything up to a five-year transition period towards internal self-government. To their surprise the

Map 27.2 Independence in Congo (Zaïre)

Belgians agreed to full political independence within less than six months. Totally unprepared, political parties mushroomed throughout the country: 120 different parties contested the parliamentary elections for 137 seats in May 1960. So long oppressed by poverty, forced labour, heavy taxation and racial discrimination, the Congolese electorate were swept away by the wildest of expectations for the coming independence, expectations which could not possibly be met.

The problems of regionally-based parties quickly came to the fore in the negotiations to form a coalition government for independence on 30 June. Only Lumumba's MNC favoured a single centralised government. The other, regional, parties wanted a federal constitution which would guarantee them domination of their own local self-government. With the style of constitution still undecided, Lumumba headed a very shaky coalition as prime minister with Kasavubu as formal president. Within days, the newly independent state began to fall apart. The army mutinied against the continued presence of Belgian officers and Katanga declared itself a separate state.

Lumumba's government was paralysed. It had lost both its main source of income, taxes from the Katangan copper-mines, and control of the army with which to enforce the law. Into the chaos which now ensued, the United Nations (UN) sent a peacekeeping force. But, under pressure from the

United States, the UN force refused to intervene against Katangan secession. Some time between November 1960 and January 1961, Lumumba was murdered in Katanga. Meanwhile, the army commander, General Mobutu, was, with strong US backing, emerging as the main power behind the series of shaky governments in Kinshasa.

The reality of independence and neo-colonialism

The lesson of this traditional version of events was that the Congolese were not ready for independence. The Belgian fault was that they had not prepared the Congolese for political power over a longer period, or that they should have delayed the process for a number of years. Recent historical research, however, has turned this version on its head. The historical revision has been led by a Dutch writer, Ludo De Witte, whose work (see Suggestions for further reading, p. 488) has been based upon access to the UN archives in New York and to the Belgian government archives and memoirs by key Belgian figures of the time. From this research a very different story emerges.

The Belgian government's sudden move to independence was not at all a panic move, but rather a deliberate attempt to forestall the build-up of a radical agenda among Congolese nationalists. The Belgians believed that if they moved quickly, they would be able to keep control of the government behind the scenes, primarily *because* the Congolese politicians were so inexperienced. It was believed that even the radical nationalist figure of Lumumba could, in practice, be contained. Shortly before the general election of May 1960, the Belgian government changed the Congolese constitution to allow the six provincial governments virtual complete autonomy. This was a deliberate safeguard so that in the event of the central government falling into the 'wrong' hands, such as those of Lumumba, the richest province of Katanga would be able to act independently, and even secede. Within Katanga, Belgian settlers and officials had joined Tshombe's CONAKAT and had even drafted the party's manifesto. Tshombe was to prove a willing tool of Belgian interests.

At the independence ceremony on 30 June 1960, the Belgian king, Baudouin, made a paternalistic speech referring to Belgium's noble 'civilising mission' and praising his predecessor, Leopold II (see above pp. 322–3, 344–7) as a genius! He urged the incoming government not to indulge in 'hasty reforms', but rather to heed the advice of their Belgian administrators and technocrats. This anticipated a 'neo-colonial' future for the Congo: the colonial system of economic exploitation would remain, with minimal change, apart from a small elite of African politicians as figureheads at the top. Lumumba, however, defied protocol and replied with a radical speech that castigated the brutality and injustice of Belgian rule. He declared the Congolese people finally free from 'the humiliating slavery that was imposed on us by force'. Some have argued that this speech sealed Lumumba's fate. De Witte, however, believes that it was not so much the speech that condemned him in Belgian eyes – politicians say many things to gain popularity – but rather the fact that he followed it up a few days later with action to implement his promises.

When the army mutinied (5 July), an event which De Witte refers to as a 'strike', Lumumba intervened on the side of the soldiers, dismissed the Belgian senior officers and asked the African soldiers to put forward their own choice of officers as replacements. Thus Mobutu became a colonel and chief of staff. In Katanga Belgian officers refused to accept dismissal, and when Congolese soldiers rebelled against their defiant Belgian officers, the Belgian government sent in paratroopers to disarm them (10 July). Tshombe, now under the protection of Belgian forces, felt free to proclaim Katanga's independence from central government (11 July 1960). Immediately, the Union Munière paid Tshombe's government a year's worth of taxes in advance, to ensure the state's financial viability. Further Belgian troops were flown in to secure the other major Congolese cities in the days that followed (including the capital, Leopoldville, on 13 July). They came ostensibly to protect Belgian property and civilians, subject to attack during the initial mutiny of 5 July.

When Lumumba appealed to the United Nations for help against this external aggression, which he regarded in effect as an attempted re-colonisation, he got no sympathy or support. On the UN Security Council, the United States and Britain supported the Belgian cause and distrusted Lumumba as likely to promote a socialist transformation of the country. The UN Secretary General, Dag Hammarskjöld, concurred, and thus the UN troops that arrived in the Congo in August 1960 had a mandate merely to help restore 'law and order'. Although the Belgians were persuaded to withdraw and hand over to the 'Blue Berets', the UN made no attempt to remove the Belgians from Katanga, or to end that province's secession. Indeed, when elements of the Congolese army loyal to Lumumba tried to end the secession, UN troops provided a barrier to prevent them entering Katanga.

Belgian plans, supported by the United States and the UN Secretary General, were to undermine and destroy Lumumba's nationalist government and they were prepared to use Katangan secession as a means to achieve that. Rather than reincorporate Katanga into the rest of the Congo, the Belgians aimed to rebuild the Congo from their base in Katanga. The major obstacle to Belgian and US plans was Lumumba. By this time the United States, Britain and Belgium were all agreed that Lumumba, the democratically elected prime minister, should be removed, permanently. The US Central Intelligence Agency (CIA) persuaded President Kasavubu to dismiss the prime minister, whereupon Mobutu, acting for the CIA, dismissed the elected parliament and placed Lumumba under house arrest on 5 September 1960. The UN stood by and did nothing to protect Lumumba, even when he was transported to Katanga in December 1960. On 17 January 1961 Lumumba and two of his closest aides were shot by firing squad, with the full approval of Tshombe and in the presence of three Belgian officers.

Katangan secession lasted two-and-a-half years. It was supported and financed by the Belgian controllers of the Union Munière copper-mining company and other Belgian business interests in the region. Tshombe's Katangan military force was assisted by a motley crew of white mercenaries made of up former Belgian soldiers and adventurers from Rhodesia and South Africa. It was not until towards the end of 1962 that the United Nations finally intervened decisively in Katanga and ended Tshombe's secession in January 1963. Ironically, for a while during 1964–5, Tshombe himself became prime minister of the newly unified Congo government. But Tshombe's rule was soon discredited, partly for corruption and finally for his use of white mercenaries and American and Belgian paratroopers during the suppression of a major rebellion in the Lumumbist heartland of Kisangani.

Figure 27.6 Ghanian UN troops in the Congo 1961

Mobutu's coup d'état *and the* Republic of Zaïre

In November 1965 General Mobutu finally seized power in a bloodless *coup d'état*. The only surprise was that he had not done so earlier. He had, perhaps, needed the intervening time to consolidate his hold over the redisciplined army. Mobutu re-established strong central government control, helped by a temporary but rapid rise in the international price of copper. The old discredited politicians were gradually squeezed out as Mobutu established his own very personal style of presidential government. In the early 1970s, in a move to symbolise a new beginning, the province of Katanga was renamed Shaba, while the name of the country itself was changed to Zaïre.

Rwanda and Burundi

Belgium ruled the joint territory of 'Ruanda-Urundi' as a League of Nations/United Nations Mandate and, in contrast to the Congo, was under obligation to the Trusteeship Council to prepare the countries, separately, for internal self-government. Thus, during the 1950s, political activity was allowed and numerous political parties were formed.

As seen earlier (p. 216), in pre-colonial times 'Hutu' and 'Tutsi' were social and economic terms rather than ethnic distinctions as such. Hutu meant peasant or servant while Tutsi, originally 'pastoralist', on the eve of colonisation was equated more generally with wealth and status (of which cattle ownership was often an important part). German and Belgian colonisers hardened these flexible terms into rigid ethnic identities, enshrined in law and recorded on every person's identity document. They recorded Tutsi myths of distant origin, transmuting them into historical fact and confirmation of Tutsi superior racial identity. After two generations of colonial rule, these distinctive Tutsi and Hutu identities were widely accepted and entrenched in people's minds. Thus those identified as Tutsi were a small privileged elite that was co-opted as a junior partner in colonial rule. The majority, classified as Hutu, were a subservient underclass, subject to forced-labour demands and with less access to education or social privileges. This colonial legacy, that defined the whole of society in terms of ethnicity, was to harden with political independence into bitter ethnic enmity and conflict.

In Rwanda political parties were ethnically based from the start. The Tutsi elite demanded immediate independence in order to preserve their privileged position of domination. Newly emerging Hutu intellectuals, led by Grégoire Kayibanda, demanded that majority rule should precede independence. Amid mounting inter-ethnic violence, the Belgians backed the Hutu intellectuals, replacing many Tutsi chiefs with Hutu nominees. The latter organised a general persecution of Tutsi, rich or poor, regardless of their elite or common status. Persecution turned into a series of massacres between November 1959 and October 1960 that has been described as a Belgian-sponsored revolution. Hundreds of Tutsi were killed and tens of thousands were driven into exile in Burundi, Tanganyika and Uganda. During 1961 small bands of Tutsi exiles – called *inyenzi,* 'cockroaches', by Hutu – began to launch attacks from neighbouring Uganda.

It was against this background that Kayibanda led the PARMEHUTU (Parti de l'émancipation du peuple Hutu) to electoral victory in 1961, and Rwanda to independence as its president in 1962. Kayibanda, however, added regionalism to ethnicity and packed his government with Hutu from central Rwanda, to the exclusion of those from the north. In 1973 he was ousted in a coup staged by Juvénal Habyarimana, a Hutu from northern Rwanda. The conflict and genocide of the 1990s will be discussed in the final chapter (pp. 475–7).

In Burundi, by contrast, the widely respected leadership of King Mwambutsa IV (1915–1966) established a level of non-partisan cooperation between Hutu and Tutsi that was enshrined within the most prominent political party UPRONA (Union pour le progress national). It was founded in 1958 by the king's son, Louis Rwagasore, but the latter's assassination in October 1961 unleashed pent-up ethnic tensions. Fearful of the massacres of Tutsi that had occurred in Rwanda during 1959–60, the Tutsi leadership purged many Hutu from UPRONA and ensured that it was a predominantly Tutsi government that took the country to independence in 1962. A military coup in 1966 further strengthened Tutsi control, purged Hutu from state employment and set the pattern of military rule, massacre and rebellion that has dominated Burundi since independence.

Independence on the islands

Réunion

Réunion became a *département* of France in 1946, with the right to send representatives to the French National Assembly. This secured the sugar-plantation economy firmly in the hands of French companies. Dissatisfaction with Réunion's high levels of unemployment has been muted by financial subsidies from France, including social security and unemployment payments. With this high level of economic dependence, there have been no widespread demands for political independence.

Mauritius

The British took Mauritius from the French in 1810. After the abolition of slavery in 1834–5, the former slaves, of African descent, left the sugar plantations *en masse,* which prompted the British to import indentured labour from India. Over the next 50 years, tens of thousands of Indians arrived in

Mauritius, transforming the ethnic makeup of the population to the extent that by the early twentieth century, people of Indian descent (mostly Hindu) made up two-thirds of the population. It was from this rural working class that the Mauritius Labour Party, founded in 1936, drew its main support. As the Labour Party, under the leadership of Dr Seewoosagur Ramgoolam, pushed for independence in the 1950s and early 1960s, they were vociferously opposed by a largely Creole-supported PMSD (Parti Mauritien social démocrate) who feared independence would expose them to 'Hindu domination'. They preferred to retain a Réunion-style link with Britain. Ramgoolam, however, skilfully steered the country through a difficult decade, marred by inter-ethnic violence, to win a series of elections and achieve independence from Britain in 1968.

Madagascar

The Malagasy never really came to terms with foreign occupation by the French. While open resistance to conquest was suppressed in the decade before the First World War, secret societies were formed during the inter-war years to keep alive nationalist aspirations. French assimilation policies co-opted only a very small pliant minority of Malagasy into the colonial system. The decision by the colonial administration to support the French Vichy government in 1940 (see p. 384) led to a British and 'Free French' occupation in 1942. This serious blow to French colonial prestige encouraged Malagasy nationalists, whose cause was strengthened further by wartime food shortages, especially rice, leading to famine in 1943–4.

In line with other French African colonies, in 1946 indigenous Malagasy gained the right to elect two delegates to the French National Assembly. These two, Joseph Raseta and Joseph Ravoahangy, founded the MDRM (Mouvement démocratique pour la rénovation malgache); but their call in Paris for immediate independence was rejected. Meanwhile, French settlers tried to suppress the rising tide of nationalism in the island. MDRM leaders were arrested and workers who were believed to sympathise with the party were ill-treated or sacked. Few were surprised when the 'Great Rebellion' broke out on 29 March 1947. In the initial months of the rebellion several hundred Europeans and their Malagasy 'collaborators' were killed as rebels seized control of eastern parts of the country. Over the following year, however, the French suppressed the rebellion with ruthless brutality, leaving at least 90,000 killed.

Despite the failure of armed rebellion, the spirit of Malagasy nationalism lived on. In 1953 the Catholic Church gave official support to aspirations for independence, hoping to forestall the spread of communism. A new wave of political activity began with the French move to allow internal self-government in its African colonies in 1956. In Madagascar a new 'moderate' strand of nationalism came to the fore in the form of the PSD (Parti social démocrate) under the leadership of Philibert Tsiranana. The PSD campaigned successfully to remain within a 'French Union' in the referendum of 1958 and Tsiranana led the country to independence in 1960.

Comoros

The Comoro islands are peopled primarily by Muslim Swahili-speakers, with only the island of Mayote having a significant population of Malagasy Christians. There was no particular demand for independence from France until the violent French suppression of a school strike in 1968. In 1974, following a series of referenda, the islands voted for independence, although the French claimed that Mayote had voted to remain part of France. In July 1975 Ahmed Abdallah, leader of the Union démocratique des Comoros (UDC) declared the Comoros independent, with himself as its first president. In December that year the French recognized the independence of Grand Comore, Anjouan and Moheli, but continued to insist that Mayote remained part of the French 'territorial community'. By then Abdallah had been overthrown by Ali Soilih, who expelled all French nationals. He in turn was overthrown in 1978 by Bob Denard, a French mercenary, who invited Abdallah to return as president.

Seychelles

The movement towards independence in the Seychelles began in 1964 with the formation of the islands' two principal political parties. The SDP (Seychelles Democratic Party), led by James Mancham, favoured continued ties with Britain. The SPUP (Seychelles Peoples' United Party) was led by France Albert René, a lawyer and trades union organiser who sided with the interests of the poor, and quickly came to believe that radical social transformation could only be achieved through complete independence from Britain. The British, however, were not prepared to follow the French example and told Mancham that if he wanted to secure his country from René's socialism, he had better campaign for independence. Elections in the 1970s showed the two parties fairly evenly matched with Mancham financially supported by the United States and local landed and business interests. (The US and Britain saw the islands of the Indian Ocean as of strategic importance in the Cold War, and in the 1960s Britain leased the Chagos islands to the US to build a military air base on Diego Garcia, and leased a site on Seychelles' main island of Mahé for the US to build a satellite-tracking station.) By contrast, René's radical social programme got him the financial support of the Liberation Committee of the OAU (Organisation of African Unity) (see pp. 453–5).

The British, hoping to rein in René, persuaded the two parties to form an alliance in 1975 in preparation for independence the following year, at which point Mancham became executive president with René as prime minister. It was an uneasy alliance: Mancham believed the future of the islands lay in luxury tourism and providing an off-shore tax haven for his millionaire friends; René wanted a socialist revolution. Less than a year after independence, René staged a coup and established a one-party socialist state. Despite this, he was pragmatic enough to keep the Americans on board: the dollar rent for the US tracking station paid for the country's annual oil imports.

28

The winning of independence (3)

Federation and independence in British Central Africa

British Central Africa suffered the problem of a resident white-settler population. Most of the whites lived in Southern Rhodesia (150,000 in 1950, rising to 200,000 by 1960). There they dominated the African majority with South African-style segregationist legislation. A third of the territory, the best land, was reserved for white ownership, while most of the country's four to five million Africans were restricted to the poorest third of the country. Rigid 'pass laws' restricted the movement of workers in the towns and other racist laws reserved all the better-paid jobs for whites. Since the 1920s the white settlers of Southern Rhodesia had ruled the colony through their own system of elected parliamentary government. Africans only ever had very limited representation. African political parties were quickly suppressed as soon as they were formed.

Federation

In the late 1940s the white settlers of the Rhodesias and Nyasaland proposed that the three territories be amalgamated into a central African federation. It was a deliberate attempt to pre-empt the emergence of an African independence movement. It would enable the whites of Southern Rhodesia to benefit from the enormous tax revenues arising out of the Northern Rhodesian Copperbelt. And Nyasaland would continue to provide their farms and new manufacturing industries with a ready supply of cheap labour. The enlarged state would then be economically powerful enough, like the whites in South Africa, to resist all moves towards African majority rule. This would encourage new British investment in the region, which in turn would further strengthen the white-dominated state.

The Africans of Southern Rhodesia did not stand to be so immediately affected by federation as those in the northern territories. They already suffered all the disadvantages of white racial domination. In the longer term, however, it affected them deeply in the sense that any strengthening of the white position would postpone still further the date of their eventual liberation. The Africans of Northern Rhodesia and Nyasaland, on the other hand, stood to suffer an immediate loss by the proposed federation. They were still technically ruled as British 'protectorates' rather than settler colonies. The number of white settlers was much smaller than in the southern colony. Racial discrimination, though widely practised in the protectorates, was not yet enshrined in law.

Map 28.1 Independence in British Central Africa

African nationalists, particularly from the northern protectorates, protested vigorously against the proposed federation. Dr Hastings Kamusu Banda and Harry Nkumbula summed up their fears in a written protest to the British government. Banda, born in Nyasaland, had qualified as a medical doctor in the United States and Britain. Though practising medicine in Britain, he kept in close touch with political developments in his home country. Nkumbula, a former teacher from Northern Rhodesia, was at the time (1949) studying at the University of London. They wrote:

> of all the Europeans of Central Africa, those of Southern Rhodesia have the worst antipathy towards Africans ... . They look upon the Africans as inferior beings, with no right to a dignified and refined existence and fit only as hewers of wood and drawers of water for Europeans ... . In all their dealings with the Africans they always assume the attitude of conquerors ... . It is these Europeans ... who will rule and govern the federation ... . Under the Government provided by Southern Rhodesia, the relationship between us and the authorities will be one of slaves and masters, and the cardinal principle ... domination.
>
> (From a memorandum dated 1 May 1949, quoted in R. I. Rotberg, *The Rise of Nationalism in Central Africa*, Harvard University Press, Cambridge, MA , 1964, p. 224)

Despite vigorous African protest, federation was pushed through by the British government and white settlers in 1953. With it came all the effects of increased racial discrimination that African nationalists had feared. The immediate impact was an economic boom for whites while Africans suffered the effects of frozen wage levels in the face of a rising cost of living. Strikes, such as the Copperbelt mineworkers' strike of 1956, were severely crushed by heavy police action. A major new investment project was the building of the Kariba Dam across the Zambezi (1955–9) to provide hydroelectric power for Southern Rhodesia and the Copperbelt. The flooding of the valley behind the dam led to the forced removal of 30,000 Africans from the north bank of the river. Significantly, the power station was built on the south bank, under full control of the Southern Rhodesian authorities.

The rise of African nationalism and demands for independence

The failure of the nationalist movements to prevent federation led to their discredit and a temporary falling-off of African political activity. But new racist legislation, to strengthen still further white domination of government, revived African political protest in 1956. It was led by Nkumbula and the Northern Rhodesian African National Congress (founded 1948) and by the Nyasaland African Congress (founded 1944). They staged a series of boycotts, strikes and demonstrations in the northern territories. African political activity was severely suppressed in Southern Rhodesia. Partly inspired by the example of newly independent Ghana, African political leaders sought alternative African names for their own future independent states. Zambia (adapted from Zambezia) was adopted as the African name for Northern Rhodesia. Malawi, commemorating the seventeenth-century empire, was chosen for Nyasaland. African leaders in the southern colony chose the obvious name Zimbabwe to replace the hated name 'Rhodesia' which commemorated the white-settlers' founder, Cecil Rhodes.

African political demands were rapidly stepped up during 1957–9, especially after a number of political leaders had attended the All-African Peoples' Conference at Accra in December 1958 (Figure 28.1). Government reacted by trying to suppress protest, banning political parties and imprisoning their leaders. But as fast as parties were banned, others were founded to replace them. Political protest had by this time become so widespread that no amount of imprisoning of leaders would stop the movement. The new

Figure 28.1 The opening session of the All-African People's Conference in Accra, Ghana, 8 December 1958. The banner above the platform reads: 'Hands off Africa! Africa must be free!'

Figure 28.2 Front page of the *Nyasaland Times* at the time of the 'state of emergency', 1959

Zambia African National Congress was banned in 1959 to be replaced immediately by the United National Independence Party (UNIP). Kenneth Kaunda, an outspoken critic of federation and the racism of colonial rule since the early 1950s, became its president on his release from prison in 1960. Following Dr Banda's return to Nyasaland in 1958, a campaign of protest demonstrations, strikes and riots led to the declaration of a State of Emergency in 1959 (see Figure 28.2). The banned Nyasaland African Congress was quickly reformed as the Malawi Congress Party, with Banda as its leader. Meanwhile, in Southern Rhodesia the African National Congress had in 1957 been revived by the trades union leader Joshua Nkomo. After a series of bannings and imprisonments, it finally re-emerged as the Zimbabwe African Peoples' Union (ZAPU) in 1962.

Independence for Zambia and Malawi and Rhodesian UDI

By 1960 the British government was finally forced to pay heed to the strength of African protest. Realising that the 'winds of change' were sweeping across Africa, the British saw it would be futile to continue supporting white minority rule in a Central African Federation. (The famous phrase 'wind of change' was coined by the British prime minister Harold Macmillan on a visit to Ghana in January 1960. It was most famously repeated in a speech made to the white South African parliament in Cape Town a month later. Needless to say, his racist white audience were more than a little annoyed by the tone of this speech.) There followed three years of constitutional negotiation with the African politicians of the two northern protectorates before the break-up of federation at the end of 1963. Thereafter, Zambia and Malawi quickly moved to political independence in 1964.

In Southern Rhodesia, however, white settlers remained firmly in control, determined to resist all moves towards African majority rule. African politicians grew frustrated by Nkomo's failure to commit the party firmly to the obvious need for an armed guerrilla struggle. As a result, Ndabaningi Sithole, Robert Mugabe and others broke away from ZAPU in 1963 to form the Zimbabwe African National Union (ZANU). But lack of clarity in planning, and regional rivalries between ZAPU and ZANU, tragically reduced their effectiveness during the crucial time of the break-up of the federation. In November 1965 Ian Smith, leader of the new white Rhodesia Front Party, made a unilateral declaration of independence (UDI). He thereby illegally declared white-ruled 'Rhodesia' to be an independent state, free from any British colonial control. The British government protested but took little effective action to stop them. It was clear to the leaders of ZANU that their commitment to armed struggle was indeed the only way forward.

The international community declared a policy of economic sanctions against the illegal Smith regime. But South Africa and Portuguese-ruled Mozambique ignored the instructions of the United Nations and continued to trade with Rhodesia. Even British multinational oil companies secretly continued to supply the Smith regime. Ironically the main victim of sanctions was Zambia, most of whose trade had hitherto passed through Rhodesia.

Zimbabwe's liberation war, 1966–80

The first clash between ZANU guerrillas and Rhodesian security forces took place at Chinhoyi in northern Rhodesia in April 1966. The guerrillas were easily outgunned and seven were killed, but, coming so soon after Rhodesian UDI, it was a warning to the Smith regime of the struggle that was to come. There followed a number of incidents in the late 1960s, but ZANU and ZAPU were still torn by personal and ideological disputes in their exile in Zambia.

In 1971–2 the Mozambican liberation movement, FRELIMO, occupied much of the Tete district of Mozambique and, thereafter, ZANU guerrillas were able to infiltrate in large numbers into the north-eastern districts of Rhodesia. The war now began to enter a new, decisive phase as the guerrillas ensured themselves of local rural support before launching attacks against settler farms, police posts and security forces. The latter found it increasingly difficult to get local people to inform on the guerrillas. FRELIMO's victory in Mozambique in 1974–5 (see below) enabled ZANU guerrillas to enter Rhodesia all along the country's eastern border zone. Robert Mugabe took over the leadership of ZANU in 1975 and set about strengthening the party,

Figure 28.3 Political 'education' in ZIPRA (Zimbabwe Independence People's Revolutionary Army) training in Zambia in the 1970s

committing the movement to the achievement of a socialist revolution in a liberated Zimbabwe. The war entered its final decisive phase in 1977. By then ZANU political cadres had been preparing the ground by winning the support of the rural people for up to five or six years. ZAPU, by contrast, though heavily supplied with Soviet-made weapons in their training camps in Zambia, made few effective incursions into the western half of the country until this final phase of the war.

The Smith regime reacted to the gathering onslaught by attacking ZANU and ZAPU bases and refugee camps in Zambia and Mozambique. Among other tactics, the Rhodesians financed and armed a group of dissatisfied Mozambicans whom they called the Mozambique National Resistance (MNR or RENAMO). These were used by the Rhodesian security forces to penetrate deep into Mozambique, blowing up bridges, cutting powerlines and attacking villages. The idea was to cripple newly independent Mozambique's economy and so 'persuade' FRELIMO to abandon its support for ZANU. In the event Rhodesia's RENAMO tactics failed as FRELIMO support for ZANU never faltered, and ZANU went on to win power in Zimbabwe. Following Zimbabwe's independence, South Africa took over sponsorship of RENAMO in an attempt to assert its own political and economic domination of the region.

In its dying months (1978–9), the Smith regime, under pressure from South Africa, tried to bypass the guerrillas and reach an internal settlement. There were a number of influential Africans in Zimbabwe, churchmen and chiefs, who wished to end the suffering of the war but feared the outright victory of a socialist-orientated ZANU. They were therefore prepared to compromise their complete independence. Under an agreement signed in 1978, Bishop Abel Muzorewa became prime minister of what was called 'Zimbabwe-Rhodesia'. The name itself indicated the reality of compromise. Whites retained a strong political voice and still remained in control of the economy. The guerrilla fighters were not prepared to accept this kind of compromise, and the war went on. Muzorewa, unable to stop the war, found his government fighting his fellow Zimbabweans and he was soon discredited.

By late 1979 the guerrillas of both ZANU and ZAPU controlled the majority of the country outside the main cities. The Smith/Muzorewa regime was forced to acknowledge defeat. Under an agreement signed in London in December 1979, both sides agreed to stop fighting while full and free elections were held in February 1980. These resulted in a resounding victory for ZANU, and Robert Mugabe became prime minister of an independent Zimbabwe in April 1980.

The winning of independence in Portuguese-ruled Africa

Portugal, ruled by a fascist dictatorship, was a poor state in European terms. Her African colonies, Guinea-Bissau and Cape Verde, Angola and Mozambique, were seen as vital props to the Portuguese economy. The Portuguese government, therefore, was determined not to give way to demands for independence. The Africans of the Portuguese colonies were equally determined to win their independence. Violent Portuguese suppression of African protest in all three territories soon made it clear that African liberation would only be won through prolonged guerrilla struggle. The lead was taken by the smallest colony, Guinea-Bissau and Cape Verde.

Guinea-Bissau and Cape Verde

In 1956 a Cape Verdean, Amílcar Cabral, founded the PAIGC (Partido Africano da Independência da Guinié e Cabo Verde). He began building up membership and devising a strategy for gaining independence. In 1959 PAIGC prompted a major strike by dockworkers in the port of Bissau. The strike was brutally crushed by colonial police, leaving 50 workers shot dead. This was the turning-point. Cabral dedicated the PAIGC to a full-scale liberation war in order to create a socialist state. (For the role of socialism in independent Africa, see the following chapter.) The war began in 1963 and over the next decade the rural people of Guinea-Bissau were gradually won over to support the cause. As rural areas were liberated, schools, health clinics, roads, agricultural projects and trade were built and maintained – all the trappings of a government of grassroots socialism, based on the needs of the people. By September 1973 so much of mainland Guinea had been liberated that PAIGC was able to declare an independent state. This was beginning to receive worldwide recognition when Cabral was assassinated in January 1974. Tragically, he did not live to see the final withdrawal of Portuguese troops in September 1974.

During his term of duty as Portuguese commander in Guinea-Bissau (1968–73), General Spinola became convinced that the war could not be won by Portugal. He realised that the continuing war in Guinea-Bissau, Angola and Mozambique was draining the Portuguese economy dry. It was thus largely the African liberation wars which prompted Spinola and a group of army officers to topple the Portuguese dictatorship in a military *coup d'état* in April 1974. This in turn led directly to military withdrawal from Africa and the independence of Angola and Mozambique in 1975.

Angola

The principal liberation movement in Angola was the MPLA (Movimento Popular de Libertação de Angola) founded by Agostino Neto among the urban working class of Luanda in December 1956. In early 1961, with most of the MPLA leaders in gaol awaiting trial, a revolt erupted among peasants objecting to compulsory cotton cultivation and forced-labour practices. The rising quickly spread to the urban poor of Luanda who tried storming the prison to release their leaders. The Portuguese police and armed forces reacted with predictable brutality, indiscriminately killing hundreds of Africans around Luanda. The rising spread to northern Angola under the direction of Holden Roberto's Bakongo-based FNLA (Frente Nacional Libertação de Angola).

It was the beginning of a lengthy and bitterly fought liberation war which only ended with Angolan independence in 1975. But the struggle was marred by the interference of foreign powers. Most of the guerrilla fighting was borne by the MPLA which, with its socialist programme for Angolan reform, managed to secure training and weapons from the Soviet Union. The FNLA, based in Zaïre (Congo), took little effective part in the struggle until the war was nearly won. Then, with Zaïrean and US backing, fighting was

Map 28.2   Independence in Angola, Mozambique and Zimbabwe

aimed against the Soviet-supported MPLA. Another late entry to the war was Jonas Savimbi's UNITA (União Nacional Para a Independência Total de Angola), based among the Ovimbundu of south-eastern Angola. Like the FNLA, UNITA was more concerned with fighting the MPLA than with fighting the Portuguese. In 1974 UNITA even formed an anti-MPLA alliance with the Portuguese. UNITA was heavily backed and supplied with weaponry by South Africa who sought to install it as an alternative government to the MPLA. The South Africans feared that an MPLA government in Angola would provide support for the SWAPO liberation movement that they themselves were fighting in Namibia.

As the Portuguese withdrew during 1975, Angola found itself in a state of civil war. The MPLA had secured the capital, Luanda, and had the widest level of support in the rural areas. In the crucial early months of 1975 the MPLA received a small assignment of weaponry from the tiny, newly independent state of Guinea-Bissau. It was more a sign of socialist solidarity from the PAIGC than a significant contribution to the struggle. Angolan independence was scheduled for November when Neto's MPLA expected to assume control. In an attempt to prevent this happening, the South African army invaded Angola from Namibia and pushed northwards towards Luanda. At the same time the United States equipped the FNLA for an invasion from the north. This was supported by the Zaïrean army, Portuguese irregulars and assorted white mercenaries. Neto went ahead and declared independence on behalf of the MPLA and hastily summoned the aid of 13,000 Soviet-equipped Cuban troops. These, together with MPLA forces (now the national army of Angola), managed to expel the South Africans and the FNLA and its allies by the early weeks of 1976. UNITA, meanwhile, was pushed back to its bases in the hilly south-eastern country of Moxico province.

Angola was now officially united and independent under an MPLA government. But Savimbi's UNITA continued through the 1980s to prove a thorn in its flesh as the South Africans and Americans continued to support their protégé with money and weapons and periodic South African invasions.

Figure 28.4 Portuguese soldiers talk with an Angolan man during a patrol on September 10, 1974 near Santa Eulalia. After independence, Angola was the scene of an intense civil war from 1975 to 2002, with the MPLA government opposing the FNLA and UNITA

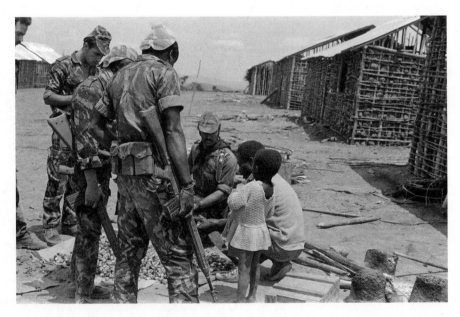

Mozambique	Mozambicans managed to unify their liberation movements in 1962 with the formation of FRELIMO (Frente de Libertaçao de Moçambique) in the Tanzanian capital of Dar-es-Salaam. They too had suffered the rude shock of Portuguese methods with the shooting of several hundred protesting peasants in northern Mozambique in June 1960. Eduardo Mondlane and his deputy, Samora Machel, led FRELIMO's struggle in Mozambique with an official declaration of war in September 1964.

As the war progressed, Mondlane and FRELIMO grew increasingly convinced of the need for a socialist transformation of the country. 'We are not replacing a foreign ruling class with a Mozambican one,' wrote Mondlane. 'Our movement must be a revolution.' The mass of the peasantry were to be the base of that revolution. Like PAIGC in Guinea-Bissau, FRELIMO set up alternative local government in the liberated zones of Mozambique. But tragically, also like PAIGC, FRELIMO lost its inspirational leader, Mondlane, to an assassin's bomb in February 1969. It was left to Samora Machel to take up the leadership of the liberation movement and lead FRELIMO to victory and Mozambique to independence in 1975.

The struggle for freedom in southern Africa

South Africa in the post-war era	As we have seen so far in this and the previous chapter, wherever there have been colonies of substantial white settlement in Africa, those colonists have done all in their power to resist moves towards African majority rule. Not surprisingly, in South Africa, the country with the largest population of white settlers, resistance to African majority rule was firmest. By the 1970s South Africa had a population of four million whites who ruled over and dominated a population of up to 20 million blacks. (The country contained two million people of mixed-race and Asian origin.) South Africa, however, was not, strictly speaking, a colony in the same sense as the other colonies of Africa. Since 1910 the Union of South Africa had internal self-government, though the nominal head of state was (until 1961) still the British monarch. But it was self-government by and for the white minority. The small number of black people who had the vote were deprived of that right in 1936. In no sense would any European decolonisation bring African independence to South Africa. African majority rule in South Africa would have to be achieved through the internal efforts of South Africans themselves. It was this which South Africa's whites were determined to resist.

The white people of South Africa were helped by the fact that their country was economically the most powerful in the continent. That strength originated from the mineral revolution of the 1870s and 1880s (see pp. 328–32). During the Second World War South Africa's industrial base was broadened by the rapid development of manufacturing industry. Deprived of wartime imports from Europe, South Africa manufactured her own consumer goods. South African industry was helped by British wartime needs for ship repairs and supplies from South African ports. South African industrial growth during 1940–5 provided important new job opportunities for blacks. Driven off their land in the rural areas (see pp. 376–7), blacks poured into the towns in search of wage employment.

In the years after the war the Afrikaner National Party played on white fears that blacks, left uncontrolled, would soon come to dominate the urban

Map 28.3 Southern Africa: independence and resistance

areas and the growing industrial economy. Then the movement for black freedom, which was gathering pace across the continent, would be impossible to stop, even in South Africa. Playing on white fears with blatant racist propaganda, the National Party won an overall majority in the whites-only general election of 1948.

The development of the **apartheid** *state*

The National Party government reinforced the segregationist system developed over the previous 50 years. It introduced a series of laws to establish a more clear-cut racist system designed to guarantee permanent white domination in South Africa. It was called *'apartheid'*. meaning, literally 'separateness'. The ultimate aim of *apartheid*, as developed during the 1950s, was to make blacks 'foreigners' in the 86 per cent of South Africa which was officially designated 'white'. Blacks were to be restricted to the poverty-stricken and overcrowded 'reserves' (later designated 'homelands') unless they were in the direct employ of whites.

The *Population Registration Act* (1950) classified people according to race, dividing them basically into white and 'non-white'. Under the old imperial principle of 'divide and rule', 'non-whites' were subdivided into 'coloured' (mixed-race), Indians (descendants of contract labourers brought to the sugar plantations of Natal in the nineteenth century) and 'Bantu' (the majority black population). The latter were in turn even further subdivided into various ethnic groups: Zulu, Xhosa, Tswana, Venda, Sotho and so on. It was a deliberate attempt to weaken African unity and destroy any countrywide sense of African nationalism. The *Group Areas Act* (1950) determined the places where the various races could live. These two Acts formed the cornerstone of the *apartheid* system. A wide range of further *apartheid* laws affected every aspect of South African social life, banning sexual relations between the races and segregating public places, buses, schools. Basically, however, it was an economic system, designed to restrict blacks to the position of a permanently subordinate, low-paid working class.

All African trades union activity was banned, thus enabling white employers to enforce very low wage levels. In contrast, white workers, whether skilled or unskilled, received wages which were ten times or more those of blacks. One of the most hated features of the *apartheid* system was the *Bantu Education Act* (1953). This withdrew black education from control of the missionaries. It forced blacks into government schools to study syllabuses which were designed to emphasise ethnic differences and to teach them only the bare skills needed to work for whites.

African protest and resistance to **apartheid**

The introduction of new, harshly racist legislation provided new stimulus to African protest and resistance in South Africa. There was a wave of resistance to new pass laws, agricultural restrictions and 'Bantu Authorities' in the rural areas, as well as a number of spontaneous strikes, boycotts and demonstrations in the towns. The ANC (see p. 359) was boosted by the leadership of a new generation of young, educated Africans, among them Johannesburg lawyers Nelson Mandela and Oliver Tambo and trade-unionist Walter Sisulu.

During 1952 the ANC staged a 'Defiance Campaign', deliberately defying *apartheid*'s segregationist laws and refusing to carry passes. By January 1953 thousands of their members had been arrested and the campaign fizzled out. In 1955 at a large public meeting south of Johannesburg the ANC joined with Indian, 'coloured' and radical white political groups in forming the 'Congress Alliance' and adopting the 'Freedom Charter' – a blueprint for creating a new, non-racist and partially socialist South Africa. The government, meanwhile, used harsh new laws to suppress all opposition, declaring it to be 'communist' and directed by the Soviet Union. In 1956, 156 Congress Alliance members were put on trial for treason, but the prosecution failed to prove that the Freedom Charter was a treasonable document and all the accused were eventually acquitted. By then a split had occurred in the ranks of the ANC. There were those who felt that African freedom would only be achieved by a purely African movement. They resented the influence which they felt that white liberals and black and white members of the South African Communist Party exercised on the leadership of the ANC, and in particular on the Freedom Charter. In 1958–9 the 'Africanists' broke away from the ANC to form the Pan-Africanist Congress (PAC) under the leadership of Robert Sobukwe.

1960, the 'Year of Africa', dawned in South Africa with none of the signs of impending liberation being experienced by Africans over so much of the rest of the continent. The executives of ANC and PAC were determined to push things forward with a year of massive peaceful protest in South Africa. But they had not reckoned on the response of the police. At Sharpeville, south of Johannesburg, on 21 March 1960, police opened fire on unarmed demonstrators, killing 69 and wounding 180, most of them shot in the back as they fled.

The Sharpeville massacre marked a new phase in the struggle for freedom in South Africa. Fearing revolution, the government swiftly banned the ANC and PAC, and thousands of their members were arrested. The South African government received worldwide condemnation. Newly independent African and Asian states at the United Nations called for economic sanctions to be

Figure 28.5 The Sharpeville massacre, 21 March 1960, marked a turning point in the political history of southern Africa; for while it temporarily halted the peaceful march of political freedom in South Africa, it hastened the decolonisation of South Africa's neighbours, Botswana, Lesotho and Swaziland

imposed against South Africa, though this was vetoed by South Africa's main trading partners, Britain and the United States. The prestigious Nobel Prize for Peace (1961) was awarded to Albert Luthuli, president of the now-banned ANC. But the South African government defied international condemnation, withdrew from the Commonwealth and declared itself a republic.

Pushed underground, the ANC executive reluctantly admitted the need for armed resistance. It formed an armed wing of the party, Umkhonto we Sizwe (MK) ('Spear of the Nation'), and sent Oliver Tambo into exile to organise support. In 1963, after several successful sabotage attacks, the high command of Umkhonto was captured on a farm in the northern suburbs of Johannesburg. In the trial that followed Nelson Mandela read a statement to the court, tracing the ANC's long but fruitless history of non-violent protest. He concluded in the now famous words:

> During my lifetime I have dedicated myself to this struggle of the African people. I have fought against white domination, and I have fought against black domination. I have cherished the ideal of a democratic and free society in which all persons live together in harmony and with equal opportunities. It is an ideal which I hope to live for and to achieve. But if needs be, it is an ideal for which I am prepared to die.

Mandela, Sisulu, Govan Mbeki and six others were sentenced to life imprisonment.

The struggle continues

Confident that it had averted black revolution by brutally suppressing all opposition in the early 1960s (see above), the South African government pressed ahead with its *apartheid* policies.

Resistance re-emerged in the early 1970s in the form of widespread, spontaneous strikes for higher pay by black workers, especially in Natal. The success of early strike action led to further strikes until the government was forced to legalise limited black trades unionism. Simultaneously, there developed amongst black students a new 'Africanist' movement known as 'Black Consciousness'. Like the *Négritude* movement in French colonial west Africa (pp. 375–6), the aim of Black Consciousness was to restore black self-respect. It re-awoke black determination to achieve their own liberation without the help of white liberals and others.

Black school students had long chafed against the inferior quality of black education, which received barely one-tenth of the level of funding spent on education of the white minority. On 16 June 1976 police opened fire on a peaceful demonstration by 15,000 school children in the Johannesburg suburb of Soweto. It was the spark that set off a fire of revolt right across the country. Rioting, school boycotts and police oppression followed for much of 1976–7 leaving at least 600 dead and countless thousands wounded or imprisoned. Among those beaten to death in police custody was the Black Consciousness leader Steve Biko.

In the early 1980s, black protesters in the townships of the eastern Cape and the Transvaal effectively boycotted white-owned shops and businesses, schools and municipal housing rents. The government responded by setting up black-run township councils in the belief that they would be more effective in controlling the townships and collecting rents. But these were quickly discredited as government stooges, and as such became targets for the people's anger. Radically minded, unemployed and out-of-school youths – self-styled 'comrades' – set up alternative 'civic associations' in the townships. They established their own people's courts to try known petty criminals as well as to enforce the boycotts and condemn police spies.

By July 1985 the townships had become ungovernable and President P. W. Botha declared a 'State of Emergency' in selected townships around the country. Hundreds died and thousands were detained in the security clampdown that followed. At the same time the security forces encouraged conservative blacks – mostly migrant-worker hostel-dwellers, who were fearful of the revolutionary youth – to act as vigilantes to break the township boycotts and the power of the radical comrades. From September 1985 bands of vigilantes attacked and burned the homes and squatter camps that housed known sympathisers of the boycotts while the security forces looked on.

Meanwhile the international news media relayed television coverage of the conflict in the townships, in particular the ruthless way the security forces fired live ammunition into crowds of unarmed demonstrators. It was clear that the South African government's much vaunted 'reforms' were meaningless to the black majority and the level of state violence was unacceptable to world opinion. Western governments, which had hitherto paid little serious heed to the iniquities of *apartheid*, could no longer justify their old position. Foreign capital began to flee the country and between August and November 1985 South Africa's currency, the rand, fell to a third of its 1984 value.

At about the same time a number of prominent white businessmen travelled north to the Zambian capital, Lusaka, to meet the ANC in exile. This was followed in 1986 by further visits from South African politicians and academics, mostly Afrikaners. Clearly the government of the Afrikaner National Party was rapidly losing credibility, even among its own supporters. But it still would not recognise the fact and responded by extending the State of Emergency to the whole country in 1986, combined with widespread banning and detentions through 1987. For the South African state, however, it was Namibia that proved to be the final straw that broke the camel's proverbial back.

Namibian independence

Namibia had been occupied and ruled by South Africa ever since the South African army had conquered the German colonists in 1915 during the First World War. From 1919 the country became a League of Nations' Trust territory, with the Mandate to rule being officially granted to Britain, who transferred the role to its Dominion, South Africa. When, following the Second World War the Trust was handed to the League's successor, the United Nations, the South African government refused to honour the terms of the Trust and prepare the country for independence. It treated the largely-desert territory of Namibia ('South West Africa') as a fifth province of South Africa and applied to her peoples all the oppressive legislation of *apartheid*.

In 1960 the South West Africa Peoples' Organisation (SWAPO) began its long campaign of guerrilla activity against the occupying forces of South Africa. We have already seen the lengths to which South Africa was prepared to go to cut off support for SWAPO in the emerging independent republic of Angola (see above, p. 424). Meanwhile, as South African occupation of Namibia continued in defiance of UN resolutions, South African-based mining companies systematically stripped the country of its vast natural mineral resources, including diamonds, copper, uranium and many other valuable minerals. Clearly a future independent Namibia would inherit greatly depleted mineral reserves.

By the late 1980s the situation was reaching a crisis. For years the South Africans had fought SWAPO, the Angolan MPLA government and their Cuban allies in the southern Angolan bush. A major South African invasion of southern Angola in 1987 was related to the government's need to convince its white electorate that it was taking the security war to the real enemy, the foreign black 'communist hordes' of its propaganda imagination. By this time, however, the Cuban-trained Angolan airforce had gained command of the skies above southern Angola and by mid-1988 the South African invasion force was cut off and trapped at Cuito Cuanavale. The South African government was finally forced to the negotiating table and, with American mediation, it agreed to end its long-term illegal occupation of Namibia in exchange for the evacuation of its troops from Cuito Cuanavale and the phased withdrawal of Cuban troops from Angola. Once accepted, this led

Figure 28.6 Frontline leaders at a conference on Namibia held in Lusaka, 1980: left to right, Sam Nujoma leader of South West Africa People's Organisation (SWAPO), President K. Kaunda of Zambia, President Samora Machal of Mozambique, President Julius Nyerere of Tanzania, Prime Minister R. Mugabe of Zimbabwe, President Jose Eduardo dos Santos of Angola. The other key Frontline President, Seretse Khama of Botswana, was too ill to attend the conference: he died a month later

fairly quickly to free elections in Namibia, won by SWAPO in 1989, and Namibian independence under President Sam Nujoma on the 21 March 1990, the thirtieth anniversary of the Sharpeville massacre.

South Africa's liberation elections

In 1989 President P. W. Botha suffered a stroke and was forced to retire. F. W. de Klerk took over as president and leader of the National Party. Though formerly a hard-liner in the Cabinet, de Klerk was forced by the realities of power into a reassessment of the whole situation. He took the bold step of repealing the Population Registration and Group Areas Acts, lifting the state of emergency, unbanning the ANC, the PAC and other political parties, and releasing a number of prominent political prisoners. On 11 February 1990 the most important political prisoner of them all, Nelson Mandela, was finally set free after 27 years in prison.

There followed four long years of intensive and dramatic negotiations between the various political parties, principally Mandela's ANC and de Klerk's National Party government, as they thrashed out the guiding principles for a future constitution. Negotiations were played out against a background of rising violence in the country. Thousands lost their lives as rival political forces sought to fill the power vacuum being created by the weakness of transitional government. Old hostilities between hostel-dwellers and township residents in the Transvaal and the Cape were stoked by elements in the security forces who still regarded the ANC as the old communist enemy. Similarly, in Natal the Kwa-Zulu Chief Minister, Mangosuthu Buthelezi, with support from right-wing elements in the security forces, used his Inkatha Freedom Party as a vigilante force to curtail the influence and support of the ANC among the Zulus of Natal. Meanwhile, right-wing Afrikaners rumbled in the wings with threats of armed revolt and vague calls for an independent Afrikaner homeland.

In spite of the persistent violence, an agreement was eventually reached. South Africa's first non-racial election was held over four days in April 1994. The ANC won 63 per cent of the vote and on 10 May 1994 Nelson Mandela

Figure 28.7 In one of the crowning events of twentieth-century Africa, South Africans of all races queued for many hours at polling stations across the country for the right to cast their vote in the country's first non-racial national election, spread over four days, 26–29 April, 1994

was sworn in as president to head an ANC-dominated 'government of national unity', with two vice-presidents: Thabo Mbeki and F. W. de Klerk.

Botswana, Lesotho and Swaziland

When the Union of South Africa was formed in 1910, it was assumed by British and South African governments that the British Protectorates of Bechuanaland, Basutoland and Swaziland would in due course be joined to the Union. Bechuanaland and Basutoland were regarded as little more than labour reserves for the expanding industrial development of South Africa, while more than half the land in Swaziland was owned by white South Africans. In all three countries colonial officials relied upon traditional chiefly authorities to run much of the local administration, including the collection of taxation.

The emerging political crisis of the 1950s in South Africa undoubtedly had an influence upon local demands for more democratic accountability in the 'High Commission Territories'. This could be interpreted as a criticism of the abuse of chiefly power as much as a criticism of colonial over-rule. Despite the hardening of *apartheid*, however, British colonial authorities still saw the political future of Bechuanaland, Basutoland and Swaziland as falling within some sort of union with South Africa. It was not until the Sharpeville crisis of March 1960 that all notion of future amalgamation with South Africa was finally abandoned. Britain then allowed the development of African political parties and began the process of constitutional reform that would lead to independence.

The people of Bechuanaland were used to the concept of accountable government through their traditional *kgotla* system, whereby a chief was accountable to his people, so they found no problem with the form of representative parliamentary government put forward by the British. The transition to independence was eased by the fact that the largest political party was led by Seretse Khama, the uncrowned king of the largest Batswana group. He became President of the Republic of Botswana in 1966.

In Basutoland the multiplicity of chiefs were eager not to lose power through the emergence of political parties and they formed their own party to appeal to traditionalist values. There was plenty of tension between chiefs and commoners (mostly trades unionists radicalised by experience in South Africa) in the run-up to independence. After a closely fought election, the party of Chief Leabua Jonathan emerged the victor, he became prime minister, and at independence in 1966 the Paramount Chief became King Moshoeshoe II of the independent Kingdom of Lesotho.

In Swaziland King Sobhuza II had remained a dominant force, with British support, throughout the colonial period. With the approach of independence in the early 1960s, Sobhuza formed his own political party to counteract the emergence of any alternative political force. Through the traditional patronage of district chiefs, Sobhuza's party swept the board at the independence elections and he himself, in effect, became executive head of state of the independent kingdom of Swaziland in 1968.

chapter 29

Africa since independence (1)

The problems that Africans and their governments have had to face since independence have, very largely, been the product of their history. This is not to suggest that the misdirection, corruption or incompetence of some African leaders or even ecological factors have not been partly to blame for Africa's continuing underdevelopment. But the roots of many of Africa's recurrent problems in the final decades of the twentieth century and the early years of the twenty-first are to be found in the period of colonial rule of the previous eighty years or more.

The political legacy of colonial rule

It was only on the eve of independence that Europeans had imposed upon Africa their own systems of parliamentary democracy with all its inappropriate European ceremony and formality. By then Europeans preferred to overlook the point that colonial rule had been largely established and sustained in Africa by brutal military conquest. The real political legacy of colonial government in Africa was that of an alien dictatorship, benevolent at times, but always prepared to crush outspoken opposition. Many of Africa's independence leaders had suffered periods of detention without trial for daring to speak out against the unjust and arbitrary nature of colonial authority.

The boundaries of the countries themselves were mostly totally artificial. They had been created at the whim of European politicians with little or no regard for Africa's multitude of pre-colonial nation-states and small-scale village communities. Peoples of widely differing languages and political and cultural traditions had been cobbled together for European convenience. The widespread colonial use of 'indirect rule' (see pp. 367–70) further served to emphasise the differences. These people were now suddenly expected to feel at ease with systems of multi-party parliamentary democracy that had only evolved in the nation-states of Europe after centuries of conflict.

The artificiality of Africa's national boundaries caused serious problems of 'national' unity after independence. African politicians may have been united in their anti-colonial sentiments, but they were yet to think of themselves as part of a single nation. Zambia's often-repeated political slogan, 'One Zambia, One Nation', was not so much the expression of a sense of national pride as a desire by the ruling party to *create* a sense of nationhood among the multitude of Zambia's differing language groups. And citizens of, for instance, the colonially created state of Nigeria were in their own minds

Map 29.1 The modern countries of Africa

primarily Yoruba, Igbo, Hausa or whatever, rather than 'Nigerians'. Countries with a single dominant party headed by an inspiring national leader such as Senegal under Senghor or Tanzania under Nyerere were not so plagued by problems of national unity. But for most African countries with multi-party systems at independence, political parties were based more upon the personal ethnic or regional origins of particular politicians than upon differing economic ideologies to guide the country's future development.

The dual legacy of authoritarian rule and artificial nation-states was to bedevil political stability on the continent in the early years of African independence. We have already seen in the previous chapter the chaos that it brought to the Congo in the early 1960s. Most newly independent African states were plagued to a greater or lesser extent by some form of 'regionalism'. In Nigeria it culminated in an attempt by the Igbo of the south-east to secede as the 'Republic of Biafra' in 1967. There followed a harrowing two-and-a-half years of bitter civil war before national reconciliation could be achieved in Nigeria.

But why were Africa's independence rulers so determined to uphold the boundaries of the artificially created nation-states which they had inherited from the period of colonial rule? The basic reason was summed up in a few short words by the military ruler of Nigeria, General Gowon, when addressing the Nigerian people in his hour of victory over the 'Biafran rebels':

> Our objective [in crushing the rebellion] was ... to maintain the territorial integrity of our nation, *to assert the ability of the Black man to build a strong, progressive and prosperous modern nation, and to ensure respect, dignity and equality in the community of nations for our prosperity.* We welcome with open arms ... all those who were led into futile attempts to disintegrate the country. Long live one united Nigeria.
>
> (Quoted in R. Oliver and A. Atmore, *Africa since 1800,* third edition, CUP, Cambridge, 1981, p. 338) (my italics)

Subsequent attempts to reconcile Nigeria's rival regional interests resulted in a federal constitution with a multiplicity of regional states. In Chad and Sudan regional disputes have been fuelled by mutual distrust between Muslim and non-Muslim and have flared into incessant civil war. But the vast majority of African governments have succeeded in holding their sometimes fragile states together.

One-party states

Most of Africa's ruling politicians quickly rejected the multi-party parliamentary system as unworkable. They pleaded the particular circumstances of their country's crying need for national unity in order to achieve rapid social and economic development. Within a few years of independence most African governments had established some form of 'one-party state'. Among those countries that became independent in the 1960s only Botswana and Mauritius, both with a low population of about one million people, had maintained an unbroken record of multi-party parliamentary democracy since independence. The argument in favour of a one-party system was that parliamentary opposition based upon regional ethnic interests was destructive rather than constructive opposition. Democratic choice, it was argued, could just as easily be exercised within a single-party system.

In some one-party states, such as Tanzania and Zambia, elections showed that unpopular government ministers could indeed be voted out of office. But an awful lot depended upon the political integrity of the party leader and his ability to control the enthusiasms of local party members. More commonly the one-party system led to an abuse of state power. In countries such as Nkrumah's Ghana, Banda's Malawi or most of the former French colonies, the one-party system was used to give the ruling party dictatorial powers in suppressing any criticism of the government. Many worthy critics of one-party governments found themselves imprisoned without trial or forced into exile in fear for their lives. Regional rebellion or military *coup d'état* was often seen as the only means of overthrowing an incompetent or unpopular government. The role of the military in African politics will be considered later in the chapter. It is worth observing here that a number of the broadly-based, one-party states under widely respected leaders survived without military intervention. Notable among them were Senegal under Senghor, Côte d'Ivoire under Houphouët-Boigny, Kenya under Kenyatta, Tanzania under Nyerere and Zambia under Kaunda. Senghor went on to introduce a modified form of multi-party rule in Senegal in 1975 while Kenya and Tanzania witnessed peaceful transitions to new civilian presidents on the death of Kenyatta in 1978 and the retirement of Nyerere in 1986. The rebirth of multi-party politics in the 1990s will be considered further in the final two chapters.

The economic legacy of underdevelopment and dependency

European colonial governments left Africa with a mounting economic crisis that had been the end-product of 80 years of colonial misrule. The African economies, such as they were, had been directed towards exporting cheap agricultural raw materials and unprocessed minerals to Europe and in return importing relatively expensive manufactured goods (see Chapters 23 and 24). There had been little or no attempt to develop African economic self-sufficiency, for that would have defeated the purpose of Europe's possessing colonies. Not only the nature of the products, but also the 'terms of trade' were determined by Europe at the expense of African interests. Prices for Africa's export commodities were controlled in the so-called 'developed economies' of Europe and north America. Thus in times of European depression Africa was paid less for her exports, and in times of European inflation Africans had to pay more for their imports. Each year more and more African effort had to be turned to producing cash crops for the European market in order to import the same amount of manufactured goods. As a result of these 'adverse terms of trade', Africa was a net exporter of wealth to Europe and north America.

At the same time, as more effort was put into cash-crop production and labouring in the mines, subsistence cultivation for Africa's basic food was neglected. By the 1950s Africa had become a net importer of food. In other words Africans on average were growing less than half of their own food needs. The crisis was heightened by the growing level of urban unemployment. From the late 1940s and early 1950s more and more people migrated to the towns in a desperate attempt to escape increasing rural poverty or forced-cropping and forced-labour schemes.

Another poor legacy from the colonial period was Africa's transport systems which were totally inadequate for the continent's internal development. Most of the railways had been built around the turn of the century to ease the export of the continent's wealth to Europe. By independence they were badly in need of repair and simply linked a country's mines or main source of cash crops to the sea; for instance, Senegal and Mali's groundnuts and cotton, Ghana's gold, Nigeria's tin and groundnuts, Uganda's cotton, and the Congo's and Zambia's copper. Roads were poorly developed and most of Africa's road and rail networks showed no concern for a country's internal development. Furthermore, there were virtually no regional road or rail links to help promote trade between one African country and another, unless as a route from a land-locked country to the sea. Telecommunications were the

MEDITERRANEAN

MOROCCO
TUNISIA
WESTERN SAHARA
ALGERIA
LIBYA
EGYPT
Aswan Dam
Tropic of Cancer

MAURITANIA
MALI
NIGER
CHAD
SUDAN
ERITREA

SENEGAL
THE GAMBIA
GUINEA-BISSAU
GUINEA
SIERRA LEONE
LIBERIA
BURKINA FASSO
Volta
Akosombo Dam
CÔTE D'IVOIRE
GHANA
TOGO
BENIN
NIGERIA
Kainji Dam
Niger
Lake Chad
CENTRAL AFRICAN REPUBLIC
ETHIOPIA
SOMALIA
Equator

EQUATORIAL GUINEA
CAMEROON
GABON
CONGO
Inga Dam
CONGO/ZAIRE
Congo River
UGANDA
Owen Falls Dam
KENYA
Lake Victoria Nyanza
TANZANIA
White Nile
Blue Nile

ATLANTIC OCEAN

ANGOLA
Zambezi
ZAMBIA
Kafue
Cabora Bassa Dam
Kariba Dam
ZIMBABWE
MOZAMBIQUE
Tropic of Capricorn

NAMIBIA
BOTSWANA
SWAZILAND
LESOTHO
Vaal Dam
Orange River
SOUTH AFRICA
INDIAN OCEAN

Key: sources of Africa's major mineral exports

Al = Bauxite (Aluminium)
As = Asbestos
Au = Gold
C = Diamonds
Ch = Coal
Cr = Chrome
Cu = Copper
Fe = Iron
Mn = Manganese
P = Petroleum oil
Ph = Phosphates
Po = Potash
Pt = Platinum
Sn = Tin
U = Uranium
Zn = Zinc

Principal cash crops

Coffee
Cocoa   Tobacco
Palm oil   Groundnuts
Cotton   Fruit and wine

0   400   800   1200   Kilometres

N

Map 29.2 The main features of Africa's export economies, showing principal sources of the major minerals and cash crops

437

same. Internal rural networks were almost non-existent, and it was easier to telephone from Africa to Europe than it was to telephone from one African capital to that of a neighbouring country.

African governments inherited two particularly repressive economic policies from their colonial predecessors: the poll tax and agricultural marketing boards. The former was charged on all adult males regardless of income. The latter paid fixed low prices to farmers, while selling their produce for higher prices abroad and keeping the difference as government revenue. Both repressive policies provided such important sources of government income that they were initially retained in many countries after independence.

The lack of education was a further debilitating legacy of the colonial period. Across most of tropical Africa barely 10 per cent of the population was literate at independence.

The early drive for economic development

Around the time of independence there was a temporary boom in the world prices paid for Africa's principal mineral and agricultural exports. This factor initially disguised the full extent of the colonially created economic crisis. The continent's new inexperienced rulers had high expectations of what could be achieved with political independence. But their dreams were soon shattered as the depth of the underlying economic crisis became apparent. To make matters worse, the new rulers of independent Africa made the initial mistake of modelling their development programmes upon the industrialised economies of western Europe and north America. In this they were strongly advised by European economic 'experts'. The theory was simple: Europe was 'developed': Africa was 'underdeveloped'. Therefore, to rectify the problem, Africa must copy the European model of urban-centred industrialisation. African leaders accepted the model because they saw rapid industrialisation as the means to achieve economic self-sufficiency. If African countries industrialised, then they could manufacture their own consumer goods, which up until then had been imported from Europe. This, in due course, would shift the 'adverse terms of trade' in Africa's favour and so halt the drain of African wealth to the already 'developed' world. But it did not work out like that.

On the one hand, early schemes for industrialisation were far too ambitious and often inappropriate for the needs and resources of the country. On the other hand, Africans had to import all the expertise, technology, machinery and building materials from Europe and north America. The same applied to the improved health, education and transport facilities which Africa's new leaders were determined to provide for their people.

Within a very few years African governments had run up huge new debts with the 'developed' world. The result was the need for ever-greater exports of cash crops and minerals to finance the debts. The old colonial trading pattern was continued, and the adverse terms of trade got worse. The industries set up with European and American capital and expertise were those which suited Europe and America rather than Africa. The history of the Ghanaian Valco Aluminium Company clearly illustrates the problem. The Ghanaian government provided it with very cheap electricity in the belief that it would use its factory to process Ghana's own bauxite (aluminium ore). But the American company which controlled Valco used its Ghanaian factory to process its own bauxite which it transported to Ghana from Jamaica. When in the early 1980s the price of electricity to Valco was increased to nearer its real cost level, the factory closed down.

Even where African governments partially or wholly nationalised mining companies, as many did, the marketing and prices paid for exports were still controlled from the financial centres of the 'developed' world. The Ghanaian leader Nkrumah coined the term 'neo-colonialism' to describe Europe's continuing economic control over politically independent Africa.

The French in particular maintained close control over the economies of their former tropical African colonies, with the exception of Guinea which had voted '*Non*' to de Gaulle in 1958 (see p. 395). The other French-speaking countries remained part of the financial French franc zone. While this made it easier for them to attract outside investment, it tied their trading priorities to the former 'mother-country'. This was particularly important to France, to whom Africa was a major source of vital minerals such as uranium for nuclear fuel from Gabon and Niger, phosphates from Mauritania and potash from the People's Republic of Congo. Important to France also were Africa's cotton from the Sahel, timber from the tropical forests of Gabon and Côte d'Ivoire, and the tropical fruits and vegetable oils of Côte d'Ivoire and Senegal. France, as the major aid donor and source of loans for these countries, exercised considerable control over development projects. These were thus geared towards the continued export of raw materials to France. A number of Francophone African governments provided France with important military bases and the French government was not beyond intervening directly where it decided French interests were at stake. French troops, for instance, played a direct role in propping up pro-French regimes in Zaïre, Gabon and Chad. And in a surprising about face, French troops helped oust the notorious regime of self-styled 'emperor' Jean-Bedel Bokassa from the Central African Republic.

By the mid-1960s it was becoming clear that independent Africa had, in the words of a French economist, made a 'false start'. The governments of those countries that had achieved independence around 1960, especially in west Africa, had spent lavishly upon expensive industrial and prestige projects with insufficient concern for their appropriateness. Ghana's Akosombo Dam was a case in point. This huge hydroelectric project saddled Ghana with a crippling international debt and in the short term provided little practical advantage for the majority of Ghanaian people. For various reasons, much of it to do with failures in central government's long-term planning and the inappropriateness of European 'expert' advice, Ghana's anticipated industrial revolution failed to take off. Nevertheless, despite the debt and some technical difficulties with power generation and the falling levels of Akosombo Lake in times of drought, Nkrumah's long-term vision did to some extent pay off. It made possible the widespread electrification of Ghana's rural towns in the 1990s.

Meanwhile, the Ghanaian government had failed to encourage investment in the country's former great economic success story, cocoa farming. By the 1970s Ghana's ageing cocoa trees were past their most productive. Virtually no new trees had been planted since independence and the government had failed to encourage the country's young to seek a future in the cocoa industry. Thus Ghana was unable to achieve economic recovery during the boom in cocoa prices which so benefited her neighbour, Côte d'Ivoire, in the late 1970s.

Figure 29.1 Ghana's Akosombo Dam. Intended to provide electricity for Ghana's industrial revolution, the dam and power station (bottom left of picture) was opened by President Nkrumah in February 1966, in what turned out to be his last official duty before he was overthrown in a coup. The lake created behind the dam was at the time the largest man-made lake in the world

At independence the vast majority of Africa's population was still based in the rural areas, dependent at least partially upon subsistence farming. But governments, dominated by an educated urban elite, often scorned the rural peasant as backward and unproductive. And yet they themselves failed to invest surplus government funds or expensive foreign loans in that one sector of the population which in the past had ensured some level of economic self-sufficiency. On the contrary, they maintained the restrictive agricultural marketing boards which they had inherited from colonial regimes. These continued to ensure that small-scale peasant farmers who produced a food surplus received little reward for their product. The example of Zambia amply illustrates the trend.

The independent state of Zambia had been born in 1964 with, in the later words of President Kaunda, 'a copper spoon in its mouth'. With soaring copper prices from the 1950s through to 1973, Zambia at independence had huge reserves of foreign exchange. But this was at the expense of an over-reliance upon the single industry of copper mining. Copper in 1970 accounted for 92 per cent of foreign earnings and 53 per cent of total government income. Zambia spent lavishly upon free education and health and a whole range of prestige urban building projects. But there was little effort to diversify the economy and no effective investment in peasant food cultivation. In fact, the retention from colonial times of government-controlled marketing boards actually stifled peasant farming initiatives. The civil service boomed and the rapid expansion of non-technical education drained people away from life in the rural areas. Almost without realising it, Zambia – a huge, formerly self-sufficient, agricultural country with low population – quickly became a net importer of food. In 1970 the Zambian government nationalised the copper-mines, paying the multinational mining companies a large part of the country's foreign exchange reserves for a 51 per cent stake in the industry. Kaunda and his colleagues believed it was in the interests of national security for the government, and hence in theory the people, of Zambia to gain control over the nation's principal industrial resource. Soon after that had been achieved, however, in 1973, Chile broke away from the international copper marketing cartel and the world price of copper collapsed. Combined with the effects of the oil price rises of the same year and of economic sanctions against its former close trading partner, 'Southern Rhodesia', this set Zambia on a spiral of decline and indebtedness from which, in the new Millennium, it is only just beginning to recover.

Meanwhile, in much of tropical west Africa, it was plain for all to see that corruption within government had become widespread. While the majority rural population remained relatively poor and urban unemployment continued to rise, government ministers, civil servants and other branches of the minority educated elite were becoming increasingly wealthy. Indeed, it has been argued within some African countries that the educated elite of the post-independence era had, in practice, done little more than replace white colonial rulers with black 'colonial' rulers!

The apparent inability of many of Africa's new political masters to do much beyond enrich themselves coincided in the mid-1960s with a dramatic fall in world commodity prices for Africa's principal agricultural exports. Manufactured imports, upon which Africa had become so dependent, thus became relatively much more expensive. Many countries now had to cut back on imports, no matter how much they needed them. Inflation rose rapidly and there were shortages of goods in the shops. Everybody but the politicians seemed to be getting worse and worse off. Was this the development and prosperity which politicians had promised at independence? With parliamentary opposition already largely suppressed, the spate of military takeovers which swept western and central Africa in the mid-1960s was, in the circumstances, hardly very surprising.

The role of the military in African politics

Most of the French-speaking states, with the notable exceptions of Guinea, Senegal and Côte d'Ivoire, went over to military rule during the 1960s. Togo and Dahomey (renamed Benin in 1974) suffered frequent military coups and counter-coups. From November 1965 coup followed coup with frightening regularity, taking in Nigeria and Ghana in early 1966. By the early 1970s military rule had become a serious African political option. It remained the most frequent means for change of government through the 1970s and 1980s.

As a serious political option, a number of interesting features can be observed about Africa's military regimes. Firstly, it should be remembered that the military had often played a powerful role in the politics of the major pre-colonial states. Secondly, the armies inherited at independence had generally been founded originally as part of the process of initial colonial conquest. And, apart from the two world wars, Africa's armies in the colonial period had mainly been held in reserve for internal use against potential rebellious subjects rather than for defence of the country against potential hostile neighbours. At independence they had little initial role to play beyond being part of the trappings of an independent nation-state. An interesting exception was the Seychelles, where there had been no army at all at independence. Prime Minister René staged his coup in 1976 with only a handful of colleagues who seized the police armoury. It was only *after* the coup that Seychelles needed an army, to defend itself from potential counter-coups!

In general in the 1960s, military *coups d'état* were reactions against inefficient and corrupt civilian regimes. As such most coups against civilian regimes were initially welcomed. At least until they got into power, the military were known to be well-disciplined and usually free of corruption. A couple of examples must suffice to show the trend.

In Nigeria the widespread belief that the elections of 1964–5 had been rigged finally destroyed the credibility of civilian government. But the first army coup of January 1966 was followed by another in July, amid fears of ethnic domination by Igbo south-easterners or Hausa northerners. The massacre of 20,000 Igbo living in the northern region led directly to the 'Biafran' secession and subsequent civil war of 1967–70. It was thus General Gowon, who had seized power in the counter-coup of July 1966, who steered Nigeria through the consequences of its political inheritance, which squabbling multi-party civilian politicians had done nothing to improve.

Though Gowon achieved a remarkable level of post-war reconciliation, during the early 1970s his government grew increasingly inefficient and divorced from the needs of the country. This led to his overthrow by General Murtala Muhammed in July 1975. Muhammed restored moral authority to the government. He embarked on a series of reforms of the administration and set a timetable for a return to civilian rule in 1979. At the same time he began to tackle the corruption and inefficiency which had led to the crippling backlog of cargo ships in the port of Lagos. The vulnerability of African governments to military intervention was starkly revealed, however, when this popular and widely respected military leader was assassinated by a group of envious middle-ranking officers in February 1976. Their attempted coup was in fact foiled and General Obasanjo took over. He continued Murtala Mohammed's reforming policies and returned the country to civilian rule in 1979.

The Nigerian civilian government of 1979–83 was the time of greatest freedom in Nigerian history in terms of the press and toleration of official opposition. But it was also the time of greatest freedom for systematic state corruption, the enrichment of politicians and the wasting of Nigeria's huge new oil revenues. Within a few years the personal greed displayed by individuals in civilian authority crippled what should have been a thriving Nigerian economy. Once again, the return of the military in 1983 was initially welcomed as a restoration of moral authority and discipline in public life. This time, however, an increasingly corrupt and unpopular military was to remain in power through a succession of rulers until 1998.

Similarly in Ghana, corruption, lavish spending and intolerance of criticism led to the welcome overthrow of Nkrumah in February 1966. For some time there had been a growing feeling among Ghanaians that Nkrumah was directing too much of his energies into being an international statesman and that he was ignoring his own country's mounting economic problems. But there were additional specific military grievances leading to the February coup. These were related to proposed cuts in the defence budget, the effects of inflation upon the declining wages of army officers, and alleged government interference in the day-to-day running of the army. Furthermore, there were fears among the military that the army, which had served with the United Nations in Congo, might be going to be sent to 'Rhodesia' to fight against the Smith regime, which had declared UDI in November 1965.

Having forced Nkrumah into exile in Guinea and purged the civil service of his political supporters, the military regime in Ghana was the first in independent Africa to 're-civilianise', in 1969. The government of the veteran 'Gold Coast' politician Dr Kofi A. Busia, however, proved quite unable to solve Ghana's mounting economic problems in the face of a further sharp fall in the world price of cocoa. The army returned to power under Colonel Ignatius Acheampong in 1972.

Once again, specific military grievances, including further cuts in the military budget, seem to have prompted the army into action. Though unable to halt Ghana's overall economic decline, Acheampong's noted achievement was 'Operation Feed Yourself', aimed at reducing Ghana's dependence upon expensive food imports. But it was not enough. Ghana, like most other African countries, was hit by the huge rise in oil prices in 1973–4. With rapidly rising inflation and the blatant wealthy living of certain army officers, Flight-Lieutenant Jerry Rawlings seized power in 1979 in what proved to be a brief 'cleansing exercise'. Three former military heads of state were executed for corrupt practices and the country returned to civilian rule within three months. Once again the new civilian government was not up to the urgent task of halting the country's decline. Ghana needed an inspirational leadership it could trust and a broadly-based economic policy which would benefit more than privileged party and urban elites. In December 1981 Rawlings seized power again, this time proclaiming a 'people's revolution' and a purging of the old elites. For the next decade Rawlings provided the leadership and much of the harsh economic restructuring that was needed, but at a heavy cost in terms of individual human rights and democratic freedoms.

It should not be concluded from the above that the military in African politics was necessarily a positive force for African development. Military rulers were just as likely to be corrupt and tyrannical as their civilian counterparts. The year 1979 saw the downfall of three of Africa's most corrupt and tyrannical regimes, that of General 'Emperor' Jean-Bedel Bokassa of the Central African Republic (1966–79), Field-Marshal 'President for Life' Idi Amin of Uganda (1971–9) and civilian president-dictator Francisco Marcías Nguéma of Equatorial (former 'Spanish') Guinea (1968–79). Bokassa squandered huge sums of his poor country's revenue upon himself and his friends, including his own notorious imperial coronation and his gift of diamonds to the president of France. Amin and Marcías Nguéma were both responsible for the torture and death of untold thousands of real and imagined opponents of their brutal dictatorial regimes. Amin's regime is generally credited with having looted and destroyed what was once regarded as one of Africa's most thriving, agriculturally-based economies.

Socialism and self-reliance: the Tanzanian course

So far we have seen African independence governments struggling with and generally failing to overcome the problems of uneven development and the export-orientated economies which they had inherited from colonial regimes. It was left to Nyerere of Tanzania to chart a bold new course and to try to take African development in an entirely new direction. It began in February 1967 with what is known as the Arusha Declaration. In it Nyerere laid down the principles by which he sought to reverse the trend of African development based upon the European model of capitalist industrialisation.

The early years of independence had shown that the European model depended upon huge foreign investment. This increased African indebtedness, in effect continuing to drain African wealth in the direction of the 'developed' capitalist economies of western Europe and north America. At the same time, as Africa grew poorer and less able to feed itself, private greed was increasing class divisions within African society. Nyerere was determined to end this 'fattening of the elite'.

Nyerere's vision of a future Tanzania was of a prosperous, self-reliant and classless society. He called it 'African socialism'. The idea had evolved among African nationalists of the 1950s as a reaction to the capitalist exploitation of colonial rule. But most independence leaders, with the notable exception of Guinea's Sekou Touré, paid little more than lip-service to African socialist principles. It was left to Nyerere to draw up a blueprint for its practical implementation. Nyerere claimed that Africans had no need to be taught the principles of European socialism as evolved by Marx and others in nineteenth-century Europe. With a rather idealistic view of pre-colonial African history, Nyerere argued that 'traditional' African village society operated on its own socialist principles of communal cooperation.

Tanzanian socialism was to be based on local resources rather than imported, high-technology industrialisation. The country's main banks and foreign-owned capitalist companies were to be 'nationalised', that is, taken over by the state on behalf of the people. A 'Leadership Code' banned political leaders from accumulating private wealth. The main emphasis of government was to be upon rural development, leading to self-reliance.

Nyerere proposed the gathering-together of Tanzania's mass of small remote rural settlements into larger, more effective villages. This would make it easier for government to provide better roads and rural markets combined with agricultural advice and improved technology. Better water, health and education facilities could also be provided more efficiently to larger, centralised villages. The policy was known as *ujamaa*, variously translated as 'familyhood', 'self-help' or 'mutual cooperation'. It was based upon the

Figure 29.2 Tanzanian *ujamaa* village committee

ancient African tradition of family and clan self-help at times of communal need, such as harvest or the clearing of new land. A vital aspect of *ujamaa* was thus the promotion of the 'African socialist' principles of communal labour for the benefit of the community. Applied to the new large villages it would, Nyerere believed, increase agricultural productivity, enabling communally cultivated fields to produce a surplus for sale to the towns or for export. At the same time, the socialist principles of *ujamaa* would ensure that greater rural prosperity would be communally shared. This would avoid the sharp divisions of wealth between the masses and the few, which had been a characteristic of colonial and early independence rule.

However fine the theory, Tanzania's *ujamaa* had a built-in contradiction. It was self-help imposed from above. In practice peasant cultivators were reluctant to move from areas where their ancestors were buried and where their families had successfully grown crops for generations. They were also reluctant to give up the personal security of private plots for the sake of communal ones. When persuasion would not work, government turned to compulsory 'villagisation'. They were helped by severe drought in 1973–4 which persuaded many villagers that a move was worth a try. Between 1973 and 1976 some five million people were moved into *ujamaa* villages. There were 8000 such villages by 1977.

Compulsory villagisation, controlled by urban bureaucrats, was sometimes oppressive and often inefficient. Peasants were sometimes moved before roads, markets and public welfare facilities in new villages were ready. There followed severe rural shortages of basic commodities such as paraffin, soap and sugar. Government and party officials portrayed peasants as backward and ignorant, not able to understand and accept the advantages of villagisation. But peasants understood only too well. Levels of production on communal lands in *ujamaa* villages were not noticeably higher than overall peasant production previously. Some families had been moved off good land on to poorer. The new agricultural 'experts' did not necessarily 'know best'. By the 1980s peasant knowledge and experience were gaining greater respect. Government was forced to ease up on the rigid dogma of the early 1970s. Non-communal, individual peasant farmers were allowed to continue, some becoming prosperous petty-capitalists, growing cash crops for export.

On a national scale, Tanzania in the 1980s remained one of the poorest countries in Africa. It had huge foreign debts and was still dependent upon exporting agricultural raw materials – coffee, cotton, sisal – at prices controlled outside Africa, in exchange for increasingly expensive manufactured imports. But its production of food crops had not deteriorated, as in many other parts of Africa. It had avoided the massive accumulation of landless rural poverty which characterised its nationally more prosperous neighbour Kenya. And Tanzania had succeeded in providing the mass of rural people with vastly improved welfare services: clean water and free health and education facilities.

The governments of those countries which had achieved independence through guerrilla struggle – Algeria, Guinea-Bissau, Angola, Mozambique and Zimbabwe – based their subsequent development on various local adaptations of basically socialist principles. Algeria was fortunate in having great oil wealth which could be used for diversifying the economy. The building of a giant Algerian steel mill in the 1970s was an important step in Africa's growing industrialisation. The regime in Guinea-Bissau unfortunately

Figure 29.3 Women weeding crops in Zimbabwe. Women are the predominant agricultural workers in Africa, a point often overlooked by agricultural 'experts' and government planners

became increasingly dictatorial and largely lost contact with its original grass-roots support. Angola had great economic potential as its basically rural economy was supported by substantial mineral wealth, especially in oil. But like Mozambique, Angolan development was persistently disrupted by the military activity of South African-backed rebels, determined to prevent the establishment of thriving socialist economies so close to South Africa's borders.

In Zimbabwe the road to socialist development was fraught with difficulties. The ZANU government of Robert Mugabe, while committed to long-term socialist transformation, had no desire to disrupt the economically productive capitalist industries and commercial agriculture established during earlier white settler regimes. Education was seen as an important avenue for the eventual establishment of socialist principles within Zimbabwe. But meanwhile, certain members of the already educated elite were eager to emulate their former white rulers in accumulating private wealth at the expense of the majority. Mugabe's return to anti-colonial rhetoric and the collapse of the Zimbabwean economy in the late 1990s and early 2000s will be discussed in the final chapter (pp. 478–9).

chapter 30

Africa since independence (2)

The dilemmas of development: debt, climate change and international aid

Historians of the future, looking back on the early decades of African independence, are likely to highlight its achievements. They will be able to contrast its levels of health, education, economic, social and political development very favourably with the neglect, oppression and exploitation of the previous hundred years. Nevertheless, there is no denying that Africa faces very grave problems in the second decade of the twenty-first century.

Two major factors stifling African development have been international debt and the vagaries of climate. Africa's indebtedness can be traced back to the adverse terms of trade established in the colonial period. Some, such as Walter Rodney (p. 182), have argued that it stemmed right back to the era of the slave trade. The situation was not helped by the lavish spending of independence governments. Since then, however, African governments of every persuasion have, with very few exceptions, struggled to curb their lavish spending, increase self-sufficiency and reduce their foreign debts. But still the debts rise.

Indebtedness in the 1970s reached crisis proportions. At the root of the problem lay the continuing adverse terms of trade that saw the value of Africa's exports consistently falling in relation to the cost of manufactured imports. The descent into chronic indebtedness, however, was hastened dramatically by the oil crisis of 1973–4 that left sub-Saharan African countries critically short of foreign exchange.

In response to the Arab–Israeli war of 1973 the oil producers of western Asia and north Africa deliberately cut oil exports to the industrial world that had supported Israel in the war. Accounting for 40 per cent of world oil production at the time, their action led to a serious world shortage and sent the world price of oil soaring – it tripled during 1973–4. The industrial world of western Europe and north America went into temporary recession, and immediately prices that they were prepared to pay for Africa's raw material exports fell still further than they had in the 1960s. Furthermore, the inflation that characterised the industrial world's economic recovery in the 1970s increased the price of Africa's imported consumer goods, at the very time that income from her exports was falling. At the same time Africa was itself suffering from the hike in oil prices of 1973–4. (This was before the west African oil boom of the 1980s. Nigerian oil was only just beginning to come on stream.) Most African countries imported all their oil requirements, paid for in foreign exchange that was every month becoming more and more expensive in terms of what it would buy. By contrast, international banks, fed by a decade of high inflation and high interest rates, were overflowing with funds looking for places to lend. African governments, verging on bankruptcy, found themselves with little alternative but to run up huge foreign debts; and they found the international banking system only too eager to lend them money, with a recklessness and lack of security that would not be seen again until the early 2000s.

By 1980 many countries had simply run out of foreign exchange, even 'self-reliance' ones like Tanzania. They began to turn to the IMF (International Monetary Fund) for emergency foreign exchange and for further loans to help pay the interest on loans which were already too large for them ever to pay off. The trouble was that the IMF and its associated World Bank, both Washington-based, are financed by the banks of the 'developed' capitalist economies of western Europe and north America. Their priorities have reflected the interests of the capitalist West which is only just, in the twenty-first century, beginning to regard Africa as anything more than a source of raw materials for its own developed industries.

Structural adjustment programmes

Access to IMF and World Bank funds were tied to certain sets of preconditions known as Structural Adjustment Programmes (SAPs). These 'conditionalities', applied universally, were modelled on the practices of developed capitalist systems rather than on the specific needs and best interests of the individual African countries concerned. What were presented as solutions to underlying problems carried with them even greater problems of their own.

Firstly, governments were required to balance their budgets: a reasonable requirement on the face of it. In theory it meant a cut in the annual growth of government debt. In practice it meant a growth in unemployment and poverty as thousands of public employees were laid off and drastic cuts were made in the provision of health and education services and public-housing programmes. The second, and often most dreaded precondition, from an African viewpoint, was a devaluation of the currency. On the one hand, this ensured that producers of export crops and minerals got better prices on the world market for their commodities. The other side of the same coin, however, was a rise in the cost of imports. This included most consumer goods, fuel oil and even food to feed burgeoning urban populations. Thus for most Africans, devaluation meant a dramatic increase in prices on the streets.

A third precondition for IMF and World Bank financing was a liberalisation of capital controls. Africa's greatest economic weakness, next to its adverse terms of trade, has been its lack of adequate indigenous capital to invest in its own industry, agriculture and other forms of production. In colonial times Africans had been denied access to credit banks. Business and its profits had remained almost exclusively in European hands. In the first two decades of independence, African governments had restricted capital movement in an attempt to ensure that foreign capital and its profits stayed within the country and were reinvested. The removal of these restrictions in the 1980s and 1990s was supposed to encourage greater foreign investment in Africa, by assuring potential investors that they would be free to remove their capital and their profits as and when they wanted. As a result, Africans lost a large measure of control over their own economies, and liberalisation of capital controls

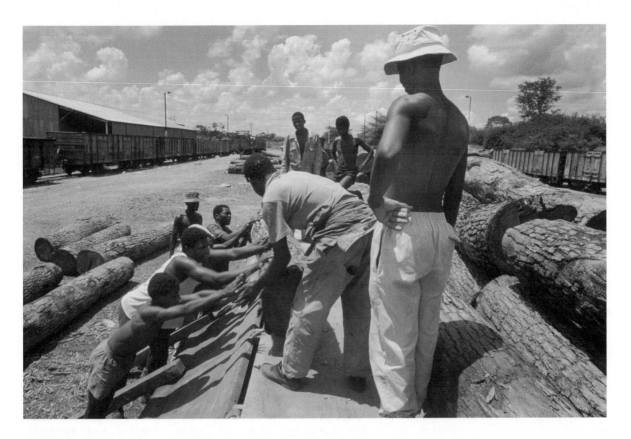

Figure 30.1 Loading hardwood for export at the Victoria Falls marshalling yard, Zimbabwe

did little to solve the real structural problem – shortage of indigenous capital. Predictably, the foreign capital that did come in was mostly invested in primary, extractive industries, such as gold in Ghana, oil in Nigeria, copper in Congo/Zaïre or timber in Gabon.

Declining world prices for African commodities during the 1980s and the consequent drastic shortage of foreign exchange had pushed most sub-Saharan African countries into Structural Adjustment Programmes by the early 1990s. And, as we saw above, international financiers were more concerned that SAPs should increase exports to pay off foreign debts rather than help the continent as a whole to become regionally self-sufficient. This meant a continuation of the old colonial pattern: concentration on cash crops for export at the expense of food crops for local consumption. The best agricultural land and expensive new irrigation schemes were thus set aside for export crops. In the sub-Saharan region, subsistence farmers were pushed on to marginal lands previously used for pasture, while pastoralists were squeezed ever-closer to the margins of the desert. 1984 was a year of severe drought in the Sahel. Yet, Sahelian countries, such as Niger, produced bumper crops of cotton, while local food crops failed and pastoralists lost up to 90 per cent of their livestock. A small local minority gained some prosperity, interest was paid to foreign banks and the bulk of the population faced starvation. Through the international debt system, Africa in the early twenty-first century was still a net exporter of her wealth to Europe and north America. That means: every year Africa spends more of her precious foreign exchange in debt repayment to foreign banks than she receives in foreign aid.

The CFA franc zone   The majority of Francophone African countries have had a slightly different economic experience since independence in 1960. Although the basic over-dependence upon raw material exports and foreign investment has been the same, the former members of the French west and central African empires have had a common currency, the Communauté Financière Africaine (CFA) franc. From 1947 until January 1994 the CFA franc was tied to, and inter-changeable with, the French franc at the fixed rate of 50 francs to one French franc. This provided the 14 African countries concerned with a degree of economic stability in terms of dependable foreign investment. At the same time, however, it tied them financially and economically to France and it was thus French interests which predominated. Africans in the CFA zone sold their cocoa, coffee, cotton, groundnuts, timber, oil, uranium and manganese to France. They received considerable French investment, but it was almost exclusively into those primary industries. At the same time, since 65 per cent of CFA foreign reserves had to be held in French francs, the CFA countries received virtually all their consumer imports from France. It was 'neo-colonialism' par excellence. It was also a serious barrier to greater economic integration across the west African region. Only 7 per cent of CFA trade in the 1980s was within the west African zone.

By the early 1990s the CFA franc had become seriously overvalued, especially in relationship to neighbouring Anglophone countries. This meant that producers of export crops were being underpaid in CFA francs, while at the same time imports from France were relatively cheap. The latter had led to an over-dependence upon French consumer goods, at the expense of local industry, and a high proportion of foreign exchange was spent on luxury French foods for the urban elites of Dakar, Abidjan and Yaoundé. Meanwhile, French interest in Africa was waning as it concentrated its economic energies upon European integration. With less investment capital coming from France, governments of the CFA zone were obliged to turn to the IMF. It was thus under pressure from the IMF, and with the approval of the Bank of France, that Francophone African governments hesitantly accepted a dramatic devaluation of the CFA franc by 100 per cent in January 1994. The political instability which followed the overnight doubling of import prices was predictable and almost inevitable.

Globalisation   By the dawn of the new century a new word had come to replace SAPs in the industrial world's prescriptions for Africa – 'globalisation'. This was an insistence that in the new electronic age of the internet, capital and goods must be allowed to flow freely around the world with no trade barriers between states. As we saw earlier in this book with regard to Britain as the dominant world power in the nineteenth century (p. 312), the dogma of 'free trade' is the freedom of the powerful to pursue their own economic interests anywhere in the world. It was argued by the world's most powerful industrial nations, the G8 (the USA, Canada, Britain, Germany, France, Italy, Japan and Russia), that globalisation would benefit the poorer nations of Africa because they would be able to sell their goods in the rich markets of the industrial world. African countries would thus 'trade' their way out of poverty. In practice it did not work like that. In order to gain access to these rich markets, African countries have had to open up their own economies and services to foreign private competition. They have had to remove trade barriers designed to protect weak emerging industry and agriculture and force them to compete openly with the 'world market'. Thus, for example, Mauritania was persuaded to lease its valuable Atlantic fishing grounds to Spanish industrial fishing fleets. The government received money for the lease, but local Mauritanian fishermen were driven out of business and were no longer able to feed their families on their own fresh fish. This practice was repeated in many coastal countries around the continent.

Globalisation was not only 'neo-colonialism' in new clothes; it has also been hypocritical; for while African farmers were thrown open to world competition, the farmers of the European Union and north America were heavily protected and subsidised. They have thus been able to produce more than they needed and have dumped the surplus on the world market, driving African farmers out of business.

Within this globalisation climate, in the twenty-first century, global capitalist investors, especially from Britain and America, have been buying up vast tracts of African land – across the tropical continent, from Senegal to Mozambique. And they have been doing it with the cooperation of weak African governments. The investors expect to make large profits, especially from the growing of crops such as palm oil for bio-fuels. Meanwhile China and some of the oil-rich nations of western Asia have for some years been buying up land in countries such as Sudan and Tanzania in order to grow food for their own populations. All of this 'land-grabbing' activity takes valuable land out of the hands of African producers, driving ever-more former farmers into urban shanty-towns while others become employees of multi-national agri-corporations. Though providing some local employment, this further reduces Africa's chances of gaining control over her own self-sufficiency in food – a basic requirement of any meaningful development.

International aid

The subject of international aid has become a controversial topic where discussion of Africa's economic development is concerned. It is often pointed out in Western political forums that Africa has received a huge amount of aid over the past half-century and yet there is precious little to show for it. The implication of this scenario is that Africans are to blame for not using their aid more wisely. Why, Western politicians and voters ask, does Africa keep needing emergency aid to cope with famines, such as that affecting Somalia in 2011?

Too often in these discussions general international aid to Africa is equated with emergency aid. The two are quite distinct. Emergency aid undoubtedly saves many lives in famine situations. The main criticism levelled at emergency 'disaster relief' aid is that a predictable situation, often associated with armed conflict in a marginal environment, is left to fester into a disaster before international emergency funds are raised to deal with the result. Furthermore, the amount of publicity given to international fund-raising, with harrowing pictures of starving children, helps to reinforce in the world's media a very negative image of Africa as a whole. Nevertheless, disaster aid will still be needed for as long as there are still disasters. What Africa needs is development that will *prevent* disasters. So why has general international aid over 50 years not achieved this?

At independence in the 1950s and 1960s Africa's new leaders demanded aid from their former colonial masters. They needed capital in order to make the kind of physical infrastructure and educational and health investment that the colonial powers had neglected to do during the 70 years that they were in control. It was, in effect, a debt owed to Africa as compensation for the blatant exploitation of colonial rule. The arrangement suited the former colonial powers, for it enabled them to ensure that their former colonies remained dependent upon them and it guaranteed them continued access to Africa's resources.

The way it has developed since then stems from the fact that government to government (bilateral) aid has never been intended to develop complete independent self-sufficiency for the recipient African nation. Much of the aid has been in the form of loans, which laid the basis for Africa's chronic indebtedness. The reckless lending by international banks in the 1970s has already been commented upon. Since the IMF and the World Bank stepped in in the 1980s, too many African governments have become addicted to automatic inflows of international aid. This has cushioned them from the harsh realities of what their country can really afford. At the same time it has divorced them from accountability to their own people. In line with the old maxim: 'He who pays the piper calls the tune', major aid donors tend to dictate Africa's development goals.

It can be argued that African countries are poor because the international trading and commodity market system of globalisation does not pay African producers enough for their hard-won resources. And if this means that impoverished Africa must receive aid from the developed industrial world, then that is merely compensation for the low prices paid for Africa's raw materials. It has already been observed that even in the twenty-first century Africa pays out more annually to Western banks than she receives from Western aid donors. In effect, this means that international aid to Africa, far from compensating Africa for past underdevelopment, in fact acts as a subsidy to multi-national banks.

It is for reasons such as this that some African economists now argue that international aid to Africa must be brought to an end; and African governments must focus on planning for development *without* international aid. Under these circumstances, African politicians would be much more answerable to their electorates. And this greater accountability could only lead in the long term to greater political stability.

Climate change

Since the 1950s there has been a slight but noticeable fall in the average annual rainfall in many parts of the continent. Recent research points to the possibility of general world climatic change, probably caused by increasing pollution of the atmosphere in the industrialised northern hemisphere. The net result for Africa has been an increasing incidence of extreme oscillation between drought and flood, especially in the Sahelian and savannah zones of seasonal rainfall. Added to the disruptive effects of drought have been those of civil war in some of the worst-affected areas: Chad, Sudan and Ethiopia. The military regime that overthrew Haile Selassie in 1974 was, by the mid-1980s, spending half of Ethiopia's annual revenue upon arms to fight 'rebels' in Tigray and Eritrea. And this at a time of severe drought and widespread famine in the war-torn regions of the country. Similarly, warfare waged by South African-backed 'rebels' in drought-stricken Mozambique in the 1980s caused havoc in that fertile country, formerly able to feed itself.

That drought does not necessarily lead to famine is illustrated by the case of Botswana. Perched as it is on the edge of the Kalahari Desert, Botswana experienced the drought of 1981–6 and 1991–2 just as badly as anywhere

Figure 30.2 The 'youth group' of Dlaba on their community-owned field hoeing the soil between millet plants by hand, accompanied by live music

else. But Botswana had a stable economy based upon cattle and the export of diamonds and it had a stable political democracy. It was thus able to use its well-developed infrastructure and its economic reserves to establish effective drought-relief projects and thus ensure that although people suffered from the drought, starvation was averted and the country held together.

As early chapters of this history, have revealed, Africans have in the historic past coped with climatic changes and have evolved new pastoral and agricultural techniques for coming to terms with their environment. But in those days population levels were a fraction of what they are today. Today's climate change and its increasing incidence of drought and flood are happening in a very different world, with rapid population growth, combined with mobility restrictions imposed by modern state boundaries. There is a growing awareness amongst African governments of the need to devise their own locally evolved solutions to their countries' problems. Whether these local solutions can keep up with the increasing volatility of global weather patterns is another matter.

International cooperation and the Organisation of African Unity

We saw in an earlier chapter (p. 415) that the Pan-African movement helped awake in early African nationalists an awareness of the common plight of Africans in their struggle against colonial domination. The first Pan-African meeting held on African soil was the All African People's Conference hosted by Nkrumah in newly independent Ghana in 1958. Nkrumah and Sekou Touré were among Africa's most dedicated Pan-Africanists. Nkrumah was greatly influenced by his educational experience in the United States of America. He believed that the only way to achieve complete economic as well as political freedom from European domination was to create a powerful new 'United States of Africa'. Then, through continent-wide cooperation, Africa would really be able to take its place on the world economic and political stage on terms of equality. In unity, Nkrumah saw strength, but in practical terms his dream proved illusory. At home in Ghana, Nkrumah himself only achieved the appearance of internal political unity by suppressing regional Asante opposition. On the wider continent, individual African states and their newly independent governments had too many of their own immediate problems to take political union seriously. Even the attempt to federate Ghana, Guinea and Mali in 1961 fell apart within months.

In May 1963 the 32 heads of state of then independent Africa came together in the Ethiopian capital, Addis Ababa, to form the Organisation of African Unity (OAU). Falling far short of a 'United States', it was more along the lines of an African 'United Nations'. Its aim was to promote political and economic cooperation between independent states and to help speed the decolonisation of the rest of Africa. Two important principles accepted at its founding were a recognition of international boundaries as existing at independence and an acceptance of the principle of 'no interference' in the internal affairs of member states. A further founding principle was a commitment to help complete the decolonisation of the continent. To this end the OAU's Liberation Committee played an important role in the 1970s and 1980s (Figure 30.3). The main beneficiaries of Liberation Committee financial support were the exiled politicians and 'freedom fighters' of southern Africa – Zimbabwe, Angola, Mozambique, Namibia and South Africa – especially those that gathered in Dar-es-Salaam as guests of President Nyerere of Tanzania. On the whole they did not receive enough financial support to buy weapons, but enough to run an office, support exiles and promote their political cause abroad.

A major weakness of the OAU was the fact that it had no legal sanction to enforce its resolutions. It was thus frequently criticised for being little more than 'a talking-shop'. Nevertheless, the OAU was a useful forum for international African cooperation. Its regular meetings of ministers and heads

Figure 30.3 The OAU summit in Tripoli, August 1982, was boycotted by one-third of the African heads of state, who supported Morocco's claim to the Western Sahara. Most leaders who turned up at Tripoli saw themselves as 'radical', 'socialist' or 'revolutionary', including seated here: President Moussa Traore of Mali, *left*, and President Julius Nyerere of Tanzania, photographed with Colonel Gaddafi. The Tripoli boycott ensured that there was no quorum and so the host, Gaddafi, could not be elected Chairman of the OAU for the coming year, 1982–3

of state were helped to generate a greater awareness of other countries' problems. There were of course disagreements between states and groups of states, but its common purpose was cooperation and the OAU survived to the end of the century with no permanent split.

The African Development Bank, which grew out of the OAU in 1967, became an invaluable tool for mobilising world finance for African development projects. The idea of coordinating and mobilising international capital for the benefit of Africa was of particular value during the 1970s and early 1980s. With the ending of the Cold War (1989–90) and break-up of the Soviet Union (1991), however, world finance lost much of its former interest in African investment. African leaders were forced to recognise a harsh new reality. Africa was going to have to rely upon its own internal resources for its future development. This meant more trade *within* Africa and, ultimately, greater economic integration: in other words, moves towards Nkrumah's vision of a 'United States of Africa', at least, initially, in the economic sphere. In recognition of this, at their annual conference, in the new Nigerian federal capital of Abuja, in June 1991 the OAU heads of government signed a treaty initiating moves towards an African Economic Community. A decade later the OAU itself was formally converted into the African Union, launched in South Africa in July 2002 as the first step in the eventual economic and political union of the continent. Although a long way from becoming a reality, the declaration of intent was significant. In the meantime, the greater initial hope for economic integration lay in the regions.

Regional groupings: ECOWAS, SADC and the EAC

In 1975 the Economic Community of West African States (ECOWAS) was founded in Lagos. This new regional grouping of west Africa's 16 states was particularly significant because it cut across the artificial and disruptive barriers of Anglophone and Francophone west Africa. Wisely, it did not try to embark upon an over-ambitious political union. In the spirit of the OAU, ECOWAS preferred to concentrate on gradually increasing regional economic cooperation, starting with transport and telecommunications and moving on to greater financial and commercial interchange. The origins of SADC can be traced to 1980 and the independence of Zimbabwe. Founded originally as the Southern African Development Coordination Conference (SADCC), it brought together the independent states of southern Africa other than South Africa, with the specific aim of breaking its members' historic economic dependence upon *apartheid* South Africa. Namibia joined the SADCC fold when it gained its political independence from South Africa in 1990.

SADCC and ECOWAS enabled their respective regions to coordinate long-term development planning and to produce a united front when negotiating for foreign aid and development loans. Since 1990 both organisations have shown a willingness to increase their levels of regional cooperation. SADCC, looking to the future incorporation of a free South Africa, began moves towards establishing a regional economic and trading network and in 1992 it changed its name to the Southern African Development Community (SADC). The aim now was greater economic integration of the whole southern African region.

With the entry of South Africa into SADC in 1994, the southern African organisation assumed greater regional significance. With its secretariat in Gaborone, the capital of Botswana, the most stable country in the region,

Map 30.1 Regional groupings: ECOWAS and SADCC/SADC

cooperation across many spheres was generally very good. There remained, however, a certain level of tension between South Africa and Zimbabwe. The latter, under the leadership of Robert Mugabe, had, until 1994, been the dominant political and economic partner in the grouping. From 1994 Mugabe's Zimbabwe was rather eclipsed by South Africa under the leadership of a charismatic statesman of world renown, Nelson Mandela. An example of the tension came in 1997 when South Africa decided to intervene in Lesotho to sort out an army mutiny. The South Africans persuaded Botswana to send some troops to back up their intervention and thus give it the legitimacy of a SADC operation. Mugabe, however, was chair of the defence portfolio of SADC and he had not authorised it. Instead, he chose to intervene in the evolving civil war in the Congo, joining Angola and Namibia under the cloak of a SADC operation to prop up the recently installed government of Laurent Kabila in Kinshasa. Further tension within SADC emerged from 1998 and into the 2000s as the Zimbabwean economy spiralled out of control, amid mounting political violence (see below, p. 479). Mandela's successor, President Thabo Mbeki, faced the unenviable task of trying to put pressure on Mugabe to negotiate with his political opposition and halt his country's economic collapse from destabilizing the whole region.

ECOWAS, meanwhile, took a bold initiative which, indirectly, revitalized the whole concept of political and economic cooperation in west Africa. In August 1990, ECOWAS assembled and landed a peace-keeping force, called ECOMOG, in civil war-torn Liberia (see pp. 464–6). The ECOMOG initiative was particularly significant because it collectively broke the long-standing OAU taboo about non-interference in the internal affairs of a fellow member state. ECOMOG initially played a fairly passive role, a spectator to the rising tide of violence in Liberia. After a time, however, the financial strain of an open-ended commitment to the crisis began to tell on the ECOWAS member states that came under increasing domestic pressure to wind up the Liberian operation. ECOMOG was dominated by troops from the west African giant, Nigeria, which was itself under military rule at the time and seemed only too happy to find a valid external role for its armed forces. In 1992, ECOMOG went on the offensive and forced the principal rebel leader, Charles Taylor, to the negotiating table in 1993.

That was not the end of the Liberian conflict (see pp. 466–7), but ECOWAS was revitalized by ECOMOG's apparent success in Liberia. On the economic front, member states began negotiating towards a united currency that would enable them to form a real, effective trading bloc across the whole west African region. The principal bar to currency union was the old Francophone–Anglophone divide. The Francophone countries already had a single currency – the CFA franc (see p. 450) – and they were reluctant to surrender this to domination by the Nigerian *naira*, which they believed would happen with full economic union. Nevertheless, the region began the new century with intra-regional trade barriers loosening and cross-invest-ment and political and economic cooperation on the increase. Meanwhile, ECOMOG was called on to intervene in other conflict areas, most notably Sierra Leone (see Chapter 31, pp. 465–6).

The East African Community (EAC) has in many ways been the most successful of Africa's organisations for regional integration. It is much more clearly focussed on the economy than either SADC or ECOWAS. Inaugurated in 2000 by Kenya, Tanzania and Uganda, the EAC was joined by Rwanda and Burundi in 2007. Its long-term aim is to establish economic, political, social and cultural integration. Enthusiastically pushed forward by Uganda's President Museveni, economic integration has progressed well. It is working towards the establishment of, first, an effective common market, then a monetary union and, finally, a political federation of its member states. In 2010 the Common Market Protocol was ratified by all member states amid high hopes that this would be effectively implemented. Negotiations for a monetary union commenced in 2011, although in the world financial climate of the time, establishing an effective monetary proto-col was a far harder task.

31

Contemporary Africa (1)

Democratic progress in the 1990s

To outward appearances most of Africa was politically transformed in the early 1990s, as military dictatorships and one-party states almost universally gave way to multi-party systems of democracy. A number of factors, both internal and external, combined to bring this about. The most important external factor was the ending of the Cold War between capitalist West and communist East, most dramatically symbolised by the destruction of the Berlin Wall in 1989. Africa was no longer the tropical playing field for global strategic power games. Corrupt and ineffective governments or longstanding dictators, such as Siad Barré of Somalia (1969–91) or Mobutu Sese Seko of Zaïre (1965–97) were no longer supported with external funds or arms supplies simply because they declared themselves to be anti-communist or anti-capitalist.

Hitherto, with the notable exceptions of Botswana and Mauritius, no African country which had gained its independence in the 1960s had maintained a completely unbroken record of multi-party parliamentary democracy. Botswana, it could be argued, was a special case as its governing political party had never seriously been challenged at the ballot box, at least until the 1990s. Mauritius, on the other hand, had shown great political maturity when its multi-ethnic electorate had successfully replaced a longstanding government in a dramatic 'Sixty-Zero' general election in 1982, a feat it repeated in the 1990s. By contrast, most African heads of state, when faced with electoral defeat, had simply suspended the constitution, secure in the knowledge that they would receive external recognition and support from one side or other in the Cold War conflict.

By the early 1990s, however, a whole new generation of Africans had reached their forties and early fifties as beneficiaries of the great educational expansion of the 1960s. They had lived their young adult lives as witnesses to the failures of successive African governments – multi-party, one-party or military dictatorship. They no longer looked back to colonial shortcomings, but drew instead upon their own experience of Africa's political and economic woes. The mounting economic crisis of the 1980s added a sense of urgency. Armed with a determination to find their own solutions to Africa's problems, the much-abused African electorate decided it was time to call their governments to account. This was where the drive for the new African democracy was born.

Between 1990 and 1994, African governments, one after another, were dragged, sometimes kicking, to the constitutional negotiating table. In a small number of cases like Zambia, Malawi or Benin, where the opposition remained united, a successful change of constitution and government was achieved through the ballot box. In others, such as Mali, the constitutional conference assumed unto itself the sole legitimacy of government, drove out the incumbent head of state and redrafted the constitution. In Zaïre (Congo), where constitutional delegates tried the same type of tactic and appointed an interim prime minister, head of state Mobutu, impervious to the mounting violence he provoked, counteracted by appointing a new prime minister of his own. This left a rapidly bankrupting state with two parallel governments, even two currencies, and no peaceful solution in sight (see below p. 477).

Flight-Lieutenant Jerry Rawlings, who had come to power in Ghana (for a second time) by coup in 1981, made one of the more respectable transformations from dictatorship to democracy in 1992, helped largely by divisions

Figure 31.1 Mathare informal township, Nairobi, Kenya, December 2010

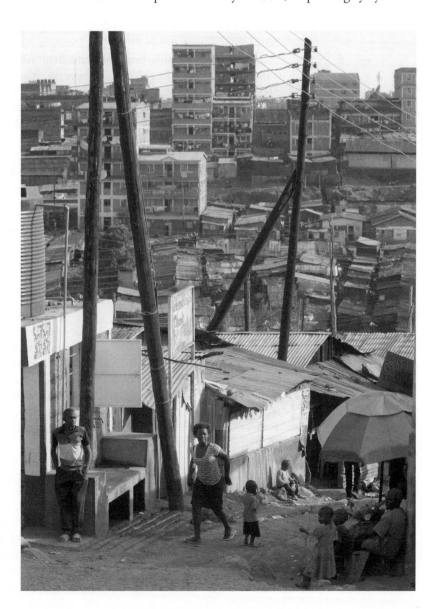

and weaknesses in the ranks of the opposition. In Kenya, the reluctant democrat, President Moi, managed to get himself and his party re-elected in a ballot that was widely condemned as far from 'free and fair'. His example was emulated in a number of other former one-party states where the incumbent president managed to strong-arm his own political party back into power in what was a purely nominally 'multi-party' system. The most spectacular failure in the democratic process was Nigeria, which, after years of preparation, suffered the ignominy of seeing its presidential election of 1993 cancelled by General Babangida just as the results were beginning to emerge.

The forms of democracy reborn in the early 1990s did not necessarily fulfil the hopes and aspirations of the ordinary electorate, who yearned for a change of government to bring in new and fresh ideas. They did, however, re-establish a basic democratic principle, which had been brushed aside too easily in the past: namely, that governments were ultimately answerable to their electorates. In the 1990s even military dictators such as Captain Strasser of Sierra Leone (1992), General Abacha of Nigeria (1993), Lieutenant Yahya Jammeh of The Gambia (1994) or Ibrahim Maïnassara of Niger (1996) were quick to recognise this principle and promise a prompt return to constitutional civilian rule. In the case of Nigeria, it soon became clear that General Abacha, who had replaced Babangida soon after the cancelled elections of 1993, had no intention of fulfilling his initial promise. The west African giant (Nigeria) was only relieved of his brutal and kleptocratic rule by his sudden death in 1998.

On the whole the new continent-wide democratic movement, whatever its limitations, opened a new era of direct African involvement in the search for African solutions. Governments acquired a new legitimacy which, combined with the concept of greater regional economic integration, opened up whole new horizons for the continent's long-term future. Whatever the long-term potential, however, there was no easy road to a better future, as the following regional survey will show.

North Africa

North Africa as a whole did not follow the democratic path more typical of sub-Saharan Africa after 1990. Here the economic pressures and high levels of unemployment, partly resulting from structural adjustment programmes, prompted a religious upsurge in the two most populous and industrialised countries, Algeria and Egypt. Muslim brotherhoods and clerics vociferously rejected the 'Western' culture of free-market capitalism and multi-party democracy espoused by the World Bank and IMF. They wanted nothing to do with the 'godless culture' of 'globalisation'. They promised a fairer, less divisive, less corrupt and more morally guided society that would result from the widespread adoption of *sharia* law. As we have seen throughout this history, promises of an idealised Islamic society have been made at various times in Africa's past, although the promised ideal rarely emerged and seldom lasted for long. On this occasion the 'Muslim fundamentalists', as they were branded by their enemies, were confronted by powerful governments that had ample external backing and were determined to thwart them.

In the early months of 2011, however, the Arab world of north Africa and western Asia was set alight by what rapidly became known as the 'Arab

Spring'. The fuse that lit the fire of revolt began to burn in supposedly stable Tunisia.

Tunisia

Through the 1990s the authoritarian government of President Zine al-Abidine Ben Ali had managed to avoid the sort of violence that bedevilled its neighbour Algeria. Despite high levels of unemployment, the weakness and divisions of the political opposition had enabled Ben Ali to win successive contested elections. The oppressive nature of the Tunisian state, which is often a feature of long-serving governments, however, added to the tension that had been heightened by the rapidly rising food and fuel prices triggered by the world financial crisis of 2008.

State oppression was symbolised by the abuse meted out by police to a young Tunisian fruit-seller named Muhammad Bouazizi, whom they beat up for trading without a licence. In despair Bouazizi burned himself to death on 17 December 2010. Tunisians spontaneously took to the streets in protest at this wanton police brutality. Simmering resentment of the forces of government by the general populace quickly spiralled out of state control as mass demonstrations called for President Ben Ali to step down. On 14 January 2011 in the face of mass public protest, Ben Ali stepped down and went into exile.

It was the Arab world's 'Berlin Wall' moment as the Tunisian people's achievement inspired similar mass protests in Egypt and elsewhere in the Arab Muslim world of western Asia.

Meanwhile, in Tunisia a provisional government took over with a promise of elections for a constitutional forum scheduled for late July 2011. In the event the election took place in October 2011. It was won by the Islamist party, Ennahada, with 41 per cent of the vote; but tensions remained as Islamists, secularists and the military eyed each other with distrust. Clearly, the establishment of a stable democracy that better embraced the needs of all the peoples of Tunisia was a lot more difficult than the holding of a single election.

Egypt

Egypt was ripe for the 'Arab Spring'. The most populous country in north Africa, Egypt had developed an overdependence upon oil exports and suffered the consequences of a fall in oil prices in the 1980s. Earlier wars against Israel (ended in 1979) had left the government with a huge military infrastructure to sustain; and decades of neglect of the agricultural sector in favour of industrialisation meant that by the 1990s, Egypt had to import 80 per cent of its food requirements.

President Mubarak, a former military officer, maintained an authoritarian regime. Although in theory a multi-party electoral system since before President Sadat's assassination in 1981, Egyptian politics was dominated by the governing National Democratic Party. Mubarak was intolerant of most political opposition, the press was heavily censored and political and personal freedom was curtailed. Heavily supported by US aid, and World Bank and IMF loans, the Mubarak government followed structural adjustment policies, cutting food subsidies and reducing general government expenditure. The result was a lowering of living standards, even among the huge, salaried civil service and professional classes. Only a small minority of entrepreneurs and their political supporters seemed to thrive in these conditions. With well over 50 per cent of the 70 million population living in urban areas, two-thirds of them in Cairo, there was a huge underclass of urban unemployed who had fled the rural areas only to find greater poverty in urban slums.

The government kept a tight rein on Islamic groups, hoping to co-opt 'moderate' Islam into the political fold. Through the 1990s, however, radical Islamic groups attacked the government and its policies through the tourist industry, a major source of foreign exchange. The terror-tactics of killing Western tourists decimated the tourist industry for a while. The government clamped down hard, arresting thousands of Islamic radicals and by the turn of the millennium, opposition appeared to have been suppressed. Mubarak's government continued to receive vital diplomatic and financial support from the United States, but the fundamental economic problems, in the face of a rapidly rising population, remained to be resolved.

The Egyptian populace saw their opportunity for freedom in the Tunisian example of January 2011. Tahrir Square in central Cairo quickly became the focus for widespread protest and everyday life in the Egyptian capital was brought to a standstill. This was not a revolt by organised opposition. There was no leadership as such for Mubarak's security apparatus to attack, and even the Islamists kept a low profile. Within a remarkably short four weeks, Mubarak was forced to step down on 11 February 2011. The military took over with a promise of constitutional reform. Protestors who had been camping in Tahrir Square dispersed, believing, or at least hoping, that the military promise meant meeting their demands for real democratic freedom and reform. Months later, however, little had been delivered and attempts to re-establish protest in Tahrir Square were suppressed by army and police. With the political future of Egypt still uncertain, the Muslim Brotherhood re-emerged on the political scene, on occasion harassing protestors who were demanding democratic elections. In the medium term, whatever constitutional arrangement emerged, poverty, unemployment and rising prices would remain the primary concern of the majority of Egypt's population.

Algeria

In Algeria the ruling Front de Libération Nationale (FLN – 'National Liberation Front') had ruled the country as a one-party 'socialist' state since independence. Colonial Chadli Benjedid succeeded President Boumédienne following the latter's death in December 1978. Through the late 1980s Benjedid followed structural adjustment programmes that cut government spending in the face of falling oil prices (Algeria's biggest export) and rising unemployment. The government's violent suppression of rioting in Algiers in October 1988 left 500 dead and prompted the emergence of radical Islam as a major political force. Benjedid hoped to divide and defuse opposition by agreeing to multi-party elections; but the local government elections of June 1990 were won overwhelmingly by the radical Front Islamique de Salut (FIS – 'Islamic Salvation Front'). With national elections scheduled for December 1991, the FIS campaigned openly on the promise that if elected, they would abolish multi-party democracy and establish an Islamic state based on *sharia* law. Despite a security clampdown and the imprisonment of its leaders, the FIS won nearly half the seats in the first round of elections in December 1991. The army reacted by overthrowing Benjedid, suspending the elections, banning the FIS and imprisoning thousands of its members and supporters. It did this in the name of 'democracy and freedom' and as such was strongly supported by France and the United States.

Deprived of power by peaceful political means, Islamic radicals turned to violence and the government responded in kind. In the civil war that followed the Islamists claimed wider popular support than they in fact enjoyed, partly because of their targeted use of violence to control the rural areas. Government-funded militias replied with similar atrocities – each side blaming each other for massacres of rural non-combatants. In 1998, with 60,000–100,000 killed, a shaky ceasefire was established. Thereafter levels of violence declined, but the fundamental issue of *sharia* law versus liberal democracy remained unresolved.

Algeria was not immediately affected by the 'Arab Spring'. Despite unemployment, endemic corruption and a severe urban housing shortage, people were reluctant to revolt. They had a freer press than elsewhere in north Africa and perhaps they were influenced by their experience of the 1990s. Strikes and protests were widespread in April 2011; but President Bouteflika wisely ordered his security forces not to use violence against the strikers and protestors. Indeed, he withdrew the 'State of Emergency' that had been in place since 1992. With large foreign reserves accumulated from gas exports, Bouteflika was able to stave off an Algerian 'Arab Spring' by promising huge public expenditure on infrastructure projects to create jobs. Whether this would be successful, or whether the increased involvement of the state in the country's economy would store up economic problems for the future, remained to be seen.

Libya

In the early years of the new millennium the Libyan leader Muammar Gaddafi became one of the driving forces behind the new African Union (AU). Seen for many years as a divisive and unpredictable force in African politics, Gaddafi had previously given Libyan petro-dollars to virtually every radical anti-Western movement in Africa and beyond. Now, however, he appeared to sense the mood of the new millennium and provided much-needed financial backing to the emerging African Union. International political action such as this, however, was not going to save Libya from its own 'Arab Spring'.

While Gaddafi had freely used the country's petro-dollars abroad to support his own political whims, he had been sparing of using them to support widespread social and economic development at home. His system of the de-centralisation of power to local people's councils had defused any coherent opposition to the central control that he and his family exercised over Libya's oil wealth. Following the fall of Mubarak, popular protests started in Bengazi in the east of the country. Gaddafi appeared to be taken by surprise. For a few weeks he was hesitant to appear in public and when he did so, he protested that the Libyan people loved him. Then, when the protests clearly would not go away and it became obvious that they were not the work of outside agitators, he unleashed the full power of the military against the Libyan people in Bengazi.

When it looked as though Gaddafi's forces might be about to flatten Bengazi and all hope of regime-change in Libya, interested Western powers, especially France and Britain, persuaded the UN Security Council to allow the West's military alliance, NATO (the North Atlantic Treaty Organisation), to establish a 'no-fly' zone over Libya. The UN resolution got the backing of other Arab states because it was ostensibly to protect Libyan civilians from attack by Gaddafi's airforce. But the wording of the resolution was kept deliberately vague and thus open to varied interpretation. With the United States not wanting to become too embroiled in yet another unwinnable war, France and Britain were soon interpreting the resolution as clearance to attack all Libyan military installations in what appeared to be an attempt to force Gaddafi out of power. With the assistance of NATO, irregular forces were able to take Tripoli and finally, in October 2011, Gaddafi's home town of Sirte, where Gaddafi himself was captured and summarily killed. The first part of the Libyan revolution was now over; but with the country awash with firearms, numerous armed factions distrustful of each other and no clear national leadership, the future for Libya looked very unstable.

Morocco

In Morocco King Hassan II initiated cautious political reform during the 1990s that culminated in direct universal suffrage and the recognition of trade unions in 1998. Hopes that his son and successor Mohammed VI (1999) would finally settle the Western Sahara issue faded as he failed to initiate a referendum on the future status of that territory. Indeed, he continued his father's policy of settling Moroccans in the occupied Western Sahara.

In February 2011 'Arab Spring' peaceful protests spread to Morocco, with the 'February 20 Movement' demanding that the king relinquish most of his powers and become a figurehead, constitutional monarch. On 9 March the king promised constitutional reforms and on 1 July a referendum endorsed a new constitution, but youthful protestors felt these reforms did not go nearly far enough. The king still chaired cabinet meetings, could dismiss parliament and continued to control the army, the judiciary and religious affairs. With these issues not addressed, the February 20 Movement continued to organise protests in Rabat, Tangier and Casablanca.

West Africa

West Africa since the 1990s has been a region of stark contrasts. It has witnessed stability and peaceful electoral change of government in Benin (1991, 1996), Mali (1992, 2002), Ghana (2000, 2008) and Senegal (2000); but at the same time it has experienced some of the worst civil conflict on the continent in recent times. The latter has occurred principally within and between Liberia and Sierra Leone.

Liberia and Sierra Leone

Ironically, in more stable times these two countries had formed the Mano River Union (1973) aimed at eliminating barriers and increasing cooperation between them. This had been joined by Guinea in 1980. Relationships soured from 1985, however, as a failed coup in Liberia was blamed by President Samuel Doe on dissidents based in Sierra Leone. Doe closed the border, effectively ending the era of cooperation signalled by the Mano River Union. In December 1989 Liberian dissident Charles Taylor invaded Liberia from neighbouring Guinea. He was assisted by Sierra Leonean dissidents who hoped that a victorious Taylor would help them overthrow the APC government in Sierra Leone. As we saw above (p. 457), ECOWAS intervened, with varying degrees of success, in Liberia's civil war, which rumbled on past numerous 'ceasefires' through the 1990s. Taylor was finally elected president in 1997 by an exhausted electorate who seem to have believed that putting him in power was the only way to end the fighting.

Meanwhile, conflict had broken out in Sierra Leone, where Taylor provided weaponry to the Revolutionary United Front (RUF) in exchange for diamonds. The Sierra Leonean army was unable to contain the RUF rebellion and felt neglected and let down by Momoh's corrupt APC government. In 1992 Captain Strasser staged a coup with promises of a quick resolution of the war in the east. Strasser promised a return to elected constitutional government in 1996; but he was unable to deliver on the war and was himself overthrown a month before the scheduled elections. The latter was won by Ahmed Tejan Kabbah of the Sierra Leone People's Party (SLPP), the veteran Independence party of the Margai brothers, Sir Milton (prime minister 1956–64) and Sir Albert (1964–7). By the end of the year a peace agreement had been reached with the RUF and hopes were high for Sierra Leone's recovery. In the diamond-rich east of the country, where most of the fighting was concentrated, local villagers formed vigilante militias known as 'Kamajors' to protect themselves from the indiscriminate looting, mutilation and limb amputations that characterised the RUF rebellion. The RUF leader, Foday Sankoh, felt that Kabbah's Sierra Leonean army was in league with the Kamajors, and in any case he was clearly never going to be content with a constitutional route to power. He formed an alliance with a faction in the army led by Major Johnny Koroma. In May 1997 Koroma overthrew Kabbah in a coup and set up an Army Forces Revolutionary Council (AFRC).

With little help from the wider international community, West African leaders sent in ECOMOG to expel the AFRC/RUF from Freetown. In March 1998 President Kabbah was able to return to the capital and a UN peace-keeping force of 6000 was assembled, but it had no firm mandate to take the fight to the enemy and the war continued in the region beyond Freetown. The 'international community', as expressed through the UN

Figure 31.2 Abdoulaye Wade, elected president of Senegal in 2000, addressing the World Economic Forum in Davos, Switzerland, January 2004, at which he reminded the major industrial powers of their responsibility to give active economic support to the 'New Democratic Wave' in Africa

465

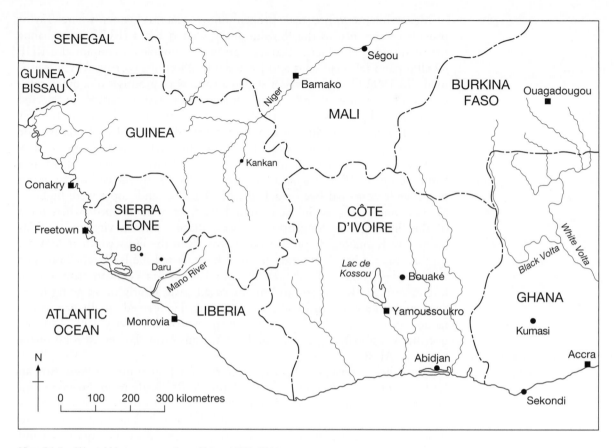

Map 31.1 West African zones of conflict, *c*.1990–2011

Security Council, clearly had little stomach for a firm military commitment in Sierra Leone and President Kabbah came under intense international pressure to come to terms with the RUF and bring Sankoh into government. The subsequent peace treaty, signed in Togo in July 1999, however, was quickly violated by the rebels who now pushed into Freetown itself. The city was saved by firm ECOMOG and British intervention. This action helped turn around the war as ECOMOG took the fight to the enemy and British military advisers trained up a new Sierra Leonean army. Sankoh was captured and subsequently died in prison and the Abuja ceasefire of November 2000 marked the beginning of the end of the conflict. In January 2002 President Kabbah celebrated the formal ending of the war by ceremonially destroying a large stockpile of weapons that had been surrendered over the previous two years.

In May 2002 Kabbah's government was re-elected and a Special Court was set up to try war criminals. In June 2003 the Special Court indicted President Charles Taylor of Liberia for crimes committed by his instigation of the RUF rebellion. This action helped precipitate the fall of Taylor himself.

Taylor had for years played a pivotal role in stirring up regional conflict and his former actions and alliances soon came back to haunt him. In 1999 Liberians United for Reconciliation and Democracy (LURD) launched an attack from Guinea, with the support of President Conté whose country had for years suffered from the conflicts in both Sierra Leone and Liberia. They were joined by newly disarmed Kamajors from Sierra Leone. Tens of thousands of people were displaced as the LURD rebels pressed towards Monrovia. Regional pressure mounted for Taylor to step down before new elections and this was achieved by the Accra Agreement of June 2003. Two months later Taylor went into exile in Nigeria on the understanding that he would not be extradited out of the country to stand trial.

In 2006, however, Nigerian President Olusegun Obasanjo agreed to Taylor's extradition to the Liberian capital Monrovia. In the meantime, in 2005 economically crippled Liberia had elected Ellen Sirleaf Johnson as President. In January 2006 Sirleaf Johnson took office as Africa's first and only female elected head of state. Despite her surname, which her father had adopted from the then-serving Liberian president, Sirleaf Johnson came from a poor indigenous rather than Americo-Liberian background. An economist, with wide international financial experience, there were high hopes that she, if anyone, could steer Liberia through a much-needed economic recovery. Her first symbolic task, to get the electricity back on in the capital, was achieved by the middle of the year. She was then confronted with what to do with Taylor, amid fears that he may not receive a fair trial in either Sierra Leone or Liberia. She wisely backed plans mooted at the UN to have the Special Court transferred to The Hague in The Netherlands. In due course Taylor was transferred to The Hague and his lengthy trial commenced there in January 2008.

In October 2011 Sirleaf Johnson was jointly awarded the Nobel Prize for Peace and went on to win the first round of the presidential election the following week. Her main opponent, William Tubman, however, condemned the vote as fraudulent and boycotted the run-off the following month, leaving Sirleaf Johnson's re-election unopposed.

The inter-linked civil wars of the Mano River region of Liberia and Sierra Leone had lacked any clear political, economic or philosophical direction. Fed by extremes of inequality, poverty and despair at the ineffectiveness of corrupt government, the conflicts were characterised by ethnic enmity, brutality, personal ambition, distrust and greed. The latter was fed by the spoils of war, especially from the misuse of diamonds, a resource which, as shown in the case of Botswana, has the potential to play a very positive role in the achievement of civil stability and development. The illicit sale of so-called 'blood diamonds', however, had been financing brutal civil conflicts in Angola, the Congo and the Mano River region for many years. To counter this, DeBeers, the world's biggest diamond marketing organisation proposed the setting up of what became known as the Kimberley Process Certification Scheme. The process enabled experts to identify the geological origins of illicitly acquired diamonds and thus prevent them from entering the legal diamond market. Backed by the UN, the scheme came into effect in 2003.

Côte d'Ivoire

Neighbouring Côte d'Ivoire had for years been flagged as the symbol of stability in the region. During his long presidency (1960–93) Houphouët-Boigny had actively encouraged immigrant labour and farmers from Côte d'Ivoire's poorer northern neighbour Burkina Faso. The general principle that the land belonged to those who worked it attracted many Burkinabe to the country's thriving cocoa and coffee sector. By the turn of the century there were an estimated two and a half million people of Burkinabe origin in

Côte d'Ivoire, besides many other immigrants, many making vital contributions to the country's success. Indeed, Houphouet-Boigny's prime minister, Alassane Ouattara, was the Muslim son of a Burkinabe immigrant. He had presidential ambitions and hoped to succeed Houphouët-Boigny. On the latter's death in December 1993, however, in accordance with the constitution the president of the National Assembly, Henri Konan Bédié, a southern Christian, became president.

Serious economic problems in the 1980s had already obliged the then prime minister Ouattara to introduce the harsh restrictions of a structural adjustment programme. In the 1990s falling coffee and cocoa prices and the devaluation of the CFA franc combined to confirm that the era of post-independence prosperity was definitely over. Despite contributing so much to the country's economic success in times of plenty, the 'immigrant community' was made the scapegoat when the economy suffered a serious downturn. Bédié allowed the crude ethnic concept of 'ivoirité' to intrude into Ivoirian politics. To be northern and Muslim was to be suspect and 'foreign'.

In December 1999, with ethnic tension mounting and Bédié's government unable to solve the country's economic problems, General Robert Guei seized power in a coup. Mass street demonstrations, however, forced him to step down and hold presidential elections in October 2000. Ouattara, a 'Burkinabe foreigner', was barred from standing and the veteran opposition politician Laurent Gbagbo won the election. The exclusion of Ouattara and the subsequent sacking of Guei and others from the army added to ethnic tensions within the country. Although a coup attempt by a group of soldiers in September 2001 was foiled, the rebellious soldiers seized control of the central garrison city of Bouake and the country slid dangerously towards all-out civil war. The rebels had no more coherent demands than the LURD or RUF of Liberia and Sierra Leone, but they threatened the economic and political stability of the whole region. Côte d'Ivoire was responsible for 40 per cent of the GDP of the whole of the CFA zone, and Mali and Burkina Faso in particular were heavily dependent upon Ivorian economic stability. France too had an important stake, with 60 per cent of her exports to west Africa passing into or through Côte d'Ivoire.

An emergency ECOWAS summit was held in Accra and France brokered a peace deal in Paris in January 2003. French forces were stationed at various points in the country; but the rebels were not disarmed, in line with the peace deal; they remained in control of the north; and there were no moves towards an inclusive government. Early in November 2004 Gbagbo's government launched an attack on the rebel stronghold during which nine French soldiers were killed. The French retaliated by destroying the entire Côte d'Ivoire airforce on the ground in Abidjan. This provoked anti-French riots and the smashing of French business premises. When the French responded by shooting dead some fifty unarmed demonstrators, they lost all credibility as peacemakers; whereupon the African Union in the person of South African president Thabo Mbeki stepped in. His intervention ensured that the year ended with calm restored to north and south of the country. Fighting over the ensuing years, however, continued on and off until a peace agreement was finally signed in 2007.

Presidential elections were supposed to have occurred in 2005, but they were frequently postponed because of the on-going civil war. With this now ended, elections were due to take place in 2009, but they were again postponed until late 2010. After the second-round run-off between incumbent Laurent Gbagbo and former Prime Minister Alassane Ouattara in November 2010, the Independent Electoral Commission announced that Ouattara had won 54 per cent of the vote. This announcement was challenged the following day by the chairman of the Constitutional Council, who claimed that Gbagbo had won the election. Amid rising violence, especially perpetrated by supporters of Gbagbo in Abidjan, the ground was set for a classic stand-off between the representative of the north and the representative of the south. ECOWAS, with UN backing, implied that it would use force if necessary to ensure the true winner, Ouattara, was installed. Gbagbo was supposed to have stood down by March 2011. When this did not happen, Ouattara's forces, with French military support, swept down into Abidjan and Gbagbo was arrested. An uneasy peace settled over Cote D'Ivoire.

Nigeria

The giant of the region, Nigeria, finally returned to civilian rule in May 1999, under the presidency of the former military ruler (1976–9) Olusegun Obasanjo. Although military rule had by this time been hugely discredited, as much for its corruption as for its authoritarianism and violence, the road to political and economic stability in Nigeria was strewn with pot-holes. The run-down oil industry failed to fulfil its development potential, while the adoption of *sharia* law by a number of northern states sparked inter-ethnic violence between Christians and Muslims that threatened the political security of the whole federation. Nevertheless, for the first time in nearly forty years (since 1964) and for only the second time in its independent history, Nigeria saw out a whole governmental term and re-elected Obasanjo to the presidency in 2003. The real turning-point for Nigeria, however, was set by the election of Goodluck Jonathan in 2011.

When Obasanjo's successor, President Yar'Adua died in office in May 2010, Vice-President Goodluck Jonathan was sworn in as president. A Christian from the south, Jonathan then defied the People's Democratic Party's tradition of allowing the presidency to alternate between north and south of the country after the completion of two terms. He stood for election in 2011 and won a resounding victory. It appeared that the people of Nigeria were ready for a new era in the country's politics. However, a failed oil industry, combined with institutional corruption and inter-religious distrust that consistently verged into episodes of extreme violence, were such deep-seated problems that elections alone could never be expected to solve them.

chapter
32

Contemporary Africa (2)

Eastern and Central Africa

Figure 32.1 Mwai Kibaki, leader of the National Rainbow Coalition (NARC), elected President of Kenya in 2002 on a platform of anti-corruption, free primary education and economic renewal, is greeted warmly by President Thabo Mbeki of South Africa in Pretoria, August 2003. Kibaki did not live up to his anti-corruption rhetoric, with disastrous consequences for the country

The history of eastern and central Africa since the 1990s has been largely overshadowed by the spectres of civil war, ethnic conflict and genocide. Against this negative backdrop Tanzania remained poor but relatively stable.

Kenya

Kenya managed to outlive the autocratic rule of President Moi and elect an opposition politician, Mwai Kibaki, to the presidency in December 2002. Kibaki's National Rainbow Coalition launched a five-year economic recovery plan that showed some early promise. Its commitment to uncover and fight corruption, however, was a grave disappointment. Disillusionment soon set in. High unemployment, crime and poverty were still widespread as graft continued, alongside ethnic favouritism. Widespread ethnic violence that left

1300 dead followed the general election of 2007 when it looked as though the Orange Democratic Movement of Raila Odinga had won the election, but President Mwai Kibaki refused to step down. The ethnic violence was finally ended when a peace deal was brokered in January 2008 by former Secretary-General of the United Nations Kofi Annan. But the power-sharing deal that left Kibaki as president, alongside Odinga as prime minister, set a dangerous precedent: namely, that a defeated politician could remain in power if his supporters used enough violence, as happened in Zimbabwe later in the year (see below). As we saw above, ECOWAS refused to countenance such a deal when Cote D'Ivoire's defeated incumbent refused to step down in 2011.

Even a power-sharing deal, however, failed to sort out Kenya's endemic corruption. Kenyans use the metaphor 'eating' to refer to corrupt politicians feeding off the state, and with no politician found guilty of corruption, the saying by 2010 was: 'They are all eating together.' The International Criminal Court (ICC) in The Hague, however, took action against those accused of instigating the ethnic violence of 2007. In April 2011 the ICC indicted six of Kenya's most prominent political leaders, including Uhuru Kenyatta, the son of Kenya's founding president, Jomo Kenyatta.

The Horn of Africa   The peoples of Ethiopia and Eritrea won their freedom from the Marxist dictatorship of Mengistu Haile Mariam as a result of a prolonged civil war. The Eritreans had begun their war for independence from Ethiopia as early as 1964 (see above, p. 400). After Mengistu took control of Ethiopia's ruling military *derg* in 1977, he gained the support of the Soviet Union whose massive supply of weaponry enabled Mengistu to defeat the Eritreans almost totally. During the 1980s, however, the Soviet input decreased and the Eritrean People's Liberation Front (EPLF) regained control of most of Eritrea outside of Asmara. By the late 1980s numerous Ethiopian rebel movements had joined the war against the Mengistu regime, particularly the Tigray People's Liberation Front (TPLF). In 1989 they united under the Ethiopian People's Revolutionary Democratic Front (EPRDF), fighting in alliance with the Eritreans against a common enemy. By 1990 the EPRDF and the EPLF controlled most of the north of the country, with the Oromo Liberation Front active in the south.

In 1991 Mengistu fled to exile in Zimbabwe. The EPRDF took over the government in Ethiopia and the EPLF did likewise in Eritrea. Following an earlier agreement and a referendum, Eritrea seceded from Ethiopia and became independent in 1993. Unfortunately, recovery from decades of conflict, hardship and drought was disrupted in 1998 by a border dispute that escalated far too quickly into a full-scale border war between the two former allies. It was only brought to an end by a devastating Ethiopian military victory in 2000. In 2006 Ethiopia was drawn into another international conflict as, with United States' backing, it invaded its neighbour Somalia.

In Somalia the vacuum created by the departure of Mohammed Siad Barré in 1991 had opened the way for clan-based militias to effectively destroy the nation-state. In May 1991 the northern region (former British Somaliland) seceded as the independent 'Republic of Somaliland', but it failed to gain international recognition. The remainder of Somalia disintegrated into ten or more clan-controlled territories, largely under the rule of 'war lords' and ill-disciplined militias. For a while in the early 2000s, local religious leaders established some semblance of stability in an attempt to take the guns off the streets. As they gained control over more areas they came together to form the Islamic Courts Union (ICU). This, however, was in the aftermath of the 9/11 attacks on the World Trade Centre in New York.

In President George W Bush's 'War on Terror', Somalia was suspected of harbouring 'Islamic terrorists'. Consequently, in December 2006, the United States instigated an invasion of Somalia by Ethiopia. The aim was to establish a Transitional Federal Government (TFG) that would bring stability to Somalia and root out Islamic extremism from the country. The invasion effected the opposite. It radicalised members of the ICU and led to the founding of *Harakat al-Shabaab al-Mujahideen* ('Movement of the Warrior Youth'), popularly known as 'al-Shabaab'. As Ethiopia withdrew, the African Union became involved in support of the TFG, sending in an armed peacekeeping force, the African Union Mission in Somalia (AMISOM). Through 2008–9 al-Shabaab began capturing territory and setting up rudimentary local government structures. The TFG's claim to be a 'government' was shown to be totally hollow and AMISOM was soon involved in direct armed conflict with al-Shabaab in the streets of Mogadishu. As drought and food shortages hit the region in 2009–11, al-Shabaab was unable to cope with the food needs of the people, but was distrustful of the World Food Programme and other international relief agencies. Thousands of starving Somalis fled across the border into Kenya as the United Nations declared a famine in the region and instigated emergency relief. Outside observers condemned al-Shabaab for its authoritarian violence; but the TFG did not appear to offer a viable alternative. Under these circumstances, the situation in this strategically important country remained critical.

Sudan

Apart from an 11-year hiatus (1972–83), civil war has been a feature of Sudan's history since the year before independence in 1956. Traditionally portrayed as a war between Arab/Muslim north and African/Christian or traditional-religion south, the reality is that there have been several interconnecting and conflicting civil wars devastating Sudan, particularly since the 1980s. The Sudan People's Liberation Army (SPLA), under the leadership of John Garang, has, for the most part, dominated the southern struggle for independence from the north. But there have been numerous other groups in rebellion against the central government, both southern and northern Muslim. For its part, the Khartoum government has generally been dominated by northerners who would see themselves ethnically as part of the Arab Muslim world.

There has been a long history of northerners exploiting and raiding the resources of the south – in the form of slaves, ebony and ivory through the nineteenth century (see above, pp. 289–90). But in the late twentieth century a new resource entered the fray in the form of huge oil reserves located just to the south of the traditional administrative border of northern and southern Sudan. A return to civil war in 1983 disrupted the full exploitation of the oil reserves, but the government made its intentions clear by building an oil pipeline straight to Port Sudan, thus preventing the south from gaining direct benefit from its own resource. The other major natural resources of Sudan are its water and its fertile soil, most of which are also to be found in the south. This provides the impetus for the determination of successive Khartoum governments to maintain and strengthen their control

Map 32.1 Sudan/South Sudan, *c*.1990–2011

473

of the south. Part of their means of doing this has been the implementation of *sharia* law. But this in turn has sharpened the SPLAs determination to separate from the north.

The government of Ahmad al-Bashir first came to power through a coup in 1989. Supported by the Muslim Brotherhood's National Islamic Front (NIF), al-Bashir's government stated its determination to turn Sudan into an Islamic state. In 1991 *sharia* was officially abolished in the south; but this concession failed to relieve war tension as it strengthened the SPLA's determination to be separated from the north where *sharia* still applied. In 1993 Sudan officially returned to civilian rule, with al-Bashir as the elected president. Through the 1990s oil revenues enabled the government to purchase massive armaments and a search for a lasting peace agreement began in 1997. The government attempted to isolate the SPLA by making overtures towards the Nuer-based South Sudan Defence Force (SSDF) which dominated the struggle in the region of the oil fields. 'Arab' nomad militias were widely used by the government in its war in the south. Early in 2003 the rebel movements in Darfur, the Sudan Liberation Army and the Justice and Equality Movement, realised they were being excluded from the tentative negotiations that were going on between Garang's SPLA and the Khartoum government. But as they stepped up their rebellion in Darfur through 2004, the government unleashed its militias, known as the Janjaweed. Backed by government air attacks, these 'Arab' militias wreaked havoc in the western region of north Darfur, taking the opportunity to 'ethnically cleanse' rival Muslim 'African' pastoralists from their traditional grazing lands. While international eyes were focused on the real prospects of peace between central government and the SPLA, up to a million people were displaced in the west, with 100,000 of them fleeing into neighbouring Chad.

By the early months of 2004, an accord between Khartoum and the SPLA had been brokered by the Kenyans which set out a political framework for peace, if not yet a firm and complete ceasefire. The accord provided for a six-year transition period of limited 'power-sharing' before a referendum on the independence of the south. A power-sharing agreement that brought John Garang into government as vice-president was formally agreed in January 2005. Garang died shortly afterwards in a helicopter accident, but the power-sharing agreement survived the shock. When the time for the long-awaited referendum finally came in 2011, the south voted almost unanimously for separation from the north. There were still armed clashes over disputed territory in the border area, but the Khartoum Government did not halt the process leading to independence , as many feared, and on 9 July 2011 Africa's newest state, South Sudan, was born.

Uganda

Following the Tanzanian invasion and overthrow of Idi Amin in 1979, Uganda made a poor start at political and economic reconstruction. The old divisions of the 1960s resurfaced and Obote was returned to power in a flawed election in 1980. Yoweri Museveni, who had been among the first to commit himself to guerrilla warfare against Amin, took to the bush again, determined to transform the Ugandan political scene by force. His National Resistance Army finally won power in 1986. Thereafter, Museveni established a non-party 'movement' system of political accountability and, with important Western backing, revitalised the moribund economy, at least in the south. Prosperity in the north was thwarted by a disparate group of 'bandit' rebels, who operated out of southern Sudan. They remained a constant thorn in the side of the Museveni regime and a drain on its 'all-inclusive' credibility. In 2005 Museveni, who had made a virtue of the claim that he was 'not like other presidents', changed the constitution so that he could be elected for more than two terms. Continuing to be elected in successive elections, Museveni became more intolerant of opposition the longer he stayed in power, introducing restrictive laws on freedom of expression and association. In a 'Walk to Work' peaceful protest against rising fuel prices in April–May 2011, people abandoned cars and taxis and thronged the streets of Kampala. Insisting that this was not a 'Tahrir Square moment', Museveni's police used heavy-handed tactics to disperse the protesters.

Rwanda

The regime of Juvénal Habyarimana, in power since 1973, was a northern regional and family affair, to the exclusion of other Hutu elites. He established a civilian one-party state in the 1980s that lasted until the emergence of a multi-party system in 1991. By then a civil war had begun with an invasion by Tutsi exiles from Uganda. The soldiers of this Rwanda Patriotic Front (RPF), under the leadership of Paul Kagame, had learned their guerrilla warfare by fighting for Yoweri Museveni's National Resistance Army (NRA) in Uganda (1981–6).

Habyarimana had initially reacted to the invasion by clamping down on Tutsi in Kigali. This was followed by the recruitment and training of thousands of Hutu militias that went by the name of *Interahamwe* ('those who stand together'). Habyarimana's army and the militia were trained and armed by the French who were determined to hold on to influence in this little bit of 'francophonie' and prevent it from falling to the 'Anglos' of the Ugandan-educated RPF. The Interahamwe underwent secret political indoctrination that prepared them for a 'final solution' – an act of genocide against all Tutsi in Rwanda and any Hutu 'traitors' who opposed the Hutu regime.

In 1992 international pressure mounted on Habyarimana to reach a settlement with the RPF, and the Arusha Accord of 1993 allowed for limited power-sharing with the RPF. But this was seen by Hutu hard-liners as a betrayal. Habyarimana's years of rule through his northern family clique had distanced him from wider Hutu support and he was no longer trusted to protect exclusively Hutu interests. When neighbouring Burundi's new and only Hutu president, Melchoir Ndadaye, was assassinated by Burundi's largely Tutsi army in October 1993 the die was cast. Lists of targets for assassination were secretly drawn up in the Rwandan capital Kigali and the Interahamwe were primed by the notorious Radio Télévision Libre des Mille Collines to ready themselves for the imminent destruction of the Tutsi '*inyenzi*'.

The shooting-down of Habyarimana's plane as it approached Kigali airport on 6 April 1994 was taken as the signal for the genocide to commence. The main political figures of Habyarimana's government were killed within hours, the killing of hundreds of thousands of Tutsi civilians all over the country took longer. Nevertheless, at a chilling rate, over approximately 100 days an estimated 800,000 Tutsis were killed, many by machete, by their known neighbours, often herded into churches where they received little or no protection from the clergy.

The genocide was brought to an end by the RPF's occupation of Kigali in July 1994. The Interahamwe fled westwards to the protection of Mobutu's Zaïre (Congo), taking some two million Hutu civilians with them

Map 32.2 East-central Africa, *c.*1990–2011

for protective cover. The general exodus was overseen by a French intervention force. This allowed the Interahamwe and remnants of the Hutu army to regroup and provide an on-going threat to the security of the new RPF government in Rwanda.

In 1995 Kagame's Rwandan army raided the Hutu refugee camps of eastern Zaïre, seeking out the Interahamwe and driving the bulk of the Hutu refugees back into Rwanda. It was the start of Rwanda's involvement in a regional war in the Congo that was to last officially until 2003.

Democratic Republic of Congo (Zaïre)

The Rwandan government did not see itself as secure until it had rid eastern Zaïre of all trace of potential-rebel Hutu. It saw its chance in a rebellion in eastern Zaïre in 1996. The Rwandan army supported the rebellion in what effectively became an invasion of its neighbour, and culminated in a general rout of Mobutu's army and the fall of Mobutu himself in 1997. The Rwandans installed the veteran Congolese rebel Laurent Kabila in power in Kinshasa; but the new government of the renamed Democratic Republic of Congo failed to provide the border security hoped for by Rwanda and its ally Uganda. Fearing that Kabila's government was actually supporting their Hutu and other enemies in eastern Congo, Rwanda and Uganda switched their allegiance in 1998 and sent in occupying armies to support anti-Kabila rebels in the east of the Congo.

The internationalisation of the Congolese civil war was heightened by the entry of Angola, Namibia and Zimbabwe on the side of Kabila's government. While Angola, Uganda and Rwanda could legitimately claim strategic security interests in their intervention, and Namibia was there out of loyalty to Angola, Zimbabwe's intervention was more dubious. There have been strong allegations that Zimbabwe was mainly attracted by the promise of diamond concessions and a desire to distract attention from its own internal problems. As the war continued through several years, however, similar allegations – the pursuit of mineral wealth, as well as human rights abuses – have been levelled at the Ugandan and Rwandan armies. The assassination of Laurent Kabila by his own bodyguard in January 2001 brought his son Joseph Kabila to the presidency. After many false starts, a regional peace accord was finally signed in December 2002 that provided for the withdrawal of all foreign troops during 2003. More than three million Congolese had died over the five years of civil war, and full peace, stability and recovery still remained little more than a hope for the future in the Congo.

The looting of eastern Congo's minerals, especially coltan, that valuable ingredient of mobile cell phones, remained a strong incentive for banditry and militia violence. And a decade after Joseph Kabila came to power a low-level war rumbled on, with mass-rape being used as a weapon of terror by militias and government troops alike.

Southern Africa

South Africa

The main theme of Mandela's one term in office was reconciliation between the races, and certainly in that respect South Africa since liberation has been enormously successful. On the economic front the judgment has not been so clear-cut.

Since the first overtures towards the exiled ANC by South Africa's white business community in the mid-1980s, it had become clear that an ANC government was not going to inaugurate the socialist revolution outlined in its Freedom Charter and subsequent propaganda. This was understood by de Klerk when he took his momentous decision to enter formal negotiations with the ANC. Mandela, his successor Thabo Mbeki, and the ANC establishment generally, put their faith in the retention of the capitalist system.

They believed that the removal of the racial factor would enable the black majority to share in the economic growth that would follow political liberation. More than a decade on from South African liberation the reality of the *apartheid* version of capitalism lay exposed: it was as much about retaining class privilege and control as it ever was about race. Class distinctions remained, but with a new prosperous African middle class joining the white elite in their segregated suburbs. A huge amount was achieved by the ANC governments of Mandela and Mbeki, in the provision of electrification, water and housing, but for the huge poor majority progress was desperately slow. In the meantime class and wealth divisions between rich and poor grew.

As Mbeki entered his second five-year term in office there began developing within the ranks of the ANC a feeling that the president was too remote from the harsh realities of life as experienced by the mass of the people. This perhaps accounted for the growing popularity of his charismatic and populist deputy-president (1999–2005) Jacob Zuma. At the ANC conference in Polokwane in December 2007, Zuma challenged Mbeki for the leadership of the ANC and won. The presidency of South Africa was based upon the leader of the largest party at a general election, and Zuma's move had in effect left Mbeki as president without a party. In many other African countries the incumbent president would have found a way to stay on, but Mbeki recognised the constitutional impossibility of his situation and stepped down in September 2008. Following a brief interim presidency by the ANC's deputy president Kgalema Motlane, Jacob Zuma was elected president of South Africa at the general election of May 2009.

Angola and Mozambique

The liberation of South Africa brought immediate relief to her two formerly Portuguese-ruled neighbours, Angola and Mozambique. For both it meant the end of South African sponsorship of 'rebel' movements that had no political programmes beyond destabilising South Africa's 'socialist' neighbours. Peace enabled Mozambique to move fairly smoothly to multi-party democracy. The rapid economic growth there that accompanied post-war reconstruction was only temporarily interrupted by the hugely destructive natural flooding of the Zambezi in 2000 and 2002.

In Angola attempts to bring rebel UNITA leader Jonas Savimbi into constitutional democracy failed in 1992. When he realised he had lost the election, Savimbi took to the bush again and restarted the war. He was encouraged in this by the failure of the United States (his former backers) to recognise immediately the electoral victory of the nominally 'Marxist' MPLA government. US recognition was crucially withheld for six months pending the successful outcome of negotiations between US oil companies and the Angolan government. UNITA's rebellion, now partly funded out of illegally traded Angolan and Congolese diamonds, continued until Savimbi's death in February 2002. Angola was finally able to get on with the task of national recovery and development, funded from its vast oil wealth, although the Dos Santos regime had by then developed a reputation for large-scale corruption.

Zimbabwe

The principal outstanding issue facing Robert Mugabe's government following Zimbabwe's political liberation in 1980 was that of land ownership. The vast majority of the country's viable arable land was in the hands of a tiny minority of white settlers. It was the issue that most of the veterans of the liberation war of the 1970s had fought for. Mugabe had believed the verbal assurances of the British government that it would raise a fund to buy out white farmers, whose predecessors had seized the land, without compensation, during the original British colonisation of the 1890s (see above, pp. 334–5). But the fund did not materialise. Initially, Mugabe did not press the matter as the tobacco products of the white-owned commercial farms were Zimbabwe's principal foreign-exchange earners. In the late 1990s, however, rising unemployment in the urban areas put Mugabe's ZANU/PF government under increasing political pressure from a well-educated, articulate, urban electorate. It was in these circumstances that Mugabe chose to return to the 'unfinished business' of land redistribution. With ZANU/PF encouragement, self-professed 'war veterans' (many too young to have fought in the war) occupied white-owned land, forcing most of their owners to abandon their farms. The anarchic manner of the 'land redistribution' enabled ZANU/PF youth to terrorise the rural areas and thus ensure ZANU/PF victory in subsequent elections. On the other hand, agricultural production was seriously disrupted, foreign capital fled the country, currency exchange-rates and inflation soared and the economy virtually collapsed. Mugabe, however, in denial about the economic chaos around him and the political violence that was keeping him in power, stuck to anti-colonial rhetoric and blamed the British government for most of Zimbabwe's woes.

Political violence by party activists and police against perceived critics of the regime increased through the mid-2000s. In spite of this ZANU/PF finally lost its majority to the opposition Movement for Democratic Change (MDC) in the parliamentary elections of 2008. In the presidential elections MDC leader Morgan Tsvangirai won more votes than Mugabe, but not enough for outright victory. With a second round scheduled, the level of ZANU/PF violence grew so great that Tsvangirai withdrew his candidacy. International pressure forced Mugabe to accept a power-sharing deal whereby he remained as president, but with Tsvangirai as prime minister. With Mugabe in his late eighties in 2011 and in failing health, a revised constitution approved and a new electoral register in the offing, signs were optimistic for freer and fairer elections in 2012–13.

The HIV/AIDS pandemic

From the mid-1980s Africa's youthful population was particularly hard hit by the HIV/AIDS pandemic. The initial trouble was that this new sexually transmitted disease was widespread in the heterosexual population of central and eastern Africa before the disease was even recognised. From the mid-1980s to the mid-90s it spread devastatingly through much of central, eastern and southern Africa – often carried initially by migrant workers and long-distance transport drivers. In the absence of a vaccine, new drugs were developed in the industrial West to suppress the virus; but they were too expensive for African health budgets. Governments, therefore, either remained in denial of the seriousness of the crisis or focused upon preventive programmes of public health education. The latter was developed effectively in Uganda where infection rates had begun to drop by the late 1990s. Some sceptics believed that this was because infected people were dying and were thus falling away from the statistics. Nevertheless, there is no doubt that public health education did play a positive role in raising people's awareness that it was a preventable infection

Figure 32.2 A health education poster in Botswana, 1997. Following the relative success of Uganda's example, Botswana (with one of the continent's best infrastructures for health clinics, schools, clean water and political stability) has embarked upon a pro-active campaign of public information and peer-education to combat the pandemic of HIV/AIDS

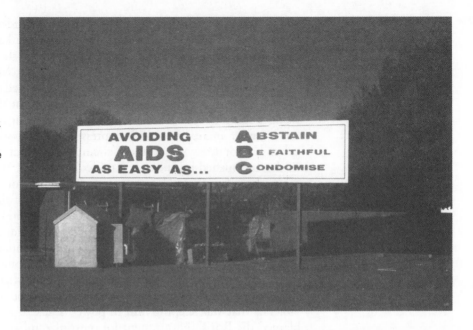

and rates of new infection have begun to fall elsewhere. As the accompanying illustration shows, Botswana, with particularly high rates of infection in the mid-1990s, followed Uganda's example and embarked upon a pro-active campaign of public health information and peer-education to combat the disease. Nevertheless, the virus had by then cut a swathe through the generation that had grown to maturity since independence and upon whose shoulders so much of the hope for the future had been placed.

Since the turn of the millennium the price of drugs to suppress (but not cure) the virus has been brought down and a number of countries have been able to make these drugs available to some of the infected population, focusing particularly upon pregnant women to prevent the spread of the virus to the next generation. These, however, have been the more fortunate, stable countries, such as Botswana, Namibia, South Africa, Uganda and Senegal. Others, such as the Democratic Republic of Congo, plagued by widespread warfare and mass-rape, and with little effective infrastructure, are likely to continue to be devastated by the pandemic for many years to come.

China and Africa

The previous edition of this book (published in 2005) concluded that Africans in the first decade of the new millennium had much to be hopeful about. Most of the civil wars that plagued the continent in the 1990s had, by local African commitment and effort, been brought to peaceful conclusions (Sierra Leone, Liberia, Sudan, Angola, to some extent Congo, though not Somalia). And with the pan-African spirit of the new African Union, and the greater economic integration of regional organisations, Africa might well be at the beginning of a genuine renewal. That was written before the significance of China in Africa had become widely apparent.

Since its withdrawal from direct trading contact with the east African Swahili coast in the fifteenth century, China had no direct links with Africa until the 1960s. Then the Chinese communist government was prepared to provide a small amount of finance to what it perceived to be socialist governments – such as Nyerere's Tanzania – and to provide small-arms weaponry to radical African liberation movements. The only infrastructure project of note was the TAZARA (Tanzania Zambia Rail Authority) railway, built with an interest-free Chinese loan in the early 1970s to link the Zambian Copperbelt with the port of Dar-es-Salaam. Since the turn of the millennium, however, as China has emerged on the world economic scene as the world's fastest growing industrial economy, this situation has changed dramatically. In 2005 China was still a minor player in Africa. Six years later she was the continent's largest single trader and investor, eclipsing the former European colonial powers and the United States in both value and volume of trade and investment in Africa. China's rapid industrial growth has been drawing in mineral resources (especially oil and precious metals) and other raw materials from Africa on a scale of growth that exceeds even the early colonial period. Which raises the question: is China Africa's new neo-colonial master? The consensus answer appears to be 'No', based upon two points: the scale of China's infrastructure investment and the fact that China pointedly has nothing to do with Africa's politics. This latter point means that she turns a blind eye to dictatorships and abuses of democratic rights – hardly surprising in the light of China's own political system. Where Western investors hesitate to tread, such as Sudan or Zimbabwe, China moves in with massive investment.

China has chosen South Africa as its principal investment base, from which to advance northwards, and in 2011 she invited South Africa to join the BRIC (Brazil, Russia, India, China) group of emerging industrial nations.

The bilateral investment projects that China is most involved in are to do with transport, not only roads, but in particular railways. All over the continent rail construction has returned, with Chinese capital and expertise, on a scale not seen since the early years of the twentieth century. And this is not just Chinese state investment. Although many of the larger financing agreements are bilateral, government to government, most of the Chinese investment in Africa is by private Chinese companies, investing in particular in mining. At times their treatment of their African work forces has given rise to unease and protest, as on the Zambian Copperbelt, and whether the Chinese presence in Africa comes to be widely resented remains to be seen. It will probably depend on the success of African economic growth and employment.

As was written at the end of this book's previous edition, 'Africa might well be at the beginning of a genuine renewal.'

Suggestions for further reading

General histories and regional surveys

The most comprehensive general reference works, in order of publication are:
The Cambridge History of Africa, 8 vols (CUP, Cambridge, 1975–86)
UNESCO General History of Africa, 8 vols (Heinemann, London, 1981–93; abridged paperback editions, James Currey, Oxford, 1990–9)
Historical Atlas of Africa, J. Ajayi and M. Crowder (eds) (Longman, Harlow, 1985)
Africa, T. Falola (ed.), 5 vols (Carolina Academic Press, Durham NC, 2000–3)
Encyclopedia of African History, K. Shillington (ed.), 3 vols (Fitzroy Dearborn/Routledge, New York, 2005)

Single-volume general histories include:
A History of African Societies to 1870, E. Isichei (CUP, Cambridge, 1997)
The Making of Contemporary Africa: The Development of African Society since 1800, B. Freund, 2nd edn (Macmillan, Basingstoke, 1998)
The Civilizations of Africa: A History to 1800, C. Ehret (James Currey, Oxford, 2002)
Africa Since 1800, R. Oliver and A. Atmore, 5th edn (CUP, Cambridge, 2004)
Africans: The History of a Continent, J. Iliffe, 2nd edn (CUP, Cambridge, 2007)
A History of Sub-Saharan Africa, R. O. Collins and J. M. Burns (CUP, Cambridge, 2007)
A History of Modern Africa, 1800 to the Present, R. J. Reid (Wiley-Blackwell, Oxford, 2009)

Detailed regional surveys include:
A History of the Maghrib in the Islamic period, J. M. Abu-Nasr (CUP, Cambridge, 1987)
Trans-Saharan Africa in World History, R. Austin (OUP, Oxford, 2010)
History of West Africa, J. Ajayi and M. Crowder (eds), 2 vols, 3rd edn (Longman, Harlow, 1985–6)
The Great Lakes of Africa: Two Thousand Years of History, J. P. Chrétien (Zone, New York, 2003)
History of Central Africa, D. Birmingham and P.M. Martin (eds), 2 vols (Longman, Harlow, 1983)
The Cambridge History of South Africa, C. Hamilton, B. K. Mbenga, R. Ross, A. K. Mager and B. Nasson (eds) 2 vols (CUP, Cambridge, 2010–11)

Useful books on method and theory are:
J. Vansina, *Oral Tradition as History* (James Currey, Oxford, 1985)
D. P. Henige, *The Chronology of Oral Tradition: Quest for a Chimera* (Greenwood Press, Westport, 1987)
S. Howe, *Afrocentrism: Mythical Pasts and Imagined Homes* (Verso, London and New York, 1998)

A controversial and influential challenge to Eurocentric views of world history remains:

C. A. Diop, *The African Origins of Western Civilization* (Lawrence Hill Books, Chicago, 1974)

Within this theme: M. K. Asante, *The History of Africa: The Quest for Eternal Harmony* (Routledge, New York, 2007)

Important general thematic books, covering a long time-frame:

G. Connah, *African Civilizations. Precolonial Cities and States in Tropical Africa: An Archaeological Perspective* (CUP, Cambridge, 1987)

J. Iliffe, *The African Poor: A History* (CUP, Cambridge, 1987)

P. R. Schmidt and R. J. McIntosh (eds), *Plundering Africa's Past* (Indiana UP, Bloomington, 1996)

D. M. Anderson and R. Rathbone (eds), *Africa's Urban Past* (James Currey, Oxford, 2000)

D. L. Hodgson, *Rethinking Pastoralism in Africa* (James Currey, London, 2000)

Continent-wide academic journals containing articles based on some of the most up-to-date research on African history as well as extensive book reviews:

Journal of African History (Cambridge, 1960–)

International Journal of African Historical Studies (Boston, 1968–)

History in Africa (Los Angeles, 1974–)

African Archaeological Review (Cambridge, 1983–)

Other journals relating mostly to modern or contemporary affairs include:

African Affairs (formerly Journal of the Royal African Society, since 1901) (Oxford, 1944–)

African Studies Review (Atlanta, 1956–)

Journal of Modern African Studies (Cambridge, 1963–)

For more detailed works on specific themes and periods see the following:

Human origins (Chapter 1)

Barham, L. and P. Mitchell, *The First Africans: African archaeology from the Earliest Toolmakers to most Recent Foragers* (CUP, Cambridge, 2008)

Berger, L. with Brett Hilton-Berber, *In the Footsteps of Eve: The Mystery of Human Origins* (National Geographic Adventure Press, Washington DC, 2000)

Stringer, C. and R. McKie, *African Exodus: The Origins of Modern Humanity* (Jonathan Cape, London 1996)

Prehistory: from Stone Age to Iron Age (Chapters 1 to 4)

Barich, B. E. P., *Water and Grain: The Beginnings of Domestication in the Sahara and the Nile Valley* (L'Erma di Bretschneider, Rome, 1998)

Blench, R. M. and K. C. MacDonald (eds), *The Origins and Development of African Livestock: Archaeology, Genetics, Linguistics and Ethnography* (UCL Press, London, 2000)

Ehret, C., *An African Classical Age: Eastern and Southern Africa in World History, 1000BC to AD400* (James Currey, Oxford, 1998)

Hassan, F. A. (ed.), *Droughts, Food and Culture: Ecological Change and Food Security in Africa's Later Prehistory* (Kluwer Academic/Plenum, New York, 2002)

Herbert, E. W., *Iron, Gender and Power: Rituals of Transformation in African Societies* (Indiana UP, Bloomington, 1993)

Keine, B., and D. Nurse (eds), *African Languages: An Introduction* (CUP, Cambridge, 2000)

Kent, S. (ed.), *Gender in African Prehistory* (Altamira Press, Walnut Creek, 1998)

Lane, P., A. Reid, A. Segobye, *Ditswa Mmung: The Archaeology of Botswana* (Pula Press and Botswana Society, Gaborone, 1998)

Lewis-Williams, D. and T. A. Dowson, *Images of Power: Understanding Southern African Rock Art* (Southern, Johannesburg, 1999)

Marshall, F. and E. Hildebrand, 'Cattle before Crops: The beginnings of food production in Africa', *Journal of World Prehistory*, 16:2 (2002), 99–143

Neumann, K., A. Butler, S. Kahlheber (eds), *Food, Fuel and Fields: Progress in African Archaeobotany* (Heinrich-Barth Insitutue, Köln, 2003)

Perigrine, P. and M. Ember (eds), *Encyclopedia of Prehistory: Africa* (Kluwer Academic/Plenum, New York, 2001)

Pwiti, G. and R. Spear (eds), *Aspects of African Archaeology* (University of Zimbabwe Publications, Harare, 1996)

Shaw, T., P. Sinclair, B. Andah, A. Okpoko (eds), *The Archaeology of Africa: Food, Metals and Towns* (Routledge, London, 1993)

Sutton, J. E. G. (ed.), *The Growth of Farming Communities in Africa from the Equator Southwards* (British Institute in Eastern Africa, Nairobi, 1995)

van der Veen, M. (ed.), *The Exploitation of Plant Resources in Ancient Africa* (Kluwer Academic, New York, 1999)

Ancient Egypt, Kush and Meroe (Chapters 2 and 3)

Bord, K. A., *Encyclopedia of the Archaeology of Ancient Egypt* (Routledge, London, 1999)

Clayton, P. A., *Chronicle of the Pharaohs: The Reign-by-Reign Record of the Rulers and Dynasties of Ancient Egypt* (Thames & Hudson, New York, 1994)

Davies, W. V., *Egypt and Africa, Nubia from Prehistory to Islam* (British Museum Press, London, 1991)

Dodson, A., *The Hieroglyphs of Ancient Egypt* (New Holland, London, 2001)

Manley, B., *The Penguin Historical Atlas of Ancient Egypt* (Penguin Books, London, 1996)

Midant-Reynes, B., *The Prehistory of Egypt: From the First Egyptians to the First Pharaohs* (Blackwell, Oxford, 1999)

O'Connor, D., *Ancient Nubia: Egypt's Rival in Africa* (University of Pennsylvania Museum, Philadelphia, 1993)

Smith, W. S., *The Art and Architecture of Ancient Egypt*, 3rd edn (Yale UP, New Haven, 1998)

Török, L., *The Kingdom of Kush: Handbook of the Napatan-Meroitic Civilization* (Brill, Leiden, 1997)

Tyldesley, J., *Rameses the Great* (Viking, London, 1999)

Welsby, D. A., *The Kingdom of Kush: The Napatan and Meroitic Empires* (British Museum Press, London, 1996)

Wildung, D. (ed.), *Sudan: Ancient Kingdoms of the Nile* (Flamarion, New York, 1997)

North and northeastern Africa to 1000 CE (Chapter 5)

Brett, M. and E. Fentress, *The Berbers* (Blackwell, Oxford, 1996)

Cherry, D., *Frontier and Society in Roman North Africa* (Clarendon Press, Oxford, 1998)

Pearson, B. A., *Earliest Christianity in Egypt* (Institute for Antiquity and Christianity, Claremont, 1997)

Phillipson, D. W., *Foundations of an African Civilisation: Aksum and the Northern Horn, 1000BC–AD1300* (James Currey, Oxford, 2012)

Raven, S., *Rome in Africa*, 3rd edn (Routledge, New York, 1993)

Shaw, B. D., *Environment and Society in Roman North Africa* (Variorum, Aldershot, 1995)

The Sahara and west Africa to the sixteenth century (Chapters 6 and 7)
Austen, R. (ed.), *In Search of Sundiata: The Mande Epic as History, Literature and Performance* (Indiana UP, Bloomington, 1999)
Connah, G., *African civilizations. Precolonial Cities and States in Tropical Africa: an Archaeological Perspective* (CUP, Cambridge, 1987)
Insoll, T., *The Archaeology of Islam in Sub-Saharan Africa* (CUP, Cambridge, 2003)
Levtzion, N. and J. F. P. Hopkins (eds), *Corpus of Early Arabic Sources for West African History* (CUP, Cambridge, 1981)
Levtzion, N., *Ancient Ghana and Mali* (Methuen, London, 1973)
Lovejoy, P. A., *Salt of the Desert Sun* (CUP, Cambridge, 1986)
Lovejoy, P. A., *Transformations in Slavery*, 2nd edn (CUP, Cambridge, 2000)
Savage, E., *The Human Commodity: Perspectives on the Trans-Saharan Slave Trade* (Frank Cass, London, 1992)

Eastern, central and southern Africa to the sixteenth century (Chapters 8, 9 and 10)
Chrétien, J. P., *Burundi: L'histoire retrouvée* (Karthala, Paris, 1993)
Galaty, J. G. and P. Bonte (eds), *Herders, Warriors and Traders: Pastoralism in Africa* (Westview Press, Boulder, 1991)
Garlake, P., *Great Zimbabwe Described and Explained* (Thames & Hudson, London, 1973)
Hall, M., *The Changing Past: Farmers, Kings and Traders in Southern Africa, 200–1800* (David Philip, Cape Town, 1987)
Henze, P., *Layers of Time: A History of Ethiopia* (Hurst, London, 1999)
Horton, M. and J. Middleton, *The Swahili* (Blackwell, Oxford, 2001)
Huffman, T. H., *Snakes & Crocodiles: Power and Symbolism in Ancient Zimbabwe* (Witwatersrand UP, Johannesburg, 1996)
Kent, R. K., *Early Kingdoms in Madagascar, 1500–1700* (Holt, Rinehart & Winston, New York, 1970)
Kusimba, C. M., *The Rise and Fall of Swahili States* (Altamira, Walnut Creek, 1999)
Schmidt, P. R., *Iron Technology in East Africa* (James Currey, Oxford, 1997)
Schoenbrun, D., *A Green Place, A Good Place: Agrarian Change, Gender and Social Identity in the Great Lakes Region to the 15th Century* (Heinemann, Portsmouth NH, 1998)
Wilmsen, E. N., *Land Filled with Flies: A Political Economy of the Kalahari* (University of Chicago Press, Chicago, 1989)

North Africa to the eighteenth century (Chapter 11)
Abu-Nasr, J. M., *A History of the Maghrib in the Islamic Period* (CUP, Cambridge, 1987)
Cornell, V. J., *Realm of the Saint: Power and Authority in Moroccan Sufism* (University of Texas Press, Austin, 1998)
Daly, M. W. (ed.), *The Cambridge History of Egypt*, Volume 2, *Modern Egypt, from 1517 ...* (CUP, Cambridge, 1998)
Getahun, S. A., *History of the City of Gondar* (AWP, Asmara, 2006)
Le Gall, M. and K. Perkins (eds), *The Maghrib in Question* (University of Texas Press, Austin, 1997)
Nicolle, D., *The Mamluks, 1250–1517* (Osprey, London, 1993)
Strathern, P., *Napoleon in Egypt* (Vintage, London, 2008)
Walker, E. P., *Exploring an Islamic Empire: Fatimid History and its Sources* (I.B. Taurus, London, 2002)

The Slave Trade and west Africa to the nineteenth century (Chapters 12, 13 and 16)

Alie, J. A. D. A., *A New History of Sierra Leone* (St Martin's Press, New York, 1990)

Anstey, R., *The Atlantic Slave Trade and British Abolition, 1760–1810* (Macmillan, London, 1975)

Barry, B., *Senegambia and the Atlantic Slave Trade: Senegambia Before the Colonial Conquest* (CUP, Cambridge, 1998)

Bay, E. G., *Wives of the Leopard: Gender, Politics and Culture in the Kingdom of Dahomey* (University of Virginia Press, Charlottesville, 1998)

Djata, A., *The Bamana Empire by the Niger: Kingdom, Jihad and Colonization, 1712–1920* (Markus Wiener, Princeton, 1997)

Hawthorne, W., *Planting Rice and Harvesting Slaves: Transformations along the Guinea-Bissau Coast, 1400–1900* (Heinemann, Portsmouth NH, 2003)

Law, R., *The Slave Coast of West Africa, 1550–1750: the Impact of the Atlantic Slave Trade on an African Society* (Clarendon Press, Oxford, 1991)

McCaskey, T., *State and Society in Pre-Colonial Asante* (CUP, Cambridge, 1995)

Roberts, R., *Warriors, Merchants and Slaves: The State and the Economy in the Middle Niger Valley, 1700–1914* (Stanford UP, Stanford, 1987)

Shick, T., *Behold the Promised Land: A History of the Afro-American Settlers in Nineteenth-Century Liberia* (Johns Hopkins UP, Baltimore, 1977)

Solow, B. L. and S. L. Engerman (eds), *British Capitalism and Caribbean Slavery: the Legacy of Eric Williams* (CUP, Cambridge, 1987)

Thornton, J., *Africa and Africans in the Making of the Atlantic World, 1400–1800* (CUP, Cambridge, 1998)

Webb, J. L. A., *Desert Frontier: Ecological and Economic Change along the Western Sahel, 1600–1850* (University of Wisconsin Press, Madison, 1995)

Williams, E., *Capitalism and Slavery* (University of North Carolina Press, Chapel Hill NC, 1944)

Eastern, central and southern Africa to the nineteenth century (Chapters 14, 15, 17 and 18)

Elphick, R. and H. Giliomee, *The Shaping of South African Society, 1652–1840*, 2nd edn (Maskew Miller Longman, Cape Town, 1989)

Etherington, N., *The Great Treks: The Transformation of Southern Africa, 1815–1854* (Longman, Harlow, 2001)

Hamilton, C. (ed.), *The Mfecane Aftermath: Reconstructive Debates in Southern African History* (Witwatersrand UP, Johannesburg, 1995)

Harms, R., *River of Wealth, River of Sorrow: The Central Zaire Basin in the Era of the Slave and Ivory Trade, 1500–1891* (Yale UP, New Haven, 1981)

Hassen, M., *The Oromo of Ethiopia: A History 1570–1860* (Red Sea Press, Trenton NJ, 1994)

Hilton, A., *The Kingdom of Kongo* (Oxford UP, Oxford, 1985)

Larson, P. M., *History and Memory in the Age of Enslavement: Becoming Merina in Highland Madagascar, 1770–1822* (James Currey, London, 2000)

Miller, J. C., *Way of Death: Merchant Capitalism and the Angolan Slave Trade, 1730–1830* (University of Wisconsin Press, Madison, 1988)

Newitt, M., *A History of Mozambique* (Hurst, London, 1995)

Reid, R., *Political Power in Pre-Colonial Buganda* (James Currey, Oxford, 2002)

Sheriff, A., *Slaves, Spices & Ivory in Zanzibar: Integration of an East African Commercial Empire into the World Economy, 1770–1873* (James Currey, Oxford, 1987)

Spear, T., *Mountain Farmers: Moral Economies of Land and Agricultural Development in Arusha and Meru* (James Currey, Oxford, 1997)

Vansina, J., *Antecedents to Modern Rwanda: The Nyiginga Kingdom* (UWP, Madison, 2004)

Vansina, J., *Paths in the Rainforests: Toward a History of Political Tradition in Equatorial Africa* (James Currey, Oxford, 1990)

Nineteenth century and colonial conquest (Chapters 19, 20, 21 and 22)

Ageron, C. R., *Modern Algeria. A History from 1830 to the Present* (Hurst, London, 1991)

Clark, A. F., *From Frontier to Backwater: Economy and Society in the Upper Senegal Valley, 1850–1920* (University Press of America, Lanham, 1999)

Cole, J. R. I., *Colonialism and Revolution in the Middle East: Social and Cultural Origins of Egypt's 'Urabi' Movement* (Princeton UP, Princeton, 1993)

Fahmy, K., *All the Pasha's Men: Mehmed Ali, His Army and the Making of Modern Egypt* (CUP, Cambridge, 1997)

Gewald, J.-B., *Herero Heroes: A Socio-Political History of the Herero of Namibia, 1890–1923* (James Currey, London, 1999)

Gray, R., *Black Christians and White Missionaries* (Yale UP, New Haven, 1990)

Hastings, A., *The Church in Africa, 1450–1950* (OUP, Oxford, 1995)

Landau, P. S., *The Realm of the Word: Language, Gender and Christianity in a Southern African Kingdom* (James Currey, London, 1995)

Marsden, P., *The Barefoot Emperor [Tewodros II]: An Ethiopian Tragedy* (Harper Perennial, New York, 2008)

Nasson, B., *The South African War, 1899–1902* (Arnold, London, 1999)

Olusoga, D. and C. W. Erichsen, *The Kaiser's Holocaust: Germany's Forgotten Genocide and the Colonial Roots of Nazism* (Faber & Faber, London 2010)

Pakenham, T., *The Scramble for Africa, 1876–1912* (Random House, New York, 1991)

Pennell, C. R., *Morocco since 1830: A History* (New York UP, New York, 2000)

Porter, A., *European Imperialism* (Macmillan, London, 1994)

Ross, K. R. (ed.), *Christianity in Malawi: A Source Book* (Mambo Press, Gweru, 1996)

Shik-Abdi, A., *Divine Madness: Mohammed Abdulle Hassan (1856–1920)* (Zed, London 1992)

Shillington, K., *Luka Jantjie: Resistance Hero of the South African Frontier* (Aldridge Press, London/Palgrave, New York/Wits UP, Johannesburg, 2011)

Worden, N., *The Making of Modern South Africa: Conquest, Segregation and Apartheid*, 2nd edn (Blackwell, Oxford, 2000)

Zewde, B., *A History of Modern Ethiopia, 1855–1974* (James Currey, Oxford, 1991)

Colonialism in Africa (Chapters 23, 24 and 25)

Abdullahi, M. D., *Culture and Customs of Somalia* (Greenwood Press, Westport, 2001)

Anderson, D. M. and D. H. Johnson (eds), *Revealing Prophets: Prophecy in Eastern African History* (James Currey, Oxford, 1995)

Beinart, W., *Twentieth-Century South Africa*, 2nd edn (OUP, Oxford, 2001)

Buchert, L., *Education in the Development of Tanzania, 1919–1990* (James Currey, Oxford, 1994)

Chichester, D., *Savage Systems: Colonialism and Comparative Religion in Southern Africa* (University Press of Virginia, Charlottesville, 1996)

Digre, B., *Imperialism's New Clothes: the Repartition of Tropical Africa, 1914–1919* (Peter Lang, New York, 1990)

Falola, T., *The History of Nigeria* (Greenwood Press, Westport, 1999)

Friedrichsmeyer, S., et al. (eds), *The Imperialist Imagination: German Colonialism and Its Legacy* (University of Michigan Press, Ann Arbor, 1998)

Gershovich, M., *French Military Rule in Morocco: Colonialism and its Consequences* (Frank Cass, Portland, 2000)

Harrison, C., *France and Islam in West Africa, 1860–1960* (CUP, Cambridge, 2003)

Hochschild, A., *King Leopold's Ghost: A Story of Greed, Terror and Heroism in Colonial Africa* (Houghton Mifflin, New York, 1998)

Jankowski, J., *Egypt: A Short History* (One World, Oxford, 2000)

Klein, M., *Slavery and Colonial Rule in French West Africa* (CUP, Cambridge, 1998)

Lewis, I., *Understanding Somalia and Somaliland* (Hurst, London, 2008)

Lunn, J. H., *Memoirs of the Maelstrom: A Senegalese Oral History of the First World War* (Heinemann, Portsmouth NH, 1999)

Maloba, W. O., *Mau Mau and Kenya* (Indiana UP, Blomington, 1993)

Manning, P., *Francophone Sub-Saharan Africa, 1880–1995,* 2nd edn (CUP, Cambridge, 1998)

Miers, S. and M. Klein (eds), *Slavery and Colonial Rule in Africa* (Frank Cass, London, 1999)

Moore, H. L. and M. Vaughan, *Cutting Down Trees: Gender, Nutrition and Agricultural Change in the Northern Province of Zambia, 1890–1990* (Heinemann, Portsmouth, 1994)

Nelson, S., *Colonialism in the Congo Basin, 1880–1940* (Ohio University, Athens, 1994)

Ochieng, W. R. (ed.), *A Modern History of Kenya, 1895–1980* (Evans, London, 1989)

Ranger, T., *Are We Not Also Men? The Samkange Family and African Politics in Zimbabwe, 1920–64* (James Currey, Oxford, 1995)

Thomas, M., *The French Empire at War, 1940–1945* (Manchester UP, Manchester, 1998)

van Beusekom, M., *Negotiating Development: African Farmers and Colonial Experts at the Office du Niger* (James Currey, Oxford, 2002)

Warburg, G., *Islam, Secularism and Politics in Sudan since the Mahdiya* (Hurst, London, 2003)

Wright, J., *Libya, A Modern History* (Croom Helm, London 1982)

Zewde, B., *A History of Modern Ethiopia, 1885–1991* (James Currey, Oxford, 2001)

The winning of independence (Chapters 26, 27 and 28)

Baker, C., *State of Emergency: Crisis in Central Africa, Nyasaland, 1959–1960* (I.B.Tauris, London, 1997)

Birmingham, D., *Kwame Nkrumah: The Father of African Nationalism,* revised edition (Ohio UP, Athens, 1998)

Birmingham, D., *The Decolonisation of Africa* (Ohio UP, 1995)

Cooper, F., *Decolonization and African Society: The Labor Question in French and British Africa* (CUP, Cambridge, 1996)

de Witte, L., *The Assassination of Lumumba*, trans. A. Wright and R. Fenby (Verso, London, 2001)

Geiger, S., *TANU Women: Gender and Culture in the Making of Tanganyikan Nationalism, 1955–65* (Heinemann, Portsmouth NH, 1997)

Heywood, L., *Contested Power in Angola, 1840s to the Present* (University of Rochester Press, Rochester NY, 2000)

Kanza, T., *Conflict in the Congo: The Rise and Fall of Lumumba* (Penguin, London, 1972)

Legum, C., *Congo Disaster* (Penguin Books, Baltimore, 1961)

Ogot, B. A. and W. R. Ochieng (eds), *Decolonization and Independence in Kenya, 1940–93* (James Currey, Oxford, 1995)

Pennell, C. R., *Morocco: From Empire to Independence* (One World, Oxford, 2003)

Poggo, S. S., *The First Sudanese Civil War: Africans, Arabs and Israelis in the Southern Sudan, 1955–1972* (Palgrave Macmillan, Basingstoke, 2009)

Rathbone, R., *Nkrumah and the Chiefs: The Politics of Chieftaincy in Ghana, 1951–1960* (James Currey, Oxford, 2000)

Sampson, A., *Mandela: The Authorised Biography* (Harper Collins, London, 1999)

Tignor, R. L., *Capitalism and Nationalism at the End of Empire: State and Business in Decolonizing Egypt, Nigeria, and Kenya, 1945–1963* (Princeton UP, Princeton, 1998)

Vaillant, J. G., *Black, French and African: A Life of Léopold Sédar Senghor* (Harvard UP, Cambridge MA, 1990)

Africa since Independence (Chapters 29, 30, 31 and 32)

Cooper, F., *Africa since 1940: The Past and Present* (CUP, Cambridge, 2002)

Coquery-Vidrovitch, C., *African Women: A Modern History*, trans. B. G. Raps (Westview Press, Boulder, 1997)

Cowen, M. and L. Laakso (eds), *Multi-Party Elections in Africa* (James Currey, Oxford, 2002)

Mamdani, M., *Citizen and Subject: Contemporary Africa and the Legacy of Late Colonialism* (James Currey, Oxford, 1996)

Nugent, P., *Africa since Independence: A Comparative History*, 2nd edn (Palgrave Macmillan, Basingstoke, 2012)

North Africa

Al Aswamy, A., *On the State of Egypt: What Caused the Revolution?* (Canongate, Edinburgh, 2011)

Badran, M., *Feminists, Islam and Nation: Gender and the Making of Modern Egypt* (Princeton UP, Princeton, 1995)

Lemarchand, R., *The Green and the Black: Qadhaffi's Policies in Africa* (Indiana UP, Bloomington, 1988)

Malley, R., *The Call of Algeria: Third Worldism, Revolution and the Turn to Islam* (UCLA Press, Berkeley, 1996)

Martinez, L., *The Algerian Civil War, 1990–1998* (Hurst, London, 1999)

Mojuetan, B. A., *History and Underdevelopment in Morocco: The Structural Roots of Conjuncture* (Lit Verlag, Heinburg, 1995)

Murphy, E. C., *Economic and Political Change in Tunisia: From Bourguiba to Ben Ali* (Macmillan, London, 1999)

Reudy, J. (ed.), *Islamism and Secularism in North Africa* (St Martin's Press, New York, 1994)

Vandewalle, D. (ed.), *Libya since 1969: Qadhafi's Revolution Revisited* (Palgrave Macmillan, Basingstoke, 2011)

West Africa

Adebajo, A. and A. R. Mustapha (eds), *Gulliver's Troubles: Nigeria's Foreign Policy after the Cold War* (University of KwaZulu-Natal Press, 2008)

Bingen, J. et al. (eds), *Democracy and Development in Mali* (Michigan State UP, Lansing, 2000)

Hirsch, J. L., *Sierra Leone: Diamonds and the Struggle for Democracy* (Lynne Rienner, Boulder, 2000)

Hutchful, E., *Ghana's Adjustment Experience: the Paradox of Reform* (James Currey, Oxford, 2002)

Osaghae, E. E., *Crippled Giant: Nigeria since Independence* (Hurst, London, 1998)

Richards, P., *Fighting for the Rain Forest: War, Youth and Resources in Sierra Leone* (James Currey, Oxford, 1998)

East Africa

Barkan, J. (ed.), *Beyond Capitalism vs. Socialism in Kenya and Tanzania* (Lynne Rienner, Boulder, 1994)

Behrend, H., *Alice Lakwena and the Holy Spirits: War in Northern Uganda, 1986–97* (James Currey, Oxford, 1999)

Dommen, E. and B. Dommen, *Mauritius: an island of success, 1960–1993* (James Currey, Oxford, 1999)

Eide, O. M., *Revolution and Religion in Ethiopia, 1974–85* (James Currey, 2000)

Gordon, C., *The Horn of Africa* (St Martin's Press, New York, 1994)

Hansen, H. B. and M. Twaddle (eds), *Developing Uganda* (James Currey, Oxford, 1998)

Johnson, D. H., *The Root Causes of Sudan's Civil Wars* (James Currey, Oxford, 2003)

Legum, C. and G. Mmari (eds), *Mwalimu: The Influence of Nyerere* (James Currey, London, 1995)

Lewis, I. M., *A Modern History of the Somali*, 4th edn (Uhio UP, Athens, 2002)

Central Africa

Daley, P. O., *Gender and Genocide in Burundi* (James Currey/Indiana UP, 2008)

Lemarchand, R., *Burundi: Ethnic Conflict and Genocide* (CUP, Cambridge, 1995)

Prunier, G., *The Rwanda Crisis: History of a Genocide, 1959–94* (Fontana, Kampala, 1995)

Reyntjens, F., *The Great African War: Congo and Regional Geopolitics, 1996–2006* (CUP, Cambridge, 2009)

Scherrer, C. P., *Genocide and Crisis in Central Africa: Conflict Roots, Mass Violence and Regional War* (Praeger, Westport, 2002)

Southern Africa

Hodges, T., *Angola: Anatomy of an Oil State*, 2nd edn (James Currey, Oxford, 2001)

Lodge, T., *Politics in South Africa: From Mandela to Mbeki* (Indiana UP, Bloomington, 2003)

Robins, S. L. (ed.), *Limits to Liberation in South Africa: Citizenship and Governance after Apartheid* (Ohio UP, Athens, 2004)

Scones, I. et al., *Zimbabwe's Land Reform: Myths and Realities* (James Currey, Oxford, 2010)

Seekings, J. and N. Nattrass, *Class, Race and Inequality in South Africa* (Yale UP, New Haven, 2005)

Tvedten, I., *Angola: Struggle for Peace and Reconstruction* (Westview Press, Boulder, 1997)

Index

ABAKO (Alliance des Ba-Kongo)
  408
Abacha   460
Abbas, *khedive*   356
Abbasids   83
'Abd al Mu'min   98
'Abd al-Qadir   281–2
'Abd al-Rahman al-Sa'di   1
Abdallah, Ahmed   415
Abdallah ibn Yasin   96–8
'Abdallahi, *khalifa*   291
Aborigines Rights Protections Society
  362
Abu-Bakr   97–8
Abyssinia   379, *see* Ethiopia
Acheampong, Ignatius   443
Acheulian handaxe   12, 14, 23
Acholi   20
Adal   120–22, 170–1
Adulis   77–9
Adwa, battle (1896)   295, 380
Afonso I   204–5
Africa, origin of name   71
African Lakes Company   302
African National Congress, *see* ANC
African Union (AU)   455, 463, 468,
  472, 480
African Development Bank   455
Afrikaans/Afrikaners   340–2, 376
Afrikaner nationalism/National Party
  274, 342, 376, 425–6, 429, 431
African Association   304–5, 311
Africanus, *see* Horton; *see also* Leo
  Africanus
Afro-Asiatic-speaking peoples   18–19,
  26–7
Afrocentricism   3
Agaja, King of Dahomey   199–200
Agbome   199
Age-regiments/age sets   171, 217,
  227, 229, 254, 256, 263–4,
  266–8
Agostino, *see* Neto
agriculture   8, 23–6, 29–31, 35–6,
  71–3, 76–9, 83, 86, 88–90,
  101–3, 113–14, 144–5, 151–2,
  155, 192, 194, 203–4, 208,

  212–13, 215–17, 287, 402,
  448–51, 453
  Iron Age   43–6, 49–68
Aha (Namer, Menes)   33,39
Ahmad ibn Ibrahim   121–2
Ahmed al-Mansur   174–5, 187–8
Ahmadu Seku   317
Aid, international   401, 449, 451–2,
  455
Aïr   110, 187, 191–3
Aja   199
Ajayi, *see* Crowther
Akan   105, 177, 200–2, 348
Akosombo dam   439–40
Aksum   54, 76–9
Akwamu   201
al-Sudan   1
  see also Sahel; Sudan
Alassane, *see* Ouattara
Alawid dynasty   175
Alexandria   69, 71, 73, 78, 81, 115,
  128, 283, 287–8
Algeria   55
  French occupation   280–2, 362,
    368, 374
  liberation war   395–8, 405
  modern republic   445, 460, 462–3
Allada   197, 199
All African People's Conference (1958)
  408, 418, 453
Almeida, Francisco d'   139–41
Almohad Empire   98, 100
Almoravids   93, 94, 96–8, 100, 230
Aloma, *Mai* Idris   191
Alvaro I   206
Alwa   170
Amandebele, *see* Ndebele
Ambaquista   249
America(ns)   238, 245–6, 287, 298,
  327, 328, 344, 353, 375, 447–9;
    War of Independence   237, 243,
    283
  see also United States
American Colonisation Society
  245–6, 299
Amhara   115, 122
Amin Dada, Idi   405, 443, 474

ANC (African National Congress)
  359, 427–9, 477–8
Anglo-Boer War, *see* South African War
Angola   145, 147, 149, 247–8, 323–4
  Independence   422–4, 430
  modern republic   445, 454, 456,
    477, 478, 480
Annan, Kofi   471
Antalaotra   143
Anti-Slavery Squardon   238–40, 244,
  256–7
apartheid   263, 376, 426–9, 431–2,
  455, 478
APC (All People's Congress)   464–5
Apolo, *see* Kaggwa
Arabic language   1, 80, 87, 93, 98,
  134, 163–4, 281, 304
Arabisation of north Africa   98–9,
  163–4, 169
Arabs, conquest of Egypt   76, 80–1
  in east Africa   403–4
  in north Africa   81–3, 90, 128,
    130, 134–6, 256–8, 302
  'Arab Spring'   460–4
archaeology   9–13, 15, 17, 21, 37,
  45, 54, 57, 59, 61, 75, 77,
  122–4, 130–2, 144, 151, 196,
  335
architecture   33, 37–8, 42, 51, 71,
  105, 115–16
Arma   188–9
artforms   33, 38, 51, 71, 94–5, 100,
  115
Arusha Declaration (1967)   443–4
Asante   2, 182, 200–2, 241, 300,
  318–19, 393, 454
Asantehene   201–2, 319
Askiya dynasty   110–13
  see also Muhammad Ture
Aswan dam   31, 349, 400
Ateker (Karamojong)   127, 216
Atlantic Charter (1941)   386
Augustine of Hippo   75
Australopithicines   10–11
Austronesians   130, 143
Awdaghust   90, 93, 96, 98
Ayyubid dynasty   166

Azania   128–30
Azikiwe, Nnamdi ('Zik')   373, 393

Babangida, Ibrahim   460
Badarian period, Egypt   31
Baganda   261, 325, 404
Bakongo   323, 408
Bakri, al-   91–2
Balewa, Abubakar Tafawa   393
Bamana (Bambara)   104, 189, 200,
   235
Bambandyanalo   153
Bambara, see Bamana
Bambata pottery   65
Bambuk goldfields   90, 92, 94, 101,
   108
Bambuti   21
Banda, Dr Hastings Kamusu   417,
   419–20
Bantu-speaking people   21, 30,
   57–68, 123–5, 127, 130, 134,
   143, 161–2, 217
Banu Hilal   164
Banu Kanz   169
Banu Sulaym   164
Barawa   130, 140
Barotseland   335
   see also Lozi
Barré, Siad   401, 458, 471
Barth, H.   307–8
Barwe   158
Bashir, Ahmed al-   474
Basutoland   432
   see also Lesotho; Sotho Kingdom
Battuta, see Ibn Battuta
Batwa   21
BDS (Bloc Démocratic Sénégalais)
   394
Bechuanaland   303, 333, 335, 340,
   353, 362, 432
   see also Botswana
Bédié, H. K.   468
Belgian Congo   382, 407–9
   see also Congo, Democratic Republic
      of; Congo Free State; Zaïre
Belgium/Belgians   259, 309–10,
   407–13
Bemba   150, 252, 254, 336
Ben Ali, Zine al-Abidine   461
Ben Bella, Ahmed   398
Benin, city/kingdom   46, 177, 182,
   196–9, 296, 320
Benin, Republic (formerly Dahomey
   Republic)   199, 459, 464
Benjedid, Chadli   462

Berbers   18, 42, 55, 72–5, 81–3,
   86–7, 90, 93, 96–8, 100, 164–5,
   280, 282
Berlin West Africa Conference
   (1884–5)   314, 319, 321–2, 324
Biafra   435, 442
Biko, Steve   429
Bisa   150, 208, 252
Bismark, Otto von   314–16, 324
Bito   125–6, 213
Black Consciousness movement   429
'blood diamonds', see Kimberley
   Process
Blyden, E. W.   298–300
Boer Trek   274–9
Boer War, see South African War
Boers   220–4, 228, 267, 271–7, 279,
   303, 311, 328, 330–2, 340–2
Bokassa, Jean Bedel   439, 443
Bonapart, see Napoleon
Borno   113, 187, 190–1, 232–3, 234,
   307, 318
Borno-Kanem   189–91, 233
   see also Kanem
Botha, P. W.   429
Botswana   432, 435, 452–3, 456,
   458, 480
   see also Bechuanaland
Boumedienne, Houari   398, 462
Bourguiba, Habib   396
Bouteflika   463
Brazil, and slave trade   180, 184, 201,
   206–7, 238, 240, 247–8, 256
Brazzaville   382, 384, 388
Bridewealth/brideprice   68, 151
Britain/British   463–4, 466
   abolition of slavery/slave trade
      237–41, 257, 413
   colonial administration   367–70
   and Congo   411
   and Egypt   287–9, 291
   and Ethiopia   294, 382–3
   imperialism   299–300
   and Independence   390–3,
      398–400, 402–6, 413–5, 479
   'scramble' for Africa   196, 259,
      289, 311–15, 319–21, 324–7
   and South Africa   271–4, 278–9
British Central Africa   416–20
British South Africa (BSA) Company
   303, 323, 334–6, 340, 343
Broken Hill, see Kabwe
bronze(s)   41–2, 43–4, 46, 55, 94–5,
   195–6, 198
Bruce, James   303, 306

Buganda   2, 126, 213–15, 254, 261,
   289, 303, 324–5, 404–5
Bunkeya   259, 323
Bunyoro   126, 213–15, 289, 325,
   350
Bure goldfields   93, 101, 236
burial practices   33, 36–8, 42, 48, 51,
   54, 76–8, 91, 95, 196
Burkina Faso (formerly Upper Volta)
   467–8
Burton, Richard   306–7, 311
Burundi   126, 215–16, 360, 370,
   412–13, 457, 475
Busoga   350
Buthulezi, Mangosuthu   431
Busia, K. A.   443
Butua   157
Byzantine Empire   80–1, 135

Cabral, Amilcar   422
Caillé, René   306, 311
Cairo   81, 105, 166–7, 174, 190,
   283–4, 371, 462
Calabar   241
camel(s)   55, 70, 73, 81, 85–7,
   106–7, 163, 187
Cameroon   314, 347, 355, 384
Cape Colony   219–24, 228, 267–9,
   271–4, 267–9, 301, 303, 328,
   330, 333, 335, 340–2
Cape Verde   422
Cape/Xhosa 'Frontier' Wars   224,
   272–4
capitalism   2, 186, 237–8, 448, 460,
   477–8
Caprivi Strip   315
Capsian peoples   18
Caribbean and slave trade   178,
   180–1, 184, 237–9, 283, 298
Carthage   55, 71, 81, 85–6
cash crops   287, 347–50, 362–4, 366,
   436, 449
cattle(-keeping)   22, 25–8, 35,
   49–53, 85, 120, 125, 144, 150,
   162, 171, 219, 226–9, 249,
   352–3, 355, 412, 453
   and political power   124, 151–4,
      160–1, 215–16
   domestication   19, 26
Central African Republic   439
   see also Ubangui-Chari
Cetswayo   331
Ceuta   99
CFA (Communauté Financière
   Africaine) franc   450, 457, 468

Chad (Lake) 4, 20, 26, 94, 347, 384, 394, 435, 439, 452, 474
Chagga 217
Chagos islands 415
Changamire dynasty 157, 211–12, 255
   see also Rozvi
Cheikh anta Diop, see Diop
Chewa 145, 150, 336
Chibunda Ilunga 147
Chikunda 253–4, 258
Chilembwe, John 354–5
China 132, 136, 153, 155, 257, 401, 451, 480–1
Chokwe 248–9, 323
Christian Crusaders 165–6
Christian missionaries 245, 269, 272, 296–303, 353, 371–2
Christianity 99, 111, 186, 353
   and Aksum 78–9
   in Ethiopia 114–18, 121, 171–3, 292–4
   independent Churches 353–5, 374, 376
   in Kongo 204–6
   in Madagascar 262
   in north Africa 73–5, 81–3
   in Nubia 75–6, 81, 169–70
   in South Africa 301–2
   in West Africa 243–5, 298–301
   see also Donatists; Monophysites; Missionaries; 'Ethiopian Church' movement
Chuma 308
Church Missionary Society (CMS) 298–9, 303, 373
Chwezi dynasty 125–6, 213
civil war 452, 456, 463–8, 470, 472–3, 477, 480
Cleopatra 42
climate, climate change 3–4, 9, 10, 13, 14, 18, 21, 25, 30, 447, 452–3
CMS, see Church Missionary Society
cocoa 348–9, 374, 385, 450, 467–8
coffee 385, 450, 467–8
Cold War 401, 415, 455, 458
colonialism 2, 182, 330, 353
colonisation/colonial conquest 258, 261–2, 280–91, 301, 307, 310, 312–27, 330–42, 357
   resistance to 256, 262, 330–42
colonial administration 344, 350, 367–70
colonial development strategies 389–90

colonial legacy 433–5, 436–8
'Coloured', Cape 223, 272–3
coltan 477
Comoros Islands 131, 135, 414–15
Conté, L. 466
CONAKAT (Confédération des Associations Tribales du Katanga) 408, 410
concessionary companies 321, 343–7
Confederacies, Fante and Accra 300
Congo Basin/forest/river 4–7, 10, 18, 21, 30, 59–62, 144–5, 149, 180, 203–4, 259, 309, 314, 321–3, 335, 344–7
Congo Free State 314, 322–3, 344–7
   see also Belgian Congo
Congo (Brazzaville – Moyen (Middle)) 347, 408
   see also Zaïre
Congo, Democratic Republic of (Zaïre) 409–12, 434, 436, 449, 456, 459, 477, 480
Convention People's Party (CPP) 392–3, 402
copper 31, 39, 41, 43–5, 55, 62, 95, 146, 148–50, 153, 157–8, 177, 186, 195–6, 218–19, 251, 254, 430, 436, 441–2, 449
'Copperbelt' 146, 208, 251, 323, 365, 374, 416, 418, 481
Coptic Church 70, 75, 81, 83, 115
Coptic language 75, 82, 83
corruption 401, 411, 458, 465, 469, 470–1, 478
corsairs 173, 281
corvée, see labour, forced
Côte D'Ivoire 319–21, 347, 356, 362–3, 394, 436, 439, 467–9, 471
cotton 26, 46, 111, 128, 136, 157, 164, 184, 186, 192, 248, 252, 261, 283, 287, 349–50, 385, 389, 436, 449–50
coups d'état 398, 401, 405, 412, 413, 415, 423, 435, 441–3, 459, 464, 468
cowries 105, 111, 177, 199–200, 308
CPP, see Convention People's Party
crafts/craftsmen 38, 43, 53, 67, 124, 136, 146, 148, 157–8, 192–3, 195–6, 204, 207, 210, 212, 243, 245
Creoles 245
Crowther, Revd Samuel Ajayi 245, 298–9

Cuba 240–1, 397, 424, 430
Cugoano, Ottobah 238
currency 62, 77, 100, 105, 111, 112, 135, 146, 150, 158, 164, 177, 200, 251, 450, 457, 459, 479
Cushitic-speaking people 18, 28, 61, 115, 119, 124, 127, 170, 217

Dahomey, Kingdom 182, 199–200, 241, 319, 368
Dahomey, Republic (1960–75) 199, 441
   see Benin Republic
Darfur 169, 289, 291, 356, 371, 474
Darwin, Charles 9
De Beers (diamond mining) 328–9
De Brazza, S. 321
De Klerk, F. W. 431–2, 477
debt 281, 287–8, 367, 438, 444, 447–50, 452
democracy 388, 432–3 435–6, 443, 453, 458–62, 464–5, 467, 469, 474, 478
Denkyira 201–2
development/underdevelopment 2, 182–3, 433, 435–41, 443–7, 452
diamonds 279, 301, 312, 328–9, 430, 443, 465, 467, 477–8
Difaqane 263, 268, 274, 278–9
Dinar, Sultan Ali 356
Dingane 267, 276–7
Dingiswayo 229, 264
Dinka 20, 289
Diocletian persecution 74–5
Diop, Cheik Anta 3
Dithakong, battle (1823) 270
Djenne, *see* Jenne
Djibouti 7, 295, 327, 401
Doe, Samuel 464
Dogali, battle (1887) 295
Dombo 211
   see Changamire
domestication 19, 22, 25–6, 28, 30, 45
Donatism/Donatists 74–5, 83
   see also Christianity
Dongola 75, 286, 290
Drakensberg 6–7, 161, 227–8, 265–7
drought 24, 90, 145, 152, 160, 168, 187, 205
Dube, Revd John 377
Dutch and slave trade 180, 206–7, 218

Dutch East India Company   219–21, 271
Dyula traders   104–5, 200, 235–6

East African Community (EAC)   457
East African Protectorate   350
   see Kenya
Eboué, Felix   384
ECOMOG (ECOWAS Monitoring Group)   457, 465
ECOWAS (Economic Community of West African States)   455–7, 464, 468, 471
Edo-speaking people   196
education   262, 298–9, 301
   colonial 245, 348, 353, 367, 370, 372–4, 407, 412, 427, 429, 438
   pre-colonial   371–2
   post-colonial   445–8, 458
Efik   241
Egypt   18, 94, 105, 327
   ancient   1, 3, 30–42, 43–4, 284
   Arab invasion   76, 80–1
   Fatimid   84, 114, 135, 164–5
   Mamluk   165–9
   Ottoman   168–9
   French invasion   283–4
   Muhammad Ali 'dynasty'   284–7
   British occupation   288, 314, 349, 359, 398
   Independence (1922)   376
   World War II   383
   post-war revolution   398–400
   21st century   460–2
Egyptology   3, 284
Embu   405
English, *see* Britain/British
environment   3–8, 10, 12, 14, 18, 24, 54–5, 93, 117, 152, 157, 161, 195, 203, 263
EPLF (Eritrean People's Liberation Front)   471
EPRDF (Ethiopian People's Revolutionary Democratic Front)   471
Equiano, Olaudah   238–9, 243
Eritrea   76, 295, 380–1, 383, 400, 452
Ethiopia(ns)   1, 6–7, 28, 71, 76, 114–22, 170–3, 291–6, 323, 327, 360, 380–3, 387, 401, 452, 454, 471–2
'Ethiopian Church' movement   353

ethnicity   2, 216, 258, 332, 412–13, 426, 434–5, 458, 467, 470, 472–5
Equatorial Guinea   443
evolution, human   9–15
Ewuare   196
Ezana   54, 78

Fadl Allah ibn Rabih   317
   see also Rabih ibn Fadl Allah
Fante   201, 300, 309, 319, 393
farming, origins of   21, 22–30
   see agriculture
Fasiladas   173
Fatimid dinar   164
Fatimid dynasty   84, 100, 164–6
   see also Egypt
Fayum   30, 40
Fazari, al-   91
fellahin   167, 285, 287
Fernando Poo   367
Fezzan   94, 190, 233
FIS (*Front Islamique de Salut*)   462–3
firearms, *see* guns
Firestone Rubber Company   367
fishing   15–17, 20, 24, 35, 66, 89, 108, 144–7, 203, 451
FLN (Front de Libération Nationale)   397–8, 462
FNLA (Frente Nacional de Libertação de Angola)   423–4
floodplain   30–1, 35–6, 46, 49–50, 52, 71, 75, 104, 111, 126, 226, 249–51
Foday, *see* Sankoh
Fodio, *see* Usman dan Fodio
Fokeng   227, 270
Fon   199
'Four Communes'   367
Fourah Bay College/University   299, 373
'Fourteen Points'   357, 359
France   463–4, 468, 475–6
   and Algeria   280–2, 462
   and 'assimilation'   367–70, 376, 414
   and Egypt   169, 283–4, 287–9
   and Independence   390, 393–8
   and Madagascar   262
   and 'scramble' for Africa   311, 314, 316–19, 321, 327
   and Senegal   235–6, 309, 316
   and slave trade   180, 194, 207, 237, 240
   World War I   355–6
   World War II   384, 388

FRELIMO (Frente de Libertação de Moçambique)   420–1, 425
'Free French'   379, 384, 388, 414
French Equatorial Africa   344, 347, 363, 372–3, 383–4, 393–6
French West Africa   316–19, 363, 372–3, 384, 393–6
Fu'ad   376
Fulbe (Fulani, Peuhl)   113, 182, 188, 230–3
Funj Sultanate   170, 289
Futa Bondo   317
Futa Jalon   182, 230–1, 235–6, 368
Futa Toro   113, 231, 234–5

Gabon   318, 321, 347, 389, 439, 449
Gaddafi, Muammar   454, 463–4
Galadewos   122, 296
Galla, *see* Oromo
Gambia, The   393, 460
   see also Senegambia
Gambia River region   180, 189
Gao   101, 105, 107–8, 111, 174, 188
Garamantes   56, 85
Garang, John   472–4
Garvey, Marcus   375, 391
Garenganze   323
gathering (wild food)   16–18, 21–4, 28, 67–8, 144, 218, 222, 225
   see also hunting
Gaza state   267, 337
Gbagbo, Laurent   468–9
Ge'ez-speaking people   77–8, 115
gender   2, 17, 23, 30, 35, 38, 66–8, 92, 124, 151, 176, 183, 204, 227, 248, 259–60, 266, 269–70, 298, 364–5, 372, 382
genocide   352, 413, 470, 475–6
geography   3–8, 305
Germany   298, 412
   in east Africa   256, 316, 324, 351–2, 355, 360
   and 'scramble' for Africa   312, 314–16, 324
   in South West Africa (Namibia)   302, 333, 338–40, 352–3, 355, 360, 430
   in west Africa   314–15
   World War I   355–6, 358, 360
   World War II   379, 382–4
Ghana, ancient empire   46, 88–93, 96–8, 176
Ghana (Gold Coast)   2, 202
   colonial rule   348, 356, 362–4, 374, 382, 389

Independence 391–3, 396
   Republic 408, 418, 420, 435–6,
      438–9, 441–3, 449, 453–4, 464
Gikuyu 405–6
globalisation 450–1, 460
Gobir 192, 231–2
Gojjam 114
Gokomere-Ziwa pottery 65
gold 296, 312, 449
   Akan and Asante 105, 177, 187,
      191, 200–2, 241
   and Kilwa 135–7
   and South Africa 279, 331–2, 340
   and Zimbabwe 152–5, 157–60,
      210–12, 333–5
   and trans-Saharan trade 55–6,
      86–7, 90–3, 98, 100–1,
      104–5, 107–8, 110–13
   see also Bambuk; Bure
Gold Coast 181, 300, 309, 319
   see Ghana, colonial rule
Goldie, George 320
Gondar 173, 291, 303, 306
Goodluck Jonathan, see Jonathan,
   Goodluck
Gordon, Charles 289–90
Gouveia 337–8
Gowon, J. 435, 442
Gqunukhwebe 218, 224
Gran, see Ahmad ibn Ibrahim
'Great Trek', see Boer Trek
Great Zimbabwe 65, 154–9
Greeks, in Egypt 42, 51, 69–71
Griqua 223, 225, 268–71, 275, 328
Griqualand West 328
groundnuts 29, 194, 241, 347–9,
   356, 363, 385, 389, 436, 450
Guei, R. 468
Guinea 231, 241, 362, 364, 374,
   389, 395, 441, 444, 454, 464, 466
Guinea-Bissau 422–5, 439, 445
guns 173, 182, 186–8, 191, 193, 196,
   199, 202, 205, 208–9, 220, 222,
   235–6, 243, 248–9, 253–4, 258,
   261–2, 268–71, 277, 279, 281,
   284–6, 290–2, 295, 301, 312,
   318, 324, 338, 458, 464–5, 472
Guruuswa 157

Habyarimana, Juvénal 413, 475
Hadza 21
Haile Selassie (Ras Tafari) 381–3,
   400–1, 452
Haiti 239, 283
Hajj Umar, al-, see Umar, al-Hajj

Hamed bin Muhammed (Tippu Tip)
   258–60, 322–3
handaxe, see Acheulian
Hassasn II 464
Hausa 95, 110, 187, 191–4, 197,
   199, 231–3, 320, 348, 434, 442
Hehe 256, 324
Helm, Revd 303, 334
Herero 149, 218, 225, 302, 338–40,
   352–3
Herodotus 37, 71
hieroglyphics 33–4, 70
   see also literacy
Hima 126, 215–16
historians 1–3, 11, 34, 40, 57, 62,
   91, 109, 122, 128, 187, 263,
   267, 274, 285, 288–9, 312, 328,
   367, 447
historiography 1–3, 408
Hitler, Adolf 379, 382–4
HIV/AIDS 479–80
Hlakoena 270
Hlubi 267–8
Homo, evolution of 10: habilis
   11–12; erectus 12; heidelbergensis
   12–13; neanderthalus 12–13;
   sapiens 11–15
'Horn of Africa' 18, 42, 119
Horton, James Africanus 299–300
Houphouët-Boigny, Felix 394–5,
   467–8
housing 17, 23, 28, 35, 52, 66, 76,
   91, 106–7, 113, 116, 131,
   135–6, 143, 151, 154, 161, 189,
   192, 196, 228, 478
hunting 10, 12, 22, 24, 28, 40, 45,
   49, 53, 61, 67, 88, 124, 144–5,
   147, 150, 155, 203, 210–13,
   221, 223, 225–9, 248, 251,
   253–4, 258–61
Hurutshe 227
Hutu 216, 412–13, 475–7
Hyksos invasion of Egypt 41–2

IBEA (Imperial British East Africa
   Company) 324–7, 343
Ibn Battuta 100, 105–7, 132, 137
Ibn Khaldun 100
Ibrahim, Ahmad ibn, see Ahmad ibn
   Ibrahim
Ibrahim bey 283–4
ICU (Industrial and Commercial
   Workers' Union) 377–8
Ifat 120–1
Ife 46, 195–6

Ifriqiya 81
Igbo 241–2, 245, 321, 347, 368,
   434–5, 442
Igbo-Ukwo 94–5, 196
Ijo 241–2
Ila 251
Ilorin 232, 320, 370–1
Ilunga Kalala 146
   see also Chibunda Ilunga
Imbangala 147, 207, 210, 249
IMF (International Monetary Fund)
   288, 448–50, 452, 460–1
'indirect rule' 367–70, 404, 433
industrialisation 202, 304, 356–7,
   377, 385–6, 438–40, 444–5,
   448, 450, 460–2
influenza pandemic (1918–19) 357
Ingombe Ilede 157–8
Inkatha Freedom Party 431
Interahamwe 475–6
iqta (tax-farming) 164–8, 284–6
Iron Age, early 43–68, 127, 144
   later 66, 124, 127, 144–62, 218,
   329
iron-working 44–7, 53–4, 59, 62,
   67, 89, 123–5, 146–7, 151, 161
irrigation 30–1, 35–6, 40, 77, 79,
   164, 287, 349, 389, 400, 449
Isandhlwana, battle (1879) 331
Islam 79–80, 191
   and Berbers 81–3, 90, 96–8
   in east Africa 128, 130–1, 135–6,
      137
   and education 230–1, 233, 371–2
   in Egypt 80–4
   law 230–2, 282, 460–2, 469, 474
   and literacy 233, 371
   in Maghrib 173, 176–7, 281
   in north-east Africa 118–21
   and politics 435, 461–3
   in west Africa 92–3, 187, 189,
      370–1
   see also Muslim brotherhoods
Islamic Courts Union 472
Isma'il, khedive 287–8
Italy, and Eritrea 294–5, 327, 380–1
   and Ethiopia 295, 379–83
   and Libya 356
   and Somalia 327, 401
ivory 39, 41–2, 48, 51, 56, 86–7,
   114, 119, 128, 131–2, 137, 150,
   153, 155, 158, 195–6, 198,
   208–10, 218, 229, 248–9,
   251–4, 257–61, 266, 271, 289,
   302, 312, 351

Jabavu, J. T.   301
Jaga invasion   205–6
Jaja   320
Jameson, L. S.   340
Jammeh, Yahya   460
Janjaweed   474
Jantjie, Luka   301, 332
Jenne   46, 105, 188, 371
Jere-Ngoni   255
Jibril ibn 'Umar   231
Jo-Bito clan, see Bito
Johannes IV   294–5
Johnson, Ellen Sirleaf   467
Johnson, Samuel   2
Johnston, Harry   336
Jolof   193
Jonathan, Goodluck   469
Jonathan, Leabua   432
Juhayna   169

Kaarta   235
Kabaka Yekka Party   404
Kabalega   325
Kabbah, Ahmed   465–6
Kabila, Laurent   456, 477
Kabila, Joseph   477
Kabwe   12
Kadalie, Clements   377
KADU (Kenya African Democratic
    Union)   426
Kagame, Paul   475–7
Kaggwa, Apolo   2
Kalahari Desert   4–7, 151, 218,
    225–6, 338, 353, 452
Kalala, see Ilunga Kalala
Kalenjin   217
Kalonga dynasty   150, 209–11
Kamajors   465, 467
Kamba   217, 254
Kamerun, see Cameroon
Kamwana, Eliot   345–5
Kanbalu   132, 135
Kanemi, Muhammad al-   233–4
Kanem   94–5, 190–1
    see also Borno-Kanem
Kano   191–3, 232–3
KANU (Kenya African National
    Union)   406
Kanuri-speakers   94, 190, 233
Karamojong, see Ateker
Kariba dam   448
Kasanje   147, 207, 249
Kasavubu, Joseph   408–9
Katanga (Shaba)   344, 347, 408–12
Katsina   232

Kaunda, Kenneth   419, 430, 436,
    440
Kazembe's Lunda   208–9, 251–2,
    254, 259
Kebbi   192, 232
Kenya   324–7
    colonial   350–1, 368, 383, 385,
        389, 401, 403
    Independence   405–6
    Republic   436, 445, 457, 460,
        470–1
Kenyatta, Jomo   387, 406–7, 436,
    471
Kenyatta, Uhuru   471
Kerma   49–50
Kgatla   227
Khaldun, see Ibn Khaldun
Khama III   301, 303
Khama, Seretse   430, 432
Khami   157
Kharijite movement   83
Khoekhoe (Khoikhoi)   162, 219
    (map)
Khoesan (Khoisan)   17, 19, 21, 25,
    28, 68, 161–2, 218–24, 228,
    272, 300–1
Khufu   38
Khumalo   266, 270
Kibaki, Mwai   470–1
Kikuyu   217, 254, 261, 327, 368,
    385
    see also Gikuyu
Kikuyu Central Association   406
Kilwa   131, 135–7, 140–1, 211, 252,
    256
Kimbangu, Simon   374
Kimberley Process Certification
    Scheme (diamonds)   467
kingship   34–5, 53, 78, 101–3, 105,
    110–11, 143, 144–7, 150–1,
    155, 158, 195, 199, 201, 209,
    213, 250–1
Kirina, battle of (1235)   101
Kisale   145–6
Kiswahili   128, 134, 136, 403
Kitara   125–6
Kiyabanda, Grégoire   413
Koena   227
Kololo   251, 254, 335
Kongo   145, 149–50, 181, 296, 309,
    323
Kora (Koranna)   223, 268–9, 328
Kordofan   20, 289–90
Koroma, Johnny   465
Kru   367

Kruger, Paul   340–1
Ksar Kebir, al-, battle (1578)   174
Kuba   204
Kumbi-Saleh   91–3
Kunda   146
Kush (Nubia)   39, 48–9, 76
Kwale pottery   62
KwaZulu Natal   265
Kwena   227

labour   271–2, 276, 279, 328, 330,
    351, 406
    forced   223, 285, 321, 327, 332,
        340, 347, 367–8, 385, 389,
        409, 412
    migrant   2, 276, 329, 331, 337,
        352, 365–6, 373, 429, 432
    see also slavery
Lagos (lagoon, colony)   196, 241,
    311, 314, 319
Lalibela   115, 117–18
Lamtuna Berbers   96–7
Lamu islands   130, 134–5
land   272–4, 277–9, 282, 286, 293,
    329–40, 342, 351, 385, 398,
    406, 432, 451, 478–9
    see also settlement, white
Lander brothers   306, 311
languages of Africa, ancestry   18–21
    as evidence   57–9, 122–3, 125,
        143, 161
Leabua, see Jonathan, Leabua
League of Nations   360, 381–2, 412,
    430
Lebna-Dengel   121
Leo Africanus   111
Leopard's Kopje culture   152–4
Léopold II   309–10, 314, 322–3,
    344–7, 410
Lesotho   227, 432
    see also Basutoland; Sotho Kingdom
Lettow-Vorbeck, Paul von   355, 358
Lewanika I   250–1, 335–6
Liberia   243, 245–6, 298–9, 301,
    318, 380, 457, 464–8, 480
Libya   42, 71, 356, 380, 383–4,
    463–4
literacy   33–4, 49, 51, 91–2, 96, 98,
    100, 103, 122, 134, 163, 298,
    301, 305, 336, 371–3, 386, 407,
    438
Livingstone, David   258, 307–9, 311
LMS; see London Missionary Society
Loango   204
Lobedu   227

Lobengula 303, 334–5
London Missionary Society (LMS) 298, 300–1, 303
Lozi 226, 249–51, 335–6
  see also Barotseland
Lualaba River 145, 149
Luanda 206, 249
Luba kingdom/empire 146–7, 150, 259
Lubosi, see Lewanika
Lueji, see Rweej
Luena 147
Lugard, Frederick 320, 324–5, 368
Luka Jantjie, see Jantjie
Lumumba, Patrice 408–11
Lunda (Empire) 147, 207–8, 248, 252, 408
  see also Kazembe
Lunda titles 147, 250
Lundu dynasty 209–10
Luo 126
Lupemban tradition 21
LURD (Liberians United for Reconciliation and Democracy) 466–8
Luthuli, Albert 428
Luyana 147, 249–50
Lwo-speakers 125
Lydenburg 65

Maasai 127, 216–17, 254, 261, 324, 326
Machel, Samora 425, 430
Mackenzie, Revd John 303
Madagascar 5, 61, 143, 221, 262, 396, 414
Magdala, battle (1868) 293–4
Mahdi, see Muhammad Ahmed
Mahdist Sudan 290–1, 318
Maherero 339–40
Mahmadu Lamine 317
Maïnassara, Ibrahim 460
maji-maji 324, 351–2
Makanga 258, 338
Makoko 321
Makonde 337
Makurra 75, 81, 169
Malagasy, kingdoms 262
  language 143; people 414
Malawi 418–20, 435, 459
  region 145, 150, 255, 301–2
  see also Nyasaland
Malawi Congress Party 419
Malebo Pool 149–50, 204–6, 310, 321, 344, 346–7

Mali, Empire 93, 100–8, 192, 200, 235–6, 318
Mali, Republic 394, 436, 454, 459, 464, 468
Malindi 136, 139
Malinke 93, 200, 235
Mamluks 165–6, 283–6
  see also Egypt
Mancham, James 415
'Mandate' territories 360, 401, 412, 430
Mande 88, 100, 182, 235
Mandela, Nelson 427–8, 431, 456, 477–8
Mandinka 235–6, 317–18
Mane migration 182
Manganja 150, 209
Mano River Union 464
Mansur, see Ahmed al-Mansur
manufacturing 33, 144, 146, 149–50, 158, 192, 248, 252, 262, 385–6, 436, 439, 447
Manyika 158, 211
Mapela 152
Mapungubwe 153–4
Maravi 150, 209–11, 254, 418
Margai, Albert 465
Margai, Milton 465
'Maroons' 238, 244
marketing boards 385, 393, 438, 440
marriage 17, 68, 151, 224
  see also gender
Marxism 2–3, 471
Mashonaland 334
Masina 234–5, 317
Massangano 258
Massawa 168, 171, 294–5
Massingire 258, 338
Massinissa 72
Masudi, al- 132, 135
Matabele, see Ndebele
mathematics 33–4, 99
Matiwane 267, 269
Matope 158
Mau Mau, rebellion 405–6
Mauritania, region 55, 72–3, 82
  Republic 397
Mauritius 256, 262, 413–14, 435, 458
Mawanga, kabaka 213
Mazoe 157, 159
Mazrui 326
Mbanderu 225, 340
Mbanza Kongo 150

Mbeki, Govan 428
Mbeki, Thabo 432, 456, 468, 470, 477–8
Mboya, Tom 406–7
Mbukushu 226
Mbundu 145, 147, 149, 207, 323
MDC (Movement for Democratic Change) 479
medicine 300, 307
Menalamba revolt (1895–7) 262
Menelik II 294, 327, 381
Menes, see Aha
Mengistu Hailie Mariam 401, 471
Merina kingdom/empire 262
Meroe 49–54, 69, 75–6, 78
Meru 405
Mfecane 263, 267, 274, 279
  see also Difaqane
microliths 11–15, 21
migrancy, see labour
military rule 435, 441–3, 457, 458–60, 464–7, 469
mineral revolution 328–32, 425
mining 53, 56, 144, 146, 251, 328–9, 331–2, 364–6, 581
Mirambo 261
missionaries 269, 296–303, 351, 353, 403, 427
  agents of imperialism 301–2
  see also Christianity; Church Missionary Society; London Missionary Society
MK, see Umkhonto we Sizwe
Mlozi 261
MNC (Movement National Congolais) 408–9
Mobutu Sese Seko 410–12, 458–9, 475, 477
Moffat, Robert 270
Mogadishu 130–1, 135–6
Mohammed VI, of Morocco 464
Moi, Daniel arap 406, 460, 470
Mombasa 136, 139–42, 257
Momoh, Joseph 465
Mondlane, Eduardo 425
Monophysites 75, 78, 115
  see also Donatists
Morocco 6, 105, 174, 280, 356, 368
  Independence 396, 464
  invasion of Songhay 174–5, 187–9
  see also Western Sahara
Moshoeshoe 268–9, 278, 301
Moshoeshoe II 432

Mossi   108–11
Moyen (Middle) Congo   321
   see also Congo (Brazzaville)
Mozambique   131, 141, 159,
   210–11, 221, 256, 344, 445–6,
   451–2, 454, 478
   Independence   390–401, 402–15,
   417–27, 453
Mpande   277
Mpangazita   267
MPLA (Movimento Popular de
   Libertação de Angola)   423–4,
   430
Mpondo   267
Msiri's Yeke Kingdom   259, 322–3
Mswati I   267
Mthetwa   229, 263–5
Mubarak, Hosni   461–3
Mugabe, Robert   420–2, 430, 446,
   456, 478–9
Muhammad, The Prophet   79, 80,
   83, 84, 232
Muhammad V, of Morocco   396
Muhammad Abdile   327
Muhammad Ahmad, el-Mahdi
   290–1
Muhammad Ali, pasha of Egypt
   284–7, 400
Muhammad Bello   232, 234
Muhammad Ture   109–13, 187
Mukhtar, Umar al-, see Umar
Mungo Park   189, 305, 311
Munhumutapa (Mwene Mutapa)
   158–60, 211, 296
Munyigumba   256
Murad bey   283–4
Murphy, Revd J. B.   344–6
Murtala Muhammed   442
Musa, Mansa   102, 104–6, 304
Museveni, Yoweri   457, 474–5
Muslim brotherhoods   281, 290, 371,
   376, 460, 462, 474
Mussolini, Benito   379–80, 382
Mutapa state   157–60, 210–11, 254,
   296, 333
Mutesa I, kabaka   261, 404–5
Mutota   158
Muzorewa, Abel   422
Mwaant Yaav, see Mwata Yamvo
Mwambutsa IV   413
Mwanga, kabaka   315, 325
Mwata Yamvo (Mwaant Yaav)   147,
   207–8, 252
Mwene Mutapa, see Munhumutapa
Mzilikazi   266, 270–1, 334

Nama   225, 302, 338–40, 352–3
Namer, see Aha
Namib Desert   4–7, 225, 338
Namibia   218, 225, 302, 314,
   429–30, 454–6, 477, 480
Nandi   127, 327
Napata   49–51, 54
Napoleon Bonaparte   280–1
NATO (North Atlantic Treaty
   Organisation)   463–4
Narmer, see Aha
Nasir, Abd al- (Nasser, Abdul)
   398–400
Natal   267, 277–9
nationalism, African   2
   in Egypt   288, 359, 376
   pre-colonial   299–301
   anti-colonial   352, 354–5, 359,
   374–8
NCNC (National Council of Nigeria
   and the Cameroons)   393
Ncome River, battle (1838)   277
Ndadaye, Melchoir   475
Ndebele   255, 265, 269–71, 275–6,
   303, 334–6
Ndongo   147, 149, 181, 206
Ndwandwe   229, 263–5, 267, 270
Ndzinga   206
Necho   42
Négritude   375–6, 394, 429
neo-colonialism   182, 410, 439,
   450–1, 481
Netekamani   54
Neto, Agostino   423–4
Ngamiland   225
Ngola   149, 206
Ngoni   254–6, 267, 271, 336–7, 356
Nguéma, Marcias   443
Ngungunyane   337
Nguni-speakers   161, 218, 224,
   227–9, 263, 265, 270
Ngwane   263–4, 267, 268–9
   see also Sobhuza
Niani   100–1, 103
Niger   364, 394, 439, 449, 460
Niger River   5–7, 304, 306, 311, 314
   'Inland Delta'   7, 26, 30, 46, 234
   Niger Bend   7, 20, 175, 189, 307
   Delta   7, 180, 241, 298–9, 307,
   309, 319–20
Niger-Congo languages   20–1,
   29–30, 57–9, 88, 113
Nigeria   319, 343, 347–8, 355–6,
   362–4, 366, 368–71, 373, 382,
   389

Independence   393
   civil war   393, 435, 442
   Republic   433–5, 441–2, 449, 457,
   460, 469
Nile River   4–6, 18–19, 26, 30,
   49–50, 311
Nilo-Saharan languages/peoples
   18–20, 26–8, 94, 125
Nilotic-speaking peoples   125–7,
   216–17
Njimi   94, 189
Nkomo, Joshua   419–20
Nkongolo   146
Nkore   126, 213, 215–16, 325
Nkrumah, Kwami   374, 387, 391–3,
   404, 435, 439, 442, 453–5
Nkumbula, Harry   417–18
Noba   54, 75, 81
Nok culture   46, 48, 95, 196
Northern Rhodesian African National
   Congress   418
NPC (Northern People's Congress)
   393
NRA (National Resistance Army)
   474–5
Nubia(ns)   18, 33, 39, 42, 45–50, 54,
   75–6, 81, 164, 168–9
Nuer   20, 474
Nujoma, Sam   430–1
Numidia   71–3, 75
Nupe   232
Nyamwezi   217, 254, 259–61
Nyanga   150, 336
Nyasaland (Malawi)   336–7, 354–5,
   383, 389, 416–20
   see also Malawi
Nyasaland African Congress   418
Nyerere, Julius   402–4, 430, 434,
   436, 443–5, 481
Nyungu   261

OAU (Organisation of African Unity)
   454–5, 457
Obasanjo, Olusegun   442, 467, 469
Obote, Milton   404–5, 474
Odinga, Raila   471
Oduduwa   195–7
Ogaden   383, 401
Oginga Odinga   406
oil (petroleum)   241, 420, 441, 445,
   447, 449–50, 472–4, 478, 481
'Oil Rivers'   306–7
Olaudah, see Equiano
Oldowan tools   11
Omdurman, battle (1898)   291

one-party states   435–6, 458, 460, 462, 475
Oorlams   223
Opobo   320
Opoku Ware I   202
oral tradition   1, 2, 100, 109, 122, 146–7, 150, 157–8, 372
Oromo   122, 170–3, 295, 327, 471
Osei Kwadwo   202
Osei Tutu   201–2
Ottobah, *see* Cugoano
Ottomans   121, 171, 187, 355–6
   in Egypt   168–70, 284, 287
   in north Africa   174, 191, 281, 380
Ouattara, Alassane   468–9
Ovambo   149, 218, 225, 325, 340, 353
Ovimbundu   159, 249, 257
Oyo   182, 194, 197, 199–200, 241

PAC (Pan-Africanist Congress)   427
PAIGC (Partido Africano da Independência da Guiné e Cabo Verde)   422, 424–5
PARMEHUTU (Parti de l'émancipation de people Hutu)   413
palm oil   29–30, 200, 241–3, 245–6, 248, 319, 347, 356, 385, 451
Pan-Africanism   299–300, 374–5, 387, 391–2, 453–5
   see also PAC
Park, *see* Mungo
'pass' system   363, 377, 527
   see also labour
pastoralism   21–8, 40, 43, 52, 54–5, 59, 67–8, 73, 79, 86, 93–4, 113, 120, 122–7, 149, 161–2, 163–4, 170–1, 215–16, 218–19, 222–5, 230–1, 261, 449, 452, 474
peasantry   2, 33, 35, 52, 82–3, 187, 191, 200, 232, 291, 347–51
Pedi   227, 276, 330–2
Pemba   132–3, 135, 257
Periplus of the Erythraean Sea   77, 128, 130
Peters, Carl   315
Peuhl, *see* Fulbe (Fulani)
pharaohs   34–42
Phelps-Stokes Commission   373
Phiri clan   150
Phoenicians   54–5, 71, 85
plantation system   177–8, 180, 184–6, 199–200, 237–41, 256–7, 259, 262, 282–3, 344, 348, 350, 363

Plaatje, Sol   301, 377
PMSD (Parti Mauricien Social Democrate)   414
Pokot   127
Polisario Front   397
   see also Western Sahara
political parties, formation of   359, 376, 378, 391–4, 397, 402, 404, 406, 408, 412–15, 416–25, 427, 432
polygamy, *see* gender
pombeiros   206–7
population   18, 23, 46, 52, 54, 144, 147, 157, 168, 183, 185, 196, 219, 221, 224, 226, 228, 232, 238, 278, 282, 285, 304, 329, 353, 367–8, 393, 397, 400, 416, 435, 445, 461–2, 467
Portuguese, in Angola   206–7, 311, 323–4
   and Christianity   296
   colonial administration   369–70
   decolonisation   422–5
   on east African coast   137–42, 218, 252–3, 257
   and Ethiopia   121–2, 296
   and Independence   388
   and Kongo   150, 204–6
   in Mozambique   252, 258, 337–8
   and Mutapa   159–60
   in north Africa   99–100, 173–4
   and slave trade   177–80
   and West Africa   177, 180, 196
pottery   38, 75
   late Stone Age   23, 26, 28
   early Iron Age   46, 51, 59, 61–5, 130–31, 144, 150
   later Iron Age   124–5, 144–6, 153
prazeros   211–12, 253–4, 258, 337–8
Prempe, Asantehene   319
Príncipe   177
Ptolemaic dynasty   42, 69, 71
Punt   42, 76
pyramids, in Egypt   37, 38, 40, 42
   in Meroe   51–3
Pyramids, battle of the (1798)   283–4

Qadhdhafi, *see* Gaddafi
Qadir, *see* Abd al-Qadir

Rabih ibn Fadl Allah   233, 318–19
race, racism   2, 14, 71, 83, 186, 263, 300, 303, 375, 378, 379, 403, 408, 412, 416, 426–7, 477–8, 481

railways   287, 314, 327, 344, 347, 450, 357, 365, 374, 385, 436
rainfall   3–4, 22, 25, 49–50, 52, 66, 67, 161, 195
Rameses II   452
Ramgoolam, Seewoosagur   414
Ras Tafari, *see* Haile Selassie
raw materials   304, 312, 343–8, 356, 385–6, 390, 436, 445, 447, 481
Rawlings, J. J.   443, 459
RDA (*Rassemblement Démocratique Africain*)   394
'recaptives'   244–5, 298–9
Reindorf, Carl Christian   2
religion, indigenous African   2, 12, 13, 21, 23, 25, 34, 49, 51, 91–2, 95, 96, 101–3, 110, 124, 144–5, 147–50, 154, 156–7, 195, 199, 201, 204–5, 226–7, 231, 396–8, 301, 335, 351, 372
   see also Christianity; Islam
RENAMO (Mozambique National Resistance)   421
René, F. A.   415, 441
resistance, primary   281–2, 312, 314, 316–21, 323–7
   secondary   344–7, 350–3, 427–9
Réunion   256, 262, 413
Rhapta   128–9
Rhodes, Cecil   328, 331, 333–4, 336, 340–1, 418
Rhodesia (Zimbabwe)   340, 343, 355, 361–3, 365, 383, 389, 416–22
   see also British Central Africa; Zimbabwe
Rhodesia, Northern, *see* Zambia
Riebeeck, Jan van   220–1
Rift Valley   5, 7, 123, 217, 254, 351
rinderpest   327, 332, 340, 352, 355
Rio d'Oro *see* Western Sahara
rock art   15, 17, 27–8, 55–6, 85
Rodney, Walter   2, 182
Rolong   227, 271, 275–6
Romans, in Egypt   42, 51, 54
   in north Africa   71–5, 86
Rosetta stone   70
Royal Niger Company   320, 343
Rozvi   211–12, 255, 271, 333
RPF (Rwanda Patriotic Front)   475–7
rubber   248–9, 312, 324, 344, 347, 367, 385
Rubusana, Revd Walter   377
RUF (Revolutionary United Front)   465–6, 468

Rwagasore, Louis 413
Rwanda 126, 213, 215–16, 355, 360, 370, 412–13, 457
Rweej (Lueji) 147

SADC (Southern African Development Community) 455–7
SADCC (Southern African Development Coordination Conference) 455
Sa'dids 174
Sabaean-speaking people 77
Sadat, Anwar 461
Sahara 4–6, 10, 15, 25, 26–8, 40, 55–6, 72–3, 82, 85–95, 164, 191, 304, 316, 449, 452
Sahel 86, 304, 316
Saifawa dynasty 94, 189–91, 233
Salah al-Din ibn Ayyub (Saladin) 165–6
salt 55–6, 67, 85, 87, 90, 92, 94, 104–6, 108, 146, 149, 187, 191, 202, 208, 251, 308
Samburu 217
Samori Touré 235–6, 317–18, 319
Sandawe 21
Sanhaja Berbers 86, 90, 96–7, 106–7, 164
Sankoh, Foday 465–6
Sanusiyya brotherhood 356, 380
São Tomé 177–8, 180, 205–6
SAPs, see structural adjustment programmes
Sarsa Dengel 171
Savimbi, Jonas 424, 478
'Scramble for Africa' 237, 243, 246, 284, 289, 291, 295, 311–16, 327, 337, 380
SDP (Seychelles Democratic Party) 415
Sebetwane 251, 270
segregation 276–8
Segu 189, 235, 317
Sekeletu 251
Sekou Touré 295–6, 444, 453
Selassie, see Haile Selassie
Sena 158–9, 210–11
Senegal 316–17, 367, 372, 393
    Republic 434, 436, 439, 441, 451, 464, 480
Senegal River 3, 5–7, 90, 180–1, 309
Senegambia 193–4
Senghor, Léopold 375–6, 394–5, 434, 436

settlement, white, in Algeria 281–3, 397
    in Kenya 350–1, 361–3, 405–6
    in Malawi 336
    in Namibia 339–40, 352
    in South Africa 218–24, 263, 268, 271–9, 303, 329–32, 425
    in Tanzania 402–3
    in Zambia 336–7
    in Zimbabwe 334–5, 361–3, 478–9
Seychelles 256, 319, 325, 376, 441
Seyyid Said 257
Shaba, see Katanga
Shabaab, al- 472
Shaka 264–7, 269
Shambaa 217
Shangane 337
    see also Soshangane
Sharpville massacre (1960) 427–8, 431–2
Shi'ite movement 83–4
Shilluk 20, 289
Shimbra-Kuré, battle of (1529) 121
Shirazi 135
Shoa 114, 118, 121–2
    Sultanate 119–21
Shona 155, 158, 211–12, 227, 254–5, 271
Siad Barré 401, 471
Sidama 295
Sierra Leone, founding 182, 236, 243–5
    colony 244, 298–301, 318–19, 356, 373–4, 382
    Independence 393
    Republic 460, 464–8, 480
Sijilmasa 90, 94, 97–8, 105–6
Sirleaf, see Johnson, Ellen
Sisulu, Walter 427–8
Sithole, Ndabaningi 420
slavery/slave labour 3, 54–5, 72, 77, 82, 92, 104, 111, 167, 174, 176–9, 189, 192, 200, 202, 221, 223, 231, 233, 248–54, 256–62, 272, 285, 287, 290
slave trade, abolition 237–41, 243–5, 247–8, 257, 262, 297
    African dimension 181–2
    Atlantic 177–86, 194, 196–7, 199–200, 204–7, 247–8, 256
    east African 114, 119–20, 132, 137, 256–62
    European dimension 182, 185–6
    Nile valley 165, 169, 171

profits from 185–6
    and racism 186
    scale of 180–1
    South African 221, 268
    trans-Saharan 92, 94, 113, 173, 175–7, 189–91, 237–8
SLPP (Sierra Leone People's Party) 465
smallpox epidemic 222
Smith, Ian 420–7
Sobhuza's Ngwane 229, 264, 267
    see also Swazi
Sobhuza II 432
Sobukwe, Robert 427
socialism 401, 411, 415, 421–3, 425, 427, 444–6, 462, 477–8, 481
Sofala 132, 135–7, 141, 159–60
Soga, Tiyo 301
Sokoto 231–4, 236, 307–8, 317, 320, 368–70
Solomonid dynasty 115–19
Somalis/Somalia 120–1, 295, 327, 380–2, 400–1, 451, 458, 471–2, 480
Songhay 1, 20, 101, 107–13, 174–5, 187–9, 191–2, 232
Songye 146, 259
Soninke 88, 90, 92–3, 96–8, 100, 109, 200
Sonni Ali 108–9
Sonni Sulayman Dandi 108
Sorko 108
Soshangane 267
Sosso 93, 101
Sotho 225, 227, 251, 267–8, 271
    Kingdom 268–70, 277
    see also Basutoland; Lesotho
Sotho-Tswana 160, 161, 218, 225–8, 270
South Africa 263, 301, 311, 353, 355, 360, 416, 420–2, 424–32, 452, 455–6, 477–8, 480–1
    Union of 342, 360, 376–8, 383, 385–6, 425, 432
    see also Cape Colony
South African War (1899–1902) 340–2
South Sudan 474
    see also Sudan
South West Africa 302, 314, 315, 340
    see also Germany in South West Africa; Namibia
Soweto uprising (1976) 429
Soviet Union 396, 400–1, 421, 423–4, 427, 455, 471

UNITA (União Nacional para a Independência Total de Angola) 424, 478
United Arab Republic (Egypt) 400
United Nations (UN) 409–11, 412, 420, 427, 430, 463, 465–7, 469, 472
United States (USA) 240–1, 246, 287, 298, 312, 357, 364, 367, 373–4, 386, 391, 400–1, 410–11, 415, 417, 423, 430, 450, 453–5, 462, 464, 471–2, 478, 481
UPC (Uganda People's Congress) 404
UPRONA (*Parti de l'Union et le Progrès National*) (Burundi) 413
Upemba 148
Urabi, Ahmad 288
uranium 430, 450
urbanisation 8, 46, 50, 90, 194, 357, 373, 385–6, 405, 425, 436, 438, 440–1, 448, 451, 461–2, 479
Urewe pottery 62, 124
Usman dan Fodio 231–2, 234
Uteve 158, 160
Uvinza 67

Van Riebeeck, Jan, *see* Riebeeck
Vandals in north Africa 73, 81
Vansina, Jan 2
vegetation 3–8
Venda 227, 276, 332
Versailles Conference (1918–19) 259–60
Voortrekkers, *see* Boers
Von Lettow-Vorbeck, *see* Lettow-Vorbeck
Von Trotha, Lothar 352–3

Wadai 233
Wade, Abdoulaye 465
Wafd party 359, 376
Walaswa dynasty 120
Wangara, *see* Dyula
'War on Terror' 472
Watchtower movement 354–5
Waterboer, Nicholas 328
weapons 41, 43, 45–6, 53
    see also guns
Wegbaja 199
welfare associations 386
Wesleyan missionaries 298
Western Sahara 396–7, 454, 464
Whydah 199
Wilson, Woodrow 357, 359
Wingate, R. 356
Witbooi, Hendrik 339–40, 353
Witwatersrand 331
    see also gold in South Africa
Wolof 193–4
World Bank 288, 448, 452, 460–1
World War I 327, 353, 355–60, 374, 386, 414, 430
World War II 2, 373–4, 375–88, 389

Xhosa 218, 224, 228, 272–4, 301, 330

Yahya ibn Umar 97–8
Yao 252–3, 256, 259, 302, 324, 336–8, 348
Yasin, *see* Abdallah ibn
Yei 226
Yeke, *see* Msiri's
Yoruba 2, 95, 195–9, 232, 245, 319, 320, 434
Yoruba Action Group (YAG) 393
Yusuf ibn Tashufin 98

Zaghlul, Sa'ad 376
Zagwe dynasty 114–15, 120
Zaïre 309, 412, 423, 458–9, 475, 477
    see also Congo, Democratic Republic of
Zambezi river/valley 5–7, 158–60, 209–12, 226, 249–56, 270
Zambia, region 61
    colonial 336, 365, 374, 416–20
    Republic 433, 435–6, 440–1, 459
Zamfara 192, 232
Zanj, *see* Zenj
ZANU (Zimbabwe African National Union) 420–2, 479
ZAPU (Zimbabwe African People's Union) 419–22
Zanzibar 131, 135–6, 139, 254, 256–7, 259, 323–4, 326, 403
    see also Tanzania
Zaria 192, 232
Zazzau 192
Zenata Berbers 86
Zenj (Zanj) 130–2
Zimba 210
Zimbabwe 418, 422, 445–6, 454–6, 471, 477, 478–9, 484
    see also Great Zimbabwe; Rhodesia
Zimbabwe plateau 65, 135, 141, 152–8, 254–5, 275, 333–4
Zimbabwe-Rhodesia 422
Zulu (Kingdom) 229, 264–7, 271, 276–7, 330–1
Zululand 331
Zuma, Jacob 478
Zwangendaba 254–5
    see also Ngoni
Zwide 229

Speke, Hanning 307, 311
SPLA (Sudan People's Liberation Army) 472–4
SPUP (Seychelles People's United Party) 415
Stanley, H. M. 215, 258, 260, 309–10, 311, 314, 321, 346
Stone Ages 11
stone tools 9–17, 23, 60–1, 67, 123–4, 144
stonemasonry 65, 75–6, 115–16, 152, 154, 156–7
Strasser, Valentine 460, 465
structural adjustment programmes (SAPs) 448–50, 460–2
Subiya 226
sudd 126
Sudan 285, 289–91, 389
    al-Sudan 87, 93, 167
    Independence 400
    Republic 435, 451–2, 472–5, 480–1
    Southern Sudan 125–7, 289, 382, 472–5
    see also South Sudan
Suez Canal 287–9, 327, 382–3, 400
sugar 256, 283
Sulayman, Mansa 105
Sumaguru 101
Sundjata 100–2; The Epic 1, 100
Susenyos 172
Swahili 1, 128, 134–41, 164, 256, 258–61, 302, 322–7, 336, 351
    see also Kiswahili
SWAPO (South West Africa People's Organisation) 430–1
Swazi (Kingdom) 267, 276–7, 331
Swaziland 432

Tabora 259, 260–1
Taghaza salt mines 87, 90, 105, 110, 112, 187
Takrur 94, 108
Tambo, Oliver 427–8
Tadmekka 101, 105
Tahrir Square 462, 475
Tanganyika 259, 316, 324, 360, 389, 413
    Independence 402–3
    union with Zanzibar 404
TANU (Tanganyika African National Union) 402–3
Tanzania 127, 217, 254–6, 261, 251–2, 355
    Independence 402

Republic 404, 425, 434–6, 443–5, 448, 451, 454, 457, 470, 474, 481
Tar'rikh al-Sudan 1
Tashufin, see Yusuf ibn
Taung 227, 270
Tawfiq 288
taxation 33, 35–6, 40, 52–3, 71–3, 79, 81–3, 103–4, 111, 147, 150, 155, 159, 160, 164, 167, 188–9, 195, 199, 230–2, 251, 276, 291, 318
    colonial 331, 347–51, 354, 362, 365
    see also iqta
tax-farming, see iqta
Taylor, Charles 457, 464–7
TAZARA (Tanzania and Zambia Rail Authority) 481
Tel el-Kebir, battle (1882) 288
Temne 244
'terms of trade' 436, 478, 444, 448
terracing 152, 157
Teso 217
Tete 158–9, 210–11, 338
Tewodros II 292–4
Thebes 38, 42, 49
Thembu 269
Tigray 76, 173, 452
Timbuktu 1, 101, 104–5, 107–9, 111–12, 174, 188–9, 304, 306, 311, 371
Tio 204, 321
Tippu Tip, see Hamed bin Muhammed
Tlhaping 270
Tlokoa 227, 268
Togo 355, 360, 441
Tondibi, battle (1591) 188
Tonga 160
tools/tool-making 9–17, 23, 41, 43–9, 51, 62
    see also stone tools; Iron Age
Toro 325
Torwa state 157, 211
tourism 462
Toussaint L'Ouverture 239
Toutswe tradition 59, 151–2
TPLF (Tigray People's Liberation Front) 471
trade 23, 33, 38–42, 43–4, 49, 54, 67, 144–55
    Indian Ocean 69, 76–80, 105, 114, 118–19, 128–43, 152–3, 155, 157–9, 150, 164, 168, 208–11, 256, 262, 480

'legitimate commerce' 240–3
long-distance 204–5, 208–9, 217, 218, 229, 248–9, 251–4, 258–61, 304, 403
trans-Saharan 54–6, 85–95, 98, 100–1, 105–13, 173, 187–92
trades unions 374, 377–8, 427–8, 432, 464
Transvaal 65, 227, 274, 331, 340–2
Trekboers, see Boers
'triangular trade' 185
tribute, see taxation
Tripoli 94, 174, 191
Trotha, Lotha von, see Von Trotha
tsetse fly 26–7, 66–7 124, 197, 390
Tshombe, Moise 408–11
Tsiranana, Philibert 414
Tsonga 218, 255
Tsvangirai, Morgan 479
Tswana 218, 225–7, 270–1, 276, 301, 328, 332
Tswapong hills 151
Tuareg 86, 107–10, 164, 173, 187–8, 191–2, 230–1, 356
Tukolor 231, 235–6, 316–18, 368
Tunisia 55, 174, 288, 374, 384, 396, 461–2
Turkana 217
Tutankhamun 38, 40–1
Tutsi 126, 215–16, 412–13, 475

Ubangui-Chari 321, 389
    see also Central African Republic
UDI ('unilateral declaration of independence') 420
Uganda 127, 303, 324–7, 349–50, 363, 413
    Independence 402, 404–5
    Republic 413, 436, 443, 457, 474–5, 477, 479–80
UGCC (United Gold Coast Convention) 391–2
uitlanders 340–1
ujamaa 444–5
Ujiji 259, 261
'Umar, see Jibril ibn
Umar, al-Hajj 234–5, 317
Umar al-Mukhtar 380
Umar, Yahya ibn, see Yahya
Umkhonto we Sizwe (MK) 428
Undi dynasty 150, 209
UNIP (United National Independence Party) 419
Union Minière 347, 365, 411